SHATTERED DREAMS,
INFINITE HOPE

SHATTERED DREAMS, INFINITE HOPE

A Tragic Vision of the Civil Rights Movement

BRANDON M. TERRY

THE BELKNAP PRESS OF
HARVARD UNIVERSITY PRESS
Cambridge, Massachusetts
London, England
2025

Printed in the United States of America

Second Printing

EU GPSR Authorised Representative LOGOS EUROPE,
9 rue Nicolas Poussin, 17000, LA ROCHELLE, France
E-mail: Contact@logoseurope.eu

Library of Congress Cataloging-in-Publication Data

Names: Terry, Brandon M. author
Title: Shattered dreams, infinite hope : a tragic vision of the civil
rights movement / Brandon M. Terry.
Identifiers: LCCN 2025002197 (print) | LCCN 2025412018 (ebook) |
ISBN 9780674271289 cloth | ISBN 9780674299702 epub | ISBN 9780674299719 pdf
Subjects: LCSH: Civil rights movements—United States |
African Americans—Civil rights—History—20th century |
Collective memory—Political aspects—United States | Civil rights—Philosophy |Civil
rights movements—United States—Historiography
Classification: LCC E185.61 .T325 2025 (print) | LCC E185.61 (ebook) |
DDC 323.1196/0730904—dc23/eng/20250422
LC record available at https://lccn.loc.gov/2025002197
LC ebook record available at https://lccn.loc.gov/2025412018

CONTENTS

SHATTERED DREAMS, INFINITE HOPE

INTRODUCTION

> Is there any one of us who has not faced the agony of blasted hopes and shattered dreams?
>
> —Martin Luther King Jr.

TIME IS A CRUEL arbiter of the enduring significance of human action. Even in societies that compulsively archive the detritus of the past, few human events or personalities escape the fate of obscurity. Fewer still insinuate themselves into common thought and practice. Yet in the United States, and indeed much of the world, the twentieth-century revolt against racial and social injustice led by African Americans known as the civil rights movement has attained this stature, becoming an exemplary event in the political culture of the present.

To describe the civil rights movement as exemplary is to suggest that it serves as a touchstone of ethical, social, and political thought.[1] Bridging the particular and the general, exemplarity shapes and structures disagreement around many of the identities, ideals, and concepts we rely on to understand or critique our forms of life. It is invoked or mobilized to help us define and communicate values, understand other events and phenomena we encounter, guide our imagination, and disclose or order our normative and political judgments. Therefore, to anoint something as exemplary is to insist that it is productive and purposive. We expect to learn something valuable from engaging with or even emulating it. In doing so we aim to clarify what we should value or reject, pursue or avoid, strive for or disavow in our lives and traditions. We may even expect it to bring us nearer a defensible answer to that most existential of questions: What may I hope?

The philosopher Alessandro Ferrara describes exemplarity as one of the "three great forces" that shape our world, alongside the force of *what is* and the force of *what ought to be*.[2] The force of what is may best be captured in the experience of resistance or finitude we undergo as we act in pursuit of specific purposes.[3] Throughout our lives, each of us confronts obdurate and imposed social facts, dynamic social systems, and complex ecologies that disclose the limits of will and comprehension or mock the professed sovereignty of human action.[4] By contrast, the force of what ought to be involves those ideals and principles that we use in exercises of critical evaluation and imagination, especially in moral reasoning. Among our experiences with this force are flights of imaginative enthusiasm, flashes of righteous indignation, or feelings of profound disappointment. Our capacity to experience this sense of what ought to be seems stunningly resilient. Even in the face of repeated violations of our greatest hopes or grueling confrontations with skepticism, many of us continue to invest ethical ideals with great significance, making tremendous sacrifices in their name.

We should not, however, treat these two forces as exhaustive. Doing so forces us into "an unbridgeable gap between these two realms." Falling into a portrait of the world "as split between facts and values, facts and norms . . . is and ought, descriptive and normative accounts," Ferrara argues that we are misled "into overlooking the specific relevance and force of *exemplars:* namely, of entities, material or symbolic, that are as they should be . . . where *is* and *ought* merge and, in so doing, liberate an energy that sparks our imagination."[5] To speak of this "spark" is to strain language to capture an explosive idea—that accounts of exemplarity allow us to bridge the ethical and the epistemological, achieving illustration, demonstration, reimagination, and guidance in light of the unique congruences that exemplars seem to enact between ought and is.

Appeals to civil rights movement history in argument—whether made in the overlapping scholarly fields of philosophy, political theory, jurisprudence, and African American studies or in the rough-and-tumble world of politics beyond the academy—often presume that it is an event that entails these qualities. Many expect that its invocation, at least when performed properly, will help us judge clearly and think critically about a variety of social practices and political phenomena. This is especially true of those that involve the demands of democratic citizenship and civic freedom, the struggle against racial injustice and discrimination, judgments of protest and dissent, and the ethical valence of inequality and oppression.[6]

The movement also seems, for many, to speak to the vital question of the morphology, or practical form, of our attempts to enact political morality. The historian David Burner goes so far as to describe the civil rights movement as "about as close to moral perfection as American political action has ever come."[7] Civil rights history is often treated as a touchstone for the practical question of how we might successfully embody or productively strive toward ideals and norms we take it to exemplify, even if, ultimately, we wish to argue that those standards are obsolete or inadequate.[8] Such claims get reliably and passionately raised during the appearance of contentious social movements like Black Lives

Matter, Occupy Wall Street, antiwar protests, or even the right-wing Tea Party movement.[9] Julian Bond, a founder of the Student Nonviolent Coordinating Committee and a former chairman of the National Association for the Advancement of Colored People (NAACP), noted proudly during the fight for constitutional recognition of same-sex marriages that "our movement"—the civil rights movement—"has provided so much inspiration for others . . . [and] has been so widely imitated, and that our tactics, heroes, heroines and methods, even our songs, have been appropriated as models for others."[10]

We should not understand this emulation and enthusiasm in narrowly strategic or instrumental terms. It is often charged that various gestures toward the civil rights movement are dishonest, confused, or even cynical. It is not often enough admitted that such criticism remains question-begging in a profoundly important way. Why, we must remember to ask, do even cynical actors appear compelled to pay the tribute of hypocrisy that vice pays to virtue? And what would it mean for even this compulsion to disappear from our political life?

The civil rights movement raises, in addition to more familiar political matters like democracy and justice, other far-reaching ethical and existential questions of peoplehood, authenticity, and hope. The movement is commonly understood as a historical inflection point where decisive questions regarding the "self-reassurance" of American civilization, African American traditions, or even the modern age itself are raised with dramatic significance, revealing fundamental insights about what we may hope for from the forms of life we have inaugurated under these descriptions, or the capacities for political action available to us.[11]

President Barack Obama's remarks at the 2011 dedication of the federal memorial to Rev. Dr. Martin Luther King Jr. on the National Mall in Washington, DC, are instructive. On that occasion, the first African American president argued that the nation honored King "because he had faith in us" and represents, even in memory, something "quintessentially American." Rhetorically forged into a metaphor of American peoplehood, King's memory and an implicit interpretation of the civil rights movement are meant to buttress the self-reassurance that American civilization is, and perhaps always has been, a project worthy of affirmation and continued investment rather than one whose self-undermining flaws make it unworthy of the confidences its celebrants project into the future:

> For all the hardships we've endured, for all our sometimes tragic history, ours is a story of optimism and achievement and constant striving that is unique upon this Earth. And that is why the rest of the world still looks to us to lead. This is a country where ordinary people find in their hearts the

> courage to do extraordinary things; the courage to stand up in the face of the fiercest resistance and despair and say this is wrong, and this is right; we will not settle for what the cynics tell us we have to accept and we will reach again and again, no matter the odds, for what we know is possible. That is the conviction we must carry now in our hearts. . . . As tough as times may be, I know we will overcome. I know there are better days ahead. I know this because of the man towering over us.[12]

Such rhetoric is exceptionalist but not exceptional. It is not only, as some critics rightly note, that King and the civil rights movement are conscripted here to provide spurious defense of American geopolitical hegemony and the financially profligate and democratically unaccountable militarism required to sustain it.[13] Far more striking is how claims of "knowledge" that invoke the history of the movement play an altogether more fundamental and near-theodicean role in the political and philosophical epic of America. In this "time-space of epic proportions," the civil rights movement is called on to play a climactic role in a grand narrative of the "epochal struggle" of a uniquely modern nation and its constitutive commitments against a despotic past of irrationalism and evil.[14] America's alleged victories in this confrontation with Jim Crow, arguably even more than the slavery-compromised founding of the nation, are what represent for many politicians and intellectuals the nation's greatest claim to a vanguard position at the normative horizons of modernity.

It is rare to see a historical event around which such extraordinary political longings and philosophical energies coalesce. To venture an argument about certain essential questions of our shared political and ethical life—the legitimacy of religious arguments in a pluralist democracy, the permissibility of dissent and disobedience, the politics of identity and exclusion, the ethics of representation and reparation, or questions of faith and hope—is to expect, or even invite, an avalanche of appeals or references to the civil rights movement or its key personalities. Indeed, simply to use some of the abstract concepts or norms we rely on to orient ourselves toward such questions (e.g., "civil disobedience" or "racial progress") is already to cast our lot, wittingly or unwittingly, with some understanding or account of the movement.

But why should this be the case? "The degree to which life requires the service of history at all," as Friedrich Nietzsche mischievously put it, "is one of the supreme questions and concerns in regard to the health of a man, a people or a culture."[15] He infamously warned that certain modes of historical consciousness or representation might contribute to our unfreedom, even as they claim to do the work of emancipation or edification. Such skepticism raises these difficulties in our own time as well. Why do we compulsively invoke the exemplarity of the civil rights movement to explain who we are or orient us to face our present dilemmas? How should we understand the consequences of this practice on the education of our judgment, the formation of our concepts, and the possibilities for thought and action we might open or foreclose? Why should a particular event from the past, however dramatically compelling or historically consequential, speak to moral and political judgment here and now? Or, to take our bearings from the divinely paradoxical admonishment issued to the women gathered at Jesus's empty tomb, "Why seek ye the living among the dead?"[16]

These questions are at the heart of *Shattered Dreams, Infinite Hope*. To venture an answer worthy of their difficulty, I offer not a new history of the civil rights movement in a conventional sense but a critical theory of the movement's exemplarity with implications for philosophy and political theory *writ large*. Embracing this practice of excavation and disinterment focused on the problem of exemplarity is one of the central tasks for African American political thought and contemporary critical theory in our cacophonous present. We must bring out of the concealment of habit and thoughtlessness those accumulated experiences, judgments, and accounts of the past at work when people treat the civil rights movement as exemplary in politics and philosophy.

To do so, however, is to immediately raise the vital question of narrative, which is the essential form of historical discourse. It is narrative that facilitates the movement of examples in the broader culture, creating an economy of exemplarity marked by circuits of exchange between historiography, popular culture, public political argument, philosophy, and social and political theory. Once we take narrative and storytelling itself seriously as a problem for how we understand and argue about exemplarity in political thought, we will find that competing narrative modes come to structure the way we perceive our practices or the patterns of justification and understanding we find persuasive. These stories, and the particular forms they take, can prefigure the terms of debate and help order our frameworks of interlocking judgments, concepts, and understandings. They shape what we judge as urgent and significant, and even what is, as a matter of politics, sensible, intelligible, and visible to us.[17] In the course of circulation and repetition, different narratives of exemplary events authorize divergent notions of reality, styles of attention toward meaning, and judgments of value. Grasping the form and force of narrative modes raises a still underappreciated "aesthetic" problem for modern politics, philosophy, and history, troubling the commonsensical empiricism many take for granted when thinking about the past.[18]

To carefully capture the larger ethical and political stakes of how we narrate and exemplify the past, we need to keep pace with the movements of this economy of exemplarity and make judgments about which narrative mode speaks best to pressing concerns across politics, ethics, and epistemology.

This requires a practice of critical political theory in an unapologetically interdisciplinary mode, combining insights from philosophy of history, literary theory, aesthetics, history, and the broader social sciences. *Shattered Dreams, Infinite Hope* is an argument—by example, one might say—in defense of critical theory's insistence that we should not cordon off the vital work of analytical reconstruction and normative argument constitutive of mainstream political philosophy from these other modes of inquiry in cultural and interpretive criticism. The traditional normative concerns of political theory should be pursued within "a larger critical enterprise . . . pursued in a self-consciously interdisciplinary manner."[19]

It bears noting that scholars of black critical theory and African American philosophy long ago set out on this interdisciplinary path.[20] In that pathbreaking text of African American philosophy, *Prophesy Deliverance!* (1982), Cornel West offered the argument that "the major function of Afro-American critical thought" is "to reshape the contours of Afro-American history and provide a new self-understanding of the Afro-American experience which suggest guidelines for action in the present."[21] While West's account seems largely to emphasize the import of African American history for African American thought narrowly construed, I want to insist on, and demonstrate, the far-reaching implications of any reshaping of this history for political thought and practice across a wider range of traditions—especially contemporary liberalism.

I also want to chasten any hubris about how and when such "reshaping" is practically possible or politically efficacious. When exemplary events are entrenched within authoritative narratives and interpretive schemas, they have a kind of intuitive character, appearing as a largely frictionless part of our common sense. Criticisms may be made, but all too often fall, as W. E. B. Du Bois worried *The Souls of Black Folk* might, "still-born into the world wilderness."[22] Even our practical interaction with the world seems to reflect back to us the obviousness of these stories and schemas, or at least steadily drums our episodic doubts into submission.

This need not, however, be permanent or inevitable. As Ludwig Wittgenstein insisted, "it is not single axioms that strike me as obvious, it is a system in which consequences and premises give one another mutual support."[23] And as certain premises fall into disrepute, or actions seem unable to generate their expected consequences, authoritative interpretations and narrative conventions also lose some ability to compel genuflection, orient effective understanding, or generate reliable affective response.

This does not mean, however, that these conventions cede the stage peacefully to other actors any more than scandal reliably dethrones a tyrant. Wendy Brown powerfully details how even though the authority of some of the "constitutive narratives of modernity"—progressive history, for instance—has eroded in the face of sweeping social, political, and epistemological changes, such stories stagger along. Even in their ostensibly weakened state, they still elicit melancholic attachment, habits of acquiescence, and unruly affects of "insecurity, anxiety, and hopelessness." Nevertheless, Brown is right to insist that other "political and epistemological possibilities" may emerge from the shattering of hegemonic narrative and the new modes of judgment and understanding that are unleashed in its wake. These shattered dreams compel us to grapple with a new indeterminacy—"*so much* history and *so many* histories"—that suggest "uncharted potential" for reorientating our politics and self-conception.[24]

We cannot expect to predict, a priori, when our constitutive narratives might fall into crisis, but the resulting disorientation can spark genuine creative and intellectual ferment. Revisionist historiography blossoms in such circumstances, even if it is prone to mistaking its own arguments for the sole cause of its persuasive power and cultural resonance. Likewise, fights erupt in philosophy and politics over the meaning of exemplars, including, in some quarters, a determined interest in a more totalizing rejection rather than revision. The pressing problem in such moments—our moment, I will argue, regarding the civil rights movement—is not simply understanding exemplarity, narrative, and judgment in the abstract as philosophical puzzles. Instead we find ourselves faced by the problem of whether we have the capacity to judge, with critical clarity, the intellectual inheritance, political practices, and normative architecture with which our narrative accounts of exemplarity are entangled.

Can a theory of exemplarity help orient us within this space of narrative uncertainty, both to clarify the stakes of our crisis and to motivate new imaginings of African American history that are politically emancipatory without being epistemically indefensible? Or—and we must take the possibility deathly seriously—does the contemporary crisis of our once authoritative stories about the civil rights movement bolster the case for nihilism? How do we confront the allegation that this particular investment in historical exemplarity not only fails to give warrant to reasonable hope for a better world but also no longer even casts light on the future or gleans a feasible path out of our present obscurity?[25]

The Exemplarity of the Civil Rights Movement in Politics, Culture, and Philosophy

Thinking through the exemplarity of the civil rights movement is a central preoccupation of African American intellectual writing, black political life, and antiracist social movements. "Many of the most heated battles in the arena of the black freedom struggle," scholars Leigh Raiford and Renee Romano remind us, "revolve around how the civil rights movement should be remembered," with skirmishes ranging from "memorials to art exhibits, advertisements, community celebrations, legislative battles, and even street names."[26]

These fights are largely an inheritance from an earlier generation of scholars, artists, and intellectuals, many of whom either participated in the student wing of the movement, were contemporaneous critics (e.g., black nationalists), or were part of its first generation of chroniclers. The intimate tone of their research, relying heavily on oral histories and personal reminiscences of movement participants, amounts to a heart-wrenching blend of apostolic faith and postmortem investigation. The former involves the question of who can authoritatively interpret revelations of truth from the past, keeping faith "against false claimants on behalf of rightful heirs."[27] The unmistakable aim of the latter is to evaluate what we did right, where it went wrong, and whose fault it all was.[28]

Our era, however, is decades into the building of both a grand edifice of civil rights memorialization with universalist aspirations and a stubborn regime of post–Jim Crow racial inequality whose burdens fall far more narrowly. Unsurprisingly, our commentary reflects this disorienting and imposing cultural milieu. Critical reflection cannot speak without first breathing in the vast circulation of images, invocations, and reflections related to the civil rights movement. Any iconoclastic opinion must swim doggedly against currents of convention and canonization. Dying is the sense of intimacy; the tone of defensiveness and embattlement soldiers on.

As Adolph Reed Jr., who was eighteen when the Voting Rights Act became law, writes, his generation—one that includes my mother and father—is "basically the last, black or white, for which the Jim Crow regime is a living memory." As those with "intimate knowledge" of "everyday life of the segregation era" pass from the world, Reed rightly worries about whether we have replaced a collective "sense of how the segregationist regime was held together, what practical purposes it served and for whom, what it ultimately *was*" with a series of "abstractions" that distort our judgments of past and present alike.[29]

Looming over these contentious discussions of the civil rights movement, especially within black political life and antiracist social movements, are ongoing debates about the sources and significance of black disadvantage in American society, the values by which we should assess the continuities and discontinuities in social inequality and racial orders, and the appropriate place and performance of protest and activism in contemporary politics.[30] Such debates, once seemingly curdled into exhausted melancholy in the late twentieth century under the weight of "underclass" discourse and laments about the "crises" of "black leadership," flickered with new life and urgency in the aftermath of Barack Obama's historic election to the American presidency and the successive, highly publicized police and vigilante killings of unarmed African Americans that led to a flurry of protest, organizing, and social criticism. Both events occasioned intense comparison to, and reflection on, the exemplarity of the civil rights movement.[31]

This should not be surprising, for at least two reasons. The first is that one of the central roles of philosophical reflection on politics, at least according to John Rawls's influential account, is the task of orientation. This means contributing "to how a people think of their political and social institutions as a whole, of themselves as citizens, and of their basic aims and purposes as a society with a history."[32] It also involves asking questions like, What does it mean to be a citizen, or better yet, an *equal* citizen? Does it make sense to speak of our political and social institutions as a democracy, or as basically just? What is the significance of the history of this society—between slavery and abolition, Jim Crow and civil rights, mass incarceration and the Obama phenomenon—for our basic aims, purposes, and obligations as a political people?[33] For many, the civil rights movement is an event where something profound about the answers to such questions is uniquely disclosed. They expect to clearly discern the contours of our civic ideals, moral principles, and other concerns through the aperture of this history.

This leads to a second, even more fundamental concern with the ethical and existential problematic of tradition: the question, "How do we stand with respect to all that comes down to us from the past?"[34] This is related, but not ultimately reducible to, the question of civic orientation. And despite the disciplinary jealousies of political theory, we should avoid flattening the philosophical and practical navigation of the epistemological crises and experiences of renewal and disruption that shape the inheritance of black political traditions forged in domination to the civic domain alone. After all, within black political life and antiracist social movements, the possible redemption, continuity, and legitimacy of the American polity are axes of intensive debate rather than axioms that serve to place strict limits on the space of argument and aspiration. Although the motto of Martin Luther King Jr.'s Southern Christian Leadership Conference—"To Save the Soul of America"—announced their goal in a sagacious blend of Cold War realism and evangelical enthusiasm, King's band of ministers was nevertheless compelled to recognize and respond to dissenting voices in Black America skeptical that the nation's putative soul was either capable or worthy of a rescue mission.[35] Other more fundamental questions often took precedence.

The persistence of such thoroughgoing political and existential disputation in African American traditions is what leads the conservative political theorist Herbert J. Storing to celebrate their exhilarating political philosophical significance. "Black Americans," Storing incisively argues, "are like a revolutionary or, more interestingly perhaps, a founding generation. That is, they are in the difficult but potentially glorious position of not being able to take for granted given political arrangements and values, of having seriously to canvass alternatives, to think through their implications, and to make a deliberate choice."[36] The deepest wells of dynamism within the black political thought traditions are fed from this volatile emphasis on experimentalism, receptivity, and radicalism about value and praxis.

The interpretive challenge that this instability represents is exacerbated by a fundamental incongruity between the tradition's remarkable capaciousness and those habits of historical reflection that construe the animating questions of black political thought as narrow, stable, and readily subsumed under familiar categories. Yet, as Robert Gooding-Williams powerfully contends, failure to attend to the vicissitudes of the questions that orient inquiry and debate or investigate the significance of changing descriptions of problems leads too often to systematic distortions of a tradition and an uncritical self-satisfaction with our philosophical tools of trade.[37] Rummaging through the past as if it were a ready-to-hand storehouse of stable question-and-answer positions easily subsumed under abstractions like "inequality" and "inclusion," we lose history and tradition's most powerful capacities to unsettle the thematic vocabularies, conceptual models, and vocational self-conceptions that we inherit without critical reflection or treat as axiomatic.

In other words, we unhelpfully turn our gaze away from the "subversive" power or "otherness" of tradition—namely, "the idea that what comes down to us in tradition, what tradition preserves or rather entails, is not a deposit of familiar meanings but something strange and refractory to interpretation, resistant to the present, uncontainable in the given world in which we find ourselves at home."[38] Proceeding without appropriate critical reflection on how the questions and answers we take as constitutive of our traditions were formulated or what alternatives are possible (even from within the canonical texts and exemplars), we can become ensconced in "irrationality, obsolescence, contradictoriness, or dysfunctionality."[39] We lose our ability to grasp the myriad ways we are deceived from the "inside out" and are unable to adequately respond to the problems besetting our present "forms of life."[40]

Such interpretive failures are made more pernicious and pronounced by professional incentives and pressures. The arduous quest for the disciplinary legitimacy of scholarship on black political thought, or at least détente from the hostility and humiliation that has traditionally been the lot of (mainly black) scholars in political science and philosophy, exerts a strong temptation to subsume the concerns of African American thinkers and antiracist movements under the dominant idioms and questions of the field's mainstream preoccupations (e.g., equal citizenship, democracy, and inequality). That the once ubiquitous, now frantically disavowed, call for "diversity and inclusion" in the profession might be answered on terms that would require only minor rearrangement was understandably alluring. This is perhaps especially true in a field uniquely defensive among humanistic and social scientific disciplines about its canonical thinkers and texts. Yet students of the black political thought tradition should be wary, especially in seasons when the Negro passes from in to out of vogue, that the ostensible triumph of disciplinary legitimacy is not purchased at the long-term cost of philosophical mutilation.[41]

Much of the recent enthusiasm for the study of African American political thought in professional political theory, for example, has been invested in the contributions and clarity it might offer to democratic theorists in an age of anxiety about their project. While this hope for a timely rescue is understandable, one would be remiss to wholly subordinate black traditions' broad thematic preoccupations with questions of white supremacy and racist ideology, resistance and solidarity, or the possibilities of black dignity and emancipation under conditions of injustice under this vocationally familiar but philosophically restricted category.[42] Beyond the normative underpinnings, imaginative design schemes, and highly valent rhetoric of democracy, there are questions of political life consistently explored within black intellectual traditions concerning what is to be done—existentially, ethically, and practically—in the face of profound social evil and cultivated cruelty.[43] The grammars of these traditions spill over and outside the vocabularies developed by mainstream academic political philosophy, at least as the latter has evolved in the late twentieth and early twenty-first centuries. Basic quandaries for African American political thought—including the wisdom and justice of various practices of resistance, the character of virtue and vice amid damaged forms of life, the relation between expressive cultural tastes and political judgment, and the unique duties and burdens of living intimately and in political solidarity with others in an atmosphere of oppression—cannot necessarily take the prospect of democratic redemption as a stable horizon or even central presupposition. Within the domains of African American political thought, black political life, and antiracist social movements, for instance, there is far less anguish about defending the democratic legitimacy of various modes of protest than there are concerns about whether such practices could be truly self-assured responses to the scale and substance of the challenges at hand—purposive rather than quixotic, meaningful rather than alienated, life-affirming rather than nihilistic.

The exemplarity of the civil rights movement, therefore, is a key site for thinking through both enduring civic concerns about both the meaning of democratic equality and justice as well as the broader epistemic, existential, and ethical problems germane to the dynamic process of inheriting and renewing political and cultural tradition as such and black traditions of struggle in particular.[44] Cognitively, civil rights exemplarity invites us to make intelligible distinctions between past and present, thematizing elements of continuity and discontinuity within traditions of political response to white supremacy and their practices. Ethically and politically, it clarifies that our problem is consequently about "getting right the proportion of continuity and discontinuity in the forms of life we pass on."[45]

To put the problem this way is to emphasize, again, an active relation to tradition. How should practices and presuppositions that may have been self-assured, axiomatic, and efficacious in the resistance to the mid-twentieth-century racial order be evaluated in a world that has been reconfigured in the wake of that resistance and a vast array of other transformations? Which semantic resources, cultural practices, political institutions, and philosophical ideals associated with this rebellious past do we identify as our own, treating them as especially worthy of study and curation, renewal and attachment, and which do we disavow as inadequate to the futures we imagine, to be discarded as best as possible on the other side of a temporal break we take as a vital reference point for politics and understanding?

That such questions would be so constitutive of the practice of black political life and political thought reflects the long shadow that the battle against Jim Crow (including "Jim Crow North") casts on the present.[46] Even for those, like Eddie Glaude, who have despaired at times that the imaginative resources in black political life have been too "captured by the symbolic significance of the black freedom struggle of the 1960s and 1970s," the problem of exemplarity endures. Not only does Glaude concede, and even celebrate, how the lives of King, Malcolm X, and other civil rights activists might "model a standard of excellence that encourages excellence in our own lives," but his familiar interest in the horizons of a post-soul African American politics presumes nothing more fundamental than an epochal break occasioned by "the major legislative victories of the civil rights movement."[47]

The very application of the prefix *post-* to organizing motifs like *soul* in culture, *civil rights* in politics, *Jim Crow* in law, *black* in art criticism, and *racial* in sociology and philosophy treats the cultural and political transformations that the civil rights movement wrought (or that today are lived as haunting and disappointment) as still axiomatic to the problem of orienting black political thought *now* amid dynamics of continuity and change that require the careful parsing and judgment of tradition.[48] Mark Anthony Neal's influential account of "post-soul" culture and politics, for example, aims to track and diagnose the late twentieth-century paradigm shift in black cultural and political life from "urban industrialism to deindustrialism, from segregation to desegregation, from essential notions of blackness to metanarratives on blackness."[49] Or, as the critic Nelson George, who coined the phrase, has colorfully put it, the shift from "the we-shall-overcome tradition of noble struggle, soul and gospel music, positive images, and the conventional wisdom that civil rights would translate into racial salvation" toward "a time of goin'-for-mine materialism, secular beat consciousness, and a more diverse, fragmented, even postmodern black community."[50]

Paul Taylor connects this "posterizing impulse" to other efforts to theorize and periodize the "postmodern" or "postcolonial," noting that each of these formulations share commitments to "highlighting the emergence of a new-found diversity in some domain; using the historic shift, break, or rupture marked by this new pluralism in order to establish distance from some older way of proceeding . . . and expressing suspicion or skepticism about our ability to understand current and emerging practices and experiences in the older vocabularies we have available. Posterizing is all at once a gesture of repudiation, of indebtedness, of skepticism, and of openness—done with an eye toward the inexorability of change over time."[51] What is distinctive about the race-related "posts," however, is that they all take as their referent "the particular regime of race-thinking and racial formation processes that gave us the civil rights era" and involve figuring the civil rights movement as a "break" or "opening" in history that calls for the ambivalent gestures described above.[52]

In this way, a metahistorical debate about the exemplarity of the civil rights movement imposes on many of the central disagreements of contemporary African American political thought and philosophy and explains why they incessantly wrestle with the politics and legacies of the civil rights movement, positing various stances toward this fragment of the past. Such debates include the political roles of religious institutions and faith; the ethics and scope of solidarity (e.g., racial, national, or even transnational); whether racial integration or constitutional reform are imperatives of justice; the possibilities and limits of rights-based ethical and political discourse; the evaluation of competing modes of leadership; and the ethics of various informal, formal, and rebellious modes of political resistance, some of which include violence.[53]

Even arguments about the nature of a good life, the morphology of moral action, and the proper response to deviance are often anchored in appeals to the civil rights movement within black political life. At a 1995 Martin Luther King Jr. Day celebration, Eric Holder, the US attorney for Washington, DC, who would later go on to become the country's first black attorney general under President Obama, declared that "Dr. King would be shocked and disheartened by the condition of his people in 1995—and I, for one, would be ashamed to reveal to him what we have let happen to our community. . . . Did Martin Luther King successfully fight the likes of Bull Connor so that we could lose the struggle for civil rights to misguided or malicious members of our own race?"[54] The appeal to civil rights memory as a source of virtuous example, cultural authority, and covenantal sacrifice with which to exhort African Americans to moral and cultural reform was so widespread in the mid-1990s that the lawyer and legal scholar James Forman Jr. hardly exaggerates when he writes, "It was difficult to attend a Martin Luther King Day sermon . . . without hearing a minister or other speaker invoke King's memory in order to denounce crime and violence in black America."[55]

The twenty-first century has not yet dispelled this habit. In 2006 *The Boondocks,* an animated television show based on Aaron McGruder's popular comic strip, aired "Return of the King," a satirical answer to the recurring question, What would Martin Luther King think of the present? In the show, King does not die by assassination in Memphis but rather falls into a nearly four-decades-long coma before waking up to find his place among post-9/11 political currents. In the episode's climactic scene, King's determined efforts to begin an independent political party deteriorate into chaos as its opening convention is hijacked by "hustler preachers," fights in the crowd, and a carnivalesque air of hedonistic irreverence and cynical commodification. Losing his preternatural calm, McGruder's King launches into an abusive tirade meant to shame the black audience into self-transformation. Punctuating his sermon with sweeping condemnation of the derivative character of black expressive culture and the supposed degeneracy of post–civil rights black cultural norms and vices (lack of ambition, procrastination, hypocrisy, captiousness, and profligacy), an exasperated King shouts, "Is this it? This is what I got all those ass-whuppings for? I had a dream once. It was a dream that little black boys and little black girls would drink from the river of prosperity, freed from the thirst of oppression. But lo and behold, some four decades later, what have I found but a bunch of trifling, shiftless, good-for-nothing niggas."[56]

Despite the episode's nostalgic preoccupation with imagining the power of King's singular charismatic leadership and its impossibility in our political and cultural milieu, it is important to acknowledge that the episode does not end with King's heroic reinstallation to the vanguard. Instead an exhausted King abdicates his leadership role altogether. Riffing on the famed "I've Been to the Mountaintop" speech delivered the evening before King was shot dead in Memphis, McGruder's King proclaims, "I've seen what's around the corner! I've seen what's over the horizon! And I promise you—you niggas have nothing to celebrate. And no, I won't get there with you. . . . I'm going to Canada." Stunned into a moment of silent self-inventory by the righteous disappointment and defection of their secular saint, the masses of African America swiftly turn to cultural and political revolution, evidenced by plummeting dropout rates, antiwar boycotts organized by professional athletes, and an uprising at the White House. What is remarkable, then, about "Return of the King" is that rather than invest further in the collective mourning after King's death that led to widespread and deeply gendered longing for a suitable inheritor to take up the envisaged role of spokesman, strategist, and tribune for "the race" (as many did with Ralph Abernathy, Stokely Carmichael, Louis Farrakhan, and Jesse Jackson), King's example performs the work of mass moral and political transformation even in his absence.

Although *The Boondocks* may be an especially irreverent and imaginative entry into the conversation on civil rights exemplarity, it is by no means an outlier in its gestures to movement history and the citation of the movement's leading lights who teach the public about the ethical commitments that should constitute civic ideals and political peoplehood. In their individuality, such invocations often aim to inspire and inform or (like McGruder) deliver a stern lesson to a captive audience. Collectively, however, references to the civil rights movement amount to a centripetal force within black intellectual life, politics, and philosophy.

While competing appeals to civil rights exemplarity are most conspicuous in black political life and in circles of antiracist organizing and debate, it is surprising, and thus even more striking, how widely the movement appears in the canonical literatures of mainstream political theory and philosophy, disciplines whose leading practitioners are not normally understood as especially concerned with problems of racial injustice or the role of racial ideology in American historical and political development.

Take, for example, the work of John Rawls, the towering liberal philosopher of the latter half of the twentieth century in whose shadow an enormous swath of professional philosophy still labors, for better or for worse.[57] Despite the reverence accorded to Rawls in most precincts of political theory and philosophy, the most influential reading of him on the problem of race is the indictment offered by Charles W. Mills alleging that Rawls had "nothing to say about racial injustice, the distinctive injustice of the modern world."[58] As part of his attack on Rawlsian theory's alleged inability to understand racial injustice, much less offer effective guidance in the battle against it, Mills suggests that a major source of these failures is that the "postwar struggle for racial justice in practice and in theory and the Rawlsian corpus on justice are almost completely separate and non-intersecting universes."[59]

For all the stridency of Mills's objection that Rawlsianism is silent on questions of race and the postwar struggle for racial justice, however, his sweeping charge ignores the existence and import of the recurrent surfacing of the civil rights movement as an exemplary event in Rawls's texts and the debates to which Rawls remains central. It is one of the major arguments of *Shattered Dreams, Infinite Hope,* developed at length in Chapter 6, that the critical philosophy of race cannot rest contentedly with strategies of reading and interpretation whose frameworks and keywords (e.g., *silence*) subtly train us to be inattentive to and uncritical of the surfacing of important instances of exemplarity across philosophical argument. What I hope to show throughout the book, but in this chapter on Rawls and Mills specifically, is that sustained attention to these appearances, scattered throughout political and philosophical discourse, can excavate the deeply embedded narratives of African American history *within* the conceptual constellations, considered judgments, orienting pictures, and animating anxieties of recent efforts in political philosophy.

This is an insight inspired by Toni Morrison rather than prevailing currents in professional political theory or philosophy. Morrison criticized the conceit, once as dominant among US literary historians as it is among contemporary political philosophers, that "traditional, canonical American literature is free of, uninformed, and unshaped by the four-hundred-year-old presence of, first, Africans and then African-Americans in the United States." This assumption that "black people signified little or nothing in the imagination of white American writers," Morrison argues, is demonstrably false if we take seriously the metaphorical and narratological practices, self-reflexive or allegorical themes—and, I will add, archival traces—through which white writers engage and invoke African American presence and imbricate their work with judgments about race and its politics.[60]

Building on Morrison's pathbreaking insights in literary criticism and hermeneutics, a critical theory of exemplarity abjures, or at least holds provisionally at bay, popular keywords of contemporary critical theory like *silence* or *absence.* Instead it insists that we patiently observe and critically excavate the oft-overlooked African American presence in philosophy and political thought. Even where references to the civil rights movement seem marginal, rote, or even tool-like in service to abstract conceptual or normative judgments, the philosophical stakes of exemplarity are often deceptively significant. "It would be a pity," Morrison warns, "if the criticism of [American] literature continued to shellac those [canonical] texts, immobilizing their complexities and power and laminations just below its tight, reflecting surface, . . . too polite or too fearful to notice a disrupting darkness before its eyes." Following Morrison's insights, my wager is that the critique of exemplarity allows us to productively plumb this disruptive darkness. Anticipating her critics (and perhaps mine), Morrison is worth quoting at length: "Surely, it will be said, white America has considered questions of morality and ethics, the supremacy of mind and vulnerability of body, the blessings and liabilities of progress and modernity, without reference to the situation of its black population. After all, it will be argued, where does one find a fulsome record that such a referent was part of these deliberations? My answer to these questions is another: where is it not?"[61] Morrison's argument was meant to operate as a sweeping interpretive lens for American literary history *writ large*. For all its insights in that domain, however, I want to insist that it is arguably on even more solid footing and of greater political and philosophical urgency with regard to the civil rights movement given its exemplarity in political thought and judgment.[62]

In *A Theory of Justice* (1971), for instance, Rawls influentially characterized his defense of civil disobedience as an attempt to "set . . . the sort of conception" offered by Martin Luther King Jr.'s 1963 "Letter from a Birmingham Jail" into "a wider framework."[63] Rawls's interpretation—or as I will argue later, his conscription—of King as an exemplar for his philosophy of civil disobedience was swiftly absorbed by a field stubbornly resistant to competing interpretations of the movement and too narrow in its self-description to carefully interrogate the range of questions animating King's own sophisticated efforts in public philosophy and political theory.[64]

A handful of Rawls's contemporaries tried to push their colleagues to rethink their reading of the movement's exemplarity, arguing that his invocation of King and the civil rights movement reflected a deep mischaracterization of American society and that it relied on dangerous conceptual confusions of black activist arguments (treating, for example, the acceptance of arrest and punishment as expressing a more comprehensive fidelity to the extant legal order).[65] Dramatizing the profound tensions between King's thematization of civil disobedience and Rawls's account, these critics charged Rawls with obscuring the contentious and radical character of King's politics and reifying an ideal of protest that would discredit significant and defensible modes of dissent or wrongly preclude egalitarian justifications for protest against structural forms of injustice. A more recent wave of theorists and critics, writing in the wake of Black

Lives Matter and Occupy Wall Street, has taken up this earlier critique, exploring the history of ideas and the construction of prevailing narratives to understand (and often defend) a wider range of disobedience and justifications of protest that strain beyond liberalism.[66] Yet more fundamentally challenging to liberal political philosophy and its theory of protest is where the critique of Rawls's particular account of civil rights exemplarity reveals its subtle role and traces in the broader architecture of Rawlsian liberalism, including formulations about the relationship of the burdens of political judgment to the lexical priority of distinct principles of justice, the theodicean tasks of political philosophy, and even the normative demands of public reason.

In the last case, for example, Rawls's arguments about public reason are developed through the concepts of *public speech* and *civility* that he pioneered within his discussions of civil disobedience and legal obligation. In those earlier formulations, Rawls famously argued that when deliberating on matters concerning the society's constitutional essentials and most fundamental institutions, citizens and public officials must avoid appeals to religious reason or "comprehensive" moral doctrine.[67] By restricting one's public justifications for political decisions principally to public political values (e.g., reciprocity, equal political and civil liberty, fair value of opportunity, or fair rules for assessing evidence), Rawls argued that democratic citizens could show respect for our fellow "free and equal" citizens and avoid subjecting them to exercises of power justified solely by worldviews to which they could not reasonably be expected to assent.

When circulating this argument in draft form, however, Rawls was challenged to rethink this "exclusive" view as too strict, in part on the grounds that it would objectionably exclude from the acceptable boundaries of public reason the arguments of abolitionists and civil rights activists who appealed to prophetic Christianity to wrest the possibility of justice from an enslaving and an apartheid society, respectively.[68] Approvingly citing the example of Martin Luther King, Rawls developed an inclusive view that allows one to make religious arguments that aim to establish political justice in a specific condition of injustice—where a society is "*not* well ordered and there is profound division about constitutional essentials."[69] Pushed by critics like Michael Sandel to further consider whether this account of public reason sufficiently appreciated the distinctive public philosophical contributions of figures like King or others in the civil rights struggle, Rawls revised his view once more.[70] His last considered position (which he called, following his student, the philosopher Erin Kelly, a "wide" view of public reason) allowed for reasonable religious arguments to be advanced at *all* times if citizens justified their arguments "in due course" through public, political reasons.[71] The exemplars anchoring the revision were, once again, familiar. There could be "no better example to illustrate the force of public reason in political life," Rawls suggests, than the tradition of prophetic agitation in defense of racial justice that he associates with Abraham Lincoln, nineteenth-century abolitionism, and the civil rights movement.[72]

Bracketing, for now, the persuasiveness of Rawls's particular claims or the historical interpretations from which he constructs them, I want to draw attention simply to the intimate rhetorical and conceptual relationship to the example of the civil rights movement. A pattern of reasoning pervades contemporary political thought: the example of the civil rights movement drives an elaborate theoretical architecture toward revision and reconciliation to its exemplarity, generates new conceptual categories and norms, or is invoked as ideally illustrative or disclosive of some crucial matter of political or ethical judgment. Similar mappings of civil rights exemplarity could be produced about the role of affect in politics, the alleged tension between political demands for recognition and those for redistribution, the ethics of dissent and disobedience, and the politics of constitutional interpretation.[73] This is to be expected insofar as grappling with exemplarity allows us to communicate in the absence of shared standards, organize what may come into view for evaluative judgment, and generate new norms.

The underlying contention here, to put a finer point on it, is that "examples do not merely illustrate, but produce knowledge and condition its production."[74] In other words, to take something as an example or as exemplary is not to engage in pure description. Instead it "already implies comparison and differentiation, that is, a linguistic structuring of perception, be it in the form of concepts or of narrative."[75] It is not so much that examples betray us by virtue of their being fixed (which in fact, they are not) but that in embodying presuppositions they tend to structure our understanding, put pressure on our evaluative judgment and concept formation, and habituate us to certain presumptions or conventions.

To speak in the language of exemplarity, at least in critical theory, means to take notice of this curious phenomenon. It means to subject to critical attention how particulars come to "*mingle* the singular with the normative" and to try to understand the kind of force they exert over and through our judgment as they circulate through thought, discourse, and other forms of symbolic practices.[76] Doing so requires that we take seriously Hannah Arendt's allegation that "most concepts in the historical and political sciences . . . have their origin in some particular historical incident," which "we then proceed to make . . . 'exemplary'—to see in the particular what is valid for more than one case."[77] It then demands that we accept the task of unraveling the epistemological, ethical, and political consequences of this oft-unstated genealogy, hoping the resulting discoveries offer not just a more faithful account of our interlocutors' arguments and excavation of their presuppositions but also disclose precise pressure points for more efficacious and self-reflexive practices of critique.

In this view, practicing the critical philosophy of race in the present entails something more than the inclusion of forgotten figures or lost histories. More fundamentally, it means unraveling the ideological uses and abuses of African American history that already circulate through political philosophy (often in the examples embedded in narratives, metaphors, and archival gestures favored by liberalism) so that we might avoid being conscripted into ways of philosophically proceeding that are ultimately self-undermining. The goal is instead to clear this treacherous ground for more emancipatory efforts in theory and praxis.

This conception of the tasks of critical thought also shares a great deal with that advanced by the philosopher Thomas McCarthy, who argues that normative political theory and political philosophy

> always [rely] upon implicit background assumptions drawn from some preunderstanding of contemporary society's structures, dynamics, potentials, and dangers. These implicit "images" or "models" of society tacitly enter into normative-theoretical constructions and often play a covert role in what appear to be purely normative disagreements. . . . These considerations strongly suggest that such understandings, images, or models of society, which are always at work, though usually only tacitly, in normative theorizing, have to become an explicit theme if political theorists hope to avoid exalting intuitive preunderstandings of their social contexts into universal ideals.[78]

An essential and productive site for excavating what McCarthy calls "background assumptions" and "preunderstandings" are precisely those moments in rhetoric and text where the appeal to historical exemplarity is meant to anchor normative judgment, give content to or serve as a vector for conceptual abstraction, and scaffold our arguments and ideals, expectations and commitments.

Even where exemplary events appear in the guise of a ready-at-hand "mere" example whose import is presumed so obvious as to warrant nothing but brief mention, they nevertheless draw on larger practices of signification that may profoundly shape and thematize the imagined terrain and boundaries of abstractions like democracy, freedom, citizenship, and disobedience, as we shall see in the civil rights movement case. Further, exemplary events and figures play an outsize, if not always well-understood or explicitly thematized, role in the hard ethical-existential quandaries that politics raises. Discussions of "soulcraft"—the education of virtue, the disciplining of affect, the morphology of moral action—often draw on civil rights exemplars like King or Rosa Parks to persuade us and guide our judgments about character and praxis. Stories about the putative end of slavery or the heroic sufferings of civil rights activists, moreover, often have a way of emerging when we confront hard questions about what we owe to each other and whether our societies (here, America in particular) can bear reasonable hope of overcoming injustice, furthering vital ideals, or validating our allegiances and sacrifices to collectivities or struggles larger than ourselves. Exemplarity, in this context, thus functions as an obscured force within our political imaginations, partially authorizing and constituting the judgments, rules, and principles we generate and defend in the course of moral and political argument. Irene Harvey illuminates this point, pushing each of us as readers to ask, "How do the examples betray what they are supposed to exemplify or reproduce? Are they in fact productive and creative rather than reproductive? Are they pre-text that only appears in the guise of a postscript, seeming to come after the fact as accidental appendages to the theory, but are in fact its progenitors, its unacknowledged city fathers?"[79]

A compelling answer to this line of questioning and this search for our "unacknowledged city fathers" must scrutinize the appearance of historical reference in political and public philosophy even as "mere" example. Indeed, it must do so even where historical examples do not appear under the banners of realism or republicanism, perhaps the traditions in contemporary political theory that flaunt their citation of history most ostentatiously.[80] This interpretive approach is perhaps best characterized as *excavation* insofar as it aims to disinter those gestures and references to exemplary events scattered throughout philosophical and political discourse. The aim is to interrogate the uses to which these invocations get conscripted, the abstractions they appear to authorize, and their prismatic function as structuring nexuses for common discourse, disagreement, critique, and judgment. The hope is that in reconstructing this economy of historical exemplarity within texts and discourses, we might make interpretive advances in understanding various intellectuals or traditions and better grasp the significance of historical imagination's structuring hold on political thinking. This, I aim to show, is crucial for the practice of critique with an emancipatory interest in black flourishing and freedom.[81]

The Crisis of Civil Rights Exemplarity

Before we go any further, it is crucial to underscore the above point that exemplarity is not fixed, nor is it unmediated or necessarily uncontested. Admittedly, where exemplary events are embedded within authoritative traditions of interpretation, they can become so familiar and our judgments concerning them so reflexive as to become intuitive, passing without attention or extensive comment. This is perhaps why talk about the exemplarity of the civil rights movement can at first glance appear all too obvious or even trite. The civil rights movement remains arguably the most celebrated political phenomenon of twentieth-century American history, likely competing only with the Allied forces' defeat of the Third Reich in World War II.[82] In our contemporary political moment, where extreme partisan polarization is parasitic on, and amplified by, racialized distrust and hostility, it is especially conspicuous that a wide swath of ordinary citizens routinely cite civil rights movement luminaries like King, Parks, and John Lewis as their most admired Americans while commentators of all stripes invoke the words and deeds of movement heroes in political argument and civic celebration.[83]

The very landscape of American communities, many of which commemorate movement events through a built environment of streets, schools, memorials, museums, and other structures that bear the names of movement heroes, seems to root this exemplarity in the relevant permanence of asphalt, concrete, and bronze. Well over a dozen major monuments and museums across the country already commemorate the civil rights movement, and even in the midst of the Great Recession's severe consequences for state finances, legislatures in the former Confederate states of Alabama, Florida, and Mississippi appropriated funds to open civil rights museums.[84] While absorbed in our daily concerns and ordinary purposes, these monuments may occasionally fail to attract sustained attention, appearing as mundane features of the world around us; yet the very habits of navigating this landscape "allows a certain vision of the past to be incorporated into the everyday settings and activities of the city, structuring the very language that people use" in the everyday practices of navigation and description.[85]

At the groundbreaking ceremony for the historic King monument in Washington, DC (currently the only one on the National Mall dedicated to an individual who did not serve as president), then-President George W. Bush celebrated the memorial's location "between the Jefferson and Lincoln Memorials" as "unit[ing] the men who declared the promise of America and defended the promise of America with the man who redeemed the promise of America."[86] Later, in an address to the NAACP, Bush offered a rapprochement in his long-standing feud with the nation's most legendary civil rights organization by proclaiming not only the "heroic" legacy of King and the civil rights movement but also the movement's status as a veritable second founding of the United States.[87]

Memorialization suggests, as two prominent geographers argue, "that a memorial's message enjoys a measure of orthodoxy," allowing "a particular interpretation of the past" to accrue "the power of the norm."[88] Yet if the statues of Confederate rebels toppled and defaced in the 2020 wave of anti-racist protest and rebellion could testify to anything beyond the thoughtlessness of their creators and the cruelty of their commissioners, they would be among the first to remind us that memorialization and commemoration do not permanently settle conflicts of interpretation and judgment. Even where, in their symbolic power, they seem to deter a coming storm, monuments cannot prevent such reckonings through magnitude or majesty.

Thus, we should not be altogether caught off guard to find that in recent years, beneath the apparent concord of civil rights celebration lies a bubbling torrent of dissent, skepticism, and perhaps outright cynicism toward the dominant tropes and themes that govern interpretations and representations of the movement. A growing number of activists, professional historians, and progressive commentators on problems of race and disadvantage suggest that our culture's compulsive references to the civil rights movement are less a furtherance of the movement's genuine ideals and greatest achievements than a veritable parade of "distortions, embellishments, and omissions."[89] This is the subject of Part Two of this book, which diagnoses the collapse of the exemplarity of the master narrative and its authoritative pillars before I defend a new philosophy of civil rights historiography.

Following Julian Bond, the civil rights activist turned politician and intellectual, critics of mainstream civil rights narratives argue that popular civil rights talk (and a good deal of canonical historiography) trafficked in misrepresentation and illusion for so long that there now exists a master narrative of civil rights memory that has become the basis of a new national mythology. As Bond neatly summarizes this master narrative,

> Traditionally, relationships between the races in the South were oppressive. In 1954 [with the *Brown v. Board of Education* decision outlawing mandated segregation in schools], the Supreme Court decided this was wrong. Inspired by the court, courageous Americans, Black and white, took protest to the street, in the form of sit-ins, bus boycotts, and freedom rides. The protest movement, led by the brilliant and eloquent Dr. Martin Luther King Jr., aided by a sympathetic federal government, most notably the [John F. and Robert F.] Kennedy brothers and a born-again Lyndon Johnson, was able to make America understand racial discrimination as a moral issue. Once Americans understood that discrimination was wrong, they quickly moved to remove racial prejudice and discrimination from American life, as evidenced by the Civil Rights Acts of 1964 and 1965. Inexplicably, just as the civil rights victories were piling up, many African Americans, under the banner of Black Power, turned their backs on American society.[90]

In the master narrative, which spans from the famed bus boycott in Montgomery, Alabama, to King's assassination in Memphis, Tennessee, it is a spasm of militancy and "identity politics" that crested under the sign of Black Power after King's death that marks the embittered denouement of the civil rights movement. While lamenting how the black movement lost its way in the wake of its significant victories, however, these accounts treat the profound national mourning unleashed in the wake of King's death as consolidating the gains of civil rights lawmaking and the decisive defeat of Jim Crow.[91] The triumph of the civil rights movement, in this view, ushered in a purified legal order, a dramatic transformation of racial attitudes, and an unprecedented era of black opportunity. While, for complex and contested reasons, many blacks are still unable to seize the new opportunities of the age, the successes of the civil rights movement and the redeemed American civic ideals they represent reflect an epochal political transformation most fully reflected in the historic election of Barack Obama as the first African American president.[92]

Some scholars, surveying the vast reach of this master narrative and its imagery, have gone so far as to describe it as a kind of consensus memory in American life.[93] The thematic foci, periodization, central cast of characters, political vocabularies, and ethical visions that anchor the master narrative of civil rights history enjoy pride of place in the broader public sphere. Popular culture and museum exhibitions, state monuments, and viral internet content—even political rhetoric and school curricula—reflect and reproduce its influence and treat it as central to civic identity.[94]

The master narrative plays a central role in what the political scientist Rogers Smith calls American "stories of peoplehood."[95] As bearers of particular interpretations of history and social structures or as accounts of collective identity and purposes, these stories of peoplehood provide motivating accounts of what binds us to others in and across political communities and other forms of solidarity. Performing the vital work of constituting political subjects and our orientation to our society, these narratives shape our judgments about what we owe to each other or what counts as honorable or heroic forms of action for people like "us," defining the contours of political collectives in the process.[96]

Obama, it is important to note, routinely invoked a similar version of civil rights history as a central theme of his articulations of American civic identity and its tasks in the present. At the funeral of the legendary civil rights activist and long-standing Georgia Congressman John Lewis, Obama argued that the movement, and Lewis's life in particular, "redeemed" and "vindicated the faith in our founding." Lewis and the civil rights movement, Obama contended, exemplify the "most American of ideas"—namely, "that any of us ordinary people without rank or wealth or title or fame can somehow point out the imperfections of this nation, and come together, and challenge the status quo, and decide that it is in our power to remake this country that we love until it more closely aligns with our highest ideals."[97] This idea, a recurrent theme in Obama's speeches, led him elsewhere to render Martin Luther King Jr. as not simply a heroic figure or moral exemplar but "quintessentially American." For Obama, King's exemplarity is meant to remind Americans that "for all the hardships we've endured, for all our sometimes tragic history, ours is a story of optimism and achievement and constant striving that is unique on this Earth . . . [and] why the rest of the world still looks to us to lead."[98]

Obama's rendering of the exemplarity of the civil rights movement, with its strident optimism about racial reconciliation, the egalitarian horizons of American capitalist democracy, and the implications of US global dominance, was met with fierce criticism in important corners. The philosopher and activist Cornel West has argued that Obama's gestures toward King hypocritically obscured the strident anti-imperialism, antimilitarism, and economic egalitarianism of King's political philosophy. Asked by *The New York Times* to imagine what he would say given thirty seconds alone with Obama, West, the most visible critic of the administration from the black Left, focused his fury on the contrast between the president's symbolic envelopment in the legacy of the civil rights movement and the domestic and foreign policy actions issued from the Oval Office. As West exclaimed, "Look at that bust of Martin Luther King Jr. in the Oval Office and recognize that tears are flowing when you let Geithner and others shape your economic policy, when you refuse to focus on poor and working people or when you drop the drone bombs that kill innocent civilians. [Secretary of the Treasury] Tim Geithner does not represent the legacy of Martin King."[99]

West's denunciations provoked a vicious backlash. Some insisted that racial solidarity and political realism obliged black critics of President Obama to be more circumspect in their disagreements.[100] But rather than be distracted by the tone of West's criticisms of Obama or the proxy defenses by the former president's allies, we should note how West's critique is noticeably immanent. In other words, even as it embraces radically divergent conclusions, it begins from an overlapping considered conviction about the enduring *exemplarity* of King and the civil rights movement.

Perhaps in subtle recognition of his vulnerability to immanent criticism on the terrain of exemplarity, Obama devoted a large section of his 2009 Nobel Peace Prize address to distancing himself from what he described as King's "idealized" views on war, while insisting that the normative expectations of his role as commander in chief meant that he could not "be guided" by Mahatma Gandhi's or King's "examples alone."[101] Even for those sympathetic to Obama's appeal to the genuine ethical and structural constraints on the occupant of the White House, however, such role distinctions could not settle the philosophical merits of the disagreement.[102]

Even while rejecting out of hand the idea that an American president could ever, given the demands of the office, truly "represent the legacy of Dr. King," the social scientist Glenn Loury nevertheless insists that determining the rightful "heirs" to the "prophetic" tradition of which King and many civil rights activists are a part is a critical political and intellectual project. The integrity of our memory of the tradition's exemplars, Loury argues, is a "precious resource" for Americans of all backgrounds, one not to be sold cheaply "on the auction block of Obama's political ambitions," lifted up where convenient and disavowed when not.[103] Such remarks, and the passions excited by this debate, disclose some measure of the profound significance many of us ascribe to the task of curating, clarifying, and debating the precise contours of civil rights exemplarity in political and philosophical disagreement.

Haunting such debates, as should be clear, are metatheoretical issues concerning competing proprietary claims over the authority to publicly interpret, inherit, and invoke the movement's legacy. One of the more unexpected legacies of the civil rights movement is that appeals to its exemplarity seem to extend across nearly all meaningful principles of socioeconomic and political differentiation, with the exception of the most strident authoritarians and unreconstructed white supremacist hate groups.[104] Desmond King and Rogers Smith, for instance, contend that the extreme partisanship of the past three decades of American politics is due in large part to polarization stemming from, or at least in great part underwritten by, divisive debates over racial policy between advocates of race-conscious and color-blind politics and public policy. Yet despite the deep political and social disagreements that characterize the contemporary scene, King and Smith acknowledge that "both sides of this debate have long presented themselves as the true heirs of the preceding, triumphant civil rights movement."[105]

Roughly thirty years after the Civil Rights Act of 1964, for instance, some of the most prominent leaders of the Christian Right attempted to reframe their movement as the struggle of an aggrieved and marginalized minority against the intolerance of the wider society and thus as a "descendant of the African American civil rights movement."[106] More farcically, in 2010 the far-right propagandist Glenn Beck, infamous for alleging that Obama, despite his white mother, "has a deep-seated hatred for white people or the white culture," took the occasion of the forty-seventh anniversary of the March on Washington for Jobs and Freedom to host his own "March on Washington."[107] Nearly fifteen years later, President Donald Trump's second inauguration fell on Martin Luther King Jr. Day, and in his address he obligingly thanked "the Black and Hispanic communities" for their electoral support before declaring that in Dr. King's "we will strive together to make his dream a reality."[108]

To put it exceedingly politely, there are glaringly obvious reasons to treat the words and acts of such political figures as falling far short of sincerity. Yet the charge of disingenuousness only goes so far. The rhetoric occasioned by such ceremonial and symbolic occasions reflects, at the very least, even the demagogue's expectations of their audience and the broader public. These utterances and initiatives anticipate, therefore, that huge numbers of Americans want, in some respect, to identify with this historical event and that some significant cohort treats its example as significant to the articulation of their principles and purposes and orientation in narratives that connect the past to judgments about the present and its possible futures. It is in recognition of this import and the dangers inherent in it that the historian Jacqueline Dowd Hall used her presidential address to the Organization of American Historians as an opportunity to issue a clarion call to scholars and storytellers, pleading for a new civil rights movement history, one "harder to celebrate as a natural progression of American values. Harder to cast as a satisfying morality tale. Most of all, harder to simplify, appropriate, and contain."[109]

The Critique of the Master Narrative: Ideology and Alienation

Answering Hall's call to arms, a rising wave of historians and critics have come to condemn this orthodox Montgomery-to-Memphis master narrative of civil rights history, claiming that it is "built on a number of misleading representations of modern US racial history" that indulge "fallacies about the South as an exception to national racial norms," fail to "recognize the historical depth and heterogeneity of black struggles against racism," and unduly narrow the political scope and geopolitical contours of black agency.[110] The master narrative, they argue, is too easily pressed into the service of falsely triumphalist judgments about American society, tragic blindness toward our civilizational pathologies, and the reflexive condemnation of contemporary movements for social justice. This is especially true of the iconography around King. Although implicit, this argument discloses some of the consequences of exemplarity. To the extent we are prone to invoke, analogize, or appeal to the civil rights movement when thinking or acting politically (including reasoning about abstract ideals like equality, citizenship, solidarity, and antiracism), our practices and judgments will reflect some measure of the particular understanding of "the civil rights movement" we bring to bear.

Translated into the language of philosophy and critical theory, the charges they press against the master narrative are that it is *ideological* and *alienating*. To describe the master narrative as ideological, at least in the pejorative sense developed by critical theorists, is to claim that it has epistemic defects, oppressive functions, and a pathological etiology that serve to buttress injustice and frustrate the practice of emancipatory politics.[111] Revisionist critics, therefore, see one of their tasks as to unmask the ways that relevant facts about civil rights figures and events, or race and American political development, are distorted, obscured, misrepresented, or manipulated, revealing how such illusions contribute to maintaining an objectionable social order.[112]

Particularly vexing to revisionists like Hall is how what they consider to be narrowly rendered depictions of movement demands regarding racial injustice (e.g., the end to formal legal inequality, invidious racial classification in law, and public expression of explicitly racist insult) provide valuable scaffolding for reactionary or quiescent politics in the present. It may seem odd to ascribe such power to historical representation, especially in a country where basic civics and historical knowledge are abysmal, but for over four decades, the rhetoric of American politicians, social movements, and public figures have been reliably laden with references and encomiums to the civil rights movement. Their appeals to the civil rights movement aim beyond establishing or reiterating legal and bureaucratic precedents of civil rights law to enact a broader civic pedagogy. The narration of movement history and the citation of its leading lights are meant to teach the public about the ethical commitments that should constitute civic ideals and American peoplehood. It aspires, in part through ubiquity, repetition, and ritual, to train the citizenry to adopt a particular orientation to our social and political institutions.[113]

For President Jimmy Carter, the chief lesson of the civil rights movement was the need for, and virtue of, a kind of prophetic trust in democratic ideals and American government, "even in its darkest days." The challenge of the present, he declared in 1979, was for citizens and the government to "stay true to the trust placed in America by the civil rights movement and Martin Luther King Jr. He trusted our country. He trusted our Government. He trusted our people, even when an objective observer would say in complete truth, there were times when our Government, its laws, and many of its people didn't deserve to be trusted."[114] Celebrating how King's actions "prevailed," Carter argued that the civil rights movement secured America's moral leadership across the globe on questions of human rights and justice. "We can speak out now," he proclaimed, "as a nation with one voice on the sensitive issue of human rights all around the world, because Martin Luther King Jr. and the civil rights movement helped to liberate all Americans from the chains of official racism here at home."[115]

Echoing and radically extending Carter's judgment that the achievements of the civil rights movement ultimately redound to the greatness of American civilization, his successor, Ronald Reagan, signed into law in 1983 the federal holiday honoring Martin Luther King Jr. On the occasion, Reagan celebrated the self-correcting nature of American democracy and its commitment to basic liberties of speech and dissent, proclaiming that "as a democratic people, we can take pride in the knowledge that we Americans recognized a grave injustice and took action to correct it. And we should remember that in far too many countries, people like Dr. King never have the opportunity to speak out at all." While Reagan privately and obliquely criticized King's personal life, alleged sympathies with communism, and support for expansive civil rights protections, in public he packaged King to speak to the essential goodness he identified at the core of American civic life. "Ultimately," Reagan argued, "the great lesson of Martin Luther King Jr.'s life was this: He was a great man who wrested justice from the heart of a great country, and he succeeded because that great country had a heart to be seized."[116]

For historians like Hall and Jeanne Theoharis, another incisive critic of civil rights memory, such statements wrongly treat racial injustice as aberrational rather than enduring and offer a false, flattering picture of American democracy as akin to a "self-cleaning oven, powerful, strong, and constantly self-improving."[117] By rendering the civil rights movement a largely successful battle over the American heart that could not genuinely have ended otherwise, or as a war against invidious legal classification rather than the pursuit of economic justice and sociopolitical reconstruction, the master narrative has paradoxical consequences. It tends, on their view, to support a misguided turn toward cultural deviance as the chief explanatory factor in persisting forms of black disadvantage while licensing the demonization of so-called race-conscious or "progressive welfarist" public policies meant to further reparative justice and the fair value of equal opportunity for African Americans.[118] These policies, too, get tarred with the stigma against invidious racial discrimination.

The coup de grâce for the neoconservative reaction, in this account, was the discovery that by treating so-called color blindness as the normative and constitutional horizon of the civil rights movement, they could rhetorically portray affirmative action and reparative justice policies as a new iteration of (anti-white) racist discrimination while claiming the mantle of the movement for themselves.[119] While the term *color-blind* comes from Justice John Marshall Harlan's well-known dissent in the 1896 Supreme Court case *Plessy v. Ferguson,* where he lambasted the constitutionality of "separate but equal" racial segregation, neoconservatives rarely miss an opportunity to conscript King's image to their cause.[120] American conservatism, at least in the wake of the master narrative, found itself for decades compulsively repeating the line from King's 1963 address to the March on Washington for Jobs and Freedom in which he expresses hope that his children "will one day live in a nation where they will not be judged by the color of their skin but by the content of their character."[121]

Such distillations of King's political philosophy are so at odds with his explicit endorsement of race-conscious redress, from affirmative action to school integration, that they raise the suspicion of outright cynicism among critics. More sympathetically, however, it seems that at least the following must be true: such readings clearly confuse King's prophetic advocacy for the utopian ideal of a fair, truly color-blind society with their own desire to impose color blindness as a legal and normative standard in the present without first—as King and other movement activists insisted—attempting to ameliorate the background injustices of a society indelibly shaped by black oppression and exploitation.[122] The consequences, according to critics, have been devastating. Insofar as the master narrative undergirds this politics, it "impoverishes public discourse, discourages investment in public institutions, and undermines our will to address the inequalities and injustices that surround us now."[123]

One way to think of the political philosophic legacy of the Black Lives Matter movement is that it marries this critique of ideology with a less familiar charge of *alienation* in order to discover new vectors of agency and political organization. In the view of many Black Lives Matter–era intellectuals, prevailing representations of the civil rights movement can diminish our contemporary sense of our own agency or delude us with illusory pictures of social change, conflict, and American political development.[124] The inspiration it engenders, too saccharine for lasting effect, leaves the imbibers of the master narrative careening from euphoric imitation to exhaustion and depletion.

The master narrative, they charge, has the insidious effect of refracting contemporary acts of protest, politics, and even personal conduct in the present through hallowed but hagiographical and mythic images of the civil rights movement. Seeing and judging the political demands of the present through evaluative standards, ideals, and exemplars refracted through the distorted lens of the master narrative leaves us unnecessarily demoralized or ultimately unable to find proper bearings in the present. The cultural dominion of the master narrative, in this argument, leads too many of us to imagine ourselves as perpetually falling short of our ancestors' impossible standard, prone to derivative, impotent imitation or worse, cruelly attached to illusory forms of political optimism that no longer should have warrant.[125]

Drawing on the philosopher Rahel Jaeggi's careful reconstruction of the alienation concept, we might say that the revisionists contend that the power of the master narrative creates a distorted relationship to ourselves and the world, posing a serious obstacle to our ability to achieve productive forms of identification, meaning, or self-realization in our practices, social roles, and scripts of identity.[126] Estranging us from our desires and actions or making us powerless to act meaningfully at all, they charge the master narrative with paradoxically deepening our contemporary political despair and paralysis. It is a form of exemplarity that leaves us incapable of effectively accessing the profound ethical, cultural, and political resources they insist are still contained within a "usable" past of the civil rights movement. This past, which they endeavor to narrate, is one shorn of illusions that have grown thick and suffocating.

The problem of civil rights exemplarity swelled into a matter of palpable angst and urgent public debate with the eruption of Black Lives Matter. This complex, sprawling, and at times inchoate movement of activists, dissidents, rebellious citizens, artists, entertainers, and others coalesced in the wake of a series of high-profile police and vigilante killings of African Americans that began during the Obama presidency. Almost immediately, one of the central axes of debate about the movement concerned its degree of fidelity to, or apostasy from, the imagined exemplarity of the civil rights movement.

Glenn Loury, for instance, once again raised the specter of civil rights exemplarity, this time to rebuke the mass mobilization of racial justice advocacy around the 2014 killing of Michael Brown in Ferguson, Missouri, by Darren Wilson, a white police officer. Although Brown's killing, followed by the Sophoclean indignity of his corpse lying in the August sun for over four hours, was the immediate impetus for public mourning and grief, the Ferguson Police Department's militaristic repression of dissent sparked open rebellion against a city government organized as a near-colonial enterprise of economic exploitation and racial discrimination.[127] Reflecting on the early Black Lives Matter movement, Loury suggests that sober reflection on the civil rights movement should cast doubt on the wisdom and viability of contemporary antiracist organizing. Characterizing Brown as the aggressor in the incident and declaring him, therefore, "no Rosa Parks," Loury warned that organizing in the face of the ambiguous circumstances of Brown's death and conduct would tether too many critical political goals to the unfavorable facts of his case. Further, unlike the struggle against Jim Crow segregation, Loury contended that Black Lives

Matter activists had neither a clearly unjust, racist law to oppose nor a "legislative agenda activists can point to as a plausible remedy for the conditions we all lament." Instead of treating "structural problems—too few jobs, concentrated poverty, failing schools" as "issues of race," Loury argued, activists would be better served by focusing on "common maladies" across the color line and recognizing that "issues about crime, policing, and poverty cannot be addressed in the ways that traditional civil rights issues could."[128]

Ironically, many leading Black Lives Matter activists shared, in broad contours, Loury's account of the civil rights movement, complaining that the movement's exemplarity is unduly suffocating of the kind of radical egalitarianism and thoroughgoing critique that the present demands. Seeing in arguments like Loury's a kind of "respectability politics" and accommodation to antiblack ideology, they seek to rhetorically and symbolically distance themselves from prominent imaginings of the civil rights movement. Opal Tometi, Alicia Garza, and Patrisse Khan-Cullors, the three founders of the #BlackLivesMatter organization (which does not include all forms of solidarity forged under the description "Black Lives Matter"), proudly describe their organization as one "full of leaders from the margins" that "rejects the compromise and respectability politics of the past."[129] The Christian activist and writer Rahiel Tesfamariam, who was prominently arrested in Ferguson protests, similarly counts respectability politics as among the authoritative criteria of civil rights–era activism that the contemporary struggle rightly rejects. "For this generation," she writes, "there's no need to hide behind a veil of purity or wear a suit to have an authoritative seat at the table. This is a movement that encourages all to 'come as you are.' Natural. Bohemian. Rebellious. Tatted up. Provocative. Ratchet."[130] The rapper-activist Tef Poe, of Hands Up United, who famously pronounced that "this ain't your grandparents' civil rights movement," described the Ferguson uprising as a vigilant fight against "all forms of respectability politics."[131] Elsewhere he forcefully argues that "we live in a world where people are telling us to be respectable to targets that just aren't respectable. There's nothing respectable about white supremacy, there's nothing respectable about oppression, there's nothing respectable about sexism and misogyny, and rape and murder and pillage."[132]

Reflecting on such discord, a growing number of historians and scholars have grown more publicly vexed. How have we forgotten, for instance, that King's "I Have a Dream" speech proclaims that "we can never be satisfied as long as the Negro is the victim of the unspeakable horrors of police brutality" or "as long as the Negro's basic mobility is from a smaller ghetto to a larger one"?[133] Or how should we parse the argument in King's posthumously published *A Trumpet of Conscience* (1968), in which he describes the "historic social contribution" of youth activists in the civil rights movement as when they "threw off their middle-class values" and status symbols (e.g., "Brooks Brothers attire"), placed their "careers and wealth in a secondary role," and "cheerfully became jailbirds and troublemakers"?[134]

What about *Organizing Manual No. 2*, the pamphlet written largely by the leading movement organizer, Bayard Rustin, summarizing the goals and strategy of the 1963 March on Washington for Jobs and Freedom? There the focus is precisely on those structural problems that Loury describes as somehow outside the bounds of traditional civil rights or black movement concerns. Rustin writes of "the twin evils of racism and economic deprivation," which "rob all people . . . of dignity, self-respect, and freedom." They "impose a special burden on the Negro," however, who is "denied the right to vote, economically exploited, refused access to public accommodations, subjected to inferior education, and relegated to substandard ghetto housing." To combat these problems, march leaders demanded not just antidiscrimination laws but also "a massive federal program to train and place all unemployed workers—Negro and white—on meaningful and dignified jobs at decent wages," as well as a national minimum wage act.[135] The way leading depictions erase or flatten complex intramovement debates about virtue ethics and respectability, or justice and political economy, have led some historians to complain that the "inspirational stories [of the civil rights movement], with their distortions, embellishments, and omissions," have become the worst kind of "national fable," one that is itself "a potent obstacle and bludgeon used to diminish contemporary efforts" to achieve racial and economic justice.[136]

The Long Civil Rights Movement

The leading response thus far to these objections against the master narrative, at least among historians, has been the call to produce a new periodization and narrative of civil rights history they call the *long* civil rights movement. Their project, taken collectively, represents a concerted attempt to overthrow the traditional, classical frame of the civil rights movement that unfolds largely within the South, "from Montgomery to Memphis." This historiographical revolt, however, should not be construed as a simple debate about periodization; it seeks nothing less than to rewrite the story of the most famous popular movement in American history—its chronology, cast of characters, and central concerns—against a broader context and competing interpretation of American and world history.[137]

Long civil rights movement historians begin their accounts with the first great wave of northern and urban migration by African Americans following World War I and concurrent with the Bolshevik Revolution of 1917. This massive wave of urbanization and migration was followed by the explosion of leftist labor organizing by communists, socialists, civil rights organizations, black nationalists, and others from the 1920s until the 1940s that inaugurated the long civil rights movement. This first peak of movement activism is said to have reached its highest point in concert with the New Deal's articulation of economic rights, the emergence of mass consumer capitalism, and the overthrow of laissez-faire jurisprudence articulated in article 1, section 8, clause 3 of the Constitution (the so-called commerce clause), before staggering under the weight of popular anticommunism, divisions within and between organizations on the left, and other strategic missteps. In long civil rights movement historiography, the transition into World War II and the immediate postwar era is reinterpreted in light of this history and a related focus on the emerging geopolitical context. Thus, attention is drawn to the exemplary evil of the Holocaust, the formation of the United Nations and evolution of human rights discourses, the domestic and international politics of the Cold War, and so-called Third World anticolonial struggles—all of which contextually revise the interpretation of conventionally recognized events and actions in the civil rights movement while revealing new spaces of inquiry, undertheorized intellectual traditions, and overlooked normative ideals and conflicts. The upshot is a far more sprawling history of the civil rights revolt, a more complicated sense of the movement's relation to Black Power, and a sense that any account of the meaning of this movement and its much celebrated victories must be judged in light of the more radical freedom dreams that animated its most far-seeing visionaries.[138]

The central events and themes of the master narrative—school integration and *Brown* or the expansion of voting rights following the campaign in Selma, Alabama—yield pride of place in long civil rights historiography to a more arduous and halting struggle punctuated with unfamiliar characters and partial victories, the redemptive inquiry into outright defeats, and reflection on the roads not taken that, in light of the present, have themselves become exemplary. As Glenda Gilmore puts the point, "In the simplified stories that the media told of the movement, civil rights came to mean school integration, access to public accommodations, and voting rights." This narrative, moreover, has tragically "erased the complexity of a drive to eliminate the economic injustices wrought by slavery, debt peonage, and a wage labor system . . . [taken] residential desegregation off the agenda, apparently once and for all . . . [and] swept away connections among civil liberties, labor rights, and civil rights that liberals and radicals had carefully forged."[139] Or, as Nikhil Singh writes, "Many of the valuable insights derived from the ethics and politics of living and overcoming Jim Crow are now being squandered" by a "national forgetting of what Frederick Douglass called the standpoint of the victims in American history."[140]

In this commitment, long civil rights movement historians self-consciously follow in the pathbreaking footsteps of W. E. B. Du Bois, who at the end of his monumental tome *Black Reconstruction in America* (1935) distilled his long-standing critique of the American historical establishment's scholarship on slavery and emancipation into a merciless attack on what he rightfully called the "propaganda of history." In his brief bibliographical essay on sources that concludes the book, Du Bois, a trained historian who was the first African American to receive a doctoral degree from Harvard University, turned an obligatory scholarly ritual into an earth-shattering "arraignment of American historians and an indictment of their ideals."[141] Surveying the dominant historiography of slavery and post–Civil War Reconstruction, then led by the historians John Burgess and William Dunning and their students, Du Bois argued that the field's prevailing interpretations could be plausible only from within an epistemology presumptive of black inferiority and an ethics predicated on white supremacy.

Surveying monographs and monuments alike, Du Bois documents how the interpenetration of antiblack ideology, the interests of property owners, and narrow methodological convention led to the systematic burial of the actions and voices of African Americans underneath "silence and contempt," allowing "the most unfair caricatures" of black capabilities to stand in their stead.[142] In doing so, he argued, historians and other stewards of public memory did more than bury the Negro under an avalanche of degrading images and speculative race science. They also unduly diminished the scope and significance of the democratic strivings provisionally defeated with the collapse of the Reconstruction experiment. By obscuring the efforts of enslaved persons to win their freedom—first in flight from bondage, next in military battle, and then, tragically, in the aborted attempt to remake the political and economic foundations of American life through land redistribution, public education, and participatory parity—Du Bois alleged that the dominant histories of Reconstruction missed what he provocatively called "the real plot of the story"—namely, the vicissitudes of abolitionist and democratic struggle led by African Americans themselves in the wake of war.[143]

Narrative, Emplotment, and Historical Imagination

For all of its insight into the pernicious implications of the master narrative and exciting recovery of African American political history, long civil rights movement historiography is still not self-reflexive enough about a fundamental aspect of its canon and expression: its own narrative form or "plot." The shifts it makes in narrative mode and figurative language from the key texts of the master narrative reflect deeper ethical, epistemic, aesthetic, and political philosophic commitments that are not always clearly rendered or effectively defended. It evades this self-reflexivity in part because it frames its critique of the master narrative on a model of ideology and alienation critique that juxtaposes the "illusory" against the "real," suggesting that this collision will unmask the former as false and the latter as the true depiction of what is and what was.[144]

The problem with this approach is twofold. On the one hand, the zeal for a final unmasking of the master narrative as ideology contains a fervor for negation that, on historiographical grounds alone, need not stop at the revisionist stories of roads not taken and lost possibilities that undergird long civil rights movement historians. Negating the master narrative, in other words, underdetermines where one goes from there. It leaves the door ajar for subjecting even the above nods to redemptive hope and historical memory to unforgiving forms of critique.

This possibility, and the profound stakes of this critical indeterminacy, have become clearer with the emergence and consolidation of so-called Afropessimism among a small but influential group of critical theorists, social scientists, and historians.[145] Their views, which surged in influence amid a wave of unpunished police and vigilante killings of African Americans that started and stymied Black Lives Matter, are diametrically opposed to the master narrative. They refuse, in other words, to treat the civil rights movement as a moment of moral progress and emancipatory promise. Instead they see it as a moment where the fundamentally racist structure of US society was reconstituted and other forms of subjection (like class hierarchy or patriarchy) reentrenched. At odds with long civil rights movement historians, they argue not only that every ostensible possibility for black emancipation or multiracial democratic equality is always already foreclosed but also that in light of this judgment the so-called victories of civil rights agitation are less than partial; they are, in essence, nonevents.

Propelled both by the internal compulsion of negation and disappointments engendered by despair in the present, this judgment seeks justification within historical narratives that eschew the chronological ordering of conventional historical discourse. Constantly juxtaposing and rearranging judgments about the past, present, and future, the accumulated weight of stories of African American history is meant to dramatize what they judge to be unwavering domination underneath *apparent* political contingencies and victories. The aim is to show—as the historian Leon Litwack ironically described the steady state of black political history in his *How Free Is Free?*—how "it is all very different. It is all very much the same."[146]

Drawing on this narrative rendering of African American history, such figures defend models of self-conduct that enact self-professedly nihilist disavowals of political hope and practical faith. They reject, as fatally compromised, cruelly impossible ideals of black emancipation, egalitarian citizenship, social justice, and civic freedom.[147] This historical dynamic, once unmasked by their criticism, spills ever backward into the past; the failures of the civil rights movement are said to mirror earlier failures of emancipation from slavery. Indeed, such narratives regularly frame even emancipation as a nonevent: "Formally the Black subject was no longer a slave, but the same formative relation of structural violence that maintained slavery remained—upheld explicitly by the police (former slave catchers) and white supremacy generally—hence preserving the equation that Black equals socially dead."[148] Or, as Frank Wilderson puts it, "1865 is a blip on the screen" when compared to the "continuum of slavery-subjugation that Black people [continue to] exist in."[149] This approach to historical imagination is, as Saidiya Hartman writes, a kind of "recombinant narrative," which "weaves present, past, and future . . . in narrating the time of slavery as our present."[150]

The stridency of this school of criticism leaves the long civil rights movement narrator in a bind. How can they argue against the picture of the world offered up by the master narrative and at the same time contend with the more thoroughgoing negation of that narrative from the pessimists, a form of totalizing critique that threatens to sweep them right along with the tide? How do they explain the fact that the pessimists, too, draw on similar sources of discontent and similar skepticism about the adequacy of the interpretive keywords that hold the master narrative intact? In such a case, the assertion of the "truth" of the matter is necessary but insufficient.

The kinds of certainty that would compel agreement here are not forthcoming. This is not a disagreement, for instance, about whether Martin Luther King was assassinated on April 4, 1968. It is one that ranges across far more indeterminate grounds of judgment: What is the value of a defeated cause in retrospect or the significance of counterfactual thinking? How should we weigh the psychic costs of racial integration or the notable shift in white racial attitudes against the material circumstances of economic opportunity for African Americans? What are the criteria of significance that should govern what we include in our narratives of the "civil rights movement" or what we should leave out? What counts as a heroic or a wasted life or makes an investment in hope illusory and unjustified? And what makes us confident that the vocabularies and concepts we use to get a grasp on such questions—*race, racism, Jim Crow, blackness, democracy,* and *resistance*—are not self-defeating? Insofar as historical discourse, especially about exemplary events, presumes such answers in the complex arrangement of judgments that make up its narrative output, the idea of unmasking such questions as untrue and illusory from a neutral ground, much less one solely within historiography, seems implausible.

To find a way out of this bind, we need to turn back to Du Bois's idea of the "real plot" and not treat it as mere rhetorical gloss. The language of plot raises a number of profound questions about historical understanding that bear on the relationship of history, judgment, and political thinking generally and our concerns regarding the exemplarity of the civil rights movement more specifically. I want to insist not just on the fact of competing histories, or even the necessity of making judgments between them, but also that such evaluation must deal with the vehicles of *plot*—namely, stories and storytelling. In this I follow Du Bois's intimation of the extensive entanglement within historical representation between narrowly "scientific" historiographical questions like factual accuracy and interpretive plausibility and knottier epistemological, aesthetic, and ethical questions about the practice of storytelling, its possible relationships to the moral and ethical significance of its subject matter, and the place of peculiarly impactful stories in the web of narratives that constitute our life in common.

Du Bois's formulation of the problem suggests that the familiar historiographical question of better or worse ways of telling stories of the past, and even the more strident charge that some ways of talking about the past are ideological or alienating, all need to take seriously the problem of plot and all it entails regarding narrative structure, rhetorical figuration, and criteria of significance in historical discourse. To recover this less familiar thread and speak forthrightly of the "plot" of historical writing is immediately to draw attention to the fact that history, too, is a species of storytelling, where various facts of the past must be arranged, emphasized, and excluded to produce a narrative that can be understood.

As the philosopher and historian Hayden White has famously argued, "The historian confronts a veritable chaos of events already constituted, out of which he must choose the elements of the story he would like to tell . . . by including some events and excluding others, by stressing some and subordinating others," and—perhaps most important—by presenting them in story form "as a comprehensible process with a discernible beginning, middle, and end." For White, the question of what makes stories followable raises the issue of what kind of story is being presented. The question of how a particular story might be evaluated alongside other possible stories that might be told also raises this problem. Coining the concept of "emplotment" to capture this problematic, White pushes us to ask what kinds of archetypal plots, generic conventions, aesthetic motifs, tropes, and narrative modes are at work in the production and apprehension of narrative meaning in history.[151] What interpretive tools and categories do we need at our disposal to best orient ourselves to and within the historical imagination if, as White suggests, the question of emplotment is inextricable from questions of ethics, politics, and critique?

In this spirit, *Shattered Dreams, Infinite Hope* interrogates how exemplarity—in its articulations of the general or universal in politics and philosophy (e.g., conceptual constellations, normative commitments, idealizations, and abstractions) is often tethered to particular historical judgments and consequently implicated in practices and conflicts of historical narration. The far-reaching import of this entanglement between exemplarity, narrative, and judgment means that struggles over narrative or crises of narrative coherence have an unruly and contagious character for our thinking. Crises of exemplary narrative not only reflect broader problems that beset contemporary forms of life but also represent vital opportunities to become "insightfully aware of a previously uncritical relation to the past" and to use the occasion of narrative contention "to rethink our commitments to certain ideals and practices, perhaps to break free of them, by imagining previously untried or uncovering previously suppressed possibilities."[152]

In drawing attention to the link between historical example and historical narrative, I build on the claim, pressed most trenchantly by White, that historical accounts do not merely discover the "true story" or the unmediated "real" and simply relate it to us with rhetorical finesse. Instead histories organize events through narrative form and rhetorical figures and then produce imaginative representations of historical reality that entail various political, ethical, aesthetic, and ontological commitments. Historical discourse involves inevitably selective judgments about the inclusion and exclusion of events and characters, as well as the overarching development of a "structure of relationships"—including where a narrative begins and ends—through which "the events contained in the [historical] account are endowed with a meaning . . . as parts of an integrated whole."[153]

Even when political figures or theorists briefly invoke historical examples, they often arrange (or rely on others' arrangements of) various constitutive elements into the historical event or exemplar they invoke, enabling us to understand such invocations as situated within, or constituted by, *stories*. Moreover, insofar as stories are intelligible, coherent, and meaningful, they will necessarily deploy specific criteria of significance irreducible to positivistic attempts of causal explanation. These criteria will authorize, often implicitly, the inclusion, priority, and placement of particular events, personalities, and developments over others that might have plausibly been included or emphasized in alternative ways. Given this, White argues, it becomes incumbent on critical and philosophical accounts of historiography and historical narration to ask what notions of reality, criteria of significance, or styles of attention to the world authorize the construction of both particular narratives (or, for White, narrative *as such*).[154]

As W. B. Gallie has argued, "If it is true that in the physical sciences there is always a theory, it is no less true that in historical research there is always a story."[155] If being capable of following a story is constitutive of historical understanding, we must not only pay close attention to historical-explanatory arguments about causality embedded in particular accounts but also attend to the plot structure of historical narrative. We want to know how narratives' often implicit criteria of significance authorize certain moves of inclusion, emphasis, priority, or closure. Far from being purely descriptive or analytical, these ostensibly formal or aesthetic dimensions of narration are part of the imaginative production of meaning. As White explains, "The 'content' of the discourse consists as much of its form as it does of whatever information might be extracted from a reading of it." Thus, "to change the form of the discourse might not be to change the information about its explicit referent, but it would certainly change the meaning produced by it."[156] That historical narration works this way is a necessary consequence of the *underdetermining* character of historical facts and archival traces for narrative construction, as well as the fusion of horizons that cause judgments about the past to be shaped by judgments about the present and imaginings of the future.

Rhetorical or figurative elements inhere in the practice of narration.[157] If historical discourse relies on the story form, the ability to narrate and follow these stories' means is powerfully shaped by our immersion within a cultural horizon where we inherit and repeat certain story forms and narrative modes, with characteristic figurative and symbolic effects. To follow a story often means to follow it as a particular type or genre of story, with all the patterns of expectation that entails. As Martha Nussbaum writes, "The selection of genre" is one of the features of narratives that "expresses a sense of life and of value, a sense of what matters and what does not, of what learning and communicating are, of life's relations and connections."[158] Nussbaum's interests here are primarily literary, but the implications of her claims extend far beyond into the more diffuse realm of narration as such.

Genre provides dynamic expectations and conventions to guide interpretation and the production of meaning within a particular genre and—necessarily—in relation to and differentiation from other genres and their identifying traditions or conventions.[159] Apart from the formal efforts of demarcation by critics, the practical experience of generic interpretation reveals an intuitive or, better yet, habituated structure to our understanding that we imbibe through the rich languages of human expression. These traditions have a pervasive effect on what we find intelligible, appealing, and persuasive in stories. Our understanding reflects deeper (usually implicit and often intuitive) commitments to particular significance criteria that mediate between plot, meaning, and explanation.[160] These narrative elements convey a "representation of reality" and involve literary devices that procure for them a sense of meaning, closure, or at least intelligibility based in part on aesthetic, ethical, and figurative grounds.

This approach is especially helpful in grasping the ethical and political stakes of revisionist historiographical movements, including the one currently raging in civil rights history. The most prevalent, powerful, and influential plot forms circulating among historians and other political thinkers overlap with those available to other imaginative writers: romance, tragedy, comedy, irony, melodrama, epic, and the like. What appears, prima facie, to be a debate about periodization—the revisionary advocates of the long civil rights movement paradigm against the defenders of a classical civil rights movement narrative—involves evaluative claims, normative ordering, judgments of significance, analytical frameworks, and political commitments that are best disclosed through a focus on genre and narrative mode. In a broader public and philosophical discourse where these invocations of the civil rights movement serve as key reference points or as presumed terrain for agreement and disagreement, unraveling the generic presuppositions and narrative modes at work is tremendously important to prevent critique and judgment from going awry.

The Genres of Civil Rights History: Romance, Irony, and Tragedy

The leading historical imaginaries of the civil rights movement can be reconstructed from this interdisciplinary vantage according to their narrative modes as *romantic, ironic,* or *tragic.* In Parts Two and Three of this book I examine how each narrative form in its way lays claim to civil rights exemplarity and informs political philosophy and thought.

Romantic narratives are devoted to the portrayal and description of forms of unity—national, familial, ideological, and so forth—in a temporal process of becoming and overcoming. Relying heavily on metaphorical and symbolic representation, romance—as a style of attention to political and social life—organizes judgments about the periodization of history, the significance of particular events and figures, and the specific themes around the dramatization of emergent forms of consensus, conciliation, and inclusion. Moreover, this emphasis on unity and becoming is moralized by a narrative structure that dramatizes heroic transcendence over division and the struggle of higher-order virtues and goods against ultimately transitory or inessential obstacles of vice, injustice, and unfair circumstance.[161]

Akin to many efforts in theodicy, romance presupposes a world (or cosmos) that is not fundamentally at odds with realizing the higher purposes or ideals it treats as the subject of its inquiry. In Chapter 4, I show how Taylor Branch and other popular historians, as well as Barack Obama, rely on a romantic narrative of the civil rights movement, specifically anchored in biblical tropes, American nationalism, and a particular rendering of Martin Luther King as the central character and metaphor for the story. Through a close reading of Obama's speeches and writings and, in Chapter 5, the political philosophy of John Rawls, I show the objectionable *political* implications of this romantic vision, specifically in the ways that it privileges metaphors of inclusion/exclusion to understand injustice, imposes a nationalist frame on political and ethical judgment, and systematically discourages and discredits radical protest politics (e.g., civil disobedience) aimed at economic justice. This chapter shows how romantic histories are prone to redescribing politics that aim at radical transfiguration or reconstruction into narratives that flatten them into a less decentering politics of fulfillment, rendering the exemplarity of moments like the civil rights movement ripe for ideology in the pejorative sense. At times, romance longs to transcend genuinely contentious politics altogether.

Beyond this critique of romantic narrative, I also offer a diagnosis of why, after a long period of cultural and intellectual authority, the romantic narrative appears to be in crisis, allowing other genres to emerge, emboldened. Following an insight of Fredric Jameson into the history of genres, I pursue the hypothesis that "the failure of a particular generic structure . . . to reproduce itself not only encourages a search for those substitute textual formations that appear in its wake" but also demands analysis of "the historical ground, now longer existent, in which the original structure was meaningful."[162] To this hermeneutical end, I argue that the crisis of romantic narrative is intimately tied to a broader crisis of "authority" in black political life, where certain ideas and formulations that were once intuitively appealed to for understanding no longer compel such adherence. These authoritative pillars are *racial realism* (the idea that political, cultural, or solidaristic commitments flow inexorably from the "fact" of race); *church vanguardism* (that the black church is the core institution of black political life); the *integrationist/nationalist dichotomy* (that black political debate should be primarily understood on this binary axis), and the politics of cultural representation (that a crucial element of black politics involves practices of cultural representation that defend "the race" from inferiorizing and harmful depictions, while also articulating and protecting a shared black cultural identity that can sustain group flourishing and compel recognition and respect from others).

After detailing how Rawls's liberalism can be profitably understood as bewitched by a romantic narrative of civil rights history, I turn in Chapter 7 to exploring the strident attempt to negate the romantic master narrative with what I describe as "ironic" narratives of African American history and the "Afropessimistic" critical theory its most extreme version engenders. These ironic narratives eschew the chronological ordering of conventional historical discourse and constantly juxtapose and rearrange judgments about the past, present, and future to dramatize what they see as "the changing same": ironic phenomenon of unwavering domination underneath apparent political contingencies and victories. I offer a sustained reconstruction of this element of Afropessimistic theory's historical imagination, showing through a genealogy of ironic critique in Black studies that Afropessimism is distinguished from other skeptical or radical traditions not by its acceptance of a thesis of permanent antiblackness but by its embrace of nihilism as a response to the historical contradictions and disappointments of black political and cultural striving. Further, I show that despite the frequent claim by Wilderson and others that Afropessimism's social ontology of antiblackness takes place at a level of abstraction that is too high for narrative and the logic of storytelling, its arguments are in fact predicated on this mode of "ironic" history and historical narration, evident in Afropessimists' own uses of civil rights exemplarity to attack what they describe as "redemptive" narrative alternatives.

Focusing specifically on the defense of nihilism they think follows from this historical analysis, I offer a therapeutic critique that takes Afropessimism's predication on the practice of *ironic history* as a productive point of entry to disclose four major flaws of its picture of the world: its incoherence regarding race and reference, its self-undermining and ontologically essentialist conception of "politics," its implicit and metaphysical commitment to purity and permanence, and its pathological attachment to a conception of the vocation of black intellectualism that has collapsed in the post–Jim Crow era.

This therapeutic criticism is my entry point into Chapter 8, which takes up Cornel West's claim that African American philosophy and political thought involves "the interpretation of Afro-American history, highlighting the cultural heritage and political struggles, which provides desirable norms that should regulate responses to particular challenges presently confronting Afro-Americans."[163] With this imperative in mind, I offer a philosophical reconstruction of the revisionist historiography of the long civil rights movement, revealing it not simply as a periodization or presentist debate among historians but as reflecting a *tragic* vision of African American and civil rights movement history with keys to overcoming the weaknesses of romantic and ironic narrative modes.

Rejecting both the confident teleology of romantic narratives and the paralyzing resignation of irony, the tragic vision insists on confronting the complexity, contingency, and conflict inherent in human struggles for justice. At its core, tragedy grapples with weighty conflicts—conflicts that do not lend themselves to resolution by compromise or rational reconciliation but instead reveal the deep tensions between competing goods, ethical commitments, and the structures of power and domination. This framework reclaims the significance of defeat, arguing that losses are not merely setbacks or occasions for despair but vital sites of meaning and reflection. They force us to contend with a world in which the reasonable and just are often overpowered by the irrational and unjust, while still holding open the possibility of future transformation. To narrate the civil rights movement as tragedy is to see it as a series of intertwined victories and defeats, shaped by the profound contingency of history. Human action, for all its power and promise, unfolds in a world of unpredictability, shaped by fleeting opportunities and structural constraints. The tragic vision teaches us to remain alert to these missed opportunities, to understand how history could have turned out otherwise, and to draw lessons for the present from the roads not taken. Its practitioners hope to understand and reengage the past through a historical discourse that treats defeat as a poignant and often mournful glimpse into past ideas, efforts, and opportunity structures that might inspire ethical and political action today.

Against its competing genres, the tragic vision of the civil rights movement aims to train and refine our judgment, enabling us to identify potential opportunities, tensions, and ruptures for emancipatory action, rather than allowing this capacity to deteriorate under the belief in a seamless narrative of negativity or an unbroken arc of moral progress. At its heart, therefore, tragedy affirms the resilience and responsibility of moral agency rather than resignation. Even in the face of overwhelming odds, individuals and movements bear the weight of moral choice and judgment, particularly when navigating tragic dilemmas in which all available options involve some measure of moral compromise. This sense of responsibility, far from breeding acquiescence, underscores the stakes of action and judgment.

My account of this vision draws heavily on the long tradition of reflections on tragedy, but also on figures like A. Philip Randolph, W. E. B. Du Bois and Martin Luther King Jr. who defend a tragic yet hopeful stance toward history and struggle. My tragic vision of civil rights history recovers the lost realism of civil rights internationalism—a tradition of sharp-eyed assessments of geopolitical constraint and moral suasion's limits, rather than in moralized or romanticized cosmopolitanism. I then turn to A. Philip Randolph's idea of "reconstruction" as a radical rethinking of "integrationism" shaped by labor politics, democratic constitutionalism, and a tragic understanding of American history's reversals and betrayals. Together, these efforts challenge attempts like Richard Rorty's to Randolph and the movement into an explicitly romantic national narrative. From Du Bois, I adopt an insistence on memory as a moral and political obligation, a belief in the deep reservoirs of ethical and political insight among the defeated, and a commitment to recovering and renarrating suppressed histories as privileged resources for critique. King's notion of shattered dreams, from which this book draws its title, embodies a tragic vision's acknowledgment that unfulfilled hopes are not failures but the inevitable companions of a relentless pursuit of justice. For King, these disappointments are not a verdict on the futility of struggle but a summons to press forward, demanding that we embrace a deeper resolve and sustain a faith that endures beyond the limits of immediate victories. The struggle against racial injustice is, as Du Bois so eloquently described, a "long siege," marked by unpredictable confrontations with aspects of our societal structure that resist rational critique or straightforward prediction—namely, ideology, capital, and violence. Despite these obstacles, however, politics remains suffused with contingency, complexity, and collective memory, and our goal must be to try to reconcile ourselves to the nonsovereign character of human freedom and association in light of these truths.

Ultimately, the tragic vision deepens our understanding of the civil rights movement as a site of ongoing conflict, aspiration, and reflection. In this way, the tragic vision does not simply narrate history; it calls us to responsibility, asking us to reckon with the ever unfinished work of justice and injustice alike. It is a vision that can cultivate a disposition attuned to loss that, nevertheless, resists despair, sustaining commitments to dignity and emancipation in the dark times ahead.

Toward a Critical Theory of Exemplarity and Judgment

Before we wade into the heated debates over narratives of African American history and the political significance of their exemplarity, we must first develop a methodological and interpretive approach adequate to the task. After all, while the civil rights example is unique in the breadth of its impact and the intensity of its influence, our investigation of its uses will inevitably raise broader questions concerning how political theorizing is profoundly entangled with how we understand, argue about, and incorporate exemplary events and figures. This problematic demands a critical theory of exemplarity and a phenomenological account of its experience. These tasks, admittedly of more disciplinary interest to political theorists than many historians, are the main tasks of Part One of *Shattered Dreams, Infinite Hope*.

In eras of political theorizing more self-conscious of the significance of exemplarity, this methodological prelude may not have seemed as strange as it perhaps does now. On some accounts, the enterprise of political theory began as "almost entirely a collection of examples" curated and distilled from literary, historical, and religious texts by intellectuals whose aim was to educate judgment, provide models of virtue and vice, and produce perceptive generalizations about political life.[164] Yet with the ascendancy of modern science in Enlightenment Europe helping entrench a new hierarchical ordering of knowledge, the theorization of rule- or lawlike generalizations and predictions displaced the intellectual authority once embedded in the retrospective exemplars of tradition. Where philosophers most fully mimicked the advance of reasoning in the natural sciences, the exemplary events of political history were recast as being, at best, merely illustrative of more general laws of "universal" history and progress.[165] The idea of an exemplar lost much of its richly textured and tradition-bound specificity and took on the character of equipment, a step stool that might help reach the heights of abstraction, but which could be cast aside without consequence.[166] As Denis Diderot, the eighteenth-century French *philosophe,* would describe this philosophical and cultural transition, "Philosophy knows only the rules founded on the nature of beings, which is immutable and eternal. The last century furnishes us examples; it is up to ours to prescribe the rules."[167]

Despite the self-conceit of Enlightenment intellectuals, this dismissive stance toward the idea of exemplarity collapsed under its own weight. It was unable to grapple effectively with key phenomenological experiences of exemplarity, and especially those moments where an authoritative interpretation of the example breaks down or where something is exemplary for us in light of its *innovative,* rule-exceeding quality rather than its easy fit with *embedded* convention. This problem of how to understand our experiences with exemplarity as a dynamic and often transformative encounter in a space between the particular and the general is the subject of Chapter 1, where I turn to phenomenology to step back from our habits and sedimented interpretations and, as Hannah Arendt might put it, "think what we are doing" when we invoke, reflect, and argue through exemplarity.[168]

This phenomenological account serves as an entry point into a more sustained reflection on the relationship between historical exemplarity and judgment, which takes its starting point from Immanuel Kant, whose illustrative and informative ambivalence about exemplarity and the power of judgment to navigate its terrain is the subject of Chapter 2.

In the *Critique of Pure Reason* (1781) Kant begrudgingly acknowledged that the "great utility of examples" is their ability to "sharpen the power of judgment"—especially for those who lack "natural talent."[169] In *Groundwork of the Metaphysics of Morals* (1785) he further conceded that examples are important for encouragement insofar as they can temper inevitable doubts about the practicability of successfully carrying out our moral duties.[170] At the same time, however, he worried aloud that examples posed an inherent danger to true understanding or genuinely moral judgment. One could not "give worse advice to morality," Kant argued, "than by wanting to derive it from examples."[171] While examples could help navigate the applicability of moral rules in real life, Kant thought the specificity of any complex example makes the attempt to absorb them into abstract concepts or rules a feat prone to error. Worse yet, in the realm of practical reason, compelling exemplars could seduce the immature among us to aspire only to rote mimicry of others rather than live up to the maxim of Enlightenment: "use your own understanding."[172]

Later, however, as Kant pursued his ongoing inquiry into the relation between nature and freedom onto the difficult terrain of aesthetic judgment, he became fascinated by ways of thinking about the significance of exemplars and the relationship between exemplarity and validity in ways other than determining or subsuming them under a priori cognitive rules or moral laws.[173] Natural and artistic beauty, Kant insisted in *The Critique of the Power of Judgment* (1790), could not work that way. In such instances, "no rule" (or law, concept, etc.), as one reader of Kant puts it, "is available before we encounter the example, and no exemplar points toward a rule we have known all along."[174] In these cases, it is something particular that confronts us, and any universal or general qualities it instantiates must be found through the exercise of what Kant called reflective judgment.[175]

What was "remarkable" about this practice, Kant thought, was that it revealed a kind of "universal validity" to our judgments about particular objects that were not logically coerced by antecedent concepts or rules ready at hand.[176] Although principally focused on art and natural beauty, Kant shifted the terrain to pose, with unprecedented clarity, difficult questions about the intersubjective validity and truth value of examples, the role of imagination in producing examples for judgment, and the relationship between inheritance and originality in emulating the exemplary. In doing so he alighted on the ways exemplarity might occasion *new* patterns of sensibility, sociability, solidarity, and value.

In the wake of Kant's intervention, however, continuing to speak in the vocabulary of exemplarity demands more than merely noting the curious way that thinking and talking about art—or, more to our purposes, political and historical examples—seems to converge on particular events, personalities, or actions to treat them as bearers of general evaluative and practical significance. To treat exemplarity as a site of post-Kantian critical inquiry means to inquire into how the exemplary comes to "mingle the singular with the normative" and to how it comes to clarify the difficulties of making evaluative judgments in a world of pluralism and disagreement.[177] To make headway in this direction, however, we must break with the facile, reflexive opposition of aesthetics and politics in order to be attentive to how traditions developed to understand problems of "aesthetic experience and response" (e.g., the possibility of the new, the relationship between the ordinary and extraordinary, and problems of judgment and receptivity) can help us theorize similar phenomena in the political realm, especially where an exemplary event or personality seems to inaugurate new vistas for, or manifestations of, our normative orders, core concepts, or political ideals.[178] Broadly aesthetic terms like "authenticity, beauty, perfection, integrity, charisma, aura, and many other names" have tended to describe what is in fact a *broader phenomenon of exemplarity*—namely, the "quality of bringing reality and normativity, facts and norms not just to a passing, occasional, and imperfect intertwining but to an enduring, nearly complete, and rare fusion."[179]

On the value of such an approach, Hannah Arendt is a vital interlocutor, influentially insisting that as a matter of political and moral judgment, we are "in the same situation in which the eighteenth century found itself with respect to mere judgments of [aesthetic] taste."[180] Like many European intellectuals writing conspicuously and self-consciously in response to totalitarianism and the Holocaust, Arendt argued that these epochal horrors constituted "a break with all our traditions" and "exploded our categories of political thought and our standards for moral judgment."[181] In the wake of this crisis, Arendt argued that Kant's aesthetic theory offered a way of salvaging good moral and political judgment, with its account of how we can freely make judgments about particulars devoid of a priori rules without abandoning ideals of validity or of common sense among people of divergent tastes and perspectives. Chapter 3 interrogates her formative contribution.

If the twentieth century crystallized the collapse of formerly authoritative banisters to Western thought in metaphysics, ontology, ethics, and politics, the consequences seemed to Arendt to be perhaps the most profound challenge we inherited from that catastrophic century. The crisis in authority and its consequent crisis of understanding could, as she alleged in the case of the Nazi bureaucrat Adolf Eichmann, exacerbate barbaric (if nevertheless banal) forms of evil. On the other hand, if attended to thoughtfully, the crisis could present the extraordinary opportunity to rethink, in dialogue with others, our inherited traditions to resist the consequences of nihilism and unfreedom alike. By disavowing the reflexive reliance on "false universals," illusory teleologies, or sedimented habits of interpretation that no longer provide adequate purchase on the world or our duties, Arendt thought we might be able to meet "the phenomena [of the world], so to speak, head-on, without any preconceived system."[182] This led her back to exemplarity as the key to mediating between the particulars of our lives and this expansively general or universal outlook of "normativity." Examples, she writes,

> are indeed the "go-cart" of all judging activities, are also and especially the guideposts of all moral thought. . . . We judge and tell right from wrong by having present in our mind some incident and some person, absent in time or space that have become examples. . . . Our decisions about right and wrong will depend upon our choice of company, of those with whom we wish to spend our lives. And again, this company is chosen by thinking in examples, in examples of persons dead or alive, real or fictitious, and in examples of incidents, past or present.[183]

Judgment, the faculty of relating the particular to the general, here takes on a dual character, both dimensions of which are crucial for *Shattered Dreams, Infinite Hope.* Historically, judgment involves imaginative reflection on particular events of the past with an explicit concern as to their enduring significance (e.g., ethical, explanatory, and evaluative) but without reliance on the integrity of tradition to guide us. This fragmentation of tradition makes possible, however, new freedom in our descriptions and narratives of the past, opening the possibility of presenting or reassessing exemplary events from the perspective of struggles and strivings long lost or suppressed. Arendt—who was especially fond of quoting Cato the Elder's statement "The victorious cause pleased the gods, but the defeated one pleases Cato"—was especially attuned to how, in the exercise of judgment, past ideas or moments of rupture can become more than curious roads not taken but "precious fragments" scattered amid the "debris" of history awaiting the imaginative rediscovery, curation, and storytelling of historians and political thinkers.[184]

Part of what the link between company, exemplarity, and judgment involves is what Kant, in his discussion of genius, called "succession": the treatment of something exemplary (his example is an author) as a meaningful precedent that we keep as a model, inspiring us "to create from the same sources." Or, in Arendt's words, it is only through becoming "manifest in the guise of an example" that a philosophical truth becomes practically inspiring and persuasive, or "verified as well as validated," in the realm of politics.[185] Yet insofar as judgment is preoccupied with and attuned to interpretive possibilities and potentials beyond the brute facts of a historical event or a person's outcomes—the victorious cause, so to speak—the retrospective exercise of judgment can be profoundly disruptive. As in the encounter with a dramatically innovative work of art, some judgments of the past may rise to the level of "genuine re-cognition: seeing differently, as though for the first time, something familiar or taken for granted." Insofar as we can be coaxed or persuaded in light of historical examples to see things or speak about things in a different way, it becomes especially clear and urgent that we face an ethical-existential problem of judging what precisely we want to pass on, or disavow, in the forms of life we have inherited.[186]

The practice of judging particulars helps constitute a "common world" and the values that can come to shape it.[187] They can become reference points that are presuppositions of the communicability of disagreement constitutive of politics and that shape what we judge so significant or relevant about our shared life together that it becomes the terrain on which we stake many of our arguments and self-interpretations.[188] The idea of exemplarity, as a concept, serves to focus our attention on these shared objects of concern, without, however, prematurely foreclosing our appreciation for the plurality of interpretations and perspectives that might be brought to bear on specific examples.

Where a commonsense exemplar shatters into fragments, however, sparking struggles over how to describe ourselves and the world, the commons of exemplarity becomes a battleground where the question of what "company" we keep is pitched with intensifying ferocity. The survivors—some bearing scars from the collapse, others bleeding from wounds untended and ignored—do battle with the shards at hand. Amid the confusion and disorientation, however, something new may appear in the wreckage if we angle ourselves for the right reflective light.[189]

If there is a benefit to this disorienting scene, it is that from the vantage of crisis, the political and philosophical consequences of our most familiar examples and their underlying *narrative modes* seem especially clear and open to revision and recommitment. The collapse of what we thought we knew makes possible a reckoning with the terrible truths we have long avoided, even as this forces confrontation with those self-assured pessimisms that insist that despair is the only law.[190] Armed with a tragic vision and the strange discipline of hope it strives to cultivate, we may instead heed the call to reassemble the fragments into something more honest and enduring for the long, dangerous road ahead.

I

A CRITICAL THEORY OF EXEMPLARITY, JUDGMENT, AND NARRATIVE

CHAPTER 1

ON EXEMPLARITY AND DISCLOSURE

The Experience of Exemplarity

> Any real change implies the breakup of the world as one has always known it, the loss of all that gave one an identity, the end of safety.
>
> —JAMES BALDWIN

IN HER REMARKABLE REFLECTIONS on the *vita contemplativa* and its implications for political judgment and action, Hannah Arendt raised a serious worry about how "clichés, stock phrases, [and] adherence to conventional, standardized codes of expression and conduct" can function to distract or otherwise deter our ability to stop and think critically about the events and facts of the world.[1] "Thoughtlessness," Arendt argued, stems not only from "heedless recklessness or hopeless confusion" but also from the "complacent repetition of 'truths' which have become trivial and empty"—a habit that she complained was "among the outstanding characteristics of our time."[2] Yet resisting the soporific effect of cliché on critical thinking is easier said than done. The familiarity and ubiquity of the clichéd example are a remarkably absorbing part of our everyday cultural background, and our engagements with it are often habituated and unreflective.

This is not philosophically inconsequential. Samuel Fleischacker argues that we "can never so much as identify a concept properly without giving some example of its use." If the very possibility for identifying concepts as such depends on being able to distinguish between group similarities manifested in distinct intuitions and drawing boundaries between those that are included in the concept and those that are not, then example-giving plays a fundamental role in thinking and communication. This holds especially true, Fleischacker argues, for evaluative discourse and practice where abstract concepts like "'justice,' 'equality,' and 'well-being,'" not to mention ontological categories like that of "human being," are continually contested and redescribed.[3]

Part of the problem, however, is that in both everyday explanation and understanding and formal theoretical argument, examples often seem to reveal themselves to us as mere tools ("equipment"), "ready at hand" for instrumental purposes.[4] Their possible meanings are often thoughtlessly structured and constrained by sedimented habits, and calcified into familiar symbols within a narrowly conventional scope of meaning and significance.[5] We do not, in this instance, encounter these deployments of examples as especially open, or as inviting us to engage in reflection or evaluation of other possibilities that a given example could manifest. This is an exemplarity that aspires to function as epistemically closed—the example as practical fact with transparent significance from which knowledge about other related propositions or judgments can be reliably deduced.

When broader social and cultural conditions seem to throw these conventions and expectations into crisis, however, with growing factions finding prevailing appeals to exemplarity or uses of examples intolerable or unintelligible, the resulting communicative breakdown calls for self-conscious criticism. We must somehow develop or retrieve strategies capable of effectively reading, interpreting, and evaluating what might be called an economy of exemplarity: the fact that certain gestures, images, citations, references, appeals, and invocations circulate specific representations of exemplary events or personalities across disparate contexts of thought, discourse, and action. To treat exemplarity as a category of critical analysis is to call us, as readers and listeners, to become more highly vigilant to how appeals to exemplary events (including what appear to be mundane uses of them in the giving of examples) surface along a vast range of performances, texts, and discourses in politics and philosophy. What world-constituting work are these examples asked to perform? What abstractions and concepts do they scaffold? What judgments do they appear to authorize? How do they serve as points of departure as we attempt the perilous crossing of thinking and striving from debatable past to agonized present, and onward to a future worthy of our affirmation?

Following this path of inquiry requires that we step back and deliberately resist our familiar ways of practically engaging with civil rights exemplarity or even the familiar ways of trying to think critically about what we do when we invoke "the civil rights movement." The hope is to try to disclose something more immediate concerning how we experience historical exemplarity, the capacities it engages, and the forms in which it is articulated.[6] It calls us, as Arendt might put it, "to think what we are doing," and I might add, what we are *experiencing*.[7]

This approach to critique has many virtues. By rethinking our *interpretive practices* we can make visible the often overlooked connective tissue binding political philosophy, political rhetoric, historical imagination, and narrative. Attention to these overlaps allows us to bundle together texts whose powers of persuasion and underlying commitments are more effectively disclosed in combination, and only via tools usually sequestered by discipline. A sustained inquiry into exemplarity also allows us to raise essential questions about the relationship of a particular exemplary event to general or universal claims ostensibly advanced by reference to representations of it. This approach pushes us to understand the faculty of judgment that allows us to navigate this dynamic relation between particular and general without skirting challenging issues of representation, validity, authority, and normativity that bedevil our exercises of judgment in historical reflection and present-day politics.

In pursuit of this sort of critical theory, this chapter offers an extended philosophical and phenomenological account of the nature and argumentative force of exemplarity to lay the groundwork for such an approach. I distinguish between two forms of exemplarity—embedded and innovative—and focus my account on the latter, as it is less familiar. The aim is to draw out its key elements of illumination, disclosure, and rupture with special emphasis on the connection between exemplarity and founding, an important entry point for political theorists.

Exemplarity and Examples Between the General and Particular

A judgment of exemplarity involves a claim about something particular *and* its relation to something more general beyond itself. It is not intuitively clear, however, how it is possible to move from the particularity of a given event, experience, or object to a more general normative claim, theoretical principle, or descriptive account that remains valid even as it extrapolates from its origins in the particular. To answer this question, we are perhaps well served by thinking through what it means to be an example or exemplary in the first place.

The *Oxford English Dictionary*'s account offers a helpful starting point to pick out key meanings of the word *example* for philosophical reflection. We note first that exemplarity is characteristic of a relationship between a particular ("a typical instance," "a particular instance," "a single instance," "a parallel case," "a precedent") and something beyond that particular, which could be a general rule, category, or quality, a set of similar cases, or some nonidentical range of human actions, cognitions, and dispositions influenced by a given particular.[8] I can identify my pet dog as an example of the breed category of German shepherd, for example, or this pot of boiling water as an example of the general rule that water boils at one hundred degrees Celsius at sea level. In more complicated cases, I can identify specific instances as exemplary of general qualities—civil rights activists facing down high-pressure fire hoses and those aforementioned German shepherds employed as police dogs, for instance, as exemplifying the virtue of courage. Although the specific event, action, or historical person cannot precisely be repeated, the general quality we recognize as manifest in their character or the event's unfolding seems to project a standard beyond itself in meaningful ways.

We can also identify a certain degree of normativity or evaluation embedded within the concept of exemplarity. When, for instance, the late historian Manning Marable hailed Malcolm X as "a definitive yardstick by which all other Americans who aspire to a mantle of leadership should be measured," we understand that he is making at least two claims.[9] First, Marable articulates an "ought" claim about the qualities or characteristics of leadership that we should want from political leaders and that they should aspire to manifest. Second, he advances a descriptive claim about their exemplary instantiation in the form of leadership practiced by Malcolm X.[10] Here the example—Malcolm X—serves as a standard, however debatable, by which to judge a broad category of political action and aspiration.

This is one way that exemplarity can entail evaluative judgment, but it is not the only way. Normativity of a sort also arises when we attempt to identify the *typical* case in a given set or the instance that best captures the essential characteristics or qualities of a broader category. In these cases, claims of exemplarity rank and measure some subset of the manifold qualities of a particular instance and make a claim as to the significance of the particular instance's specific combination of these qualities for its relationship with something beyond itself. This judgment brings with it implicit or explicit evaluative claims.

In describing a typical example of an animal species, for example, one might consider the mean value of the weight, height, and length distributions across the species population; the modal, or most common, foodstuffs consumed by individual organisms; observational data about the geographic distribution of the population; and knowledge of animal scientific classification schemes based on the evaluative premise that these are most important to describing the typical member of a species. From here we may construct or discern an exemplary individual case that comes closest to fitting the outlaid criteria, with the notion of "best fit" necessarily reflecting evaluative claims about the significance of particular qualities and the relative insignificance of others. Therefore, these relevant criteria, and thus the notion of exemplarity (the typical) itself, depend on purposes of human interpretation and the judgments we exercise. The criteria sketched above may be appropriate for describing the typical brown bear for an audience at the city zoo but unhelpful for describing the typical brown bear for a population geneticist trying to map bear genomes. The types of information relevant to satisfying the purposes of the search for exemplarity can be quite different, even when we are prima facie concerned with the same "object."

A kind of evaluative judgment also arises when exemplarity is understood less as the identification of the typical than as the highest-order illustration of a concept or set. Consider Orlando Patterson's much-discussed concept of slavery. He defines slavery by the presence of three elements: an extreme relationship of coercion between persons ultimately maintained by direct violence; a condition of "natal alienation" that denies the slave "all claims on, and obligations to, his parents and living blood relations . . . his more remote ancestors and on his descendants" grounded in the extreme refusal of social recognition respect that Patterson calls "social death"; and generalized dishonor.[11] We could recognize, as Patterson does, many societies with widespread social relationships that manifest these constituent elements and judge that they cross the relevant interpretive threshold of systematicity—including the antebellum United States, ancient Greece and Rome, and early modern West African societies. We might also, however, identify a slave society as *exemplary* insofar as it not only manifests these three constituent elements but also realizes each of them to such a degree or in such a combination that it could be said to be "the most like what it is"—that particular instance that best reveals, in comparison with other cases, the constitutive elements or significant features of something (a concept, a style, a genre, a social arrangement, etc.) that we can recognize as a more general phenomenon.[12] In both the sociology literature and public debates on social movements, the civil rights movement is often considered exemplary among social or protest movements in this fashion.[13]

Alessandro Ferrara captures the spirit behind these sorts of claims when he describes the exemplary as the "enduring, nearly complete, and rare fusion" between reality and normativity and locates the "force" of the example as arising precisely from this "singular and exceptional congruence that what is exemplary realizes and exhibits between the order of its own reality and the order of the normativity to which it responds."[14] Drawing on concepts more familiarly associated with aesthetics, existentialism, and virtue ethics, Ferrara argues that "authenticity, beauty, perfection, integrity, charisma, aura, and many other names have been attributed to this quality of bringing reality and normativity, facts and norms not just to a passing, occasional, and imperfect intertwining but to an enduring, nearly complete, and rare fusion."[15] This is the register, as I noted in this book's Introduction, in which the historian David Burner describes the civil rights movement as "about as close to moral perfection as American political action has ever come."[16]

Embedded Versus Innovative Exemplarity

Building on Ferrara's account, we might say that exemplarity can exist in two distinct forms: *embedded* and *innovative*. The former reflects instances in which we are conventionally committed to certain normative principles or considered judgments and readily recognize those particular cases, actions, and the like that best conform to them or achieve them to the greatest degree. This exemplarity might manifest in a virtuoso athletic performance, great statesmanship, professional practice (medicine, law, teaching, etc.), or some other excellent performance of a role conventionally understood.[17] Medical doctors, for instance, have a widely accepted obligation to do no harm, tend to the ill, and heal the sick and wounded under their charge as best they can. The general recognition of this normative obligation makes it possible to consider certain physicians exemplary by how well they fulfill these obligations, especially in a particularly demanding context or scenario.[18] Being thrown into this "concrete situation," we find ourselves "attuned to a cultural and historical context where things already count in determinate ways in relation to a community's practices."[19] We can call this embedded exemplarity.

When Secretariat is described as an exemplary racehorse, the prevailing evaluative standards in the practice of horse racing—namely, that the best horse is the one that, under a jockey's control, runs the fastest over a predetermined distance—and our deep cultural familiarity with the practice render exemplarity more determinate and even intuitive.[20] This force of the example is perhaps most clearly felt within traditional practices (e.g., horse racing), those forms of cooperative human activity that have internal goods (e.g., winning the race) that are realized primarily in the very course of "trying to achieve those standards of excellence which are appropriate to, and partially definitive of," the form of activity that makes up the practice itself.[21] This force of the example that is experienced as intuition or norm is powerful and often appears as natural, even instinctive, although the categories and standards mobilized in recognition are often based in patterns of acculturation and socialization that can extend generations.

The second form of exemplarity diverges from the embedded by being so "pure and *innovative* that we first vaguely sense it by drawing on the analogy with past experiences, and only *subsequently* do we succeed in identifying the normative moment so forcefully reflected on or discerned in the object or action at hand."[22] In philosophy and literature, this sort of judgment has occasionally (and most profitably) been pursued in the wake of tremendous social upheavals (e.g., the American, French, and Haitian Revolutions), epic military conflicts (especially the American Civil War and World War I), and horrific human atrocities (especially the Holocaust).

More consistently, however, this is an experience that philosophers traditionally have tended to confine to the realm of aesthetic experience, and specifically to the "sublime" (as opposed to the "beautiful," which we might see as more consonant with embedded exemplarity). Here the shattering force of experience more chaotically precedes a coherent apprehension and account of its exemplarity. We feel that our full powers of understanding or reason are overwhelmed, at least initially, by an encounter with an object or event that appears to transcend our present capacity to grasp its significance. We can call this innovative exemplarity.

This "normative moment" at work in innovative exemplarity seems to consist of three main achievements that are analytically distinct but not mutually exclusive: an illumination of novel ways of transcending existing limits; a disclosure of the world that opens new dimensions of normativity; and a rupture, following an action, event, or appearance of a work, in the continuity of tradition and time that compellingly (if perhaps only symbolically) suggests new normative aims in a future no longer inevitably encumbered by what in the past was experienced as limit (a founding is an especially potent form of rupture that involves an aspiration to establish another order that endures). The apparent "rare fusion" or "exceptional congruence" of these elements that Ferrara describes is a substantial part of what makes the exemplary a touchstone for judgment and a model for action, especially insofar as it seems to expand our sense of what is possible and open up our hope and imagination for the future. I will discuss each of these three elements in turn.

Illumination

One of the insightful features of Ferrara's account of exemplarity is that he foregrounds *forceful* experience. Recall that the first "great force" that Ferrara describes as shaping the world is "the force of what is," those natural and social facts that we experience, at least when we attempt to resist or overcome them, as having some coercive force not reducible to or immediately subject to our individual will. Émile Durkheim, in his influential account of social facts, deftly highlights the experience of this facticity:

> Of course, when I fully consent and conform to [these social facts], this constraint [of coercion] is felt only slightly, if at all, and is therefore unnecessary. But it is, nonetheless, an intrinsic characteristic of these facts, the proof thereof being that it asserts itself as soon as I attempt to resist it. If I attempt to violate the law, it reacts against me so as to prevent my act before its accomplishment, or to nullify my violation by restoring the damage. . . . If I do not submit to the conventions of society, if in my dress I do not conform to the customs observed in my country and in my class, the ridicule I provoke, the social isolation in which I am kept, produce, although in an attenuated form, the same effects as a punishment in the strict sense of the word . . . even when I free myself from these rules and violate them successfully, I am always compelled to struggle with them . . . they make their constraining power sufficiently felt by the resistance they offer.[23]

Illumination entails some sort of transformation (not necessarily an overcoming) in how we experience such social or natural facts as specific limitations to our ethical aims, practical ends, or the contours of our imagination. Hannah Arendt judged the 1957 launch of Sputnik 1, the Soviet Union satellite, "second in importance to no other [event]," in part because the use of human ingenuity used to escape Earth's atmosphere cast doubt, for better or for worse, on the presumption that "the earth is the very quintessence of the human condition."[24] One might even take other moments of technological innovation and achievement in this fashion—the Wright brothers' flight at Kitty Hawk, North Carolina, for instance—as fundamentally altering not the physical force of gravity but the way that human beings had once related to it *practically* as binding them to terrestrial earth in their movements through time and space.

Illumination can also unfold beyond the natural or social facts immediately involved. A shift in our experience of one specific "limitation" may enable other experiences, clear the path for new pathways of imaginative thought, open terrain for rethinking our evaluative judgments (e.g., what justice requires), and create new vocabularies. These can all coagulate into a broader shift in our relation to, or cognizance of, myriad features of the world.

Through illumination, we alter our capacities for receptivity. We "come to notice not only what is always happening but, all the more important, to notice what is not happening, and so to notice what gets in the way of something new happening, what gets us in the way of a new beginning."[25] It is a way of describing the discernment or reconceptualization of the existing order of things such that we discover ways to avoid or surmount certain forms of limitation or misunderstanding, unmask assumed limits as illusory or unnecessary, or undermine the authority that reinforces the power of social facts and insulates them from critique. In an account of *historical* exemplarity, this quality is made manifest by demonstrating, through narrative representation, the achievement of these feats in the past and accounting for its relation to us in the present.

Disclosure

The second element of innovative exemplarity is what Ferrara describes as the expansion of "the reach of our normative understandings" or the disclosure of "new dimensions of normativity."[26] As Nikolas Kompridis helpfully explains, the question of disclosure involves our very "conditions of intelligibility" and understanding. It speaks to the thematization and criticism of the way that ordinary practices "constrain what can show up as significant and relevant,"[27] affecting our interpretive frameworks and judgments of value and possibility: "The world is first disclosed to us through our prereflective receptivity and attunement to things and our practical involvement with them. One might think of this as first-order disclosure. But there is also a *reflective* mode of disclosure, where through second-order practices—philosophical, artistic, aesthetic, narrative, and collective—we redisclose the world, opening up and articulating possibilities that were not already there, or buried or disguised meanings, or as Wittgenstein and Heidegger showed in their philosophical practice, disclosing the background conditions of intelligibility as such."[28]

Kompridis's account of reflective disclosure also further distinguishes between disclosures that lead toward "refocusing" or "decentering" our preunderstandings of the world, ourselves, and our actions. These distinctive phenomena, as we shall see, must be retroactively and processually described. This inevitably raises questions about narrative and judgment.

Refocusing involves making us more aware of obscured, inarticulate, or "unthematized" connections within our "shared pre-understanding of the world." The aim is to uncover and rearticulate our deepest shared values and commitments and, in doing so, repair "breakdowns" in attention, interpretation, and judgment that appear to threaten these values and the coherence of our self-understanding. Decentering, on the other hand, "can critically introduce meanings, perspectives, interpretive and evaluative vocabularies, modes of perception, and action possibilities that stand in strikingly dissonant relations to already existing ways of speaking, hearing, seeing, interpreting, and acting . . . [and] cannot but disturb the unreflective, taken-for-granted flow of our self-understanding and social practices." We undergo a decentering when there is a "scrambling" or "defamiliarizing" of our preunderstandings and practices, and a push, ultimately, to "enlarge and transform" them in a new direction.[29]

Whether refocusing or decentering, disclosure in the realm of historical exemplarity involves becoming "insightfully aware of a previously uncritical relation to the past" and recognizing that this change in orientation "would have to make us more accountable to, more responsible for, the proportion of continuity and discontinuity in the forms of life we pass on."[30] While Kompridis concedes that it is often not easy to distinguish clearly between these two modes, he neglects to emphasize that part of this dilemma comes from the fact that disclosure is theorized and recounted *narratively*.

The reliance of the idea of disclosure on notions of crisis and breakdown, discontinuity and novelty, continuity and recovery seems to require narratives that synchronically organize and retrospectively integrate these features into a story, often with a dramatic arc.[31] This reliance on retrospective narration is especially apparent in the case of an exemplary historical event being treated as a site of disclosure (or when reflection on such an event is part of an attempted redisclosure). Indeed, whether exemplary events should be understood as refocusing or decentering is one of the central axes of our most important ethical and interpretive disputes, which, as we will see, is often adjudicated via narrative form itself. The civil rights movement is a case in point.

Refocusing Disclosure and the Civil Rights Movement: The Evolution of Myrdalism

Many contemporary commentators treat the exemplarity of the civil rights movement as a moment of refocusing. Cass Sunstein describes the (classical) civil rights movement, in language evoking the idea of exemplarity, as a unique "period of public punctuation" that "helped transform our understandings of constitutional principles" and whose "political and moral claims . . . helped spur legislation that continues to raise foundational issues about our constitutional order." Reflection on the "appropriate characterization—and evaluation—of the movement," he suggests, continues to be an important issue in the public sphere and "connects to our understanding of our constitutional heritage." In undertaking a bit of this reflection himself, Sunstein argues that the character of the civil rights movement is ("surprisingly," he notes, for rhetorical effect) essentially "conservative and backward looking." In other words, the "defining aspirations" of the movement "came from America's own stated ideals" (i.e., the freedom from desperate conditions, the opposition to caste, and equal citizenship as defended in key documents by the Founding Fathers and later national leaders' restatements) and the courageous insistence that "the nation should live up to them."[32] In this account, the innovative character of the civil rights struggle was less about instantiating any transformation of American society's values than about dramatizing the depth of their violation, rhetorically and performatively rearticulating what is at stake in their moral and political affirmation.

Sunstein's argument nests neatly within the picture of African American politics influentially advanced by the Swedish social scientist Gunnar Myrdal in *An American Dilemma,* his pivotal Carnegie Foundation–commissioned study of the so-called Negro Problem published in 1944. In the book's famous thesis, Myrdal explains the social facts of enduring racial inequality, racial discrimination, and various interracial "tensions" as "a problem in the heart of the American," a problem that boils down to an "ever-raging conflict between, on the one hand, the valuations preserved on the general plane which we shall call the 'American Creed,' where the American thinks, talks, and acts under the influence of high national and Christian precepts, and, on the other hand, the valuations on specific planes of individual and group living, where personal and local interests; economic, social, and sexual jealousies; considerations of community prestige and conformity; group prejudice against particular persons or types of people; and all sorts of miscellaneous wants, impulses, and habits dominate his outlook."[33]

Myrdal identifies the "American Creed" as a set of ethical valuations broadly shared in differing constellations and intensities by Americans of all backgrounds. It consists of values Myrdal associates with the (European) Enlightenment—rationalism, liberty, equality, justice, fair opportunity, and the consent of the governed—but that are charged with culturally unique emotional and authoritative force through their alchemical mixture with America's ecumenical and democratic tradition of Christianity.[34] The titular dilemma arises insofar as the hearts and souls of white Americans are affectively and intellectually torn between these ideals of the American Creed and the hostilities, status interests, base impulses, and reflexive habits that, according to Myrdal, are constitutive of race prejudice and stigma.

It is not often enough noted that Myrdal's argument turns on a sweeping universalist claim about moral psychology and, perhaps, metaethics that "in America as everywhere else people agree, as an abstract proposition, that *the more general valuations—those which refer to men as such and not to any particular group or temporary situation—are morally higher.*" The purportedly universal values of the American creed, therefore, are supposedly experienced and understood by everyday actors as ethically prior and morally superior to those valuations that are essentially ethnocentric but which are also widely held. After all, Myrdal argued that white Americans *also* practically achieved sweeping consensus on the "rank order of discrimination," or which forms of discrimination were most urgent, sacrosanct, and ethically defensible, with those sex and egalitarian interracial social relations being the most taboo and vigilantly enforced, even by self-described liberals.[35]

How Myrdal attempts to square these two forms of contradictory consensus is by noting that the latter valuations "are commonly referred to as 'irrational' or 'prejudiced,' sometimes even by people who express and stress them" and are often "defended in terms of tradition, expediency or utility" as opposed to principles or doctrines of right.[36] The collision between these two valuations and the short-circuiting of the correct decision procedure to navigate them results in forms of cognitive dissonance and moral-psychological strain that Americans allegedly cope with by sublimating them below active consciousness and mutilating their perceptions and beliefs concerning social reality.[37] In other words, white people avoid their culpability in creating and reproducing the Negro Problem by downplaying its scope, mythologizing its origins, or altogether denying its existence.

Solving the problem, in this view, demands not only rational argument and education to beat back race prejudice but also political action designed to force this sublimated conflict in the American conscience to the surface. Then it may be resolved by refocusing us on the more deeply held, more well-reasoned, and more universal commitments of the American creed. Accordingly, Myrdal understood black politics as constituted almost entirely by the strategy of trying to "play on the conflicting values held in the white majority group" and the philosophical identification of "the Negro cause" with "broader issues in American politics and social life and with moral principles held dear by the white Americans." This is why African American political thought, for Myrdal, was essentially a contradiction in terms: "Negro thinking is almost completely determined by white opinions, negatively and positively. It develops as an answer to the popular theories prevalent among whites by which they rationalize their upholding of caste. In this sense it is a derivative, or secondary, thinking." "Negro thinking in social and political terms," Myrdal continues, "is . . . *exclusively* a thinking about the Negro problem," chiefly concerned with the proper balance between "accommodation" and "protest" and defending which "social class or group among the whites is chosen as a prospective ally."[38]

Myrdal regarded the supposed imitative and opportunistic quality of Negro thinking as exceedingly rational and, frankly, fortunate. "The Negroes, the new immigrants, the Jews, and other disadvantaged and unpopular groups," he concluded, "could not possibly have invented a system of political ideals which better corresponded to their interests" than the liberal principles he claimed to discern as the bedrock American creed. Indeed, where black thinkers veered off script from creedal liberalism (i.e., into black nationalism or leftist radicalism), flummoxed social scientists of the Myrdalian breed tended to turn to the language of therapeutic psychology for assistance. Such positions were more likely to be described in the diagnostic concepts of rage, frustration, and make-believe than in a philosophical register demanding reasoned argument or generous reconstruction.[39]

For thinkers shaped by something like this social and political theory, the exemplarity of the civil rights movement tends to be understood as an instance of *refocusing*. It is characterized, as in Sunstein's account, as a series of dramatic political actions that brought into stark relief what Myrdal called the "hundred-year lag" between American ideals and the prevailing practices of American society, forcing these concealed and sublimated contradictions to the foreground and offering an opportunity to repair a cultural breakdown that could bring the order of things in American society more in line with the deepest wellsprings of its authentic order of normativity. In this account, the civil rights movement occasioned a self-reflexive ethical transformation that restored the American creed to pride of place and compelled white America to extend its promises and entitlements to African Americans and subsequently to other nonwhite groups, sexual minorities, and women. It is not unlike the language that Charles Taylor uses in a different context to describe as the refocusing power of disclosure: "What I bring out to articulacy is what I 'always knew.'"[40]

The Myrdalian analyses of American political development generally and of race specifically have come under widespread critique in contemporary social science, but little attention has been paid to the ways that their core claims of deep consensus embodied in the American creed underwrites an image and narrative of black subordination as a problem of exclusion and black politics as a "quest for inclusion."[41] I use *image* and *narrative* deliberately to evoke the multivalent character of political ideas. It is important, when reflecting on political ideas and arguments, to think through their *aesthetic* dimensions—the "images they present, the impressions they emit, and the connections they ascertain [that] all point to strata of value that extend well beyond their value as a philosophical argument."[42] These features of political ideas are often conveyed through metaphors, which Danielle Allen poignantly describes as "vehicles for the imagination no less than institutions." Metaphors help us build crucial political concepts (e.g., "the people") while shaping our understanding of the core insights, obligations, and institutional forms that flow from thinking of politics in the ways these pictures or figurations suggest.[43]

It is this sort of multivalent analysis that reveals how the language of "exclusion" and "inclusion," particularly when treated as a kind of master concept that fundamentally organizes egalitarian politics, coheres with a certain picture of the world, one governed by "metaphors of 'lines' that can be crossed and horizontal notions of 'inside and outside.'"[44] As Allen brilliantly elucidates, this particular metaphor is misleading insofar as it tends to suggest "a door closing someone out from some desirable 'indoors,'" lending unjustified credence to the presumption that "those who perpetrate injustice can nonetheless have, among themselves, mostly healthy and just forms of political practice . . . inside an essentially healthy political sphere."[45] The solution to injustice that this seems to suggest, therefore, is incorporating the excluded into this healthy political sphere and the mainstream of social life, a process that involves instructing them to its existing habits, norms, and practices rather than endeavoring to understand how "the political cultures and forms of citizenship belonging to both groups are diseased" due to the arbitrary subjection that structures the polity and the habits and arrangements required to sustain it.[46] After all, as one historian writes, "Jim Crow was a world of intimacy," with highly developed, regulative forms of etiquette, social performance scripts, and customs for a vast range of interpersonal interaction, in the background of which loomed a violent enforcement apparatus of state and vigilante violence.[47]

Allen's argument helps illuminate a tension in the rhetoric of the civil rights movement that has subsequently been reproduced in competing accounts of its exemplarity. Often enough, activists would speak in something like the vocabulary Allen decries, and these utterances are, it must be admitted, ready at hand for characterizations of the movement as refocusing. Rev. Dr. Martin Luther King Jr., in a 1964 interview with the writer Robert Penn Warren, described the civil rights movement as a "revolution to get in . . . a revolution calling on the nation to live up to what is already there in an idealistic sense."[48] Lodging a modest dissent against even King's description of the movement as a "Negro revolution," Roy Wilkins, the executive director of the National Association for the Advancement of Colored People (NAACP), argued that even this was misleading, for "we are trying to get the government, as expressed by a majority of the people, to put into practice its declared objectives. . . . In other words, the Negro wants in."[49] As the psychologist Kenneth Clark, who helped conduct the famed children's doll study cited in *Brown v. Board of Education* (1954) as evidence of the psychic wounds occasioned by racial segregation, writes,

> In regard to the American civil rights movement, it is significant to observe that the civil rights groups—the NAACP, the Urban League, and to some

> extent a pre-McKissick CORE [Congress of Racial Equality]—are essentially conservative organizations in terms of the extent of change they require of the American social, political, and economic system. Without evaluation or bias one may call these groups conservatives, because they are not requiring, they are not demanding that the social system, the power system, be changed fundamentally. They were not even requiring that it be modified too significantly, except from the point of view of the resistant extreme white. They were merely asking that it include the Negro.[50]

The Myrdalian view that black political thinking is essentially derivative and functionally conservative finds a comfortable abode in such statements. Especially when the speaker claims to channel the voice of "the Negro," these utterances suggest a near-consensus view that African Americans are striving in a broadly united direction toward incorporation into what already exists and that what must be overcome is racial exclusion based on unreconciled values among white people. Under this description, all but the most incorrigible social scientist might be expected to concentrate their talents on unraveling the mysteries of white moral psychology and racial attitudes, presuming that in these beliefs lie the most important phenomena in the study of American race politics.[51] The idea that black political action might aim at something beyond a national refocusing is, if not quite unthinkable, certainly insignificant and inconsequential.

For Allen, the overdetermination of our thinking by the exclusion image (and I would add, its rendering in the Myrdalian tradition), leads us astray because it guides us toward notions of citizenship that can be pictured as a healthy "in" or negative "out" to be repaired by inclusion (via legal status or duties). Instead, she asks that we understand society as constituted by "deep rules" or "habits of interaction [that] give form to public space and so to our political life." When these allow for domination, we should see these habits as *diseased* and ourselves as implicated in ways unlikely to be mapped by the rhetoric of "inclusion."[52] This is the philosophical analogue to James Baldwin's impassioned pronouncement near the end of his 1963 classic, *The Fire Next Time,* where he laments that he "cannot accept the proposition that the four-hundred-year travail of the American Negro should result merely in his attainment of the present level of the American civilization. . . . White people cannot, in the generality, be taken as models of how to live. Rather, the white man is himself in sore need of new standards, which will release him from his confusion and place him once again in fruitful communion with the depths of his own being."[53]

Or, as Allen clarifies, drawing on the writer Ralph Ellison,

> If exclusion is the basic injustice perpetuated by segregation, the segregating regime is a fundamentally sound political order, but for the unfortunate exclusion of black people. . . . If, however, one sees that segregationist

> regime in terms of domination, as Ellison did, the matter is otherwise. The dominated are inside the political sphere already . . . with its two complementary forms of citizenship, one for the dominators and one for the dominated. . . . From Ellison's perspective, the central question for an effort to craft new citizenly techniques, then, is how to integrate into one citizenship the healthy political habits of both the dominators and the dominated . . . to refashion the meaning of citizenship for everyone.[54]

For Ellison, "What is needed in our country is not an exchange of pathologies, but a change of the basis of society. This is a job which both Negroes and whites must perform together. In Negro culture there is much of value for America as a whole. What is needed are Negroes to take it and create of it 'the uncreated consciousness of their race.' In doing so they will do far more, they'll help create a more human American."[55]

This, too, is a crucial dimension of the political thought and rhetoric of the civil rights movement. Much in Allen's argument is anticipated, for instance, in the 1964 remark by Whitney Young, executive director of the Urban League, that "my concept of integration doesn't mean that any group gives up all that it has and adopts all that another group has. My concept of integration is that we explore and identify, within each group, the positives that have been developed out of that group's culture." Like Allen, Young criticizes the "meanness, the selfishness, the inability to give up privilege and advantage" in white Americans as a constituent feature of political life in need of transformation.

Yet, in Young's view, this remaking of norms and civic habits from African American insights is justified in part by its potential service to corporate profit. "The Negro," he insists, "out of suppression, has developed a kind of compassion and humanness, certainly a kind of patience and tolerance that General Motors could use."[56] But important parts of Ellison's corpus—especially from the 1940s—suggest more radical elaborations of Allen's critique than Young's vision of a 1965 Buick Skylark built with the input of the Negro's world-historical forbearance.

Ellison, in his enduring critique of *An American Dilemma,* gives a different diagnosis of what Allen once described as the "two complementary forms of citizenship" of Jim Crow America. Mocking Myrdal for evading "class struggle" and "the economic motivation of anti-Negro prejudice which to an increasing number of Negro intellectuals correctly analyzes their situation," Ellison argues that *American Dilemma* "avoids the question of power *and* the question of who manipulates that power." Any talk of "the American *ethos,*" he suggests, needs to be located "in terms of its material manifestations" in class conflict and political economy, which will ultimately reveal that "there exist *two* American moralities, kept in balance by social science" and its mystifying ideologies.[57]

As it stands, Allen's critique of the inclusion paradigm and emphasis on civic habits and democratic sacrifice proceeds without sustained attention to the ways that political economy might structure and constrain the habits of "bad citizens." While there is nothing approaching the corporate boosterism of Young's comment in *Talking to Strangers,* Allen's early work does not yet link her theory of domination or reading of the civil rights movement with radical questioning of the structure of asset ownership, the oligarchic concentration of decision-making authority, socioeconomic interests created by existing municipal boundaries and tax law, and the cynical uses of race conflict by forces aiming to suppress labor unions and labor costs.[58]

Raising these concerns helps us pose, with better clarity, just how much conflict Myrdalism and the inclusion paradigm can obscure. How much of what appears, prima facie, as endorsement of, or refocusing on, the American creed contains divergent interpretations of this society and its contradictions, accounts that link interracial hostility to systematic distortions of economic and other interests? Where does the rhetoric of "exclusion," while seeming to capture something like discrimination in the job market, lead us to persistently misdescribe and even ignore what Shatema Threadcraft calls "intimate injustice" suffered by black women domestics in the Jim Crow era? What is concealed of the ways that such women were coerced by structural injustice to perform both typically masculine labor and "work *within* the white intimate sphere . . . that served to meet the bodily needs of white families often at the expense of care for the bodily needs of their own" and under persistent threat of sexual and physical violence?[59]

This approach seems to consistently lead us to produce, in our retrospective analyses of the civil rights movement, normatively laden accounts of history that try to distinguish legitimate or praiseworthy struggles for inclusion that are constitutive of the *authentic* civil rights movement from radical departures that seek, wrongly, to challenge more fundamental structures of American civilization. In narrative form, as we shall see, the Myrdalian inclusion synthesis buttresses stories about the civil rights movement as functionally complete or, by the late 1960s, as in *intellectual* decline, without raising the essentially dialectical question of how to understand movement participants' persistent return to radical economic egalitarianism, internationalist agitation, and experiments in civil disobedience over the decades. Are these, as countless histories of the 1960s suggest, a misguided departure from the American consensus, or can they instead be more fairly characterized as crisis-driven, progressive learning processes about the problem of racial injustice from *within* the movement whose more adequate apprehension of the problems and implications for justice are blocked by competing social forces, obsolete forms of interpretation, and one-sided historical narratives?[60]

Under the refocusing lens of Myrdalism, casual analysts of black politics are led toward subsuming what is "significant" in black political life neatly within traditions of American liberal democratic politics (or to conceiving of African American political life as a contest between heroic integrationist-assimilationist strategies of inclusion and misguided nationalist-separatist tendencies that worsen exclusion).[61] The historical exemplarity of the civil rights movement remains narrowly construed. Against the sordid past of a bounded problem (antiblack racial discrimination and formal exclusion, mainly in the South), here is a moment of nationally bound, heroic overcoming that refocuses American civic identity, successfully expands democratic equality to its neglected others, and realizes a "more perfect union."[62]

But if that is the case, what do we do with the fact that by the end of his life, Martin Luther King no longer described the "black revolution" to which he gave his life as a revolution for Negroes to "get in" but as "much more than a struggle for the rights of Negroes"? In King's description, the movement was, in function if not always in intention, "forcing America to face all its interrelated flaws—racism, poverty, militarism, and materialism. It is exposing evils that are rooted deeply in the whole structure of our society. It reveals systemic rather than superficial flaws and suggests that radical reconstruction of society itself is the real issue to be faced."[63] To develop an account capable of meeting this interpretive challenge, we must turn to the concept of *decentering* disclosure.

Decentering Disclosures: Rethinking the Exemplarity of the Civil Rights Movement

Recall the claim that decentering disclosures lead us to adopt "new" perspectives and normative judgments on our ways of life. But what does it mean to genuinely think anew? How is it possible to disturb our very self-understandings and to inject dissonance into our existing modes of being, and why would we even desire such transformation? This, I wager, can best be answered by thinking through the experience of crisis.

It has long been part of the self-conception of critical theory that the diagnosis of crisis is an essential task. The etymology of *crisis* draws our attention to the medical connotations of the term in the Middle Ages as the "stage in the development of a disease that is a turning point and during which the decisive diagnosis concerning the healing or worsening of the patient is reached." This philological insight, preserved in the medical vocabulary of "critical condition," reveals the connection between the "process of social and natural disturbance and subjective judgment" that remains at the heart of crisis diagnosis in critical social and political theory. As Seyla Benhabib powerfully reminds us, the demand to theorize crisis, at its most comprehensive, combines arguments about the "objective" or "dysfunctional" character of systemic breakdowns (e.g., economic recessions or state collapse) and also *lived* experience (often through disorientation, anomie, alienation, anxiety, aggression, or suffering).[64] In myriad ways and with varying degrees of consciousness, these subjective experiences are grasped (at least by some) as rooted in "an awareness of things going, or having gone, terribly wrong" in the broader society.[65]

Kompridis, following in this tradition, argues that both refocusing and decentering disclosure (but especially the latter) are indispensable responses to crisis. When reflective disclosure is represented as refocusing, the operative metaphor for response to crisis is one of repair. We see, as in the accounts of the civil rights movement above, claims that some action or speech excavated our strong evaluative or ontological commitments from burial, inarticulacy, or breakdown to make them more immediately present and actionable in the face of unforeseen or previously unacknowledged problems. This recovery, understood as a return to who we most authentically are, decisively overcomes and even dissolves the crisis at hand by reintegrating the formerly fractured or disoriented subject of disclosure, whether collective (e.g., a political people) or individual.[66] We are not likely to experience this sort of disclosure as a radical dislocation in self-understanding or as a disassembling of identity. Indeed, the normative force of its exemplarity comes from its sense that an event was required to achieve authentic relation with our identity and realign with what it means to flourish under a given description (e.g., our national identity).

Decentering disclosure, on the other hand, entails a qualitatively different experience. As Kompridis writes, "Genuine experiences of self-decentering involve and challenge all of our cognitive and affective capacities, our whole sensibility. . . . It is not something that we can master; if anything, it masters us. Genuine decentering is genuinely uncomfortable, unsettling, which is why, understandably, it is resisted. And it is resisted because it demands our willingness as much as it tests our capacity to expose and suffer our vulnerability, not just the fallibility of our beliefs."[67]

The vulnerability that Kompridis alludes to exceeds epistemological questions about what we know and strikes at the heart of the existential-ontological question of identity: who we are. Who do our practices, commitments, and values make us? The challenges these sorts of experiences pose are of a depth and character that shake the very coherency and contiguity of self-understanding and the concomitant feeling of understanding and orientation, or being at "home in the world," as Arendt puts it.[68] The transformations they affect in our horizons of significance and the commonsense pictures we have of the world are not subtle revisions around the edges or restoration operations launched from their deepest foundations; they are more like jarring leaps beyond. They shake the central pillars of our normative and epistemological orientations, and in doing so rephrase what Kompridis calls the defining question of modernity—"the problem of getting right the proportion of continuity and discontinuity in the forms of life we pass on"—as a more insistent and impatient query, one that refuses even to take the contours and content of identity, the "we" at hand, as settled business.

Paradoxically, these moments can lead us to a greater recognition of being subject to forces outside ourselves while also threatening and tempting us with an enlarged sense of our own (collective) freedom. Here, as is so often the case, James Baldwin puts it best:

> Any real change implies the breakup of the world as one has always known it, the loss of all that gave one an identity, the end of safety. And at such a moment, unable to see and not daring to imagine what the future will now bring forth, one clings to what one knew, or thought one knew; to what one possessed or dreamed that one possessed. Yet, it is only when a man is able, without bitterness or self-pity, to surrender a dream he has long cherished or a privilege he has long possessed that he is set free—he has set himself free—for higher dreams, for greater privileges.[69]

These contentions are what the idea of decentering attempts to explain. It refers to those events or moments that inaugurate a crisis in the continuity of social identities by deeply challenging their narrative and other foundations but that cannot be reduced to the decision of an agent alone. These events strike on the other side, if you will, of the dynamic nominalism that produces identities, undermining a particular way of being.[70] They interrupt our settled habits and expectations by revealing new possibilities for seeing, acting, and being in the world. Moreover, they redescribe or reveal new accounts of problems that challenge existing paradigms challenging problems and subject the narrative coherence of existing identities and traditions to critique.

Decentering overflows the control of individual subjects—and even polities and peoples, for that matter. There are occasions when our existing identities and their constitutive horizons of significance are confronted with events that lodge a sense of inadequacy, longing, frustration, or dissonance in our pictures of the world and render us skeptical that the scripts we have inherited and the self-understandings we have constructed are adequate to carrying on. In retrospective judgment, however, we can potentially regain our footing and exercise a degree of freedom precisely in the ethical-existential sense that Kompridis suggests, deciding what in this inheritance to carry on and what to leave behind. When we judge certain acts or events as central to this sort of experience and in orienting us to beginning anew, they tend to have the stature of the exemplary.

A Decentering Account of the Sit-In Movement

One such dramatic redisclosure could be argued to have begun on February 1, 1960, when a group of four black students from North Carolina Agricultural and Technical Institute (later known as the Greensboro Four) orchestrated a sit-in demonstration against the segregationist practices of a Woolworth's lunch counter in nearby downtown Greensboro, sparking a wave of imitative and radicalizing protests. These demonstrations, in the civil rights activist Ella Baker's memorable phrase, were "concerned with something much bigger than a hamburger or even a giant-sized Coke."[71] They were an attempt to reflectively disclose a new picture of citizenship and dignity.

Politicians and political thinkers have traditionally understood citizenship as being defined by rights or practices of formal political participation (voting, for example, or holding office), the criteria of recognized membership in a given polity (nationality), or, at least among left-leaning liberals, civic standing linked to social rights of employment, education, and welfare.[72] Excepting the brief moment of antidiscrimination statutes for public accommodations in Reconstruction era jurisprudence, the solidity of these conceptual boundaries for citizenship made it difficult to imagine a constitutional pathway to refusing the expansive privileges of discrimination claimed by business owners as constitutive of their property rights.[73] For most of American history, guaranteeing access to, or dignified treatment within, spaces of consumer society would not appear to be a prerequisite of equal citizenship. As former President Harry S. Truman, who issued the executive order to desegregate the US military, responded in an interview to the sit-in demonstrations by claiming, "If anyone came to my store and sat down, I would throw him out. Private business has its own rights and can do what it wants."[74]

The sit-in movement activists, however, were creating and committing themselves to a dissenting picture of citizenship that grasped the spaces of consumer society and their constitutive practices of hiring, customer treatment, and pricing as among the vital domains of citizenship and dignity in the modern world.[75] It is in these spaces, made all the more important by rapid growth and diversification in the postwar period, that many of the deep habits of interaction and membership are learned and reiterated, shaping far-reaching norms about who is owed recognition and respect and what forms of conduct would authentically enact and reliably signal such regard.[76]

As King argued, "The 'sit-ins' represent more than a demand for service; they represent a demand for respect."[77] To realize this demand, however, required not simply the dismantling of state-mandated segregation statutes. It also demanded a higher-order realization that the discriminatory practices of private consumer enterprise are a legitimate public matter of *justice.* From the lunch counters of dime stores and department stores, thousands of courageous students and their allies attempted to redescribe the meaning of citizenship and dignity, disclosing how deeply the whole political community—its civic habits, notions of freedom and fairness, constitutional traditions, and practices of law enforcement—are always already implicated in something as seemingly minor as who can be served a hamburger and how.

One difficulty in retrospectively grasping the force of their protest is the exclusion metaphor. Although the paradigmatic Jim Crow image is arguably the "Whites Only" sign that suggests pure prohibition and separation, Jim Crow capitalism—at least its consumer-facing side—is more accurately described as a complex and often conflicting admixture of commitments.[78] Proprietors sought to balance the imperatives of profit, the obligations of law, and the mores of white supremacy. Too wedded to a facile notion of exclusion, we can easily lose sight of how a great many businesses navigated Jim Crow capitalism in more ad hoc configurations, navigating a rather unstable context of anticipatory judgments about how white customers or politicians might respond to any specific partitioning of the races in a store.[79]

This complexity stems in large part from the imperatives of profit. Stores like Woolworth's did not turn away the patronage of Southern black people outright. Instead they came to the same conclusion that, as Malcolm X acidly recalled in his *Autobiography,* white organized-crime figures alighted upon in running vice and gambling in Harlem years before—that there are "fortunes being made in . . . 'nigger pennies.'"[80] Jim Crow capitalism was not a sweeping logic of total exclusion but rather one that created a confusing archipelago of attempts to incorporate rigid hierarchies and ritual humiliations into the everyday American drama of buying and selling without sacrificing too much in the way of income or the power of ownership.

Thus, at this Woolworth's, Negroes could freely purchase school supplies at the store counter, but they could not purchase and consume food at the dining counter. At this restaurant, Negroes could order food, but they had to be served in the back. At this department store, Negroes could purchase clothing, but they could not try on items before they purchased them. At this movie theater, Negroes could attend the film screening, but they could only sit upstairs in the balcony—the "Crow's Nest" in mocking Jim Crow parlance. At the amusement park, Negroes could ride the carousel, but only on the annual Negro Day.[81]

The goal of such enterprise was often less to "exclude" African Americans from consumer life in a categorical sense but instead to incorporate the reassertion of intractable and categorical racial difference and the humiliating deference of black semicitizens to white citizens into forms of profiteering that appeared to accommodate a stable racial hierarchy. In many respects, the practices of postwar segregation in consumer spaces and public accommodations targeted by sit-in activists were downstream evolutions of the plantation store. In that earlier and more extreme institutional vehicle of Jim Crow domination, the sharecropper and his family were compelled—by interminable debt, state- and vigilante-restricted freedom of movement and contract, geographic isolation, and lack of education—to buy goods on exploitative terms (e.g., crop liens) or with company-issued "currency" from the owners of the land on which they worked.[82] The advent of local merchants and migration to urban centers began to destabilize this particular consumer regime, erecting the unstable commercial world of Jim Crow capitalism that is more familiar from the classical phase of civil rights protest.

In descending on spaces of consumer life like Woolworth's with the tactics of direct-action protest, the sit-in activists sought to press their claim that the practice of Jim Crow consumer capitalism were corrosive to democratic citizenship and injurious to human dignity as such. Moreover, the performative dimension of a sit-in dramatized the description of lunch counters and shopping centers as political spaces. They impugned any imagining of the polity that excluded these arenas, a priori, from political contestation on the grounds of the public-private distinction and challenged claims about rights of contract and association that served functionally to obscure the relations of domination, acquiescence, and collective violence undergirding these practices.

The sit-in movement also revealed, perhaps most clearly for its participants, the extent to which Jim Crow consumption required a careful balance of public acquiescence and police enforcement. Part of why contemporary observers consistently note how protestors grew "more determined and confident all the time, surprised by their own strength" was that they discovered, through nonviolent noncooperation, that the mechanisms to enforce the existing order were more limited than had been expected.[83] Narrating his experience as a white Presbyterian minister and professor protesting alongside black college students in Knoxville, Tennessee, Merrill Proudfoot wrote that when the store lunch counter frantically shut down in response to their arrival, "what I felt was inferiority and resentment contradicted by a sense of new power. If the presence of four Negroes could cause a restaurant seating eighty people to close, what power was placed in our hands?"[84] Proudfoot's account draws on familiar tropes of the sublime to describe this new disclosure, which—as we shall see in Chapter 2—is a powerful vocabulary for this kind of political experience.

What Proudfoot and others discovered was that spontaneous, sprawling mass participation, with willingness to resist arrest and refusal to post bond created logistical nightmares for police repression. The nationalization of the issue, through dramatic press coverage, solidaristic black and liberal voters, and the corporate consolidation of firms like Woolworth's (as opposed to stores that only were local outlets), restrained the kinds of violent reprisals available to Jim Crow's regional enforcers. And the demands of profit made the initial response of permanently shutting down stores untenable. The students' conspicuously nonviolent protest, combined with their reflection on prevailing understandings of duty, freedom, and power, had critically disclosed a new set of once-suppressed possibilities for politics and for self-understanding.

The spectacle of black students disrupting the calcified habits of Jim Crow capitalism in the name of citizenship shattered the settled boundaries of the political and the widespread expectation of black acquiescence. In the former register, the students redisclosed an insight—long a truism in the labor movement that pioneered a version of the sit-in, known as the sit-down strike—that while "the law tends to declare rights—it does not deliver them." As King argued, "A catalyst is needed to breathe life experience into a judicial decision by the persistent exercise of the rights until they become usual and ordinary in human conduct," and the sit-in movement participants "offered their energies, their bodies to effect this result."[85]

This radically participatory notion of lawmaking, as King pointed out, involved not only a rejection of conventional jurisprudential thinking but also the prevailing technocratic and elitist conception of black and antiracist politics as strategies decided and carried out by NAACP lawyers and lobbyists. As Ezell Blair, one of the Greensboro Four recollected,

> We wanted to sort of destroy the old idea that Negroes had to be told everything we do, by the NAACP or CORE . . . we realized that [the NAACP] had been the forerunner of the civil rights movement for a long time, and we respect the organization very much for what it has done, but we felt that it was time for new action to be taken in the South. You see to us, it appeared that it was something like the hierarchy, maybe something like the Catholic church—and no offense to the Catholics in that—you know in Italy giving all of the orders, you know, and none of its affiliates in other countries will make a move until maybe the ideas or suggestions . . . were approved by the head office in Italy . . . and so we thought the NAA[CP] was organized on the same basis, and we felt that many times Negroes felt discouraged in the South because it took too long for [the] NAACP to make up its mind what to do.[86]

This disruptive action made its impact felt on existing notions of political obligation and national destiny, inspiring one of the great participatory peaks of activism in American history. In doing so these activists also compelled the support of a critical segment of white Americans, especially students, who came to see the fate of civil rights activism as deeply entangled with the fortunes of their nation and themselves and as disclosing a new set of possibilities for democratic, nonviolent world making.[87] King distilled this enthusiasm with characteristic eloquence: "Not long ago the Negro collegian imitated the white collegian. In attire, in athletics, in social life, imitation was the rule. . . . Today the imitation has ceased. The negro collegian now initiates. Groping for unique forms of protest, he created the sit-ins and freedom rides. Overnight his white fellow students began to imitate him. As the movement took hold, a revival of social awareness spread across campuses from Cambridge to California. It spilled over the boundaries of the single issue of desegregation and encompassed questions of peace, civil liberties, capital punishment and others."[88]

The contagious character of this protest movement, and the sense of entanglement and implication it raised, is crucial to interrogate. How did it help push people to call into question features of their societies that they had, theretofore, treated as certainties? Perhaps it poses, in the political domain, a question akin to Ludwig Wittgenstein's query in *On Certainty:* "Why is it not possible for me to doubt that I have never been on the moon? And how could I try to doubt it? First and foremost, the supposition that perhaps I have been there would strike me as idle. Nothing would follow from it, nothing be explained by it. It would not tie in with anything in my life. When I say 'Nothing speaks for, everything against it,' this presupposes a principle of speaking for and against. That is, I must be able to say what would speak for it."[89]

The Wittgensteinian idea of an "idle supposition" that "nothing speaks for" suggests a proposition or argument that, within a certain picture of the world, lacks explanatory, normative, or utilitarian significance. It simply does not cohere with, or provide critical purchase on, the narratives that shape my self-understanding or the practices that I suppose constitute my life. Wittgenstein's point is that for us to have a genuinely new and critical relation to what we once "knew" or took for certain, challenges to our certainties must not have this character of "idle suppositions." However they redescribe our past or project us toward a set of possible futures, our critical and practical interventions must somehow *change* what counts as evidence and adjudication. This is done by disclosing, speaking to, and plausibly addressing a sense of crisis, often through practical action that disrupts the habits of our forms of life. The question, of course, is, what does it take to recognize something as genuinely raising the problem of crisis, or as challenging us at the scale of conceptual or systematic error rather than being the kind of phenomenon that is simply unthreatening, anomalous, or spurious?

Indeed, a striking feature of early responses to the sit-ins is the allegation that they were "another college fad of the 'panty-raid' variety," insinuating that the youthful protestors simply enjoyed the carnivalesque disruptions of hierarchy that their protests managed to briefly achieve, or that the demonstrations could have been thwarted with "a ham sandwich" begrudgingly offered on the first day.[90] Their spread and persistence in the face of both danger and token concession, however, obliterated this interpretation, which relied on settled expectations about Negro passivity and cowardice. The rise and fall of that stereotype, one of the few that has effectively ceased to be a controlling image of blackness, reflects nothing so much as the way the sit-ins tore and strained at the epistemic and political certainties that once held Jim Crow in place.[91]

James Baldwin, in an interview with Kenneth B. Clark, put it trenchantly:

> One of the things I think that happened . . . is that in the first place, the Negro has never been as docile as white Americans wanted to believe. That was a myth. We were not singing and dancing down on the levee. We were trying to keep alive; we were trying to survive a very brutal system. The Negro has never been happy in "his" place. What those kids first of all proved—first of all they proved that. They come from a long line of fighters. And what they also prove—I want to get to your point, really—what they also prove is not that the Negro has changed, but that the country has arrived at a place where he can no longer contain the revolt.[92]

My insistence on taking habits and enduring practices seriously stems from the ways that, as Baldwin contends, our habits come to generate propositions about what the world is like, cultivate forms of (in)attention to phenomena, our ability to remember and forget, and what we feel entitled to expect from others.[93] Coming to depend on the world's being a certain way influences social norms (e.g., trust) and scripts of identity, becoming through the circuitous pathways of habit part of the normative order and structure of feeling within a form of life.

The sit-in movement, on the decentering account, therefore, was not simply about securing rights. It involved uprooting an imposing edifice of settled expectations that structured the lifeworld of American civilization and consumption, disclosing alternative ways of being in the world, new forms of identity, and new emotional experiences and practices of sympathy and solidarity. Activists put fatal pressure on the existing narrative conventions of civic identity and the practices of civic life under Jim Crow. Disclosing a competing picture of the power relations, group identities, and ethical-political possibilities inherent in the American racial order, the sit-ins turned a localized blaze into a full-blown critical conflagration, setting fire to the constructions standing on nearby terrain as struggles about gender, sexuality, peace, environmentalism, and so on spread from Greensboro.

But here we must sound a note of caution that later chapters will flesh out. Drawing attention to the fact that intentional collective action may be involved in something like reflective, decentering disclosure is not meant to buttress a long-discredited fantasy of sovereign control over such experiences. Unsettled expectations of the sort that would change political propositions and moral axioms from idle to vital, in Wittgenstein's sense, involve breakdowns in what he calls a broader "system in which consequences and premises give one another mutual support."[94] Seemingly unrelated developments (e.g., the growing cultural importance of television and the nationalization of department stores and consumer enterprises as firms) or judgments (e.g., the epistemological weight given to filmed brutality versus testimonial accounts of brutality) can become central features of redisclosure, even though no one intended them to be put to the purposes they were appropriated for. A complex background of processes, cultural drifts, and experiences can weaken the mutual supports that hold a picture of the world together in ways that are unthematized or inaccessible until a decisive moment is *retroactively judged*. Any story of decentering (and it must be a story) will involve a broader context of structural and cultural rupture as well as the forms of receptivity necessary to make sense of it. These cannot be captured solely by the concept of "action" in the narrow sense of intentionalist or sovereign control.

Rupture: Exemplarity, Narrative, Judgment

My insistence on nonsovereignty does not mean that we should therefore abandon questions of freedom or evaluative judgment concerning our possible ethical-existential need for or response to decentering experiences of rupture in how we see and inhabit the world. While refocusing disclosure emphasizes continuity, decentering elicits a variety of responses that try to make sense of what, retroactively, seems best narrated and grasped as a dramatic transition.

We may try to expunge traces of our earlier form of life from ourselves and the world. Or we may construct cultural and institutional bulwarks against slippage back to a path now judged as a grand, even world-historical, mistake. We might explore and experiment with the potentials of a life newly aligned by the dynamics of disclosure, or move to persuade others to see things the way we do. In a reparative mode, we might investigate how harms constitutive of the old form of life have generated obligations and injuries in this one. What underlies all these possibilities,

I want to suggest, is a dimension of freedom best described as the ability to forge and found a new beginning with others.[95] This enactment of freedom, however, requires *exemplarity, narrative,* and *judgment.* Whatever else a description of reflective disclosure involves, it requires a narrative of continuity and discontinuity.

Where decentering disclosure seems an apt description, critics often reach for the language of founding to connect an account of crisis and breakdown to the emergence of something exemplary that anchors an enduring way of being, seeing, and doing in the world. This is, I think, a better way of grasping what Sunstein rightly notes is King's frequent reference to the American founding, but without the broader context of his citation of it within a series of other revolutionary or liberatory struggles. Describing the courage of students and their allies facing state repression, King proclaimed, for example, that

> with the punishments [of sit-in activists], something more is growing. A generation of young people has come out of decades of shadows to face naked state power; it has lost its fears, and experienced the majestic dignity of a direct struggle for its own liberation. The young people have connected up with their own history—the slave revolts, the incomplete revolution of the Civil War, the brotherhood of colonial colored men in Africa and Asia. They are an integral part of the history which is reshaping the world, replacing a dying order with modern democracy. They are doing this in a nation whose own birth spread new principles and shattered a medieval social society then dominating most of the globe.[96]

This notion of an iterative tradition of founding and refounding is widespread. In art, for example, we tend to recognize particular works as moments of founding when they inspire other artists to take art's aesthetic achievements as a model or standard for an incipient artistic practice and aesthetic philosophy that confronts the limits of other paradigms. These moments found—or are, at least, thought capable of founding (or refounding)—artistic traditions (e.g., cubism, impressionism, and surrealism). They render what might not have even seemed possible before being eminently so and change what counts (to channel Wittgenstein) as giving an account of beauty, meaning, sublimity, and the like. They instantiate, seemingly out of themselves and their inheritors, a different way of thinking about meaning and validity, and retrospectively judging the traditions and exemplars that will be our heritage.

Political revolutions can also manifest this sort of innovative exemplarity. Arendt described revolution effectively, if too singularly, as "the only political events which confront us directly and inevitably with the problem of beginning." Revolutions, in this account and eventually in their own self-understanding, sweep away some expansive measure of the extant political order to found a new body politic.[97] In his *Reflections on the Revolution in France* (1790), Edmund Burke expressed utter dismay at just this process, lamenting that the "very idea of the fabrication of a new government, is enough to fill us with disgust and horror."[98] Part of Burke's horror, however, stemmed from one of the central difficulties of revolutionary political action: the difficulty of reestablishing, through acts of human freedom, political authority in a new form after the collapse of the old regime.[99]

Many modern revolutionaries appealed to the idea of natural right to articulate and preserve the fragile authority of this new social order, but as Arendt notes, it would eventually become "the act of foundation itself, rather than an Immortal Legislator or self-evident truth or any other transcendent, transmundane source, which eventually would become the fountain of authority in the new body politic." In other words, the very act of foundation, when it inspires affirmation and iterative action, becomes exemplary. In its exemplarity, it serves as a touchstone for reflections about politics and policy, and interpretations of its spirit or significance serve as guides for actors who to varying degrees of self-awareness appeal for understanding and principle to what, in their interpretation, it has disclosed. Reflecting on the US Constitution—in the dual sense of the founding itself and the document that enshrines the principles of the founding—Arendt found herself "tempted . . . to predict that the authority of the republic will be safe and intact as long as the act itself, the beginning as such, is remembered whenever constitutional questions in the narrower sense of the word come into play."[100]

This claim should not be misinterpreted as an endorsement of either the so-called originalist school of constitutional law or the constitutional fundamentalism of populist right-wing activists.[101] These modes of remembrance turn their fetishism for the alleged original intent of the Founding Fathers into an interpretive dogmatism that sprouts from faulty epistemological and hermeneutic premises.[102] More important, at least for the purposes of understanding the innovative exemplarity of political revolution, these impoverished modes of remembrance hollow out the significance of freedom—the human capacity to act in the world, in concert with others, in pursuit of novel aims—that is a crucial dimension of the dual meanings of *constitution*.[103] In their most extreme forms, they represent bad-faith denials of contemporary capacities for freedom and action in the present and abdicate the responsibility of good judgment to a sacralized, deified vision of the Founding Fathers whose eighteenth-century pronouncements are expected to reveal the right and final verdict on the permissibility of citizens' aims and government's projects in perpetuity. Abandoning judgment, they lead to imitation rather than action or cynicism masquerading as covenantal commitment.

This contrast allows us to revisit an important point about exemplarity where human action is concerned. When we invoke an example for ourselves or others, we are offering a model or interpretation of something more generally significant, but it is only a touchstone, not a strict rule, or an interpretation, not a conclusive fact, and its guidance will always require judgment to make sense of. In the very selection of one example (or the interpretation of an example) over any number of others, we reveal the inescapability of judgment. To then conceal this freedom, rooted in our capacity for judgment, by treating the example as if it were a rule or order that we have no choice but to follow strictly is to commit a kind of violence against our capabilities and the import of exemplarity. We abdicate the responsibility to ourselves and others to give an account of the why and the how that must normatively govern the examples we invoke for action.

Moreover, we deny, at some level, that the example and our own actions exist in different historical spaces, times, and contexts that can, by definition, never be entirely congruent. Every appropriation of an example is interpretive and adaptive and thus retains an ineliminable dimension of human freedom. Genuine exemplarity involves a subjectively meaningful relation with the example that does not extinguish this freedom.[104] This seems especially true of innovative exemplarity, where a constitutive feature of the example is the very ability to disclose what we take to be a truly novel beginning or transformation in the midst of history—an ability perhaps not reducible to, but inexplicable without, reference to human freedom.[105]

Another set of dangerous interpretive tendencies bears noting. I have suggested throughout that there is an inescapably historical-temporal dimension to disclosure, since it marks, and is experienced as, the movement or development of a form of life (and its constitutive identities) over time. Reflective disclosure is inevitably historical insofar as any instance of disclosure is necessarily in the past yet is alleged to be significant (and thus, an object of reflection) in the present. The (historical) reflection on disclosure, which the judgment of exemplarity involves, demands that we give an account of these transitions in time through narrative, the basic grammar of historical thinking.

Insofar as this transition alters our relationship with the past bedrocks of our identity or forms of life, however, we are confronted with a metanarrative problem. We become people who had once assumed certain things about the world and ourselves as part of our basic orientation, or had these assumptions as part of our heritage, but now do not or cannot. The question is, How do we assimilate such a shift to our stories about ourselves and our peoplehood? The dilemma is that in constructing a narrative account of disclosure, we are perpetually tempted by three interpretive dangers.

The first is a retrospective overestimation of continuity of identity, modes of being, and practices over time. This occurs especially where a posteriori justifications for changes actually made to social practices are misguidedly assumed to be a priori reasons or motivations and thus are presented as having too much explanatory weight in the account of disclosure's happening. This is one of the main reasons one might characterize a decentering disclosure as a refocusing one.

The second is an underestimation of the breadth and depth of the occasioning crises and the significance of historical moments of indeterminacy in the relevant traditions where alternative political paradigms, social practices, or philosophical pictures were considered. Here the purported repairing of the deep values of a society can be wrongly assumed to have been an essentially inevitable historical process or have not even been subject to serious contestation and possible amendment by other visions. Perhaps the most powerful recent critique of this sort of tendency is in Adom Getachew's *Worldmaking After Empire,* which rediscloses the era of decolonization not as overdetermined by a telos of national sovereignty but as riven by debates over other possible postcolonial arrangements, including regional federations, refounded global governance institutions, and transnational political movements (e.g., Pan-Africanism).[106]

Finally, there is the misguided assumption that all disclosures represent a universal or total gain in understanding and ethical wisdom. Even if a given disclosure refocuses us on some significant phenomenon about the social world or powerfully extends normativity within a cultural horizon, it is also possible that it conceals or levels other features of our context. The price of certain gains represented by an ascendant disclosure might, in time, be revealed to be deficiencies or lacunae concerning other important practices or judgments. This, we will come to see, is one of the great insights of tragedy and its vision of human existence.

In the immediate case of the sit-ins, for instance, it is difficult to avoid the retrospective judgment that it was nearly impossible to offer, all at once and in the midst of anticommunist hysteria, the critique of white supremacist and libertarian conceptions of property, liberal-formalist notions of citizenship, and the resistance to civil disobedience and nonviolence noted above, alongside an ethical critique of consumerism as a form of life and a sweeping vision of economic reconstruction. One enduring paradox of the sit-in movement, therefore, is the way that notions of civic standing and freedom were entangled with ideas of consumer standing and freedom in both emancipatory and self-undermining ways. Not only did access to consumer spaces mean little without economic resources that portended far more sweeping structural changes, as King often noted, but the dramatic symbolism of the sit-ins also layered African American consumption (especially of products symbolized as "white" or "exclusive") with an increasingly ideological veneer of subversive memory and collective effervescence. The legacy of this symbolic charge has, in popular even more than political culture, helped produce a steady stream of self-valorizing musical and visual paeans to black consumption whose celebrations of the counterhumiliation of black wealth or hollowing out of the language of "black excellence" seems finally, hopefully to have reached the point of exhaustion.[107]

In the remaining chapters of Part One, I continue to pursue a critical theory capable of navigating these problems of exemplarity, narrative, and judgment. I begin with an investigation into the judging faculty through Immanuel Kant's arguments concerning aesthetic judgment in the *Critique of the Power of Judgment.* This account will help explain how we rely on judgment to apprehend examples, give interpretive accounts of their significance, offer them up as valid or rightly imitated to the world, and orient our practical freedom around them. I show how Kant's interest in aesthetic judgment led him to develop notions of historical and political judgment connected to his discoveries in the aesthetic realm.

I then turn to Arendt's idiosyncratic but inspirational attempt to appropriate Kant's third *Critique* for her concerns with political, moral, and historical judgment. I sympathetically reconstruct her argument to address recent criticisms that her theory of judgment is a radical misreading of Kant, normatively deficient, and insufficient to address questions about the general validity of particular judgments. Specifically, I buttress her arguments with a closer reading of her divergences from Kant and their significance, considering the connections between aesthetic, political, moral, and historical judgment. I then sketch an account of the validity of reflective judgment that foregrounds dignity while preserving this form of judgment's inextricable link to practices of freedom and narrative representation before turning explicitly to questions of narrative and critique.

CHAPTER 2

BETWEEN AESTHETICS AND HISTORY

Kant and the Problem of Judgment

IN CHAPTER 1, I OFFERED an account that tried to step back from the routinization of exemplary events through their mobilization as examples in everyday discourse in order to redisclose and thematize the *experience* of exemplarity, especially in its most innovative sense. In what follows I want to deepen this phenomenological inquiry by delving into the conditions and capabilities that make such experiences possible. How do we come to apprehend or imagine exemplarity in our encounters with particulars and their representations? How do we treat judgments about these particulars as generally (or even universally) valid, extending our claims about exemplarity beyond our private subjective feelings? How is it that through our judgments about exemplary objects or events, we find our way toward forms of sense making, horizons of significance, and ideals that appear to exceed what exists and establish norms that transcend their local origin? How might pondering or pursuing instances of exemplarity train our powers of judgment, dispositions, and relations to one another? These questions undergird our larger concern with whether we can legitimately treat certain historical events as exemplary—as touchstones for judgment, action, and imagination—even when we lose confidence in determinant categories or totalizing narratives.

Despite the importance of such questions for understanding how we represent and think through problems of politics and history, investigations of this sort have arguably been pursued with the greatest sophistication in modern aesthetic philosophy. This philosophical partitioning is due, above all, to aesthetic philosophy's fascination with problems of *judgment*. "The power of judgment," as Immanuel Kant described it in his essential *Critique of the Power of Judgment* (1790), is "the faculty for thinking of the particular as contained under the universal" ("Introduction," IV:179).[1]

Judgment allows us to recognize, interpret, and evaluate particular cases in light of principles, categories, norms, and rules. We also, however, make judgments even when a rule is not readily available. Judgment allows us to discern and even generate new evaluative interpretations, norms, and categories by imaginatively reconsidering, comparing, and giving novel accounts of particulars such that they become exemplary in the innovative sense. These are the kinds of judgments occasioned by works of art—Pablo Picasso's *Les Demoiselles d'Avignon* (1907) or Ornette Coleman's *Free Jazz* (1961) might come to mind—that seem to break with familiar rules or mechanically imitative standards and invite claims that they manifest a novel sense of rightness or order out of themselves, a normativity that serves an exemplary purpose for others "as a standard or a rule for judging" (§46, 308).[2] To paraphrase the poet William Wordsworth, some works of art seem capable of creating the taste by which they are to be enjoyed.[3]

To describe these phenomena, cultural critics and philosophers of aesthetics have clung to terms like *charisma, genius,* and *originality* rather than abandon them to the reflexive suspicion of scholars of politics. In speaking unironically of genius or originality, however, inquiries into aesthetic experience capture more fully how paradigm-shifting artworks seem to radically transform our sense of beauty or even what art itself might look like or mean. In political and social theory, though rarer, the ability to speak without paralyzing suspicion of charisma is to admit a similar concern with how particular actions, events, and personalities might create new forms of authority or standards, inspiring emulation through their incisive challenge to "the givenness of the present, its powers and routines, its compass points and assumptions . . . with an alternative orbit of meaning."[4]

Judgment is how we come to posit, evaluate, and communicate these possible relations. It is the capacity through which we answer questions like, What are we encountering, and why should we see it *this* way rather than another? How does this encounter make me feel, and is this feeling only idiosyncratic to me or suggestive of something more universal? What are the possible forms of meaning, significance, understanding, and imagination that my encounter with an object of judgment might occasion or elicit? How might specific modes or exercises of judgment change our experiences of the world and our relation to, and claims on, one another?

It is, at least since the seismic intervention of Kant's third *Critique,* far more common for philosophers of aesthetics to wrestle with problems of judgment so construed. Thinkers concerned with traditionally "aesthetic" questions (e.g., the beauty of art and nature) came decisively to grapple with how it could be that a particular object or happening (e.g., a work of art or an instance of natural beauty), created and subjectively experienced in a specific context, could nonetheless occasion a judgment like "This painting is beautiful" that expects general, or even universal, agreement in a way that an utterance like "I like the taste of this meal" does not (§22:239). Somehow, as Michel Chaouli puts it, "the singularity" of aesthetic experience "reveals itself as a strange form of universality," without, however, being able to compel universal agreement as in a mathematical proof or logical judgment.[5]

Although, as Kant concedes, "every art presupposes rules" of possibility (e.g., sculpture must be three-dimensional), the judgment as to the beauty of an aesthetic object—especially if it is to involve a certain *feeling* of aesthetic pleasure—cannot be predetermined by or compelled by these rules, or any rules for that matter (§46:307). As Christian Helmut Wenzel notes, "There may be techniques that have to be learned, and the artist can explain some of the ideas he or she had in mind while creating the object," but there are nonetheless "no rules for beauty, no rules for beautiful art, and also no rules for the production of beautiful art."[6]

For Linda Zerilli, arguably the leading scholar of the implications of Kantian aesthetics for political theory, this fundamental quandary of aesthetic judgment is "the heart of the matter" and the key question that makes Kant's account of judgment so vital for political theory. "How," she asks, "can a judgment that is not subject to validation on the basis of proofs possibly make a claim to the agreement of all?"[7] How, in other words, can we adjudicate better and worse judgments without relying on a priori rules or determinate concepts that would compel our assent?

In posing this question in pursuit of political matters, Zerilli follows a path cleared by Hannah Arendt, who provocatively argued that Kant's inquiry into the faculty of judgment and effort to think with particulars amounted to a pathbreaking political philosophy capable of grappling with the most fundamental issues of history and politics, even if these are not obviously headlining themes in the *Critique of the Power of Judgment.*[8]

This chapter offers a brief reconstruction of the influential Kantian account of judgment in pursuit of our larger critical theoretical goal of understanding exemplarity. I consider the aims of Kantian aesthetics, especially its attempt to defend a notion of general validity for subjective feelings of pleasure and judgments of beauty. After focusing on central notions of common sense and the free play of our cognitive faculties, I discuss Kant's ideas of purposiveness without purpose and the distinction between determinant and reflective judgments. I close with an investigation of Kant's drift from aesthetic judgment into historical speculation and the significance of his notions of beauty, sublimity, and teleology in this domain. These controversial speculations on history, nature, and theology will serve as an important building block for this book's central concern: the critique of the content of narrative form in civil rights historiography and its implications for political thinking which appeals to the validity of civil rights exemplarity.

Kant and the Endeavor of Modern Aesthetics

Before Kant, leading work in the philosophy of aesthetics, at least as practiced in western European traditions, was dominated by empiricist ambitions derived from the natural sciences. Intellectuals entertained great hopes for the prospect of a *science* of the beautiful. They eagerly anticipated the discovery of sufficiently a priori standards capable of adjudicating questions of beauty in a standardized, law-governed fashion or a definitive indexing of the causal relationships between the sensible qualities of various objects and the psychological and physiological reactions that cohere into "aesthetic" taste.[9] Edmund Burke's 1757 effort, *A Philosophical Enquiry into the Origin of Our Ideas of the Sublime and the Beautiful,* was characteristic in its attempt to catalog a set of necessary psychosomatic responses to objects, articulate rules for perception and judgment, and generate a priori concepts that, if followed, would allow anyone to recognize correctly or make valid claims about what was beautiful, ugly, or sublime in art and nature.[10]

As conceived by this empiricist tradition, the quest for a science of beauty is now widely considered a failure, even on its own terms.[11] "The Germans," Kant complained in the *Critique of Pure Reason,* "are the only ones who now employ the word 'aesthetics' to designate that which others call the critique of taste. The ground for this is a failed hope, held by the excellent analyst Baumgarten, of bringing the critical estimation of the beautiful under principles of reason, and elevating its rules to a science. But this effort is futile."[12] Over a century later, Max Weber, who traced the origins of the scientific method and "the rational experiment" in European modernity to the Renaissance artists of the fifteenth and sixteenth centuries, argued that in the "artistic experiments of the type of Leonardo [da Vinci] and [Renaissance] musical innovators" practiced, "*science* meant the path to true art, and that meant for them the path to true nature." Surveying the failure of treating art and artistic evaluation as fully continuous with science from his "disenchanted" vantage in 1918, Weber could only conclude that "'science as the way to nature' would sound like blasphemy to youth. Today, youth proclaims the opposite: redemption from the intellectualism of science in order to return to one's own nature and therewith to nature in general. Science as a way to art? Here no criticism is even needed."[13]

Kant's and Weber's open mockery reflects how the sweeping cultural and epistemological transformations of the modern age (especially the spread of modern science itself) decisively discredited the hope for a "scientific" aesthetics and transformed how we make sense of the world and find (or fail to find) meaning in different practices. The purported rationalization of modernity charted by Weber and, more recently, Jürgen Habermas, is constituted chiefly by this process of differentiation in value, meaning, and knowledge. Practices they alleged were congruent or indistinguishable in the comprehensive systems of meaning characteristic of traditional, "pre-Axial age" cultures—religion, science, art, morality, politics, and economics—have, in the modern age, undergone a dramatic fracturing into distinctive value spheres where "what is rational from one point of view may well be irrational from another."[14]

"In contexts of communicative action," Habermas argues, "we call someone rational not only if he is able to put forward an assertion and, when criticized, to provide grounds for it by pointing to appropriate evidence, but also if he is following an established norm and is able, when criticized, to justify his action by explicating the given situation in the light of legitimate expectations."[15] When rationalization breaks apart the integrated unities of traditional cultures into differentiated value spheres, the conditions for the validity of claims concerning one domain are no longer congruent with validity conditions in another. Indeed, part of how we differentiate between practices is by the type of validity claims or patterns of support for persuasive arguments we find intelligible and meaningful within them.[16]

If we are leaving the local movie theater and I utter, "I enjoyed the film *Selma*," the validity of my claim might rest principally on my sincerity or truthfulness in giving this account of my pleasure. If "I enjoyed *Selma*" is all I offer, such an utterance has no force on its own as a claim that *you ought* to like the film, especially if "ought" here is construed, implausibly, as a matter of moral duty or virtue. For that sort of moral argument to intelligibly get off the ground, as some arguments about the kind of art African Americans should produce and consume might suggest, further argument is required: how my enjoyment of the film might reflect my refined ability to appreciate and emulate certain depictions of heroic political resistance, or whether I appropriately cultivated my character to take dutiful pride in the political achievements of African Americans and the elegant depiction of those achievements by talented artists.[17]

Indeed, even my enjoying the film is not presumptively valid as an aesthetic judgment about beauty properly understood. Just because I liked the film and found it enjoyable (or "agreeable," to use Kant's preferred term) does not quite mean that I judge it beautiful and expect you to do so too.[18] I might, on reflection, realize that my predilection for the film is based on self-interested and incorrigibly partial feelings, not the kind of judgment of taste I expect to be universally communicable.[19] This is the kind of distinction we usually use when we speak of our tastes as guilty pleasures—artworks we might enjoy but doubt would elicit broader agreement as to their aesthetic qualities.

Modernity, on the neo-Kantian and Weberian/Habermasian view, is characterized by the fragmentation of these various patterns of reasoning. What kinds of utterances we find valid, as requiring the assent of all rational subjects, tend to be deeply tied to the value sphere in which they are best contextualized and do not easily traverse such boundaries. That a work of art depicts moral goodness, for instance, is not enough to compel judgments about its beauty.

This problem bedeviled empiricist, scientistic approaches to aesthetics. While we might find a mathematician's demonstration of quantifiable fractal geometric patterns in a work of popular abstract art to be a genuinely notable scientific discovery, many would resist that such information would be necessary or sufficient to render valid the claim that I *ought* to find the painting beautiful, even if, as the evidence seems to suggest, many people do consistently judge artworks with these patterns to be so.[20] As Kant writes, neither popularity nor any other "empirical *ground of proof*" will compel rational agreement about taste:

> The judgment of taste is not determinable by grounds of proof at all, just as if it were merely *subjective*. If someone does not find a building, a view, or a poem beautiful, then, first, he does not allow approval to be internally imposed upon himself by a hundred voices who all praise it highly. He may of course behave as if it pleased him as well, in order not to be regarded as lacking in taste; he can even begin to doubt whether he has adequately formed his taste. . . . But what he does see clearly is this: that the approval of others provides no valid proof for the judging of beauty . . . what has pleased others can never serve as the ground of an aesthetic judgment [for me]. (§33:284)

This holds, too, even for determinate rules produced by esteemed aesthetes and critics of taste. One can "adduce all the rules they established as proofs that [a] poem is beautiful; certain passages, which are the very ones that displease me, may even agree with rules of beauty (as they have been given there and have been universally recognized): I will stop my ears, listen to no reasons and arguments, and would rather believe that those rules of the critics are false or at least that this is not a case for their application than allow that my judgment [of taste] should be determined by means of a priori grounds of proof" (§33:284–285). This arresting image of a person with (presumably) lousy taste, unwilling and unable to hear the claims of eminent and reasonable judgment, represents a now familiar worry that this solipsistic fate of aesthetic taste is the apotheosis of a "slide to subjectivism" characteristic of the dialectical movement of modernity's liberatory ideals (e.g., freedom and authenticity) into a malaise of skepticism, nihilism, and disorientation.[21] It represents a concern that evaluative judgments as such (not just aesthetic ones) might now be merely subjective or riven by culturally incommensurate values and thus incapable of rational adjudication or effective criticism.

Such anxieties about subjectivism and value pluralism raise problems for any self-consciously critical theory of exemplarity. How is it possible, without an integrated tradition, comprehensive worldview, or determinate set of categories that would determine the outcome of our reasoning about examples with authority, to move persuasively from the particularity of a given event, experience, or object to advance a more general evaluative or analytical claim about its significance that could be valid or meaningful for all addressees?

This problem takes on heightened significance in light of the fact that each of us finds ourselves thrown into a cultural life whose vocabularies and conditions of intelligibility seem knitted together, in part, by a vast archive of "recorded actions and utterances" purporting to represent the past, and which reveal themselves to us as "an almost inexhaustible source of analogies and resemblances in terms of which to express our understanding of ourselves or to interpret to others our purposes and actions . . . [and] current circumstances." This cultural swirl of "practical pasts," as the philosopher Michael Oakeshott describes it, seems to be a chaotic but "indispensable . . . condition of articulate practical activity."[22] We inherit a universe of mythical and historical referents, and by adding to them or redescribing them, we imagine and narrate the past through telling stories that give expression to our practical judgments of approval and disapproval.

But even Oakeshott's account, while rightly drawing attention to the practical significance and constructed character of our representations of the past, nevertheless remains question-begging with regard to the unique problem of exemplarity. It offers little guidance for understanding why *specific* events become exemplary in an enduring sense and others do not. Indeed, Oakeshott treats the idea that history can teach by example as a mode of relating to the past that thoroughly renders it a "matter of *indifference*" whether putatively historical references are even real at all. It would do just as well to point to "scenes from a mythology, products of poetic imagination or [other] alleged bygone exploits."[23] Yet conceding this indifference makes it challenging to offer a perceptive account of the relationships between representation and experience that might answer the question of "how and why we may become fascinated by our collective past," much less give us any reasoned guidance between interpretations and judgments of particular iterations of exemplarity.[24]

Indeed, this worry goes so deep as to raise the question of whether subjectivism and value pluralism leave us without enough shared commonality to speak coherently of exemplary particulars as shared or common objects of judgment that we are engaged in a genuine argument about. This destruction of this "common" space, as we shall see, was one of Hannah Arendt's urgent concerns, which she saw manifest in the well-known academic custom to grant "each of us . . . the right 'to define his terms.'" For Arendt, making this concession in the domain of the social sciences suggests that vital terms of analysis and understanding, such as "'tyranny,' 'authority,' and 'totalitarianism' have simply lost their common meaning, or . . . we have ceased to live in a common world where the words we have in common possess an unquestionable meaningfulness" rather than meaning relegated to private language games or local subcultures.[25] In light of such anxieties, we might worry that talk of historical exemplarity just identifies the form that competing deities take as they speak past one another despite sharing nominal referential terms. The outcome, perhaps, would be a self-undermining spiral of "emotivism, decisionism, and irrationalism."[26]

To meet this challenge of evaluative judgment in aesthetics, Kant pursued a theory of judgment that, while grounded in the analysis of the *subjective* feelings at the core of aesthetic experience, retained the possibility for some degree of *reasoned adjudication* and *general validity*.[27] This alternative path leads from subjective feeling to the possibility of intersubjective validity and the instantiation of a common sense that grounds the aforementioned normative aspiration that others "*should* agree" with genuine judgments of taste (§22:239). In doing so Kant landed on "the core dilemma of all speech about aesthetic experience, thus of all criticism"—namely, that while my aesthetic experience is first-personal and subjective, it nevertheless remains "responsive to the presence of others and occurs only within a field of intersubjective relations" where we make normative and evaluative claims on one other and aspire to produce a world in common.[28]

For Kant, serious reflection on the experience of coming to the judgment "This is beautiful" reveals that despite our inability to settle arguments about beauty by reference to fixed concepts, proofs, or deductions, we should still hold that "wherever it is supposed to be possible to argue, there must be hope of coming to mutual agreement; hence one must be able to count on grounds for the judgment that do not have merely private validity and thus are not merely subjective" (§56:338). The *Critique of the Power of Judgment* aims to give this intuition systematic demonstration and support. Such insights will be crucial for resolving this tension in historical and political judgment when, as in Parts Two and Three, we excavate the "aesthetic" qualities of narrative form and genre in historical discourse about the civil rights movement.

Pleasure, Purity, Play, and Purposiveness

Through the aesthetic experience of beauty, Kant argues, "I come to know something in myself, a singular form of pleasure, that surpasses my familiarity with myself, and this something that is not wholly mine opens the experience to a public dimension and makes it available to others." This "singularity reveals itself as a strange form of universality" that we can reconstruct.[29] By reflecting appropriately on certain feelings of pleasure and displeasure and rethinking what it is we do when we argue about judgments of taste, Kant insists that we can make sense of the expectation that judgments of beauty have hopes of reaching agreement, and we can rightly make claims about the exemplary validity of certain judgments of beauty, sublimity, and the like (§18:237).

How should we grasp this contention about the singularity of feeling that somehow opens to a "strange form of universality"? And without the kinds of proofs that, on principle, should settle disagreements, what kind of arguing can be done about our judgments of these particulars? Crucial to any exposition of Kant, on feelings or otherwise, is an acknowledgment of his commitment to characterizing the mind as comprising three distinct faculties: cognition, pleasure, and desire. Each of his three *Critiques* is motivated by an attempt to find the a priori principles that determine the claims and limits of validity in and between the exercise of these three faculties. While he claimed to have discovered the a priori principles governing theoretical reason (in the *Critique of Pure Reason*) and practical reason (in the *Critique of Practical Reason*), Kant had long harbored a deep skepticism about the possibility of finding similar a priori principles in the realm of pleasure and displeasure. By 1787, however, Kant was confident in the extension of his systematic, transcendental "critical" philosophy to this realm and embarked on what would eventually become the *Critique of the Power of Judgment.*[30]

Fundamentally, Kant associates pleasure with attaining and achieving ends ("Introduction," VI:187–188). These ends need not be practical (nor even consciously grasped); indeed, given the frantic state of the human mind, the most persistent ends we have and attainments we realize are cognitive—the aims of thinking. From this foundational attribution of pleasure to achieving the ends of cognition, Kant sought to discover the possible operation of rationality and validity in the experience of pleasure itself. Following the precedent of his arguments concerning cognition (knowledge) and desire (will) in the preceding *Critiques,* Kant pursued the transcendental deduction of a "pure" case of feeling to build his critique of "taste" or aesthetic judgment (§§13–14).

Kant uses the distinction of "pure," idealized judgments of beauty from judgments about "the agreeable" or "the good" to theorize judgments of beauty at their most "disinterested" and, on his account, most free. When we primarily relate to something as agreeable, we have a subjective interest in the sensory pleasures it produces. It gratifies us, sometimes intensely (as do alcohol and fatty foods), and we may develop an interest in experiencing its sensory pleasures again in a matter that seemed, to Kant, akin to coercion. This interest, in other words, distorts or usurps our freedom and undermines our capacity to be discriminating (which is central to genuine judgment). "Everyone says that hunger is the best cook," Kant asserts, "and people with a healthy appetite relish everything that is edible at all; thus such a satisfaction demonstrates no choice in accordance with taste. Only when the need is satisfied can one distinguish who among the many has taste or does not" (§5:210).

Likewise, when we discern something as good (under the moral law, for example), Kant claims that it commends itself to us by reason. We recognize that which is inherently good through rational reflection on its concept. As an end posited by reason, all rational beings are interested in its realization (§§4–5:207–210). This claim about our interest in morality is a logical outgrowth of Kant's commitment to the existence of objective moral laws accessible through the exercise of practical reason. "Where the moral law speaks," Kant proclaims, "there is, objectively, no room left for free choice with regard to what is to be done. . . . It contains *a command* and produces *a need*" (§5:210, emphasis added).

Kant, however, claims that pure judgments of taste are distinctive because they judge representations of objects by the subjective feeling they produce "*apart from any interest*" (§4:211, emphasis added). This condition is supposed to mitigate against undue impositions on our judgment from two directions. The first are agreeable pleasures or pains; my attraction to a flower's scent might draw me to it, but it does not determine my sense of its beauty. The second is cognitive, since I can experience cognitive "pleasures" through acts of correct cognition. Yet the pleasure I experience in correctly identifying what species of flowering plant I have encountered is, if not irrelevant, woefully inadequate to aesthetic judgment. Instead I freely take in the flower's form and reflect on the pleasure I experience in doing so.

Freedom is a significant part of what allows Kant to break decisively with the British aesthetic philosophers and their empiricism. "One way of characterizing the difference between the pleasure in the agreeable and the beautiful," Michel Chaouli explains, "lies in the fact that I understand the former to come about thanks to the objects I encounter, while the latter arises thanks to *my imaginative work* . . . how my free and productive—my poetic—imagination joins together what I perceive and know and feel."[31] We take pleasure, Kant surmises, in this feeling of freedom "to make anything into an object of pleasure ourselves" (§5:210). This is an experience and practice of freedom insubordinate to the "extortions" of approval or the "needs" that come inexorably from our inclinations toward desire or respect for moral law.[32]

Kant thinks that since the pleasure I feel in judging something to be beautiful in this pure instance of aesthetic judgment is not derivative of any empirical-sensible or cognitive interest, it must be "*within* consciousness."[33] Three faculties constitute Kantian consciousness: (1) understanding, the faculty of theoretical cognition; (2) reason, the faculty of knowledge from a priori principles that determines desire and will; and (3) the imagination, the key faculty for the workings of judgment ("Introduction," IX:195). The interaction between understanding, reason, and imagination might sometimes be nebulous, but Kant claims to have discerned its key, which involves hierarchical and harmonious relationships.

Where cognitive judgments about empirical facts are the aim, the power of the imagination to produce and order our intuitions into representations is limited by the specific cognitive task at hand and its determinant rules (e.g., this dog is a German Shepherd). There are, however, instances where cognitive rules and subsumptive categories or norms are not determinate, either because of the indeterminable character of what they are trying to grasp, or because we have adopted a self-consciously "aesthetic" approach to judgment that refuses this kind of closure or determinacy.[34] In these instances, our faculties can come into a different, more unrestricted arrangement. For Kant, aesthetic judgment presents just this sort of instance—it is not governed by determinant rules of cognitive judgment. Instead the relationship between the faculties can enter into what he calls a "free play, since no determinate concept restricts them to a particular rule of cognition" (§9:217).

For Kant, the moment of primary interest is where the imagination and the understanding seem to spontaneously coincide and generate representations that, without a strict determination by our cognitive faculty, nevertheless achieve a kind of coherence with it. Put more clearly, the creative projections of our imagination approximate the expectations of formal unity that ground the cognitive rules Kant associates with our understanding—the things we *know* as determinant facts. In this way, these products of our imagination appear purposive—they seem to manifest or suggest a fittedness for—determinant ends. But we can only sense this, not deductively or logically prove it.[35] They are, in the Kantian vocabulary, *purposive* without a determined purpose.[36]

This may, at first glance, appear strange. We usually understand purpose through the desire or will of an agent. Yet Kant insists that there are objects or phenomena that we may encounter in the exercise of judgment that, while they do not permit us to deduce a will or an end as something we *know* is there, are nevertheless only intelligible and explicable for us insofar as we think with the *assumption* of its having purposes or as being the causal effect or aim of purposive action (§10:220). This assumption of purposiveness is a regulative idea, or what John Zammito calls a "cognitive order." We (necessarily) use such ideas to render the world intelligible, to refract it through the lens of design and purposive action, reflecting our own practical engagements in the world.[37]

Intelligibility, however, does not ground objectivity; we can "attend to the appearance of design, which does not necessarily entail its actuality." The result of this interpretive move enables Kant to speak of "purposiveness without purpose," or the subjectively pleasurable and uncoerced apprehension (again, not objectively) of an appearance of recognizable, intelligible form of purpose in an object of judgment. This feeling helps underwrite Kant's conception of judgments of beauty as not just free but impartial, and therefore capable of expecting validity beyond the individual judging subject because we all share a "common sense" rooted in these cognitive faculties.

"It would be easy," Chaouli writes, "to think of this activity as a failure, and thus of aesthetic judgment as an aborted (or otherwise defective) form of cognition. . . . But Kant declines this option, for reasons we know: aesthetic experience is a distinct mode of experience that consists in a form of feeling and thinking not reducible to the sort of propositions we know from cognition. It does both less and more; it speaks in a different register."[38] This "form of feeling and thinking" is part of what Kant identifies as the subjective ground of the judgment of beauty, which, nevertheless, points toward an intersubjective, *exemplary* necessity whose condition is a sensus communis (§§18–20).[39] "The reason my particular feeling of aesthetic pleasure dares to make a claim on your assent," Chaouli argues, "is that it is not mine alone . . . its structure partakes of something beyond myself"—namely, "a feeling of the purposeful arrangement of the cognitive powers, even though no purpose I could name controls that arrangement." Where a work of art occasions this aesthetic experience and judgment of beauty, then it is our encounter with this object that also "generates the logic of exemplarity," tying the exemplary necessity of the judgment to the exemplarity of the artwork that occasioned it and which brings forth a community of aesthetic experience.[40]

But what is this different register, and how do we avoid this free play of thinking and imagining from spiraling simply into nonsense? How can such freedom or free play from the very determinant concepts we consider crucial to thinking still ground the expectation of mutual agreement on matters of taste and the possibility of intersubjective validity? And, more important for our larger aims of understanding *historical* judgment, how should we think about the most controversial feature of Kant's account—namely, that the feeling of pleasure that accompanies these judgments and experiences of beauty, this spontaneous accord in our faculties, suggested for him something more than the delight of objects in the world accidentally according with human consciousness? Indeed, they intimated the far more significant possibility that, although we cannot *prove* such a contention in Kant's strictest terms, these communicable experiences of beauty are the best evidence we have that the world and cosmos may be purposefully designed to fit the highest ends of human freedom, feeling, and reason.[41]

Determinant and Reflective Judgment

To grasp Kant's answers, and ultimately our own, we must go back to essentials. Recall that the problem of judgment generally is "the faculty for thinking of the particular as contained under the universal" ("Introduction," IV:179). This relationship, Kant explains, can move in two directions: the first Kant calls "determinant"; the second he calls "reflective."

If a universal principle, law, or category is already cognitively and appropriately available to the judging subject, judgment is a matter of subsuming the particular appropriately under the corresponding universal. This subsumptive process Kant calls "determining" (also translated in the literature as *determinant* or *determinate*) judgment, as it "merely subsumes" under "universal transcendental laws" given by understanding ("Introduction," IV:179). The Kantian understanding is the active cognitive faculty first explored in his *Critique of Pure Reason,* which has the power to form the a priori and empirical concepts and categories we use to cognitively process sense data, with the help of the imagination's representations, into theoretical knowledge (§§29, 31).[42]

"The concept of dog," explains Kant by way of example, "means a rule according to which my imagination can always draw a general outline of the figure of a four-footed animal, without being restricted to any particular figure supplied by experience or to any possible image which I may draw in the concrete."[43] The disciplined imagination in determinate judgment works by producing schemas that organize particulars (or perhaps more precisely, their "sensible impressions") according to the rules dictated by conceptual boundaries.[44] In this sense, our imagination serves "judgment and cognition as a stepping-stone between the abstract content of a concept" (the concept of *book,* for example) and "the various objects that, despite their many differences, instantiate it" (the hundreds of individual books in my library).[45]

Determinate judgment, unlike aesthetic judgment, is distinguished by the governance of the cognitive-conceptual faculty of understanding "which legislates the form of appearance," while "the schematizing mediations of imagination *subserve* the aims of cognition." These, for Kant at least, are the production of objective knowledge.[46] The various books in my library are objectively (according to our linguistic-conceptual conventions) books. There is a harmony here among the faculties of mind, to be sure, and the recognition of empirical concepts would be impossible without it. Still, the hierarchical order of understanding over imagination and the subsequent determinate aim of objectively valid, cognitive judgments leave little room for the freedom Kant associates with exercising aesthetic judgment. If at any point in our lives we learned the concept *book* and the schema used to judge instances of books correctly, it would be nigh impossible for us to apprehend a book at first glance as anything else.[47] And while I might be free to judge these books to be something else (sculptures perhaps, or repositories for talking spirits), given the global consensus about "bookness," I would be roundly criticized as behaving irrationally, disingenuously, fantastically, or stupidly.[48] For Kant, choice or freedom does not seem to be appropriate to an account of determinate cognitive judgments of this sort.

More promising where freedom is concerned is *reflective* judgment, which we rely on when there is no readily available, well-fitting, or coherent determinate concept or rule under which to subsume an object or event we experience. We must instead find "the universal" (§15). Maurizio D'Entreves describes reflective judgment as an exercise in judgment "without the mediation of determinate concepts *given in advance.*"[49] But the nuance here is crucial. It is not clear how anything could be consciously thought without some reference, even if initial, provisional, inadequate, or limited, to determinate concepts of the sort laid out above. We should not understand Kant as arguing that we somehow are thinking without concepts altogether.[50] As Samuel Fleischacker argues, to "think without a 'definite' or 'determinate' concept might be best understood," at least attitudinally, "as using concepts without defining or determining precisely which concept one is using: to allow a range or array of concepts to play with the contents of one's imagination instead of fixing one of them determinantly to that content."[51] In cases where this is less an approach borne solely of a certain attitude and instead one of interpretive necessity—where the object in question "exceeds the grasp of our current categories and so resists cognition under determinative judgments"—the description of reflective judgment as "the effort to give structure and meaning to the uncanny" is incisive.[52]

A comparison from the world of art might help clarify this point. At the turn of the twenty-first century, Marcel Duchamp's 1917 work from his "readymade" collection, *Fountain,* was voted by a panel of art critics affiliated with the prestigious Turner Prize as the most influential work of modern art.[53] It was and remains somewhat controversial in large part because it broke decisively with artistic conventions of the period. The piece is a porcelain urinal purchased from a New York plumbing supply store, rotated ninety degrees so that it sits on its back. It contains the sole physical alteration of a pseudonymous signature reading "R. Mutt 1917." As a matter of determinant judgment, we might quickly come across *Fountain* and say, simply and certainly, "This is a urinal." The particular urinal we know as *Fountain* is, whatever else we might say about it, quite straightforwardly a urinal subsumed under the empirical concept. Shorn of its art gallery setting, with the artist's signature erased, we would tend to encounter little resistance in recognizing it as such and instead confront it as a familiar, ready-at-hand tool for mundane excretory purposes.

Yet the subtle touch of the artist's signature and the gallery setting presents a difficulty for judgment insofar as they seem to represent, given cultural conventions about artistic production (i.e., artists sign their work, art is shown in art galleries or art fairs, etc.), an invitation for us to perceive some other set of purposes or features in this particular urinal beyond the obvious truth rendered by the subsumptive judgment above.[54] When we perceive a work of art, our imagination "intuitively takes up, goes through, recollects and recalls what we see; and it is our understanding that tries to grasp and decide what is depicted or what it all means."[55] In adopting a reflective attitude, despite the obvious allure of the determinant judgment, we release the imagination from domination by understanding and allow it to more freely wrestle with the possible interpretive meanings gleaned from its representations of this object and the various concepts proffered up by a more free-ranging attempt to understand what else this more-than-urinal or other-than-urinal could possibly be.

Our faculties might, for example, come to feel a gratifying harmony between imagination and understanding in a judgment of beauty that declares *Fountain* an opportunity for us to recognize the understated formal beauty of modern engineering—the feelings that curving lines, clean porcelain finishes, or convergences between form and function might evoke in us if not concealed by the mundane character of everyday life or our disgust at the scatological functions of the human body. Perhaps our attempts at conceptualizing this piece or coming to any spontaneous judgment of beauty are so repeatedly frustrated that we eventually come to recognize some "aesthetic idea" at work. Perhaps we make sense of *Fountain* with reference to the idea that our concept of "art" is too unduly influenced by the power relationships and bourgeois pretensions that control access to the art world, or we interpret it as a self-undermining joke about the status-oriented pretensions of high art production and consumption destined to be absorbed and diffused by the same culture of decadence.[56] The conclusions suggested here are, for our purposes, beside the point; the important thing to note is that one might come to any of them through an adjustment in approach toward a given object, even one that once seemed as ill fitted to aesthetic judgment as the urinal.

It is essential to distinguish between two potential outcomes when we engage in reflective judgment, especially in judgments of exemplarity. In one, there are objects that we encounter without available and acceptable concepts under which to subsume them, simply because of our ignorance.[57] A more purely reflective judgment, however, is one where the finality of determinant subsumption is resisted, proves futile, or misses the significance of the experience we have and expect others to have in our encounter with particular objects.

This helps explain why it is that in Kant's meditations on and exercise of reflective judgment he moved explicitly to evaluative arguments about history and politics, domains characterized by this indeterminacy. This convergence of aesthetic judgments of beauty and sublimity with matters of politics and history, even in Kant, allows us to pursue a final discussion that teases out the political implications of reflective judgments of beauty versus those of the sublime. This account will prepare the way for understanding the philosophical foundations of competing narratives of civil rights movement and African American history, especially given the ways that they draw on ideas of beauty and unity or sublime rupture to dramatize and characterize what is at stake for human freedom and other values.

In Search of a Beautiful History: Philosophy of History, Humanity, and Teleological Judgment

Given Kant's reputation as purely "formalist" in his aesthetic philosophy, this claim about its relevance to political and historical matters may seem surprising. Yet Kant's interest in pure judgments of beauty is driven more by his attempts at transcendental argument than his persistent and more phenomenological interest in describing our more common exercises of judgment. Kant, for instance, is also interested in "dependent" beauty, where "a concept of what the object should be" and a relative notion of "perfection" plays a significant role (§16:229). There Kant's talk of purposiveness without (determinant, proven) purpose links the judgment of beauty and its feelings of pleasure with the intimated appearance of perfection in purpose or design in things like organic forms.

In raising this judgment of dependent beauty, Kant also opened the door to questions that were "fundamentally ontological and theological and [found] their expression precisely in an investigation of teleology."[58] Inspired by his sense that organic forms suggested an internal organization ("intrinsic purposiveness") by which "everything is an end and reciprocally a means as well" (§66:376), Kant moves shockingly swiftly to wondering whether he might be able to justifiably extend a similar systematic argument about the fit of parts to the organismic whole beyond *specific organisms* to their ecosystems, and eventually, to *nature as a whole* ("extrinsic purposiveness"). To determinantly establish the purposes of even a segment of this massive web of nature, Kant conceded, would require him to know the ends of nature as such, a prospect he surrenders for now to the realm of the "supersensible" beyond the capacities of determinant, cognitive judgment (§§66–67). Instead he turned to reflective judgment, and in doing so, he defended the necessary *regulative* use of a principle assuming the systematic, organized unity of nature, a patently metaphysical maxim that proclaims, "Everything in the world is good for something, that nothing in it is in vain; and by means of the example that nature gives in its organic products, one is justified, indeed called upon to expect nothing in nature and its laws but what is purposive in the whole" (§67:379).

Reflecting the anthropocentric bent of much Enlightenment philosophy, Kant proclaims that we have sufficient cause to consider the human being as "the ultimate end of the creation here on earth, because he is the only being on earth who forms a concept of ends for himself and who by means of his reason can make a system of ends out of an aggregate of purposively formed things" (§82:426–427).[59] While Kant incessantly invoked the caveat that his teleological judgments were only "regulative" and "reflective," Susan Neiman's assessment as a reader is apt: "Kant repeated such lines often enough to be boring, and his repetition suggests a guilty conscience. Though no one worked harder to show that the question of whether the world is made for us cannot even be properly formulated, no one seems more tempted to give it a positive answer."[60] Something of the same tendency appears at work in an age that has scandalized the very question of theodicy but projects the same answers onto the exemplary events of the past.

While many of the most enduring and exciting implications of Kant's teleological arguments are in the realm of environmental science and evolutionary biology, our concern with historical exemplarity and narrative must lead us to focus on Kant's powerfully influential, interlocking accounts of the natural and sociopolitical histories of the human species, expounded in the *Critique of the Power of Judgment* and a series of essays across the 1780s and 1790s.[61] In the earliest, "Idea for a Universal History with a Cosmopolitan Purpose" (1784), Kant proclaims what, roughly, is the core aim of his career in the philosophy of history, that the philosopher's view of history must attempt to "discover a purpose in nature behind [the] senseless course of human events." In "Idea" he already argues that all species inherently develop toward their full capacities and that humanity holds a unique place in the natural order because of its capacity for reason. From these two premises and the expectation of natural purposiveness, Kant unfurls a narrative of human history in a teleological mode that suggests various ways that nature has ordained the development of humanity according to the full flourishing of its distinctive capacities at the species level.[62]

This history, it must be admitted, is not a peaceful process. Kant claims that the physical weakness and vulnerability of human beings compared to their counterparts in the animal world is further evidence that nature wanted us to develop, under the motivating threat of nonsurvival, the only characteristics that could secure our survival in, and later, dominion over, the world: reason and "rational self-esteem." In addition to physical hardship, Kant also contends, in "Idea" and elsewhere, that nature generated in human beings an "unsocial sociability," an internal psychological propensity for desiring both enriching social intercourse with others and an unfettered, individual autonomy rooted in aggressive self-assertion.[63] This "unsocial sociability" creates an atmosphere of competition and conflict between humans and their groups. Ironically, it in turn encourages—to the ultimate benefit of reason—everything from the origins of culture and art in status-seeking individuals looking for distinction to mutually protective pacts to create civil society and constitutional government, the counterintuitively positive development and migration caused by war and other ills, and the development of culturally based forms of discipline (norms) and skills (instrumental rationality and technology) capable of habituating us to more ethical behavior. Finally, Kant hopes, it will lead to the establishment of a global federation of republics, and ultimately the "final end" of a "Kingdom of Ends" that merges global, cosmopolitan civil society with a robust, virtuous moral community.[64] Particularly on this last point, Kant saw human history as a "bridge between nature and freedom," the milieu in which "raw human nature is gradually cultivated to the point at which the realization of a moral world in nature/history becomes not a certainty but a *rational hope*."[65]

The significance of this sort of narrative, particularly once Kant abandoned his intimations toward objective validity in favor of reflective and regulative judgment, was less about the quality of the historical explanation it offered than about its pedagogical value for his audience. Indeed, by 1798's *The Contest of Faculties,* Kant explicitly characterizes his historical reflections as "prognosticative or prophetic . . . a history of future times" that begins with speculative reflections on the past and present.[66] Consistently throughout his philosophy of history, Kant expresses worry that without progressive and providential conceptions of history of the type he offers, we and our political leaders will frustrate what we have considered reason to think is nature's plan. Our failure will only prolong the awaited realization of our species' final ends. Moreover, without the rational hope provided by such history, we are more likely to suffer from pervasive despair and pessimism. We will lose faith in the world's hospitality to our natural ends, its amenability to our moral purposes, and its intelligibility for scientific investigation and human understanding. These will all exercise a harmful effect on our development as a species.

When Kant, in the *Critique of Pure Reason,* suggests that the question "What may I hope?" is central to reason, he is conceding its irrepressible character and gesturing toward the inevitable need for a defensible and persuasive answer to it. Thus, the sort of beautiful philosophical-prophetic history he produced in the 1780s and 1790s might be better understood as a response to this epistemic-existential query, in full acknowledgment of its practical seriousness: a provocative, if often vexingly fantastic, blend of providential theology, anthropocentrism, progressive history, natural science, and theodicy meant to shore up hope against the persistent threat of deep skepticism and moral despair. In my view, we must take seriously Kant's description of the distaste or revulsion engendered by a notion of human history that lacks a unifying and positive purpose. The notion of human history as a senseless course is aesthetically charged, not just in Kant's deployment of a language of disgust but also because it draws us into a reflective judgment in a mode of negative feeling and reveals the disappointment and displeasure experienced when our faculties cannot attain any purchase on an idea or object so seemingly crucial to our flourishing whose indeterminacy nevertheless is so extreme it cannot be thought in any meaningful form.

Faced with that abyssal possibility, Kantian notions of beautiful history serve as a countervailing or centripetal force, holding our actions—past, present, and future—in deceptively orderly, comprehensible rotation and drawing any disjointed feature of the world back toward its gravitational center whenever its fittedness to our imagined ends emerges as a crisis. Beautiful history presents a vision of reality whose manifest unity, subjectively evoked by regulative principle and the narrative representation of a beautiful order, secures our confidence in the very idea that there can be a fundamental unity in the purposes of human beings among each other, over time, and in accordance with the world. Perhaps most important, it erects matrices of judgment where even the worst atrocities, injustices, and disappointments can be slotted back into an overarching order that appears to remain obstinately amenable to realizing our highest purposes.

Hayden White once worried that the claim to be able to explain and understand historical developments at all relied too heavily on a problematic conception of history modeled on the beautiful. He argued that "insofar as historical events and processes become . . . explainable, as radicals believe them to be"—and as White associates with beautiful order—"they can never serve as a basis for a visionary politics more concerned to endow social life with meaning than with beauty." In other words, White worried that to the extent we endorse visions of history that present its "manifest confusion [as] comprehensible to either reason, understanding, or aesthetic sensibility," we will make the mistake of depriving "history of the kind of meaninglessness" that he thought was all that could "goad living human beings to make their lives different for themselves and their children, which is to say, to endow their lives with a meaning for which they alone are fully responsible."[67] In response, White offered a competing vision of historical representation based on the sublime as an alternative capable of more steadily bearing a radical, transformative politics.

White claimed to find a productive notion of the "historical sublime" in Friedrich Schiller, the German artist-intellectual and Kant contemporary. In his "On the Sublime," Schiller writes,

> Away then with falsely construed forebearance [*sic*] and vapidly effeminate taste which cast a veil over the solemn face of necessity and, in order to curry favor with the senses, counterfeit a harmony between good fortune and good behavior of which not a trace is to be found in the actual world. . . . We are aided [in the attainment of this point of view] by the terrifying spectacle of change which destroys everything and creates it anew, and destroys again. . . . We are aided by the pathetic spectacle of mankind wrestling with fate, the irresistible elusiveness of happiness, confidence betrayed, unrighteousness triumphant and innocence laid low; of these history supplies ample instances, and tragic art imitates them before our eyes.[68]

That Schiller's tortured cries might bolster criticism of what I have called beautiful history is, I think, clear enough. What is not apparent, however, is that turning to the sublime forces us into a conception of history as meaningless. Indeed, Kant's own notion of the sublime can point us toward a way out of his teleology and the allure of the beautiful, even if he did not always avail himself of those full possibilities of that route.

History and the Sublime

The British philosopher and statesman Edmund Burke famously describes the sublime as "whatever is fitted in any sort to excite the ideas of pain and danger . . . whatever is in any sort terrible, or is conversant about terrible objects, or operates in a manner analogous to terror." This terror of the sublime is, according to Burke, "the strongest emotion which the mind is capable of feeling." In its "highest degree" this terror becomes sheer "astonishment," or "that state of the soul in which all its motions are suspended, with some degree of horror." Burke's brief account of what precisely engenders this sort of terror in man turns principally on two features that relate to our aspirations for control being overwhelmed: infinitude and power. When we contemplate the idea of an omnipotent God ("the Deity"), the experience is inevitably sublime: "To be struck with his power, it is only necessary that we should open our eyes. But whilst we contemplate so vast an object, under the arm, as it were, of almighty power, and invested upon every side with omnipresence, we shrink into the minuteness of our own nature, and are, in a manner, annihilated before him . . . no conviction of the justice with which it is exercised, nor the mercy with which it is tempered, can wholly remove the terror that naturally arises from a force which nothing can withstand. If we rejoice, we rejoice with trembling."[69] This agreeable sensation or ability to rejoice that we find, perhaps paradoxically, in the terrifying experience of the sublime is what takes hold of our imaginations. It compels us to pursue an understanding of these vast complexities.

For Kant, this was the most crucial consideration of sublime experience. He followed Burke in distinguishing the beautiful and the sublime and adopted much of the latter's account of the feelings of infinity and power associated with it.[70] "The mind," Kant argues, "feels itself set in motion in the representation of the sublime in nature; whereas in the aesthetic judgment upon what is beautiful therein it is in restful contemplation." Kant describes this feeling as a "movement" that "especially in its inception, may be compared with a shaking, that is, with a rapidly alternating repulsion and attraction produced by one and the same object" (§88:258). Reflection on this feeling, Kant insisted, would reveal it to be caused by a similar free play of the faculties as in judgments of the beautiful. Instead of the harmonious relationship between the imagination and the understanding, however, we find a dissonant relationship between the imagination and reason.

In judgments of the sublime, something of complexity and magnitude (including the idea of *possibility*) excites reason toward an idea, but our imagination falters under the weight of the impossible task of presenting the totality of this in a whole intuition. In Kant's conception of the mathematical sublime, he (like Burke) offers "infinity" as one illustrative example. Infinity is an idea of reason; we use it in logical argument and everyday discourse to connote something without limit. Yet any attempt to honestly imagine infinity, to apprehend it and comprehend it in intuition, leaves the imagination defeated; Kant describes it as like "an abyss in which it fears to lose itself" (§88:258). But in this feeling of being overwhelmed, Kant discerns another, more powerful feeling: enlargement and respect.

This feeling arises out of awe of incomprehensible magnitude and from an appreciation of the expansion of the imagination and a more profound respect for the powers of reason. In other words, we do not need sensibility to provide a fully unified intuition of infinity to apprehend it through analytical reason. Our reflection on sublime objects of judgment sets the imagination and reason on such a course that even though imagination eventually falls behind, its powers have been enlarged, and reason has not been deterred. This play of faculties allows us to think "supersensible" ideas, in part through the production of metaphors and other imaginative projections capable of bearing interpretations of these ideas. It is in this sense that viewing the horizon from the shores of an ocean beach can lead one to a judgment of the sublime. While we, like Burke, often attribute the power of the sublime to the object itself (i.e., the horizon), Kant insists that this is a mistake. As we look out into the vast ocean, the feeling we undergo is appropriately occasioned by the jarring reflection on an idea—infinity, perhaps, or possibility—and the appreciation for our capacities that this engenders. The horizon is not infinite, but it has brought us to the *idea* of infinity and the possibilities and limits of our powers of our reason.

This insight is perhaps even more potent in the case of what Kant calls "the dynamical sublime." Here the same general sequence of feelings occurs, but the mind is thrown onto a respect for its practical reason. When we contemplate such natural terrors as "thunder clouds towering up into the heavens, bringing with them flashes of lightning and crashes of thunder, volcanoes with their all-destroying violence, hurricanes with the devastation they leave behind, the boundless ocean set into a rage, a lofty waterfall on a mighty river," Kant suggests that we can judge these to be sublime because our reflection on them leads us to "discover within ourselves a capacity for resistance of quite another kind, which gives us the courage to be able to measure ourselves against the apparent all-powerfulness of nature." In the crux of the trembling of "physical powerlessness" we feel as natural beings embodied and fragile, we come to realize that we have "a capacity for judging ourselves as independent of [nature]." In a striking passage, Kant insists that this leads us to "call forth our power (which is not part of nature) to regard those things about which we are concerned (goods, health and life) as trivial, and hence to regard its power (to which we are, to be sure, subjected in regard to these things) as not the sort of dominion over ourselves and our authority to which we would have to bow if it came down to our highest principles and their affirmation or abandonment" (§28:261–262).

In other words, the sublime wrenches us from the illusions of being determined by nature through an exaltation of the powers of human reason, will, imagination, and judgment. Kant's interest is in how we can sustain the resolve (§16:230) we need to keep track of "the superiority of moral law to considerations of material gratification, even that of life itself."[71] He wants to defend the notion that even in the face of "the force of what is," we can reason, will, imagine, and judge in the mode of "what ought to be." The force of the example is less akin to a causal force of nature than to that power that raises us above nature so that we might also think of ourselves as free. Kant's critical insight here is that even in the shadows cast by the towering "might" of "what is," human imagination and freedom remain resilient and can transform the world and our capacities within it.

Whereas most of Kant's writing on the philosophy of history tries to shore up this resilience on the grounds of beauty and teleology, at least one fascinating feature of his work suggests another way of thinking about history and politics: his reflections on the French Revolution and European reactions to it. In his perpetual quest to discern phenomena in the world that might be evidence for the progressive conception of human development to which he remained normatively committed, Kant returned, near the end of his career, to the question, "Is the Human Race Continually Improving?" Through this essay Kant has elevated what was once a brief aside in closing (the impact of a progressive philosophy of history on political leaders) as the central theme and explicitly characterized his history as a "history of future times"—a prophetic history.[72]

The exemplarity of the Hebrew prophets here is no empty stylistic gesture. Evading more mystical interpretations of the prophetic tradition, Kant argues that their prophecies came to occasional fruition because the prophets and political leaders were one and the same and, thus, the architects of the very fate they prophesied.[73] He draws an analogy to contemporary political leaders, who counsel against reform and transformation on the supposedly realist grounds that they are taking men as they are without acknowledging that these people were made this way "by unjust coercion." To the extent, then, that these political leaders (including, in Kant's time, church authorities) rule with anticipation of historical decline or stagnation, it is in large part because they have created the very conditions for the catastrophe over which they claim to discern, and have no intention in changing their actions to produce a different result.[74] Human progress, he concludes in the essay, will in large part depend on top-down guidance of wiser political and ecclesiastical leadership. Therefore, it would be best if these rulers adopted a more progressive understanding.[75] This advice illustrates a shift in Kant's thinking from plans of nature and abstract speculation about popular moral transformation toward a more straightforwardly political and humanistic account involving revolutions and statecraft inspired by historical consciousness.

Indeed, Kant even anticipates the narrativist philosophy of history that will concern us in later chapters of this book, suggesting roughly three narrative forms to discuss human history: (1) the *terroristic* (decline), (2) the *eudaemonistic* (progressive), and (3) *abderitism* (no essential movement). As Hayden White and others would later insist, Kant argued as early as the 1790s that the facts gathered by historians would bear multiple interpretations and narrative genres, particularly because future events could radically alter any interpretation.[76] The future, Kant insists, is a problem for *historical judgment* because such judgments are addressed to an audience in the present and thus ultimately concern "freely acting beings to whom one can dictate in advance what they ought to do, but of whom one cannot predict what they actually will do." Without determinate recourse to providence or metaphysical proof of man's inherent goodness, we are left only with human freedom, "that man has the quality or power of being the cause and the author of his own improvement," and our *pragmatic* assessment of when the particular "circumstances which help to shape it *actually arise.*"[77]

For Kant and a host of other eighteenth- and nineteenth-century politicians and commentators, the French Revolution in 1789 was one event in which inspiring human action and contingent circumstance collided.[78] What is unique about Kant's account, however, is that his focus is not mainly on the revolutionaries themselves—the Declaration of the Rights of Man or their founding of a new political order against feudalism; it was instead the "attitude of the onlookers as it [revealed] itself in public." In observing reactions around a world with unprecedented interconnection across public spheres, Kant identified "universal yet disinterested sympathy for one set of protagonists against their adversaries . . . bordering on enthusiasm."[79]

What makes Kant's claims perplexing is that in an accompanying footnote, he reiterates his long-standing moral argument against the right to revolution on the grounds that revolutionary means violate moral law. The best way to make sense of this apparent contradiction, and Kant's interest in worldwide enthusiasm, is to turn to his notion of judgments of the sublime.

In the *Critique of the Power of Judgment*, Kant explicitly defines enthusiasm as the "idea of the good connected with affect." Enthusiasm for Kant is a sublime feeling that is "a stretching of the powers through ideas, which give the mind a momentum that acts far more powerfully and persistently than the impetus given by sensory representations" (§29:272). In spectators of the French Revolution, Kant identifies two "ideas of the good" at work: "the right of every people to give itself a civil constitution of the kind that it sees fit" (self-determination) and the inherent good of a republican constitution designed to prevent war.[80] These ideas are the ones that are "connected with affect" in the enthusiasm Kant identifies. Reflection on this feeling, Kant continues (along the pattern of judgments of the sublime), shows it to be "disinterested," not only because spectators are not participants in the French Revolution but also for the more robust reason that in many places, showing enthusiasm in public for the revolution was to provoke retribution from political authorities. This disinterest and Kant's claim that the purposes that excite enthusiasm in this instance are inherently moral secures the universal validity of this judgment for him. The morality of a constitution governed by natural right is given further evidence in affective response, and this affect is engendered by evidence that human freedom can indeed bring about the existence of an idea of the good in the world.

Perhaps most fascinating about Kant's account of the revolution, and what links it most with the sublime, is the contention that it marks the decisive intervention of something new in history that would take extraordinary effort to reverse and that, therefore, indelibly marks the future course of the species. Part of Kant's shift from his more thoroughly providential conception of history is the appearance (*disclosure*) of something radically unprecedented and irrevocable. The French Revolution "revealed in human nature an aptitude and power for improvement of a kind which *no politician could have thought up by examining the course of events in the past.*"[81] This is, as we saw in Chapter 1, an instance of *decentering*.

This revelation, moreover, is an indelible mark of a different kind of progress. Here, at least in the first instance, Kant builds his commitment to progress not on the grounds of a natural plan but on the collective memory of humanity. He suggests that "even if the intended object behind the occurrence we have described were not to be achieved for the present, or . . . to fail, or if, after . . . [the occurrence] had lasted for a certain time, everything were to be brought back onto its original course," the event would still manifest its sublime force. A "phenomenon of this kind which has taken place in human history," Kant proclaims, "can never be forgotten. . . . The occurrence in question is too momentous, too intimately interwoven with the interests of humanity and too widespread in its influence upon all parts of the world for nations not to be reminded of it when favorable circumstances present themselves and to rise up and make renewed attempts of the same kind as before."[82] In other words, the circuits of public discourse and historical memory will be drawn toward an exemplary event so tightly tied to the interests of humanity in freedom that whenever the moment presents itself, people will pursue similar ends guided in part by that example.

These exemplary events are touchstones of judgment insofar as they expand the imagination of what is possible and renew a respect for human freedom (and perhaps even morality). Moreover, the memory of these events can underwrite a more tempered and fragile notion of "progress," one where it is not nature's plan that guarantees the expansion of human freedom or the flourishing of a moral community but dogged memory and unprecedented acts of human freedom inspired by examples from the past. This is, in the realm of historical judgment, the creative and pedagogical power of exemplarity—its ability to inspire and elicit emulation and teach us, as aesthetic education does the artist—"to create from the same sources" (§32:283).

The most sublime dimension of this vision of history comes in the enthusiastic reflection on the revolutionary or transformative action of the past with awe in the power of human action. So too in reflection, finding that its purposiveness should not be reduced to one or two determinant aims but instead enlarges our imagination for what is possible and confronts us with the scope of our own freedom. It is this last confrontation that, ultimately, would be the source of the sublime feeling—a frightening apprehension of the world-creating and world-destroying capacities of humans acting in concert along with the thrilling, if no less scary, recognition that we, too, have the freedom we often mistakenly render as a metaphysical property of the politics and personalities of the past. This point, which Kant emphasizes in his distinctions between aesthetic autonomy and heteronomy (allowing others to determine our judgments of taste) or between creative succession and mechanistic imitation, is critical to retaining a compelling notion of freedom within an account of exemplarity (§32:283).

By now I hope we can discern the outlines of an approach to historical consciousness and judgment that takes up the aesthetic charge of the sublime but that looks nothing like White's meaningless slog of historical time awaiting existentialist irruption. Instead this is a sublime history marked by exemplary events that spark a unique enthusiasm even for spectators and future generations. Enthusiasm, in Kant's words, is a kind of "astonishment that does not cease when the novelty is lost" (§29:272).

In the raging storm that confronts us with Schiller's "pathetic spectacle of mankind wrestling with fate," the apprehension of exemplarity is akin to discovering a life raft amid this unforgiving sea—what Ralph Ellison called, after Mark Twain's literary example, a "raft of hope."[83] The salvation offered by a raft is provisional: one hopes it remains afloat until more effective help comes along or that it can be piloted toward safety's shores. In the midst of a storm that has sunk the vessel that one arrived on, however, a raft may be the essential vehicle—indeed, the only vehicle—for carrying on, coming to terms with the meaning of our experience, and beginning anew. If, in the depths of disappointment, frustration, or terror, we can discern some example that inspires us to renew our ideals or generate powerful new ones, we can reaffirm the power of human action in the face of powerlessness, inspiring struggles to build a world more hospitable to freedom and justice.

Let us suppose that the civil rights movement plays a similar role to the one Kant ascribed to the French Revolution. In that case, we are perhaps on the precipice of the challenge that Ellison set for his fiction, which should read differently in the wake of our discussions of exemplarity, common sense, particulars, and the sublime. "My task," Ellison writes in the idiom of exemplarity, "was one of revealing the human universals hidden within the plight of one who was both black and American, and not only as a means of conveying my personal vision of possibility, but as a way of dealing with the sheer rhetorical challenge involved in communicating across our barriers of race and religion, class, color, and region . . . [which] prevent what would otherwise have been a more or less natural recognition of the reality of black and white fraternity."[84]

What is imperative to note about these passages is that the terror of a history of oppression, for Ellison, is affectively jarring in part because it reveals how much of our flourishing remains entangled and dependent on the actions of others. Whatever freedom we have is not commensurate with sovereignty. Yet this disclosure does not issue in despair. Ellison, reflecting on the persistence of racial inequality thirty years after the publication of his landmark novel *Invisible Man* (1952), is worth quoting at length:

> If the ideal of achieving a true political equality eludes us in reality—as it continues to do—there is still available that fictional vision of an ideal democracy in which the actual combines with the ideal and gives us representations of a state of things in which the highly placed and the lowly, the black and the white, the Northerner and the Southerner, the native-born and the immigrant combine to tell us of transcendent truths and possibilities such as those discovered when Mark Twain set Huck and Jim afloat on the raft. Which suggested to me that a novel could be fashioned as a raft of hope, perception and entertainment that might help keep us afloat as we

> tried to negotiate the snags and whirlpools that mark our nation's vacillating course toward and away from the democratic ideal.[85]

I want to suggest that historical exemplarity can do this work as well, and perhaps because it relies on narrative form, it also involves some of the same interpretive, aesthetic, and affective questions that the novel does. But we are getting ahead of ourselves. For now, we must turn to Hannah Arendt to further explain this problem of judgment, tackling more straightforwardly the problem of exemplary validity and the difficulties of translating Kant's aesthetics into a language more capable of bearing the unique questions of intersubjectivity and interpretation at the intersection of politics and history. From there we will emerge with a conception of judgment that will guide our larger purpose: a critical reflection on the historiography and popular narratives of the civil rights movement considering its exemplarity in political theory and public philosophy.

CHAPTER 3

THE DEFEATED CAUSE

Judgment, History, and Narrative

OUR PATH THUS FAR suggests that Immanuel Kant's reflections on aesthetic judgment have significance far beyond traditionally aesthetic concerns with the beauty of nature or the sublimity of fine art. This argument not only tried to draw out the intimate relation between Kant's arguments about aesthetic judgment and his exercises of historical judgment (especially his divergent accounts of beauty and sublimity) but also pointed to the ways that he sought to speak to pressing ethical-existential questions of hope, meaning, and self-assurance by adjudicating competing narrative approaches to history. My line of inquiry thus far takes its deepest inspiration from the political theorist Hannah Arendt, who idiosyncratically insisted on the incisiveness and significance of Kant's *Critique of the Power of Judgment* for thinking through problems of historical reflection and politics. Although Arendt died in the midst of writing her considered treatment of judgment, she left behind a series of essays, books, and lecture notes that amount to a scattered but compelling set of arguments that have been profoundly important for two generations of political theorists struggling with questions of particularity and universalism; pluralism and public reason; democratic action and spectatorship; and ideas of exemplarity and validity across aesthetics, morality, politics, and history.[1]

I make no effort here to provide a comprehensive reconstruction of Arendt's thinking on these matters; nor do I attempt to resolve all of the ambiguities and contradictions in her theory of judgment. This would require its own book, and admirable ones have already been composed in pursuit of that important project.[2] I hope instead to use Arendt as, in my reading, Arendt used Kant: as a spur to understanding the interpretive and political dilemmas of judgment that she understood herself as inheriting. For Arendt, this was the crisis of disorientation and understanding in the wake of the (negative) exemplary historical event of the Holocaust and the collapse of authoritative traditions of political philosophy that genocidal totalitarianism seemed to crystallize.

This Arendtian model of thinking can help us understand the fragmented exemplarity of the civil rights movement and the crises of authority in American liberalism and African American political life. As I will show at length in Chapter 4, our inherited and formerly authoritative narratives and interpretative categories for understanding the civil rights movement are in decay. The ruling romantic narrative and its interpretive pillars no longer compel intuitive genuflection, and we are losing a certain commonsensical relation to tradition "which selects and names, which hands down and preserves, which indicates where the treasures [of the past] are and what their worth is," as Arendt put it in another context.[3] This collapse of authority, in its immediate unfolding, means not only the fracturing of consensus around "the validity of historical claims and the significance of events" but also, as Part Two of this book details, the intelligibility of concepts, patterns of political thinking, and even political philosophical edifices built on once familiar judgments about history.[4]

I propose that we see this as nothing less than a breakdown of a whole structure of Arendtian common sense, with the practical disorientation and theoretical vertigo that this portends. This breakdown is no mere loss, however, nor does it mean that the civil rights movement will necessarily recede into oblivion or a failure of memory, leaving the American landscape littered with civil rights monuments as hauntingly meaningless as Ozymandias's sand-covered statue in Percy Bysshe Shelley's famous poem.[5] On the contrary, the *question* of the civil rights movement's meaning surges forth with all the more force and urgency.

As some seek to shore up the old romance through ritual commemoration or seize the opportunity of crisis to take the hammer of skeptical criticism to the teetering pillars of romantic narratives, it is difficult to avoid the sense that we are at a strange inflection point of historical memory and imagination. Amid the warring factions seeking to domesticate or decimate the exemplarity of the civil rights movement, we are called to judge. Yet we find ourselves, to borrow Wendy Brown's formulation, "spinning without tether or illumination, without certain knowledge about what to affirm and negate, without temporality or directionality for a motion of history," conditions that leave our "purpose and judgment alike . . . stripped naked."[6]

If our inherited judgments have collapsed under the pressures of the present, however, we can do worse than recall what is arguably Arendt's greatest insight—namely, that judgment is the paramount human capacity that allows us to find our bearings, to make a new world and new way of going forward out of the ruins of the old. "Even though we have lost yardsticks by which to measure, and rules under which to subsume the particular," she argues, "a being whose essence is beginning may have enough of origin within himself to understand without preconceived categories and to judge without the set of customary rules."[7] Elsewhere, she describes this as "thinking without a banister," and it is this capacity, intellectually and politically, that allows us to enter into this abyss, construct new narratives, retrain our judgment, and enact anew the demands of freedom, justice, and solidarity.[8] To do so, Arendt thinks, requires breaking from the "worn-out coins and abstract generalizations" I described in Chapter 1 and instead rethinking and rearticulating the exemplary "political experiences which originally gave rise to political concepts."[9] We will get to these narrative breakdowns and the perils and possibilities they engender, but first we need a sense of the stakes at play and the importance of a theory of judgment for navigating them.

The immediate difficulty that confronts us is that any account of Arendt's thinking about judgment involves unraveling her patently unconventional interpretation of Kantian philosophy. Surveying Kant's prolific corpus, replete with its works on cosmopolitanism, republicanism, constitutional law, and world history—not to mention his account of the subordinate relationship of politics to moral law—Arendt nonetheless dismissively concludes that Kant's political philosophy is "nonwritten."[10] To find "the greatest and most original aspect of Kant's political philosophy," she suggests, we need not sift through the "marginal" essays that are usually offered up as its constitutive elements; instead we should turn to the ostensibly aesthetic text, the *Critique of the Power of Judgment*.[11] This is a radical departure from standard assessments of Kant or conventional strategies concerning the interpretation of his texts, and it leads Arendt to conclusions that have been vexing to students of her thought.[12] But despite—and occasionally, because of—her infidelity to Kant's expressed intentions, Arendt helps illuminate critical dimensions of the faculty of judgment and its indispensable role in our inevitably overlapping and mutually constitutive reflections on history, morality, and politics.

The argument advanced here defends Arendt's conception of (reflective) judgment as the faculty that allows us to deal with the particular and the contingent and to do so in a way that is not determined a priori by rules, laws, concepts, or imperatives. This faculty has important purchase in the realms of history, politics, and morality, where ineliminable conditions of particularity—indeterminacy, creativity, unpredictability, singularity, and human plurality—appear to be constitutive factors of the phenomena we are trying to understand. Arendt was especially interested in how our powers of judgment might be important for wrestling with history, not only because of the crisis of tradition and the collapse of its interpretive keys to historical experience that she so powerfully tried to disclose across her corpus but also because of the more fundamental interpretive indeterminacy of historical events and constructs like "the civil rights movement."

In Kant's aesthetics, indeterminacy is associated with "the free play of faculties" and the invigoration of the imagination. Following that Kantian intuition, I want to accent, perhaps even more than Arendt did, the creative and productive role of the imagination, which is especially crucial for thinking, communicating, and constructing stories about "what is absent," like the events of the past.[13] Defending a long-standing insight of philosophical hermeneutics, I want to insist (with Arendt) that part of the indeterminacy (or indeterminability) of historical judgment and interpretation stems from our imaginings of the past always being subject to reinterpretation, redescription, and re-thematization in light of what we do in the present and the imagined futures that orient us. This explains part of the interpretive controversies over civil rights history and memory.

In drawing attention to the imagination, however, I do not want to abandon Arendt's evident and rightful interest in the intersubjective validity of judgments. How can we make sense of the notion of better or worse judgments about the past? I follow the train of thought in her discussions of this problem, buttressing her idea of a sensus communis (or common sense) that makes it possible to think of judgments having more than subjective validity, pursuing three efforts at philosophical reconstruction. The first involves fleshing out her famous notion of "thinking from the standpoint of others." The second excavates the role of narrative understanding in judgments about the past. The last recovers the underappreciated import of her occasional claims concerning the importance of considerations of human dignity in judgment.

These considerations matter greatly for historical judgments about exemplary events, as we can discern from a careful reading of Arendt's various reflections on historiographical problems. I end, however, by going beyond Arendt to extend her insistence on the import of narrative into a systematic inquiry. Turning to the insights of philosophical hermeneutics and Hayden White, I argue that we must understand historical judgment as involving a fusion of horizons and aesthetic problems of representation that inhere in the narrative modes and genres that shape historical argument and representation about events like the civil rights movement. By drawing out the relation between the content of narrative form and the traditional problems of understanding in hermeneutics, we clear a new path for identifying and critically evaluating the ethical, epistemological, and political stakes of narrative modes like romance, irony, and tragedy in civil rights and African American history.

The Break in Tradition

Though long interested in different elements of the problem of judgment, Hannah Arendt turned to Kant's theory of reflective judgment to answer a set of questions that became especially pressing after she covered the 1961 trial of Adolf Eichmann for *The New Yorker.* Eichmann, the high-ranking Nazi bureaucrat tasked with organizing the logistics of Jewish extermination, had been captured by Mossad agents from Israel while hiding in Argentina after World War II. Arrested and extradited to Israel, Eichmann was tried in Jerusalem for crimes against the Jewish people and against humanity.[14]

For Arendt, the trial raised, in an acute form, a version of familiar problems of legal judgment. The normal dilemma of how to apply (and even create) legal categories and attribute responsibility was exacerbated by a case that was so world-historic and unprecedented that it strained the inherited categories of law and tradition.[15] Perhaps even more unsettlingly for Arendt, Eichmann's testimony and the horrific regime and crimes it tried to defend also raised the deeper question of the nature of thought and action in modern society, calling into question traditional philosophical approaches to authority, morality, truth, and history.[16] "Totalitarian domination . . . in its unprecedentedness," Arendt wrote, "cannot be comprehended through the usual categories of political thought, and [its] 'crimes' cannot be judged by traditional moral standards or punished within the legal framework of our civilization. . . . It has broken the continuity of Occidental history."[17]

Through Eichmann, Arendt saw the relationship between the horrors of modern society and the prevalence of habituated rule-governed thinking and action come out of concealment. The power of judgment appeared capable of meeting the dangers of this catastrophe, but only if it could be *reflective,* drawing on and instantiating a common sense that was not overdetermined by lawlike, unconditional rules. Arendt became persuaded that this power of judgment, despite only being discovered by philosophy in the realm of aesthetics, was nevertheless the chief human faculty that might allow us to navigate the human condition in the wake of the Holocaust and the collapse of traditional authority.

Was it possible, however, in the absence or abeyance of a priori or determinant rules or authoritative tradition, to communicate our opinions to others and elicit agreement on the basis of exemplary instances? How should we navigate the problem and possibility that "the unprecedented, once it has appeared, may become a precedent for the future"?[18] How, "under these conditions," could we compose a defensible "story that would once again reorient the mind in its aimless wanderings . . . [and] reclaim the past so as to build the future?"[19]

Arendt worked out these thoughts with special force in her treatment of what she described as the collapse of, or "break" in, tradition and its related crises of authority. This is one of her grander arguments, and it is pursued above all in the contention that nearly the whole of political philosophy, from Plato to Karl Marx (and his contemporary adherents), can be characterized as preoccupied with politics as rule, constituting it as the dominant intellectual tradition of the West.[20] For Arendt, Plato's cave allegory represents the inauguration of a tradition that severely disparaged the value of ordinary human affairs and judgment as fundamentally ignorant and mired in an epistemological darkness.[21] The general populace is stuck in interminable confusion, lacking knowledge of what is truly significant about reality or life, and offering no hope of their finding this crucial knowledge in their everyday engagements with each other. What is needed is the philosopher, who through the power of intellect and will removes themself from this context, elevating beyond this benightedness to discover the transcendent "truths" that alone can dispel the myths of the cave. In revealing reality, they may compel recognition of the proper beliefs and purposes of mankind.[22]

The relationship of this mode of philosophy to politics, Arendt insists, is principally occupied with thinking through how to apply the transcendent or external standards discovered by the philosopher or the sovereign who wields them to the realm of politics in ways that would *compel* agreement, adherence, or simply obedience from those subjected. "It is only when [the philosopher] returns to the dark cave of human affairs to live once more with his fellow men," Arendt argues, "that he needs the ideas for guidance as standards and rules by which to measure and under which to subsume the varied multitude of human deeds and words with the same absolute, 'objective' certainty with which the craftsman can be guided in making and the layman in judging individual beds by using the unwavering ever-present model, the 'idea' of bed in general." This picture of politics as analogous to the work of the craftsman "degrades political action into the category of means and ends" and treats human beings as instrumentally as the logics of work and science treat nature.[23] In Arendt's account, this tradition's longing to discipline action and routinize its consequences betrays a recurrent desire for compulsory norms, predictability, and universal agreement that is not only at odds with the nature of action itself, but the human freedom and plurality that is emergent in it.[24]

The persistence of the picture that Arendt criticizes demands, of course, a diagnosis. What are the assumptions, motives, and attachments that hold this vision in place? Arendt's analysis is, in part, existential. In pursuit of our own private or local purposes, it is a matter of "elemental simplicity" that many of us grow aggravated with the irreversibility, relative anonymity, and fundamental unpredictability of the consequences of our speech and action. Facing these frustrations, all manner of human beings have tried to imagine how we might find "shelter from action's calamities in an activity where one man, isolated from all others, remains master of his doings from beginning to end."[25]

This fantasy underwrites the philosophical and political attractions of sovereignty, which Arendt defines as "the ideal of uncompromising self-sufficiency and mastership." Yet, for Arendt, sovereignty is an illusion in the pejorative sense, especially where people commit the "basic error" of confusing sovereignty with freedom.[26] Against this conflation, her objections are unequivocal:

> If it were true that sovereignty and freedom are the same, then indeed no man could be free, because sovereignty, the ideal of uncompromising self-sufficiency and mastership, is contradictory to the very condition of plurality. No man can be sovereign because not one man, but men, inhabit the earth—and not, as the tradition since Plato holds, because of man's limited strength, which makes him depend upon the help of others. All the recommendations the tradition has to offer to overcome the condition of non-sovereignty and win an untouchable integrity of the human person amount to a compensation for the intrinsic 'weakness' of plurality. Yet, if these recommendations were followed and this attempt to overcome the consequences of plurality were successful, the result would be not so much sovereign domination of one's self as arbitrary domination of all others, or, as in Stoicism, the exchange of the real world for an imaginary one where these others would simply not exist.[27]

The reference to Plato is significant.[28] Arendt offers a kind of origin story for philosophy's anxieties about plurality in Socrates's execution for corrupting the youth of Athens and its ostensible lesson that the denizens of the polity will not simply ignore but violently reject the pronouncements of the philosopher, perhaps even turning on him in violence.[29] In Plato's search for a relationship between philosophy and politics that would prevent the horror of Socrates's punishment, he sought to place authority and coercive force on the side of the former (even if this must be done surreptitiously). Arendt saw this leading to a conception of politics as rule, a vision based on a model of making and manufacturing akin to what the craftsperson knows and practices rather than the unruly picture of politics as argument, persuasion, and action among equals Arendt aimed to retrieve and defend.[30]

The "concept of rule," Arendt argues, is a hallmark of attempts to denounce and avoid that messy realm of public political debate and action dramatized, at its best, by tragic theater.[31] Commitment to politics as rule tends to betray "exasperation" with the unpredictability of political action, as well as its (tragic) irreversibility, the relative "anonymity" of participants in democratic politics, and the resilient fact of human plurality. The concept of rule also often presupposes "the notion that men can lawfully and politically live together only when some are entitled to command and others forced to obey," a notion Arendt traces to the petty despotism of property-owning males in ancient Athenian households and the claims to superior knowledge by the philosopher-kings who serve as the guardians of Plato's *Republic*.[32]

Arendt's notion of rule, however, goes beyond the epistocratic designs of Plato or the monarchical claims of Thomas Hobbes. Most innovative in Arendt's account is her insistence that the metaphysics underlying this deterministic view of craftmanship or making is present across a range of political and social theories, and especially teleological theories of history (e.g., Marxism). She finds it also in excessively causal accounts of historical processes in the social sciences, and even those forms of moral philosophy, like Kant's *Metaphysics of Morals* or strict utilitarianism, that seek to provide rules or determinately render orders under which *all* political action can be a priori interpreted, evaluated, or logically subsumed. For Arendt, this "tradition," despite these disparate branches, has long provided the basic metaphysical and interpretive roots of debate and philosophical reflection within which our political orders and actions are evaluated, understood, and defended. It is only in the late modern age, represented philosophically for Arendt by critical intellectuals like Søren Kierkegaard, Karl Marx, and Friedrich Nietzsche, that this paradigm buckled under its accumulated strains, a prelude to the advent of totalitarianism which brought about the irrevocable collapse of its authority.[33]

Paradoxically, because of the rule-bound character of political thought in this modern tradition, the breakdown of the tradition's authority was not fully visible. In Arendt's view, this picture of—and approach to—the world did not leave most intellectuals in a position to genuinely recognize a truly new phenomenon or event when they encountered it.[34] This dilemma, which Linda Zerilli describes as "the problem of the new," is entangled in the broader tradition's understanding and experience of causality, determinism, and teleology.[35] In Arendt's view, philosophers and political theorists are ill equipped to grapple with radical novelty, as they are ensnared in a worldview that ensures every action is understood as an extension of a prior series or mere continuation of the past. In this deterministic continuum, everything that appears is shackled by its own historical and logical preconditions, stifling the emergence of the truly new.

Against this picture of the world, Arendt wants to defend the significance of contingency in social ontology and social theory, as well as a notion of freedom that is not derived from the dangerous fantasy of "freedom as sovereignty"—"the ideal of a free will, independent from others and eventually prevailing against them" in ways "incompatible with the existence of society"[36] Sovereignty and its derivatives, insofar as they imply control, predictability, and solipsism, contradicts the contingency, spontaneity, and plurality that define genuinely *human* freedom.

Zerilli underscores the importance of judgment in navigating the political space between what is new and what is given, a space characterized by a productive, and ineliminable, tension between the creation of new institutions or practices and the maintenance of existing ones. In her neo-Arendtian view, political judgment is not about applying predetermined rules or logical deductions but about recognizing and responding to the contingencies and particularities of our situation. This requires forms of practical wisdom and world building that can foster conditions where the unpredictable and emergent nature of human action is possible, while cultivating the receptivity and attunement necessary to evaluate the meaning and significance of what appears without reducing it fully to its causes, a historical process, or an existing rule. This interpretive demand offers a threat and a promise: "The threat was that, confronted with this new phenomenon, we would not judge but attempt to explain it in terms of the old, especially through the use of inherited ideas of causality, which, like logical reasoning, deduces what is from what was. The promise was that the very loss of the 'yardsticks by which to measure, and rules under which to subsume the particular' would prompt us to recognize what is new in the phenomenon of totalitarianism, which is to say, prompt us to judge it, for the rules under which to subsume that phenomenon no longer exist."[37]

This is how to better understand, for instance, Arendt's argument in *The Origins of Totalitarianism* that the Holocaust was a manifestation of radical evil with no equivalent in human history.[38] "All parallels," Arendt argued—including coerced labor regimes, forced expulsion or migration, and slavery—"create confusion and distract attention from what is essential" in reflecting on the Nazi concentration camps.[39] This refusal to assimilate the comparison to other social phenomena manifesting utter cruelty, naked brutality, and wholesale degradation of human life suggests that the nature of the Holocaust's evil did not, for Arendt, consist primarily of any of these unfortunately familiar characteristics. At least in her early work, Arendt described radical evil as the destruction of human life and dignity in a fashion that totally overwhelms our capacities for understanding, largely because of a lack of any apparent instrumentally rational purpose (e.g., economic exploitation) for the devastation.[40] In a Kantian register, she searched for purposiveness and found her judgment utterly and entirely frustrated (at least in the third-person perspective) by the exorbitant irrationality and excess of the concentration camp. In the camps and killing fields, no custom, settled wisdom, or authoritative experience remained as a limit. "We actually have nothing to fall back on," Arendt lamented, "in order to understand a phenomenon that nevertheless confronts us with its overpowering reality and breaks down all standards we know."[41]

In the wake of totalitarianism's collapse of tradition, it was now imperative to discover some way of retrieving from this rubble the power of moral and political judgment, a sense of the world held in common, and a way of reconciling ourselves with it. Kant's aesthetic judgment, with its emphasis on judging without rules and its insistence that this did not necessitate a loss of universal validity, seemed to her to hold this promise. It also seemed to be hospitable, unlike almost all of the now fragmented tradition, to the ideals of nonsovereign freedom and plurality that Arendt so defiantly sought to defend. My suspicion is that this extreme case, and Arendt's formulations from it, speak to a broader problem of the economy of exemplarity and the exercise of judgment in the wake of crises of authority.

Responsibility and Judgment Against Thoughtlessness

One reason for this hope is the way Arendt figured the relationship between rules, judgment, and responsibility. Kantian aesthetic judgment, unlike the compulsory force of logical judgments, demands that each of us identifies with, and accepts responsibility for, the particular judgments of taste we make. Each of us is responsible to think and evaluate in the spirit of *autonomy* rather than *heteronomy*.

This distinction between autonomy and heteronomy in moral judgment came most prominently to the fore in Arendt's reflections on the Eichmann trial. David Cesarani, noting the small coterie of books and other popular accounts of Eichmann's life that appeared immediately after his capture, recounts their insistence on his "broiling fanaticism" and "sadistic brutality" and the "prurient glee" they evidently took in recounting the sexual "kinks and perversions" in the Nazi bureaucrat's past. These popular biographies, Cesarani argues, "reflected the fashionable understanding of Nazi perpetrators as losers or depraved criminals that derived from the psychological theories of Fascism and Nazism developed in the postwar period."[42] Against such expectations, the figure that Eichmann cut at trial was, at least in Arendt's account, a disappointment. "It would have been very comforting indeed to believe that Eichmann was a monster," Arendt argued, but the "trouble with Eichmann was precisely that so many were like him, and that the many were neither perverted nor sadistic, that they were, and still are, terribly and terrifyingly normal."[43] In spite of the prosecution's attempts to present a "diabolical and fanatical" Eichmann and attribute to him "near comprehensive responsibility for the Holocaust," commentators widely remarked that he looked like "a faceless bureaucrat," describing him as "a balding civil servant" and "a myopic middle-aged clerk."[44]

Ironically, it was the trial format itself that exposed Eichmann's all-too-human characteristics. As Arendt would later reflect, the trial "inevitably confronts you with the person and personal guilt, with individual motivation and decisions, with particulars, which in another context, the context of theory, are not relevant."[45] As it turned out, with the sole exception of "an extraordinary diligence in looking out for his personal advancement," Arendt concluded that Eichmann "had no motives at all."[46]

The backlash to this thesis was intense and widespread. Leading international Jewish organizations, including the Anti-Defamation League of B'nai B'rith, the Council of Jews from Germany, and the World Jewish Congress, either attacked her directly or sponsored criticism. Irving Howe described the reception of her book among Jewish intellectuals in New York as a "civil war." Alongside the matter of the biting ironic tone in which much of the book was written, many critics were also incensed by Arendt's audacity in declaring a high-ranking official of the Nazi regime—whose official function was specifically the mass deportation of Jews for extermination—"normal," and the evil that he represented "banal," with all its connotations of the mundane and unexceptional. While more recent evidence suggests that Eichmann held far more viciously anti-Semitic attitudes than Arendt seemed to countenance, and self-consciously performed some of his alleged "banality," one might still conclude, with Christopher Browning, that Arendt "had the right type but the wrong guy." "There were all sorts of people like Eichmann was pretending to be," Browning contends, "which is why his strategy worked."[47]

With her account of banality, Arendt attempted to link the moral dangers of "thoughtlessness" to the problem of judgment and responsibility. Earlier, in her book *The Human Condition,* Arendt described "thoughtlessness" as "the headless recklessness or hopeless confusion or complacent repetition of 'truths' which have become trivial and empty." The more she observed Eichmann, the more she thought he represented this "outstanding characteristic of our time" in the extreme. "The longer one listened to him," observes Arendt, "the more obvious it became that his inability to speak was closely connected with an inability to think, namely, to think from the standpoint of somebody else."[48] The failure to think was itself the failure to exercise good judgment—or, frankly, any reflection worthy of the term *judgment.* Devoid of judgment, Eichmann was obstinately unresponsive to the claims of the countless lives he brought to catastrophic end in a vacuous climb up the Nazi hierarchy.[49]

Thoughtlessness was Arendt's attempt to capture this shallow, surface-level engagement with the world and others while underscoring its paradoxical connection to evil. In a 1963 letter to Gershom Scholem she wrote,

> It is indeed my opinion now that evil is never "radical," that it is only extreme, and that it possess neither depth nor any demonic dimension. It can overgrow and lay waste the whole world precisely because it spreads like a fungus on the surface. It is "thought-defying," as I said, because thought tries to reach some depth, to go to the roots, and the moment it concerns itself with evil, it is frustrated because there is nothing. That is its "banality." Only the good has depth and can be radical.[50]

Thoughtlessness is a bit like proceeding as if the world were already fully and completely cognized or insignificant. Nothing new can appear, no event or instance can press itself on our reason in a way requiring that we know it for what it is. There are no reflective judgments to make at all. This is the height of immorality because it is the abandonment of responsibility for determining one's own actions and commitments.

Totalitarianism raised Arendt's anxiety that this thoughtlessness was a general feature of modernity.[51] The Nazi regime might have cultivated it to an especially intense degree, to the point of creating an entire society saturated with the same self-deceptions that left Eichmann "shielded against reality and factuality."[52] But this thoughtlessness was already latent, and traceable to the way we understand reasoning, morality, and responsibility in the modern age.

Indeed, this is why Arendt was so shaken by Eichmann's surprising invocation of Kant's categorical imperative during his controversial testimony. In court Eichmann stated proudly that he had tried to live his entire life according to the Kantian categorical imperative, which he expounded to mean that "the principle of my volition and the principle of my life must be such that it could at any time be raised to the principle of general legislation." The judges, as one might expect, incredulously interrogated Eichmann's claim, concerned with how Kant's categorical imperative to treat other persons not merely as means but as ends in their own right and to hold one's own actions to the standard of a universal law in the hypothetical Kingdom of Ends could possibly permit operating the machinery of racist mass murder. Eichmann conceded as much, strictly speaking, but in the "exceptional times" of the Nazi regime, Eichmann thought himself not only within the bounds of the Kantian categorical imperative ("the categorical imperative for a small man's domestic use," he called it) but duty bound to remain "true to the law, obedient" and to live so his personal life would not "come into conflict with the law" as it stood.[53]

As Arendt wrote, "He had not simply dismissed the Kantian formula as no longer applicable, he had distorted it to read: Act as if the principle of your actions were the same as that of the legislator or of the law of the land . . . act as though one were the legislator of the laws that one obeys."[54] Consequently, as responsibility in Kantian deontological morality accrues to the self-legislating autonomous actor, for Eichmann, his "subjection" to the legislation of Nazi Germany—the dictates of the führer's will—meant that the responsibility for actions carried out in accordance with this law were therefore displaced onto the "higher authorities" who created it.

Arendt was aghast. Simply concluding that Eichmann had interpreted Kant incorrectly was not enough. She thought she had found a deep tension in Kantian moral philosophy between the paean to independent thinking, intellectual responsibility, and political judgment in "What Is Enlightenment?" and the rule-governed, lawlike morality of the *Critique of Practical Reason* and *The Metaphysics of Morals*. This "emphasis on rule-following," Bryan Garsten argues, was seen by Arendt as "too easily turned into excuses for non-judgment" and too ready to turn "obedience," rather than freedom, into "a human virtue."[55]

Understanding morality as rule following was irresponsible not just because it was thoughtless but because it made a kind of fetish out of the imperative form of moral law. This was visible in how quickly Germans traded one comprehensive moral system for another. After Germany's defeat in World War II, "the Nazi doctrine did not remain with the German people. . . . [Adolf] Hitler's criminal morality was changed back again at a moment's notice." The world did not simply witness "the total collapse of a 'moral' order" but witnessed it *twice*. "It was," Arendt incredulously wrote, "as though morality suddenly stood revealed in the original meaning of the word, as a set of mores, customs, and manners, which could be exchanged for another set with hardly more trouble than it would take to change the table manners of an individual or a people."[56]

This wholesale substitution of moral orders left Arendt deeply skeptical of the character of the nature of the postwar return to normalcy and what it might disclose about the underlying relationship to moral norms in modernity. Arendt thought that totalitarianism revealed that morality was experienced by all too many as a kind of external rule, or lawlike imperative.

For such persons, moral life requires little in the way of judgment: just the apprehension of rules and the sterility of obedience.

But in the horrific world opened up by Nazism (and, one might add, in the Jim Crow regime that inspired it), *disobedience* was the authentic enactment of moral judgment and action. Thus, Arendt became fascinated with those individuals who, in contrast to Eichmann, "never doubted that crimes remained crimes even if legalized by the government . . . [and] acted according to something which was self-evident to them even though it was no longer self-evident to those around them."[57] Or, as Martin Luther King Jr. put the point, narrating a tradition of civil disobedience, "We must never forget that everything that Hitler did in Germany was 'legal.' It was illegal to aid and comfort a Jew. . . . But I believe that if I had the same attitude then as I have now I would publicly aid and comfort my Jewish Brothers in Germany if Hitler were alive today calling this an illegal process. . . . So I think these [sit-in] students are in good company, and they feel that by practicing civil disobedience they are in line with men and women through the ages who have stood up for something that is morally right."[58]

But if morally responsible action required not just rule following but the personal exercise of judgment (and action) against existing rules, from where might we expect such judgments? "Could the activity of thinking as such, the habit of examining whatever happens to come to pass or to attract attention, regardless of results and specific content," Arendt wondered, "be among the conditions that make men abstain from evil-doing or even actually 'condition' them against it?"[59] What stock of experience, evaluative claims, or styles of attention to the world could guide us in such contexts? For Arendt, this was a question of orientation, understanding, and imagination and it pointed to a profound connection between judgment and the world-constituting role of examples. Exemplary validity, she argued, channeling Kant, could produce the common sense through which individuals might resist the "erosion of Common Sense" and the loss of the "world conditions" through which judgments discover a shared character.[60] But what, without rules or shared standards, could make these judgments and their constitutive interpretations of experience valid or even exemplary enough to matter?

A Kantian Prelude: Common Sense (*Sensus Communis*)

To answer these questions, Arendt draws our attention to Kant's discussion of judgments of taste (discussed at length in Chapter 2). It should now be clear why this is so. For one, unlike the abdication of responsibility she associated with Eichmann, Kant's account of aesthetic judgment *requires* "that the subject judge for himself" without making "the judgments of others into the determining ground" of their own taste (§32:282).[61] Further, Kant's theory of reflective (aesthetic) judgment deals with particulars where the determinate concept or universal rule is not given but must be found. In Arendt's view, historical and political events generally admit of similar treatment. They are contingent events whose possible meanings are tethered to the unpredictability and nonsovereignty of human freedom, tied in various ways to what happens in the present and future and whose utter complexity leads to some indeterminacy and the possibility of being described and interpreted in many different ways. This importance of reflective judgment only heightens "when one communal tradition no longer provides the overarching framework that can direct interpretation," precisely what Arendt describes as a break in tradition.[62]

Reflective judgment, in other words, is a source of hope. Even in the face of our disorienting crisis of tradition, we have, in principle, the capacity to make and attune judgments that reach toward a level of general, intersubjective validity beyond subjective preferences. In doing so we appeal to and further cultivate a communal sense, or sensus communis, that "aims at a future community" and, through judgment, "projects a reflective consensus to be arrived at."[63] By collectively practicing certain habits of mind, caring for the publicity and plurality that allows objects of judgment to "appear" for us at all, and by reflecting sensitively and self-critically on our and others' affective and cognitive reactions to various phenomena in the world, we can move closer to a kind of general validity. Yet this can never be compelled in the fashion of determinant logic. We are *free* to be persuaded, and part of this persuasion will involve considering matters from the standpoint of others and selecting and appropriately characterizing examples.

This account of persuasion is a form of reasoning most familiar to aesthetics. It guides rather than definitively proves, and it deepens descriptions and offers styles of attention so that one might see the matter under judgment like *this,* rather than like *that,* and respond according to the distinctions drawn.[64] With regard to historical examples, such descriptions and redescriptions, as we shall see, rely heavily on narrative to do this work. Part of how we come to know a judgment or set of judgments has succeeded in persuasion and reorientation, therefore, is that people repeat, reiterate, and rely on certain exemplary stories to situate themselves and their judgments in the world. Or, as in artistic tradition, they emulate them, especially by treating orienting examples and reflections on them as exemplary, enacting new rules, ideas, qualities, and practices that are themselves worthy of emulation (§49, 318).[65]

What buttresses these various claims is the Kantian notion that the communicability of our judgments, the expectation that they elicit the assent of others, and their ability to move from the particular to the universal and general are all related to a "common sense." It is this sense that serves a "pivotal role in [Kant's] account of what makes judgments of taste possible," as well as Arendt's.[66] "Taste," Kant writes in the *Critique of the Power of Judgment,* "is a kind of sensus communis," which is to be understood as

> the idea of a *communal* sense, i.e., a faculty for judging that in its reflection takes account (*a priori*) of everyone else's way of representing in thought, in order *as it were* to hold its judgment up to human reason as a whole and thereby avoid the illusion which, from subjective private conditions that could easily be held to be objective, would have a detrimental influence on the judgment. Now this happens by one holding his judgment up not so much to the actual as to the merely possible judgments of others and putting himself into the position of everyone else, merely by abstracting from the limitations that contingently attach to our own judging. (§40:293–294)

Kant's conception of common sense is multifaceted and somewhat ambiguous. At different points in his work, he characterizes it as a principle, norm, feeling, and faculty, sometimes seeming to suggest its role as a "constitutive principle" of experience and transcendental psychology; at other times, he treats it as a regulative principle.[67] Generally, however, Kant aims to deduce the plausibility of positing the existence of something like a common sense from the very structure or modality of judgments of taste.

Insofar as the judgment of taste "ascribes assent to everyone" and judgments of beauty entail the normative expectation "that everyone *should* approve of the object in question and similarly declare it to be beautiful," Kant thinks that it raises a condition of "necessity" (§§19–20:237–238). Yet the necessity of agreement that we posit in judgments of taste, as has been detailed at length, cannot be grounded by objective determinant principles or rules. Further, in the case of "mere sensory taste" or agreeable sensations, the question of intersubjective necessity wouldn't arise at all (§20:237–238). What Kant thinks *must* instead be the case is that there exists a "subjective principle" that determines what is pleasurable through feeling (rather than concepts), yet still entails a kind of "universal validity" located in a common sense that is itself dependent on "the underlying similarity of our cognitive faculties" (§21:238–239).[68]

Part of his confidence in this claim stems from clues within his analysis of determinate judgments of knowledge. Kant argues that if we recognize that our arrival at determinate cognitive judgments requires a proper functioning of our faculties (the imagination subsumed under the understanding through schematic representation), then our universal agreements in cognition actually rest on an account of the proper functioning of faculties (here, a harmony of faculties involving the imagination's subservience to understanding). If it is possible to universally communicate *this* proper functioning for cognitive judgments, however, it must also be possible to communicate aesthetic judgments of beauty. After all, they are simply a different arrangement of these *same* faculties (here, "free play") and discernible through "disinterested" feelings of pleasure and the "heightening" or "energizing" of our faculties.[69] In other words, the communicability of cognitive judgments extends to the mental state that produces them, which involves a universally communicable feeling when optimally proportioned. If judgments of taste are similarly communicable, then there must be an aesthetic common sense that allows these judgments to aspire to universal agreement, mirroring the role of cognitive common sense in cognitive judgments.[70] Kant permits himself the conclusion that "just as the judging of an object for the sake of cognition generally has universal rules, the delight of any one person may be *pronounced as a rule for every other*" (§31:281, emphasis added). The judgment is *exemplary* in this respect (§19:237).

As Samantha Matherne powerfully argues, however, part of what Kantian common sense must make possible is enabling us "to reflect on the grounds of our judgments [and feelings] from a universal point of view" and treat that aspiration as normative. This ability to discriminate between kinds of pleasure to abstract from charm, emotion, determinant concept, and whatever else "pleases us [only] privately" in order to "take into account what pleases universally" is an *ability* that can be *educated* and *trained*.[71] In other words, Kant helpfully moves from this abstract account of (transcendental) psychology to maxims by which we can make better or worse purposive use of our cognitive faculties generally and our judging ability in particular. These are "1. To think for oneself; 2. To think in the position of everyone else; 3. Always to think in accord with oneself" (§40:294).

These maxims, which would take on enormous importance for Arendt, require training and education through exemplarity. Kant remarks,

> There is no use of our powers at all, however free it might be, and even of reason (which must draw all its judgments from the common source *a priori*), which, if every subject always had to begin entirely from the raw predisposition of his own nature, would not fall into mistaken attempts if others had not preceded him with their own, not in order to make their successors into mere imitators, but rather by means of their method to put others on the right path for seeking out the principles in themselves and thus for following their own, often better, course. Even in religion, where, certainly, each must derive the rule of his conduct from himself, because he

> also remains responsible for it himself and cannot shift the guilt for his transgressions onto others, whether as teachers or as predecessors, general precepts . . . never accomplish as much as an example of virtue or holiness . . . among all the faculties and talents, taste is precisely the one which, because its judgment is not determinable by means of concepts and precepts, is most in need of the examples of what in the progress of culture has longest enjoyed approval if it is not quickly to fall back into barbarism and sink back into the crudity of its first attempts. (§32:283)

As Matherne elucidates, examples "can help us overcome our crude aesthetic tendencies . . . [and] reflect on the grounds of our aesthetic judgments from a universal, rather than a merely private, point of view" because "when we treat them as examples, we treat them as stand-ins for what, at least allegedly, pleases not in a purely private fashion, but universally." In her words, exemplarity draws us "out of ourselves" and our "egoism" and toward the universal, eliciting a kind of thinking from the standpoint of others in anticipation and response.[72] For Arendt, "the highest aspiration of communicability" embodied in this regulative ideal reached out toward the "idea of humanity itself."[73]

Toward Arendtian Judgment

Arendt responded powerfully to Kant's idiosyncratic mix of subjectivity, autonomy, and sociability in his account of aesthetic judgment, treating it as a vital aid to her struggle against the pathologies of the (now broken) tradition of political philosophy and its anxieties about human plurality, the public realm, and the nonsovereign character of action.[74] For Arendt, "the world" (in the Heideggerian sense of human involvements) should be understood as a realm of human plurality, where the particularity of human beings is enacted and articulated within a horizon of significance mediated through language and action. Through speech and action, Arendt argued, "men distinguish themselves instead of being merely distinct. . . . [They] appear to each other, not as physical objects, but qua men."[75] But the condition for the phenomenological appearance and apprehension of this particularity is a space where such speech and action between people can appear without being foreclosed by violence or coercion that disrupts these self-disclosing and communicative possibilities. A great deal of Arendt's political theory is, therefore, committed to the preservation of the political realm's ability to remain a "space of appearances" where speech and action as she understands them not only flourish but can be judged, a practice constitutive of that flourishing. The biggest threat to the existence of this space of appearances are those coercive forms of politics—rule, totalitarianism, bureaucracy—that attempt to destroy human plurality and control the shape and outcome of human action, if not eliminate it (in Arendt's technical sense) altogether.

What Kant's theory of aesthetic judgment accomplishes, then, is to provide Arendt an alternative model for politics. She reads Kant's account of aesthetic judgment as counseling attention to the unprecedented and the particular, as avoiding reliance on a priori rules or determinant concepts, and, above all, as dependent on the existence of plurality. This is because Kant's notion of aesthetic judgment seems to presuppose the public and nonhierarchical exchange of individual opinions concerning shared (aesthetic) objects that cannot be resolved through demonstrative, logical proofs, but nonetheless seem to admit the possibility of uncoerced, intersubjective agreement and shared validity.[76] For Arendt, political judgment—even more so than aesthetic judgment—suggests that we are engaged in "an anticipated communication *with others with whom I know I must finally come to some agreement.*"[77]

Trained in the traditions of Martin Heidegger and Karl Jaspers, however, Arendt seized on Kant's regulative maxims to take his theory of judgment in a less transcendental and more hermeneutical and phenomenological direction. She was concerned to figure out "how it is that citizens get certain objects into view as objects of judgment at all," and how we come to a sense of "realness" and relevance about "'objects' for judgment [and] matters of common concern."[78] Crucial to this is her aforementioned insistence on the importance of "thinking from the standpoint of others" as fundamental to judgment.

Arendt argued that the common-world criteria of significance and validity of judgment turn on the extent to which we can achieve an "enlarged mentality" that "abstract[s] from private conditions and circumstances" by imaginatively projecting the potential or possible judgments of others on matters of common concern and taking them into account as part of the exercise of one's own judgment.[79] Expanding beyond the aesthetic limits of Kantian judgment to the realm of the political, Arendt sees the faculty of judgment as transposing similar concerns with impartially ascertaining novelty and originality (in human action, not art), interpreting significance, and making the import of the object of judgment present for others through considerate, persuasive formulations of my own.[80]

Here Arendt channels Kant's maxims for judgment and his insistence that we can argue about (if not logically dispute) taste. She quotes with unbridled approval her translation of his third *Critique* that the judging person can only "woo the consent of everyone else" and not compel it.[81] Agreement may appear as a regulative ideal—but not agreement based on compulsory, objective truths and conclusions that politics cannot provide.[82] Arendt suggests that if we practice certain habits of mind collectively—caring for the publicity and plurality that allows objects of judgment to "appear" for us at all, or reflecting sensitively and responding self-critically on our and others' affective *and* cognitive responses to various phenomena in the world—we can do the work of persuasion and be free to be persuaded ourselves. All this involves considering matters from the standpoint of others, including selecting and appropriately characterizing examples to elicit and perhaps educate these interlocutors' judgment toward the furtherance of a "common sense" and anticipated agreement.[83] The expectation is that others will find good judgment and well-rendered examples a practical advance over other ways of thinking (or not thinking, for that matter) about an object, event, or action.[84] The key, however, is that this evaluation cannot be anticipated ahead of it being elicited and exercised.[85]

For Arendt, this is akin to judgments of beauty insofar as "ascriptions of the predicate 'beautiful' are in fact placeholders that call for further investigation into the significance of particular exemplar . . . [and] to make a normative claim voiced in an imperative mood: 'consider what this phenomenon manifests.'"[86] In the freer play it gives to imagination, reflective judgment allows us to make present what is absent and venture new ways of considering or thinking about the world (including from the perspective of others) without subjecting them to a priori determination by extant rules or concepts.[87] We can indulge in the free play of faculties and see what ideas, examples, or figurations may be disclosed that unexpectedly enlarge our understanding, redirect the aspirations of reason, or reshape our (common) sensibilities. These are not invoked as proofs per se but "as part of a larger strategy to light up an aspect of an object previously unseen."[88]

To substantiate this anticipated agreement about—and mode of argument through—examples, Arendt homes in on the Kantian notion of "exemplary validity." In her lectures on Kant, Arendt defends his aforementioned notion of exemplary validity through an analogy with the conceptual schemas used in cognition. If my particular dining room table, for instance, is related to the corresponding concept *table* by which I already recognize it as such, it is because this concept—according to Kant—has a corresponding schema (a "merely formal table shape," in Arendt's words) in our imaginations that every particular table conforms to and can be subsumed under. This is how determinate judgment relies on schemas.

Reflective judgment, by contrast, must bring us to concepts or perceive a universal in the particular.[89] Arendt's account moves quickly and is vague here, but it seems that in exercising reflective judgment, we inevitably come to rely on examples to illustrate affinities, draw distinctions, emphasize significant ideas, reveal inconsistencies, and guide our normative conclusions. We do so even if these are always somewhat indeterminate and open to revision from better judgments.

For Kant, as we have seen, reflective judgment is driven by an expectation of purposiveness (as in his philosophy of history) and an aspiration to imaginatively produce the comprehensive unity and systematicity that are the aim of reason. Despite reflective judgment's inability to produce a "completed, unified understanding," the imagination attempts to produce a unity, or coherence in the object(s) under consideration that is emulative of rationality even if it can never achieve its most stringent demands. As Kirk Pillow reminds us, however, the case of paranoia—the pathological manufacture of coherence out of supposedly hidden affinities—shows that the validity claims embedded in reflective judgment must be demanding if they are to have the intersubjective import that Kant and his followers are searching for.[90] Otherwise, we would have no means of evaluating the imagined unities, perceived contradictions, or new principles and categories proffered by reflective judgment against anything much beyond the subjective imagination that produced them.[91] The internal standards of systematicity, unity, coherence, and noncontradiction are not quite enough.

Indeed, in one sense, these standards are in tension with the regulative ideal of purposiveness without purpose. This eye to the multiple interpretive possibilities that we can recognize (or imagine others recognizing) in an object means that we can give multiple accounts of its meaning. By arranging and rearranging the manifold characteristics of a given object, our interpretations might manifest systematicity, unity, coherence, and noncontradiction to persuasive degrees, but so do competing interpretations. Without other grounds for validity (excluding, of course, determinate concepts or rules), the choice between competing interpretations of examples would appear to be an existential one largely unmoored from a stringent responsibility to evidence and incapable of providing reasons for how one's judgment could be valid for others—assuming these judgments would be communicable at all.[92]

How then, do critics, they of presumably cultivated taste in such matters as contemporary art or music, persuade us of their judgments? This is akin to the problem of judgment haunting competing interpretations of the civil rights movement and, for Arendt, it broadly inflects political and historical matters as well. Why, for instance, think that the interpretive chaos around the civil rights movement expresses anything more than the private feelings of contemporary critics engaged in a war of nonadjudicable, even incommensurate, "practical pasts"? It is unclear just how to distinguish—given these presuppositions—arbitrary, subjective preferences from a subjective response that has wider validity and is worthy of emulation.

Arendt on Validity

Arendt's proposed solution is to develop a regulative ideal for our judgments. Instead of offering up our private, self-referential opinions and preferences, which could never be valid beyond ourselves, we are expected to think in the "place" of the others with whom we share or wish to share a common world. As Arendt proclaims, "I form an opinion by considering a given issue from different viewpoints, by making present to my mind the standpoint of those who are absent. The more people's standpoints I have present in my mind while I am pondering a given issue, and the better I can imagine how I would feel and think if I were in their place, the stronger will be my capacity for representative thinking and more solid my final conclusions, my opinion."[93]

Not only is the particular project of intersubjective validity, therefore, not viable without this thinking in the place of others, but Arendt claims that reflective judgment, properly speaking, is impossible in "isolation or solitude." This thinking from the standpoint of others is supposed to facilitate the "enlarged mentality" that Kant tried to appeal to with his ideal of the sensus communis while also constituting the limits of the validity of our judgments.

Our validity claims, Arendt argues, can "never extend further than the others in whose place the judging person has put himself for his considerations."[94] Still, they must place a prohibition on solely subjective validity claims that presumably extends to all members of the political community, and thus, even our thinking from others' standpoints should also avoid *their* purely subjective validity claims. If this is the case, then the only referent of an anticipated agreement could be those objects of judgment that are considered as public concerns, potentially to be shared generally, albeit from different perspectives.

At this point it is natural to worry whether Arendt has provided any real solution to her own problem. If Kant's appeal to a universal, transcendental human psychology is too speculative, the sort of imaginative projection that Arendt counsels may seem equally utopian. And even if we were capable of it, it is unclear that it could secure anything other than a modus vivendi rather than a more robustly normative consensus. Iris Marion Young, for instance, criticizes Arendt for assuming that we can, by virtue of imagination, leap across stark differences in subjectivity partially constituted by differential experiences in a given social order, particularly one marred by group-based forms of domination.[95] If we project our own settled habits and expectations forged in domination into our imagined perspectives of others, we may systematically distort their standpoint. One might offer Arendt's own clumsy attempts to imagine herself from the standpoint of African American mothers in the Jim Crow South confronting the possibility of participating in desegregation struggles as evidence that she underestimated this difficulty.[96] Young suggests that the goal should instead be the institution of *actual* dialogue structured by what she calls "asymmetrical reciprocity," a form of deferential exchange (she likens it to gift giving) that does not presume one can inhabit another standpoint but instead counsels respectful listening and learning that will hopefully open up our ability to understand the needs and claims of others.[97]

Young's proposal only moves the goalpost of judgment farther downfield. We can agree with Young that Arendt's idea of an "enlarged mentality" would be on firmer ground if it were presented with more humility and was more attentive to ideology, structural domination, and group hierarchy. But unless we are willing to simply grant epistemic privilege (and thus demand deference) to victims of domination, then even this injunction to deference could not secure the validity of judgments that emerge from it.[98] We ourselves still have to judge (i.e., what happens when the "victims" disagree?). Indeed, it is a danger—one familiar from some of the more tutelary variants of identity politics—to present what we are doing as merely receiving a gift from the (communicative) gift giver as if we no longer remain responsible for our own judgments.

A more compelling defense of Arendt is offered by Bryan Garsten, who argues that "Arendt's notion of representative thinking is one in which the perspectives of others are somehow made present someplace where in fact they do not exist—inside of us." It is in this way that judgment is inextricably linked with persuasion, which Arendt sought so mightily to defend as the substance of politics. "To be open to persuasion we must be able to imagine ourselves believing something different and yet still being ourselves," a capacity that is forged in this process of imagining the opinions of others as though they could be (and sometimes making them) our own. The picture that Young presents is of identities that are too "singular or unified" and thus "remained closed to . . . the capacity to imagine oneself as something other than oneself, and yet still oneself, the capacity to represent oneself."[99]

But even if we have this capacity, it is not clear normatively where we should go with it. Who must we include in our enlarged mentality? With whom should we seek agreement? Zerilli rightly implores us not to treat this question as one that can be answered a priori. All we can do is engage in the exercise of judgment and in doing so enter into a "world-building" practice, discovering "not simply the personal preferences of other people . . . but the extent and nature of what we have in common. . . . Kinship based in the practice of judgment is something one discovers—or fails to discover—in the practice itself."[100] The demand to discover what can possibly be agreed on, or even said, in advance of saying much of anything at all, is precisely the species of pathology that Arendt warned us about in her critique of political philosophy's ambivalence toward plurality and human action, and its determination to settle the outcomes of political matters in advance.

The turn to aesthetic judgment, despite its prima facie incongruity with politics and history, draws our attention to what we are doing and what kind of arguments or criteria we are eliciting when we argue about indeterminate matters.[101] In other words, political and historical judgments have "a fundamentally anticipatory structure: we posit the agreement of others, that is, we perform an act of closure," but whether others agree "is another matter and part of the openness of democratic politics itself." Even the power of the opening claim of the Declaration of Independence, "We hold these truths to be self-evident," is, from this vantage point, realigned from emphasis on "truths" (natural law) and "self-evidence" (compulsory reason) onto the meaning of "we hold." As Zerilli writes, "We judge objects and events in their freedom. We don't have to hold these truths to be self-evident any more than we have to hold the oppression of women abominable or the rose beautiful; nothing compels us. There is nothing necessary in what we hold. That we do so hold is an expression of our freedom. In the judgment, we affirm our freedom and discover what we have—and do not have—in common."[102]

What, in the end, do Arendt's reflections on judgment and exemplary validity achieve? For commentators like Garsten and Zerilli, it redeems the practical significance of reflective judgment and its connections with persuasion, freedom, solidarity, and responsibility across a range of political matters. One of Arendt's most striking remarks is her claim that "our decisions about right and wrong will depend on our choice of company," and that "if someone should come and tell us that he would prefer Bluebeard for company, and hence take him as his example, the only thing we could do is to make sure he never comes near us."[103]

Even if we try to fill in the content of who we should engage in enlarged thought with something like "humanity" or "everyone," we run into the obvious problem that this is, ultimately, another "indeterminate" idea. As Garsten reminds us, the idea of humanity itself is a product of representative thinking "because it is not present anywhere. . . . We know humanity only through examples." We are again without determinate rules; the "ultimate criterion upon which I base my choice of company must be nothing other than my own imagined sense of humanity," for the very examples I use (or take) to present this concept "require precisely the sort of judgments that we are attempting to ground." Garsten argues that in making the moral foundations of judgment (right and wrong) so "elusive" (based on freedom, exemplarity, and judgment, not rules), Arendt's account has "the effect of preventing us from blaming the principles or dictates of reason"—as Eichmann did—for "our actions and opinions."[104]

But beyond that moral-practical achievement, Arendt's thinking also gives us something of a guide to the use, interpretation, and representation of historical events like the civil rights movement. As we now move more concretely to the accounts of the movement, it is worth gathering together what we get from Arendt and what we still have to do. Arendt provides us not just with an argument for the practical importance of aesthetic judgment in general but with a sense of the power of the exemplary. In particular, she opens up for us the importance of understanding the challenge of exemplary validity. Nowhere is this challenge more vital for us than in questions of historical interpretation.

Historical Judgment as Reflective Judgment

Historical judgments about events like the civil rights movement are instances for the exercise of reflective judgment. We must attend to and assess the particular case, absent clearly defined antecedent rules, especially when we are trying to apprehend novel events. The interpretation of those events not only explains to us what happened but establishes a new pillar for our common sense and therefore for contemporary politics. But we cannot even begin to understand this as the challenge of historical interpretation if we understand history as itself governed by lawlike necessities or as always already subsumable under inherited categories.

This is part of what drives Arendt's extreme doubts about progressive theories of history, which she thinks are guilty of this approach. Arendt puts pressure on progressive histories in two important directions that will inform our discussion of civil rights memory and historiography. The first is the way that deterministic theories of history or explanation—especially progressive ones—make it impossible to grasp and value particularity, as well as "the contingent character of processes" which collide and coincide to create reality and occasion action in complex ways. If progress was always already teleologically secure, then there would be nothing really to attend to—only the confidence or comfort in the intellectual act of subsuming particular events under general laws of historical development. What totalitarianism revealed, for Arendt, is that this meant subsuming particular human beings—vast numbers of human beings—into these logics, by force or by neglect, if they dared resist or otherwise gum up the works of the "necessary" progress of humanity.

The influence of Arendt's friend, the critic and philosopher Walter Benjamin, is crucial here. Arendt appropriates from him a critique of progress as antagonistic to human dignity. In a well-known passage from his "Theses on the Philosophy of History," Benjamin describes progress through the thought-image of the "Angelus Novus." The grand narrative sweep of historical progress leaves us, Benjamin contends, with no genuine vantage point to think from the standpoint of those actors or events that do not quite fit the storyline or whose appearance is in a subordinate role as the vanquished. These people are the "wreckage" of history, its "debris" in the storm of progress. When we let an ideal of historical progress sit in judgment over all of the happenings of history, the only criteria of significance, and the ultimate evaluative criteria of meaning, is an event or person's instrumental contribution to this end. The "thought of progress in history as a whole, and for mankind as a whole," Arendt argues, "implies disregard of the particular and directing one's attention, rather, to the 'universal' (as one finds it in the very title of the 'Idea of a Universal [General] History') in whose context the particular makes sense—to the whole for the existence of which the particular is necessary." It involves an imposition of *necessity* that is a category she finds to be a coercive imposition on human affairs. Later, in her lectures on Kant's political philosophy, Arendt puts this critique even more bluntly: "It is against human dignity to believe in progress."[105]

This leads to a second point of pressure. Part of the indeterminacy and the non-rule-governed nature of historical interpretation Arendt defends argues that our access and apprehension of the past, the only reason we can say anything meaningful about it, is that it is somehow related to our own questions, purposes, categories, and being in the present. And, as Arendt never tires of pointing out, the *tragic* character of action—its contingency, dependency, and unpredictability—means that those who come after us will always have the possibility of seeing more of the consequences and meanings of our actions than we can in the moment.

Indeed, we can even judge that whatever was "successful" in conventional categories of evaluation or leading accounts of the processes of historical development is not, upon reflective judgment, truly worthy of our affirmation. Our retrieval and memory of the defeated can, as an exercise of anamnestic reason, become a vantage point from which we can judge our history and present in a different light, opening up alternatives to the force of what is that are otherwise elusive.

Arendt associated this insight with one of her favorite quotes, from Cato the Elder: "The victorious cause pleased the gods, but the defeated one pleases Cato."[106] The gods—those who try (and fail) to survey the historical record from the Archimedean point of universal progress—are only interested in victory, but in our capacity for human freedom we can choose to honor the dignity of the defeated. We can acknowledge and honor that they shared, as human beings, the same capacity for action and beginning as the victors—and build anew on the inspiration and emulation of their exemplarity. This "essential element of the tragic" in Arendt's approach to human history, one I will build on in the ensuing discussion of the civil rights movement, insists that "in the course of history, tragedy and defeat may be as world-disclosing and world-preserving as any victory," depending on what stories we tell.[107]

Although Arendt does not ever systematically develop the insight, this requires a different approach to historical representation and judgment, one that Seyla Benhabib has characterized as "fragmentary historiography."[108] Fragmentary historiography acknowledges the connection between exemplary events, profound social changes, and the meaning of philosophical concepts. In an elegiac essay on Benjamin, Arendt writes,

> Like a pearl diver who descends to the bottom of the sea, not to excavate the bottom and bring it to light but to pry loose the rich and the strange, the pearls and the coral in the depths and to carry them to the surface, this thinking [of Benjamin] delves into the depths of the past—but not in order to resuscitate it the way it was and to contribute to the renewal of extinct ages. What guides this thinking is the conviction that although the living is subject to the ruin of time, the process of decay is at the same time a process of crystallization, that in the depth of the sea, into which sinks and is dissolved what once was alive, some things "suffer a sea-change"; and survive in new crystallized forms and shapes that remain immune to the elements, as though they waited only for the pearl diver who one day will come down to them and bring them up into the world of the living—as "thought fragments"; as something "rich and strange."[109]

For Benhabib, the thinker who uses this fragmentary historiography breaks "the chain of narrative continuity . . . [inherent in] chronology as the natural structure of narrative, to stress fragmentariness, historical dead ends, failures, and ruptures."[110] But for what purposes and with what warrant?

Arendt's uses of fragmentary historiography turn principally on three commitments, all essential. To stay with the metaphor of pearl diving, you might characterize them as why we dive, what we find, and what we "swim" through.

First, why do we dive at all? Arendt's remarks about dignity and progress are embodied in the hope "to do justice to the memory of the dead by telling the story of history in terms of their failed hopes and efforts"; these are key clues to why we dive.[111] This incorporation of a duty to show reverence to dignity into historical judgment is above all a rejection of those overarching approaches to history that refuse to consider the perspectives of "defeated causes" and their proponents on their own terms, or as Arendt might put it, to think from their standpoint or respect them as cocreators of our world. To the extent that this cannot but happen in the unfolding of new stories that contend with existing ones about the past, it also counsels a deep skepticism of those narrative forms that habituate us to determinant judgments on history and the sort of epistemic arrogance that concludes, a priori, that there is nothing worth salvaging in the so-called wreckage or defeats of history.

Here we discover a thin conception of validity in judgment. Historiographical controversies have many different sources, some of them well entrenched within existing practices of justification and others related to political projects or aims in the present. But when they have a moral or ethical dimension, it seems inextricable from some explicit or implicit advancement of the claim that the story as it stands falls short of showing the appropriate respect for the dignity of some relevant characters or acts. This contention, however, will often be inarticulate. In the following chapters, I will argue that it is often submerged in the aesthetic dimension of narrative form—how stories and their emphases, beginnings, and ends are arranged to disclose meaningful aesthetic unities—and must be disclosed by perspicacious judgment that reveals how the historian's representations of particular events seek to render various themes, "characters," and ideas generally significant. This seems to me to be an overlooked task of political theory and a promising way of rethinking the import of Arendtian judgment. The familiar divide between the judgment of the actor and the judgment of the historian or spectator is perhaps bridged by this insistence on the importance of dignity and a historical approach that seeks, in stories of the past, to recover it from burial or ignominy. The goal is to educate judgment to be attentive to ways in which we might fall short of respecting our own dignity and that of others in the present.

Second, what are the "pearls" we find? For Arendt, the words and stories we rely on for judgment, as we have seen, can be lost or can collapse over time. In such cases, although we no longer have a reliable thread or set of pillars to make sense of past experiences or even our own, judgment has the potential to break through this impasse. Through experimental and interpretive judgment, Arendt described herself as trying "to discover the real origins of traditional concepts in order to distill from them anew their original spirit which has so sadly evaporated from the very key words of political language—such as freedom and justice, authority and reason, responsibility and virtue, power and glory—leaving behind empty shells."[112]

From this vantage point we can understand historical judgments' bearing a special kind of weight. At one level, they orient the common sense of politics. When acting together, people imagine themselves thinking about the same object or aspiring to emulate the example of that object, be it a person like Martin Luther King Jr., a movement like the civil rights movement, or an event like the sit-ins in Greensboro, North Carolina (see Chapter 1). It is no wonder that the validity of these judgments are of such high stakes: people risk their lives in pursuit of the proper objects of our emulation.

At another level, historical judgments orient the common sense of politics by providing us with new concepts that exercise a special totemic force. What is or is not valid is not the event, person, or model itself but the concept or evaluative vocabulary abstracted from that event. Concepts, in other words, attempt to standardize examples. Instances can become concepts by abstracting and formalizing them, which is one of the vectors of historical thinking and judgment. We move from the instance of the civil rights movement to the concept of social movement theory, from the instance of 1963's Project Confrontation in Birmingham, Alabama, to the concept of civil disobedience. Each of those acts of conceptual standardization involves that imaginative expansion and creative play of our faculties that we now know are characteristic of reflective judgments about moments of exemplary validity. Arendt has bequeathed to us enough to recognize the nature and importance of the task, and especially the question of how to adjudicate these judgments.

But Arendt's thought trains are incomplete. For the purposes of evaluating the romantic, ironic, and tragic structures of civil rights theories, we need, somewhat ironically, *more* determinate concepts or interpretive structures. This brings us to the last question: When we dive for pearls, what are we swimming in? Arendt's most persuasive answer, at least on my account, is that we are wading through *stories*.

Our accounts of action, our examples, our exercises of self-disclosure, and even our analyses of "the break" in tradition all rely on narrative—they are conveyed through the practice of storytelling. For Arendt, the "meaning of a committed act is revealed only when the action itself has come to an end and become a story susceptible to narration." Narration, which is "ever-recurrent," is what establishes meaning and significance as well as "permanence and persistence" in our relation to the messy, contingent, particular, indeterminate, and unpredictable character of human actions. Through stories we not only make sense of our own lives but we find ourselves even further entangled in what Arendt called a "web" of narratives about the past, the broader world we inhabit, and even our possible futures. To think from the standpoint of others is, in reality, to try to imagine and inhabit stories about them, and renarrate our own in that light.[113] In this respect, stories are part of what Arendt describes as the space of appearances; the kinds of stories we tell affect what can appear as common objects of judgment and argument, what we think of as worthy of emulation, and even what identities or forms of peoplehood seem to anchor our practical reasoning.

This was especially apparent in the wake of totalitarian horror, as Arendt detailed in *Men in Dark Times*. The need for new stories—stories capable of illuminating moral questions, reorienting us to our traditions, or pointing us forward amid the ruins of what was—was gruesomely clear. But new is not enough. We lack a way of understanding the competing claims about the web of narratives that structure our increasingly fragmented and chaotic thinking around events like the civil rights movement, especially as the authoritative interpretations fall into crisis. So as we turn now to these questions of philosophy of history and the representation of civil rights history, we will find it necessary to take more seriously than Arendt did the problem of narrative itself. We will need theories of narrative structure and genre to make sense of this otherwise impossible web and its relation to meaning, politics, and human flourishing.

Philosophical Hermeneutics and the Problem of Narrative

We turn to narrative because we are concerned with the problem of historical judgment, the attempt to discern meaning in retrospective accounts of the past. If narrative is a constitutive language of historical judgment, then it will be profitable for us to turn to hermeneutics, where the study of narrative understanding has long been a central preoccupation.

The fundamental insight, arguably, of the hermeneutic tradition is the contention that "the sense or the significance of a narrative stems from the intersection of the world of the text and the world of the reader."[114] Hans-Georg Gadamer, perhaps the leading philosopher of hermeneutics, argues that our own preunderstanding and context are always already constitutively involved in the interpretation of a text (text being broadly construed)—that is, if they are ontological conditions of our understanding.[115] To even begin to find the contours of a given story intelligible, then, requires a complex background of experience, intuitive beliefs, and knowledge—whether something as fundamental and oft-unarticulated as the temporal character of experience or our engagement with the world, or something more contextual and cultural, like the assumed significance of a given author (e.g., Jane Austen or William Shakespeare).

Our hermeneutic situation, therefore, is shaped by what Gadamer calls a "forestructure of understanding": those beliefs and ideas that we inherit or are otherwise influenced by that serve as the point of departure for our understanding to gain any purchase on a text or other object of interpretation. Paul Ricœur describes what occurs in the act of reading as an unfolding of "the world horizon implicit in [a text] which includes the actions, the characters and the events of the story told" that causes the reader to belong "at once to the work's horizon of experience in imagination and to that of his or her own real action."[116] Thus, we have what Gadamer famously called the *fusion of horizons*—the coming together of the cultural and imaginative horizon of the text and the horizon of the reader. Understanding arises from the interpretive possibilities inherent in the creation and exploration of this indeterminate, in-between space, which can emerge between eras, cultures, and other similar divisions that frustrate immediate, intuitive understanding.

In fleshing out what is most relevant about hermeneutics for our present purposes, we must take seriously some core features of narrative and meaning. The first is the narrativity of human action, or the sense in which human action "call[s] for narration." For example, Ricœur argues that without the semantics of action offered to us by natural languages, we would be unable to "distinguish between action and mere physical movement" and otherwise unable to comprehend that which is signified by "project, aim, means, circumstances, and so on."[117] Far from being relevant only in the phenomenological perception of simple action, this inherent narrativity also structures self-understanding and thus shapes the contours of intentional action by providing symbolic mediation and narrative logic to our capacities for human understanding. This is even more true for complicated sequences of action, cause and effect, and so forth, which offer themselves up for narratives that are complex enough to arrange events and actions in a story that is intelligible and that provokes the imaginative and rational faculties of understanding toward the discernment of meaning.

"If indeed action can be recounted," Ricœur argues, "this is because it is already articulated in signs, rules and norms; it is always symbolically mediated . . . [which] gives an initial readability to action."[118] The symbolic mediation of action is therefore necessarily confronted in recounting. Even if hermeneutic reflection inevitably discerns meanings that might not have been available to the original actors, the process will remain tied to considerations of symbolic mediation that allow for inquiry into the original actors' possible orienting questions, intentions, self-descriptions, and so forth.

Aside from this ontological claim about the inherent narrativity of human existence (too often theorized on the idealized individual) is a question about the significance of these more complex *social* narratives, like those offered in historical writing or popular historical memory. Here Charles Taylor's concept of a "horizon of significance" draws our attention to the irreducibly social content entangled with the ethics of our self-understanding and related to preexisting narratives about who one is and ought to be, or who we as a given social group are or ought to be. The narratives and "rich languages of human expression" we inherit and inhabit provide structure, albeit flexible structure, to our cultural tastes and political commitments. Yet these languages also organize deeply held evaluative frameworks that make features of our social lifeworlds *significant,* often initially in a more intuitive, tacit, background way. As Taylor notes, "Our self-interpretations are partly constitutive of our experience, . . . [and] certain modes of experience are not possible without certain self-descriptions."[119] Put bluntly, how else can we recognize or judge an action unless we grasp it as an action of this or that kind? How would we evaluate it outside of some such description? How would we notice it without some background of significance?

Let's take as an example the 1910 victory of Jack Johnson, the first African American heavyweight boxing champion, over James Jeffries, the "great white hope" enlisted to defeat the black usurper and reestablish the white supremacist propaganda of physical and mental superiority tethered to early twentieth-century boxing. In the wake of Jeffries's defeat, we see African Americans in exuberant parades while white Americans revolted in roving murderous mobs. The intelligibility of both responses lies in deeply felt emotional outbursts rooted in a wide array of cultural background assumptions about the meaning and significance of a boxing match between two men for broader social concerns like racial hierarchy, masculinity, imperialism, segregation, racial identification, and the like.[120]

Part of the challenge of critical hermeneutic reflection, therefore, is to disclose dimensions of implicit moral, epistemological, and ethical commitments that structure and render intelligible our horizons of significance (and those of our interlocutors). We then have to subject these commitments to critical evaluation in light of other horizons and mobilize the capacities of imagination and judgment to pursue a similar task for the horizon of the historical object or event under consideration. The coming together of these horizons occasions an attempt not only to reevaluate deeply held notions of significance but also—and often more practically—to allow contemporary readers to take note of important events, ideas, and figures of the past who have become significant in new respects. Just as Arendt admonished against the abdication of judgment, so, too, can we say, with Thomas McCarthy, that the "participants and their traditions" in any given hermeneutic situation cannot have the "final say about the significance of the practices they engage in."[121] The past can continue to speak only so long as those in the present stand ready to interpret.

Narrative and Emplotment

The particular object of critical reflection in our case is the historical event and its place in, or construction through, a historical narrative. If the meaning of action arises from a narrative, the question is how narrative structure generates meaning. It does so by holding together and organizing its constitutive events in a particular way. Hayden White calls this holding together "emplotment."

Emplotment is the practice that transforms the many disparate events or actions in a given field of perception, imagination, or awareness into a structured story that conveys what is presumed relevant about its constituent parts. Emplotment produces a meaning separate from any of the singular events that constitute its complete trajectory. "It is not enough that a historical account deal in real, rather than merely imaginary, events," observes White, "and it is not enough that the account in its order of discourse represent events according to the chronological sequence in which they originally occurred." To achieve the level of narrative history, events must be "revealed as possessing a structure, an order of meaning, which they do not possess as mere sequence."[122]

White illustrates the distinction between emplotment and mere sequence through his contrasting of more familiar, contemporary narrative history with the chronicle or annals form of historical accounting prevalent in medieval Europe. The latter simply lists a series of events in chronological order, selected for an unstated criterion of significance, but with no manifestly discernible central subject—no beginning, middle, or end and no suggestive connections between one event and another clearly articulated.

To illustrate this point and take us toward the controversies of civil rights historiography, let us transpose the first chapter of Glenda Gilmore's field-defining history of the long civil rights movement, *Defying Dixie: The Radical Roots of Civil Rights, 1919–1950,* into the chronicle form.[123]

1896 In *Plessy v. Ferguson,* the US Supreme Court declares the "separate but equal" doctrine of racial segregation constitutional

1906 Lovett Fort-Whiteman matriculates to the Tuskegee Normal and Industrial Institute

1910 Howard Odum publishes *Social and Mental Traits of the Negro*

1910 The Mexican Revolution begins

1912 Woodrow Wilson of New Jersey is elected president of the United States

1913 Wilson orders the racial segregation of the federal government's operations in Washington, DC

1915 One hundred lynchings are recorded in the United States

1915 US military forces occupy Haiti

1917 The United States enters World War I

1917 Lovett Fort-Whiteman registers for the US military draft, performs *Othello*, and joins the Socialist Party of New York

1919 Twenty-six race riots occur in the United States during the summer

1919 The Commission on Interracial Cooperation is founded

1920 Howard Odum founds the School of Public Welfare and the Sociology Department at the University of North Carolina

1921 The Worker's Party of America is founded

1922 The US Senate orders "agricultural instruction" to become a curriculum in Haitian public schools

1924 Lovett Fort-Whiteman travels to Moscow and delivers speech on "the Negro Question" to Ho Chi Minh and Joseph Stalin, among others

1925 DuBose Heyward publishes *Porgy*

1925 The American Negro Labor Congress convention is held in Chicago

1927 James Weldon Johnson, executive secretary of the National Association for the Advancement of Colored People (NAACP), visits Haiti

1927 Paul Green wins the Pulitzer Prize for *In Abraham's Bosom*

1928 Harry Haywood delivers his "Black Belt Thesis" at a meeting of the Communist Party USA

1928 The Republican Party excludes black delegates from official national convention hotels

1929 Jacques Roumain leads protests in Haiti

1929 Julia Peterkin wins the Pulitzer Prize for *Scarlet Sister Mary*

1930 Marc Connelly's *The Green Pastures* is performed in theaters

1932 The Haitian Communist Party is founded

This sequence, as presented here, is disorienting and seemingly meaningless. Its inauguration—it seems odd to call it a "beginning"—commences in 1896 with a federal court decision, but no other verdicts are mentioned, while the publication dates of a few books and speeches, and the performance dates of a handful of plays, are. The list includes events that occur in

Haiti, Mexico, Russia, and the United States. Some events concern leaders of government, and others refer to political organizations or acts of violence. There are some mentions of the movements and actions of individuals for certain years, but other years and their events are not referenced at all.

Our sense of the inadequacy of the chronicle form stems in part from the fact that it represents history to us "as if real events appeared to human consciousness in the form of unfinished stories."[124] We find the chronicle form repellant (or at best, deeply unsatisfying) because the discontinuities it offers frustrate our expectations for continuity—reasons, implicit or explicit, that allow us not only to understand what these events share such that they should be emplotted together but also to assign varying degrees of importance or significance to constituent parts. Why is the founding of the Haitian Communist Party listed alongside the publication of *Porgy*? Why is Fort-Whiteman's matriculation to the Tuskegee Institute in the same sequence as Woodrow Wilson's election to the US presidency?

The power of comparing narrative with the chronicle or annals form is that it forces a radical confrontation with the "extent to which narrative strains to produce the effect of having filled in all the gaps." A historical narrative could attempt to emplot a vast array of events and occurrences. But at the upper limit this not only becomes practically impossible but also undermines any aspirations to coherence, explanation, and comprehensibility that we expect from narrative—especially historical narrative. Thus, White argues, "Every narrative, however seemingly 'full,' is constructed on the basis of a set of events which might have been included but were left out," and it becomes incumbent on the philosophy of history "to ask what kind of notion of reality authorizes construction of a narrative account of reality in which continuity rather than discontinuity governs the articulation of the discourse."[125]

Gilmore's particular chronological sequence is, in fact, held together by a narrative. It is one that explanatorily links the evolution of Jim Crow to the development of a global politics of white supremacy, including the white supremacist military regime installed in the US occupation of Haiti launched in 1915 and the contemporary international organizing efforts of the white terrorist group the Ku Klux Klan.[126] At the center of this account is President Woodrow Wilson, a trained political scientist and historian who wrote a prominent critique of Reconstruction's racial liberalism and, on arriving in Washington, installed segregation in the federal government by executive order.[127] He championed the racist Ku Klux Klan propaganda film *The Birth of a Nation* in a screening at the White House and ordered the invasion and military occupation of Haiti. The seemingly disconnected plays and novels that Gilmore references then become illustrative of the widespread cultural influence of the artistic works of white supremacist Southerners who offered up their ideas of black life and culture to an audience clamoring for their "privileged" insights on "the Negro."

The rest of Gilmore's chapter sustains the narrative coherence through a mirrorlike reflective structure. It tells the story of Lovett Fort-Whiteman, a Texas-born African American who graduated from Tuskegee before fleeing the oppressive South to live in Mexico, Cuba, and Canada before settling in New York. There he joined an emergent political struggle against this ideological-political formation of global white supremacy, first in the form of the socialist labor movement and ultimately as a prominent member of the Communist Party USA, where he split his time organizing African Americans in the United States and serving as a prominent theoretician on the "Negro Question" for the Communist International in Russia. His example serves to imaginatively complete, at least at the radical edges, a picture of the struggle between two opposing political and moral forces in the early twentieth century. These forces, Gilmore later goes on to claim, shaped the more familiar contours of the civil rights struggle through intellectual legacy, via traditions of domination and resistance, and above all in the geopolitics of the Cold War, where domestic anticommunism created a state imperative to act against racial segregation while at the same time encouraging the marginalization and suppression of formerly dominant leftist ideas and organizations in the civil rights movement.

Gilmore is trying to make sense of past events, but her narrative structure also inevitably aims at communicating something about its significance *for us.* Part of this claim of significance is related to the revisionist historiographical project of the "long civil rights movement" paradigm. Gilmore argues that her focus on the radical Left, and particularly communists, will show how their political action "redefined the debate over white supremacy and hastened its end," while also allowing us to better see "the conservative aspects of the NAACP's litigation strategy [to dismantle Jim Crow]" and the ways in which Cold War anticommunism "eviscerated postwar social justice movements and truncated the civil rights movement that emerged in the 1950s."[128] The former is a causal claim; the latter involves recovering a new ground of judgment from historical memory to redescribe an exemplarity we thought intimately familiar.

This attempt at revisionist criticism turns on more basic assumptions about the moral import of such a narrative. Revisionist narrative is recognizable as such only if there is a common object of revision. And that common object is worth revising only if it already plays some important role or has accrued some significance. For Gilmore, as for others, narratives about the civil rights movement are more than scholarly skirmish; they are part of the ethically constitutive stories that shape our sense of political peoplehood, whether that be American African American, or *modern.*[129]

Why do narratives have this constitutive power? Hayden White argues that all stories, and historical narratives among them, have as their "latent or manifest purpose the desire to moralize the events" they narrate. The very demand for a beginning and an end in narrative form, he contends, is a demand "for moral meaning, a demand that sequences of real events be assessed as to their significance as elements of a moral drama."[130] This might overstate the case, since we can imagine some stories being significant without having any direct *practical* or *moral* significance. But in the case of narratives of exemplary events, we are dealing with narratives that lay the foundations not just for distinguishing right from wrong but more robust and dense elements of self-understanding, authority, common concern, and shared fate.

It is from Rogers Smith that I borrow this language of ethically constitutive stories of peoplehood. Political peoples, in Smith's account, are those forms of human association that are imagined or understood to impose binding obligations and duties on its members that may conflict with other forms of human association and assert claims of primacy, or priority, in such conflicts. "To succeed in their mission," Smith argues, "doctrines, ideologies, visions of political peoplehood must make a certain sort of case to current and potential members . . . that given their personal origins and history and the way the world is, if they do indeed adhere steadfastly to the community thus depicted, they are likely to experience certain sorts of good things" like economic prosperity, political power, or the realization of ethical aims like cultural greatness or personal liberty that are believed to be constitutive of their membership.[131]

When they lead in the direction of racial supremacy or patriarchal domination, these stories can go awry. But they are an unavoidable part of the constitution of a political community. The normative aim behind Smith's project, therefore, is to salvage the significance of such narratives while making a plea for them to become more moderate, more liberal, and—most important—more universal in their aspirations to translate the ethical insights of particular stories into "larger constitutive stories defining the identity and interests of the human species."[132] As we have seen, much of civil rights exemplarity enacts this aspiration.

Returning to civil rights movement memory and historiography, we can see more clearly how an event figured as exemplary would become a point of contestation in ethically oriented stories about both American and African American peoplehood. In particular, the avenues for political judgment and critique they open up or foreclose are all intimately related to the implicit consensus around the civil rights movement's significance as part of a larger story that binds peoples together and shapes their aspirations. In this sense, revisionist long civil rights movement historiography is an attempt—even if that intent is implicit—to rewrite these stories and perhaps even offer up its particular insights into the nature of political ideals for universal appreciation.

Yet if narratives succeed in communicating an ethical orientation, they do so without always engaging in direct normative argument or normative propositions worked out in chains of logical entailment. Historians write narratives. What remains for us, then, is to get a sense of how narrative structures communicate ethical orientations without writing in a direct philosophical register.

Here, again, Hayden White provides important answers. If we are searching for the ethical moment or orientation of a given historical narrative, we have to attend to the plot structure of the work itself. This is missing in Arendt's talk of "webs of narrative." Far from being purely descriptive or analytical, the aesthetic form of the narrative is itself productive of meaning. This, as White explains, means that "the 'content' of the discourse consists as much of its form as it does of whatever information might be extracted from a reading of it." It logically follows, for White, that "to change the form of the discourse might not be to change the information about its explicit referent, but it would certainly change the meaning produced by it."[133]

The form is the ethical content in two interrelated ways. The first is that the story form of historical narrative is not found but imposed. This is true especially to the extent that story forms demand a beginning, a climax, and an end. What White is challenging is the notion that there are narrowly "empirical" historical and conclusive epistemic grounds for these sorts of interpretive decisions. This seems clearest in the ways that historical narratives tend to have an "ending," which White suggests is simply "a demand . . . for moral meaning" since "we cannot say, surely, that any sequence of real events actually comes to an end, that reality itself disappears, that events of the order of the real have ceased to happen." He goes on to proclaim that he "cannot think of any other way of 'concluding' an account of real events" other than "when meaning is shifted, and shifted by narrative means, from one physical or social space to another."[134]

Second, and most paradoxically, this productive imposition of narrative form on real events is underwritten by the broad availability and power of figurative discourse in human cultures. This is why meaning often feels intuitive. To follow a story means to have a deeply structured capacity for narrative understanding formed by immersion in a cultural horizon in which certain narrative conventions provide meaning.[135] To follow a story, therefore, means to follow it as a certain type or genre of story. We will often find narratives of real events sufficiently compelling or meaningful when they are represented according to prevailing forms of narrative. These narratives, in White's words, produce "truth-effects" and a "representation of reality" that we judge to be persuasive in part because of literary devices that procure for them a sense of closure and intelligibility based on ethico-aesthetic, or at least metaphorical, grounds.

But what do we do about *multiple* narratives? After all, in this book, we are concerned not just with the romantic but with its relation to the ironic and tragic narratives of the civil rights movement. One reading of White would have it that since events may be divergently emplotted in distinct narratives, multiple stories can be told and only in rare instances conflict.[136] White shows us, however, how much more complicated this story is. He is right to draw our attention to the problems of inclusion, emphasis, and narrative emplotment not because these are "merely" aesthetic choices that reflect historian's deliberate practice but because they reflect deeper commitments, styles of attention, and criteria of significance that mediate between plot and explanation. The significance of emplotment to historiography helps us recognize that the existence of multiple narratives is not an uninteresting or unexceptional "aesthetic" problem, pejoratively understood.

Where multiple narratives of the same "event" coexist unproblematically, it likely reflects shared conceptual underpinnings that can be best retrieved through focus on narrative form—and underlying generic similarity across superficially different stories. Meanwhile, when narratives do, in fact, conflict and seem incommensurable, attention to narrative form can help reveal the relevant truth-claims and social pictures that form the real sites and stakes of disagreement. This is why distinctions among genres, especially romance, irony, and tragedy, can be so illuminating: They help us argue against a whole picture of the world.

The argument advanced in the following chapters contends that recent controversies of civil rights history (especially the long civil rights movement historiographical revolution) proceed not as much through the discovery of new historical data as by a new mode of emplotment that has emerged as a powerful narrative option only through our present hermeneutic situation. In short, civil rights movement historians, critical theorists, and other commentators are attempting to supplant the romantic narrative of conventional civil rights historiography with two competing modes of narration: irony and tragedy. They do so, however, partly as response to a broader crisis of authority in black political life that is constitutive of our horizon.

But before turning to these critical views, I want to ask *what, exactly, was the romantic narrative of the civil rights movement* and what role did it play in political rhetoric and philosophy? Further, what settled judgments built up that authoritative pillar of common sense and have now come crashing down all around us, leaving us trying to retrieve some way of reorienting ourselves in its ruins?

II

ROMANCE

CHAPTER 4

THE ROMANCE OF CIVIL RIGHTS

From Red Sea to Ruins

THE CIVIL RIGHTS ACTIVIST, politician, and intellectual Julian Bond neatly summarized the narrative arc that has become "the master narrative" of civil rights history.[1] To paraphrase, it is a story of long-suffering African Americans, subjected to segregation, humiliation, and exclusion by their hostile Southern oppressors. In 1954, the NAACP argued *Brown v. Board of Education* in front of the Supreme Court, winning a unanimous decision that outlawed segregation in public schools and ruled "separate but equal" doctrine unconstitutional. Inspired by this epochal decision, courageous white and black Americans fought Jim Crow through boycotts, freedom rides, sit-ins, and other protest demonstrations. This exemplary movement, under the charismatic and rhetorically astute leadership of Dr. Martin Luther King, Jr., won the moral and political support of a "sympathetic" federal government, especially President John F. Kennedy, Attorney General Robert F. Kennedy, and, after the assassination of his predecessor, President Lyndon B. Johnson, a Southerner now converted to this great cause.

This alliance, which peaked in the 1963 March on Washington (with its famous "I Have a Dream" speech) and thrilling demonstrations in Mississippi and Alabama, crystallized for America the pressing moral urgency of race discrimination in the South. These efforts galvanized legislative and executive action, including the 1964 Civil Rights Act and the 1965 Voting Rights Act, fundamentally repairing much of the glaring hypocrisy at the heart of American democracy. Unfortunately, in the wake of these decisive successes, the heroic civil rights movement devolved into conflicts over Vietnam, Black Power, and other dilemmas (e.g., ghetto subcultures, leftist counterculture, feminism) and King, its great leader, was assassinated by a lone, racist gunman. Nevertheless, his heroic example, and that of the movement, has achieved immortality in memory and ritual celebration.

Its values and exemplarity can still orient American civilization, guide political judgment, and inspire others around the world.

What does it mean to describe this conventional story of the civil rights movement as not just a "master" narrative, but as a "romance"?

Moving our interpretation from the charges of hegemony and ideology, romance opens up subtler angles of understanding and critique. Hayden White, who pioneered this approach to reading historical discourse, describes romance as "fundamentally a drama of self-identification symbolized by the hero's transcendence of the world of experience, his victory over it, and his final liberation from it—the sort of drama associated with the Grail legend or the story of the resurrection of Christ." The plot conventions of romance emphasize the "triumph of good over evil . . . and of the ultimate transcendence of man over the world in which he was imprisoned by the Fall." It conceives of the arc of action or process that is its subject as "a struggle of essential virtue against a virulent, but ultimately transitory, vice."[2]

Romance is also motivated by a "passion for [exclusive] union" and the "desire for reciprocity," seen as the constitutive possibility to realize a posited good or goods in themselves.[3] Although now the term is generally associated with *eros,* or "romantic" love, the passion for union and reciprocity can readily attach to other ideas of human association and consolidation: race, ethnicity, neighborhood, movements, and, above all, nation and peoplehood.[4] In its *narrative* mode, romance dramatizes and represents—often symbolically, allegorically, or metaphorically—the process of becoming through which unities like these come into being. Indeed, the criteria of significance through which events, personalities, or tendencies are included and arranged in such narratives turns often on judgments of their fitness for bearing the symbolism of unity or as vehicles toward realizing the end(s) of union.

Popular civil rights historiography is largely emplotted in this romantic mode. In Taylor Branch's monumental history *Parting the Waters,* for example, the civil rights movement becomes thoroughly imbued with religious themes of deliverance and redemptive suffering culled from the biblical narrative of Exodus.[5] That foundational story of the Old Testament traces the divine deliverance of the people of Israel from bondage in Pharaonic Egypt through the trials of the wilderness toward a covenantal founding of a new nation in the Promised Land of Canaan. This nation, the emancipated Israel, is based on law, dignity, and faithful enactment of God's purposes.[6]

We should not be surprised that this myth surfaces in historical representation. Deeply cemented in the cultural lifeworlds of "the West," this exemplary Old Testament narrative is a ready-at-hand template and source of "powerful memories shaping our perceptions of the political world," and its telos has long authorized imagined futures where domination and exploitation are decisively overcome and once-oppressed people are permitted to live with dignity, their God having vanquished their enemies.[7] Breaking with ancient tales like *The Odyssey* that "begin and end at home" or "all mythic notions of eternal recurrence," the "Exodus is a journey *forward*—not only in time and space" but as a "march toward a goal, a moral progress, a transformation."[8]

It is also, it bears underscoring, a story that has become greatly entangled with the romance of *political peoplehood.* It dramatizes the forging of a divinely sanctioned political community out of disarray and disempowerment, and follows its arduous search for legal order, ethically constitutive purpose, and a territorial homeland. In America, the narrative and symbolism of Exodus have been mobilized especially to generate a "rhetoric of consensus . . . a way to constrain differences and conflicts" and consolidate notions of peoplehood—especially American peoplehood—that could manage the fractious consequences of dissent. In African America, the attractions of Exodus run especially deeply. As Eddie Glaude notes, by the 1840s, "the metaphors of Exodus had indeed sedimented as the predominate language of African Americans . . . [for] the ritual emplotment of bondage, liberation, and nationhood." The travails of enslavement and the struggle for genuine emancipation were broadly "understood within the narrative frame of Egyptian bondage, the wilderness, and the promised land."[9]

As racial oppression persisted beyond the nineteenth century, so, too, did this interpretive tendency in political culture. Long before Branch's mobilization of the Exodus metaphor, Martin Luther King Jr. spoke movingly of how "the Negro was thrown into the Egypt of segregation," and he chastised "those Pharaohs with hardened hearts, who, despite the cries of many a Moses, refused to let these people go." He even went so far as to describe, in 1956, the "world shaking decree" in *Brown v. Board of Education* as having opened up the "Red Sea" so that "the forces of justice marched through to the other side" and "segregation [was] caught in the rushing waters of historical necessity." Distilling the lesson of this theologico-historical parallel to the flights of romantic "hope" that were sometimes his wont, King proclaimed that "there is a Red Sea in history that ultimately comes to carry the forces of goodness to victory, and that same Red Sea closes in to bring doom and destruction to the forces of evil."[10]

In this respect, Branch's metaphor and narrative mode follows a venerable tradition, including its symbolic investment in King as a modern Moses and as "the best and most important metaphor for American history in the watershed postwar years."[11] This happened, of course, in King's lifetime too. In a 1960 interview with *Life* magazine, King replied to a line of questioning about his symbolism and potential martyrdom with ambivalence: "At times I think I'm a pretty unprepared symbol. . . . But people cannot devote themselves to a great cause without finding someone who becomes the personification of the cause. People cannot become devoted to Christianity until they find Christ, to democracy until they find Lincoln and Jefferson and Roosevelt, to Communism until they find Marx and Lenin and Stalin. I know that this is a righteous cause and that by being connected with it I am connected with a transcendent value of right."[12]

The nature of this connection with transcendent value still animates interrogation and narration. Virtues of nonviolence, reconciliatory love, the passion for justice, and, above all, what Christopher Lasch has called "the spiritual discipline against resentment" are personalized and symbolized in King, who is cast as the central hero in a story of the struggle of the essential virtues of the age against the prejudice, intolerance, and cruelty represented by Jim Crow and, to a lesser degree, the rage of black nationalist militancy.[13] This choice to make King the symbol of civil rights and the metaphor of an age could never simply be *aesthetic,* in the limited sense of the term we have been straining against. Conventional pictures of King as metaphor and symbolic vehicle of narrative trajectory exerts a centripetal pull on the historical drama of the civil rights movement and perhaps "America" itself. It invites us to see the past as a set of events that revolve around our depictions of him and invites judgment on the grounds of whether these events seem to "move" toward or away from a vision of America's future that can be ascribed to the rendering of Dr. King on offer. This is a remarkable tendency given that journalists in the 1960s could expect many readers to readily digest the notion that "the proliferation of Negro leadership organizations points up a significant fact of the Negro's revolution: that it has lacked any clear-cut, centralized direction." While acknowledging that King "has come closest to being the Negro's symbolic leader," it was commonly noted that "no one individual or organization has been able to presume to speak for all Negroes, nor, always, to control their triumphant surge into the streets."[14]

In the romantic mode, this historical drama often culminates in a somber but decisive victory, with King solemnly accepting his role as martyr, sacrificing his life to save the body politic from the monstrous excrescence of Jim Crow so that good might triumph and a grateful nation can reconcile around his heroism.[15] This, too, draws on some claims of the moment. In the immediate aftermath of King's death there were eulogies and speeches that attempted to place him in a Christ role in American civil religion. This was partly inspired by the fact that Palm Sunday fell only two days after King's assassination. Longtime King ally and Memphis pastor James Lawson, for example, proclaimed at a Palm Sunday rally and memorial service that "Memphis will be known for a long time as the place where Martin Luther King was crucified. Yes, crucified. We have witnessed a crucifixion here in Memphis." Days later, King's widow and fellow civil rights and peace activist, Coretta Scott King, talked about her husband's death in similar terms, exhorting the audience at a rally to make bring forth a "resurrection" that would "make all people truly free and . . . make every person feel that he is a human being."[16]

King's "resurrection," at least metaphorically, is often said to be manifest in the last great burst of civil rights legislation and antipoverty policy of the 1960s (i.e., the Fair Housing Act of 1968), the increased commitment to racial integration in higher education and public life, and, above all, in the monumental shift in racial attitudes away from the explicit doctrines of antiblack racism familiar in the Jim Crow era toward broadly professed commitments to racial equality and equal opportunity.[17]

Immediately after King's death, government and media elites began to promote his "I Have a Dream" speech from the March on Washington for Jobs and Freedom as "a mystical synecdoche" for the entirety of King's career.[18] Our commitment to King's "dream," often reductively distilled to the hope that his children might "be judged by the color of their skin but by the content of their character," is consecrated every year in a national holiday and in the deifying stock quotes of hundreds of contemporary politicians paying homage to the man that Branch has solemnly called our "new founding father."[19]

This trajectory follows what the literary critic Northrop Frye describes as "the complete form of the romance . . . the successful quest," as it moves from "perilous journey" (*agon*) to "death-struggle" (*pathos*) to, in its conclusion, "the *anagnorisis* or discovery, the recognition of the hero, who has clearly proved himself to be a hero even if he does not survive the conflict."[20] This last role, where King is duly recognized and transformed from martyr to canonized secular saint, is one that historians enact professionally and members of the polity perform as part of their civil religion.[21]

A romantic mode need not, therefore, altogether avoid death, disappointment, and defeat. Instead it *narratively* incorporates these despairing chords into a progressive or redemptive composition. While Branch inevitably takes us through the great losses of the classical phase of the civil rights movement—the murders of Emmett Till, Medgar Evers, Addie Mae Collins, Denise McNair, Carole Robertson, Cynthia Wesley, John F. Kennedy, James Chaney, Andrew Goodman, Michael Schwerner, and James

Reeb, to name a few of the era's most spectacular casualties—the effect of the narrative arc is to exalt, through peering into these depths, the commanding heights of the romantic whole.

The assassination of Malcolm X is illustrative. For Branch, who incorporates Malcolm as King's foil throughout his three-volume history of the King years, Malcolm's violent assassination has accrued a significance essentially no different than that which King attributed to it in 1965: "The assassination of Malcolm X was an unfortunate tragedy. Let us learn from this tragic nightmare that violence and hate only breed violence and hate, and that Jesus' word still goes out to every potential Peter, 'Put up thy sword.' . . . We will still suffer the temptation to bitterness, but we must learn that hate is too great a burden to bear for a people moving on toward their date with destiny."[22] For Branch, it remains a "teachable moment," to borrow today's vapid political parlance, for those who still harbor doubts about the moral and political outcomes of rage, resentment, and intolerance. The epilogue principally details, as Malcolm's afterlife, a gruesome series of internecine murders between black Muslims and the dispiriting rise of Louis Farrakhan, not the remarkable ferment that Malcolm's exemplarity inspired for the art and politics of the Black Power and Black Arts Movements. Put differently, the sweeping substance of a wide-ranging philosophical and political dispute—not simply about violence and "hate" but also about the efficacy of integrationism, the philosophical foundations of black solidarity, the nature of black ghetto poverty, and the meaning of class divisions for African America—is reduced to the minor term in the dialectical movement of American and African American history.[23]

Excavating this kind of judgment buried in narrative form brings us to the point where we may clearly state issues at stake in an analysis of the romantic vision of the civil rights movement. We must gain an understanding of how the structure and development of romantic history generated a kind of common sense about race and American political life that had authority for those seeking to address post–civil rights conflicts. Then, turning to the decline of romantic narration, we must make further headway applying our earlier theoretical work in hermeneutics, genre criticism, and the study of narrative form to explain how the crisis of romantic narrative's reproduction is generated in part by, and further accelerates, a broader crisis of authority in black political life.

This chapter walks us through these elements in sequence. Via a discussion of historians like Branch, and political figures like President Barack Obama who rely on this narrative mode, we see how the romantic vision functioned in American public life and the mode of historical consciousness and political judgment it authorizes. Obama's oratory, especially his invocations of the "Moses" and "Joshua" generations, reveals how romance can attempt to suture black struggle and sacrifice to a redemptive telos of union and national purpose. Yet, as I contend, romance as a mode of historical understanding is moving but not innocent. It can warp our understanding of political temporality and the demands of ongoing injustice, confuse compulsion with consensus, and naively treat as settled political matters that are sites of deep antagonism.

Where the self-confidence of romantic narrative erodes, it is especially prone to melancholy and nihilism, stubbornly attached to the ruins of an imagined moral and political clarity. I trace how some most committed chroniclers of the civil rights movement drift over time into a kind of historical mourning, clinging to redemptive narratives they themselves find hard to credibly sustain. Drawing on the work of Wendy Brown and David Scott, I argue that this shift reflects more than narrative fatigue or the idiosyncrasies of psychology; it marks a deeper crisis of authority.

After this account, I turn in Chapter 5 to confront this crisis of authority directly. I situate the analysis of the romantic vision of the civil rights movement within the hermeneutic framework developed at the end of Part One to explain *why* there is a crisis of authority in black political life and what that means for how we can and should approach the exemplarity of civil rights movement. I make the case that black political life has undergone its own "break in tradition," to invoke my discussion in Chapter 3 of Hannah Arendt's diagnosis of the modern age.

The crisis of black political life, I argue, is marked by the collapse of four pillars that once were authoritative, in the sense of intuitively compelling understanding and setting many of the axiomatic assumptions of our discourse. These assumptions helped give credence to notions of good decisively transcending evil, the value of redemptive sacrifice, the progressive civic nationalism of a "more perfect union," and, above all, ideas of unified black peoplehood that buttressed romantic history and its political philosophic appendages.

The first pillar, *racial realism*—the belief that shared biological, cultural, or historical-political foundations ground political solidarity—has unraveled under sharp philosophical scrutiny and the pluralizing pressures of immigration, class stratification, and identity fragmentation. The second pillar, *black church vanguardism,* or the claim of privileged political leadership by the church, has withered in the face of secularization, conflicts over gender, scandal, and theological mutations (i.e., the advent of prosperity gospel) too hollow to sustain its prophetic politics. The third pillar, an interpretive schema that mapped black political philosophy as a *binary opposition between integrationist and nationalist futures,* has also faltered. The vocabulary of integrationism has become exhausted by the stubborn realities of segregation and hollow reform, and its inability to clearly pose questions of class or culture. The vocabulary of nationalism, on the other hand, has waned under the global crisis of nationalist aspirations, as well as more local dilemmas of "intraracial" differentiation and contradiction, a vast campaign of antinationalist state repression, and its surprising susceptibility to parody and self-parody. Finally, the *cultural politics of representation* has also unraveled. It was once a set of assumptions animated by a widely held moral duty to vindicate the race with cultural production and enactment of "positive" images or to cultivate and defend a shared group cultural identity as "a people" that can compel respect from others and enact a distinctive form of *black* flourishing. Once a comprehensively moral project aimed at vindicating black humanity and shaping collective identity, the cultural politics of representation relied on artists to uplift the race and police its image. Over time, that project buckled under the pressure of expressive freedom, class antagonism, the collapse of Christian authority, and the destabilizing force of popular culture. This is crystallized especially in the growth of hip-hop, which both challenged respectability and redefined authenticity on its own terms. Today, with no stable, shared sense of the "positive" or "negative" to orient judgment about art and artistic representation distributed and dispersed across platforms, political loyalties, and micropublics, the very premise that art can or should speak for "the race" is in disarray.

I preview the argument here because I want to underscore that the fact that *historiographical* criticism of the romantic narrative appears so powerful and urgent reflects not simply the immanent force of history writing itself but a broader cultural and political collapse of the kind of presuppositions about black political life that were once intuitively authoritative for most people's judgments about the past, present, and future. This is why we have, at various points, drawn attention to Ludwig Wittgenstein's insistence that, "it is not single axioms"—or, here, narrative accounts of the civil rights movement—"that strike me as obvious, it is a system in which consequences and premises give one another mutual support."[24] As certain culturally and politically conditioned premises fall into disrepute in the present, or as our contemporary acts of imitation of the past seem unable to generate their expected consequences and experiences, it should not surprise us that these authoritative narratives have fallen into crisis. Our authoritative interpretations and narrative conventions are losing their ability to compel genuflection, orient effective understanding, or generate reliable affective responses.

To be clear, when I say that black political life is in the throes of an increasingly self-conscious crisis of authority, I do not mean that political struggle or striving has ceased but that the interpretive foundations that once gave our understanding of a certain form of coherence and direction are no longer the same. We must face up to that challenge and, where necessary, abandon the old vocabularies and role expectations they made seem intuitive. What we confront now is not only *political disappointment* in the limits and fragility of what we broadly understood the civil rights movement to have won in terms of legislation, social norms, and political hope, but a breakdown in the authority of inherited frameworks to understand our judgments about that moment and its import for us now. There is a palpable disorientation about who we are, what we owe, and where we are headed as the romance of civil rights—the mythic arc of deliverance, exemplarity, and moral progress—has lost its grip. Its heroes, at least as they are presented to us, feel embalmed. Leading narrative modes too obviously flatten dissent, obscure tragedy, and often describe modus vivendi as "consensus" and justice. Our attempts at emulation, understandably, curdle into imitation: expressive performance without genuine solidarity, protest without purpose, remembrance without renewal. This is the crisis: not the absence of politics but politics unmoored from the authority of the traditions that once made their practice meaningful. The aim is to confront this with courage and seek a way out.

Barack Obama and the Rhetoric of Romance

To describe the prevailing narrative mode of civil rights movement history and memory as romance, it should now be clear, does not mean it is akin to a shallow or superficial love story. In characterizing Branch's account as romantic, I want to emphatically emphasize that this does not amount to a charge of simple naivete. I do not, moreover, deploy the category *solely* to pick out those depictions of American political development that see race as an insignificant structuring feature of the distribution of benefits and burdens, opportunities and wealth, social esteem and social capital in American society. Nor is it an insult via the circuitous and hardly rewarding route of literary genre criticism and narratology, meant to heap further scorn on those accounts of American history that treat the practice and legacy of antiblack racism as decisively overcome in the 1960s.

I am far more interested in the apparent appeal of romance as a way of suturing together a compelling history of "progress," a contiguous set of identities and ideals that ground critical evaluative standards for the present, and an insistent faith in an imagined future that will redeem the emancipatory hopes and strivings embodied in a particular rendering of the civil rights struggle.

The powerful admixture of these elements is on full display, for example, in nearly all of Barack Obama's most renowned speeches on race. Throughout his campaigns and two-term presidential administration, Obama insisted vehemently that the civil rights movement and its aftermath had improved American racial order by any defensible moral standard and that this truth must be acknowledged in order to ward off the cynicism, resignation, and despair that he sees as fundamental obstacles to further progress along this hallowed path. In his widely celebrated 2007 "More Perfect Union" speech in Philadelphia, organized hastily to confront anxieties over his pastor Jeremiah Wright's incendiary denunciations of the American racial order and foreign policy regime. Media outlets circulated spliced-together excerpts of sermons by Wright, a devotee of James Cone's "Black Theology" and an influential United Church of Christ pastor and activist in Chicago, where he offered a strident prophetic denunciations of American civilization for its history of racial injustice and mass incarceration, and militaristic foreign policy:

> Where Governments lie, God does not lie. Where Governments change, God does not change. Governments fail. . . . And the United States of America's government, when it came to treating her citizens of Indian descent fairly, she failed. She put them on reservations. When it came to treating her citizens of Japanese descent fairly, she failed. She put them in internment prison camps. When it came to treating her citizens of African descent fairly, America failed. She put them in chains. The government put them in slave quarters, put them on auction blocks, put them in cotton fields, put them in inferior schools, put them in substandard housing, put them in scientific experiments, put them in the lowest paying jobs, put them outside the equal protection of the law, kept them out of their racist bastions of higher education and locked them into position of hopelessness and helplessness. The government gives them the drugs, builds bigger prisons, passes a three-strike law, and then wants us to sing "God Bless America." No, no, no. Not "God Bless America"; God Damn America! That's in the Bible, for killing innocent people. God Damn America for treating her citizen as less than human. God Damn America as long as she keeps trying to act like she is God and she is supreme![25]

Obama distanced himself from his pastor's controversial remarks by criticizing what he saw as Wright's "fatal mistake." The error, Obama alleged, was that Wright "spoke as if our society was static; as if no progress had been made; as if this country . . . is still irrevocably bound to a tragic past." Wright narrated the sweep of American history as defined by a successive series of profound moral "failures" that invite damnation. This reading, Obama suggested, unduly disavowed the evidence of America's ability to change and, in doing so, missed "the true genius of this nation."[26] The consequence, for Obama, was not just epistemological but ethical: We lose our sensitivity to the power of past progress to inform hope in the present.

How should we understand this invocation of the "true genius" of America, or Wright's "fatal mistake"? For Obama, much of the genius embodied in the American project is rooted in the dialectical relationship between the Declaration of Independence and the US Constitution. He chose Philadelphia, the city where both documents were adopted, as the setting of his speech to underscore this symbolism. The Declaration, in Obama's view, initiated an anchoring commitment to republican government ("We, the people"), equal liberty, and civic equality. The Constitution is where those ideas could find institutional entrenchment and elaboration, providing for "a union that could be and should be perfected over time."[27]

Later, at a commemoration of the 1965 voting rights march in Selma, Alabama, Obama would expound on this view: "Selma shows us that America is not the project of any one person. Because the single-most powerful word in our democracy is the word 'We.' 'We The People.' 'We Shall Overcome.' 'Yes We Can.' That word is owned by no one. It belongs to everyone. Oh, what a glorious task we are given, to continually try to improve this great nation of ours."[28]

As the political theorist Melvin Rogers carefully details, this conception of "the people" as having "two bodies"—an institutional and constitutional structure that claims to act in the name of the people *and* an "aspirational" space of constituent power and popular contestation of "we, the people" suggests a process by which the latter can exceed, call into question, and remake the former. As Rogers puts the point, "the idea of the people reflexively encodes openness as part of the legitimating logic of republicanism, and thus creates a productive tension between the governmental apparatus and those in whose name that apparatus claims to speak . . . the aspirational people is thus a presupposition of democratic life."[29] This is how, in Obama's view, "Americans in successive generations who were willing to do their part—through protests and struggles, on the streets and in the courts, through a civil war and civil disobedience, and always at great risk—[could] narrow that gap between the promise of our ideals"—the ideals embedded in the Declaration—"and the reality of their time."[30]

But while Rogers emphasizes (in principle) the radical reconstruction and indeterminacy made logically possible through this feature of a democratic republic, Obama more strictly anchors his judgment of the telos, or proper end, of this "aspirational" American peoplehood in a progressive politics aimed at redeeming the American Creed and enacting constitutional fidelity. The Constitution was "stained by this nation's original sin of slavery" at the time of its signing, Obama argues, but "the answer to the slavery question was already embedded within our Constitution." So, too, are the answers to all manner of racialized social problems, from segregated schools to wealth inequality to mass incarceration. The obstacle, in each instance, is that "the people" have not effectively achieved "unity" or further perfected a "union" distilled from the "common stake" in one another and creedal values that Americans share. Jarringly, Obama even insists that one of the signal differences between the era of the classical civil rights movement and the present is that we have now lost reliable grasp of, partly *because* of "the admission of minorities and women into full citizenship, the strengthening of individual liberties and the healthy willingness to question authority," those historically "shared assumptions—the quality of trust and fellow feeling—that bring us together as Americans."[31]

The demand, therefore, is to perform a kind of "refocusing" disclosure. Refocusing, as I argued in Chapter 1, involves making ourselves more aware of obscured, inarticulate, or "unthematized" connections within our "shared pre-understanding of the world." The aim is to uncover and rearticulate our deepest shared values and commitments and, in doing so, repair "breakdowns" in attention, interpretation, and judgment that appear to threaten these values and the coherence of our self-understanding. Here Charles Taylor's notion of bringing to articulacy what we always knew remains clarifying.[32] So, too, is the reminder that when this refocusing discourse is *teleological,* the historical narrative embodies and enacts the standards by which we "measure right choices" or "instantiate" the proper direction of our history.[33]

Yet Obama's civic pedagogy trains our perception and judgment in peculiar ways. His "refocusing" on creedal nationalism and constitutional veneration, to borrow Aziz Rana's incisive concepts, does not draw attention to the possible threats to the prospects for racial justice and interracial reconciliation that inhere in constitutional compromises tracing back to slavery and were defended by the architects of Jim Crow. Diffuse exhortations to unity find no institutional soil on which a critique of those features that make the presidential elections, the Senate, and judiciary appointments biased toward largely white rural areas, even permitting long stretches of minority rule, might flower.[34] Nor does this framing lead us to the question of how the Constitution permitted, and continues to permit, spaces of authoritarian experimentation at the state and local levels, most spectacularly in the form of Jim Crow.[35]

Unmoored from this kind of structural analysis, the obstacles to "a more perfect union" that Obama does emphasize are strikingly focused on political affect and social psychology. Black rage, once broadly justified in the era of Jim Crow, now is disparaged because it "all too often . . . distracts attention from solving real problems . . . [or] facing our own complicity within the African-American community in our condition."[36] The rage and resentment in the souls of black folk alienate potential allies desperately needed for progressive change. This anger, at least for Obama, has its alleged correlate among "working- and middle-class white Americans," many of whom are not descended from slave owners but late nineteenth or early twentieth-century refugees from European poverty, famine, and war. They bristle with resentment at talk of "white privilege," especially after decades of offshoring in American manufacturing, the collapse of unions and corporate pensions, wage stagnation, and cost increases for basic needs (e.g., childcare, housing, and health care). Affirmative action programs deepen these resentments, focusing inchoate frustration with an increasingly fractious and expensive scramble for elite colleges and jobs on minorities rather than the scarcity itself. Stereotypes abound on both sides, exploited by cynical commentators, talk shows, and activists who obscure "legitimate concerns" with "counterproductive" distraction.[37]

Much of what Obama defends as a response to this scenario is familiar to students of Democratic Party liberalism at the turn of the twenty-first century. He asks white Americans to reject zero-sum thinking and see their black fellow citizens as allies across a range of policy domains (e.g., employment, health care, and education). He also urges white Americans to express respect for African Americans by acknowledging how cumulative disadvantages undermine the fair equality of opportunity and distort procedural justice (e.g., criminal law). Likewise, he counsels African Americans to adopt a politics of "binding our particular grievances—for better health care and better schools and better jobs—to the larger aspirations of all Americans" while cultivating an ethos of self-help and personal responsibility. This is especially vital in child-rearing, where African Americans themselves must develop a spirit of resilience, self-confidence, and civic faith in black children.

These arguments are worthy of sustained interrogation, some of which I pursue elsewhere.[38] But most interesting for our present purposes is that Obama also recommends, for African Americans explicitly, a reorientation of *historical consciousness:* a disposition toward history that "embrac[es] the burdens of our past without [us] becoming victims of our past," mired in self-defeating rage and despair. In this respect, Obama's advice converges with John Rawls's argument that one of the key tasks of political philosophy in a democratic society is *reconciliation:* the demand that we show how our "institutions, when properly understood, from a philosophical point of view, are rational, and developed over time as they did to attain the present, rational form."[39]

Romance and Reconciliation

The explicitly Hegelian goal of reconciliation is to lead us to "accept and affirm our social world positively, not merely be resigned to it." Rawls especially wants us to reconcile ourselves to some measure of "the fact of profound and irreconcilable differences in citizens' reasonable comprehensive religious and philosophical conceptions of the world, and in their views of the moral and aesthetic values to be sought in human life." This fact of pluralism is reasonable and valuable, however frustrating, and the goal should be to affirm it rather than wish it gone. Yet Rawls also sounds a note of quiet caution. "Political philosophy as reconciliation must be invoked with care," he warns, for such a practice is "always in danger of being used corruptly as a defense of an unjust and unworthy status quo, and thus of being ideological in Marx's sense." We want to know what kinds of disagreement we should regard as reasonable, but we must also know which developments involve a "historical fate we should lament."[40]

This mission, as Rawls's reference to Hegel suggests, relies mightily on historical judgments; and, if one chooses to accept it, it entails the risk of intensifying our desire for historical narratives that seem to achieve this task and demonstrate a kind of "beautiful" consensus or movement that may not be apparent at first glance. My suggestion is that romance, as a narrative form, is exceptionally attractive to those who philosophize in this vein and, in a friendly amendment to Rawls's note of caution, an especially potent source of ideological danger.

Romantic narrative is prone to exaggerating consensus and minimizing the political and ethical content of social conflict, loss, dissent, and disruption. The critical possibilities of these moments are submerged in romance, and we must go through great hermeneutical difficulties to retrieve them. Romance can also impose narratives of mythic consensus brought into being by heroic exemplars of near-superhuman agency. These portraits of the past, inevitably debt inducing, act as a cultural compulsion to imitate these figures and events, ethically and teleologically. This can have the paradoxical impact of alienating us from the very traditions that those who invoke these histories imagine will inspire us, or educating our political judgment to unduly dismiss those forms of politics—especially *contentious* politics—that do not appear, prima facie, to conform to the expectations engendered by the romances that structure our horizons of expectation. Its strategies of historical comparison and judgment can fetter our imaginings of what is possible, tolerable, or estimable by bludgeoning us with rationalizations of the status quo. As Rawls worried, it is easier than we would like to confuse reconciliation with acquiescence to, and rationalization of, injustice.

The near-mythic suturing across time in romantic narratives is often achieved through morally charged metaphors and tropes, and we should be vigilant when we see Exodus play such a dramatic role. As early as a 2007 campaign stop in Selma, Obama echoed Branch's biblical symbolism, characterizing civil rights activists as the "Moses generation" who successfully "led a people out of bondage" to the brink of "the promised land." Obama's innovation, based on a conversation with the veteran civil rights activist and Cleveland pastor Otis Moss, was to invoke the Old Testament figure Joshua, Moses's faithful disciple, to describe his cohort of black elected officials. This "Joshua Generation," in Obama's rendering, was *proof* of the movement's heroic victories, the authentic inheritors of a people's sacred struggle for unity and equality, and the future authors of the fulfillment of our covenantal faith in unprecedented terrain. As Joshua, Moses's faithful aide and scout, was called by God to secure the Israelites' faith and obedience to the Mosaic covenant, cross the River Jordan, and conquer Canaan, so Obama insists that a new generation of black politicians and their supporters have been "called to be the Joshuas of our time . . . the generation that finds our way across this river."[41]

Here a unified African American peoplehood (modeled on the ancient Israelites) is reconciled with the aspirations of American peoplehood. The mission of the Joshua Generation involves not only the achievement of equality for an oppressed people but also the redemption and perfection of America's "common creed" of "tolerance and opportunity, human dignity and justice," enshrined in the egalitarian promise of the Declaration of Independence.[42] With the Declaration as covenantal origin and horizon-shaping telos, the civil rights movement is figured as an iterative articulation and dramatization of the deep-seated American consensus on values. It intimated what must now be realized, a more perfect union to come, and has decisively performed the hardest work of all: deliverance from Egypt.

The faith that the Joshua generation will progress toward a more perfect union, rather than wander in the wilderness, is, at least for Obama, secured by a form of historical consciousness deeply inflected by romantic conventions and aimed at achieving reconciliation. This vision of romantic historical judgment has four principal dimensions.

First, it demands that *charitable comparative reflection* on the past be incorporated into the evaluation of the justice of a social order and the question of whether one should keep faith and allegiance to it. This project takes its most provocative form, perhaps, in a thought experiment that Obama relayed in one of his last major speeches as president, at the 2016 Howard University commencement. While Obama often chose to speak at historically black colleges and universities (HBCUs) during commencement season, his choice of the illustrious Washington, DC, school seemed especially deliberate. During Obama's presidency, the Baltimore-born journalist and Howard University alumni Ta-Nehisi Coates became a public intellectual phenomenon. Consciously styling himself after James Baldwin, Coates became arguably the most famous African American essayist since the author of *The Fire Next Time* (1963). In 2015, the year before Obama spoke at Howard, Coates won the National Book Award and a MacArthur Foundation Fellowship (colloquially known as "the Genius Grant") on the heels of the epistolary writings gathered as *Between the World and Me.*[43]

Coates's popularity was wrung from a series of explosively popular essays, many woundingly personal, on the long historical durability of racial inequality and animus. From his perch at *The Atlantic,* and against the backdrop of a swirling movement galvanized by police and vigilante killings of African Americans, Coates served as an eloquent foil to the rhetoric of racial reconciliation, creedal faith, and common purpose pouring from the White House. As he succinctly argued in a debate with the liberal journalist Jonathan Chait, "Obama-era progressives view white supremacy as something awful that happened in the past and the historical vestiges of which still afflict black people today. They believe we need policies—though not race-specific policies—that address the affliction. I view white supremacy as one of the central organizing forces in American life, whose vestiges and practices afflicted black people in the past, continue to afflict black people today, and will likely afflict black people until this country passes into the dust."[44]

Perhaps sensing an obligation to respond at Coates's alma mater (Obama briefly mentions Coates in the speech), the nation's first black president declared that, despite the murmurings of pessimists, "race relations" (and other matters of basic liberty and equality) were faring better than at any time in American history. Obama pointed to the decline in antiblack racial attitudes, the weakening of racialized constraints on individual identity and expression, and the ascendancy of black elites in higher education, business, entertainment, and, of course, politics, as prima facie evidence for his contention before launching into his thought experiment. "If you had to choose one moment in history in which you could be born," Obama challenged the Howard commencement audience, "and you didn't know ahead of time who you were going to be—what nationality, what gender, what race, whether you'd be rich or poor, gay or straight, what faith you'd be born into . . . you'd choose right now."[45]

Howard graduates who studied their political theory might have wondered from their seats if Obama meant to invoke John Rawls, who was famous for a thought experiment he devised to model the values of impartiality and rationality he took to be at the heart of any defensible conception of "justice as fairness." Rawls's influential idea was that citizens should choose principles of justice on which to order society as if they were behind a "veil of ignorance" and blind to their personal characteristics, social location, and historical circumstances.[46]

If Obama did indeed intend this resonance, it bears noting that Rawls thought this way of modeling impartiality for the derivation of principles that *should* govern the social order would illuminate the worst injustices of *present* society in light of these ideals. Obama's romantic and rhetorical appropriation mostly dispenses with this task, instead constraining his audience's choice to preferences and judgments of progress made within America's sordid past. In this respect, the thought experiment pulls its participants closer to the conservative economist Thomas Sowell's Leibnizian retort to progressives—unjust compared to what?—than Rawls's utopian search for the perfectly just.[47]

A second dimension of this romantic historical consciousness is that it *narrates past political struggles as heroic sacrifices* for future generations and the project of national progress. The Moses metaphor, especially, allows Obama to ascribe a sense of "sacrifice and dignity" to forebears who "battled for America's soul . . . shed blood . . . [and] endured taunts and torment," while conceding that the journey to come will not permit the Moses generation to enter alongside into "the promised land" of genuine equality.[48] Their reparation will be symbolic and historical, not material.

Obama's Moses talk draws a direct connection, of course, to King, who eerily delivered a soul-stirring meditation on this very theme the night before he was assassinated. Speaking to a crowd of thousands, who'd braved a storm to rally on behalf of striking sanitation workers in Memphis at the city's iconic Mason Temple, King delivered an exhilarating tour of his journey in the civil rights movement, punctuated by a somber reflection on the swirl of credible death threats and assassination attempts that had become his daily bread. Confessing that "I don't know what will happen now," and offering an ominous prophecy of "difficult days ahead" for his country and himself, King nevertheless sought to stiffen his spine, his audience, and the broader movement for an awful fate he did not expect to elude much longer.

Invoking Moses's ascent to the peak of Mount Nebo in Deuteronomy 34, nearing the end of the Israelites' journey through the wilderness, King concluded his speech by declaring,

> But it really doesn't matter with *me* now. Because I've been to the mountaintop. I don't mind. Like anybody, I would like to live a long life. Longevity has its place. But I'm not concerned about that now. I just want to do God's will, and He's allowed me to go up to the mountain. And I've looked over. And I've seen the promised land. I may not get there with you, but I want you to know tonight, that we, as a people, will get to the promised land! So I'm happy tonight, I'm not worried about anything—I'm not fearing any man! Mine eyes have seen the glory of the coming of the Lord![49]

Against the backdrop of this history, ritually recounted as part of our civil religion, Obama's turn to the exemplarity of Joshua allows him to insist on a certain picture of African American peoplehood. This conception of African America is one that survived the collapse of Jim Crow through inherited prophetic, political traditions. These traditions have wide cultural investment, but are shepherded in the intergenerational transfer of leadership, often between charismatic men. Obama conjures this picture and lays claim to this leadership through the work of narrative transfiguration. By this I simply mean the narrative rearrangement and redescription of those vanquished aspirations, partial victories, tragic defeats, and even absurd sufferings of the past (especially in the civil rights era) into spiritual strivings and unintentional "sacrifices" that may yet be redeemed by the right leaders with the right project.

Obama's skill in articulating such promises and tying them to the rationale of his presidential campaign brought forth hope from many African Americans that his election would itself lead to dramatically redemptive outcomes. We find such exhilarating hopes, now so discordant to the ear, in Henry Louis Gates Jr.'s euphoric essay, published the day after Obama's decisive victory in the 2008 election. There the decorated Harvard University professor of African and African American Studies declared Obama's victory "the symbolic culmination of the black freedom struggle, the grand achievement of a great, collective dream." His thoughts drifting to centuries of black ancestors, Gates wondered aloud,

> Would they say that all those lost hours of brutalizing toil and labor leading to spent, half-fulfilled lives, all those humiliations that our ancestors had to suffer through each and every day, all those slights and rebuffs and recriminations, all those rapes and murders, lynchings and assassinations, all those Jim Crow laws and protest marches, those snarling dogs and bone-breaking water hoses, all of those beatings and all of those killings, all of those black collective dreams deferred—that the unbearable pain of all of

those tragedies had, in the end, been assuaged at least somewhat through Barack Obama's election?[50]

In a cruel irony, Gates was forced to confront that existential question about the relationship between one's own suffering of racial humiliation and injustice, and any presumed movement of history reflected by the forty-fourth president. On July 16, 2009, Gates was wrongly arrested for charges of "disorderly conduct" on the steps of his Cambridge, Massachusetts home, after a mistaken report of breaking and entering and a heated exchange with police. At a press conference ostensibly about health care reform, Obama spoke honestly and off-script in response to a reporter's question about the arrest, relaying his opinion that the arresting officer, James Crowley, "acted stupidly." Backlash to these comments was swift, unleashing a torrent of racial anxieties, resentments, and expectations in the early months of the first black presidency. As Obama would later admit, the White House's internal polling team quickly informed him that "the Gates affair caused a huge drop in [his] support among white voters, bigger than would come from any single event during the eight years of [his] presidency," and one he would never recover from.[51]

To staunch the bleeding, and do his part for the historical movement of Obamaism, Gates was implored to moderate his public indignation and instead visit the White House for a "beer summit" with Obama, the offending officer, and Vice President Joe Biden, the latter perhaps invited to avoid another dangerous visual: Officer Crowley, alone on the White House patio, outnumbered by (wealthy, successful) black men.[52] This spectacle of awkward interracial comity, whatever its concessions to racial paranoia, police union belligerents, and the professional hysterics of cable news, reveals a deeper underlying commitment of political significance.

This is the third dimension of the romantic historical consciousness elaborated by Obama: the view that romantic histories are warranted by, and commensurate with, *a practical faith in the nation's redemptive, self-perfecting capacities* that lie in the consensus under most of our political, cultural, and even metaphysical disagreements. Beneath such pronouncements as naming the activists of "Seneca Falls, and Selma, and Stonewall" as "our forebears" or his famous 2004 declaration that "there's not a liberal America and a conservative America . . . a black America and white America and Latino America and Asian America" lies a venerable liberal view that the task of public political philosophy is to discern and articulate that consensus.[53] This conception, articulated quite clearly by Rawls, sees public political philosophy's practical task in a liberal democratic society as uncovering "some underlying basis of philosophical and moral agreement" beneath "deeply disputed questions" to sustain respectful social cooperation.[54]

Even in this, Obama takes inspiration from the exemplarity of the civil rights movement. In his 2015 speech in Selma commemorating the fiftieth anniversary of the Selma-to-Montgomery marches and Bloody Sunday on the Edmund Pettus Bridge, Obama reminds his audience that the activists of that moment faced danger and denunciation, caricature and condemnation. Yet, in the face of this divisive hostility, they held fast to "the belief that America is not yet finished" and achieved a form of political action that he implores us to see as "the manifestation of a creed written into our founding documents." Their example, therefore, remains "a call to action, a roadmap for citizenship and an insistence in the capacity of free men and women to shape our own destiny"—at home and abroad. Their example teaches us that "no matter how hard it may sometimes seem, laws can be passed, and consciences can be stirred, and consensus can be built."[55]

This talk of deep agreement and practical faith raises an obvious worry. How can romance acknowledge these past conflicts, or engage disagreement in the present, while nevertheless insisting that there is a "unity" or "consensus" underneath us or just over the horizon? After all, Obama is not guilty of denying the persistence of racial injustice. His major speeches on race all acknowledge the existence of racial discrimination and the cumulative disadvantages that disproportionately burden African Americans. He explicitly cites onerous racial disparities in health care access and outcomes, quality education, economic opportunity, incarceration, employment and life expectancy. Yet how can his romantic practice of historical judgment manage the enduring injustices that raise skepticism about reconciliation?

For Obama and other progressives, the principal rhetorical-philosophical strategy is one of *anachronism.* In the romantic composition of American history, we are led to see certain enduring injustices or contemporary political opponents through a moralized prism that treats them as fundamentally *anachronistic.* Romantic narrative arranges these inconvenient social facts and forces such that they accrue a particular valence and significance from their incorporation into the overarching romantic arc. Indeed, part of how Obama means to evoke a sense of moral disgust at these inequalities and a kind of "common sense" recognition of the need to ameliorate them is through a conception of political temporality he seeks to embed in our political rhetoric and judgment.

By this I mean that Obama frequently adopts a familiar compulsion of modern political and social thought—namely, the propensity to "to demarcate and serially redefine" the competing discourses of modern politics through romantic narrative, relegating some practices (e.g., white supremacy and black radicalism) to the status of "unacceptable remnants of a past order."[56] Within the plot structure of romantic narrative, one can evoke a sense that certain forms of injustice, political belief, or rhetoric are somehow not *authentically* coeval with the broader society given the ways that political temporality is narratively organized and thematized as a time scale of collective moral learning.[57]

A key difficulty, therefore, that stems from thinking within the narrative constraints of moralized, romantic temporality is that the allure of anachronism is an attractive frame not just for condemning disparities resulting from past injustice, but also for describing one's political opponents. It is common, among progressive commentators with a romantic historical sensibility, to rhetorically present right-wing movements like the Tea Party or figures like Donald Trump as monstrous remnants of a past order, denying in some respects their coevalness. Instead of acknowledging these features and forces as part of the same space of politics, this rhetoric treats them as if a necromancer has risen the dead to walk terrifyingly among us.

It is, it must be admitted, easy to see why this rhetoric is analytically and strategically attractive. It can capture important rhetorical, political, and cultural continuities in right-wing movements while leveraging stigmas against widely disavowed movements in the past to delegitimize political actors in the present. Yet this framework seems to lead to an excess of confidence in the long-run guarantee of political victory for progressives in any given conflict. Such rhetoric suggests that opposing political coalitions are made of anachronistic "remnants," always already condemned to defeat, exaggerating their pastness rather than their emergence out of a set of institutional and cultural arrangements in the present. Ironically, anachronism can even undermine the economy of expression needed to convey the genuine urgency of resistance or prepare us for the disciplined practice of long-term political persuasion or conflict rather than expulsion or condemnation. The journalist David Graham captures this tendency in Obama's political thought and rhetoric powerfully, noting that "Obama's position represents a different sort of abdication, a chance to write off the hard work of politics—both enacting policies and trying to bring skeptics around to his position. If he's on the right side of history, why bother? Everything's coming his way anyway."[58]

The political life of romantic history and its reliance on anachronism helps explain, I think, two common progressive tendencies that seem otherwise paradoxical. The first is the ease with which progressive intellectuals, supposedly attuned to the protean nature of race and the ability of racial domination to be reconstituted in different times, were nevertheless seduced by "demography is destiny" arguments. These ideas suggested that Democrats' historical association with the civil rights movement and racial liberalism and a demographic shift toward a "majority-minority" country portended a permanent liberal majority.[59] The glee with which Democratic Party officials publicly celebrated this prediction, rarely sounding a note of tragic regret, was unseemly. It amounted to a public acknowledgment that the path to the consolidation of power involved patiently waiting for opposing voters, many of whom are judged beyond the reach of persuasion, to die and be replaced with a group who, given their racial and ethnic makeup, will see our political party as the obvious choice. The amateur political sociology of race that underpinned the bizarrely static conceptions of partisanship and "race" central to this prediction could only thrive under a worldview with a tendency toward wish fulfillment fantasies about "unity" and the final overcoming of conflict without open antagonism.

The second paradox is how progressive *rhetoric* meant to underscore the relation of contemporary right-wing factions to discredited exemplars of historical evil (e.g., Italian Fascists, Nazis, Confederates, Jim Crow supporters) does not seem commensurate with the *politics* such critics advocate or practice. If the monstrous has indeed been exhumed from the grave to stalk us once more, why are the strategies that vanquished them in the past—state repression (e.g., President Dwight D. Eisenhower federalizing the National Guard to integrate Little Rock Central High School or the Federal Bureau of Investigation infiltrating the Ku Klux Klan), mass civil disobedience (e.g., the 1963 Children's Crusade in Birmingham), and political violence (e.g., the organized self-defense used to protect Congress of Racial Equality and Student Nonviolent Coordinating Committee activists in Mississippi)—unthinkable in the discursive and institutional spaces of liberal political reason?[60] The kind of "historical" consciousness promoted wants to avail itself of the power of the progress idea to "settle" questions and place certain forms of dissent beyond legitimate advocacy and contestation yet also does not seriously entertain the demanding forms of contentious and coercive politics that secured these "settlements" when it claims that reactionary remnants have returned from their repression. In this way, romantic consciousness congeals into a structure that permits the *abdication of political responsibility* while narratively conjuring self-satisfaction and moral certitude, even in times of crises where the common sense that once made its worldview plausible erodes under our feet.

The Broken Heart of Romance: Melancholy and Nihilism

In the years since King's assassination, some aspirations associated with the "classical" civil rights movement have become, paradoxically, both more mundane (e.g., the integration of public accommodations, higher education, the election of black political officials, and norms of racial tolerance) while others have grown more remote (e.g., de facto school integration, the elimination of intergenerational black ghetto poverty, robust prosecution of employment discrimination, broad American support for government intervention to ensure economic equality, and the flourishing of an ethos of nonviolence in everyday life). Wrestling with this paradox has led, in time, more critical assessments of romance to become prevalent. Against this rising tide, romantic historians have absconded with the embalmed body of the conventional civil rights narrative to popular presses, museums, memorials, and other institutions of public memory whose political and economic constraints leave them less vulnerable to assailment by critical academics and other disillusioned commentators.[61]

Yet some historians persist. It is a notable quirk of romantic history as a genre of discourse that its teleological structure tends to connect narrator and history such that the speaker or writer sees their own writing as the further *realization* of the historical process they purport to describe. Taylor Branch, writing in 2006, eighteen years after the first volume was published, found himself lamenting that statecraft is "still preoccupied with the levers of spies and force, even though two centuries of increasingly lethal 'total warfare' since Napoleon suggest a diminishing power of violence to sustain governance in the modern world." While acknowledging the incessant return of the evils of political violence, he dutifully incorporates even those moments into a progressive historical trajectory, organized through exemplarity: South Korean student protests against an authoritarian government, the Velvet Revolution in the former Czechoslovakia, the fall of the Berlin Wall, the deadly protest at Tiananmen Square, and Nelson Mandela's post-imprisonment movement for truth racial reconciliation in South Africa. Against that narrative backdrop of successive global examples, appended as political coda to the story of the civil rights movement, Branch hopes to shore up the metaphorical world-historical significance of King as a prophet of nonviolence, love, freedom, and cosmopolitan patriotism. Quoting one of Obama's touchstone remarks from King, Branch insists that "the arc of the moral universe is long, but it bends toward justice" and implores us to mind these "treasures" that "abide with lasting promise from America in the King years."[62]

But once faith in the moral arc of the universe weakens, romantic history can curdle into melancholy. In Hayden White's account, the historian Jules Michelet, who wrote powerfully of the French Revolution as national and progressive romance, originally conveyed great confidence in the course of history. Then, looking back on the French Revolution from the vantage point of Louis Napoleon's domestic tyranny and imperial adventurism, Michelet found himself besieged by an "ironic apprehension" of history but remained committed to a romantic belief that "this eternal return of evil and division in human life" would only be "a temporary condition for mankind over the long run." By the twilight of his career, "once Michelet's faith in the triumph of right and justice began to dissipate, as the antirevolutionary forces gained the ascendancy, there was nothing left but a fall into melancholic reflection on the defeat of the ideal whose original triumph he had chronicled in his early histories."[63]

This trajectory is familiar to civil rights historians, and especially King biographers. The conservative-orchestrated political backlash against racial liberalism and its constitutional warrants, the seeming disorientation of "black politics," the "backsliding" and "degeneration" of American democracy, and, above all, the endurance of certain dimensions of racial inequality have contributed to a similarly melancholic and elegiac tone to the romantic civil rights histories of more recent vintage.[64] Stewart Burns, in a recent biography of King, recounts the pastor's faith in the transformative and forceful power of nonviolence and reminds his readers that just as King "came to accept that his own redemption would happen only after he hit bottom, so he believed that [America] would be redeemed and regenerated when doom thundered across the sky." This example is supposed to steel our resolve in our present time, which Burns describes as "uncertain terrain" stalked by "self-righteous terrorists, official or unofficial, and by masses of disempowered consumers alienated from the world and their own souls." Adrift in a sea overrun by the monsters of consumer capitalism and the terrorists of a Manichean age, Burns leaves us with only the "life raft of nonviolence" that is the "legacy of Martin Luther King Jr." and the instruction to cling to it "as determinedly as he did during the last years of his life." He can no longer, however, muster the belief in ultimate deliverance that Branch gestures toward. Burns leaves us with the hollowed romanticism that remains when every other alternative is, as he puts it, "unspeakable."[65] If this is historical narrative as jeremiad, it speaks in halting and unsure cadences rather than the thunderous confidence of the true believer.

That developments in consumer capitalism, late twentieth-century conservatism, and recent iterations of political violence figure so mightily in these historians' sense of King's significance might be surprising for those trained to think of history as commonsense empiricism about the past, bracketed from whatever action occurs when figures like King or Rosa Parks have left the stage. Yet, as I argued in Chapter 3, historical reflection and writing cannot but bring to bear the horizon of the present on its discernment of the horizon of the past. We have no unmediated access to the past. All historical narration therefore requires a fusion of horizons from the past with those of the present. This fusion not only makes sense of the basic sense data of history but also allows for new claims of significance or meaning to be advanced, either explicitly or implicitly through narrative form. In other words, these shifts in significance manifest themselves not only in data and focus but also in the very mode of what White called "emplotment," in which a set of events or personalities is represented, thematized, and told as a story.

This is certainly the case with the histories of many of the so-called new nations that emerged in the midst of anticolonial revolutions in the mid-twentieth century. The history of a nation like Zimbabwe, once under ruthlessly exploitative rule by foreigners, was widely understood in a romantic vein as triumphant exemplar of good overthrowing evil. Now, after decades of fractious political violence, despotism, exploitation, and misery, all under the leadership of the revolution, it is difficult for the generic conventions of romantic emplotment to bear this interpretive weight against competing narrative forms.[66]

Yet the example of so-called postcolonial nations also shows another more subtle influence on the shift in emplotment. Thinking primarily about the Caribbean case, and Haiti in particular, David Scott has drawn out an important consequence of the fusion of horizons in histories of political thought and action. Following White's interest in emplotment and narrative, Scott's principal concern is "to inquire into the problem of how one chooses between kinds of story forms, or how one decides that a particular story-form, a particular mode of emplotment, say, no longer yields the critical insight it once accomplished, and how one decides whether it might be usefully displaced by another."[67] To this end Scott interrogates the hermeneutic relationship of historical reflection by pressing on the present situation.

"It seemed to me," Scott writes, "that very little systematic consideration, if any, was being given to what present it is that the past is being reimaged for." For all of the insistence on what Branch called the "lasting treasures" bequeathed to us from the King years, it might be the case, as Scott suggests in the postcolonial world, that "the old languages of moral-political vision and hope are no longer in sync with the world they were meant to describe and normatively criticize." From here on, a danger arises because it is "often difficult to specify what aspect of [the present] is being illuminated [by a historical narrative] or why illuminating this particular aspect of it is of immediate (or more than academic) significance." In other words, a certain vision of what problems are important and what interventions are appropriate to those problems, taken from classical formulations in our intellectual traditions, can become "congealed into an immobile structure of implicit and unchanging determinations" that encourage us to represent the past in a certain way so that it can produce the insights that we already assume are appropriate into a contemporary situation that we presume to be commensurate in a familiar way.[68] This is a complex version of thoughtlessness that evades the need for reflective judgment in our own time.

The romantic tradition in civil rights historiography and memory has powerfully shaped the popular understanding of racism as malicious, often interpersonally violent, and based on feelings of racial ill will. It has also shaped our understanding of the effective and appropriate response to racism as theatrical direct-action protest and organized demonstrations amplified by media coverage to garner the support of public opinion and government officials or compel reformist intervention by political elites and courts. We look for, and galvanize around, events that seem to confirm this frame, and our historical work can become overdetermined by this structure such that it returns to the same incidents and same lessons, claiming to cast light on our own time in the process. We fail, often, to think and judge *analytically*—breaking the object of inquiry into its component parts, trying to understand what precise question or problem even familiar practices of civil rights protest and organizing were meant to solve, and whether they have appropriate analogues in the present.

I will try to show the stakes of these arguments in Chapter 6, where I consider some ethico-aesthetic problems of civil disobedience obscured by the way romantic narratives are taken up in political philosophy. For now, however, I want to draw attention to one last feature of Scott's extraordinary work, from which I have taken obvious inspiration.

Scott is especially concerned to map the contours of "imagined futures" in political philosophy and public life, those imaginative horizons that orient the purpose and point of moral, political, and ethical aims and project a direction for political action and judgment. In American politics and thought, these futures have ranged from Thomas Jefferson's yeoman republic and the white empire of manifest destiny, to W. E. B. Du Bois's democratic cultural pluralism, to the egalitarian welfare state of President Lyndon B. Johnson's Great Society.

Yet what happens when these futures no longer exercise a hold on our imagination? What happens when they are no longer *authoritative,* reliably inherited through *tradition,* or capable of providing *direction* in the present, frustrating attempts to transpose insight straightforwardly from then to now? For Scott, the challenge is daunting; we face the likelihood that the possible futures that were once horizons of meaning in the past are now lived as "the tangible ruins of our present."[69] Their crisis, defeat, or foreclosure not only haunts present political judgments, casting their shadow on imagination and action, but raises a further problem of *nihilism as disorientation.* As Wendy Brown poetically renders it, we find ourselves "spinning without tether or illumination, without certain knowledge about what to affirm and negate, without temporality or directionality for a motion of history."[70]

This, I argue, is what brings about both Afropessimism and the turn toward "long civil rights movement" historiography. It is as much—if not more—about the ruins of our present hermeneutic situation than an avalanche of newly discovered information about the past. Implicit in their restructurings of the plot of the civil rights movement is an awareness that ranges from explicit acknowledgment to vague gesturing at the collapse of the authoritative traditions of black political life—traditions I identify as racial realism, black church vanguardism, the imagined futures of integrationism and black nationalism, and the cultural politics of representation—in the post–Jim Crow era. The dissolution of their authority is not a result of any teleological arc of black politics. Instead it is the outcome that macrostructural trends and the political and philosophical choices made by elites and their constituencies alike that have transformed the world. Following an account of this collapse of black political life's authoritative pillars, I will then turn to a reading of the romantic narrative in the unlikely place of John Rawls's political philosophy, setting the stage for a critique of its influence in political philosophy and paving the way for further inquiry into how irony and tragedy present themselves as alternatives to this way of proceeding.

CHAPTER 5

THE TANGIBLE RUINS OF OUR PRESENT

The Crisis of Authority in Black Political Life

ARMED WITH A SENSE OF the structure of the romantic narrative of the civil rights movement and its influence on political thinking and judgment, I now deepen this narrative analysis with the hermeneutic framework developed earlier to diagnose the present crisis in black political life—a crisis of orientation and meaning. I argue that black political life has undergone its own break in tradition, echoing Hannah Arendt's account of the crisis of authority in the modern age: a collapse of the tacit, once-intuitive frameworks that undergirded interpretation across a wide range of political, cultural, and philosophical questions.

This collapse helped create and accelerate the crisis of romantic narration. We must resist any account of the historiographical crisis around civil rights movement interpretation that treats its unfolding as solely immanent to the practice of historical writing itself. These currents instead reflect a broader cultural collapse in more diffuse, taken-for-granted premises that once made such stories feel obvious, intuitive, or worth telling. Further, when these philosophical, political, and cultural underpinnings totter, the narrative modes which relied on them lose their stability as well.

This narrative crisis has implications for our political disorientation. Political striving and argument persists, of course, but the interpretive frameworks that once seemed to guide interpretation and judgment no longer compel allegiance. We find ourselves not just disillusioned by the uneven and faltering victories we describe as "civil rights reforms" but disoriented by the loss of the frameworks that once told us what those victories meant, how we might extend them, and why they were worth fighting for. Where romanticism finds dogged repetition, the appeals to heroism feel increasingly remote and pejoratively mythic, while imitative action or rhetoric fails to find its footing in the present. It is no wonder that some activists experience such invocations as culturally repressive and historians find them inattentive or obscurantist with regard the afterlives of slavery, much less Jim Crow. This, then, is the crisis—not the end of black political life, perhaps, but its disconnection from the traditions that once rendered it intuitively intelligible and the judgments we make about it compellingly authoritative. The task now is to find new ways to exercise judgment about the civil rights example, without the thread of authoritative tradition.

In this chapter, I argue that four pillars of black political life, long taken as authoritative, have fractured under the weight of philosophical scrutiny, demographic change, and political and cultural transformation. The first pillar, *racial realism*—the conviction that shared biological, cultural, or historical roots might secure solidarity and consensus—has unraveled amid migration, class stratification, and the fragmentation of identity. The second pillar, *black church vanguardism*—the presumption that the church should play the leading spiritual and organizational role in Black politics—has been hollowed by secularization, scandal, theological drift, and the atrophying of its moral authority, especially on issues of gender and sexuality. The third pillar, the interpretive mapping of black political vision and imagined futures on the binary of *integrationism versus nationalism,* is now profoundly exhausted. This is due not only to the vast dispersal of black political opinion but also the immanent ways that self-conceived integrationism has been battered by the persistence of segregation; its own failures to resolve questions of class, culture, and political economy; and its uneasy relationship with liberal norms of freedom of association and property rights. Black nationalism, on the other hand, while severely weakened by a long history of state repression and the mutations of political economy that have discredited many of the aspirations of statist nationalisms, has also suffered from its inability to meet the challenge of "intraracial" differentiation and beat back its critics in critical theory and popular culture. The last pillar, *the cultural politics of representation,* was once a set of assumptions animated by a broadly endorsed "duty" of intellectuals and artists to vindicate the race with cultural production and "positive" images or to cultivate and defend a shared group cultural identity as "a people" that can compel respect from others and achieve a distinctive form of group flourishing. Once a comprehensive bundle of ethical norms, this sense of vocation buckled under the pressure of expressive freedom, class antagonism, the collapse of Christian authority, and the destabilizing force of popular culture. This is nowhere clearer than in the ascendency of hip-hop, which defied respectability and redefined authenticity on its own terms. Without the shared sense of the "positive" or "negative" to orient judgment about art, images, and artistic representation, the very premise that art can or should speak for "the race" suffers confusion. And where its defenders cling to the project, cultural production is too widely distributed and dispersed across platforms, political loyalties, and micropublics to be as effectively policed as it may have been in the past.

In each of these pillars I discuss, I certainly do not mean that "authority" turns on consensus or universal agreement. What I mean to track is a diffuse cultural sensibility and normative order, which will always have its dissenters and critics, some of which may even get incorporated into the prevailing understanding of what the norm permits.[1] Another way of putting the point, besides the language of intuitively appealing to the norm for understanding, might be that the norms produce a sense of obliged responsiveness. What norms do we feel, even if we depart from them, obliged to give a justificatory account concerning why we do so? And to whom do we feel we owe such explanation?

While it may not be easy in real-world judgments to distinguish this sense of normative responsiveness from ordinary prudence about unwanted consequences, I want to hold on to the idea of a normative order as a framework of justification and mutual obligation through which we debate questions of legitimacy, fairness, honor, good conduct, and other ethico-political questions.[2] In the case of the authority of the cultural politics of representation, for example, talk of normative order is how we come to grasp, phenomenologically, the experience of shame or betrayal we might feel if we act, speak, or create in ways that seem to confirm negative stereotypes about our group or which are "inauthentic" to the culture.

This leads to a conceptual concern. I use the term *black political life* to refer to an expansive set of concerns and orientations. It includes but extends well beyond participation in electoral politics, or even the pithy "Who gets what and why?" formulation that includes interest groups and is focused primarily on resource distribution. Black political life is the name for a broad field of practices that attempt to formulate political obligations and rights of justification among black people qua black people; publicly claim and pursue a set of goals, practices, institutions, or grievances as worthy of action in concert; and articulate stories of peoplehood that guide judgment on questions of ethics, authority, group membership, and tradition. What ultimately makes it *black* political life is not the "racial" identity of the practitioners as such. It is instead a tradition of involvement in these practices and taking them as authoritative or at least as a set of norms one is accountable to.

If black political life is organized around a set of prominent questions, the first must be the one that dominates both the content and scholarly assessment of black political thought throughout history—namely, How should black people respond to white supremacy and its legacy? Let us call this the "white supremacy question," defining white supremacy not as the existence of Klansmen or Nazis necessarily but as a broad set of values, institutional arrangements, and policy priorities that reflect a disregard or disdain for the proposition that nonwhite and white lives are equally meaningful and thus deserving of equal regard.

Another family of questions might be gathered under the notion of "the ethics of the oppressed." Here Tommie Shelby is again helpful when he describes this as inquiring "what would constitute a morally responsible and dignified response on the part of the oppressed to intractable, oppressive conditions? The answer to this question constitutes what I will call the ethics of the oppressed. Depending on the social conditions that obtain . . . there is an ethic of resistance aimed at liberating the oppressed from injustice and an ethic of resistance aimed at living with dignity despite insurmountable injustice."[3] While the former can be subsumed under the problem of white supremacy, the latter sprawls across political philosophy, religion, and, above all, virtue ethics. Many of the confusions that come from reading African American political thought and literature stem from an inability to take the preoccupation with virtue and vice in black political life seriously or to understand the complex cosmologies, accounts of philosophical anthropology, or metaethical views in which these ideas are situated. Exemplary is W. E. B. Du Bois, whose provocative questions in *The Ordeal of Mansart* have achieved a notoriety untethered from that uneven novel: "How shall Integrity face Oppression? What shall Honesty do in the face of Deception, Decency in the face of Insult, Self-Defense before Blows? How shall Desert and Accomplishment meet Despising, Detraction, and Lies? What shall Virtue do to meet Brute Force?"[4] One last question I want to draw attention to was also posed by Du Bois in 1926, though it has grown more pressing in its significance every year since the collapse of Jim Crow. Speaking at an awards ceremony for the distinguished black historian Carter G. Woodson, Du Bois leveled a query that both went to the heart of why the response to white supremacy matters in the first place and moves beyond oppression to the horizon of human possibility that is the promise of any truly compelling political philosophy: "If you tonight suddenly should become full-fledged Americans," Du Bois questioned, "if your color faded, or the color line here in Chicago was miraculously forgotten; suppose, too, you became at the same time rich and powerful;—what is it that you would want?"[5]

This challenge represents a pointed philosophical question concerning what, if anything, there is to be learned about the ends of human association or the ends of a good life, through renderings of the African American experience on the underside of modernity, a terrain dotted by the landmarks of chattel slavery, lynching, sharecropping, sexual violence, and so forth. It is a monumentally difficult question, but it is the one that provoked Ralph Ellison's proclamation that since "this society is not likely to become free of racism," it is therefore "necessary for Negroes to free themselves by becoming their idea of what a free people should be."[6] The force of this line of questioning is that it raises ethical and existential questions about the responsibility of tradition, or what values and forms of life get preserved and passed down, and treats politics not simply as resistance but as the practice of building a world hospitable to particular values and goods.

In the course of pursuing compelling answers to these questions, black political life has generated much that is insightful and some that is inane. But as in all political and cultural traditions, certain assumptions and pathways of thinking, due to some incalculable convergence of factors, manage to accrue an authoritative force for those actors and thinkers that move within its rough boundaries. It may strike some as odd to refer to ideas as authoritative given our contemporary tendency to confuse authority with violence, law, or domination. But as Hannah Arendt tried to convince us many decades ago, authority is not these things—and, at least in the case of violence, these things may indeed be evidence of its absence. This is because authority is, in its full expression, nothing more or less than the force of those ideas that collectives of human beings intuitively appeal to for understanding. They are the scaffoldings that support and give shape to our thought and action, and because these ideas are rooted in particular histories, times, and places, it makes less sense to speak of "authority as such" than of specific forms of authority, like those that have characterized black political life until this moment.[7]

The content of these practices of black political life often revolve around black solidarity, social and political virtues, the political ethics of the oppressed, or combating racial injustice. But in principle, the indeterminacy of the concept allows us to better understand those participants in black political life that try to project aspirations beyond the horizons of antiracism.[8] It also tries to draw attention to the "world-building" and pluralist character of these practices, properly understood, and the ways that argument and judgment are fundamental to their enactment.[9]

Some words of caution are already due. Black political life, in my view, is not a demographic phenomenon; it is not any political action by black people with shared interests, or by black individuals as such, as the language of "black politics" often gets used. That seemingly straightforward demographic approach reveals a lingering essentialism, which denies black people the possibility of behaving without racial reasoning or racial consciousness, or ascribes a specious racial expressivism to the totality of their behavior. If, for example, the astrophysicist Neil DeGrasse Tyson publicly advocates for more federal funding for space travel, is that "black politics"? If he insists that the highest organizational purpose of the state is to promote scientific advances, is that "black political thought"?

Deepening the political import of this antiessentialism, this notion of black political life helps us appreciate what most people call black politics as a *formation* rather than something akin to a natural kind. It also helps appreciate the fragility of its spaces of appearances and traditions of argument. In my view, black political life did not cohere as a formation until the early nineteenth century, by which time over 95 percent of black people in the United States were born in the United States and not in Africa. By then the various cultural, linguistic, and religious differences among enslaved New World Africans merged into distinctly new syncretic cultural forms that we widely recognize today as "African American."[10] A sense of broadly linked fate between black people seems to have crystallized in this era, fostered by the cotton boom that fueled the expansion of Deep South plantation slavery, the expansionist and belligerent political program of Southern slaveholders, revolutionary enthusiasm and reactionary paranoia surrounding the Haitian Revolution, the increased curtailment of civil liberties for free blacks in Northern states, and the advent of black newspapers, churches, and "colored conventions" that articulated a sense of common oppression and ethically charged peoplehood.[11] This is to say nothing of the formative political experience of the abolitionist movement and its culture of popular politics.[12]

Specific conventions, interpretations, and institutional configurations have, as with any set of practices, become dominant over time. Here it is the four pillars: the idea of "races" as a stable foundation for politics and ontology; the idea that the black church is a vanguard spiritual and sociopolitical institution; the notion that integrationism and nationalism are the fundamental binary oppositions of black political philosophy; and the idea of a cultural politics of representation whose task is to combat negative images of the race and promote a distinctively black cultural flourishing. Understanding the so-called post–civil rights era requires grasping the collapse of these pillars as authoritative presuppositions to questions and answers within black political life.

Overall, the erosion of authority in black political life can be seen as a descent from an appeal to the natural or transcendental forces of race and religion to the more this-worldly forces of the political teleologies of separatism and integrationism and the cultural politics of representation that consolidated in the twentieth century. To speak of crisis and collapse does not mean that iterations of these once authoritative ideas no longer exist. In fact, the attempts to sustain them can become all the more frantic and disinhibited as they collapse. "With their foundation eroded but their formulas and insignias lingering," Brown perceptively writes, "values do not simply evaporate but become malleable, fungible, trivial, instrumentalizable, easily trafficked for purposes beyond themselves, and at the same time histrionic and hyperbolic."[13]

For instance, in Chapter 7, I will suggest that when Afropessimists make the hysterical claim that slavery is something that still characterizes contemporary black experience, they are engaged in a kind of frantic ransacking of decaying pillars of authority. The claim is expressive of a deeper hysteresis in the culture itself, as is the swift degeneration of "black radicalism" talk into academic incantation, corporate branding, and the empty signifier of revanchist reaction.

The story I tell here primarily revolves around two explanatory forces. On the one hand, evolutions in white supremacist doctrine and global political economy have necessarily altered the intuitive force of certain ideas. On the other hand, the intellectual and cultural achievements of arguments put forth by the would-be inheritors of the black political tradition have injected skepticism and doubt into its very heart. These parallel and intertwined developments have generated a crisis of black political life by undermining its four pillars, which once tended to reinforce one another, and now sway wildly in the unfurling storm.

Racial Realism

"Before there was any such thing as a Republican or a Democrat, we were black. Before there was any such thing as a Mason or an Elk, we were black. Before there was any such thing as a Jew or a Christian, we were black people! In fact, before there was any such place as America, we were black! And after America has long passed from the scene, there will still be black people!"[14] These remarks by Malcolm X, from a debate at Columbia University in 1961, illustrate how invocations of race tend to naturalize claims about the world and torturously explain disparate social phenomena by appeal to its influence. According to Malcolm, at least in his Nation of Islam phase, we must recognize that the prevailing political, national, associative, and religious identities that give unique meaning to our lives and that shape understanding of the world we share with others are ultimately superstructural when contrasted with the ultimate foundation of human division: race. Race, then, comes storming out of our distant past to give order to our present and to point the way toward our futures, collective and individual. It is a fact whose singularity lies in its certainty and whose political promise lies in its stability.

This notion finds its origins in *racialism,* the idea that "there are heritable characteristics, possessed by members of our species, which allow us to divide them into a small set of races, in such a way that all the members of these races share certain traits . . . with each other that they do not share with members of any other race."[15] This doctrine, as the philosopher

Bernard Boxill reminds us, "classifies people into different races on the basis of the obvious physical differences between them that it calls racial . . . and then insists that these differences are signs of built-in, important, and intractable intellectual, temperamental, and moral differences."[16] Boxill traces these ideas to early modern Europe, but it was primarily in the outposts of European empire in the so-called New World where race rose from a presumed or theorized fact about natural history, battling for authority with older biblically inspired views about descent from the sons of Noah, into arguably the most immediately salient feature of the social order.[17] The labor-starved colonies were the place where modern conceptions of race caused "ethnicity" or the cultural distinctions between peoples to atrophy and congeal into a sweeping, hardened arbiter between person and subperson, freedom and slavery, white and black.[18]

The New World slaves and their descendants, struggling to gain a foothold of freedom, were forced to make their way in a social world determined by the race concept and the material reality it helped bring into being. Thus, race existed not only as an ascriptive category—one that was projected onto individuals by virtue of public policy and social power—but also as an *identity,* replete with norms of identification that shaped individuals' self-understandings and their understanding of their life projects and meaningful affiliations.[19] As a consequence, black political life, always arrayed against antiblack racism, still operated broadly from presuppositions of race. That is, it was intuitive that certain ways of life, values, ethical commitments, and political obligations flowed naturally and organically from the fact of race or ethnicity.

The conceptions of race that served as leading pillars of black political life fell largely into three categories. The first conception claims that races are real natural kinds (often biological) in origin. Marcus Garvey—the leader of the largest grassroots mass movement in the history of black political life—is exemplary of this tradition. Garvey argued for the existence of a vast racial family scattered across the globe whose political obligations included the "redemption" of their African "fatherland," self-preservation, blood-based racial purity, and the cultivation of martial virtue in separate black institutions and states.[20] The vocabulary of family and nation saturates this discourse, and often buttresses strong duties of race solidarity accordingly.

The second also claims that races are real but asserts that they are better understood as constituted by and expressing a spiritual or cultural essence. Thus, W. E. B. Du Bois, the central black intellectual of the twentieth century and cofounder of the National Association for the Advancement of Colored People (NAACP), argued early in his career that "no mere physical distinctions would really define or explain the deeper differences [between races]"—

namely, what he saw as "the cohesiveness and continuity of these groups." Du Bois instead defined a race as a "vast family of human beings, generally of common blood and language, always of common history, traditions and impulses, who are both voluntarily and involuntarily striving together for the accomplishment of certain more or less vividly conceived ideals of life." This understanding, although departing from strong naturalist or biological notions of the nature of races and having much in common with contemporary diversity discourse and multiculturalism, still betrays a lingering sense of something deeper and primordial. "We are Americans, not only by birth and by citizenship, but by our political ideals, our language, our religion," Du Bois writes, before shifting to the *Volk* language of German romanticism and insisting that "farther than that, our Americanism does not go. At that point, we are Negroes, members of a vast historic race that from the very dawn of creation has slept, but half awakening in the dark forests of its African fatherland."[21]

Later in his career, long after disavowing the biological residues of his race concept, Du Bois defended the idea of a race as "a cultural group." Lamenting the lack of precision regarding culture talk in the social sciences, Du Bois argued that what cultural group means "in modern scientific thought is that 15,000,000 men and women who for three centuries have shared common experiences and common suffering, and have worked all those days and nights together for their own survival and progress; that this complex of habits and manners could not and must not be lost." Declaring that "persons sharing this experience formed a race no matter what their blood may be," Du Bois moved swiftly to the normative demand for the "conservation" of black cultural particularity: "This race must be conserved for the benefit of the Negro people themselves and for mankind . . . not pride of biological race, but pride in a cultural group, integrated and expanded by developed ideals, so as to form a method of progress."[22]

A third, and more recent, major tradition in race thinking for black political life tries to explain differences often attributed to biological or folk races as "ethnic" differences, which are maintained by the constrained choices of individuals, socially cultivated boundaries, incompatible cultural traits, and group affinities. Here talk about blackness or the Negro race is replaced with references to African Americans and analogies to other American ethnicities—Irish Americans, Italian Americans, Jewish Americans, and so forth. Stokely Carmichael and Charles Hamilton, in their germinal text *Black Power*, adopt such a position, arguing that, in recognition of "the ethnic basis of American politics," black people must "unite, to recognize their heritage, to build a sense of community . . . define their own goals [and] lead their own organizations."[23] Less robust but related notions of ethnic politics have emerged in demands for gerrymandered districts that ensure majority black districts, the overwhelming intraracial support for black representatives in these districts, and the host of ethnicity-based social and political organizations currently operating in America today. These political commitments are invariably theorized to arise from the historical, particular—and, notably, exclusive—transmission of ethnic traits and projects or a heritage.

Thus, whether biological, cultural, spiritual, or ethnic, race purports to bring the continuous past to bear on the defensible projects that individuals might aspire to in life and in politics. And thus, despite the early Du Bois's and Garvey's fierce enmity, they both operate from the assumption that the discovery of race, whatever it may be, will aid in discovering an authoritative foundation for black political life. This is how Du Bois ends up endorsing many of the same roughly defined goals as Garvey—"race organization . . . race solidarity, [and] race unity"—even as he maintains a less chauvinist view that allows for "the realization of that broader humanity which freely recognizes differences in men, but sternly deprecates inequality in their opportunities of development."[24]

Similarly, Martin Luther King Jr., who criticized Stokely Carmichael's Black Power as a "nihilistic philosophy" of implicit separatism that "carries the seeds of its own doom," nonetheless endorsed much of Carmichael's program of the election of black candidates, the use of ethnic bloc voting, and—most important here—the cultivation of a "deep feeling of racial pride and . . . an audacious appreciation of his heritage."[25] The debates that have heretofore characterized black political life have nearly always been imagined to entail an answer about what political commitments, cultural projects, and ethical obligations arise from the fact of race or ethnicity or from the boundaries of those categories. The need for some kind of race "conservation" (against "assimilation") and highly valent ideas of racial "authenticity" were centripetal forces in black political life and experienced often as common sense.[26]

The distinctive nature of our moment is that for the first time since the crystallization of black political life, a major pole of intellectual debate is anchored decisively and powerfully in whether these categories exist at all, and if not, then discerning the implications of these collapsing categorizations for our prevailing ideas about identity and politics. This is, perhaps, clearest in philosophy and art. In popular politics, the last substantial bastions of racial realism—culture and ethnicity—are being pulled apart by class differentiation, the new black immigration, and public pluralism giving lie to the grand hopes of classical black expressivism.

Perhaps no single individual has been more influential in the *intellectual* project of injecting a crippling doubt into the authority of race and ethnicity in black political life than the philosopher Kwame Anthony Appiah. Born in

Ghana to a British mother and a Ghanian father active in the various Pan-Africanist movements of mid-twentieth-century West Africa, Appiah was educated in England before leaving for the United States to join his friend and collaborator, Henry Louis Gates Jr. I draw attention to Appiah's unusually cosmopolitan background largely because he himself draws attention to it when advancing his arguments against race. His international jaunts and culturally diverse family, unremarkable features of his childhood as they were, led him to see the world as "a network of points of affinity" and to be skeptical of familiar claims of "insuperable cultural distance."[27]

Appiah pushed the most explosive intervention in the philosophy of race of the late twentieth century by rejecting the use of race altogether—for science, politics, culture, and identity. "The truth," he argued, "is that there are no races," and "there is nothing in the world that can do all we ask race to do for us."[28] This claim had been put forward, with limited success, by some biologists and anthropologists in the mid-twentieth century.[29] But their early position would be argued with extraordinary force by Appiah's generation of intellectuals and scientists and given additional credence by the demographic shifts in race and ethnicity occasioned by the 1965 overhaul of US immigration law and the mixed-race identity movements of the 1980s and 1990s.[30]

The impressive advances in genetics in the late twentieth and early twenty-first centuries heaped severe skepticism onto the traditional biological conception of race. We know now that individuals have a vast array of genetic characteristics whose interactions with each other and the environment create such a multitude of possible outcomes that human beings who share one trait, such as skin color, could simply not be expected to share all or most others, such as mathematical reasoning ability. As Appiah reminds us, "However you define the major races, the biological variability within them is almost as great as the biological variation within the species as a whole."[31] So while we could divide the human species into all sorts of groups based on genes, there is not any way that would meaningfully correspond to the continent-based "races" to which we commonly refer. This is, of course, exacerbated in the United States, where none of the supposed "races" has been reproductively isolated, a point most popularly advanced by Henry Louis Gates Jr. in his PBS series *Finding Your Roots,* which traces the genetic backgrounds and genealogies of American celebrities.[32] There is no essence we could point to that makes white people really "white" and black people really "black" in a categorically *biological* sense.

While some geneticists and philosophers of biology attempt to defend chastened versions of racial realism, leading work in population genetics shows that classical racial types are a poor predictive model for genetic data. As the Harvard University quantitative geneticist Alexander Gusev writes, as "human history has been highly dynamic, with extensive admixture, instances of rapid migration, geographic shifts, ancient introgression events, historic populations that no longer exist in unadmixed forms," large-scale biobank data suggest that "conventional models of race are irrelevant to the study of genetic variation, and even models of simple population relationships are proving to be fundamentally wrong."[33]

Probably due to the close association of racial biology and virulent white supremacy, many African Americans have long been eager to accept antiessentialist argument here. They not only want to close the door on speculations of natural inferiority but many, I suspect, intuit what Lionel McPherson calls a "deflationary" approach to racial metaphysics, dispensing with much of the debate given that the race metaphysics are "principally . . . an expression of antiblack ideology, pseudo-rationalizing inherited slavery, enforced segregation, and (tacitly) mass incarceration" in a social order whose hierarchies have used but never "depended on faulty beliefs and feelings about the nature of race."[34]

Yet our contemporary discourse of multicultural difference often also reflects essentialist notions of race. We have retained from strong racialism what the historian David Hollinger has called the "ethnoracial pentagon," consisting of those five standard "racial" groups on most Office of Management and Budget–approved application forms—White, Black, Asian and Pacific Islander, Hispanic/Latino, and American Indian—and recoded them as "cultures."[35] But this racial vocabulary does not respond well to any plausible definition of *culture*. Take, for example, the one proffered by Orlando Patterson: "a repertoire of socially transmitted and intra-generationally generated ideas about how to live and make judgments, both in general terms and in regard to specific domains of life . . . an information system with varying levels of specificity."[36] Even with the increasing sophistication of the sociology of culture, we often carelessly speak of cultural heritage in *racial* terms, despite knowing that the ways in which ideas, patterns of judgment, values, behavioral predispositions, and tastes are transmitted are not bounded by "race," as if jazz belongs more organically to the black teenager who has never bothered to listen to it than the alternative rock bands they listen to daily. Even more implausibly than these simple genetic fallacies, such logic habituates our minds toward segregating such obviously influential cultural artifacts as those produced by Langston Hughes and William Shakespeare and proceeding as if black people float together in some entirely different cultural ether that is largely untouched by the exchanges of the wider world rather than what Du Bois described, with a blend of realist sociology and utopian aspiration, as the Kingdom of Culture.

While talk of "black culture" is still familiar, the kinds of expansive claims made for it in the idioms of race realism have diminished. It is now far more common to see reference to cultural formations without racial designations (e.g., "hip-hop culture," "ballroom culture") or the old phrase with important qualifiers attached (e.g., "black queer culture").[37] These changes reflect underlying social and political dynamics (including the weakening authority of gatekeepers to black cultural production and norms of cultural authenticity, the proliferation of internet spaces open to narrowly curated content, and the circulation of racialized cultural practices in a highly networked and less segregated society). They also show how dramatic changes in immigration patterns have increased African Americans' familiarity with cultural differences (and social conflict) among putatively black peoples from around the globe. It is striking, for instance, that at the very site where the ethnoracial pentagon was most entrenched as a normative horizon of *identification*—elite US universities—the social fracturing and fragmentation of black "cultural" and "ethnic" identities has proceeded rapidly, manifesting in increasingly granular student organizations for all manner of "black" solidarities around sexuality, cultural tastes, professional aspirations, and, above all, ethnicity and national origin. Accelerating this cultural differentiation are material underpinnings: On one hand are the economic incentives that recent African immigrants (and their descendents) have to draw, at certain points in the life cycle—sharp distinctions between their group identities and those of African Americans. On the other hand is a moral-economic project of the sort animating efforts by the group American Descendants of Slaves to claw back affirmative action opportunities and reparative justice policies they see as *morally* justified by African American oppression while currently distributed indiscriminately on incoherent "racial" grounds.[38]

This alone does not eliminate all reasonable grounds for identifying as black. Appiah, who advocated the abandonment of racial identities earlier in his career, has since moderated his position, arguing that "the importance of an identity in social life is not automatically reduced by the discovery that one has importantly false beliefs about it."[39] We might justifiably act as black people to combat white supremacy, for example, but this need not also require that we listen only to jazz or see ourselves as committed to propagating an imagined normative "black family." Yet the foundational impact of this deconstruction of the idea of race, the demand for a flexibility in identity, and a general uncertainty concerning precisely how race matters if, as Appiah maintains, race isn't "real" reflects the erosion of the authority of conventional race realisms as pillars of black political life, which is all I aim to establish.

A further striking piece of evidence in favor of this suggestion is the 2007 Pew Research Center survey that found that nearly four in ten black people believe that "Blacks today can no longer be thought of as a single race because the black community is so diverse," a view that is most widely held (44 percent) among black people ages eighteen to twenty-nine and is likely to therefore become increasingly prevalent over time. The same poll found that 61 percent of black people believed that "in the last ten years . . . the values held by middle class black people and the values held by poor black people [had] become more different," up from 44 percent in 1986.[40] This was, one might retort, before Black Lives Matter and its dramatic mobilization of black solidarities, but political scientists who study the rise and fall of "linked fate" measures among African Americans noted—at least in 2019—that measures of linked fate were at their lowest since the 1980s. Rising support for Donald Trump among black voters under the age of forty-nine, despite the first African American vice president, Kamala Harris, running as the Democratic Party nominee, strongly suggests that this trend did not go hurtling in the opposite direction.[41]

Further study of the Black Lives Matter movement and its literature only underscores my point. While culture industries fast-tracked "black" cultural content to meet an anticipated demand for such products, and black intellectuals advance mystifications that suggest the Movement for Black Lives coalition is "a philosophical return to the source: the radicalism of Black folk culture and the plantation politics of the revolutionary Black slave," clear-eyed interpretation shows that activist arguments tend to cohere around the imagination of a shared vulnerability to vigilante and police violence rather than the kind of substantive cultural heritage imagined by Du Bois at his most strident or the revolutionary culture imagined by the Marxist-Leninist and Maoist elements in the Black Panther Party.[42] The most sustained arguments about culture—for instance, in Black Lives Matter cofounder Alicia Garza's work—are about how social movements transform mainstream popular and political culture rather than a reiteration of Black Power ethnic clientelism or black nationalist metaphysics.[43] It is no wonder, given these developments, that contemporary African American political philosophy is preoccupied with projects that attempt to defend or resist ideas of black solidarity in the absence of realism about "race."[44]

Church Vanguardism

A dissolution that seems to have started slowly, and then happened all at once, is the erosion of the once authoritative idea that the so-called black church—or, more precisely, churches largely led and attended by black Americans—must play a vanguard spiritual and institutional role in black politics. “It can hardly be questioned,” contemporary commentators on the civil rights movement reported, “that, especially in the South, the Negro church has done as much as or more than any other segment of Negro society for the Negro’s cause.” The church, they noted, “has been the Negro’s sanctuary, his tactical headquarters, and a crucial means of communication between Negro leaders and the masses.”[45]

This idea, like race, also has its roots in slavery, where the evangelical fervors of the first and second Great Awakenings first introduced American-born slaves to Christianity.[46] This evangelical outreach was so well received in part because of antimaterialistic and egalitarian themes that venerated the dignity of all individuals in the eyes of God and promised the conversion and deliverance of the downtrodden. Indeed, messianic themes in slave Christianity extended well beyond Jesus to figures as disparate as Moses and Abraham Lincoln.[47]

Aside from the paternalistic ministering of white slaveholders and missionaries, enslaved people were influenced by participation in interracial churches and their own “invisible” churches conducted outside the purview of slaveholders. In the latter, especially, they tended to combine tenets of Christianity with features of West African spirituality, rejecting mainstream Christianity’s stark distinction between the cities of God and Man, emphasizing spirit possession and demonology, and practicing a more emotive, participatory, and musical form of worship. As I discussed in Chapter 4, they particularly gravitated toward the Exodus story of the Old Testament, identifying their awful plight with that of the enslaved Hebrews and anticipating a similar emancipation that would have profound ethical consequences for the world.

Unsurprisingly for an enslaved and socially dominated people in a Christian land, theodicy—the attempt to wrestle with the problem of evil in a world supposedly overseen by a just, omnipotent God—is the central problem of black religion. It has long informed many attempts to answer questions of the ethics of the oppressed within black political life.[48] Not only was black suffering in a racialized slave society so obvious and insistent, but the collective, intergenerational, and unwarranted nature of the enslavement was imposed on black infants drawing their first breaths—some literally *bred* for this condition—and made it impossible to avoid the most unyielding confrontations with undeserved suffering.

So, too, did theodicy have to confront the fact that for enslaved African Americans, Christianity was not a religion practiced by their “people” from time immemorial. This fact was not only thrown in their face as evidence of the fittedness of their race for slavery but also raised a recurring self-assurance problem in Afro-American Christianity. In this respect, black Christianity might be an especially “modern” form of religion insofar as it must, unlike many other religious traditions, give an especially recent, historical account of how the group found its faith rather than appeal to primordial myth. To succeed, moreover, it must achieve this account in terms that are reconciliatory and not further alienating.

This distinctive religious tradition emerged largely due to the relative autonomy afforded black Christian worship, and the "invisible" churches of slavery also served as forums for resolving disputes among slaves and maintaining familial ties.[49] This was even truer among urban free black people in the North who, after being expelled from white congregations, built and maintained their own churches, which sustained abolitionist protests, Negro conventions, and other political aims. Surveying this surfeit of activity, the black abolitionist, physician, army officer, and explorer Martin Delany unexaggeratingly described the free black church as "the Alpha and Omega of all things [among black people] . . . their only source of information—their only acknowledged public body—their state legislature."[50]

In the immediate aftermath of the Civil War, black churches began to sprout throughout the South, either out of formerly "invisible" congregations or due to separatist movements from interracial churches. In this period the black church served as the overwhelmingly influential force in a budding black associative life, delivering so-called uplift projects, creating schools or other educational opportunities, resolving conflicts, and organizing collective action for politics (mostly through the Reconstruction-era Republican Party or the affiliated Union League).[51] Aside from theological reasons, the black church was simply the only institutional field controlled by black people, and this autonomy allowed for the development of indigenous leadership, more extensive control of material resources, and the type of bonding social capital necessary to spur collective action and enforce social norms—both necessary to mount a challenge to white supremacy.[52] It also had inherently useful scaffolding for charismatic leadership and the kind of exhortation to supererogatory sacrifice, service, and action that sustained communities under duress.

Perhaps the most telling testament to the authority of the black church as a pillar of black political life, however, is not an account of its political activities but of how even its black critics maintained that it was necessarily a central feature of black politics' answer to the white supremacy question. W. E. B. Du Bois, who published sociological studies of the church, was notoriously critical of the intractability of theological disputes, the resistance to unification for economic and political purposes, the character of much of its leadership, and what he famously called its "awful" emotionalism.[53] Yet he nonetheless exhorted the church to work as the "most powerful agency" in the moral development and social reform of the black masses. Later in life, working more intimately in the

Marxist tradition, Du Bois "frankly" acknowledged his "attitude toward organized religion is distinctly critical," rejecting the plausibility of doctrines of divine revelation and authority. Yet he conceded that "the majority of the best and earnest people of this world are today organized in religious groups, and that without the co-operation of the richness of their emotional experience, and the unselfishness of their aims, science stands helpless before crude fact and selfish endeavor."[54]

Likewise, Carter G. Woodson, the founder of Black History Week (later Black History Month) and a Harvard-trained historian, criticized the various divisions of the black church but was convinced of its longevity and thus advocated only internal reform to focus on more "this-worldly" political concerns. Even black leftists like A. Philip Randolph kept their criticisms of the church to the limited realm of class bias, conceding that black churches would have to continue to be instrumental in providing union organizers with meeting space, resources, and sympathetic congregations. As the historian Barbara Dianne Savage concludes when reviewing these prominent figures, there is almost no work in early twentieth-century black intellectual circles (outside of conservative denominations) that normatively argued for the irrelevancy of the church for black politics.[55] This was, of course, in stark contrast to white leftists and communists, whose atheism, rationalism, and racism combined to foster intensely dismissive attacks on Christianity generally and black religious practice in particular. The famed left-wing lawyer Clarence Darrow, who figures largely in long civil rights historiography, controversially derided black ministers as "self-hypnotists" and African American Christianity as a "narcotic," which caused some pastors to ban him from their pulpits and provoked tense relations with the leaders of the NAACP who relied on his courtroom acumen and national popularity in civil rights cases.[56]

The view that the black church should play a vanguard role in black political life reached its apex at the height of the "classical phase" of the modern Southern civil rights movement from 1954 to 1968. The powerful, mutually reinforcing relationship between local churchgoers in the South and emerging religious leaders, like King and lesser-known figures like Ralph Abernathy, James Forman, and Fannie Lou Hamer produced a frontal assault on the Jim Crow edifice of white supremacy. The blend of prophetic African American Christianity, black bourgeois aspiration, and the philosophy of nonviolent civil disobedience not only existentially sustained the fragile courage of a generation of activists but also tactically outmaneuvered the Jim Crow regime in the battle for national and global moral authority.[57] The customary anticommunist attacks on black militancy were particularly well withstood by virtue of the fact that the communist position on religion as illusory ideology simply could not easily mesh with the overwhelming and public religiosity of black civil rights activists.[58]

Yet, even at its high point, the authority of the black church as a pillar of black political life was beginning to show signs of fraying around the edges. While King spellbound audiences from the streets of Montgomery to the marble feet of a memorialized Lincoln, the Nation of Islam and its most prominent spokesperson, Malcolm X, took ready advantage of a television age that gave their withering attacks on Christian leaders as "Uncle Toms" and Christianity as a foolish "slave religion" of weakness, ressentiment, and cowardice wider circulation.[59] Although never approaching the influence of King, the Nation of Islam, and Malcolm X in particular, contributed mightily to the explosion of secular black radicalism in the late 1960s and early 1970s.

In this respect, Malcolm might be said to be the most Nietzschean figure in black political life, delivering a genealogical critique of black Christianity as an alien imposition by slave masters for ideological control; an ethical critique of Christianity as a religion that celebrates undignified postures of nonviolence, love, and forgiveness in the face of domination; and an ontological critique of Christianity as life-negating insofar as it focuses on the heavenly afterlife rather than the struggle to eke out a decent, dignified life in the world. He leveled these criticisms with extraordinary charisma, and they found a hearing (if not always endorsement) among a generation experiencing rapid urbanization, mass college education, and tentative integration. As this was the first generation granted wide access to predominantly white colleges, this decline in the authority of black church vanguardism was exacerbated by the general tendency in the broader society toward secularization through higher education.[60] While, like Friedrich Nietzsche, Malcolm's own views gained only limited adherents, his criticism and its crystallization in his personally fearless and subversive example made it difficult to proceed as before. This new generation of intellectuals, students, and activists, although influenced by Malcolm's criticisms of the church and its leaders, were equally wary of both orthodox Islam and the cult version promoted by the Nation of Islam and many gravitated toward a general skepticism with regard to religion.[61]

If it is controversial to contend that black church vanguardism had an organic Nietzschean problem, it should not be contentious to insist that it also had a Weberian problem: charismatic authority amid these social developments. One of King's lieutenants, Jesse Jackson, was on the front line of this dilemma as the Southern theater's major civil rights groups attempted to establish roots in the Northern ghettoes. Jackson was purposefully sent to Chicago to start Operation Breadbasket, a Southern Christian

Leadership Conference (SCLC) program whose goal was to mobilize boycotts to extract hiring and contracting agreements from businesses.

Taking King's media politics and charismatic leadership to their logical extreme, Jackson abandoned the SCLC to create his own organization, Operation PUSH (People United to Serve Humanity), which eschewed most grassroots organizing in favor of cultivating a national media profile for Jackson, who by this time had become a reverend.[62] Although he claimed moderate successes in his 1984 and 1988 campaigns for the Democratic nomination for president, Jackson's attempt to merge his Christian social justice mission with a media-driven corporate boycott politics necessarily gave rise to the tension between the Christian virtue of doing good for its own sake, the instrumental political and economic interests of his corporate boycotts, and the "harsh light of the public" that was a necessary consequence of this media-driven politics. This susceptibility to public scrutiny, over time, tends to make putatively Christian motivations "the object of suspicion rather than insight."[63] The widespread skepticism with which Jackson, and his more controversial protégé, Al Sharpton, are often met with even among African Americans, is in part due to these tensions, which have genuine theologico-political roots.

In classical Weberian form, many churches took the changing conditions after King's death as an impetus to move from charismatic to routinized political authority. In black church life this took the form of organizing development corporations, nonprofits, and participating in Democratic Party politics. Unsurprisingly, these acts of bureaucratic routinization weakened the moral fervor around anti-poverty politics and insurgent protest.

Many churches that had the resources to engage in solidaristic black politics seemed to harbor a barely concealed class bias toward the ghetto poor, made visceral by the fear of identification with them. The class and sexual politics of black churches, as the political scientist Cathy Cohen has demonstrated, discouraged effective responses to problems that did not appear to principally affect black middle-class constituencies, like HIV/AIDS, incarceration, drug gangs, and teenage pregnancy.[64] This ethical failure of leadership rooted in a politics of respectability and persistent strains of homophobia, sexism, and the like only served to exacerbate the growing crisis of authority for the black church in those quarters where what Cohen calls the "secondary" marginalization of black subgroups was seen as being exacerbated by church politics.[65] That black churches, like other churches in late twentieth and early twenty-first century America, faced high-profile sexual abuse scandals involving their clergy only added to the sense of decadence, corruption, and hypocrisy.[66] To this we might add the Weberian point that these judgments reflect the influence of means-end rationality among black church leadership attempting to navigate the reproduction of conventional political power rather than the fanaticism, fervor, revivalism, and prophetic furor of more charismatic religious vanguards.

Surely the account above will provoke intense disagreement, but the upshot is that every study of note shows black church attrition proceeding rapidly, directionally consistent with long-term declines in religious affiliation in the society *writ large*. Now about one in five African Americans openly identifies as atheist, agnostic, or "nothing in particular." In a 2021 Pew Survey, 46 percent of black respondents in Generation Z, 49 percent of Millennials, and 39 percent of Generation X report that they never or only seldom attend church. Of Generation Z or Millennial respondents that do attend, 44 percent and 45 percent, respectively, attend churches without primarily black congregations.[67] Repeated studies of black people who are not affiliated with organized religion have "found that the unchurched tended to be younger, male, never married, and urban residents."[68] Given the significant percentage of young black males among the prison and jail population in the United States, one might expect these surveys—given their inability to reach this large segment of the population—to understate the extent of apostasy.

Another part of this decline is the clientelist relationship that many black churches have with political parties and the state. What began with the incorporation of black churches into Chicago Democratic machine politics in the early twentieth century has presently evolved into a diffuse client relationship for the resources and social capital of social service providers; political parties; and other civil society groups that underwrite voter registration drives, candidate appearances, and social issue campaigns. Churches bid increasingly for the resources provided by federal and local governments through public-private development ventures, charitable choice funding, education vouchers, and faith-based initiatives.[69] Perhaps paradoxically, what the social science research on black churches seems to indicate is that the subjective dimension of black religiosity itself is becoming more detached from politics, while the institutional formation of the black church is splintering into apolitical, largely Pentecostal and nondenominational churches and "political" churches whose authoritative force has been eroded and displaced onto political parties, civil rights organizations, development corporations, and social service providers (occasionally in alliance with Republican elected officials).

But what might have done the most (aside from gender and sexuality politics) to undermine the authority of the black church in black political life—especially in the way that the church is or is not accommodated by the nonreligious—is the recent evolution of the media-driven church's bourgeois aspirations in the realm of the prosperity gospel.[70] While these churches are incredibly popular, their absurd gospel of material rewards in exchange for Christian faith simply cannot sustain the sacrifices and collective action needed to mount an effective politics. Moreover, their theological orientation to materialism leads the congregation to the emptiness of hedonism and conspicuous consumption while producing a leadership of limited public appeal that lacks moral authority and is extremely susceptible to the skepticism engendered by their conspicuous public lifestyles.[71] As Cleveland reverend Christine A. Smith relays in a Pew interview, "When you look at what happened in the Catholic Church with the scandal with the priests, and some of the things that have happened recently, not just African American pastors, but megachurches' pastors, or saying the Lord tells them to buy a $55 million jet, these are the kinds of things that undermine people's faith in the church. . . . There was a time when the church was such a major authority in the hearts and minds of people, but these things have chipped away at that to some degree."[72]

Binary Opposition: The Imagined Futures of Nationalism and Integrationism

In his monumental *The Crisis of the Negro Intellectual,* the cultural critic Harold Cruse argued that the two major traditions of black political thought are integrationism and black nationalism.[73] Its release coincided with the crystallization of the Black Power movement and the decision to recruit significant numbers of African American students and scholars into predominantly white universities for the first time. Projecting backward from the "new wave" of "Negro Nationalism" that he identified as the most important mid-twentieth-century development in American "race relations," Cruse insisted that tensions between figures like Malcolm X and civil rights movement liberals were part of a nationalist-integrationist contretemps dating back to the 1850s.[74] In that portentous decade of the Fugitive Slave Act, the US Supreme Court's infamous Dred Scot decision, and John Brown's antislavery raid on Harpers Ferry, West Virginia, black intellectuals like Martin Delany and Frederick Douglass openly sparred over the prospects for a multiracial republic, the wisdom of black emigration from the United States, and the nature of antiblack racism.

Yet while Cruse was undoubtedly correct to note the pliability and persistence of black nationalism, his treatment of this binary as the centripetal force in black political life ultimately flattened its vibrancy. Wide-ranging debates about political economy, imperialism, gender, and political aesthetics were shoved unceremoniously offstage or cramped into ill-fitting categories in order to shore up the distinction (e.g., sexual practices as evidence of "racial authenticity," or talk of "integrationism" without drawing adequate distinctions between pro- or anticapitalist variants). As the political scientist Michael Dawson and others have documented, there are also conservatives, Marxists, feminists, radical egalitarians, and the like who compose the vibrant landscape of black political thought, and there is much to be gained from studying their insights and failures.[75]

These flattened images of black political culture were held in place not just through the idiosyncrasies of scholarly interpretation but by deep, structural constraints on black political organizing and expression characteristic of our post-Reconstruction racial orders and the ordeal of the American Left. The pathways of black political debate were constrained by marginalization in mainstream media and public forums, systematic disenfranchisement in the South and machine capture in the North, state and vigilante repression, and widespread discrimination in civil society (including unions and universities). Consequently, the space of appearances for black political expression has long been *overdetermined* by what breaks through to public notoriety on the back of philanthropic tastes, charismatic spokespersons, and racial ideology. Under such conditions, it was easy even for thoughtful students of black political thought to reduce its crucial debate to the most effective strategies for "integration," or a rejection of such strategies altogether.

For our purposes, however, the fact that the integrationist-nationalist framework does not survive clear-eyed academic scrutiny in the present is to put the cart before the horse. What is important is that it has routinely been projected backward as the authoritative way of understanding and identifying with black political traditions from the mid-nineteenth century onward. This framework has long had outsize influence in framing the thematic organization of the study of black political life, imposing a sense of sweeping historical tradition, and populating the imagined futures to which intellectuals and black publics might aspire.

Racial integrationism, as usually formulated in African American political thought, is the belief that a commitment to some ensemble of ideals in moral and political philosophy—usually equality, justice, democracy, freedom, or community—either entails a commitment to racial integration as a means to bring it about or is inextricable from racial integration itself. Integration is usually understood as the broad incorporation of individuals who are now members of marginalized or oppressed racial groups into more expansive, egalitarian, and robust participation across the major areas of society (although for libertarians this may be qualified by the fact that we may discover that such individuals simply do not want to integrate *everywhere* and should respect those individuals' choices).

Although they are often sloppily used interchangeably, *desegregation* and *integration* should be distinguished. Desegregation, in Martin Luther King's characteristic conceptual distinction, is the dismantling of segregation laws, while integration is "the positive acceptance of desegregation" and "the welcomed participation of Negroes into the total range of human activities."[76] Desegregation, in this account, is relegated to being a necessary but insufficient step on the way toward integration. The politics of integration were committed normatively to an imagined future based on the contention that the "American racial caste system would be replaced with civil and political equality only through racial integration of schools, neighborhoods, and businesses, rather than—as a competing nationalist conception argued—through a strategy focused at least initially on building strong, autonomous Black institutions."[77]

Among integrationists, there were at least four major fault lines.

The first concerns the scope and scale of integration required—whether it concerns primarily the public realm of formal politics, the labor market, universities, and commercial spaces or also involves more intimate spaces like neighborhoods, families, and romantic relationships.

The second fault line concerns the role of racial identity—whether racial identities can be justifiably used to bring about an integrated society, whether they should be significantly altered or altogether abandoned in an integrated society, or whether they can still play a positive role in personal identity and associative life. Often the question of cultural conservation or assimilation is posed in this register.

The third fault line concerns the political ethics of racial integration. By this I mean what duties, if any, exist to carry out integration? What agents (e.g., state officials, those who practice civil disobedience) may legitimately act on an imperative of integration? What benefits and burdens can be placed on different groups in order to carry out a particular integration scheme? And, when and why may citizens legitimately resist efforts at integration (whether they be African American or not)? The overarching issue here is whether integration should be a question of moral suasion and voluntary choice or involve varying degrees of state compulsion. The former claims that racial integration can be realized only by persuasive moral reasoning in the public realm and a subsequent conversion in attitudes—including, of course, the antiblack attitudes of white people and any resentments harbored by black people. The latter argues instead that integration is a compelling state interest that should be pursued by the broadest levers of public policy, either out of a firm, actionable respect for a crucial moral imperative, an insistence on the need for the coercive force of the state to dismantle recalcitrant bases of anti-integrationist power, or, perhaps most influentially, because of the tutelary, authority-accruing effect that state action would have on otherwise intractable antiblack attitudes among nonblacks and social capital deficits among black people.

The fourth fault line involves the *social and political theory of integration,* for lack of a better term. At its most comprehensive, this would include a *predictive and explanatory* account of how the various domains of integration fit together in an imagined process, and a *normative* account of what ultimately justifies the pursuit of integration along a particular series of domains. The dominance of liberal norms and presuppositions in integrationist discourse surely accounts for the underdevelopment of these theories insofar as the liberal aversion to coercion leaves it uniquely enamored with paeans to "education" as the solution to complex social problems, especially ones that can be articulated in the language of "prejudice" or "difference."[78] Put bluntly, the integrated school has been assumed—often without serious argument—to be the prime mover behind the integration of society *writ large,* and the lack of careful scrutiny or even self-conscious articulation of that position and its social scientific warrants has contributed to the stagnation of integrationism as a theoretical project.

Black nationalism has long been seen as the most enduring foil to this sort of project and the liberalism most associated with it.[79] With roots at least as far back as the early nineteenth century, black nationalism has been associated with a host of political programs, including the black convention movement, emigration, Marcus Garvey's Universal Negro Improvement Association, twentieth-century separatist religions like the Nation of Islam, radical militants like the Black Panther Party, and cultural movements like the Harlem Renaissance, the Black Arts movement, and Afrocentrism. Black nationalists, on my account, are committed to three propositions: the need for black solidarity, the desirability of autonomous black institutions, and an ethics of primacy in which perceived obligations among black people are prior to other competing obligations.[80]

The popularity of nationalism tends to ebb and flow from the debates over emigration in the 1850s through the Black Power movement in the 1960s and 1970s and up to our own moment's conflicts over cultural groups and curriculums on college campuses. But from the clear-cut conflicts of the 1850s, where integrationists like Frederick Douglass desired to stay in America and become part of the group life of the nation and emigrationists like Martin Delany argued that at least a significant number of black people should leave the United States for more prosperous opportunities in Central America or Africa, these positions have grown increasingly muddled over time. One would not know it from the vitriol launched back and forth, but as contemporary observers of the Democrats and Republicans should be well aware, the moderation of programmatic differences does not always necessarily lead to a less combative political discourse.

Thus, while black nationalists like H. Rap Brown were taunting the venerable black preacher as "Martin Loser King" and calling Thurgood Marshall "a Tom of the highest order" and integrationists like Bayard Rustin were returning fire, declaring Black Power as empty symbolism that lacked "any real value for the civil rights movement," the substantive positions on both sides after the legislative victories of civil rights grew remarkably similar on some fronts. Both sides advocated a positive reassessment of black identity, encouraged the election of black candidates for office, and promoted the development of black business.[81] The expansion of civil rights and some economic opportunity eliminated the more extravagant proposals of many black nationalists, but in narrowing their scope, it made their criticisms of integrationism more poignant.

In the most dramatic outcomes of the "classical" phase of the civil rights movement—the integration of public schools and universities, for example—the public imagery of integration was crystallized. This was the handful of brave black people venturing into the hallowed halls of white educational privilege on behalf of their people and the American dream. This was juxtaposed with a new paradigmatic image of the failure of the American dream—the all-Negro schoolhouse, which was, by virtue of its overwhelming blackness, irrefutable evidence of its inferiority. Integration, imbued with the overwhelming moral authority of the "classical" phase of the civil rights movement and its preeminent martyr, Martin Luther King Jr., became, therefore, synonymous with a moderate amount of racial diversity. A majority black school—in the logic of civil rights integrationism—could not, by definition, be successful. Malcolm X mocked this logic in his speech, "Not Just an American Problem, but a World Problem":

> They fooled the people in Mississippi by trying to make it appear that they were going to integrate the University of Mississippi. They took one Negro to the university backed up with about 6,000–15,000 troops, I think it was. And I think it cost them $6 million. . . . This tokenism was a program that was designed to protect the benefits of only a handful of handpicked Negroes . . . [who were] eating high on the hog, rubbing elbows with white folk, sitting in Washington, D. C., [while] the masses of Black people in this country continued to live in the slum and in the ghetto . . . go to the worst schools and get the worst education.[82]

Here Malcolm draws attention to the middle-class interests that dominated much of "integrationist" thinking in practice. Henry Louis Gates Jr. remembers this moment as when "the grandchildren of the Talented Tenth—those who had been trained to succeed, geared to prosper, prepared by family and teachers to 'cross over' into the white world once the walls of segregation came tumbling down—plunged headlong into the abyss of integration."[83] Somewhere in between their respective words lies the insight that poor black people, particularly those in inner cities and rural areas, were unable, by virtue of their profound social isolation, to take advantage of integration (or its derivative regime's keyword, *diversity*) and its benefits in the realm of higher education.[84] The legal scholar Derrick Bell has taken this argument to its furthest conclusion by arguing that the *Brown v. Board of Education* decision that integrated public schools in the United States should have actually upheld separate but equal while truly enforcing the equal requirement and mandating a comprehensive overhaul in the capacities of the federal government to act affirmatively to ensure equality—whether or not integration ever occurred.[85]

In the end, however, the authoritative pillar of nationalism—always precarious—was fatally eroded by a series of calamities, some of which were due to its own excesses and all of which undermined the allure and plausibility of any black nationalist imagined future. The surveillance agencies of the federal government, as well as local law enforcement officials, reacted violently to the Black Power era and targeted black nationalist groups, especially the Black Panther Party, with particularly intense repression, harassment, and violence.[86] Part of the reason for this was the Black Power generation's introduction of revolutionary violence into black political life as a serious, agenda-determining consideration for the first time and their attempt to generate political authority and substantive political theory from a sympathetic, defensive interpretation of the urban riots of the 1960s and rising rates of ghetto crime.[87]

As flat-footed as integrationist analysis of crime and rioting could be, it nonetheless retained a beautiful symmetry. The rising problems of rioting and crime, it argued, could be understood only as the response to the social isolation of poor black people in ghetto neighborhoods, where a lack of institutional resources and little or no exposure to what we would now call social capital and role models produced the deviance that was a natural response to this sort of vacuum. Given that social isolation was the problem, integration was easily confirmed as the solution. Whitney Young Jr., of the National Urban League (NUL), for instance, argued that

> the ghettoes will continue to exist as long as the ghetto population remains intact, and inasmuch as the problems of the central cities will never be solved as long as this is so, the Federal Government should revise its present policy of non-discrimination [in housing] and, instead, *actively promote a policy and practice of seeking and encouraging, aiding and abetting direct dispersal of the ghetto population*. . . . Dispersal of the ghetto population requires not only that Negroes move out of the ghetto but also that whites move in. In one stroke, [the NUL plan] Operation Urban Survival can bring new life and vitality to a decaying part of the city. It will generate new hope

> in the slums as adults find jobs and youngsters see that education can lead to tangible results. It will generate many kinds of peripheral enterprises and development, further adding to the vitality of the community. Such projects in the hearts of the ghettos will provide visible evidence that the city cares, that neglect and abuse are at an end, and that integration is a living force in city life. Most important of all, it will end the isolation of the ghetto from the rest of the community and is essential to achieving healthy traffic in both directions.[88]

Integrationists tended to treat crime and rioting as a result of opportunity structures and social capital deficiencies that stemmed from the marginality of ghetto life and assumed they would largely disappear in proportion to the extent that state-backed integration could disperse ghetto black people more equally throughout metropolitan areas. To the extent that such phenomena appear linked to issues of residential and social isolation, the integrationist account retains an allure.

Black nationalists of this period, however, had a steeper road to travel. In the course of raising the question of revolutionary violence in the United States to a level of serious debate and consideration unseen since John Brown, Henry Highland Garnet, and militant abolitionism, some black nationalists sought to interpret the riots and rising ghetto crime alike as inarticulate signs of a rising militant consciousness and impending wave of revolutionary violence. The allure of this claim is obvious; it seems a straightforward way to procure authority as a spokesperson for otherwise indeterminate and inchoate phenomena that, nonetheless, represents a form of popular mobilization and an unavoidable public policy concern for elites. In characterizing rioting and crime as inarticulate expressions of protorevolutionary consciousness, Black Power intellectuals undermined their own ethical capacity to distance themselves from these acts on grounds other than their insufficiently strategic character (that is, the violence should be *organized*) or their violation of solidaristic duties between black people (i.e., don't burn down the black neighborhood or commit crimes against black people). Instead of the imputation of vanguard revolutionary intent to rioting and crime leading to a sustained reassessment of the sources of black criminality, the stigma of crime instead attached to the public perception of self-styled black revolutionaries and served to buttress popular support for the violent government suppression of black militant groups.

Ironically, it also allowed for the rhetoric of authenticity and rebellion to be usurped by those associated with, or drawing on, the tropes of street crime themselves. Here, the black nationalist embrace of blaxploitation films like Melvin Van Peebles's *Sweet Sweetback's Baadasssss Song* (1971) and Gordon Parks's *Shaft* (1971), while seemingly innocuous or empowering at the time, led them rapidly to a paralysis in the face of the parodies of their politics embraced by the film genre. These films took the vanguard arguments of Black Power theorists about ghetto criminals to their logical conclusion, displacing even the self-styled revolutionary as inauthentically militant (and black). This allowed the black militant to become a stock figure of American comedy, with all the erosion of authority that comes from parody and satire.[89]

Repression was by far the most significant force in the decline of black nationalism, as it frightened potential allies and contributed to a fatal air of distrust in the major organizations of the period.[90] Those that survived, eschewed the rhetoric of violence, instead moving to the realm of symbolic politics, allowing politicians to trade in signals of loyalty through black expressive culture instead of tangible policy accomplishments or the costly signal of violence.[91] Some off these survivors, like the Nation of Islam, further damaged the authority of black nationalist thought by endorsing increasingly distasteful forms of anti-Semitism, sexism, homophobia, and antiwhite racism while conjuring up exceptionally implausible theories of economic self-sufficiency involving local manufacturers, small craftworks, or segregated trade in the face of a neoliberal global economy built on underpaid service jobs, multinational corporations drawing on global labor pools and favorable territorial tax arrangements, complex international free trade arrangements, and information management.[92]

Louis Farrakhan, who led the Nation of Islam until his recent bout with prostate cancer, is especially implicated in these shortcomings. While gaining massive popularity for his broadsides against white racism and black moral laxity, Farrakhan's great achievement—the 1995 Million Man March—has only an ambivalent legacy at best. While some associate its moral proselytizing with diffuse effect of cultural transformation (even suggesting it partly responsible for the long-run decline in crime during the 1990s), it is difficult to find that the vast spiritual and financial investment from the approximately seven hundred thousand participants ever developed into an institutional or organizational ecosystem of nationalist or even communitarian revival. Indeed, arguably the greatest undeniable impact of the march was to spark an oppositional revival of black feminist organizing whose ascendency is one of the central stories of American social movement politics in the twenty-first century.[93]

The collapse of nationalism's "imagined future" did not, however, mean the full triumph of integrationism. For starters, despite the near-total public opinion shift against formal segregation, the country remains incredibly segregated. In 2004, the Princeton University social scientist Doug Massey found that "a clear majority of [all] African Americans (almost 60%) lived in a metropolitan area that was highly segregated, and a substantial minority (some 41%) lived under conditions of hypersegregation."[94] To put this in better perspective, "the de jure apartheid of South Africa produced an average dissimilarity index (the metric used to measure segregation) of ninety in South African urban areas as of 1991," while de facto segregation in Chicago, Detroit, Milwaukee, and Newark in 2002 produced dissimilarity indexes above eighty-one in each city, with Detroit's eighty-six leading the pack.[95] Even with high levels of black middle-class movement out of black poor neighborhoods, white flight is substantial enough to render even the black middle-class enclaves segregated. School populations, which follow neighborhoods, are even worse. Gary Orfield, of the Civil Rights Project at the University of California–Los Angeles, has found school resegregation to be rapidly increasing, particularly in the South, and black students are more segregated now than they have been at any time since 1970. When the intersection of race and class is taken into account, as nationalists sometimes advocated, the segregation statistics are even bleaker, with poor black people and Latinos being likely to attend a school where their group is in the majority and most of the students are poor. In Boston, for example, 97 percent of the concentrated nonwhite schools also have concentrated poverty, compared to only 1 percent of the segregated white schools.[96] And even if black students manage to make it out of these decrepit public schools, it is foreseeable that the current economic and political crises crippling colleges and the recent dismantlings of affirmative action may entrench higher levels of segregation on American campuses.

While Orfield and his colleagues have steadily trumpeted the benefits of integration for school performance and former Harvard president Derek Bok has heralded diversity's supposed benefits for college education, new evidence is challenging even that long-standing consensus.[97] The economist Roland Fryer has found that black students do uniquely poorly academically and socially in moderately integrated environments.[98] Studies of recipients of the Move to Opportunity grant that allowed public-housing residents to move to market-rate housing in other neighborhoods, while far from conclusive, have suggested less than stellar outcomes for the grant recipients and their children.[99] Most devastatingly, Robert Putnam's massive study of social capital in the United States reluctantly concluded that the greater the ethnic diversity in a given community, the less likely its members are to vote, volunteer, give to charity, work on community projects, and support extensive public funding for schools and other common goods. Far from building a beloved community, it seems that integration might—at least initially—drive most Americans to adopt a bunker mentality and be generally distrustful of their neighbors.[100]

In 2007 the US Supreme Court ruled on cases originating in Jefferson County, Kentucky, and Seattle, Washington, to declare even voluntary racial desegregation plans unconstitutional, so public policy to pursue racial integration seems off the table as long as this court maintains its current composition.[101] In his plurality decision, Chief Justice John Roberts assailed the central premise of integrationism, rejecting as unconstitutional the idea that racial balancing can be a compelling state interest, even if voluntarily undertaken. With a rhetorical flourish that will surely remain at the forefront of historical memory in Supreme Court verdicts concerning race, Roberts wrote, "The way to stop discriminating on the basis of race is to stop discriminating on the basis of race." What is interesting about this decision, outside of its legal impact, is how generally muted the outcry against it was when compared to similar cases like *Bakke v. the California Board of Regents* (1978), which involved medical school affirmative action admissions. I venture that this resignation is part of the now pervasive sentiment that *integration* is not a word through which mass political mobilization, affect, or identity can any longer be activated.

For example, Orlando Patterson once described Barack Obama as a "committed integrationist."[102] But it is not entirely clear that this means or discloses anything of consequence anymore. Obama's education policy was designed not to pursue large-scale integration schemes but to demand an increase in the quality of schools as they are (meaning, segregated) through standardized testing, charter schools, and teacher reviews. In housing policy he drove stimulus funding toward efforts like those in Pittsburgh for "right-sizing," or creative attempts to turn abandoned properties in deindustrialized cities to productive spaces like gardens or aesthetically pleasing green space—not to move poor black residents into less blighted neighborhoods.[103] The goal was to make neighborhoods—segregated as they are—more livable and successful through the policy instrument of Promise Neighborhoods, based on the "wraparound" public service model pioneered by Geoffrey Canada and the Harlem Children's Zone.[104] Finally, in the realm of higher education, Obama pushed for an unprecedented amount ($98 million) of direct federal government support for historically black colleges and universities (HBCUs) while assigning his HBCU task director to help develop and incentivize programming to remedy the obscenely low graduation rates at these institutions.[105] That he could hold these views and be a "committed integrationist" seems to say more about the contemporary incoherence of such a categorization for contemporary black political life than anything particularly clarifying about Obama.

It is a frequent description of integration in the literature that it is an "ordeal," "failure," or "crisis." The above suggests this may be so. But to this I would add that, as a political philosophy, it is essentially "stillborn." By this I mean that outside of the most naive liberals who believed that integrated schools would socialize children into interracial comity and change society gradually over time, the hard questions never reached systematic articulation and theorization: Is integrationism about democratic social movement power? Is it about repairing social capital deficits? Is it about promoting republican ideals of solidarity and community? Does it require the curtailment of American federalism or the bureaucratic integration of metropolises? Is it at odds with capitalism and private property rights, or is it the only condition under which they could be legitimate? Does it require recognition of group rights and cultural protection, or would it be best served by the erosion of cultural difference? Does it need to involve the intimate sphere, and if so, how much soulcraft can a state exercise to that end? The failure of a conference like the Haverford Discussions—where leading black "integrationists" (e.g., Mamie Clark, St. Clair Drake, Ralph Ellison, and J. Saunders Redding) were called together to produce a "manifesto" to win the hearts and minds of black youth inspired by Black Power—to pose nearly any of these questions with precision and make headway on their answers is illustrative of my indictment.[106]

My sense of the rise and fall of the integrationist-nationalist framework is that it paradoxically relies principally on the strength of black nationalism at any given moment. Where nationalism weakens, as in the 1940s or our current moment, more pluralist and granular typologies of black political thought seem to sprout from the freshly cleared soil.[107] Perhaps because nationalism involves a fundamental conflict over the boundaries of popular sovereignty and asserts such strident claims of primacy over our crosscutting political allegiances and obligations, its appearance can function among intellectuals at least, as something akin to a two-party system in electoral politics. It seems to polarize alliances around a few axes of conflict, pushes rhetoric to degrees that seem exaggerated compared to many of the practical policy disagreements, and hardens "partisan" identities. The degree to which black nationalist talk may compel all manner of liberals, socialists, feminists, and others to describe their politics in the rhetoric of "integration" is, I think, an important and as-of-yet unanswered question for the history of African American political development. But regardless of this matter of political sociology, it seems clear that the practice *obscures* or otherwise seems to paralyze the sophisticated debate on the various divides among so-called integrationists on questions of political economy, state authority, federalism, and constitutional law (e.g., property rights).

The Cultural Politics of Representation

The last pillar is what might be called, following Gene Jarrett, the cultural politics of racial representation. In Jarrett's distillation, the cultural politics of racial representation involves both the "aesthetic portrayal" of African Americans in art and literature *and* the idea that, to carry out this task, a kind of authority and set of corresponding responsibilities have been delegated to artists and creatives by the broader racial group.[108] Like other representatives entrusted with political authority on behalf of their constituents, the artist has duties that follow from this delegation.

Take, for example, James Baldwin's proclamation to a group of students: "I, Jimmy Baldwin, as a black writer, must in some way represent you. Now, you didn't elect me and I didn't ask for it, but here we are. . . . Everything I write will in some way reflect on you. So . . . what do we do? I'll make you a pledge. If you will promise your elder brother that you will never, ever accept any of the many derogatory, degrading, and reductive definitions that this society has ready for you, then I, Jimmy Baldwin, promise you I shall never betray you."[109] Traditionally, in black political life, the tasks of the cultural politics of representation have broken into two analytically distinct—but not mutually incompatible—familial approaches: *racial vindicationism,* or defense of "the race" from inferiorizing and harmful representations, and the *politics of collective identity,* by which I mean the articulation and protection of a shared group cultural identity meant to compel recognition respect from others and/or secure a distinctive form of flourishing appropriate for black people as "a people."

The first, *vindicationism,* is, as Baldwin suggests, focused on combating a cultural milieu saturated with inferiorizing racial stereotypes, racist ideas, and antiblack stigma. For some black intellectuals and activists, like James Weldon Johnson, the influence of these stereotypes and cultural valuations was paramount. Even as early as 1922, with most African Americans still suffering under a Southern Jim Crow regime of terrorism, debt peonage, and disenfranchisement, Johnson nevertheless argued that "the status of the Negro in the United States is more a question of national mental attitude toward the race than of actual conditions."[110] The stridency (or absurdity) of this formulation only helps underscore the broad degree to which many intellectuals and activists held that "mental attitude[s]" of race prejudice were a *primary* cause of racial injustice, and could be effectively targeted by cultural politics aimed at "exposing the white-supremacist, discriminatory, prejudicial, and inequitable degradation of African Americans on the basis of race" through cultural criticism and production.[111]

The simplest form of vindicationism is unmasking critique, which seeks to expose depictions of African Americans as inferiorizing, untruthful, and objectionably harmful. Characteristic culture work in this vein is Ida B. Wells's careful unmasking of the stereotypes of black men as inveterate rapists through statistical analysis, investigative journalism, and cultural criticism directed at Southern media. So, too, is the NAACP campaign to boycott and ban D. W. Griffith's 1915 blockbuster Ku Klux Klan propaganda film *The Birth of a Nation.*[112]

More complex are those efforts at vindication that are deliberately "constructive," part of what Henry Louis Gates Jr. calls the many decades-long attempt by "various schools of black political thought to invent ever more iterations of the New Negro in an attempt to confect positive images of noble black people powerful enough to brace against the maelstrom of excruciating images that the white supremacist imagination had spawned."[113] This work was both *propagandistic* and *prophylactic.*

In the former sense, we see the attempt to improve the associations and attitudes of black people in the minds of others. In the latter, they hope to provide, for black people themselves, aspirational or dignified images that would improve self-esteem and self-respect, model good character and excellence, and expand their imaginative judgment of their own possibilities. The concern is that, in absence of such images, African Americans might internalize the contemptuous scripts or images that circulate in racist society and accept imitation of them as their only plausible horizon of expectation. One might think here of the psychologist Alvin Poussaint's consultant efforts on *The Cosby Show,* the popular 1980s sitcom whose now-disgraced titular star, Bill Cosby, portrayed a wealthy black obstetrician married to a beautiful, successful lawyer, played by Phylicia Rashad, heading a thriving family in a well-to-do Brooklyn neighborhood that seemed in an entirely different world, no pun intended, from the violence, drug addiction, and other social ills that dominated news reports on black America in the period.[114]

The other wing of the cultural politics of representation understood its task as producing a collective cultural identity for black people to attain recognition respect from others and/or achieve a distinctive kind of flourishing as a unique people. Alain Locke, the great cultural philosopher of the Harlem Renaissance, described it as moving from "a common condition" to a "common consciousness."[115] For James Weldon Johnson, cultural achievement, cultural identity, and recognition respect were deeply intertwined. "The final measure of the greatness of all peoples is the amount and standard of the literature and art," he argued. "No people that has produced great literature and art has ever been looked upon by the world as distinctly inferior," because they will have demonstrated the "intellectual parity" of their group.[116]

This logic ran immediately into problems evidenced by the likes of the composer Samuel Coleridge Taylor or the poet Phyllis Wheatley. Their achievements were in cultural traditions distinctively associated with Europe and "whiteness," so they could either be dismissed as imitative, or accepted as *individually* great, but as *exceptions* to the racial rule. Influenced by W. E. B. Du Bois's appropriation of the cultural philosophy of German romantics like Johann Gottfried von Herder, the black cultural politics of representation broadly embraced the idea that black "folk" culture was unified by certain "ideals of life" and had a uniquely countermodern "message" or "gift" for the world contained in its expressions. The task of artists and intellectuals was to engage this folk culture or, later, working-class proletarian or lumpenproletarian culture, and refine it for entry into "the Kingdom of Culture" as the articulate expression of this common consciousness.[117]

This complex configuration is now collapsing under its contradictions. The first seams emerged almost right away, with the Harlem Renaissance conflict over propaganda in service of black emancipation and the individual liberty of the artist to make "art for art's sake." As Paul Taylor explains, this could veer into illiberalism, subjecting artistic content to political evaluation and refraining "from exploring the seedier aspects of black life—the reality of black crime, poverty, and immorality notwithstanding."[118] This lodged a paradox right into the heart of both vindicationism and collective identity. If political impact determined the merits of art, it would diminish its artistic standing in the eyes of art purists, undermining the goal of the artwork to produce genuine recognition respect. And if art was to do the work of protest, was it not always already other-directed, affixing the quest for "common consciousness" to the recognition refusal of white people?

A second problem stemmed from the unruly, insurgent character of artistic creativity and the inability of cultural gatekeeping elites in black political life to control what forms of expression could gain entry into mass culture and high art. This protean character of culture allowed for those otherwise marginalized in both the broader society *and* in black political life to articulate axes of difference and disagreement over values. These articulations of queer, feminist, populist, and anarchic sentiment in blues, jazz, soul, disco, and hip-hop—just to mention musical forms—became central to bringing the cleavages papered over by racially generic vocabularies out of concealment.[119] There is now, as Taylor argues, a "widespread sense that racial conditions have taken on novel configurations, and that old conceptions of a stable black identity cannot countenance or illuminate this novelty."[120] If we are living, as Dan Rodgers suggests, in an "age of fracture," much of the fracturing in black communities over class, gender, and sexuality found their voice in popular culture and art.[121]

Nowhere was this clearer than in the 1990s consolidation of hip-hop around gangsta rap. Mischievously inhabiting some of the society's most toxic stereotypes live on television, gangsta rap broke with long-standing norms about the cultural politics of representation, at least in the form laden with ethics of respectability and propriety in everything from language to sexual mores to violence. Yet these artists made persuasive claims to be at the forefront of raising issues and experiences that the larger society—including many black political leaders—wanted to ignore, including incarceration and criminalization, HIV/AIDS, youth unemployment, drug abuse, and suicide.[122] Against the so-called "civil rights" generation, which "often imposed a spoken code of moral behavior, which suggested that one should 'act right' so as not to offend the tastes of dominant White society and so as to speed up one's entrance into the mainstream while recognizing that only certain Blacks . . . would be accepted," hip-hop (especially gangsta rap) could be defiant. It celebrated "disregard for the approval of the mainstream" as both lucrative and liberating.[123]

With reference to the cultural politics of representation, hip-hop performed two crisis-inducing feats. On the one hand, it turned the rhetoric of authenticity familiar to expressivist political aesthetics into a powerfully *populist* discourse that impugned existing black leadership and moral authorities as corrupt from the standpoint of an imagined black ghetto "masses," in part through an appropriation of Malcolm X's words and image.[124] This successfully lodged a fundamental class antagonism at the heart of expressivism, amplifying it through mass culture, and accelerating the demise of group authenticity talk based on *collective* identity accordingly. This was, perhaps paradoxically, because rappers' dramatization and stylization of class difference helped make legible a distinctively "ghetto" repertoire of performances that other African Americans (and black immigrants) could use as an ethical and cultural foil. These scripts and forms of self-fashioning are so well known, and the norms of antiracism so prone to taking class misrecognition as a paradigmatic racial insult, that I suspect there is a growing sense among elite and middle-class black folks that they are not especially implicated in stereotypes that seem narrowly targeted toward the ghetto poor.[125] This may also have a material basis in class and education-based divergences *among* black people (men, in particular) on measures of incarceration and arrest.[126]

On the other hand, as rappers—especially gangsta rappers—tried to culturally invert hierarchies of good and bad stereotypes, they raised a broader skepticism about the genealogy, social function, and moral ontology of these valences in American and African American political life.[127] How can there be a reliable, consensus politics organized around the critique of "negative" images and the promotion of "positive" images when insurgent cultural formations like hip-hop call these distinctions into question, raising uncomfortable concerns about their functional relation to the marginalization of the poor, the repression of human vitality (e.g., sex, self-defense, hustle), and the self-respect of their proponents? This value "pluralism" and criticism that surfaced in the course of art makes consensus judgments about positive and negative distinctions unstable—whether we are discussing Big Freedia, Cardi B, and Flava Flav or Kara Walker and Kehinde Wiley. How—when the fields of cultural production are so fragmented, algorithmically curated, organized on local values, and in principle always able to go "viral"—could anyone restore a stable cultural hierarchy generally among African Americans regarding such matters as who or what is "positive"?

"Taken as straightforward descriptors," Racquel Gates argues, negative and positive "are limiting categories that do not allow us to access the full, complex range of images that circulate in the media, nor do they allow for the possibility of nuanced engagement with these images by the people that consume them." "To invoke these categories uncritically," she continues, "reinforces racist ideologies that use discourses of black exceptionalism to further marginalize black behaviors and people that deviate from white, middle-class, heterosexual norms."[128] I do not think it too strong to suggest, in yet another hermeneutical point, that the receptivity to and political mobility of this kind of pejorative criticism of "respectability politics" in the last twenty years is in part due to the success of hip-hop artists like these in changing the very valence of "negative" and "positive" when used in reference to some imagined collective "face" or "standing" of the race.

Given this state of affairs, many of the debates of the cultural politics of representation as I have described it suffer from palpable exhaustion. Rather than debate "positive" and "negative" images, cultural critics spend an inordinate amount of time debating the just distribution of honorifics, obstacles to "recognition" of black excellence, and questions of compensation (using, of course, more morally sanguine languages of "appropriation"). Further, as other commentators have noted, the extraordinary success of many black creatives and artists further makes traditional approaches to the cultural politics of representation seem incoherent. "Why ask culture workers to uplift and defend the race, in the minds of black folks or others," Paul Taylor thinks some of us might see fit to ask, "when the work of vindication, in aesthetics and in ethics, has already been done?"[129] To borrow from Eddie Glaude, if expressivism was one influential solution to consolidating the black Tower of Babel—the dispersive forms of black cultural, religious, and ethical difference that came streaming into cities during the Great Migration—into some kind of black solidarity and collectivity, we are now living through the return of the repressed in the wake of expressivism's crisis.[130]

If the sketch above is persuasive, then we can fill in the cultural horizon that explains how the stability of romantic narrative came to its crisis of reproduction. The fall of each of these pillars undermines some decisive element of romance: the binary valuation of good and evil; the coherence of claims about unities of race, nation, political vision, or other forms of ethical consensus in the process of becoming; or the notion that victories or reconciliations are without remainder, ignoring the plight of those marginalized or repressed in the civil rights movement itself, or in the romantic triumphalism that followed. To borrow a phrase from Nietzsche, carrying on in the conventions of romantic history has long "had conscience against it."[131]

After this break in tradition, historical inquiries into black political life are faced with the hermeneutic challenge of sifting through the material of history without the intuitive and authoritatively reliable aid of the major pillars of black political life that shaped not only much of the self-understanding of black folks during the civil rights era but also the narrative conventions and intellectual orientations of contemporary historiography, and the determinant judgments of politics. Yet this collapse allows us to rethink what we deem to be significant in the course of our historical reflection: what debates have resonance in light of our interpretations of the present, what keys to our development we might locate in the past—in other words, what appears *meaningful in this new light.*

This emergent, not always self-conscious, awareness of the collapse of meaning, in the hands of historians, has sent a generation backward, into the past, combing through a now-fragmented history for answers to questions that might illuminate the significance of events, ideas, and figures that have been obscured by the conventions of romantic African American historiography. As we shall see, a sense of tragedy is deeply connected to this kind of crisis and collapse. As Raymond Williams writes, "important tragedy seems to occur, neither in periods of real stability, nor in periods of open and decisive conflict. Its most common historical setting is the period preceding the substantial breakdown and transformation of an important culture. Its condition is the real tension between old and new: between received beliefs, embodied in institutions and responses, and newly and vividly experienced contradictions and possibilities."[132]

Indeed, one intimation of a larger tragic vision must already be apparent. The very exemplary acts taken up by past actors, acts that wrenched a kind of freedom from routinized, systemic domination, set in motion a cascading set of affairs which now confront the inheritors of that exemplarity as a kind of "destiny" or "fate" that feels estranging and alien. The sublime, decentering powers of civil rights activism seem to have issued, in light of their solemn fifty- and sixty-year commemorations, forces that could not have been anticipated. Indeed, one might be forgiven for reading the whole drama of post-civil rights history through the prism of the conception of the tragic associated with Friedrich Hölderlin and German idealism, one that dwells on the destruction of one's own particularity in pursuit of freedom and the absolute.[133]

But before turning to face tragedy directly, we must delve more deeply into the world that romance helped make. After all, it is not only participants in black political life or intellectuals whose chief goal is trying to make sense of black political experience who have relied on the romantic narrative or been affected by its disintegration. This narrative has also been partly constitutive of American liberalism and the wider national self-consciousness it helps cultivate. It has even reached into political-philosophical expressions of that liberalism itself.

The civil rights movement has stood as an exemplar for liberal political philosophers, subtly but profoundly orienting their judgment about the problems any political philosophy must address, and the romantic narrative has served as a kind of common sense for the proper answers philosophers might give. Although it has served as this kind of exemplary repository of knowledge, meaning, and normative orientation, its influence has barely been appreciated. In Chapter 6 we therefore shift registers to examine and ultimately criticize the philosophical appropriation of the romantic narrative by the most famous American liberal political philosopher of the twentieth century: John Rawls.

CHAPTER 6

BEYOND SILENCE AND ROMANCE

Rawls, Mills, and the Tasks of Political Philosophy and Critique

INSISTING ON THE SIGNIFICANCE OF exemplarity, narrative, and judgment may seem especially compelling when developing, as in Chapter 4, a critique of political rhetoric or historical discourse that invokes the civil rights movement. The vocabulary of "romance" brings out of concealment a series of mystifications and confusions in liberal politics and mainstream historiography that we can profitably subject to criticism. This has become clearer, and more politically and culturally tractable, in light of the crisis of authority in black political life; a crisis manifest in the eroding pillars of racial realism, church vanguardism, the binary interpretive schema of black political thought's imagined futures as integrationism and nationalism, and the cultural politics of representation.

When matters turn, however, to contemporary political theory and philosophy, we run headlong into a well-developed school of "critical race theory" that suggests that this talk of exemplarity is unlikely to bear fruit. These disciplines, critics warn, have grown barren of reference to matters of race and black political life through unyielding commitments to abstraction and idealization.

This tradition of critical theory, at least as influentially articulated by the late philosopher Charles W. Mills, dovetails powerfully with a set of claims that problems of race, racism, and African American presence in mainstream political philosophy are so marginal that they can be appropriately described in the language of "silence." For Mills and his followers, this judgment of political philosophy's race problem demands a new hermeneutics: an interpretive theory and practice that is capable of distilling evidence from silence and prepares the way for critique and reconstruction. Attempting to establish this methodological demand through a reading of John Rawls, the towering figure of late twentieth-century political theory whose shadow still looms largely over the field, Mills understands Rawls's purported "silences" regarding race as disclosing the pejoratively ideological nature of his method.[1] This sets the stage for the promise of a philosophical project that overcomes "white" liberalism through redemptive antiracist critique.

In place of Rawls's putative silence, Mills argues, we must assert the *real* history of racial oppression and black political resistance and produce a superior *social theory* of race and society. Indeed, the insertion of history and social theory into the alleged abyss of silence does much of the heavy lifting of critique. In self-professed "radical" political theory, Mills argues, "*it is often really the facts that are doing the revisionary work rather than the values.*" "One can mount a challenge to mainstream orthodoxy [in political philosophy]," he proclaims, "simply by contesting the hegemonic but misleading pictures of social reality and by bringing the underlying deep structures of injustice to light."[2] Only in this way, Mills surmises, will we find our way to the epistemologically "firm ground" of history and social theory from which we can stand in a "righteous position."[3]

This position, it would appear, is hostile to both my insistence on the significance of the exemplarity of civil rights history once we move to the domain of political philosophy *and* the importance of excavating and evaluating *narrative* to understand the subtle and subterranean ways that historical imagination and judgment impose on political theory. In this chapter, I take this opposition as an opportunity to clarify the stakes of my approach and to excavate the broad influence of the romantic narrative of civil rights, even where we may least expect it: in political philosophy.

Despite a profound appreciation for Mills's contributions to the critical philosophy of race and Africana philosophy as a vocation, I express skepticism about this pathway as the best avenue for the relationship of black critical theory to political philosophy. My worry about Mills's alternative paradigm is twofold. First, I contend that Mills's efforts in "critical race theory" involve a hermeneutics of suspicion that relies *too heavily* on what he calls the "evidence of silence" to make sweeping judgments about theorists' ideological complicity with racial domination. I do not think that the interpretive strategies and vocabularies developed by his theorizations of "silence" through critical race theory can bear the interpretive weight of his ideology critique of Rawls and the Rawlsian tradition. Developed out of a critique of early Enlightenment thinkers, the burdens that the preoccupation with silence places on his interpretive approach become untenable when dealing with contemporary philosophers like Rawls.

This is not simply because Rawls and his ilk disavow the explicit racism of much eighteenth- and nineteenth-century philosophy but because they also rely on historical accounts of struggles against racial injustice as *exemplary* or *authoritative* in some of their key argumentative and conceptual constructions. Despite its promising intuitions, Mills's approach wrongly trains our critical judgment away from close readings of African American exemplarity in political philosophy, leaving us desensitized to the conceptual, argumentative, and even rhetorical or aesthetic roles that economies of civil rights exemplarity play in contemporary theory and the philosophical discourse of liberalism.

To defend my criticism, I offer a novel reading of Rawls's work inspired by Toni Morrison, and drawing on Rawls's published writings, lecture notes, and unpublished archival material regarding the Vietnam War and the civil rights movement. I argue that in failing to note what Morrison has called the "disrupting darkness before its eyes," Mills's mode of critical theory leaves us saddled with a distracting debate between alleged "absences" and "presences" of race talk.[4] Instead, I contend, we must sharpen the analytical tools necessary for reconstructing and critiquing the romantic narratives and judgments about race and the African American experience condensed and sedimented in the favored examples of political philosophy.

My wager is that what I call Morrisonian critique allows for a more comprehensive analysis and criticism of intertextual economies of exemplarity, providing for a more radical unsettling of the common sense that works across fields and discourses to delimit the range of concepts, anchor the terms of debate, and constrain the imagined relationship between historical and political judgment. This, I hope to show, is clearest in the political philosophy of civil disobedience, a debate utterly transformed and enduringly anchored by the exemplarity of the civil rights movement.

Second, I find that Mills's preoccupation with "silence" and "absence" as the crucial keywords of his critique of liberal political philosophy leads him to be too self-satisfied with his efforts to purge contemporary liberalism of its "ideological" baggage. Instead, building on the discussion of the concepts in Chapter 4, we should deepen Rawls's own prescient worries that his political philosophy might be at its most ideological in its very self-conception of its tasks as requiring the work of *reconciliation* and the *practical search* for consensus. This self-conception, I will show, is deeply consonant with, and perhaps even productive of, romantic history at its most distorting, even as it understands itself as sensitive to certain facts about political life. Ironically, despite being one of Rawls's greatest critics, Mills ends up repeating Rawls's own self-undermining preoccupation with reconciliation and the practical search for consensus. Where critical race theory, as in Mills's work, retains this sense of philosophy's tasks, it tangles itself in knotty contradictions that are self-undermining to its aspirations to reconstruct a liberalism equivalent to the extraordinary challenges before it. It is our unfortunate fate that the question of liberalism's future has own grown more urgent and foreboding since Mills's untimely passing from the world.[5]

Unmasking and Reconstruction

It should not be surprising that Mills pursues his project through a critique of John Rawls. In political philosophy, there is a kind of epic romance around the Baltimore-born author of the 1971 classic *A Theory of Justice*. Over two decades after his death, Rawls and his work are still the object of ceaseless honorifics, and he stands as a symbol of a certain mode of philosophy. Samuel Freeman names Rawls "the most significant and influential political and moral philosopher of the twentieth century." Thomas Pogge celebrates Rawls for bringing forth a "dramatic revival in political philosophy." Thomas Nagel has pronounced Rawls the "greatest political philosopher of the twentieth century."[6] For many, Rawls represents the highest philosophical articulation of liberalism and a reliable guide to the tasks of political philosophy in America or any aspirationally democratic society.[7]

Once only dimly heard amid this celebratory chorus, the outer provinces of professional philosophy have long bubbled with dissent against Rawls's extraordinary influence. Recently taking a place on the front lines of this resistance was Mills, for whom Rawls represented more evasion than insight and more complacency than clarity. The central, most influential theme of Mills's work was an elaborate indictment of professional philosophy and political theory—and its Rawlsian strain in particular—from what might be called the domain of "critical race theory."

Critical race theory is often understood *solely* to refer to the eponymous tradition of scholarship on race and law whose methodological and political dissents from legal academy orthodoxy flourished in the 1980s and 1990s, or, in our era of partisan polarization and speech-suppressing propaganda, as an empty signifier through which to announce one's hostility to scholarship on race.[8] Mills, however, understands the referent of this phrase more expansively. For him, to work within the tradition of "critical race theory" means to draw analytically, normatively, and explanatorily on a "long tradition of oppositional intellectual engagement with the structures of white racial domination"—including the writings of figures like Frederick Douglass, W. E. B. Du Bois, and Ida B. Wells—"which could reasonably be dubbed critical race theory *avant la letter.*" Rightly dismissing the view that this tradition of thinking is somehow parasitic on, or subordinate to, the European tradition of critical theory represented by the Frankfurt school (e.g., Theodor Adorno, Jürgen Habermas, Max Horkheimer, and Herbert Marcuse), Mills proclaims that the "issues we now think of as defining of critical theory's concerns, were brought home to the racially subordinated, the colonized and enslaved, in the most intimate and brutal way: the human alienation, the instrumentalization and deformation of reason in the service of power, the critique of abstract individualism, the paradox of reconciling proclamations of humanism with mass murder, the need to harness normative theory to the practical task of human liberation."[9] Some met this challenge with enduring theoretical contributions, whether Europeans read them or not.

From this standpoint, Mills charges professional, mainstream political philosophy with an indefensible omission in its conceptual canon. He wonders incredulously how white supremacy, the "basic political system that has shaped the world for the past several hundred years," can elude the philosophical attention that its world-historical significance in casualties and causality deserves.[10] Contrasting philosophy negatively to other disciplines in the humanities, Mills complains that part of "what makes philosophy distinctive" is that "the conception of the discipline itself is inimical to the recognition of race." To the extent that philosophers imagine themselves working exclusively or primarily with "necessary, spiritual, eternal [and] ideal truths," scholars working on philosophical approaches to problems of race and racial justice will find themselves at a professional and methodological disadvantage given their subject's location in "the contingent, the corporeal, the temporal, [and] the material."[11]

Even in *political* philosophy, which one might expect to dispense with the conceits of eternity and exhibit more sensitivity to contingency, corporeality, and temporality, Mills argues that the field's dominant strategies of *abstraction* and *idealization* render questions of race and racial justice marginal. In doing so these approaches themselves are obstacles in the path of efficacious theorizing about justice.

Exemplary of this tendency, Mills declares, was John Rawls, who "had next to nothing to say in his work about what has arguably historically been the most blatant American variety of *injustice*, racial oppression." Nor, Mills adds, is the "remediation of the legacy of white supremacy . . . of the slightest [apparent] interest or concern for Rawls and most of his commentators and critics."[12] Recalling his first encounter with Rawls's work during doctoral study at the University of Toronto in the late 1970s, Mills remembers a feeling of "utter disconnection . . . between Rawls's work and [his own] interests, a disconnection so great that it did not even manifest itself in a feeling of disappointment."[13]

After a productive period working within analytical Marxism, Mills turned, with his polemical extended essay *The Racial Contract,* to transform this disconnected indifference into substantive critique, drawing on critical race scholarship to fully articulate the methodological, political, and ethical commitments undergirding his negative intuitions about Rawls and his forebears in the social contract tradition. There, and subsequently, he focused his criticism on the relationships between history, social theory, and political philosophy, the inheritance of social contractarianism, and Rawls's influential distinction between ideal and nonideal theory.[14]

I draw attention to Mills's intellectual trajectory, as well as to his persistent concerns with professional philosophy, to shed light on an important dimension of his work that remains underappreciated despite his late efforts to correct this misperception.[15] His work is, too often, still flattened to the widespread sense of "critical theory" *solely* as "unmasking critique."[16] This is not to deny that, of course, that writings like *The Racial Contract* enact this practice, aspiring to unmask the "universalizing pretensions" of philosophical methods, the white supremacist "*herrenvolk* ethics" of social contract theory, and the "racial-sexual" domination constitutive of modernity.[17] It is simply to underscore Mills's oft-ignored plea that critical race theory should not be consumed *only* by unmasking critique. Pursued in concert with political philosophy, it should serve as an essential step in *reconstructive* philosophy and normative argument. For Mills, in particular, unmasking is a necessary prelude to, and guiding star for, *fulfilling* the potential of liberal political philosophy and the social contract tradition.[18]

We can understand Mills's critical and interpretive construct of the "racial contract," therefore, in three ways: an attempt to elaborate a hermeneutics for a "critical race theory" capable of guiding our readings of canonical philosophers and foundational political documents; an effort to generate a critique of contemporary philosophy (especially liberalism) for its approaches to questions of racial justice; and an exercise in refounding, or reconstructing, new bases for contractarian philosophy by taking seriously the sordid history of racial domination and ideas of black radicalism now considered heretical in their focus on redressing this legacy.[19] Properly understood, therefore, Mills is no anti-Enlightenment polemicist, but as Thomas McCarthy argues, a thinker well within "the tradition of radical Enlightenment critique."[20]

Critical Race Theory, the Hermeneutics of Suspicion, and the Evidence from Silence

To understand Mills's broadsides against Rawls, it is important to situate them amid his initial salvo against the social contract tradition in *The Racial Contract*. There Mills's critique is meant to encompass the broader tradition's touchstones, including Immanuel Kant and John Locke, and the constitutions, charters, and instances of political rhetoric that bear the unmistakable influence of their ideas and figurations. The tradition they represent, at least in its own self-conception, attempts to model and/or instantiate the idea that a legitimate regime's basic political and social institutions are *justifiable* to the rational or reasonable judgment of each of its citizens. "The aim of a contractual justification," Rawls argues in his account of his lineage, "is to show that each member of society has a sufficient reason to agree to that order, to acknowledge it, on the condition that other citizens acknowledge it as well."[21]

There is, however, at least one crucial divide in the social contract tradition. While some versions of social contract theory aim at the task of constructing an account of legitimacy or political obligation by imagining what principles or arrangements people would rationally or reasonably *agree* to in an initial choice situation, other iterations are more focused on critique and subversion. These subversive forms of contract theory aim principally at showing that certain arrangements—slavery, for instance, or tyrannical absolutism—cannot possibly meet with the reasonable assent of all those subjected to them, but survive through a kind of "convention" among the beneficiaries of such domination. Since the inequalities that inhere in these conventions cannot be publicly and generally justified, they persist instead through illusion, ideology, and imposition.

Mills sees himself as following a hybrid mix of these approaches, but his most influential arguments are pitched in the latter register, taking their explicit inspiration from Jean-Jacques Rousseau's 1755 treatise *Discourse on the Origins and Foundations of Inequality Among Mankind* and, more proximately, Carole Pateman's 1988 feminist classic *The Sexual Contract*. In the former, Rousseau famously argues that "moral or political inequality" is best understood as "a kind of convention . . . established, or at least authorized by the consent of men" rather than a reflection of "natural" hierarchy. This convention, however, is authorized and affirmed only by *some* men, those who enjoy "different privileges" of honor, wealth, power, and authority (to "the prejudice of others") and who cement a self-serving hierarchy through illusory and deceptive appeals to the broader polity (e.g., to the mutually beneficiary character of inequality).[22]

Mills's racial contract idea self-consciously follows this formulation, explicating the intertwined histories of racial oppression (e.g., slavery, colonialism, imperialism, Jim Crow) around the globe as a "domination contract."[23] He defines the racial contract as

> that set of formal or informal agreements or meta-agreements (higher-level contracts *about* contracts, which set the limits of the contracts' validity) between the members of one subset of humans, henceforth designated by

> (shifting) "racial'" (phenotypical/genealogical/cultural) criteria C1, C2, C3 . . . as "white," and coextensive (making due allowances for gender differentiation) with the class of full persons, to categorize the remaining subset of humans as "nonwhite" and of a different and inferior moral status, sub-persons, so that they have a subordinate civil standing in the white or white-ruled polities the whites either already inhabit or establish or in transactions as aliens with these polities, and the moral and juridical rules normally regulating the behavior of whites in their dealings with one another either do not apply at all in dealings with nonwhites or apply only in a qualified form (depending in part on changing historical circumstances and what particular variety of nonwhite is involved).[24]

Mills presses his case in favor of both the actual, historical existence of something akin to a "racial contract" and the disclosive power of that contract as a subversive analytical construct through acts of juxtaposition. On one hand, Mills contrasts the liberal, egalitarian pronouncements of social contractarians with "the startling remarks and obscure essays on race that we [philosophers] long tended to pass silently over when discussing the classics of early modern political theory."[25] On the other, he contrasts their voluminous ruminations on liberal ideals with their jarring silence on—and occasional active participation in—slavery, colonialism, and other gross violations of justice against nonwhite people.[26]

Juxtapositions of this sort evoke a hermeneutic dilemma. How should contemporary theorists interpret prima facie contradictions between ostensibly universal defenses of liberal principles and various forms of silence on, accommodations to, defenses of, and even participation in transgressions of those principles when applied to nonwhite racial groups?[27] Mills's approach, familiar to scholars of critical race, postcolonial, and feminist theory, is to reconstruct the apparent paradoxes as more consistent than they appear.[28]

This is the critical strategy systematized with "the racial contract" device. Mills argues that these canonical philosophers are committed to theories of ethnoracial (and gender) hierarchy (racial contracts) that *qualify* the conceptual and normative boundaries of their abstract theories and eliminate the illusory "inconsistency" of racial hierarchy. There is, in other words, a racial anthropology involved that imagines a hierarchical distribution of the requisite traits or characteristics (e.g., cognitive, affective, cultural, or aesthetic) for inclusion and equal standing in the polity. Even the egalitarian liberal social contract can therefore be said to be subordinate to a *prior* contract that not only *excludes* nonwhite people as parties to the egalitarian agreement but also *subjects* them to forms of exploitation and domination by white contractors.[29]

Refreshingly forthright, on Mills's account, was the US Supreme Court in *Dred Scott v. Sandford* (1857), whose ruling opinion by Chief Justice Roger B. Taney reads,

> It is true, every person, and every class and description of persons, who were at the time of the adoption of the Constitution recognized as citizens in the several States, became also citizens of this new political body; but none other; it was formed by them, and for them and their posterity, but for no one else . . . the legislation and histories of the times, and the language used in the Declaration of Independence, show, that *neither the class of persons who had been imported as slaves, nor their descendants, whether they had become free or not, were then acknowledged as a part of the people, nor intended to be included in the general words used in that memorable instrument*. . . . They had for more than a century before been regarded as beings of an inferior order, and altogether unfit to associate with the white race, either in social or political relations; and so far inferior, that they had *no rights which the white man was bound to respect*. . . . This opinion was at that time fixed and universal in the civilized portion of the white race. It was regarded as an *axiom in morals as well as in politics, which no one thought of disputing*, or supposed to be open to dispute.[30]

Given that the classical theorists of the social contract are rarely as explicit, Mills hopes to seal the judgment of their complicity with racial domination through a combination of three alternative forms of evidence. The first is textual proof of their endorsement of forms of racial hierarchy, often in noncanonical writings like Kant's lectures in anthropology. The second is an interpretive account of how these inferiorizing accounts of racial difference might logically inflect their core normative or evaluative concepts (e.g., *person, civilized,* or *rational*). The last is whether the thinker has evidence of commitments (even nascent ones) to racial redress that could be recruited sympathetically to rebut to this otherwise damning evidence.

The importance of this last consideration, an inference from silence, for Mills's critical race theory demands closer scrutiny. For example, Mills argues that Kant's forays into physical anthropology, in which he developed a systematic theory of race and hierarchically ascribed various capacities for intelligence, initiative, and moral education to different races, are compelling evidence that Kantian ethics (at least in Kant's own formulation) must be perniciously qualified by race. This follows from these hierarchically distributed capacities' critical role in Kant's substantive understanding of "personhood."[31] Bolstering this reading, at least for Mills, is Kant's alleged "silence" concerning the injustice of New World chattel slavery and too-narrow objections to the violent abuses and forms of racialized domination unleashed by colonialism. In light of the allegation of silence, Mills confidently infers that these injustices must not have greatly unsettled Kant or registered as especially "unjust." This silence, therefore, is an important piece of evidence that Kant's vaunted "universalism" was, in fact, a herrenvolk ethics and politics—inclusive and egalitarian for the "master race but tyrannical for subordinate groups."[32]

Mills's views have argumentative force because the textual evidence, to a significant degree, underscores the interpretive problem he identifies. Kant is not only the voluminous moral philosopher of the Enlightenment but also its most systematic theorist of racial hierarchy; Locke's robust conception of natural right and natural law sits glaringly alongside his deep financial and political involvement with the owners of enslaved human beings in the Carolina colony.[33] Yet, as noted above, Mills's hermeneutics of suspicion does not stop at textual or biographical exegesis. He also asks us to consider the evidence of things not said—the deafening silence of these theorists on contemporaneous issues of racial justice and equality.[34]

The invocation of *silence* is not an idiosyncratic metaphor but a popular keyword in the myriad discourses of critical theory.[35] This approach to silence is often, as in Mills's case, rooted in hermeneutics of suspicion whose interpretations assume the social world humans have created, is "riven . . . with hypocrisy and concealment" and needs to be unmasked by a "critique of the contents of consciousness"—a critique rooted in a naturalistic and often unflattering account of the social causes of these modes of consciousness and patterns of thinking.[36] For Mills, silence regarding a significant form of injustice or social antagonism is a generative entry point into these forms of hypocrisy and concealment, and we can trace the relevant causes of this silence (and the underlying concealment) back to group-based experiences and biases structured by positions in a hierarchical and unjust social order.[37]

In his interpretations of seventeenth-, eighteenth-, and nineteenth-century political philosophy, however, silence plays only the scale-tipping role. It weights already well-nourished suspicions, for we have explicitly racialist or racist speculations (or unjust practices) at our disposal. Read alongside these utterances, the absence of pronouncements against slavery, racial injustice, and colonialism in the midst of monographs on liberty, justice, and equality accrue an odious air of hypocrisy and complicity. In *The Racial Contract,* Mills expounds on this "evidence of silence":

> Where is [Hugo] Grotius's magisterial *On Natural Law and the Wrongness of the Conquest of the Indies,* Locke's stirring *Letter Concerning the Treatment of the Indians,* Kant's moving *On the Personhood of Negroes,* [James] Mill's famous condemnatory *Implications of Utilitarianism for English Colonialism,* Karl Marx and Frederick Engels's outraged *Political Economy of Slavery?* Intellectuals write about what interests them, what

> they find important, and—especially if the writer is prolific—silence constitutes good prima facie evidence that the subject was not of particular interest. By their failure to denounce the great crimes inseparable from the European conquest, or by the half-heartedness of their condemnation, or by their actual endorsement of it in some cases, most of the leading European ethical theorists reveal their complicity in the Racial Contract.[38]

A key challenge for Mills's hermeneutics of silence and suspicion, however, is that it must bridge what appears, prima facie, to be a fundamental fracturing of the tradition of political philosophy. In the course of the historical development of the social contract tradition, there is a break between its early modern proponents and more contemporary contractarians, specifically over whether to treat the social contract as an impressionistically true, quasi-historical, anthropological account based on inferiorizing understandings of the social life of non-European peoples, or, as in John Rawls's work, on an explicitly hypothetical device of representation meant to model and generate normative judgments about human capacities and cooperation.[39]

The reasons for this break, moreover, are directly relevant to Mills's concern with racial equality. They reflect a growing unease over time with the racialized and hierarchical character of early modern political philosophy, contractarianism, and its relationship to colonial and imperial endeavor. This suggests a responsiveness to historical changes and events, including the civil rights movement and decolonization.

Contemporary contract theorists, contrary to their popular classical forebears, explicitly embrace principles of racial equality and antidiscrimination. Rawls states unequivocally in *A Theory of Justice* that "there is no race or recognized group of human beings that lack" his two attributes of moral personhood: the capacity to have a conception of the good and the ability to develop a sense of justice.[40] In his very first published paper, from 1951, Rawls criticized as pejoratively ideological any attempt to "claim a monopoly of the knowledge of truth and justice for some particular race, or social class, or institutional group" or to define competence "in terms of racial and/or sociological characteristics which have no known connection with coming to know." This is no aside; it is explicitly asserted early in the course of designing a decision procedure capable of generating viable ethical principles and judgments and treated as *exemplary* of what a procedure should produce.[41]

Moreover, Rawls's mature theory of justice emerges from a modification of this early decision procedure into his "reflective equilibrium" method, where we attempt to align our moral and political theorizing with what he calls our "considered judgments" or "considered convictions of justice." These considered judgments, although capable of revision, are core moral judgments "which we now make intuitively and *in which we have the greatest confidence* . . . questions which we feel sure must be answered *in a certain way*."[42] The two judgments of this sort, which Rawls mentions so succinctly as to convey their self-evidence, are judgments that religious intolerance and racial discrimination are wrong.

Given this evidence of overt and direct concern with racial injustice—indeed, its location among the most basic axioms of Rawls's moral and political philosophy—we might wonder why Mills still holds Rawls guilty of the basic errors he attributes to the former's forebears writing at the formative stage of European colonialism. One might reasonably question why it makes sense to classify Rawls's relationship to race and racial justice as one of silence, especially in light of what he *does* say and when compared to racial discourses of the seventeenth century.[43] Yet it is clear that, for Mills, this textual evidence alone is insufficient. Surprisingly, when explicitly racist or hierarchically racialist views are removed from the equation, the calculus of suspicion shifts ever more dramatically to the evidence of silence. Contemporary philosophy, especially in its Rawlsian form, is charged with "a silence not of tacit inclusion but rather of *exclusion* . . . the black experience is not subsumed under [its] philosophical abstractions, despite their putative generality."[44]

That Mills would turn to the evidence from silence should not be surprising given his allegiance and indebtedness to critical race theory. A key inflection point in the history of "Critical Race Theory" as a self-conscious scholarly movement, at least in the legal academy, was the 1987 Conference on Critical Legal Studies in Los Angeles, whose organizing theme was "The Sounds of Silence: Racism and the Law," a frame that Kimberlé describes as "highlight[ing] the institutional and discursive mechanisms that policed the boundaries of racial discourse both within [critical legal studies] and within the legal academy more broadly."[45] Cornel West, a fellow conference participant, likewise described a crucial contribution of critical race theory in law to be a confrontation with "the relative *silence* of legal radicals . . . who 'deconstructed' liberalism, yet seldom addressed the role of deep-seated racism in American life."[46]

Taking up this keyword and tradition in his essay "Rawls on Race/Race in Rawls," Mills undertakes a review of the textual record of Rawls's five major books and some of the landmark volumes of the secondary literature, searching for references to race, racism, racial discrimination, racial injustice, slavery, civil rights, settler colonialism, genocide, and corrective justice (reparations, affirmative action, etc.). Concluding his review in a section titled, as one might expect, "Rawls's Silences," Mills argues that the paucity of more extended remarks than the judgments referenced above show that "race, racism, and racial oppression are marginal to

Rawls's thought," and "merely consulting the indexes of these five books would be enough to establish this truth."[47] More than forty years after the publication of *A Theory of Justice,* Mills contends, the fact that "there has not been more debate on the flagrant absence of racial justice as a theme in this literature" raises the question of this paradigm's "possible intrinsic 'whiteness'" and the philosophical adequacy of the Rawlsian apparatus for theorizing racial justice.[48] On balance, the silence, or more specifically, the lack of extended discussions of issues of racial justice by Rawls and his followers, is enough to animate a level of hermeneutical suspicion that reaches down to the very conceptual bases of Rawlsian liberalism and raises the question of capability rather than will, and methodology more than sincerity.

Beyond Silence: Rethinking Rawls and Race

With this concept of silence animating his hermeneutic suspicion, Mills goes on to argue that his allegation discloses (or one might say strongly redescribes) the "tendentious conceptual commissions" of what Rawls *does* say. Focus on silence is said to unmask how, in the course of elaborating a political philosophy, Rawls remains beset by "prescriptive albinism . . . complemented by a similarly bleached-out faulty picture and corresponding descriptive/explanatory conceptual framework."[49]

Mills's strong reading of Rawls's alleged silence relies on three claims. First, he argues that Rawls's commitment to "ideal theory" leads him to marginalize race and racism as questions of justice. Especially vexing for Mills is Rawls's "fundamental concept" of a well-ordered society as a cooperative venture for mutual advantage among free and equal citizens.[50] This abstraction and normative idealization, Mills argues, turns dramatically away from the real-world existence of racial identity, racial inequality, and racial domination to distill attractive ethical and political ideals. Yet, this process of abstraction and idealization—even in service of normative theory—is self-undermining on Mills's view. It saddles Rawls's theory of justice with historically inaccurate, sociologically naive, and ontologically deficient presuppositions that make it ill suited to respond to existing forms of group domination. Theorizing from these kinds of idealized assumptions rather than social facts, warns Mills, short-circuits pressing theories of corrective justice that cannot take egalitarian standing or freedom as a given and may need to order principles of justice in a radically different, nonideal fashion.[51]

Second, Mills claims that Rawls's sense of the relationship between ideal and nonideal theory is not sufficiently action-guiding. Its silence on existing injustices, which it does not appropriately theorize, may lead us away from the sorts of remedies that these issues so urgently demand. Addressing injustice practically requires us to bring back into political theorizing the very forms of group identity and group domination, for instance, that are supposedly excluded from our thought experiments by the premises of ideal theory.

Third, and finally, Mills goes on to claim that the "postwar struggle for racial justice in practice and in theory"—a category dominated by the civil rights movement—"and the Rawlsian corpus on justice are almost completely separate and non-intersecting universes."[52] The concern here is yet another suspicion engendered by "silence." Mills advances a version of the familiar argument of critical theorists that social movements must be sites of engagement or reference points for theories of justice, if theorists' claims, actions, and interpretations are to have their fullest "emancipatory potential."[53] A failure to engage with social movements on this view makes political theory untenably reliant on interpretations of need (or other concepts) distorted by ideology and domination, thoughtlessly buttressed by habit, or too circumscribed by a narrow conversation of interlocutors.

The debate that Mills intensified over Rawls and race leads to a methodological dilemma at the intersection of critical race theory and political philosophy. The first pillar of this dilemma is interpretive: How, if at all, does Rawls think about racial injustice—particularly injustices like ghetto poverty, rather than overtly discriminatory policies like segregation or black chattel slavery? The second is evaluative and methodological: Do Rawlsian commitments to ideal theorizing and social contractarianism function *ideologically?* Do they *legitimize* or *mystify* racial injustice? Do they undermine or distract from important forms of political action necessary to fight racial injustice?

This debate, unfortunately, has focused thus far on Rawls's published work in ideal theory and contented itself with making inferences regarding its possible relation to nonideal theorizing on racial injustice. It almost entirely ignores, for example, Rawls's published and unpublished writing on questions of real-world injustices like the race and class biases of US military conscription during the Vietnam War, or Rawls's extended reflections on the political ethics and purposes of civil disobedience. This is a major interpretive mistake with important interpretive, analytical, and evaluative consequences.

Using Morrisonian critical theory, I will show that Mills's view that Rawls was silent on racial injustice or social movements against racial injustice is no longer sustainable in light of new archival evidence. The claim, central to Mills's case, that Rawls's theory is incapable of accommodating notions like racial exploitation must also be abandoned. Indeed, the archive reveals that Rawls himself developed lines of argument in his discussions of the racially unjust burdens of conscription that would eventually become central to the defense of Rawlsianism that Tommie Shelby offers in his accounts of the structural injustice of ghetto poverty and various forms of legitimate resistance to its violations.[54]

Dispensing with the charge of silence, I then turn to a more complex dimension of Mills's objection to Rawls: that the latter's conception of the relationship between ideal and nonideal theory is insufficiently action-guiding or "fact sensitive" because of its ideological commitment to practices of abstraction and idealization. Here I enter into another of Rawls's explicit engagements with race and political action—his invocation of the exemplarity of Rev. Dr. Martin Luther King Jr. for his theory of civil disobedience—in order to recover the ways that Rawls saw the problem of stability as central to the mediation between ideal and nonideal theory. Contra Mills, I argue that Rawls was deeply influenced by the civil rights movement, and his historical understanding of its trajectory operates as the formative background not only for his reflections on civil disobedience and public reason but also for significant pieces of his theoretical overture as a whole. For Rawls, part of the attractiveness of the civil rights movement and its practice of civil disobedience was that these examples seemed to play a helpful role in resolving one of the key challenges of "fact sensitivity" or realism that he put even at the heart of his *ideal* theorizing—namely, that any depiction of an ideally just order must give an account of how it would achieve not simply stability over time but *stability for the right reasons*. The stability problem played a key role in Rawls's attempt to establish the practical faith he thought political philosophy ought to sustain in the face of both nihilistic challenges and the pressures that the burdens of judgment place on our ability to sustain social and political cooperation.

A significant difficulty with Mills's approach is that in posing the problem as one of silence versus voice or presence versus absence, his hermeneutic lens does not reveal the altogether more pernicious problem of the ways in which the exemplarity of African American freedom struggles are already circulating through liberal political philosophy and conscripted into such meaningful roles. The demonstration of a constitutional order riven by pluralism and injustice not only to agree on principles of justice but also to *correct itself* and *endure* when it falls short of those aspirations is a vital task for Rawlsian political theory. From this vantage point, the *romantic* narrative of the civil rights movement presents itself as an exemplary rejoinder to this problem. In its portrayal as a "refocusing" moment that breaks with the civic and legal order only to overcome and reconcile its fractures, the civil rights movement is thought to display a beautiful symmetry of ends and means in service of overlapping consensus, an idea pioneered in Rawls's discussion of civil disobedience. The narrative resonance of civil rights romance with Rawlsian liberalism's other commitments reveals an important orientational *phronesis* to Rawls's liberalism, one that not only elicits or seeks such stories for affirmation but also disciplines political action and educates our judgment of its repertoires based on a misleading picture of Martin Luther King, civil rights protest, and the constitutive dilemmas of the movement.

I take this recovery of the African American presence and civil rights exemplarity in Rawls's work, especially in its mediation of ideal and nonideal theory, its wrestling with the problem of stability, and its forthright confrontation with the burdens of judgment to lead to a final set of considerations. The suggestion I want to conclude with is that instead of the recent concern with "ideal theory as ideology" or idealization versus fact sensitivity, we might instead follow Rawls's own anxieties about the threat of ideology hiding amid these conceptions of the tasks of philosophy. Rawls warned that the philosopher's self-conception of their role as involving calming our "frustration and rage against our society and its history" by reconciling us to the alleged "rational" core of our basic institutions and practices was especially dangerous, but one might also add to this Rawls's insistence on the "practical" task of excavating the alleged deep consensus of our (singular) public political culture or providing "orientation" based on judgments about what kind of society or political roles we find ourselves inhabiting.

Put sharply, these raise the persistent threat of the philosopher displacing conflict and dissensus over injustice through narratively laden concepts, question-begging descriptions, and historical romanticism. The consequence, in such cases, can be a kind of deep *misorientation* or "reconciliation as ideology" that undermines the utopian aspirations of political philosophy by obscuring the need to *sharpen* dissensus and transform the broader categories of our self-description and self-conception at critical moments like the struggle against Jim Crow, American participation in the Vietnam War, or our own moment of profound disorientation. This longing for consensus, nourished by romantic history, obscures the action-guiding insights that reflecting on King and civil disobedience might provide in the present.

The upshot of this argument is a critique not only of Rawls but also of Mills's *constructive* project. This puts Mills's intuitions that Rawls is too wedded to theorizing injustice as a simple "deviation" from a mostly just social order on far more solid interpretive and analytical footing. Yet it also explains why Mills's attempt to restore the action-guiding character of political philosophy, reorient our self-descriptions, and reconstruct

Rawls's original position by adding back in knowledge about racial domination is insufficient. If Rawls's mistake is to think one can secure meaningful, politically tractable consensus *and* provide a compelling account of stability through an appeal to abstract principle, Mills paradoxically repeats this mistake from the other direction, hoping that loading the original position thought experiment with "facts" will compel a similar agreement. As I have argued throughout, this expectation misunderstands not only the narrative character of historical facts but also how judgment mediates between particular facts and general principles. It is the practical activity of judgment that must orient and guide the application and generation of rules, norms, self-descriptions, and ideals. This elision is apparent not only in Mills's attempt to produce a racially conscious original position, but also in the broader, Rawls-inspired preoccupation with the *legitimacy* of civil disobedience rather than the deeper ethico-aesthetic problems that the practice raises for politics and philosophy.

Reading Race/Reading Rawls: Conscription and the Color Line

In December 1966 John Rawls challenged his colleagues in Harvard University's Faculty of Arts and Sciences with a moral and political imperative.[55] Against the backdrop of a raging war in Vietnam and the burgeoning antiwar movement on campus, Rawls called for an official denunciation of the US military's 2-S system of draft deferments for university students.[56] His appeal was neither abstract nor idealized but responsive to moral urgency and a surging social movement.

Despite the clarity and rigor of his argument, however, the resolution was defeated.[57] It is often relegated to a biographical footnote, and scholars have remarked on the motion's congruence with Rawls's larger defense of liberal egalitarianism and justice as fairness. Expecting "silence," however, scholars have ignored the range of *racial* considerations that influenced Rawls's considered position on the injustice of US conscription in the 1960s.[58] Nor have they connected these arguments to the contemporary debate over Rawlsian theory and race.

For Rawls, the Vietnam War–era draft entailed profound injustice. In his famous view, a just society is guided by two principles. The first prioritizes the protection of basic liberties, which cannot be limited or restricted for the sake of economic efficiency or some perfectionist ideal of the good. The second guarantees fair equality of opportunity and a distribution of social and economic benefits and burdens that must be justifiable and to the greatest advantage of the least well off ("the difference principle").[59]

The draft contravened these by disproportionately conscripting working-class citizens and sparing the affluent.[60] The "most overtly class-biased feature of the Vietnam era draft," as the historian Chris Appy notes, was the 2-S student deferment. It allowed full-time university students to defer draft eligibility indefinitely—a privilege largely inaccessible to poor and working-class men.[61] Leaders in the Selective Service defended the policy, at least in government circles, as performing the essential work of "channeling" youth toward professions "essential to the national interest" (especially science, engineering, and teaching) during the Cold War.[62]

Rawls condemned this tendency and its justification in an "explanatory note" attached to his 1966 motion and reprinted verbatim years later in *A Theory of Justice*. "Conscription," it reads, "is a drastic interference with the basic liberties of a free society and cannot be justified by any needs less compelling than those of national security."[63] Further, while any "burden of this magnitude," Rawls argues, must be "borne equally," 2-S deferments granted exemptions for "weak reasons of social interest." This permitted the "hardships and risks of compulsory military service [to] fall disproportionately on the poor, the less intelligent, and the less well educated."[64]

For critics like Malcolm X or the activists of the Student Nonviolent Coordinating Committee (SNCC), there was also a specifically *racial* injustice to the draft, inherent in African Americans bearing the disproportionate burdens of conscription while being refused basic political and personal liberties.[65] Martin Luther King decried this "arrogance" of American policymakers in "professing to be concerned about the freedom of foreign nations while not setting our own house in order." America was "willing to make the Negro one hundred percent of a citizen in warfare, but reduce him to fifty percent of a citizen on American soil," he observed in 1967.[66]

As King correctly noted, the early years of the Vietnam conflict (1965–1967) saw the proportion of black casualties far outstrip the proportion of black people in the US population.[67] Due to intramilitary racial discrimination, lower qualifying test scores, and financial pressures to seek out higher-paying combat roles, black soldiers were more likely to get assigned to high-casualty units. Surveying such statistics, King could only see a "cruel manipulation of the poor," and especially the *black* poor.[68]

While Mills claimed that post–World War II racial justice struggles and Rawls's thought are "almost completely and non-intersecting universes," the archive reveals that Rawls was acutely attuned to such criticisms. They are apparent in documents from 1966 and 1967 written during the high point of his antiwar activism, including statements from faculty study groups on the draft, lectures to student antiwar groups, responses to potential questions concerning the motion, and correspondence with faculty about drafts of the resolution he brought before his fellow faculty members.[69] He argued that the draft both *exposed* "background" structural racial injustice within the broader society and *violated* standards of fair cooperation that African Americans deserved.[70]

The 2-S deferments, Rawls insisted, were the entitlement of the educated and were further evidence of the "degree to which a person's social status, determines . . . the extent to which that person is simply precluded from many opportunities" and can only "exert a disproportionately weak influence on the government." "Generally," Rawls noted, "it is the Negro American and the other minority groups that are represented among the underprivileged and hence excluded from higher education."[71]

An ironic consequence of conscription was that it pulled back the veil of de facto segregation to reveal, in standardized and empirical data, the depth of deprivation among the nation's poor, and African Americans in particular. Suffering from highly concentrated, intergenerational poverty and discrimination across a range of domains, black Americans were vastly overrepresented among those who failed the military's qualification test.[72] Yet this raised a conundrum for critics of the draft's supposed racial injustice. How could a draft *unfairly* burden black Americans if the group failed the qualifying test in such disproportion? Some commentators even dismissed popular charges of racial injustice by pointing out that while black men were a disproportionately large percentage of the armed forces in the war's early years, their number of enlistees and casualties eventually leveled out toward the overall black proportion of the population.[73]

For Rawls, however, these numbers represented only "superficial equality." In a 1966 document preparing for such objections, Rawls dissolves the statistical and moral dilemmas elegantly:

> It happens that if we take all black people, that the chance of a black man entering the army is the same as that of a white man. (Or let's suppose.) Does it follow that the draft does not fall disproportionately on the poor and less well educated? No—since the relevant class is that of those who pass the tests of capacity for military service. The chances should be equal over this class (cet. par.). To see this, we could imagine a society in which every black man is drafted while only one of ten white men is. But since for reasons of poverty, etc., only one in ten blacks pass the test, while for reasons of affluence every white man passes, the risks over the whole society would be equal. Yet we would not suppose this scheme just. Two injustices—one in the draft and another in background sociological conditions—combine to give a superficial equality. It is clear that this equality is the upshot of a *double injustice:* the one keeping black people below the line of passing the tests, the other taking a larger proportion of those who manage to struggle above it (than of whites).[74]

In other words, the advent of the Vietnam draft might be said to establish racial injustice in two respects. First, it *discloses,* through widespread black failure on the qualifying tests, that what Rawls calls the "basic structure" of society is unjust. Rawls's idea of a basic structure captures how "the main political and social institutions of society"—the constitutional order, government departments, law, economy, family structure, educational system, and the like—"fit together into one system of social cooperation, and the way they assign basic rights and duties and regulate the division of advantages from social cooperation over time."[75] The basic structure can be unjust by not realizing (even approximately) a principle of fair equality of opportunity, which demands that we prevent excessive wealth and property hoarding and maintain equal educational opportunity.

Rawls's reference in his unpublished papers to "background sociological conditions" that are unjustly "keeping black people below the line of passing the tests," therefore, is easily fleshed out by the history of racial wealth inequality in the United States as well as long-standing violations of basic liberty and equal opportunity, especially in education.[76] In one memo, Rawls lays out what he calls "the social injustice" argument against deferments, noting that it is "the Negro American and the other minority groups that are represented disproportionately among the underprivileged and hence are precluded from higher education," contrasting these men's backgrounds with those of "members of the privileged classes" who "regardless of intellectual merit, have undeserved access to a college education."[77] For Rawls, this, too, is an injustice: "resources for education are not to be allotted solely or necessarily mainly according to their return as estimated in productive trained abilities, but also according to their worth in enriching the personal and social lives of citizens, including here the least favored."[78]

Second, Rawls also charged the draft with the commission of racial injustice for permitting a large proportion of white men to take *unfair advantage* of these background injustices. Instead of sharing the burdens of military service equally, deferments and exemptions allowed white upper-class and elite youth a mechanism to exit the pool of eligible conscripts, leaving behind (among others) those black Americans who did manage to overcome adversity and score adequately enough on the qualifying test to receive the disproportionate burden of conscription.

When the kind of vital interests threatened by conscription are at stake, Rawls argued, there is a strong presumption in favor of *all* sharing the burdens equally, in a way that reflects the controlling idea of society as a fair system of social cooperation among equals over time. Stability and legitimacy are threatened without the mutual assurance that others will live up to their sense of justice and mutual obligation. This principle cannot, moreover, be overridden by considerations of efficiency, productivity, or perfectionist ideals (e.g., artistic achievement). Rawls mocked what he called the 2-S deferments' "ludicrous" presumption that it is in "the national interest, in any material sense, that students in philosophy (as well as many other subjects) should be deferred while the poor and the racially discriminated against are compelled to bear the burdens of military service."[79] A just democratic society, he argued, would maintain a well-compensated volunteer army with provisions for universal conscription of young men (e.g., eighteen-year-olds) or, less optimally, a universal draft lottery in times of emergency.[80]

Reading Race/Reading Rawls: Racial Exploitation

According to Rawls, the deferment structure of the draft granted the beneficiaries of morally arbitrary talent distributions (e.g., intelligence, motivation) and morally objectionable resource allotments (e.g., the benefits of overlapping racial and class hierarchy) an *institutionalized* pathway to free ride on the contributions of the less advantaged. Insofar as this free riding is possible because of background conditions of injustice (i.e., historical wrongs, democratic disempowerment, and contemporary discrimination), it is *racially exploitative* in the sense that Mills defends as vital to theorizing racial injustice. The free riding, and the institutional arrangement that facilitates it, take systematic and unfair advantage of vulnerabilities and superior power engendered by both past and present racial injustices to enrich (in resources like security, free time, money, education, health, etc.) a favored racial group, at the expense of fulfilling duties of fairness or beneficence to the disadvantaged (or dominated) group.[81]

Thus, while Mills criticizes Rawls for failing to generate a concept of "racial exploitation," Rawls's account of racial injustice in the Vietnam era actually captures many of Mills's demands for the idea, including a demonstration of how "the relations of race play a role in the nature and degree of . . . exploitation itself," conceived here as "unjust enrichment." In what Mills calls "secondary" racial exploitation, nominal civic equality and the official disavowal of hierarchical race ideologies sit alongside practices of unjust enrichment made possible by subordinate groups' inheritance of "a disadvantaged material position that handicaps them . . . in the bargaining process or the competition in question."[82] This is, it seems, central to Rawls's critique of the Vietnam draft.

Further, as befitting Mills's aspiration for accounts of racial exploitation and white supremacy, Rawls's critique of the racial injustice of the draft strives for *systematicity* and *coherence*. In other words, it links a specific institutionally embedded unjust racial benefit (e.g., the draft exemption) with a broader account of the racial (and social) injustice of the broader social order. In doing so it does not rely on malice or discriminatory intent to characterize injustice. Nor does it rely only on an account of black disadvantage. Instead it foregrounds illicit white *advantages*. This complex, interlocking picture gives a clearer sense of what is *objectionable* about such practices. Insofar as contemporary white people born well into the development of a society founded on white supremacy are "benefited by this history" of structural injustice and accrue "a competitive advantage that is not the result of superior innate ability and effort," we are confronting a problem of racial exploitation in Mills's sense.[83]

It is important to note, against one of Mills's other concerns, that Rawls is not simply reducing racial injustice to class exploitation or injustice. Rawls does object to working-class or poor white people's exploitation by the draft, but remains attuned to idiosyncrasies produced by an unjust racial order. As Rawls notes (in a point confirmed by later comprehensive empirical study), while white college students were far less likely than other white people to be conscripted, the black people *most* exploited by the draft itself were working-class men with high school education, and *not* the most abjectly poor who often failed the early Vietnam-era qualifying tests before the standards were relaxed.[84] Whereas the compressed class differentiation of the black population in this era led many commentators to collapse poverty and blackness into each other (a habit many academics still seem unable to kick), keeping these categories conceptually distinct allows the social critic to ask where past injustice or racial discrimination might contribute to an unfair distribution of burdens and benefits for black people who, nevertheless, are not "poor" on a purely income-based distribution analysis.[85] Rawls's account shows deftness with this important distinction that Mills's criticism in no way prepares their mutual readers to encounter.

Even if Mills grants this reading, it might be objected that the case of conscription is too narrow to be generally illuminating about the problem of racial exploitation. Conscription involves severe government coercion (e.g., fines, imprisonment, etc.) and social stigma (especially in job markets). Notably, however, Rawls also objects to *volunteer* (as well as "professional and market") military recruitment against conditions of background injustice for similar reasons. He writes that "if our institutions are unjust, and a volunteer army is set-up as an escape for severely deprived groups, particularly black people, then I have certain worries about it." In one of his few explicit gestures toward "transitional" justice Rawls goes so far as to insist that any advocacy of a volunteer army and a fair draft in times of emergency (his ideal military situation) *must* be accompanied by a "press for measures which give greater social justice to black people."[86] Together these claims gesture toward the argument that the political community (as the authorizing agent of military formation) would be guilty of taking unfair advantage of historical ills and discrimination through market mechanisms, rather than fulfilling its duty to ameliorate the social injustices that burden black people qua black people. Further, it is not clear if Rawls is indeed suspicious of a professional military that recruits with monetary and status incentives against a background of racial injustice—why he would not extend that same critical stance toward other market incentives in the private sector, at least when they are plausibly characterized as *coercive.*[87]

A more prominent objection in Rawls's era was that the draft could not be racially exploitative because the ostensible "victims" actually *benefited* from conscription.[88] While circulating his memo to colleagues to solicit support for the 2-S deferment resolution, Rawls received a (hitherto unknown) critical response from the neoconservative political scientist Edward J. Banfield, one of the central figures in the late twentieth-century ascendancy of "cultural" explanations of urban poverty, crime, and deviance.[89] For Banfield, who cited Daniel Patrick Moynihan's 1966 Carnegie Foundation report *Toward Equality as a Fact and as a Result,* Rawls's racial justice objections were misguided: If African Americans were "injured" by the draft process, it was arguably because they were underdrafted.[90]

There Moynihan built on his prior reports, *One-Third of a Nation* (1964) and the more infamous *The Negro Family* (1965), which both lamented that military admission standards were too high. Increasing black participation in the military would, in his view, provide a decisive boost to racial equality and black flourishing by reducing intractable black unemployment, providing opportunities for human and cultural capital acquisition, and introducing black people to one of the only institutions where they might discover interracial relations of equal recognition. Further, Moynihan surmised, conscription could "correct," through military discipline, many of the forms of psychopathology, low self-esteem, and deviance he thought were the fate of most men growing up in "disorganized and matrifocal" black families.[91] In 1966 this vision found its way into policy when Secretary of Defense Robert McNamara launched Project 100,000, which dramatically lowered the standards of admission for the military and recruited over three hundred thousand formerly ineligible men, disproportionately poor and African American.[92]

Unsurprisingly, many of the objections to Project 100,000 have been consequentialist, disputing that it benefited participants as Banfield and Moynihan expected.[93] Rawls, however, took a different tack in a revised draft version of his "A Proposal for a Military Recruitment Policy," arguing,

> We appreciate the desire on the part of many to use conscription as an agency of social justice. Given the glaring inequities of our society and the sluggishness of the movement for change, it is tempting to use the military for social ends. It may offer to some a mode of life without racial discrimination; to others it may offer an opportunity to acquire valuable skills. It is possible that there are many desirable side-effects. But we do not attempt to weight these against the many undesirable consequences. *We feel that these considerations are irrelevant in view of the kind of justification required for compulsory service. Moreover, to maintain that these injustices are so great and the other institutions of our polity are in such a state of disarray that we must call upon the military to remedy our condition is tantamount to a confession of a social disorder so profound that were we to accept this confession as true, we should have to raise the question whether such a society has the right to conscript its citizens at all.*[94]

The argument is powerful and unforgiving. Rawls suggests that even if we concede the arguments for military conscription as an engine of social equality, such claims are either beside the point or self-undermining. Coercive ("compulsory") interventions backed by the state that interfere with the most central aspects of our basic liberties cannot be legitimate unless they strengthen "the total system of liberty shared by all" and are "acceptable to those citizens with the lesser liberty."[95] This priority rule prohibits "exchanges ('trade-offs,' as economists say) between the basic rights and liberties covered by the first principle and the social and economic advantages regulated by the difference principle."[96] This presumption in favor of the basic liberties is meant to apply in nonideal cases as well.[97] Thus, Rawls ruled out coercive, paternalistic interventions like conscription meant to reform the human capital deficits of disadvantaged African Americans for their own "good."[98]

Banfield and Moynihan suggested that since liberal reforms to improve the basic structure were not forthcoming, and that recognition as "free and equal" citizens was not likely to be extended without deviant black people undergoing profound cultural transformation, the state could impose these kinds of burdens on the least advantaged for their own benefit (and for the future benefit of a more cooperative society). *If* this "realist" pessimism about the prospects for racial justice is true, however, Rawls argues that our affluent social order is so extraordinarily unfair that not only would such arguments fail to ground a justification for the state's coercive powers, but they would raise appropriate skepticism that the state itself is *illegitimate.* A state this severely illegitimate would perhaps not have the standing to reasonably expect compliance with, or rightfully enforce, normative claims on civic duty like conscription at all.[99]

This question of legitimacy and compliance raises, of course, the question of civil disobedience. It also gives important philosophical and historical context to some of Rawls's more cryptic and perhaps radical formulations from *A Theory of Justice* like "unjust social arrangements are themselves a kind of extortion, even violence, and consent to them does not bind." Even more suggestively concerning the case of African Americans, Rawls writes that "the duty to comply is problematic for permanent minorities that have suffered from injustice for many years" and who bear "too heavily" the burdens of injustice.[100]

That these arguments—and their thematic precursors within Rawls's well-known antiwar activism—have been largely ignored reflects not simply analytical philosophy's prejudices against nonideal theory or its often myopic relationship to intellectual and political history mined from the archives but, subtly, a surprisingly broad consensus between critics like Mills and Rawls's many apologists that because questions of racial justice are rarely *explicitly* engaged in Rawls's published texts, we can conclude from that relative "silence"—to use Mills's charge—their *absence*. This fallacious inference, long a target of devastating critique from literary scholars better attuned to the subtleties of writing, still exercises a surprising hold on the history of philosophy and the reading practices of critical race theory, despite diminishing returns to the investment.

Ideal and Nonideal Theory from the Perspective of Exemplarity

If my critique of the silence hermeneutic is, thus far, persuasive, I hope it allows us to more precisely pursue the difficult charge that Mills poses regarding the relationship between ideal and nonideal theory: the inability of the former to properly inform the latter because of its fact insensitivity and ideological commitment to idealization. Following Toni Morrison's insights against "silence," I focus intensely on Rawls's invocations of the exemplarity of Martin Luther King Jr. to recover the ways that Rawls understands this mediation between ideal and nonideal theory. Contra Mills, I show that Rawls is significantly influenced by the civil rights movement, not only for his reflections on civil disobedience but also for some of the most basic commitments of his political philosophy (e.g., public reason and overlapping consensus) in its quest to defend a practical faith in a just, stable, liberal society.

In my view, ideal theory is tethered, especially through exemplary judgments it cannot usually avoid, to the nonideal. These judgments not only involve the content of concepts like *civil disobedience* but also construct what "reality" is being abstracted away from and for what purposes. What judgments inform the degree of fact sensitivity that allows so-called ideal theory to find its way back to the imperfect world it presumes to judge? The devil is in the details, to put it bluntly, and the dangers that confront abstractions that purport to conceptualize racial (in)justice or theorize possible responses will not be easily evaded by broadsides against the bankruptcy of ideal theory or the vocabulary of "silence."[101]

The division between ideal and nonideal theory, commonly associated with Rawls, has become increasingly fractious in political philosophy. *Ideal theory* refers to those approaches to ethical and political questions that concentrate primarily on working out principles that should govern intentional human action and the arrangement of basic social and political institutions given the fundamental and critical assumption of "full compliance."[102] All persons and institutions in ideal theoretical thought experiments have the capacity and tendency to comply with the principles generated by its thought experiments.

This insistence, however, at least in Rawls's version, is not strictly utopian but *realistically* utopian—a concession not often enough appreciated.[103] Ideal theory, despite its abstractions, is nonetheless supposed to be critical and constructive, helping to guide "the course of social reform." Rawls, for example, sees his task as one of developing a "conception of a perfectly just basic structure and the corresponding duties and obligations of persons" in order to judge existing institutions "in light of this conception" and evaluate them as unjust "to the extent that they depart from it without sufficient reason."[104] The constructive hope is that its exercises can be significantly action-guiding by serving as the most persuasive source of "*goals* to work toward," as "normative *standards* for judging the overall justice of particular social arrangements," and, crucially, as sources of justification for these ends.[105]

An essential part of this task for Rawls is to show, even as an exercise in "ideal theory," that a society well ordered by his principles of justice is *stable for the right reasons*. The point is to demonstrate that the ideal society theorized not only "generally maintains itself in a just general equilibrium" but "is capable of righting itself when that equilibrium is disturbed" through the "fully autonomous activity" of its members. This activity must be elicited and encouraged by the institutionalization of, and common adherence to, political principles and practices that evince mutual respect.[106]

The deep concern with stability reveals, as Paul Weithman has powerfully argued in his extraordinary work on Rawls, two projects for Rawlsian philosophy. The first is the formulation of a conception of justice "that can serve as an enduring 'foundation charter' for a well-ordered liberal democracy" and inspire affirmation from across diverse worldviews. The second is a project that Weithman aptly describes as "naturalistic theodicy."[107]

This latter task is a response to the ethical-existential anxiety, perhaps best articulated by Kant, that we will be unable to meet the daunting demands of a commitment to morality and justice—indeed, to our own freedom—if we do not see that our aims can be achieved and that our efforts are a significant part of their realization.[108] Defending practical faith in the face of this theodicean challenge involves engendering justifiable confidence that "the order of nature and social necessities" (human sociability) are "not unfriendly to" a realm of ends—in Rawls's case, a well-ordered, stably just, liberal constitutional democracy.[109] The hope is that with the appropriate balance of fact sensitivity and abstraction guided by ethical ideals, political philosophy can demonstrate through reasoned argument what a just society looks like, why we should regard it as possible, and why its pursuit is worthwhile rather than a naive evasion of nihilism.[110]

Nonideal theory, in contrast, takes its theoretical departure or primary considerations from scenarios of significant noncompliance or serious violations of normative principles of justice. There may be some confusion insofar as either approach traffics in "ideals," both normative and the kind that simplify and model social or natural phenomena. Mills, however, characterizes nonideal theory as refusing reliance on "idealization to the exclusion, or at least marginalization, of the actual." Instead nonideal theorists pursue more accurate descriptive models of actually existing phenomena or historical developments to figure in their theoretical work.[111]

Once again we see Mills's sense that the crux of debate between radicals and liberals is often factual rather than ethical. The racial contract hypothesis, he writes, "is explicitly predicated on the *truth* of a particular metanarrative, the historical account of the European conquest of the world." Therefore, Mills insists, the racial contract "lays claims to truth, objectivity, realism, the description of the world as it actually is, the prescription for a transformation of that world to achieve justice—and invites criticism on those same terms."[112] It is this history that must be placed into the abyss supposedly left open by ideal theory, filling it with thick descriptions of injustice and proceeding from there to discern suitable principles, design comparatively better institutions, or in some other way reduce the harms of the given situation (often without a perfect ideal in mind).[113]

This method, Mills argues, avoids straying too far from historical facts and intuiting indefensible descriptions of society, misguided notions about social institutions, or familiar yet conceptually inadequate philosophical ideals. Mills hoped to force ideal theory to face its limitations, as did feminist critiques of Rawls's *A Theory of Justice* that exposed his early failure to acknowledge gender injustice as a problem at the level of the basic structure of society, his paternalistic naivete about the ability of the (male) "head of household" to represent the "interest" of his household in discussions of principles of justice, and his undertheorized account of autonomy, which failed to consider the care work and socialization that go into its realization.[114]

In reading the literature on ideal and nonideal theory, however, it is remarkable that while the entire debate revolves around Rawls's distinction, it hardly engages in any robust fashion with the exercises in nonideal theory that Rawls himself pursues. This is doubly problematic for Mills given that among Rawls's most sustained discussions of nonideal theory are the account of civil disobedience in *A Theory of Justice* and the account of claim making through public reason in *Political Liberalism,* both of which explicitly invoke Martin Luther King and the classical phase of the civil rights movement as exemplary touchstones and sources of insight for reflective equilibrium. These moves, moreover, raise even further doubts about the plausibility of Mills's claims that the "postwar struggle for racial justice in practice and in theory and the Rawlsian corpus on justice are almost completely separate and non-intersecting universes" (or that Rawls is manifestly unconcerned with racial justice).[115]

This insight follows from pursuing Morrisonian intuitions toward a clearer understanding of Rawls's practice of reflective equilibrium in political theory. This imposingly named method only means that we begin reasoning about normative questions from our most considered judgments—namely, those confidently held convictions "given under conditions in which our capacity for judgment is most likely to have been fully exercised and not affected by distorting influences."[116] From this start, reflective equilibrium seeks to forge a more expansive and complete theory of justice by reconciling our various considered judgments into the most complete, coherent, and consistent scheme. It pursues this by generating moral principles from these judgments, testing them in thought experiments and decision procedures against other competing claims, discarding or revising implausible judgments, and securing the best fit for our considered commitments within a broader constellation.

Crucial to this method is that some judgments overflow the borders of moral principles strictly defined. They occur, in Rawls's words, "at all levels of generality, from those about particular situations and institutions up through broad standards and first principles to formal and abstract conditions on moral conceptions."[117] In acknowledging the importance of judgments concerning "particular situations and institutions," Rawls moves us beyond determinant rules and principles to other scenes of judgment. If reflective equilibrium, in Samuel Freeman's words, privileges "neither the general nor the particular," then Rawls's method necessarily involves more than what Kant called *determinant judgments,* or those instances of subsuming particulars under a general rule. It also must include *reflective judgments,* or those instances (as in aesthetics) where, in the absence or abdication of available and adequate general rules, *only* the particular is given and the universal must be found.[118]

Our inquiry into the faculty of judgment in Part One prepares us to see what this entails. First, given their particularity and the aesthetic elements of their representation (especially narrative), historical judgments fall largely within the orbit of reflective judgment. Indeed, historical judgments often entail narrative argument about the appropriateness—the fit—of certain actions or events to certain ends (the flourishing of a national identity or the overcoming of some unfreedom). Often, historical judgments involve claims about an event's exemplary instantiation of, or representation of, an ethico-aesthetic idea (e.g., courage or beauty).

Second, these reflective historical judgments are at work in reflective equilibrium insofar as they entail strongly held evaluative claims concerning the significance and valence of historical phenomena or personalities. These judgments, therefore, enter into reflection alongside determinant moral principles, in some cases even serving as touchstones for the articulation and revision of other moral judgments. Here judgments concerning the exemplarity of certain events are not condensed into mere examples categorized and subsumed under determinant principles; they instead retain a dimension of their force as exemplars, singularities that authorize or elicit novel normative concerns. This other dimension of exemplarity's force reveals itself best in those moments when our determinant judgments conflict with our reflective judgments of exemplary events, and instead of discarding our evaluative claims of the greatness or horror of these moments, we shift or create principles so as to cohere with these kinds of historical and ethico-aesthetic judgments.

From this perspective, it is notable that during Rawls's various invocations of Martin Luther King and the civil rights movement, the movement's positive exemplarity seems to entail a unique relationship to considered judgments about racial discrimination, civil disobedience, public reason, and protest (as does the abolitionist movement against chattel slavery). Rawls, as we shall see, attempts to fit his notion of civil disobedience to his reading of the account in King's "Letter from a Birmingham Jail." Additionally, Rawls's major revisions to the scope of his theory of public reason came on the heels of criticism from Michael Sandel and others that his normative restrictions on public reason would disallow the religious rhetoric of

King and the cohort of civil rights activists affiliated with him.[119] In response, Rawls widened his conception of the use of "comprehensive" doctrines in public reason, accommodating his view of civil rights exemplarity and returning to a crucial origin of the initial distinction.

The implication is that Rawls seems to think of the civil rights movement and certain aims or ideals of his political theory as manifesting an exemplary congruence. This congruence between meaning, principle, and exemplarity makes it difficult to untangle the normative judgment from the historical judgment of the action that instantiates it. This holds not just for Rawls but also for Bernard Boxill, David Lyons, Michael Sandel, and other theorists who treat the memory of the civil rights movement as an orienting and prestructuring reference, a shared terrain for disagreement.[120] Any theory of public reason that cannot allow for the emergence of something like the civil rights movement in the face of racial injustice is, on these assumptions, deficient. Thus the area where Mills presses most demandingly his substantive philosophical critique—the presumed inability of Rawls's ideal theory to deal effectively with the nonideal normative challenges presented by racial injustice—also ironically happens to be the place where Rawls invokes the histories of the abolitionist and civil rights movements to mediate between ideal and nonideal theory and provide justificatory grounds to his arguments. The emphasis on "silence" and "evasion" is not fine-grained enough to capture this complexity or spur us to develop a critical theory thoroughgoing enough to unravel this dense network of historical narrative, exemplarity, and judgment from the inside.

Sustained reflection on the invocation of the civil rights movement and racial discrimination as critical examples in Rawls's work and throughout political theory leads, in this interpretive stance, to a consideration of the work that exemplarity does for Rawls (and perhaps political philosophy more broadly). A benefit of this approach is that it treats the charges of idealization and abstraction not as determinant judgments of *any* ideal theoretical approach but as open questions for reflective judgments of its own concerning which particular historical narratives are conscripted for particular theoretical projects. Treating ideal theory as, by definition, ahistorical or mythic precludes us from recognizing the myriad ways that historical imagination operates in the background through gestures of exemplarity meant to secure or anchor the arguments of political philosophy, even in its ideal theoretical form. Moreover, the binary construction of ideal and nonideal theory as vice and virtue trains us to be insufficiently suspicious of the stylized, narrativized, and constructed character of nonideal theory's historical claims, taking their purported "realism" or "naturalism" at face value.

In the case of the civil rights movement specifically, it fails to capture the subtle ways in which contemporary liberal ideal theory treats a romantic narrative of the movement as a source of its self-conception and as a possible resolution to its persistent crises of practical faith. In fact, civil rights exemplarity serves as an often concealed origin or intuited moment of considered judgment for the very principles, rules, concepts, and norms that liberals hope to defend. Here we should recall Irene Harvey's incisive provocation, "How do the examples betray what they are supposed to exemplify or reproduce? Are they in fact productive and creative rather than reproductive? Are they pre-text that only *appears* in the guise of a postscript, seeming to come after the fact as accidental appendages to the theory, *but are in fact its progenitors, its unacknowledged city fathers?*"[121]

Reading Race/Reading Rawls: Civil Disobedience, Public Reason, and Overlapping Consensus

What, then, are we to make of the exemplarity of the civil rights movement and Martin Luther King in Rawls's intersecting arguments about civil disobedience, public reason, and "overlapping consensus"?[122] In September 1966, just a few months before presenting his conscription resolution at Harvard, Rawls delivered an early version of his influential paper "The Justification of Civil Disobedience" at the annual meeting of the American Political Science Association in New York City. Three years later, Rawls's essay would first appear in print, with some revision, as part of a pioneering collection of writings on civil disobedience edited by the legal and political theorist Hugo Bedau and dedicated to King's memory.[123] By 1971 Rawls's final version of the civil disobedience essay appears as part of *A Theory of Justice,* with Rawls citing King's "Letter from a Birmingham Jail" to offer a description of his own project to be to set King's "sort of conception into a wider framework."[124]

This allegedly "wider framework" is rooted in a tension. Patently admiring of the civil rights movement and conceding the wisdom, necessity, and moral righteousness of many activists' disobedient tactics in a struggle against injustice, Rawls is nevertheless concerned to answer the question of "under what circumstances and to what extent we are bound to comply with unjust arrangements."[125] His worry is that while civil disobedience is an attractive response to injustice, if justified too expansively or enthusiastically its practice will erode the stability of, and faith in, an reasonably just constitutional order. His solution is to advance a conception of "justified civil disobedience": the justificatory judgments and boundaries befitting "a public, nonviolent, conscientious yet political act contrary to law usually done with the aim of bringing about a change in the law or policies of the government."[126] He suggests that this, too, is a topic for parties in the original position as a "a way of setting up, within the limits of fidelity to [higher, constitutional] law, a *final device* to maintain the stability of a just constitution . . . a morally correct way of maintaining a constitutional regime" when it suffers from serious injustice.[127]

This way of framing the question as one principally of justification and stability stems from Rawls's philosophical account of civic obligation and social theoretical framing of "injustice." When an existing political order and its constitutional essentials are reasonably fair, civic obligations of cooperation and compliance also arise to the extent that we voluntarily accept the benefits of participating in the cooperative scheme of society or take advantage of its opportunities to pursue our interests.[128] A problem emerges, however, when normative civic obligations collide with social arrangements that deviate from the standards of justice.

Rawls thinks that injustice arises in two ways. One is when social arrangements "conform to a society's conception of justice, or to the view of the dominant class," but the society or class in question holds an unreasonable and unjust conception of justice. Rawls's exemplar here is Nazi Germany. The other is when current social arrangements "depart in varying degrees from publicly accepted standards that are more or less just." "When laws and policies deviate from publicly recognized standards," he argues, "an appeal to the society's sense of justice is presumably possible to some extent. . . . This condition is *presupposed* in undertaking civil disobedience."[129] "The problem of civil disobedience"—what he calls "a conflict of duties"—arises for Rawls only "within a more or less just democratic state for those citizens who recognize and accept the legitimacy of the constitution." In Rawls's words, civil disobedience is a form of contentious address by which "a minority leads the majority to consider whether it wants to have its acts *construed in this way,* or whether, in view of the *common sense of justice,* it wishes to acknowledge the legitimate claims of the minority."[130] A departure from reasonably just standards can elicit an ostensibly straightforward claim by proponents of civil disobedience that shared principles of justice or their constitutional manifestations are being unduly violated *and* that the citizens engaged in direct action will not comply with such wrongs. A question that we will return to is whether, for Rawls, the civil rights movement and the nation it occurred in could plausibly have been said to fit this description.

Injustices of this kind, says Rawls in a note of realism, are always possible in an actual constitutional democracy. The political process, necessarily hampered by self-interested behavior, the upper limits of human knowledge, and our burdened powers of judgment, will eternally be an imperfect, mistake-prone tool for realizing the ends of justice. Yet the virtues of constitutional democratic government and the stability of even "near justice" loom so large that Rawls repeatedly warns us to not mistake the trees for the forest. Preaching a spirit of cautious and reasonable reconciliation, he advises that must we cautiously weigh the severity and systematicity of any specific injustice against the relative justice of the constitution in a given society before engaging in civil disobedience. We have a presumptive duty toward compliance with even unjust laws solely "in virtue of our duty to support a just constitution."[131]

Given this framing, one should not be surprised to find Rawls worrying that civil disobedience can erode the "trust" and "confidence" necessary to sustain the sort of political culture—with faith in the rule and legitimacy of law—that maintains constitutional democracies over time.[132] This interest in stability, cooperation, and civility appear to underwrite Rawls's insistence that civil disobedience be nonviolent, public, and accepting of punishment. He treats violence and clandestine action as broadly incompatible with civil address, as they undermine the cooperative practice of public reasoning with threats of harm and secrecy. The demand that those practicing civil disobedience should *expect* and *accept* punishment is understood by Rawls as the best way to show, despite their lawbreaking, the depth of their convictions and their higher-order commitments to a political community bounded by law.[133] Yet if civil disobedience is so dangerous, what, then, could possibly justify its practice? It was open, after all, for Rawls to insist, as many liberals did at the time, that civil disobedience was unjustified.[134] Given that he did not take this approach, how did Rawls understand the character and logic of this mode of political action, and what kinds of injustice was it appropriate to use it to contest?

Recall Rawls's definition of civil disobedience as "a public, nonviolent, conscientious yet political act contrary to law (not necessarily a law one is protesting) usually done with the aim of bringing about a change in the law or policies of the government." It is not well enough appreciated, but Rawls treats civil disobedience as akin to "public speech," and in roughly the same terms he uses to characterize public reason broadly in later works. In other words, civil disobedience (and public reason broadly), are public, deliberative democratic speech act forms that concern the justice of the basic structure of society and speak to the widely shared conception of justice in a political community. Civil disobedience is a special version of this sort of claim making, one that the breaks the law to address the majority's "common sense of justice" and "declares that in one's considered opinion the principles of social cooperation among free and equal men are not being respected."[135]

Given this understanding, Rawls in *A Theory of Justice* argues that civil disobedience must be justified by recourse to *political* principles and not by arguments from "personal morality" or "religious doctrines." These other justifications may "coincide with and support" our political claims, but in the last instance, we must appeal neither to these private moral doctrines nor, worse, particular self-interests—only the "public conception of justice by reference to which citizens regulate their political affairs and interpret the constitution."[136] Readers of Rawls's work should readily see how much of his initial account of public reason in *Political Liberalism* was already sketched in his writing on civil disobedience and perhaps see why that discussion would elicit yet more invocations of the exemplarity of King and the civil rights movement.[137]

There Rawls famously counsels a duty of "civility" in restricting the appeals of public reason to political conceptions of justice and avoiding appeals that can only be sustained within the justificatory terms of comprehensive religious or philosophical doctrines. Public reason, then, "is elaborated in terms of fundamental political ideas viewed as implicit in the public political culture of a democratic society" that "include those mentioned in the preamble to the United States Constitution: a more perfect union, justice, domestic tranquility, the common defense, the general welfare, and the blessings of liberty for ourselves and our posterity."[138] What is fascinating about Rawls's invocation of the preamble is that alongside the values of liberty and justice, there are those whose virtue is essentially stability for the right reasons: "a more perfect union," "domestic tranquility," and the concern with "posterity."

Underlying the assumption that constraining discourse in this fashion will provide stability for the right reasons are further assumptions that these restrictions on discourse will help citizens achieve consensus on the conceptions of justice they will share and the arrangement of the basic institutions of society. Rawls sees this sort of "overlapping consensus" as central to ensuring a stable constitutional order and basic justice. Thus, the insistence on certain "guidelines of inquiry; principles of reasoning; and rules of evidence," as well as restrictions on the *content* of public reason, all are to ensure that we appeal to and further develop "overlapping consensus" on these issues. Overlapping consensus "supposes agreement deep enough [across comprehensive moral doctrines] to reach such ideas as those of society as a fair system of cooperation and of citizens as reasonable and rational, and free and equal . . . [and] covers the principles and values of a political conception (in this case those of justice as fairness) and it applies to the basic structure as a whole," especially the constitutional essentials.[139] It is a "guiding framework of deliberation and reflection which helps us reach political agreement on at least the constitutional essentials and the basic questions of justice."[140]

Although not foregrounded even by careful readers, Rawls pioneered both this restrictive strategy (appeals to political values over comprehensive doctrines) and the very concept of overlapping consensus in his account of civil disobedience.[141] Much of his "justification" for civil disobedience goes beyond arguments about the ethics of lawbreaking to articulating practical and normative constraints on civil disobedience (as he does more generally with public reason). This is, as should be clear, because civil disobedience exposes a dilemma between our moral obligation to protest injustice and our duty to support just institutions by contributing to the *order, confidence,* and *trust* needed to produce them. In light of this framework, Rawls is concerned to control the *destabilizing* power of the practice. But how?

The most reliable justification for legitimate civil disobedience that Rawls concedes is the sustained violation of equal basic political liberties—rights of freedom of speech and assembly, rights of political participation, and the like—or "barriers which contravene the . . . principle of open offices which protects equality of opportunity." Rawls's other major principle (the "difference" principle)—that all socioeconomic inequalities be arranged such that they are to the benefit of the least well off—is deliberately excluded from justified acts of civil disobedience and discouraged in public reason more broadly.[142] Why, if this latter principle is also constitutive of justice, would Rawls argue for this restrictive criterion?

The answer can be separated into two broad categories.

The first involves matters of social theory and social ontology. Recall that civil disobedience for Rawls is most appropriate to societies with *some* deviation from a basically just public conception of justice or basically just constitutional principles. This framing of injustice as "deviation" or "anomaly" is deeply resonant, rhetorically and analytically, with an influential tendency in American liberal theory and praxis. For these liberals, the power of civil disobedience lies in its congruence with an already extant, widely held conception of justice and its ability to dramatically disclose the social and political world such that it "refocuses" values we already hold.[143]

Take, for instance, Gunnar Myrdal's influential distillation of the "American Dilemma"—or the relation of "the Negro Problem" to democracy—as "primarily a moral issue of conflicting valuations." Reflecting the leading liberal opinion of mid-twentieth-century American liberals, Myrdal argued that while the so-called American Creed is the near-universally held and publicly affirmed conception of justice and civic identity, there exist "departures" (to use a variation on Rawls's term) in sentiment, idea, and practice around antiblack racism that are not commensurate with the Creed's standards. This thought image is established through metaphors of verticality and stratification that give a sense of the Creed as having greater psychological entrenchment and axiological priority than racist ideology—whether one evaluates matters morally, epistemologically, or politically. As Myrdal notes, "In America as everywhere else people agree, as an abstract proposition, that *the more general valuations—those which refer to men as such and not to any particular group or temporary situation—are morally higher.*" The latter valuations, he insists, "are commonly referred to as 'irrational' or 'prejudiced,' sometimes even by people who express and stress them," and "defended in terms of tradition, expediency or utility" as opposed to right.[144] Myrdal's framework, among other things, conveys through its hierarchical picture of public political values an optimism that creedal commitments (including those to Enlightenment rationalism) would dissolve and displace allegedly lower-order valuations of race ideology over time. "The main trend in [American] history," Myrdal triumphantly writes at the end of *An American Dilemma,* "is the gradual realization of the American Creed."[145]

President Lyndon B. Johnson's 1965 commencement address at Howard University, another ur-text of twentieth-century US liberalism, echoes both this judgment of political temporality and the power of spatial metaphors to convey that creedal norms and civic identity are at the "center" of the society's conception of justice, while racial ideology is "deviant." "American justice is a very special thing," Johnson proclaims. This is a nation that, from its founding, "has been a land of towering expectations," a nation where each person could expect to "be ruled by the common consent of all—enshrined in law, given life by institutions, guided by men themselves subject to its rule," "touched equally in obligation and in liberty," and "share the harvest" of a "more abundant promise than man had ever seen." Americans have pursued this promise of liberty, equality, and dignity "faithfully to the edge of our imperfections," but "have failed to find it for the American Negro." Calling for civil rights legislation and reparative measures, Johnson celebrates "the glorious opportunity of this generation *to end the one huge wrong of the American Nation and, in so doing, to find America for ourselves,* with the same immense thrill of discovery which gripped those who first began to realize that here, at last, was a home for freedom."[146]

Analytically distinct from these social ontology arguments are others that are more straightforwardly political. Rawls gives three such arguments for treating civil disobedience about questions of economic justice and some forms of social inequality as presumptively illegitimate: violations of basic liberty are easier to recognize than violations of fair equality of opportunity or the difference principle because they are enshrined in legal statute; the shared political values of a given *national* community will make protection of basic liberties easier to agree on; and if basic liberties are protected, social and economic inequalities will not "get out of hand." On this last point he thinks that if violations of basic liberties are "rectified, [this] will establish a basis for doing away with remaining injustices" over time. These restrictions, it is worth noting, map a claim about political temporality neatly onto the more familiar ethical claims about the lexical priority of basic liberties over questions of equal opportunity and economic inequality.[147]

What unites both families of arguments are that underneath the discourse of permissibility and justification, judgments that might properly be considered *ethico-aesthetic* and historical creep subtly into these formulations. The priority that Rawls famously gives to basic liberties over questions of inequality of opportunity, socioeconomic resources, and control of economic decision-making are revealed here not only to have a *moral* foundation but also one in ethico-aesthetic, epistemological, and historical judgments.

In Rawls's account, for instance, differentiation by legal statute is the privileged site for the phenomenological recognition of injustice, while we should be wary of the judgment of the citizenry in other domains of inequality. There the ordinary citizen may be too epistemically burdened to be broadly trusted with assessing the disruptive politics of civil disobedience reasonably. Further, Rawls's priorities incorporate an implicit judgment about a projected teleology of liberal politics such that the attainment of basic liberties in a mostly just constitutional order is expected to lead to tolerable economic inequality *without further supplement of disobedience.*

Attention to these ethico-aesthetic dimensions shows that Rawls's appeal to the lexical priority of liberty over equality has a temporal structure familiar to romance. The basic liberties draw on, and further expand, the power of a preexisting value consensus through which the promise of justice or near justice can be expected in time to be redeemed. This judgment—or, better yet, *faith*—is meant, in Rawls, to circumscribe our recourse to more contentious and disobedient forms of politics and underwrite our investments of hope in the workings of liberal constitutionalism and civility toward a telos of even economic justice.

Conscripts of Mundanity: Rawls and the Romance of Civil Rights

But to the extent that Rawls treats Martin Luther King's writings and speeches and the political actions of civil rights activists as exemplary of this conception of public reason and civil disobedience, using their exemplarity and its connotations to give the force of reflective equilibrium to his arguments, it seems he can do so only by situating King in a *romantic* narrative of civil rights history. As argued at length in the preceding chapters, historiography and political theory's invocations of historical example have an irreducibly narrativist dimension, which is inevitably shaped by conventions of narrative form and genre that shape how we judge the significance of the stories that make up our historical imagination.

Romance, we can recall, is a narrative mode disposed to the symbolic and metaphorical representation of unities or forms of consensus in the process of becoming—especially concerning values or political peoples and nations. The criterion of significance for what is included and emphasized in romantic narratives is primarily a subject's or event's fitness for bearing the symbolism of these "higher" unities or their contribution to the realization of this telos of union. Romance is also distinguished by an ideal of heroic action that transcends the world as it is to realize this guiding unity and help it flourish. Narratively, romance tends to dramatize the struggle between essential, inherent, and enduring good and the alleged anomalous obstacles of injustice, evil, and bad circumstance.[148]

The King imagined by this romantic narrative is a civil rights leader in the narrow sense. If King's action is to fit the conceptual restrictions and share the homology suggested in *A Theory of Justice,* Rawls's presupposition would have to be that the United States was already, at least since *Brown v. Board of Education* (1954), *basically* just in its "constitutional essentials" with the caveat that African Americans need be extended the same basic liberties and equality of opportunity afforded to other Americans. In this view, King's direct-action demonstrations at a site like Birmingham are meant primarily to dramatize the gap between the consensus on American ideals and these anomalous, exclusionary practices while appealing to Americans' already-extant "common sense of justice." From this perspective, the passage of the Civil Rights Act of 1964 and the Voting Rights Act of 1965 will appear to be instances of overlapping consensus in the national community, fostered in large part by King's arguments. A great transformation toward a higher-order reconciliation and an egalitarian trajectory is enacted, all well within the boundaries of Rawls's normative constraints on civil disobedience and public reason.

Given that Rawls does not explicitly discuss the United States in the text, or in his remarks about the seriousness of racial injustice quoted above, the direct application of these claims may elicit some skepticism.[149] Yet in his draft notes (ca. 1966) for his original paper on civil disobedience, Rawls explicitly described the US constitutional order as "just," relying heavily on an account of federalism to both insulate the purity of the constitution from the evils of Jim Crow and to establish his view of the practice and purpose of civil rights activism in the sit-in movement: an appeal not to a "higher law" but to "the higher lawmaking authorities to correct constitutionally *aberrant* local laws."[150] Elsewhere in his methodological notes, he treats desegregation as a settled matter of justice, best understood as a problem of "implementation."[151] These remarks suggest, as Katrina Forrester has argued, a "story of liberalism" that uses constitutionalism to educate our judgments of social movements and understand the political character of injustice. Through this vision we are led to grasp "the civil rights movement" as that assemblage of action aiming at "incremental inclusion in a basic structure that was nearly just in its constitutional essentials . . . [and] the integrity of its principles."[152] It is not, perhaps, too strong to say that in the 1960s and early 1970s, at least, Rawls intuitively relied on judgments about American political culture and law that Aziz Rana might describe as *creedal constitutionalism:* they fused a devotional faith in the essential goodness or justice of the Constitution with "the idea of the country as an unfolding project in equal liberty."[153]

While Forrester and Rana are both interested in the implications of this sort of argument for "constitutionalist" thinking, I am more concerned with how the appeal of this romantic vision and its strategies of exemplification bring us back to the theodicean aspirations that Paul Weithman reveals in his discussion of Rawls's pursuit of "practical faith."[154] The demonstration of the ability of a constitutional order marked by pluralism, not only to achieve justice but also to *correct itself* and *endure* when it falls short of that charge is a critically important task for Rawlsian political theory. From this vantage, a *romantic* narrative of the civil rights movement, especially one that is resonant with constitutional romance, presents itself as an exemplary solution to this problem, or at least a rejoinder to skepticism that it can be solved. In its portrayal as a refocusing moment in American democratic constitutionalism, it is thought to display a beautiful symmetry of ends and means that performs a reunification of the American polity on a refocused consensus. Its narrative resonance with Rawls's other commitments reveals an important orientation to Rawlsian political liberalism that prestructures his sense of the significance of political phenomena and guides his judgment in romantic directions.

If this interpretation is persuasive, I hope we can see clearly how far we have moved from the terrain of "silence." Further, I hope I have dramatized why the language of idealization versus fact sensitivity (a kind of absence versus presence distinction) must not be blind to exemplarity, the demands for theorizing stability in ideal theory, and the theodicean motivations behind Rawlsian thought in its characterization of the arguments at stake. Critique should not simply meet Rawls's abstract idealizations with "real" history as if "*it is often really the facts that are doing the revisionary work*" but instead disentangle the role that historical narrative *already* plays in his work, dislodge that historiographical vision, and rework the claims and politics of justice from a different interpretation of the exemplarity.[155] This, far more than Mills's sweeping condemnations of silence or ideal theory, is what can lead us back to "action-guiding" political theory and break with the ways that a certain picture of historical exemplarity—here, the romantic narrative of the civil rights movement—has sedimented into an ideological fetter on political imagination and judgment. I try to make good on this contention by rethematizing what it might mean to put Martin Luther King's view of civil disobedience in a wider framework of political theory informed by a competing historical vision.

Martin Luther King Jr. and Some Ethico-Aesthetic Problems of Civil Disobedience

There are several interpretive burdens that one must confront in retrieving a more comprehensive restatement of King's thought, even on an issue as familiarly associated with him as civil disobedience. One difficulty, as Karuna Mantena has also identified in the case of Mahatma Gandhi, is that King's thought is often caricatured as (naive) moral idealism when, in fact, dichotomous typologies of political thought along realist-idealist or tactical-principled axes do special violence to his philosophy.[156] Like Gandhi, King produced a political theory richly informed by traditionally realist concerns of contextualism, consequentialism, and moral psychology.

Another obstacle is that King, perhaps most prominently among famous African American intellectuals, is treated primarily as a rhetorician rather than a philosopher. His major contribution to politics, on this view, is the rhetorical restatement of the formative ideals of the American Creed, and the performative dramatization, often with his own body, of their violation with regard to African Americans. Not only does this presumption lead to a broad ignorance concerning the substance, significance, and existence of King's five published books, but it also lends intuitive credibility to a style of superficial reading of King's writings and speeches that appropriates selected phrases for aphoristic use while ignoring the comprehensive arguments behind them. Practically, and relatedly, overcoming this requires displacing, to some degree, the preeminence of 1963's "Letter from a Birmingham Jail" and "I Have a Dream" as the singular exemplars of his thinking.

Above all, thinking King beyond romance requires recovering a competing social ontology and sense of the political problems King understood his politics as meant to confront. For one, King departs from the Myrdalian view that explicitly theorizes or rhetorically and metaphorically implies that the American Creed is psychologically, politically, or ontologically *prior to* antiblack racism.[157] In *Where Do We Go from Here?* (1967) King argues that America has always had "a schizophrenic personality on the question of race," one rooted in "the 'congenital deformity' of racism that has crippled the nation from its inception."[158]

King is quick to insist that this judgment does not entail that there has never been progress on matters of racial justice, nor does it mean that white people are, as Elijah Muhammad might suggest, universally and ontologically antagonistic to that progress. Nevertheless, King is at great pains to "refute the idea that the dominant ideology in our country even today is freedom and equality while racism is just an occasional departure from the norm." Indeed, in opposition to the creedal constitutionalism of twentieth-century liberals, King reminds his readers that "of the two dominant and contradictory strains in the American psyche, the positive one, our democratic heritage, was the later development on the American continent." The first, "the doctrine of white supremacy," grew—as many ideologies do—out of "the attempt to give moral sanction to a profitable system" (in this case, chattel slavery and the regimes of agrarian exploitation that followed its formal legal abolition). Limning American history not as a story of unfolding progress but as "tragic duality" with "strange indecisiveness and ambivalence toward the Negro," King describes the society as taking "a step backward simultaneously with every step forward on the question of racial justice."[159]

When we understand the divergence in presuppositions reflected in these competing narratives of American history, we can see more clearly that King does not fit neatly with this Rawlsian rendering. This is not to deny that King's reflections on civil disobedience contain commitments to the public political charters of liberal democratic societies, to nonviolence, or to the assumption of voluntary suffering and punishment by those engaged in civil disobedience. Instead it insists that the constellation of judgments, narratives, and descriptions within which these argumentative commitments fit lead King to a radically different political vision and set of conceptualizations than Rawls endorses. The alleged "wider" framework that Rawls offers becomes, in fact, a narrowing.

Beyond America: Civil Disobedience, the Geopolitics of Shame, and the Problem of Transformation

Take, for example, how Rawls incorporates his assumption in *A Theory of Justice* that ideal theories of justice can proceed on the assumption of a bounded society of conationals, into nonideal arguments about civil disobedience. This is what leads him to confidently describe civil disobedience as speech that appeals to a public constituted by one's fellow citizens and informed by a shared conception of justice in the polity. Recent critics have argued that these "Westphalian" assumptions "proved historically more contingent than Rawls and other far-sighted liberals in the 1960s and early 1970s grasped . . . [and] now seem empirically obsolescent" in light of "postnationalization."[160] For King and other civil rights activists, however, the geopolitical and transnational dimensions of their struggle were paramount far earlier than this critical chronology suggests.

King constantly sought an audience in transnational publics while engaged in acts of civil disobedience. Partly, as many historians have now demonstrated, this was a strategic move in light of the geopolitics of the Cold War.[161] With post–World War II decolonization producing new nation-states composed primarily of nonwhite peoples and a bipolar geopolitics of Soviet Union–United States rivalry, American foreign policy officials at mid-century broadly understood themselves as locked in a struggle against potential communist insurgency at home and for the allegiance of so-called Third World or nonaligned nations abroad. Despite the hysteria of domestic anticommunism, left-liberal African American intellectuals and activists immediately recognized the political leverage (and dangers) the racial and ideological politics of the Cold War occasioned, seeking to entrench racial justice as the normative standard by which US claims to global leadership should be indexed.[162]

King's writings and speeches, throughout his career, contain many attempts to walk this tightrope. He seeks to disavow communism while nevertheless treating it as a trenchant, genuine challenge to instantiate the most egalitarian promises of left-liberal democracy. "We must not engage in a negative anti-Communism," King writes, "but rather in a positive thrust for democracy, realizing that our greatest defense against Communism is to take offensive action"—including civil disobedience—"in behalf of justice and righteousness." It is only with "positive action," he continues, that we can "remove those conditions of poverty, insecurity, injustice, and racial discrimination that are the fertile soil in which the seed of Communism grows and develops."[163]

Elsewhere King appealed directly to the moral witness of formerly colonized nations to the repression revealed by civil disobedience and protest. He proclaimed in a 1963 speech that America's "declarations that we are making progress in race relations ring with pathetic emptiness in their [the Third World's] ears. . . . As the shame of Oxford, Mississippi, and Birmingham, Alabama, flashes around the globe, the world is becoming aware of our deficiencies."[164] As late as 1968, while organizing for "mass civil disobedience" in the Poor People's Campaign on Washington, DC, King remained committed to these arguments and Third World appeals, decrying the popularity of communism in decolonizing nations as, above all, "a judgment against our failure to make democracy real and follow through on the revolutions that we [in America] initiated."[165]

It is important not to reduce the significance of these appeals to tactics or strategy in an amoral sense. King not only writes at length on his principled aversions to communism but, more important, his appeals disclose something theoretically important about civil disobedience that Rawls obscures by treating the practice as a nationally bound *dialogical* exchange between a minority and majority.[166]

Recall that Rawls describes civil disobedience as when "a minority leads the majority to consider whether it wants to have its acts *taken in this way*, or whether, in view of the common sense of justice, it wishes to *acknowledge* the claims of the minority."[167] In conditions of injustice, however, this characterization of the public sphere may be woefully inadequate because the conditions of egalitarian, genuinely dialogical exchange do not obtain. Indeed, one of the principal features of injustice (and causes of its compounding disadvantages) is often this denial of recognition respect, which entails a refusal or failure to acknowledge the authoritative standing of others as persons whose dignity or other morally relevant capacities or qualities allows them to make certain kinds of claims for treatment and consideration on us.[168] When denials of recognition respect are buttressed by particularly resilient forms of ideology or habits of disrespect, the expectation that minority claims will be acknowledged is severely undermined, as such persons do not reliably appear in public as authoritative claim makers.

King is acutely aware of this dilemma. He argues that "many white Americans," even in the North, "unconsciously, and often consciously, feel that the Negro is innately inferior, impure, depraved, and degenerate."[169] Elsewhere he describes himself as "gravely disappointed" in the white moderate's pleas for order, patience, or delay, for these counsels reveal one "who paternalistically believes he can set the timetable for another man's freedom."[170] This sort of critique, and the revelation that such stances are "more frustrating than . . . ill will" seems to me to stem precisely from the suspicion that such entreaties represent a form of *recognition disrespect* in their failure to give proper, egalitarian consideration not only to the weight of justice claims from African Americans, but also their very standing as claim makers as such.

When ideology and habitual disrespect structure public political speech to such a severe degree, it may become necessary to introduce citizens and representatives of other societies as participants in discursive exchange (even if only imaginatively and symbolically). With the introduction of mediating spectator-judges from other societies with more equal standing (or even, in some cases, a group that one's fellow citizens esteem or admire more highly than they do themselves), perhaps the kind of self-reflection, perceptual reevaluation, and apprehension of injustice that Rawls assumes can realistically be compelled. While the way that the disobedient minority wants the majority to view its claims and sufferings may not be legible to, or motivating in, nationally bounded arguments about constitutional essentials, King hoped that such matters could be apprehended through the horrified reaction of other parties, in whose eyes Americans would be diminished for failing to live up to their own political charters nor global standards of justice and decency.[171]

The disjuncture here is important. In King's philosophy and praxis, addressees of civil disobedience cannot be conceptually limited, a priori, through methodological nationalism. This forecloses the space of appearance where these challenges to national honor and pride and the ethically motivating sense of shame and the reconfiguration of civic and national identity such protest often seeks to provoke.[172] In this, King follows a tradition of black protest dating back to antislavery abolitionism that was deeply attuned to transnational cultural dynamics of recognition and contingent geopolitical arrangements of social and political leverage. Take, for example, Frederick Douglass, who toured the British Isles for nineteen months in 1845–1846, explicitly hoping to use the high cultural esteem afforded British opinion against proslavery forces in America:

> If we wish to call attention to anything we may point at Britain. We learn what is the mind of Britain by reading the writings of such men as [British author Charles] Dickens, as well as by the public press. I believe that the notice of Dickens had more effect in calling attention to the subject, than all the books published in America for ten years. This is because they have some deference for the opinions of those out of the country. Americans are very peculiar in this respect—for, like the beggar, they like to know what others think of them. (Laughter.) This good or bad trait in Brother Jonathan's character, must be made available to anti-slavery. We want to tell

> them in what light their religion and their institutions are viewed in other lands; and as they look to others we will take advantage of this disposition in effecting the overthrow of slavery in the United States. Since I came to this country I have been the means of calling more attention to the subject in America, than I could have done had I remained there twelve years.[173]

In its early stage, this black liberal internationalism was principally articulated through what Cornel West more broadly diagnoses as a "triple crisis of self-recognition." By this he means to complicate W. E. B. Du Bois's famous account of unreconciled "twoness"—being "an American" and "a Negro"—with an account of Victorian-era white (elite) Americans' intense sense of provinciality and incomplete civilization.[174] Antislavery activists like Douglass, antilynching crusaders like Ida B. Wells, and education reformers like Booker T. Washington all sought to leverage this cultural dynamic, which lasted roughly until successive world wars destroyed the cultural and political hegemony of Europe and ushered in the Cold War era that King and other civil rights activists found themselves thrown into.

With the advent of the Cold War, however, a new problem crystallized. As Rana powerfully argues, constitutional creedalism was "further joined to a series of three ideological pillars: an anti-totalitarian account of individual liberty and market capitalism, an embrace of American checks and balances, with the Supreme Court at the forefront, and a commitment to U.S. global leadership and primacy." This braided set of commitments, as Rana demonstrates, "provided an official narrative about why the Constitution promoted a just political, economic, and social order and—eventually—why it should be replicated abroad," under the sweeping global authority of the United States. Bracketing Rana's specific criticisms of the constitution or Cold War foreign policy, I mean to draw attention to the way that a certain "romance" of Cold War creedal constitutionalism could congeal into a self-image too imperious to take criticism and judgment from abroad seriously.

This, then, is yet another feature of King's repertories of justification for civil disobedience. Suggested in his work is a plea that we do not allow political and public philosophy to become so captured by constitutional veneration and nationalist presuppositions that its relation to its own self-conception and categories becomes one-dimensional. It is a dangerous practice of political philosophy that becomes so besotted with its society's own independently and immanently redemptive resources that it cannot see itself as "chagrined" by unfamiliar criticism or compelled to rethink the boundaries of the conversation of justice, its categories of analysis, or sedimented judgments and concepts.[175]

My interpretation draws on the sympathetic critique of Rawls pressed by his Harvard colleague, Stanley Cavell.[176] Cavell is concerned precisely with the ways that Rawls fails to appreciate the extent to which an existing moral consensus, or the reigning forms of identification with society and its prevailing rules, can congeal into a kind of conformity or complicity that is itself constitutive of severe injustice. Such conformity, Cavell argues, prematurely forecloses the "conversation of justice" by helping to evade, in bad faith, the suffering caused by our unwarranted certainty in the prevailing vocabularies, determinant judgments, and rules of moral encounter. Certain kinds of conformity and consensus in these domains can render particular claims of justice and the political subjects that are constituted via these claims, inexpressible or invisible. Further, given that societies will always fall short of perfect justice, this dilemma is a perpetual threat.[177]

Explicitly citing Rawls's contention that "each person possesses an inviolability founded on justice that even the welfare of society as a whole cannot override" (a claim that does a great deal of work in the case of conscription), Cavell reminded his colleague that the advantaged often do not deign to describe violation as "violation," even when urged passionately to do so. A crucial element of injustice is that the advantaged often see existing arrangements as conducive to others' *welfare,* even when the latter state grievances against it. Moreover, like Torvald in Henrik Ibsen's *A Doll's House* (Cavell's example) or Edward J. Banfield in his rejection of Rawls's claims of racial injustice in the 2-S deferment debates, the advantaged often see dissent or resistance as *unintelligible,* even *immature,* and cannot grasp how their judgment is itself a violation of the moral equality of the oppressed. Conformity or complicity with such views is itself part of a structure of injustice, part of a general set of rules, principles, definitions, and categories whose every word, Cavell writes (channeling Ralph Waldo Emerson) "chagrins us."[178]

Recall that in an aside that many read as describing his views of African Americans, Rawls writes that "the duty to comply is problematic for permanent minorities that have suffered from injustice for many years" and who bear "too heavily" the burdens of injustice.[179] Yet beyond "compliance," each of us, "permanent" minority or not, must decide how and whether to identify with societies, institutions, and practices that do not meet the standards of justice. Indeed, Rawls's practice of ideal theory—at least in its self-conception—should only sharpen and spread this weighty burden of judgment.

To the extent that we remain committed or loyal to societies complicit with serious injustice, even if only in hope of reforming them, it is possible that "at some time my sense of my society's distance from the reign of perfect justice, and of my implication in its distance, may become intolerable." Dwelling on suffering that is not receiving its full and fairest hearing, we may even experience a "disgust with or a disdain for the present state of things so complete as to require not merely reform, but a call for a transformation of things, and before all a transformation of the self."[180] This, arguably, is what characterizes Martin Luther King Jr.'s reaction to the crisis around Vietnam and his decision to break the "betrayal of [his] own silences and to speak from the burnings of [his] own heart" rather than within dominant binaries of contemporaneous social criticism (e.g., civil rights/geopolitics, domestic/international).[181]

Unlike Rawls, King came to see how the habit (familiar to Rawlsians) of framing questions of social justice (including *racial* justice) as narrowly bounded within the nation-state, or as subordinate and subsumable within attempts to speak from the space of "consensus," had become—in the gap between ideal and nonideal society, part of the practice through which alternative and more just ways of living together had been foreclosed. For King, the argument that America's prosecution of the Vietnam War was racially unjust entailed *not just two separate claims* regarding racial exploitation via the draft at home and racist justifications for usurping self-determination abroad. Instead it opened up into a *global* critique describing a shared, mutually reinforcing, and implicating ideological substrate to both practices. On this view, racial exploitation is a dangerous *global* sociopolitical and economic problem, sustained by an ideology that partitions the world into a hierarchy of races (as racialized nation-states, racialized peoples, and minorities *within* the West). In theory and practice, racial exploitation and related practices show contempt for the idea that nonwhite people have legitimate or equal claims to mutual respect, fairness, and participatory parity in global and domestic institutions of governance.[182]

Transcending the habitual partiality that would burden for decades the philosophy of global justice, these charges led King to describe the Vietnam War–era United States in terms more befitting what Rawls would later call an "outlaw state" than a liberal, "decent" one, drawing attention to human rights abuses at home and abroad.[183] In sharp distinction to Rawls, however, this did not diminish King's judgment of the need for "massive, active, nonviolent resistance" and civil disobedience at the intersection of peace and civil rights, organized along "international dimensions."[184] A globally minded struggle for racial justice from within the United States, he hoped, would attack segregation at home and apartheid abroad, distribute wealth to end global poverty, restrain the efforts of Western corporations and militaries to usurp the self-governance of other peoples, and promote peace.

It is important not to treat King's vision as guilty of the abandonment of all sense of "national pride" that critics like Richard Rorty diagnose as the great cultural-political failure of the post-Vietnam Left.[185] King continued to speak of our "beloved nation," and framed his indictments in terms of America's "failure to make democracy real and follow through on the revolutions *we* initiated." Yet his talk of "new values" or a "revolution of values" suggests a different relation to consensus and contestation within the national community.

"Our movement," he pleaded, must not be understood as one "that seeks to integrate the Negro into *all* the existing values of American society." Instead he called on the evolving civil rights movement to be a coalition of "*creative dissenters* who will call our beloved nation to a higher destiny," and who may be retrospectively *judged* in the course of history as members of "a great people—a black people—who . . . through tenacity and creative commitment, injected new meaning into the veins of American life."[186]

In Search of Creative Dissent: Conjuring the Absent Majority and Transgressing the Stigma of Minorities

King gives an account of the disobedient "minority" as "creative" of "new values," as capable of injecting "new meaning," and of providing for the very "survival" of a faltering society bewitched by "old presuppositions."[187] This is not easy to domesticate within Rawls's description of civil disobedience as when "a minority leads the majority to consider whether it wants to have its acts *taken in this way,* or whether, *in view of the common sense of justice,* it wishes to *acknowledge* the claims of the minority."[188] As in the transnational public sphere, King's view of civil disobedience anticipates and aims to provoke a deepened capacity for receptivity, the restructuring of civic identity, and reconfiguration of politics and political subjectivity. In this, his account is closer to that of J. M. Bernstein, who argues that, "civil disobedience is theatrical in that it always involves the revelation of a scene where the absent majority becomes visible in or through the dissenting minority voicing the polemical principle unheeded by the actual majority."[189]

Moving from the *actual* majority to realizing an *anticipated* majority, however, is a treacherous leap, one that King's accounts of civil disobedience and protest help us rethink. One of the features of King's writing and rhetoric that deserves closer scrutiny is how, in texts like "Letter from a Birmingham Jail" or *The Trumpet of Conscience,* he subtly deconstructs the solidity and identity of the extant "majority" to which Rawls expects the civil disobedient to appeal. In a handful of powerful passages, instead of speaking to "white people," "the white community," or the "white majority" as such, King disaggregates the racial category in what I take to be part of an anticipatory politics. These rhetorical gestures, I argue, perform important critical and reconstructive work.

Insofar as King wants to undermine existing habits and attachments of white racial solidarity, he tries to avoid arguing or protesting in ways that might *indiscriminately* reinforce reflexive commitments and attachments to white majoritarian rule and existing white identities. Thus, King frequently draws attention to existing ideological and interest-based fissures between white people. He insists, for instance, that "within the white majority there exists a substantial group who cherish democratic principles above privilege and who have demonstrated a will to fight side by side with the Negro against injustice . . . [and] another and more substantial group . . . composed of those having common needs with the Negro and who will benefit equally with him in the achievement of social progress." These descriptions model for his (mostly black) allies a way of avoiding one of King's greatest worries, which is that black people's feelings of resentment or betrayal toward *particular* white people, will be unjustly inflated to "an excess of skepticism . . . [which] becomes a fetter" in political struggle. Against separatist currents in the Black Power movement, for instance, King argues that such skepticism irrationally "denies that there can be reliable white allies, even though some white people have died heroically at the side of Negroes in our struggle and others have risked economic and political peril to support our cause."[190] While vigilance against betrayal or halfhearted commitment is warranted, it is wrong, King insists, to treat whiteness as a reliable signifier of these vices.

Elsewhere King deconstructs whiteness by amending it with other appellations that have their own substantive normative role expectations—Christian, liberal, moderate, youth, radical, and even "hippie."[191] Such gestures allow King to immanently critique his fellow white citizens by appealing to the normative content of social roles they may identify with, model new forms of inhabiting those roles, and, thus help imaginatively render their transition from an oppressive majority to a novel, emancipatory one that is not yet visible or the object of "consensus" values.

The narrative structure is worth dwelling on as it discloses new perspectival orientations toward "white" identities. When discussing the white moderate or white Christian in "A Letter from a Birmingham Jail," for example, King first expresses a deeply felt disappointment in their lack of recognition respect or motivated action and in their failure to live up to standards of judgment that one might expect them to accept insofar as they indeed identify as moderates or Christians. He then turns skepticism inward, considering the possibility that perhaps *he* is mistaken for even believing that such ethical standards might reasonably attach to these roles given the forces at work in society and human psychology to undermine these identities and their constitutive ideals. Immediately, however, he summons, as if in a flash of redeeming memory, those white individuals who have worked alongside African Americans in civil rights struggle: "Some—such as Ralph McGill, Lillian Smith, Harry Golden, James McBride Dabbs, Ann Braden and Sarah Patton Boyle—have written about our struggle in eloquent and prophetic terms. Others have marched with us down nameless streets of the South. They have languished in filthy, roach-infested jails, suffering the abuse and brutality of policemen who view them as 'dirty nigger-lovers.' Unlike so many of their moderate brothers and sisters, they have recognized the urgency of the moment."

Two features of this passage are especially important. The first is that in *naming* particular veterans of civilly disobedient action, King aesthetically stages an opportunity for an imaginative inhabiting of these new, heroic social roles. The ambition here is to short-circuit racial and racist reasoning from the standpoint of white group identity. Invoking a famous scene from Harper Lee's *To Kill a Mockingbird* (1960), where Scout Finch disperses the members of a lynch mob by identifying them by name, King suggests that nonviolent civil disobedience performs similar work of "changing the face of the enemy" and separating individual from system or group.[192] King's faith in the work of this disaggregation, and its moral power, is likely influenced by his reading of Reinhold Niebuhr's *Moral Man and Immoral Society* (1932), where Niebuhr argues that in "every human group there is less reason to guide and to check impulse, less capacity for self-transcendence, less ability to comprehend the needs of others and therefore more unrestrained egoism than the individuals, who compose the group, reveal in their personal relationships."[193]

The second is that King's demonstration of the social roles that white people can play in society purposefully tries to transfigure and revalue the existing terms of dishonor and heroism that circulate among the white majority such that even these become axes of disagreement and realignment, turning "temporary obstacles" into "potential allies."[194] This recognition that desires for social esteem, honor, and praise need are unlikely to be extinguished in any imaginable regime or time of political conflict issues in an important insight. Part of anticipating and reconstituting a new majority inevitably involves reconfigurations of cultural-aesthetic questions of value, social scripts, affective attachments, and performances of esteem and appraisal that cut across existing axes of difference and disagreement.[195] It anticipates and helps make possible new, if indeterminate, forms of life within which the transformative projects of those who practice civil disobedience might secure more powerful forms of assent and acknowledgment.

King's expansive faith in the capacity of civil disobedience to create new values rests in his sense of its unique, albeit fragile, *provocative* power in the public sphere. Once we dismiss the misleading analogy of the conscientious objector breaking specifically unjust laws, we can focus on the fact that King, Rawls, and most other theorists of civil disobedience readily concede that one can (and often should) breach laws (i.e., traffic laws) that have nothing to do with the laws or forms of injustice being protested. But once we concede this, it immediately begs the question, Why choose civil disobedience as our form of dissent at all?[196]

One could suggest that civil disobedience uniquely expresses a refusal to cooperate with the existing social scheme because of its unfair terms, but, as Tommie Shelby has recently argued, any number of actions might express this, including criminal disobedience or a refusal to work.[197] Here Bertrand Russell's argument about civil disobedience has the virtue of cutting a direct path through a lot of hand-wringing—civil disobedience is simply an especially productive route via which "people are roused to inquire into questions which they had been willing to ignore" and thus a way to puncture the fog of broader societal indifference about injustice.[198]

But, again, this begs the question of *why* and *when* civil disobedience provoke us in the necessary way. What arrests our attention or elicits the right response? This question, which is so thoroughly about appearance, sensibility, reception, and judgment is, therefore, I think impossible to answer a priori and in perpetuity, but King suggests some general clues to this phenomenon. Beyond more familiar arguments about innate horror at undeserved suffering, admiration for courageous resolve, or even the shock of naked violence, we also see in King's writings a unique appreciation of the aesthetic force of *transgressing expectations of identity*.

It is difficult now to capture, viscerally, the depth of inferiorizing racial stigmas against black intelligence, organizational capacity, virtue, courage, and self-respect that ideologically buttressed the Jim Crow regime. Against this backdrop, the direct action campaigns of the 1960s spectacularly upended calcified expectations about black capability, especially with regard to strategic intelligence and political agency. King characterized Jim Crow racism as depicting the Negro "as a clown—irresponsible, resigned and believing in his own inferiority."[199] The spectacle of disciplined, direct action confrontation with dangerous mobs and police authority, however, "dissolved the stereotype of the grinning, submissive Uncle Tom. . . . The Negro was no longer a subject of change; he was the active organ of change."[200] In our own moment, where black people are stereotypically associated with reflexive protest and the aggressive assertion of grievances, it is important to underscore just how dramatic this redefinition of blackness was. For King, the most significant and deleterious stereotype regarding black people, at least in the South, was not their irrepressible militancy or disposition toward violence but their bewildering *passivity*. "The nation," King lamented, "had come to count on [the Negro] as a creature who could quietly endure, silently suffer and patiently wait . . . whatever the provocation."[201] One can glean some measure of this transformation through the cognitive dissonance suffered by those spectators to civil disobedience that, unable to imagine black protest, could not imagine the civil rights insurgency as anything other than a Soviet plot.[202]

We need to take this jarring juxtaposition of the phenomenology of race and the phenomenology of political action seriously because it may suggest that the abstractions of majority/minority that structure liberal theories of civil disobedience too readily allow for a conflation of minorities of opinion and minorities subjected on the basis of visible identities. When Rawls, for example, implores groups with various grievances to organize among themselves to coordinate and limit acts of civil disobedience in order to preserve stability, it betrays a sense that the key dilemma of their appearance in public is quantitative rather than qualitative. In the domain of nonideal theory, however, we should have recourse to more plausible and textured readings about the various aesthetic regimes that structure it when making such claims. These ethico-aesthetic dilemmas might involve, as they did for King, morally weighty reflections on whether a visible minority whose somatic differences can be easily taken as signifiers of *natural* inferiority can afford to be overly reticent in their approach to protest *or* more familiarly aesthetic questions like the inability of street marches in large cities to pierce through the "normal turbulence of city life."[203]

This intuition gains even more significance when combined with an implication of King's thoughts about provocation as involving the unsettling of expectations of identity. One way of parsing the aesthetic allure of the transgression of expectation, is that it, ironically, fulfills a deeper cultural expectation itself—namely, modernity's compulsory drive toward the production of the new.[204] As an irreducibly aesthetic phenomenon, civil disobedience is subject to this same demand for the "new" despite whatever moral or political claims are proffered by its practitioners. To clarify my point here, an ethico-aesthetic judgment about the design, performance, or meaning of protest is inevitably subject to this cultural compulsion toward "the new," a compulsion that can only gain its concrete form against the backdrop of whatever the prevailing aesthetics of race and racial formation are at the time. Here I endorse Monique Roelofs's contention that "racial formations are aesthetic phenomena and aesthetic practices are racialized structures. A theory of the nature of race and racism . . . must address the place of the aesthetic in processes of racialization. Correlatively, a theory of the aesthetic as a philosophical category . . . must account for the ways in which structures of aesthetic exchange channel racial passions and perceptions."[205]

Far from the disarray and crisis that Rawls imagines from the repetition of acts of civil disobedience, the far more terrible truth is that our aesthetic sensibilities are arranged such that performances of disobedience that appear too derivative, too typical, or too prefigured (whether with reference to "race" or not) often appear to us as what Susan Sontag calls the "merely interesting" and thus cannot perform the attention-grabbing work that authorizes most acts of civil disobedience in the first place.[206] Perhaps the cruelest irony of all is that it is partially the historical inheritance of King's iconography, and the ways his image and memory have been domesticated in American political culture, that overdetermines and assimilates our apprehension of many acts of disobedience, leading us to treat them as "particularity already mediated by type" and thus not especially provocative.[207] It is revealing, on this account, that a great deal of the literature on the Black Lives Matter movement has been devoted to the ways that it is, or is not, a "new" civil rights movement—a question whose political-aesthetic implications are far more interesting than its sociological ones.[208]

If, as some critical theorists argue, a radical democratic perspective sees civil disobedience as a "practice of collective self-determination, as a dynamizing counterweight to the rigidifying tendencies of state institutions that attempt to absorb the constituent power of their subjects," the modality of action and rhetoric I have been elaborating might be understood as an overlooked but constitutive element of this practice: the attempt to remake the "self" or "selves" in self-determination.[209] It asks, implicitly or explicitly, Who is the *self* in *self-determination?* In King's hands, this impulse is an outgrowth of nonviolent philosophy and his ontological account of our interdependence in "a mutual garment of destiny." As Judith Butler has noted, part of what is at stake in nonviolent action is the attempt to dramatize and distill how "if the self is constituted through its relations with others, then part of what it means to preserve or negate a self is to preserve or negate the extended social ties that define the self and its world," a project that should lead us to accept "a wider regime of the self—those with whom identification is possible or who are recognized to constitute the broader social or political domain of selves to which one's own self belongs."[210] Without such an account, abstract broadsides against democratic dysfunction, political sclerosis, or collective disempowerment proceed without a critical, creative assessment of the normative value of various boundaries of political community to whom ideals of self-determination might refer. A closer look at the ethico-aesthetic problems of civil disobedience from King's vantage aids us in seeing how movement attempts to re-create the meanings of *minority* and *majority* are crucial to this process.

Civil Disobedience as Aesthetics and Epistemology: Punishment, Inequality, and Stigma

While this ethico-aesthetic problem of civil disobedience remains unfamiliar, one domain where civil disobedience's capacity for the transfiguration of value and the retraining of reflective judgment is already widely acknowledged by Rawls and other commentators: the revaluation or resignification of punishment. King, for instance, describes civil disobedience as turning jail from "a disgrace [into] a badge of honor."[211] Especially in the wake of the civil rights movement's exemplarity, the willingness of the person engaging in civil disobedience to accept punishment for transgressing the law is widely thought by political philosophers to be a key demonstration of their fidelity to the constitutional order or the prevailing conception of justice. The suffering that attends punishment is treated as a reliable signifier of sincerity or other virtues.

But this preoccupation with the meaning of punishment, for Rawls and his inheritors, is intimately related with his contractarian framework. As we have seen, a central problem of civil disobedience for Rawls is that public violations of law raise the specter of self-interested "free riding" on a complex scheme of social cooperation and threaten its stability. From this standpoint, those engaging in civil disobedience need to find ways of expressing their commitment to the underlying scheme in ways that might overcome the fact that our intentions are not transparent to our fellows nor is political rhetoric always a reliable guide to motivating reasons. This leads Rawls to treat the voluntary and peaceful acceptance of punishment for acts of civil disobedience as akin to a promissory note: a "bond" that "makes good one's sincerity" and reaffirms our commitment to the political and constitutional order. Indeed, in an assertion that uncomfortably evokes Friedrich Nietzsche's infamous genealogical connection between debt, punishment, and promising, Rawls argues as a condition of justified civil disobedience that "we must *pay a price* in order to establish that we believe our actions have a sufficient moral basis in the convictions of the community."[212]

Critics in the "new" debate on civil disobedience have largely focused on how this conception of the relation of punishment and suffering to fidelity to law or the notion of a reasonably just society diverged mightily from many activists' views on the matter.[213] There is good reason to do so. King rejected the "reasonably just" description of society and seemed to resent few charges more than the accusation of free riding. When "long-withheld rights and privileges are looked upon as prizes he seeks from impertinent greed," King writes, quoting the famous words attributed to Patrick Henry in the debates on the Stamp Act, "only one answer can come from the depths of a Negro's being. . . . 'If this be treason, make the most of it.'"[214] Michael Walzer expresses similar bewilderment at the assumption that debates about civil disobedience should expend such energy on "the purely theoretical possibility that [such] action might be universalized, that all men might break the laws or claim exemptions from them."[215]

For King, in particular, the tight linkage of suffering with sincerity and fidelity to the extant constitutional order was too narrow and conciliatory. Outside of "A Letter from a Birmingham Jail," King put far more emphasis on the expectation early in his career that witnessing undeserved suffering and punishment by resolute activists could occasion feelings of shame and make one's fellow citizens more receptive to self-transformation and persuasion. In later years he emphasized the disruptive and incapacitating dimensions of accepting punishment, and especially the effect that filling jails or refusing bail on minor charges would have on police morale, the indignation of spectators, and the capacity for repression.[216] Even when suffering is meant to underscore commitment or faith in the possibility of community and constitutional law, this commitment is perhaps best characterized as *only in principle* and as *anticipatory*.

Although perhaps anathema to the literature's tendency to increasingly champion "uncivil" forms of civil disobedience, I worry that this tendency obscures how King's politics of civil disobedience hews closer to Teresa Bejan's account of "civility" as a courageous commitment to carry on in shared, cooperative society with those whom we have radical disagreements not necessarily bridged by overlapping consensus.[217] In King's case, however, this is not "mere" civility motivated by a minimalist respect for social order but a "loving" or *agapic* civility.[218] Using the Greek notion of *agape* to distinguish his conception of love from romantic or fraternal notions, King describes *agapic* love as when "the individual seeks not his own good, but the good of his neighbor" without any discrimination. Agape finds the neighbor in every person it meets, and the willingness to suffer punishment rather than impose it indiscriminately and violently on others is meant to enact this aspiration.[219]

A question that emerges from this way of approaching is how, given the possible spaces of appearance, can one effectively instantiate and embody agapic civility and sincerity?[220] Answering this question requires breaking with the assumed connection between fidelity to law, sincerity, and punishment as intuitive and unproblematic. Philip Hart, for instance, proclaims that "any tolerance that I might feel toward the disobeyer is dependent on his willingness to accept whatever punishment the law might impose."[221] More recently, William Scheuerman bases an argument for the *sincerity* of the infamous National Security Administration whistleblower, Edward Snowden, on a lengthy list of the sufferings and costs that his decision occasioned.[222]

The more skeptical pressure we place on this supposed link between suffering, punishment, and sincerity, however, the more we find both suffering and punishment aesthetically inscrutable and difficult to fix as a stable signifier of sincerity.[223] Like the misguided expectation that torture discloses truth, we should find this presupposition far more unreliable than we do. Whatever one thinks of black nationalist criticisms of direct action protestors, their various charges of masochism, martyr complexes, desires for fame, love of praise, parvenuism, and so on, all reveal a kind of inherent difficulty in trying to solve the problem of sincerity's inscrutability through indexing it to suffering. Human intentions and desires are always, to some degree, opaque, and as Nietzsche realized, even great suffering can be revalued and assimilated to the desire and pleasure of power.[224]

The problem of the ineffability of punishment itself is a clue to the intensifying ambivalences of civil disobedience in our contemporary moment. The exemplary place of the civil rights movement in our political culture, and the move to procedurally and politically manifest a sharp distinction between criminal and civil disobedience, tends toward many police and politicians advocating minor sanctions for those who engage in such disobedience. Philosophers like Kimberly Brownlee argue that we should avoid punishing them altogether.[225] Further, because of the massive expansion of the carceral state since King's time, the effect of the stigma of arrest on social esteem has been attenuated in many communities when compared to the past.[226] And, as the cultural distinction between civil and criminal disobedience is much more resilient, the stigma of prison is not particularly likely to attach to the civilly disobedient person.

Yet because we retain, epistemically and culturally, an intuitive sense that the practice of punishment helps us to judge sincerity and conviction, the fact that these punishments are so minor mean that they have difficulty meeting the hurdle of suspicion that the very demand for punishment emanates from. The ritualization, and even rote character, of punishment for civil disobedience in our era rebalances the scales of public attention. It can make civil disobedience seem more self-aggrandizing than self-sacrificing—a naked grasp for self-righteousness and heroism which disfigures its appearance. It traps most who engage in civil disobedience in a paradoxical zone of intractable inefficacy, where they appear more like civil rights movement reenactors in the safe confines of street theater, than what King called an "active organ of change." Those acts of protest that have managed to pierce the broader public consciousness in recent years are distinguished, not coincidentally, by supplanting or superseding the expressive drama of punishment with more compelling feats of danger and endurance. I am thinking here of something like the demonstrations in Ferguson, Missouri, following the killing of Michael Brown, a young black man, by white police officer Darren Wilson in 2014. What began as local grief and outrage eventually swelled to numbers that occasioned a jarring display of militarized policing and violent repression, yet protestors and their supporters sustained their demonstrations for over a year, an astonishing organizational feat. Modes of action speak in a different, more agonistic way to the demand for "sincerity" that liberalism tends to impose on civil disobedience through the expectation and anticipation of punishment.[227]

Economic Justice and Civil Disobedience

Even if this rereading of King's reflections on the ethico-aesthetic problems of civil disobedience is generative, there is a concern that I have only made Rawls's normative case even stronger. To the extent that Rawls is worried about the burdens of judgment when confronted with civil disobedience, we seem only to have compounded their difficulty. This is perhaps most clearly demonstrated via a contrast with Rawls's sense that the dangers civil disobedience entails must be curtailed through the imposition of a presumptive restriction on its claims to precisely the kind of basic political and civil liberties that are enumerated in the US Constitution rather than problems of economic inequality and injustice.

When politics moves from correcting violations of these constitutional essentials into questions of economic inequality, Rawls warns that we should be more restrained in supporting civil disobedience. This is because debate on issues of equal opportunity and economic equality "depends upon theoretical and speculative beliefs as well as upon a wealth of statistical and other information, all of this seasoned with shrewd judgment and plain hunch," an epistemological morass that makes it difficult to convince others of our good faith and raises now-familiar problems of sincerity and free riding.[228]

The dissonance with King here is striking; he endorses no such prohibition and evinces no such concern. King concedes that, up until 1965, most of his most strident demands had "constitutional backing . . . [and] legal support from the federal courts." Yet, when confronting the enduring inequalities of racial injustice, economic inequality, and the fulfillment of fair housing, guaranteed jobs and basic income, and adequate education, King admits that "the voice of the Constitution is not clear."[229] Unlike Rawls, however, King insists that mass forms of civil disobedience are not only appropriate but also *necessary* for confronting inequality, as well as other public policy decisions that imperil its overcoming (i.e., military expenditures in unjust wars). And, far from more tentative or conciliatory, King's post–civil rights legislation arguments for civil disobedience are even more baldly coercive. In the posthumously published *The Trumpet of Conscience,* King writes admiringly of a program of "mass civil disobedience" that is not simply a "statement to the larger society" or a supplicant to "government goodwill" but which "compel[s] unwilling authorities to yield to the mandates of justice" and "interrupts [society's] functioning at some key point."[230]

Setting aside the thorny question of how King might respond more broadly to Rawls's arguments for lexical priority, it strikes me that its dissolution in the domain of civil disobedience reflects, at least, a profound skepticism about the kinds of aesthetic claims at work. While Rawls treats questions of economic justice as dangerously beset by burdens of judgment and suggests its fulfillment as part of the promise of equal citizenship, King emphasizes the multiple forms of obscurantism and obstruction through which prima facie equal citizenship is betrayed and injustice obscured.

"Throughout our history," King reflects, "laws affirming Negro rights have consistently been circumvented by ingenious evasions which render them void in practice."[231] One great benefit of the "long civil rights movement" framework is that it draws our attention to the long, arduous struggle for voting rights and the right to hold office.[232] At the level of constitutional law, African Americans have been explicitly guaranteed the right to vote since the 1870 passage of the Fifteenth Amendment to the Constitution. The problem, however, was that violations of political rights occurred through measures that did not rely on constitutional law. Instead they pursued black voter disenfranchisement through nonstate avenues like the primary elections held by political parties and economic sanction by employers, or putatively "race-blind" measures like grandfather clauses, poll taxes, literacy tests, felon disenfranchisement, criminal statutes, and the gerrymandering of districts. There was no straightforward process of demonstrating the extensive labyrinth of practices that congealed into a daunting structure of black disenfranchisement, and the relentless contestation by black people and their allies over the course of the long civil rights struggle involved the same sorts of statistical analyses, theoretical interpretations, and "shrewd" judgment to demonstrate this injustice for the wider polity and dismantle the edifice of voter suppression piece by piece, from the white primary in 1944 to fights over gerrymandering in the late 1960s. In short, even the systematic violation of basic rights and liberties requires complicated forms of unmasking, demonstration, and agitation to attain public acknowledgment. Understanding this fact of politics, King showed less hesitancy in extending civil disobedience to other questions of justice, like economic inequality and foreign policy.[233]

This confidence is also rooted in King's estimation of the aesthetic force of civil disobedience as an aesthetic spectacle. The unsettling and transformative capacities that King attributes to the best iterations of civil disobedience are best described as a form of "world disclosure," meant to "disturb the unreflective, taken-for-granted flow of our self-understanding and social practices," introducing new meanings, perspectives, vocabularies, modes of attention, and the like, whose aim is to make us, ultimately, "more accountable to, more responsible for, the proportion of continuity and discontinuity in the forms of life we pass on."[234] This point is clarified in an illuminating rendering of his plans for the Poor People's Campaign, which King imagined as a multiracial and largely impoverished wave of citizens subjecting Washington, DC, to mass civil disobedience and occupation. Here King anticipates acts of civil disobedience that violate trespassing and loitering codes in area hospitals, and that risk arrest, but which will wrench us out of our taken for granted practices and occasion a moment of anguished reflection: "If you are, let's say, from rural Mississippi, and have never had medical attention, and your children are undernourished and unhealthy, you can take those little children into the Washington hospitals and stay with them there until the medical workers cope with their needs, and in showing it your children, you will have shown this country a sight that will make it stop in its busy tracks and think hard about what it has done."[235] Rawls's focus on constitutional essentials leads him to an unduly restricted conception of the site of justice dominated by the state and the legal system. G. A. Cohen argues that "properly understood, the Rawlsian difference principle, which condemns inequalities that contradict the interests of the worst off, applies not only to the actions of the state but also to the choices of individuals that are beyond the reach of the state."[236] Hence, while Rawls's definition of civil disobedience as aimed at changing government policies and law is consonant with King's vision of civil disobedience as articulated in "A Letter from a Birmingham Jail," it ignores the fact that in Birmingham and other campaigns, King targeted business elites, civil society organizations (including churches), and citizens as such—not just the state—to live up to the principles of justice because he conceived of justice as a virtue of persons and civil society, as well as the state or the basic structure of society. Indeed, one of the key insights of the classical phase of the civil rights movement was that the two were inextricable, especially insofar as attempts to challenge the ritual humiliation and degradation of black people in the private sphere were consistently met with state opposition in the form of police intervention on the grounds of *public order* and the *stability of law,* and because the achievement of justice in a bureaucratic state depends on the personal virtues of bureaucratic functionaries.[237]

The attempt to delimit the content of public reason or the arena of civil disobedience restricts what can emerge as a consideration of basic justice. That Rawls's conception of public reason unduly restricts the unpredictability of democratic justice and its constitutive capacity for need interpretation, the articulation of new rights claims, and contested terrain of politics is a contention that has been pursued profitably by a number of critical democratic theorists, and I will not repeat their arguments here.[238] I will simply add that such strict prioritization of constitutional essentials, particularly when defended by reference to a claim that their enactment will help restrict the escalation of social and economic inequality, serves to buttress the romantic idea that the African American civil rights movement considered legal protections as the chief end of the movement, that the achievement of constitutional rights has (or should have) set us on an irreversible path to broader forms of social and economic equality, and that the violation of basic liberties exhausts the legitimacy of direct-action protest.

Ideology and the Tasks of Political Philosophy

I hope this discussion helps clarify the long-term philosophical stakes in King's and Rawls's competing approaches to political philosophy and the limits of romantic narrative. Rawls defends what he calls its "practical" role, arguing that we should seek to discover, underneath explosive and divisive disagreements in society, the deeper, shared commitments from which we might refocus our moral and political judgments to attain consensus on our governing principles. This task is aided by a second, that of "orientation," which gives an account of our "political and social institutions as a whole" and situates our "aims and purposes" and civic status in a historical account that is, crucially, that of "a nation." Further, while Rawls is concerned to disclose injustice and supports radical reforms to attain it, he is also concerned with the task of *reconciliation.* He wants to "calm our frustration and rage against our society." In other words, he thinks political philosophy should aim to show, despite the prevalence of injustice and irrationality in everyday life, that many of our key institutions, social facts, and self-conceptions have a deeper, rational core that we need to affirm from "a philosophical point of view" (e.g., that of the nation-state, religious pluralism, etc.).[239] Lastly, to make such tasks emancipatory rather than ideological, on Rawls's own explicitly hopeful account they must avoid status quo bias toward existing institutions and extend our *utopian* imagination toward the limits of practicable political possibility.

With King as foil, what would it mean to set aside the concern with "ideal theory as ideology" and instead follow Rawls's intimated anxieties about the threat of ideology hiding amid these conceptions of the tasks of philosophy? The threat of ideology, in other words, may not be ideal theory as such, but the way that the philosopher's self-conception of their tasks may lead their *judgment* awry in developing the core concepts and commitments which guide their navigation between ideal and nonideal. For instance, the presumption that the "practical" role of political philosophy in a society like twentieth- or twenty-first-century America is to excavate the alleged deep consensus of our (singular) public political culture raises the persistent threat of the philosopher displacing conflict and dissensus over injustice through narratively laden concepts, question-begging descriptions, and historical romanticism. The consequence, in such cases, can be a kind of deep "misorientation" or "reconciliation as ideology" that undermines the utopian aspirations of political philosophy by obscuring the need to *sharpen* dissensus and transform the broader categories of our self-description and self-conception at critical moments. In a society built on racial domination at home and abroad, Rawls's identification of practicality with deep consensus, and reconciliation with the search for the rational "essence" of our historical institutional development, may be especially likely to lead us to compulsively and blindly produce ethico-historical accounts of consensus that exaggerate the depth and scope of agreement in our "background" political culture or the rationality of its development, making it difficult to find "orientation" in the appropriate sense. This matters because these histories, these self-descriptions, and their conceptual underpinnings then become the grist for the abstractions and idealizations that produce the fundamental categories of political and public philosophy, papering over the alchemy of historical, political, and other judgments that authorized them at their origin.[240]

Glimpsing the legitimation crisis occasioned by the interpenetration of racism, poverty, and militarism, Rawls does not approach an equivalent philosophical or self-reckoning to King's turn. The transformative possibilities of the affect of disgust or disdain, so palpable in Rawls's response to arguments in the style of Banfield and Moynihan, remain subtly discouraged by Rawls's approach to the tasks of political philosophy. The confrontation with racial injustice in the drama of his 1966 conscription resolution is, for Rawls, a missed opportunity to occasion a rethinking of what kind of society we inhabit and what parties to the conversation of justice have claims on us.

In a brief passage in *Law of Peoples* (1993), for example, Rawls argues that when a "so-called liberal" society requires citizens to fight for economic gain, power, or empire, "it no longer honors the Law of Peoples, and it becomes an outlaw state." Elsewhere he criticizes the United States' covert efforts to overthrow democratic governments in Chile, Guatemala, Iran, and Nicaragua as unjust actions motivated by "monopolistic and oligarchic interests without the knowledge or criticism of the public" that exploited the rhetoric of "national security in the context of superpower rivalry."[241] Yet never does one get the sense that the aftermath of Vietnam led Rawls to fundamentally rethink his *orientation* to America's history of settler colonialism, imperialism, and domination or his *reconciliatory* account of our essential institutions. Nor does one get the sense that Rawls recognized, as King did in the wake of Vietnam, how deeply *race* affects these judgments of "security" and of which societies are "decent" or "outlaws."

This kind of reckoning, as we see in King, should lead toward a revision of the terms on which utopian strivings for global and domestic justice must proceed, including a consequent emphasis on the problem of self-professed liberal societies becoming "outlaw" ones under the ideological influence of racialized discourses of security, racial paranoia, and religious bigotry that are more widely dispersed than the machinations of oligarchs.[242] This would introduce a "conversation of justice," both domestically and globally, where the significance of racism and the participatory parity of differently racialized groups in all governance institutions would loom far more largely.

Conceiving of a *democratic* political philosophy's task as one principally of distilling principles from the dominant consensus and proffering reconciliation as a response to political despair tilts the scale too heavily against the kind of humility and openness, self-reproach and receptivity necessary to seriously contend with the way these problems marginalize the most vital voices in the conversation of justice. It is also not especially amenable to the militant, contentious, and, in King's word, "coercive" politics that might be necessary to restage that conversation when it is substantially disfigured by ideology and misrecognition. Doing justice, in theory and practice, depends on an ethos of vigilance and receptivity. As citizens and thinkers—indeed, as thinking citizens—we cannot be "distracted" (again, in Cavell's sense) by our conventional ideals and end, self-descriptions, or the conception of our tasks such that we fail to do the painful work of transforming these things when necessary. For Cavell, the possibility of a more perfect justice must be wrested from the provisional, ignoble settlements of cultural and political convention that do not deserve the reconciliation or philosophical genuflection that romance seems to cultivate.[243]

This criticism is not without cost, however. A romantic history of the civil rights movement, especially as it circulates in public and political philosophy, was asked to play a great theodicean role across our culture. This takes us back to the millennial hope expressed at the end of Myrdal's *American Dilemma*. Published ten years before the *Brown* decision would launch the "classical" phase of the civil rights movement, he wrote that Jim Crow and black subordination could be judged as both "America's greatest failure but also incomparably America's greatest opportunity for the future." Veering from questions of political authority abroad and justice at home toward the full-throated, prophetic rhetoric of theodicy, Myrdal goes so far as to make the resolution of "the Negro Problem" a test "fateful not only for America itself but for all mankind." He writes,

> If America should follow its own deepest convictions. . . . The century-old dream of American patriots that America should give to the entire world its own freedoms and its own faith, would come true. America can demonstrate that justice, equality, and cooperation are possible between white and colored people. In the present phase of history this is what the world needs to believe. Mankind is sick of fear and disbelief, of pessimism and cynicism. It needs the youthful moralistic optimism of America. But empty declarations only deepen cynicism. Deeds are called for. If America in actual practice could show the world a progressive trend by which the Negro became finally integrated into modern democracy, all mankind would be given faith again—it would have reason to believe that peace, progress and order are feasible.[244]

Where this faith falters, due to a poverty of deeds, the limits of modern democracy, or the collapse of its underlying picture of the world, we should not be surprised to see pessimism and cynicism erect its own philosophical tribunal and proclaim its own "tasks" for critical thought. In its mature form, this response has come to bear the name Afropessimism, and in Chapter 7 we turn to its despairing treatment of civil rights exemplarity in the narrative mode of ironic history.

III

AFTER ROMANCE

CHAPTER 7

THE CHANGING SAME

Ironic History and Its Politics in African American Critical Thought

JAMES BALDWIN WRITES,

> The conundrum of color is the inheritance of every American, be he/she legally or actually Black or White. It is a fearful inheritance, for which untold multitudes, long ago, sold their birthright. Multitudes are doing so, until today. This horror has so welded past and present that it is virtually impossible and certainly meaningless to speak of it as occurring, as it were, in time. . . . There have been superficial changes, with results at best ambiguous and, at worst, disastrous. Morally, there has been no change at all and a moral change is the only real one. "*Plus ça change,*" groan the exasperated French (who should certainly know), "*plus c'est le même chose.*" (The more it changes, the more it remains the same.) At least they have the style to be truthful about it.[1]

The more it changes, the more it remains the same. How better to invoke the sensibility ascendent within the American discourse of race—the specter of pessimism? The high tide of optimism about "race relations" or the prospects for achieving racial equality that surrounded Barack Obama's ascendency to the US presidency collapsed mightily by his administration's end and has lingered in the doldrums ever since.[2] Corey Robin argues forcefully that "a deep and abiding racial pessimism now pervades our politics, transcending the divisions of left and right"; a judgment ratified by a chorus of scholars who see such dynamics manifest in the resurgence of white nationalism and racial paranoia on the right, racial despair on the left, and paralyzing melancholia concerning the elusive search for interracial consensus and comity among liberals.[3]

While Obama presented himself as a tonic to such tendencies, his administration was notable in part for coinciding with the influence of a growing number of African American intellectuals who gained substantial popularity for their bleak diagnosis of the role of white supremacy in shaping the American social order and their even bleaker prognosis about the country's prospects for transcending what the most prominent among them, Ta-Nehisi Coates, described as its "heritage" of destroying black bodies.[4] In academia, perhaps the most striking development in this vein is the movement of philosophy and cultural criticism known as Afropessimism.

Fashioning themselves as the philosophical descendants of leading African American critical theorists like Derrick Bell, Saidiya Hartman, and Hortense Spillers, and Afro-Caribbean theorists like Frantz Fanon and Sylvia Wynter, the movement and its leading figures (e.g., Calvin Warren, Jared Sexton, Christina Sharpe, and National Book Award winner Frank Wilderson III) are unified by what the literary critic Jesse McCarthy carefully identifies as four common theses[5]:

1. *The exceptionality thesis*: Blacks are distinctive among modern peoples for the unprecedented and unrestrained violence, animus, and obsession they are subjected to around the world (perhaps especially in the United States).
2. *The immutability thesis*: Antiblackness and black subordination are permanent features of the US social order and, indeed, the modern world. Political struggles like antislavery abolitionism or the civil rights movement have not fundamentally altered this arrangement, and perhaps only "apocalyptic" collapse could.
3. *The structural antagonism thesis*: Antiblackness works at the level of social ontology to structure and overdetermine the interactive possibilities, opportunity structures, institutional forms, cultural lifeworlds, interpersonal relations, and judgments of value between "blacks" and "nonblacks." Afropessimists are notoriously disparaging toward the ideal of solidaristic, interracial politics (that is, "people of color" talk or Third Worldism) or even *analogies* between the sufferings of blacks and nonblacks. Indeed, they argue that the modern concept of the *human* is constituted by permanent reference to its enduring *other:* "the black."
4. *The abjection thesis*: Blackness has no meaning or ontological substance apart from its signification and constitution as "social death." Blackness is a mark of generalized dishonor and abjection, created by and given meaning through the Atlantic Ocean and Indian Ocean slave trades. The slave ship creates and tethers the meaning of blackness, and despite the gallantry of various black nationalist projects of cultural self-assertion or demands for cultural "recognition" or a "cultural politics of difference," these projects will always be self-defeating, repeating the terms of subjection ad nauseum.

While each element of this discourse has long circulated in black political life, two features of the Afropessimist combination are especially striking considering the history of black letters. The first is that in a marked break with other black intellectuals (including many who endorse some of the theses above), leading proponents of Afropessimism explicitly endorse nihilism as the appropriate political response to these converging judgments. Criticizing any sustained investment in politics, they argue that even political hope itself is a ruse of racial domination that must be disavowed for psychic, intellectual, and spiritual integrity.[6] Another striking feature of Afropessimism is that despite the frequent claim that Afropessimists' account of the social ontology of antiblackness "takes place at a level of abstraction that is too high for narrative and the logic of storytelling," their arguments are actually predicated on a unique mode of ironic history and historical narration as a constitutive part of their attack on what they describe as redemptive narrative alternatives.[7]

Concerned by the popularity and influence of Afropessimist thinkers and their arguments in such wide-ranging domains as Black Lives Matter (BLM) activist reading groups, high school debate tournaments, and critical theory circles, a growing number of scholars have sought to bring external standards of critique to bear against the movement, charging it with myopic ignorance regarding the truth of political economy or empirical measures of progress, an ethically indefensible solipsism, or the objectionable diminishment of other forms of oppression (e.g., settler colonialism).[8] Despite sharing these concerns, I approach the issue from another, more self-consciously therapeutic vantage point. The motivation, in other words, is not solely to unmask logical inconsistencies, insist on definitional clarity, and adduce contrary evidence to cast doubt on particular conclusions. Although these conventional philosophical strategies are indispensable, the goal of therapeutic critique is also, to use Martha Nussbaum's words, "practical," "responsive," and "value-relative." It aims to break the spell and undermine the cravings and desires, the captivating illusions and pictures, and the metaphysical and ethical commitments that undergird the attachment to Afropessimist thought.[9]

Focusing specifically on the Afropessimist defense of nihilism, I offer a therapeutic critique that takes Afropessimism's predication on what I describe as a practice of "ironic history" as a productive point of entry to disclose and immanently critique four major flaws in its picture of the world: its incoherence regarding race and reference, its self-undermining and ontologically essentialist conception of "politics," its metaphysical privileging of purity and permanence in its exercise of ethical and political judgment, and its pathological attachment to a conception of the vocation of black intellectualism that has rightly collapsed in the post–Jim Crow era.

These shortcomings should lead us to adopt a more tragic approach to the narration of, and philosophical reflection on, African American history.

Irony, Critique, and History

Irony, as scholars have long noted, is characterized in its simplest or most stable form by a capacity for negation.[10] A central element of this negation stems from creative fixation on the ever-present possibility for incongruence between what is said and what is meant that is germane to language and expression.[11] If irony exploits or is otherwise inextricably tied to this incongruity and the consequent possibility of negation it entails, radical implications may follow as these slippages and incongruities compound. Since at least the time of Søren Kierkegaard, reflections on irony have grasped its possibility to proliferate and spiral toward "absolute infinite negativity," a feature that deconstructionists like Paul de Man would later come to embrace where Kierkegaard recoiled. "Irony in itself," de Man argues, "opens up doubts as soon as its possibility enters our heads and there is no inherent reason for discontinuing the process of doubt at any point short of infinity. . . . Pursued to the end, an ironic temper can dissolve everything, in an infinite chain of solvents."[12]

In other words, ironic critique can move rapidly from the incongruity between a statement and its meaning to a critique of the contents of consciousness, to the adequacy of language to represent subjectivity or the world, to the very coherence of concepts like *world* or *subjectivity*. In this sense, some degree of irony is a basic feature of all sophisticated social or political inquiry. Insofar as we do not assume, for instance, that actors have transparent access to their own motivations or that the descriptions they give to their own actions are fully adequate to analysis, the critic already embraces some measure of ironic distance.[13]

When we move from simply the bare presence of ironic distance to a historical discourse that can be characterized as ironic at the level of narrative form, however, we are tracking something far more specific—namely, how tropes and generic conventions associated with irony are critical to forging a *narrative structure* that conveys, as its overarching meaning, the negation of progress, insisting that what *appears* as progress or improvement is more compellingly described as decline or at least stasis.[14]

My invoking of ironic history seeks to deepen the underappreciated rhetorical dimension of Albert Hirschman's famous study of the "rhetoric of reaction." Hirschman argues that the appeal of arguments about the futility of social reform rest "largely on the remarkable feat of contradicting, often with obvious relish, the commonsense understanding of . . . events [like the French Revolution] as replete with upheaval, change, or real reform."[15] Underscoring my larger argument about exemplary events, it should not be surprising that Hirschman finds himself focusing intensely on the French Revolution as an exemplar of "seemingly enormous, epochal movements" of progress. Irony is occasioned by "something else on which it might produce its negative effects"—in this case, an existing historiographical and philosophical discourse taking an exemplary event like the French Revolution as evidence of radical possibility.[16] For our era, especially in the realm of reflection on American and African American history, ironic critique is routinely occasioned by the ascendancy and entrenchment of a romantic version of history especially centered on the civil rights movement.

Ironic narratives of African American history, therefore, should be considered part of a broader tradition of thought characterized by deep suspicion of the idea of progress or progressive history.[17] Yet understanding the specificity and particular occasion of *this* ironic response requires attention to the fusion of horizons characteristic of contemporary engagement with romantic ideas and stories about the civil rights movement. One must confront, first, that there is a growing sense of crisis concerning the authoritative pillars and imagined futures of black political tradition that once provided stable hermeneutic orientation to the past and within the problem spaces of African American political life.[18] Certain assumptions that once governed inquiry into, and practical understanding of, African American politics as a unified or coherent practice, for example, are no longer authoritative in the sense that we can intuitively appeal to them for understanding.

Aside from the general hermeneutic dilemma that compelled a rethinking of black political life across the humanities, romantic narratives of African American history seem especially susceptible to forms of skepticism that appeal to the enduring injustice and marginalization that characterizes much of contemporary African American life. The sociologist Patrick Sharkey, for example, offers a battery of dispiriting statistics that testify to the endurance of racial inequality since the death of Rev. Dr. Martin Luther King Jr. in 1968:

> When one considers only Americans who have been in the United States since at least 1970, there is even less change in racial inequality [than if recent black immigrants are included]. At the start of the 1970s, about 40 percent of African Americans were in the poorest fifth of the "non-immigrant" US income distribution, compared to about 35 percent at the end of the 2000s. About 82 percent of African Americans were in the bottom three-fifths of the non-immigrant income distribution at the start

of the 1970s, compared to 78 percent at the end of the 2000s. What these figures tell us is that when we consider only families that have been in the country for the last several decades, we see virtually no progress toward racial equality.[19]

Such conditions exert a kind of downward pressure on narratives of African American history (and especially civil rights movement history) that emphasize overcoming and transcendence or reconciliation and unity. Sharkey cannot help but ask the question, "How is it that the first generation of children able to take advantage of expanded civil rights has made so little progress toward economic equality?"[20]

That a problem of the present bleeds backward into historical judgment reflects the triadic relation between past, present, and future at the heart of historical judgment, especially when concerned with exemplary events in political culture. In these special instances, where the historical example is meant to serve as a touchstone of judgment, historical narration is asked more forthrightly to bear the weight of accounts of the present and to connect in some meaningful way (perhaps even as nostalgic rebuke) to the imagined futures that animate the political and social discourse of the present.[21]

The Subcurrents of Ironic History

Part of the utility of a vocabulary harvested from literary criticism (e.g., *the ironic*) is that it helps disclose ontological, political, and ethical commitments that are too often implicit in the kinds of storytelling that historians and political theorists engage in or find compelling. The language of ironic history, in particular, helps us characterize at least three subcurrents of historical discourse that often fit together and are at present inspiring broad engagement in critical theory and social movements alike: qualified fatalism; a hermeneutics of suspicion; and intensive, inward-facing skepticism.

Let's first examine *qualified fatalism*. Ironic historical discourse reflects a deep skepticism of the possibility of redemption, especially conceived as a kind of authentic freedom, a rational (or at least nonpathological) social order, or other forms of collective transcendence (e.g., religious salvation). For Hayden White, ironic and romantic narrative modes are at odds for this reason. The former represents a "drama of diremption . . . dominated by the apprehension that man is ultimately a captive of the world rather than its master, and by the recognition that, in the final analysis, human consciousness and will are always inadequate to the task of overcoming definitively the dark force of death, which is man's unremitting enemy."[22] If a central pillar of romantic narrative is the invocation of redemptive unity, consensus, transcendence, or enlightenment, ironic narratives instead deploy history to unmask our captivity to pathology and finitude. They expose those fissures and fractures that give lie to consensus and the supposed integrity of identity.

Second, this negating skepticism is directed through an expansive *hermeneutics of suspicion* arrayed against the appeal to ethical motivations and explanations in history.[23] It seeks to find baser motives and interests behind appeals to virtue, self-conceptions based on moral or ethical ideals, and professed meanings of human action. The ironist's hermeneutics assume that behind these appearances lay egoism and self-interest, duplicity and self-deception, or concealed forms of domination waiting to be unmasked. The concerns about sincerity, authenticity, and legitimacy that this engenders help produce a broader crisis of heroism in ironic narratives that is at odds with romance. The emergence of irony, White argues, "represents the passage of the age of heroes and of the capacity to believe in heroism" by stressing not only fragility but complicity—the "destructive aspect" that inheres in or follows the hero's ostensible triumphs. Innocence lost, the ironist "looks for the worm in the fruit of virtue everywhere—and finds it," often condemning the fruit accordingly.[24]

Finally, and in line with de Man's contention that irony's absolute negativity has no natural end point, the most fully developed form of irony begins to turn its powers of negation inward on its own categories and self-conception. Subjecting our vocabularies and practical identities to *intensifying forms of skepticism* engenders increasingly radical doubts about their very capacity to adequately describe, disclose, or orient us to the world (including to one another).

The thicket of scare quotes, parentheticals, and strike-throughs (e.g., commonplace uses of "race" or ~~being~~) in poststructuralist texts registers one wing of this dilemma of understanding oneself to be burdened with a vocabulary that is judged inadequate while remaining despairing of our ability to discover—or, better yet, invent—another vocabulary capable of resisting self-undermining skepticism and still remain properly critical.[25] This sense of inadequacy not only inspires historical inquiries into the putative failures of various political discourses or ideals but also generates a further skepticism of the justifications or self-conceptions on which reconstructive critique, practical identity, and practices of politics themselves might expect to proceed.[26]

Together this combination of qualified fatalism, suspicion of motivation and meaning, and skeptical anxieties about purchase of our vocabularies and practical identities combine to forge an ironist form of pessimism that seeks out history as part of its warrant. More hopeful or empowering descriptions of the world become implausible, if not absurd, and what appears heroic or emancipatory in romantic narratives is treated as an occasion for unmasking them as illusory. Such ironic pessimism is distinguished by what White describes as "a manifest disgust with the society, but a refusal to countenance the notion that any public or private action could possibly change the society for the better" and that any authentic flourishing will be episodic, fugitive, or altogether chimerical.[27]

Irony and Its Orders of Analysis

As the preceding discussion perhaps already suggests, a key problem with understanding ironic discourse is diagnosing the order of description and explanation to which it aspires, whether aesthetic, political, cultural, ontological, or metaphysical. Ironic history, particularly in the realm of politics, seems meant to narratively dramatize particular contradictions or misalignments that reveal the above frustrations as having an ostensible logic or pattern within human affairs or human-scale temporalities. There is, however, an instability here. White argues that at their extremes, such histories reflect an "absurdist *view of the world,*" involving the intractable and inescapable frustration of human purposes, longings, and self-understandings.[28]

One need not universalize this claim to realize that White's diagnosis of the absurd reflects a genuine pattern of treating cultural or political phenomena as placeholders for a more ambitious ontological or metaphysical claim about the amenability of the world or cosmos to particular human purposes, ambitions, needs, and expectations. Indeed, these grand metaphysical or ontological speculations are often revealed not simply in the ironist's descriptions of the past but also by how ironic histories are extrapolated into projections or predictions regarding the future's fidelity to the identified patterns. The ironic histories we will assess, for instance, are far more enamored with predictions about the social world than with the resolute stance of humility and openness to unexpected possibilities that characterized, by contrast, some measure of the existentialist obsession with absurdity as the radically unintelligible, unjustifiable nature of human beings' "thrownness" into our condition.[29]

The chief difficulty, however, with discerning the order of explanation at which ironic narratives aim is that it is difficult for them to remain fixated on any particular historical moment or phenomena. Their cascading and self-undermining dynamic tends to spill over into ever-larger historical scope, in some instances transforming historical claims into metaphysical or ontological stories about the world's fundamental misalignment with human flourishing that are no longer recognizable as event-laden histories, although they may retain some tethering to temporality. This is, after all, what led Arthur Schopenhauer, in his polemical restatement of the philosophy of history, to declare,

> History is untruthful not only in its arrangement, but also in its very nature since, speaking of mere individuals and particular events, it always pretends to relate something different, whereas from beginning to end it constantly repeats only the same thing under a different name and in a different cloak. The true philosophy of history thus consists in the insight that, in spite of all these endless changes and their chaos and confusion, we yet always have before us only the same, identical, unchangeable essence, acting in the same way today as it did yesterday and always. . . . The motto of history in general should run: *Eadem, sed aliter* [the same, but otherwise].[30]

The Ironic History and Analytic of the Civil Rights Movement

These preliminary remarks, I hope, will help clarify my specific focus in this chapter, which is to sketch and understand the emergence of an ironic historiography and critique of the civil rights movement aimed at negating its romantic alternative, as well as the political and public philosophy built on its scaffolding. Fundamental to the ironic emplotment of the civil rights movement are, above all, two ideas: the ineradicable permanence and deep logic of systemic antiblackness as the foundation of the American (or global) order, and skepticism about the stability and adequacy of the vocabularies and significations we rely on to describe and disclose blackness, antiblackness, and black political life over time.

Derrick Bell and Permanent Subordination

One of the most influential defenses of the idea that African Americans' history and future would always be shaped by permanent racial subordination was advanced by the legal scholar Derrick Bell and his influential interpretation of the civil rights movement. Surveying the US historical record on race, and especially the ostensible triumph of *Brown v. Board of Education* (1954), Bell concludes with the following proposition: "Black people will never gain full equality in this country. Even those herculean efforts we hail as successful will produce no more than temporary 'peaks of progress,' short-lived victories that slide into irrelevance as racial patterns adapt in ways that maintain white dominance."[31]

Bell's argument about perpetual subordination turns principally on two claims. First, he argues that the stigmatizing symbolism of race that saturates American society makes it impossible for all but a few white people "to identify with blacks as a group." Without group identification at the social psychological level—or *solidarity,* to use the preferred term of political theory—whites cannot develop the necessary levels of civic trust or empathy for African Americans. Instead of alleviating black suffering, they will meet black demands and black participation largely with aversion or suspicion.[32] This treatment is manifestly unjust, but the power of the symbolic order of race is such that it masks, ideologically, what would otherwise readily appear as hypocritical or shameful.

Second, Bell argues that the social psychological dimension of this racial group division is ultimately reproduced through racism's powerful function as a complex mechanism for generating enough material, political, psychic, and social privileges for white Americans in order to maintain cross-class solidarity and social stability in a white-dominated polity. Black Americans, Bell argues, play a "critically important stabilizing role" in American society and history. African Americans serve as convenient scapegoats for the failure to securely establish egalitarian social policy, and their broad exclusion from higher-status jobs and other opportunities ensures genuine material and psychic privileges that white citizens have grown accustomed to and invested in.[33]

Where there *appear* to be gains made for African Americans, like the end of slavery or the civil rights legislation of the 1960s, Bell exhorts us to understand these as something other than a significant transformation of the racist foundations of American society. Instead he contends that such apparent inflection points or moments of moral awakening are really contingent instances of "interest convergence." Whenever a critical mass of white citizens adopt more racially liberal or progressive policy at the macrosocial level or behave in racially inclusive patterns at the microsocial level, close scrutiny will reveal that it was "profitable or at least cost-free" for them to do so.[34] This casts a pall of suspicion over the supposed triumphs of racial liberalism as an ethical project.

In Bell's treatment, for example, the decision in *Brown* reflects an interest convergence situation where the promotion and protection of black civil rights served the more efficacious purpose of thwarting the propaganda efforts of the Soviet Union during the Cold War, a policy goal advanced by a Cold War strategy struggling to win Third World support and operating under the presuppositions of anticommunist domino theory.[35] Indeed, in one essay, Bell goes so far as to insist that *Brown* was wrongly decided and that instead of declaring "separate but equal" inherently unequal, the court should have simply compelled state governments to genuinely equalize funding for separate black institutions (e.g., schools, universities, and public spaces).[36]

Part of Bell's skepticism of the civil rights movement stems from his account of the social conditions of the post–civil rights era, with its undeniable entrenchment of ghetto poverty, social marginalization, and political animosity. He sees these pathologies not as residues of an incomplete revolution but as a "regeneration of the problem in a particularly perverse form." The depth of this perversity becomes clearest when we learn that accepting Bell's account of the radically instrumental, egoistic, and solidaristic foundation of racial politics means not only that all racial liberalism is inherently precarious but more frighteningly that the mass sacrifice of black life is "always lurking in the shadow of current events." This horizon-shaping horror, which Bell articulates by way of speculative science fiction, is the ineliminable possibility of there being some future point where white citizens "reach a consensus that a major benefit to the nation" (e.g., the Civil War–like resolution of some deep public philosophical or political conflict between white people themselves) justifies "an ultimate sacrifice of black rights—or lives."[37] Bell's inheritors, it should be noted, differ primarily in the view that such genocidal logics require no such fictional explication; they are already at work, especially in mass incarceration and policing.[38]

Given this bleak picture of progress as precarious illusion, it is not altogether unsurprising that we see Bell begin his *Faces at the Bottom of the Well* with an appeal to existentialist ethics culled from the early work of Albert Camus and the psychiatrist-philosopher Frantz Fanon. From Camus, Bell wants us to learn "the need for struggle even in the face of *certain* defeat," and from Fanon, he hopes to educate his reader to the importance of an obligation to assume the responsibility of freedom through resistance to domination—even in the face of impossible odds.[39]

Such claims set the stage for a dramatic recasting of the ethical significance of the civil rights movement. In Bell's hands, the meaning of the civil rights movement is that it reveals, in bold strokes, both the illusory nature of racial liberalism and the existentialist heroism of black struggles against the (inevitable) triumph of white supremacy. We are far afield from Obama's portrait of King and others as a "Moses generation," for no Israelites will make it across the River Jordan into Canaan. Yet Bell's pessimism uncannily transforms civil rights movement activists into our contemporaries. They become models for the courageous among us who strive to realize Bell's repetition of Fanon's catechism: man has but "one duty alone: That of not renouncing my freedom through my choices."[40]

The Ironies of Emancipation and the Crisis of Vocabulary

Bell's near-total desiccation of any imagined future beyond existentialist struggle against a permanent and intractable white supremacy, constantly reinventing itself after peaks of "interest convergence," is an important pillar of the turn to irony in black critical thought. There are limits, however, to Bell's ironic gaze that become clearer as we turn to critiques of the civil rights movement and its historiography levied by socialists, feminists, and black nationalists and to the more sweeping skepticism introduced by poststructuralist critics. Despite their profound political differences, these critics all share an abiding concern about what forms of domination are being concealed by or instantiated through political discourse, especially in ostensibly progressive, liberal, or neutral rhetoric.

Among the central concerns of these critics is the rhetorical gesture, popular throughout the civil rights movement and once a historiographical standard, toward a collective black subject. Often identified as the collective "Negro" or "the black man" and capable of bearing romantic narratives foregrounding unity and transcendence, "his" purportedly singular interests, identity, and problems are targeted with deconstructive critique. These critics have rightly unmasked how the ostensible victories of the civil rights movement in legislation and ethical transformation nevertheless did not fundamentally uproot problems of black ghetto and rural poverty or many of the cumulative disadvantages that continue to place downward pressure on the black working class. They have also challenged the ways that practices of antiracist politics have marginalized the voices, interests, and unique vulnerabilities of black women and black queer communities, often conscripting them into forms of solidarity that reproduce subjection along other axes. Beyond this critique of the black subject or general will, these traditions also share an interest in unmasking triumphalist claims about progress and national consensus, raising doubts about the analytical and moral adequacy of prevailing vocabularies and categories of social analysis, and expressing skepticism about the functions of moral discourse and moral explanations in politics and history. Most radically, some of these critics argue that the civil rights movement's goals were not simply unfulfilled but that their rendering in the course of the movement ironically facilitated the reconstitution of injustice or its entrenchment in other domains. These ills—the marginalization of sexual violence in accounts of racial domination or the limited attention integrationists gave to the dignity of black cultural practices—are often concealed by romantic histories' investment in moral progress and their invocations of unity (nationally, or even among black people).

The Eclipse of Emancipation, or, the Prison of Language

A crucial element of this skepticism stems from the poststructuralist critique of race, which lodged a sense of the inadequacy of our linguistic capacities for representation in the heart of race talk. Illustrative of the opening days of this turn is the early work of Henry Louis Gates Jr., which sought to move the philosopher Anthony Appiah's critique of racial essentialism toward a deconstruction of the sign of blackness. "If we believe that races exist as things, as categories of being already 'there,'" Gates warned, "we cannot escape the danger of generalizing about observed differences between human beings as if these differences were consistent and determined, *a priori*"—a danger that he calls "racial reasoning."[41] From this ethical-epistemological plea, Gates's early scholarship turned toward the deconstruction of literary representations of blackness wherever they may be found to be aspiring to postulation as essences or entities.

This critical, ironist gesture is certainly aimed at patently racist representations of people of African descent. But, for Gates, it is also to be turned against oppositional discourses like the black cultural nationalists of the Black Arts movement or black political intellectuals who speak in idioms of shared interests or racial authenticity. These intellectuals, in Gates's critique, make the mistake of turning the "trope of blackness" into a "transcendent presence."[42] The search for the "blackness of blackness," he writes, using Ralph Ellison's ironic turn of phrase, is declared futile. Ellison, in Gates's interpretation, rightly "parodies the idea that blackness can underwrite a metaphysics or even a negative theology; that it can exist outside and independent of its representation."[43]

The argument, therefore, is that blackness has no essence; it just *is* this so-called play of signs, wielded not so playfully in the discursive—but dangerous—realm of racial signification and the institutional formations that serve to fix, provisionally, meaning and reference in human societies. "The vast and terrible text of blackness," Gates proclaims, "has no essence; rather, it is signified into being by a signifier." This not only complicates the stability of historical references to race as an unchanging representation but also engenders an ironic understanding of racism. Gates first defined racism as when "one generalizes about the attributes of an individual (and treats him or her accordingly)"—often taking the form of projecting physically definable or biological essences into "'metaphysical' characteristics."[44]

For some postmodern critics who emphasize the instability of these significations, unmasking and acknowledging them opens the possibility of epistemically and ethically undermining the symbolic regimes of racial difference that fuel racism. This playful conception of irony sees opportunities to reconstruct identity and enjoy contingent forms of freedom and solidarity through deconstruction.[45] Feminist and socialist critics have also sought to emphasize the need for a deconstructive politics with regard to race, although they more forcefully foreground the importance of fundamental economic and structural changes to achieve such resignifications.[46]

For the intellectuals associated with the emerging movement of Afropessimism, however, the fact that the concept of blackness accrued its original meaning in the crucible of slavery and the slave trade as a negation of the human (or its defining attributes of rationality, civilization, beauty, etc.) means that blackness and negation, or blackness and abjection, are inextricably linked, even as the precise morphology of each era's significations changes.[47] For Afropessimist intellectuals, the meaninglessness of blackness is not an occasion for joyful, subversive creativity but for furious, pessimistic meditation on a permanent condition of abjection, a fate as a perpetual outsider to the most fundamental ontological and metaphysical categories of modernity. As the editors of a recent collection of Afropessimist writings contend, "it is Blackness, and more specifically anti-Blackness, that gives coherence to categories of non-Black—white, worker, gay, that is, 'human' . . . it is Blackness that is the dark matter surrounding and holding together the categories of non-Black."[48] Or, as the Afropessimist philosopher Calvin Warren puts the point, "The very structure of meaning in the modern world—signifier, signified, signification, and sign—depends on anti-black violence for its constitution."[49]

This view has immediate social and political, theoretical consequences. For one, no extant theoretical or interpretive paradigm—not Marxism, postcolonial theory, psychoanalysis, feminism, or liberalism—would remain capable of grasping the depth of black abjection. These traditions are guilty of what Frank Wilderson charges is an "unspoken, assumptive logic" that tries and inevitably fails to "analogize Black suffering with the suffering of other oppressed beings" in a shared grammar or redemptive telos.[50] Indeed, one feature of the Afropessimist position is to attempt to move arguments about blackness out of a vocabulary that treats it as one instance among many of racial kinds, insofar as to treat blacks as one family among humans would undermine the opposition between blackness and the human.[51]

More combatively, these traditions' commitments to "redemption," Wilderson argues, are parasitic on black abjection for their coherence; the fantasy of redemption uses the abjection of blackness as its unarticulated and constitutive other. This grounds what Jesse McCarthy describes as the "structural antagonism" thesis within Afropessimism.[52] Not only is every other inhabited category of human identity defined, subconsciously, against blackness as its foil, but there is a perpetual need for nonblacks to produce, reproduce, and give sanction to forms of antiblack violence to sustain them.[53]

Antiblack violence helps reconstitute in practice and remind nonblacks psychologically that the categories on which social life is premised are ontologically real. Wilderson provocatively calls antiblack violence "not a form of racist hatred but the *genome* of Human renewal; a therapeutic balm that the Human race needs to know and heal itself . . . [to] prevent them from suffering the catastrophe of psychic incoherence." Such violence stabilizes the boundaries of society (by producing the "socially dead," society's other), the category of human, and the psychic health and coherent identity of nonblacks.[54]

Although there are black nationalisms that have approached such despairing judgments about a supposed "structural antagonism" created by antiblackness, Afropessimism is distinguished from the nationalist tradition in its refusal of the politics of recognition and redefinition. For black nationalists, the meaning of blackness and black existence need not be constituted by domination, but can become otherwise through the cultural reclamation and revolution. In Warren's view, by contrast, the "affirmation of blackness proves to be impossible without simultaneously affirming the violence that structures black subjectivity itself," a view echoed by Jared Sexton's charge that antiblack subjection is both "presupposition and consequence" of black existence.[55] These critics, in short, do not deny that the concept of blackness is fecund, but they insist that its myriad meanings find their way back to the same urtext of abjection and enslavement. In this way they square the ironist circle: race is always changing, but the fact of antagonism and domination remains the same.

Afropessimism and Ironist Historical Imagination

The most distinctive feature of Afropessimism in black letters is the combination of radically skeptical, semiotically oriented conceptions of blackness and antiblack racism and an endorsement of the permanent racial domination thesis. This juxtaposition, it must be acknowledged, appears contradictory on its face insofar as it tries to reconcile radical malleability and contingency in racial signification with a social theory that posits the intractable, totalizing permanence of antiblack racism and the association of blackness with abjection. Afropessimists, however, attempt to flesh out this contention and persuade their readers of their arguments by mobilizing what can rightly be called an ironic narrative of African American history.

The ironic historical imagination of Afropessimism seeks above all to topple the organizing motifs of romantic history: progress, unity, transcendence, and triumph. According to Wilderson, "The changes that begin to occur after the Civil War and up through the Civil Rights Movement, Black Power, and the American election of a Black president are merely changes in the weather. Despite the fact that the sadism is no longer played out in the open as it was in 1840, nothing essential has changed."[56]

Such sweeping accounts of African American history give ample lie to Wilderson's frequent claim that Afropessimism is at odds with narrative. Such confusion stems from Wilderson's insistence that only redemptive narratives count as narratives, properly construed, perhaps because they have an ending.[57] Yet even the "historical stillness" that Wilderson, appropriating Hortense Spillers, takes to be the vision of Afropessimism must take narrative form because the significations of race, ostensible civic status, or political demands of African Americans have at least the *appearance* of transformation. The Afropessimist must produce an alternative, ironic history that seeks to unmask this appearance as illusory.

It is the only way, for instance, that Afropessimists can claim to show the disingenuousness of the popular view that the civil rights movement represents progress. In their view, the "reformist ideologies" of the movement and "their disastrous integration with bureaucratic machinery" fell into the impossible trap of trying to "affirm Blackness itself without at the same time affirming anti-Black violence."[58] Calvin Warren, for example, claims to unmask Martin Luther King's appeals to the redemptive power of the spectacle of voluntary and undeserved suffering in civil rights protest as the cruelest ruse in American life—blood sacrifices for a democracy never to come.[59] To reinscribe a redemptive narrative with black suffering at its center, Warren argues, imposes on African Americans a kind of masochism and cruel optimism in which "attempts at recognition and inclusion in society will only ever result in further social *and real* death."[60]

These claims avail themselves of, and radicalize, an existing civil rights historiography that also breaks with the chronological ordering of conventional historical discourse to juxtapose and rearrange judgments about the past, present, and future in order to convey unwavering continuity underneath apparent contingency. The aim of this literature is to show how, as the historian Leon Litwack concludes in his ironist account of black political history (appropriately titled *How Free Is Free?*), "It is all very different. It is all very much the same."[61]

A closer look at the last chapter of *How Free Is Free?*, titled "Fight the Power," which covers the period from World War II to the present, may help clarify the point. Litwack renders his hermeneutical fusion of horizons explicit, moving back and forth between evocative renderings of some of the most famous events of the classical civil rights movement (e.g., the march to Selma, Alabama; the Birmingham, Alabama, campaign; the lunch counter sit-ins in Greensboro, North Carolina; and the Freedom Rides) and the contemporary ceremonies meant to recognize and honor the previously scorned activists as American heroes. This romantic move, however, ultimately reveals itself as a dramatic narrative device to occasion and deepen the sense of irony. Litwack's hermeneutic movement and implicit claim of significance turns toward the yawning distance between the redemptive symbolism of events like *Brown* and the 1963 March on Washington for Jobs and Freedom and such contemporary phenomena like the deepening of intergenerational poverty among the poorest 25 percent of African Americans, the correctional control of one in nine adult African American males, and the fact that segregation levels in US public schools have returned to what they were in the 1960s. "For all the political gains, the dismantling of Jim Crow, the mass marches, and the optimistic 'We shall overcome' rhetoric," Litwack concludes, "many of the same tensions and anxieties persisted and festered, the same desperate struggle for survival, the familiar sense of expectations betrayed, of promises not kept."[62] Warren, updating these arguments for a post-BLM era, offers the long list of African Americans infamously killed by police or vigilantes in recent years as "a fatal rupture" that "haunt[s] political discourses of progress, betterment, equality, citizenship, and justice."[63]

This controlling pattern, once unmasked by ironist critique, spills over, ever backward, into the past. The failures of the civil rights movement, therefore, mirror earlier failures of emancipation from slavery. Indeed, Afropessimists regularly refer to emancipation as a "nonevent." "Formally," they argue, "the Black subject was no longer a slave, but the same formative relation of structural violence that maintained slavery remained—upheld explicitly by the police (former slave catchers) and white supremacy generally—hence preserving the equation that Black equals socially dead."[64] Or, as Frank Wilderson puts it, "1865 is a blip on the screen" when compared to the "continuum of slavery-subjugation that Black people [continue to] exist in."[65]

Again, marshaling a contentious reading of the post-BLM present in this light, the Afropessimist goes so far as to suggest that "blackness itself is criminalized" to such a degree that "a Black person on the street today faces open vulnerability to violence just as the slave did on the plantation."[66] As Saidiya Hartman writes, this approach to historical imagination is a kind of "recombinant narrative" that "weaves present, past, and future . . . in narrating the time of slavery as our present."[67] This constant folding inward on itself is what leads Wilderson to contend, however exaggeratedly, that "Black emplotment is a catastrophe for narrative at a meta-level rather than a crisis or aporia within a particular narrative."[68]

Afropessimism and Social Theory

At the level of social theory, Afropessimism contains deep resonances with the early work of Loïc Wacquant on the historical-institutional study of the black ghetto and American prisons. There the paradox between the contingency of racial signification and permanent black subordination is resolved through an implicitly functionalist approach that takes the chronological succession of four "peculiar institutions" as evidence of an underlying antiblack logic to American civilization: chattel slavery, Jim Crow, the pre-1968 racially segregated but class-differentiated urban ghettoes of the north, and the symbiosis between the post-1968 hyper-ghettoes of concentrated poverty and extreme segregation and the expansive prison regime that has grown alongside them. This foundational white supremacy is rooted in a widespread social interest in maintaining racialized caste divisions to stabilize society enough to continue providing vast privileges and profits to elites and lesser material and psychic benefits to working-class white people, model minorities, and a somewhat integrated black managerial-supervisory class. These institutions, therefore, serve the apparently fundamental and self-perpetuating social function of defining, controlling, and confining African Americans.[69]

The inclusion of *defining* is the crucial conceptual move here, as each of these peculiar institutions are identified as the primary race-making institutions of American society—veritable signification factories that give rise to, legitimate, and revise the discourses of race to sustain the control and to confine the functions of the ineliminable American caste system through broader socioeconomic transformations (the Industrial Revolution, Fordism, deindustrialization, global corporate capitalism, etc.). The meaning of blackness, therefore, changes over time regarding the essence it references; the cowardly, submissive, pacifist slave imagined by paternalistic racism in eighteenth-century America, for example, transforms into the violent, merciless, and predominantly black super predators of late twentieth-century criminology.[70]

Afropessimists retain the implicit functionalism but abandon American exceptionalism and place more emphasis on psychic and libidinal features of racial domination. For them, the investment in antiblackness is rooted even more fundamentally in the psychic integrity and constitution of modern subjects and society, as well as in the metaphysical and ontological presuppositions of modern thought and subjectivity. For Wilderson and others, the absurd, erotic, conflicted, compulsory, and excessive character of arbitrary violence against black people exposes a commitment to antiblackness that is libidinal and ontological. The performance of antiblack violence, in this view, serves to produce, regenerate, and stabilize the boundaries of society and the psychic health and coherent identity of nonblack people.[71]

It is important to emphasize the significance of stability—or, more accurately, historical equilibrium—to the social ontology of Afropessimism. Unlike, for example, Marxist social theories that posit that capitalism will collapse under contradictions and crises generated from its own systemic dynamics, Afropessimists treat the antiblack world order as totalizing, resilient, and so intractable as to be almost certainly permanent.[72] They try to sustain this contention through an appeal to ironic history. For Warren, it is history that proves that black emancipation, defined as the disentangling of blackness from metaphysical antiblackness, is impossible. In his depiction, not only has "every emancipatory strategy that attempted to rescue blackness from anti-blackness inevitably reconstituted and reconfigured the anti-blackness it tried to eliminate" but the persistent repetition of this pattern authorizes a judgment that, even in the future and no matter the intentions behind our political strivings, "anti-blackness will escape every emancipatory attempt to capture it."[73]

Or for Wilderson, "The narrative arc of the slave who is *Black* . . . is *not an arc at all,* but a flat line, what Hortense Spillers calls 'historical stillness': a flat line that 'moves' from disequilibrium to a moment in the narrative of faux equilibrium, to disequilibrium restored and/or rearticulated."[74] The depths of this equilibrium are made apparent by the utter improbability or impossibility of the accounts that Afropessimism entertain—less as practical horizons than logical ones—of what the overcoming of antiblackness would entail. Wilderson does, for example, "believe that there is a way out," but he describes it as demanding "a kind of violence so magnificent and so comprehensive that it scares the hell out of even radical revolutionaries" and which would result in "epistemological catastrophe" that would radically overthrow human relations and even the unconscious.[75] In Warren's hands, this horizon moves from a total revolution to the apocalyptic, with a Heideggerian gloss. "Black emancipation," he writes, "is not an aperture or an opening for future possibilities and political reconfigurations. . . . It is impossible to emancipate blacks without literally destroying the world."[76]

In the Afropessimist conversation, the appeal to ironic history authorizes, as we can see, a foreclosure of practical faith in emancipatory political action, realistic utopias based on political and ethical ideals, and a devotion to the idea of progress. Commensurate with the broader tradition of pessimism, however, they seek to replace these commitments with "a philosophy of personal conduct" and not "a scheme of ideal government structure or principles of justice."[77] This element of Afropessimism is best excavated via sustained critical attention to the recurrent figures—the fugitive slave, the suicidal-matricidal slave (in, e.g., Toni Morrison's *Beloved*), and the apostate—that attain pride of place in Afropessimist writing and the modes of action they perform that these authors render as historically and philosophically significant. In what follows, I focus on the apostate.

In his provocative essay "Black Nihilism and the Politics of Hope" Calvin Warren endeavors to unmask what he considers the most insidious implication of what I have described as romantic narratives of African American political history. For Warren, the insistence on racial progress enables and authorizes a broader commitment to "political hope" that is not only illusory; it also, ironically, compels blacks to endure pointless suffering aimed at civic redemption, forge self-destructive libidinal attachments to "cruel optimism," and corrupt their capacity for hope via its attachment to a political realm that can only produce antiblack domination.[78] Political hope, for Warren, is "a vicious and abusive cycle of struggle" that conscripts black death into its obscurantist categories like "perfection, betterment, struggle, work, and utopian futurity."[79]

Warren calls instead for African American philosophy to turn away from hope and to embrace nihilism, which he treats as a "'demythifying' practice" capable of unmaking the ways that hope works to subjugate black people and undermining its status as an animating ideal of our present. He characterizes the necessary form of black nihilism as a kind of "political apostasy," which he describes as "the act of abandoning or renouncing a situation of unethicality and immorality—in this sense, the Political itself" while refusing "to participate in the ruse of replacing one idol [anti-blackness] with another." The point is not to "change political structures or offer a political program"—indeed, such investments would be worse than "pointless"—but instead to achieve a kind of spiritual retrieval. Hope must be recaptured from the grips of "the Political" and be enacted within a "spiritual practice of denouncing metaphysical violence, black suffering, and the idol of anti-blackness."[80]

Warren is surely correct to draw attention to the enduring persistence of antiblack racial ideology and various mutations of racial domination in American history. A healthy suspicion of emancipatory black politics is warranted, especially in light of criticisms of forms of marginalization *among* black people from black radical traditions of political theory and historiography. Further, Warren is to be applauded for insisting that to reduce nihilism to mere pathology, unworthy of philosophical explication, is to miss important judgments worth exploring.[81] Above all, he is also right to criticize how romantic narratives can minimize the ethical import of injustice by reifying past wrongs into an evaluative standard, intuiting the inevitability of moral progress, or insulating their guiding ideals from critique by invoking a perpetually receding "not-yet" as the appropriate horizon of judgment. Indeed, the present volume shares with Afropessimism a refusal of those forms of historical narration that recruit death and suffering into a teleological narrative and recast it as sacrifice in ways that the bearers of those lives could not and would not endorse.

In the most profound passage of Ta-Nehisi Coates's *Between the World and Me,* he echoes this sentiment, writing to his son, "You must resist the common urge toward the comforting narrative of divine law, toward fairy tales that imply some irrepressible justice. The enslaved were not bricks in your road, and their lives were not chapters in your redemptive history. . . . It is wrong to claim our present circumstance—no matter how improved—as the redemption for the lives of people who never asked for the posthumous, untouchable glory of dying for their children. Our triumphs can never compensate for this."[82]

Despite these worthwhile aims, however, Warren's project reveals much that is politically retrograde, ethically objectionable, and epistemically incoherent in Afropessimist thought, all helpfully disclosed by the focus on narrative genre. Four elements, in particular, demand attention: the problem of race and reference, a self-undermining and ontologically essentialist conception of politics, an implicit metaphysical commitment to purity and permanence, and Warren's narrative mystification.

Race and Reference

One dilemma for Warren and other Afropessimists is that in their ironic language they slip between referents for blackness that, on considered reflection, may not be available to them. As Wilderson puts the point, "Afropessimism is premised on an iconoclastic claim: that Blackness is coterminous with Slaveness" and cannot be "disimbricated from slavery" as a position within social ontology. What it means to be a slave, in this sense, is to stand in relation to human beings in two ways: as subject to forms of violence without limit or excess, or which exceeds any rational (e.g., economic) explanation; and as an implement to be used, without regard to one's own interests or benefit, and to be figured as outside the realm of mutual human recognition.[83]

But how do we substantiate the link between blackness and slaveness? There is a tension between how Afropessimists run together the view that blackness has no positive or clustered content and instead marks only a position of vulnerability to extreme violence, subjection to the status of equipment, or a locus of psychic projections of fear and abjection. If African descent, group identification, cultural traditions, or even being vulnerable to antiblackness (rather than the more radical ontology of "slaveness") are not constitutive of blackness but slaveness is, we are led to an ironic query: Who among "the blacks" is black? For Warren to treat a judgment like "black suffering is getting worse" as valid, there needs to be some more robust sense of whom the term is meant to identify and a tracking of that continuity over time for cross-temporal comparison and evaluation.[84]

To put the point more squarely in the idioms of analytical philosophy, the argument that the category of blackness was causally constructed by an antiblack practice of slavery does not entail that we are justified—analytically or normatively—in arguing that blackness is, as a matter of metaphysics, constructed by this continuum of practices. For one, modern slavery has not been abolished. If blackness is slaveness, are South Asian victims of sex trafficking in the Arab world or forced laborers in East Asian sweatshops blacker than "black" people? In other words, should jarring divergence in the lives of middle-class and wealthy African Americans in the United States versus, say, lower-caste groups suffering from debt bondage in India or Uighurs herded into containment in China raise the question within Afropessimist metaphysics of whether any putatively nonblack people have become black via their proximity to slaveness? If not all slaveness is blackness but all blackness is slaveness, the hidden necessary condition remains to be clarified, as does an explanation of why the appeal to slaveness does not run afoul of the movement's various broadsides against the legitimacy of analogy.

Wilderson has attempted to answer such questions, but the results have been confused and contradictory, eliding the complexities of class, capital, and condition.[85] On one hand, Wilderson insists that all blacks are "slaves" (in a relation of social death, subjection, and generalized dishonor) regardless of their various socioeconomic standings or self-conception. He has even proclaimed himself, in an interview and memoir, the slave of his white wife.[86] In this view, blackness is slaveness, but not all slaveness is blackness.

Yet, Wilderson seems to contend that when African Americans attain forms of social standing or mobility, they become "whiter" (perhaps achieving, individually, an intermediate zone akin to so-called colored immigrants).[87] These inconsistencies cry out for explanation, especially when we have no better evidence of violence, libidinal excess, and usurpation than empirically verifiable patterns of treatment. Retreat to subjective feelings of alienation, raising notoriously impossible standards of comparative evaluation, are not helpful. One suspects here that in perhaps the most sobering irony of all, Afropessimism represents the matriculation of black political thought into that long tradition of Western political philosophy that avails itself of loose-fitting metaphors of slavery to pursue the aims of bourgeois dissent.

Either way, these questions of race and reference raise especially difficult ethical quandaries because Afropessimists tend to focus extensively on forms of violence that in fact happen to many sorts of persons (police brutality, rape, enslavement, lynching, archival erasure, and genocide, to name just a few) but try to make distinctions between violence that are, in Wilderson's words, "gratuitous" rather than "contingent" and "utilitarian," between violence that happens to blacks and violence that happens to nonblacks.[88] Yet how are we to make these determinations? We cannot appeal to explicit justifications of antiblack violence because, even in Wilderson's accounts, these will often be disingenuous, dissembled, and in bad faith (if even truly cognized at all, rather than being motivated at the level of subconscious drives).

Settler colonial violence against Native Americans, Wilderson tells us, "recognized" and "incorporated" Native American "sovereignty" in the contents of its consciousness, even as such sovereignty was practically violated. Police violence against black people, however, is a denial of humanity as such—there is no reciprocity, only living and dead.[89] This contrast, however, borders on the absurd. Both patterns involve extensive and fatal practices of grotesque violence, often disingenuously invoke legal procedures, and show severe contempt and a lack of appropriate responsibility for the victim's form of life. Indeed, settler colonialism, where it does not even deal in the ritual of treaty or contract, may be even more radically evil than police brutality. The latter, for what it's worth, at least avails itself of the juridical categories of criminality, which might plausibly be said to have a reciprocal dimension that recognizes, however contradictorily or confusedly, familiar categories of humanism: responsibility, agency, and intention.[90] Indeed, arguably the most striking feature of law, even under slavery, is the instability of any attempt to permanently bind blackness with humanity. When the slave is supposed to be chattel or a tool, the law cannot help.

It is difficult to avoid the suspicion that antiblackness in Afropessimism functions here as a nonfalsifiable "just so" claim rooted in a totalizing conception of antiblackness. Here any violence that befalls people of African descent counts on the ledger of gratuity, contradicting the semiotically sensitive injunction to seek blackness at the site of abjection and remain receptive to so-called social death's revealing itself in unexpected domains. The persistent slippage between the self-professed method of Afropessimism and the judgments it actually arrives at raises a deeper worry that Afropessimism's ontological claims are subordinate to the political positions its proponents feel compelled to adopt.

David Scott warns that descriptions of the social world or of the "problem-space" of politics can become overdetermined by expectations that we must stake out certain kinds of familiar political answer positions. In these cases, given the narratively underdetermined nature of historical facts, we actually end up emplotting the type of story we need to justify our answer. For Scott, the paradigmatic case is the postcolonial "longing for total revolution," which surreptitiously encourages a radically romantic emplotment of Caribbean history according to which the domination enacted by colonialism is so complete and overwhelming that only "total" revolution can render history complete and redeemed. Consequently, the justification of, or compulsive repetition of, certain types of political answers or attachment to the figures that exemplify these modes have an elective affinity with how we construct historical narratives. For Wilderson (certainly) and Warren (perhaps), their current longing for "total refusal" is rooted in the defeat of an excessively romantic conception of black liberation that has now been disappointed and is lived as the ruins of the present. The consequence is that they are stunningly susceptible to empirically untethered accounts of black suffering and black political action that are blind (or dissembling) not only to basic empirical questions about black life and politics but also to how class stratifies many of the claims about suffering, deprivation, and power he ascribes to the group writ large.

Politics

This is perhaps clearest in their accounts of democracy and their treatment of the vote as its dominant feature. Warren presumptively declares voting as "an ineffective practice in gaining tangible 'objects' for achieving redress, equality, and political subjectivity." Given that he thinks these objects cannot be obtained, black folks' attachment to democratic politics is judged irrational on its own terms. Indeed, Warren characterizes black voting as a kind of displaced ritual of fidelity to the dead, a consecrating ritual for a progressive conception of history. Voting is meaningful largely as a "way to contend with a painful (and shame-full) history of exclusion and disenfranchisement" and as a mode of historical consciousness meant to fulfill debts to the sacrifices of ancestors for the progress of the present.[91]

His charge of irrationality hews closely to a conception of political participation rooted in and authorized by self-interest, narrowly conceived. This may be glimpsed, in part, via the metaphors he tries to deploy. For Warren, voting is akin to monetary expenditure. "Traditionally," he says, again without engagement with the any of the African American theorists of democracy, "political participation is motivated by self-interested expectancy; this political calculus assumes that political participation, particularly voting, is an investment with an assurance of a return or political dividend."[92] The goal, therefore, is to exchange votes for material returns and political dividends. Unreliability—the failed return on investment, to use the language of investment capital—in this process renders black voting irrational.

Warren offers a critique of politics, but what is the conception of politics that he invokes for our disavowal? Reflecting his Heideggerian influences, Warren practices what Seyla Benhabib has called a kind of "phenomenological essentialism" that presumes that "each type of human activity has a proper 'place' in which it can be carried out."[93] For example, Warren posits an ontological opposition between "the spiritual" and "the Political" and further suggests—in strikingly quantified and monetary language—that hope is a "spiritual currency" that we "are given as inheritance to invest in various aspects of existence." The problem is that "the Political" has colonized (akin to Hannah Arendt's "blob" of the social) the spiritual currency of hope, compelling and conscripting black people to investment under the idea that "politics is the natural habitat of hope itself."[94]

It would surely count toward the persuasiveness of Warren's argument if he took seriously contravening empirical accounts that purport to show the vital significance of voting for resource distribution to black communities or comprehensive studies of American politics that show that it is the policy preferences of the rich (rather than simply the white) that are most rewarded.[95] Our suspicion should be heightened further by the fact that Warren cites no major African American intellectuals, because it is not clear that any major black figure of note holds such a monist position about the value of politics as the singular, discrete, determinate hope in the struggle against antiblackness. Indeed, one of the single most distinguishing things about African American political thought as a genre of modern political thought is the ecumenical stance its participants tend to take in favor of cultural production, religious worship, virtue or perfectionist ethics, and other forms of human endeavor in order to experiment with and enlarge conceptions of "politics" beyond the enactment of solidarity, the founding of institutional orders, and the contestation of power.[96] Even the single most influential work of political theory in the African American tradition, W. E. B. Du Bois's *Souls of Black Folk* (1903), is an enactment of, and defense of, hope in cultural creativity, political struggle, affective intervention, and a perfectionist ethics (for ourselves and others), all as elements of a democratic politics of redemptive refounding. This mélange is best exemplified in Du Bois's immediate turn from the claim that "there are to-day no truer exponents of the pure human spirit of the Declaration of Independence than the American Negroes" to a reflection on black music and folklore as ethical resources of democratic renewal.[97]

It is important to note, however, that this consumerist standard of evaluation for political participation is itself an artifact of nihilism, not its justification. This conception of politics, while appealing to those promoting the thinnest and most exchange-oriented defenses of democracy, is actually corrosive of many of the ideals that make democracy possible: the ethos of sacrifice; the cultivation and protection of common goods and public things;, and the kind of political friendship that involves learning from, being changed by, and taking pleasure and pride in the flourishing of those with whom we share a form of life.[98] A closer reading of democratic theory from within the civil rights movement illuminates this point.

The legendary civil rights organizer Ella Baker, for example, departs dramatically from this market model of democratic participation whose failure would only underscore her judgment that radical democratic praxis is the most important weapon against the hopelessness, self-doubt, and despair engendered by domination. Baker championed a "developmental style of politics" in which committed activists and volunteers would help cultivate among historically disempowered citizens a sense that they have the right to define the needs and problems that structure politics, the capacity to shape their own destiny, the moral authority to hold representatives and institutions accountable, and the dignity to declare their equal moral worth.[99] The right to vote was considered paramount—but as *part* of these broader ethical aims. This work inspired the community organizing wing of the Student Nonviolent Coordinating Committee (SNCC) that Baker helped found as they attempted to build a militant civic movement to uproot the byzantine and brutal obstacles to black voting in the South.

SNCC activists envisioned subjecting vast dimensions of civil society to a demand for the participatory parity of ordinary, everyday people, operating without subjection to vanguards, elites, charismatic leaders, or experts.[100] This form of grassroots democracy, according to Baker, would perform the work of recognition respect, showing genuine acknowledgment and enthusiasm for the moral agency, equal standing, and civic potential of all citizens. It would also further the work of empowerment, allowing ordinary people to undermine relations of domination, resist evolving forms of oppression, and contest the unjust usurpation of their prerogatives over important domains of human life, including politics itself.[101]

This democratic ideal, Baker provocatively argued, was incompatible with forms of charismatic, messianic, or autocratic political leadership even within civil rights organizations ostensibly organized to deepen democracy. These features of movement politics, she claimed, disavowed valuable local knowledge and culture, arbitrarily marginalized important voices (especially women and working-class or poor black people), distorted deliberation, and corroded citizens' capacities for taking initiative and articulating their needs.[102] "Instead of the leader as a person who was supposed to be a magic man," Baker argued, "you could develop individuals who were bound together by a concept that benefited the larger number of individuals and provided an opportunity for them to grow into being responsible for carrying out a program."[103] Tightly tied to practice, this developmental, community-organizing vision relied heavily on open-ended deliberations among SNCC members, informal education initiatives (e.g., workshops, Freedom Schools, etc.), and the development of alternative political practices and rituals like independent elections and parties (e.g., the Freedom Ballot).

Much of the late twentieth-century enthusiasm for "participatory democracy" in political theory and left politics can be traced to these efforts.[104] A number of SNCC activists, for example, went on to be prominent within the New Left and its principal organization, Students for a Democratic Society (SDS). Tom Hayden, for example, after joining the Freedom Rides and reporting on SNCC projects in Albany, Georgia, and McComb, Mississippi, drew on his interpretations of SNCC culture to produce the initial draft of SDS's Port Huron Statement, arguably the most influential statement of "participatory democracy" as an ideal.[105] Distilling their sense of how SNCC's organizing style cultivated a passion for democracy and enhanced the capabilities for negotiation, argument, and analysis among the most dispossessed, Hayden and the SDS argued for an entire society where problems would be generalized, clarified, and deliberated on and political decisions would be made by "public groupings," asserting that such participation builds communal solidarity and public freedom alongside individual fulfillment and independence.[106]

In stark contrast to the ideals of SNCC and the SDS, Warren's short-term market model of democratic consumerism does not take seriously either the content or time horizon that informs this Bakerist conception of democracy or the philosophical significance of its attempt to build intergenerational communities of memory and struggle. It also misreads the moral import of African American defenses of formal political participation and the democratic practice of ordinary life defended by Baker and others. These theorists view formal political participation as striving to model a practice of freedom as nondomination, nurturing its sustained existence in the world of ideas and its link to a conception of political rights and participation as expressive of dignity and dignified conduct.[107]

Perhaps most at odds with the Afropessimist interpretation, forms of democratic practice like Bakerism are also understood as seeking to avoid total complicity with injustice.[108] In this view, black voting is explained less by a theory of "indebted consciousness" to past generation's sacrifices than by a democratic tradition based on the self-respecting commitment that racial domination should not reproduce or extend itself with our complicity. Similarly, the democratic self-reflexivity at the heart of Baker's suspicion of hierarchy, patriarchy, and charisma insists that the norms that should characterize organizing and movement building are also aimed at cultivating a stance of personal political integrity, rooting out habits, forms of affect, and ideological dispositions that engender complicity with forms of structural and interpersonal injustice.[109]

Metaphysics and the Problem of Judgment

These counterideals of democracy, which reject the simple consumerist model, also help underscore a more profound anxiety about plurality that haunts Afropessimist discourse. This problem sits at the heart of Warren's distinctions between the spiritual and the political and Wilderson's thematization of redemption, grounding the pessimism of both accounts and providing the foundations of their professed apostasy and nihilism.

Warren, for instance, criticizes political hope on the grounds that it promises to lead one "beyond extant structures of violence and destruction" to a foundation where love, hope, and meaning are built on grounds of selfhood and society that are not "subject to shift, transform[ation], and decay."[110] For Wilderson, politics is defined "as a very rational endeavor" with prediction and modeling at its heart. Indeed, one of his charges against Marxism is that it is incapable of "predict[ing] the structural violence of slavery in its performative manifestations."[111] But to hold spiritual and societal strivings to a standard of purity and permanence that is immune to crisis and conflict or change and unpredictability is to imagine a standard beyond any possible world. This impossibility holds not just for black people but for all human beings.

This is especially true given that our lives unfold in a state of being with others who have the capacity for action.[112] We inhabit a world shaped by the actions and reactions of those who precede us. The philosophy of nonviolence was articulated by movement intellectuals like King, James Lawson, and Bayard Rustin, who incorporated into their politics the ontological claim that, as King put it, we are caught up in "an inescapable network of mutuality . . . a single garment of destiny." While extended and exacerbated by the interpenetrating structures of global capitalism, imperial projection, mass media, and the climate dynamics of the Anthropocene, this mutuality—or "plurality," to use Arendt's term—is a recalcitrant feature of the human condition.

This existential fact excites understandable resentment, fear, and anxiety—even horror (to use Warren's favored affect). The temptation to envision a realm where this is not the case, to picture a pure self-sufficiency that transcends not just the world as it is but the human condition is a crucial source of Afropessimist nihilism. It even appears in Wilderson's attempts to categorically distinguish antiblackness from other identities or oppressions on the basis of workers and (nonblack) colonized peoples having a prehistory to their oppression, which he treats as the site of their distinctive "plenitude . . . before the Enclosures . . . *before the settler.*"[113] The despair that pervades Wilderson's broadsides against narrative and redemption stems from his fixation on, and disillusionment with, a specific kind of romantic narrative sequence that moves from a time of purity and plenitude to the fall of domination to restorative redemption.

These ideals loom silently behind the politics of refusal and nihilism proffered by the pessimists and structure a picture of the world animated by the certainty that African American history is profane, ironic, and without meaning. There is an implicit exasperation with the unpredictability, irreversibility, and tragedy of political action, and Warren's talk of apostasy and withdrawal reflects what Arendt called the desire to seek "shelter from action's calamities in an activity where one man, isolated from all others, remains master of his doings from beginning to end."[114] This picture, which ennobles sovereign agency, the philosophy of the will, and an apolitical epistemology, may simply—like the view from nowhere or the fantasy of total consensus—be a picture that holds the pessimist captive, leading them to bludgeon the hard-won victories of the world as it is with the image of a world that belongs more to God than to beings like us.

The consequence of this stance is an unearned and unwarranted confidence in Afropessimism's ability to project a permanent future of antiblackness. This epistemic arrogance is sustained, as Theodor Adorno wrote of such doctrines, "by the false inference that because there has been no progress up until now, there will never be any."[115] While Warren excoriates the romantics for shielding themselves from critique by appealing to an unknown and unknowable future, his futural gestures toward the "impossibility" of alternative political arrangements are similarly insulated in a posture devoid of epistemic humility. This is especially bewildering given that, for Warren, black abjection is not ordained by God, written into cosmology or biology, forged in a messianic transformation, or even the necessary outcome of human history. The antiblack order, insofar as one can discern from his account, is the artifact of a complex, interdependent web of decisions, ideas, practices, desires, and other myriad strivings and sayings of human beings that coalesced to create the African slave trade, imperialism, and antiblack racial ideology. If this web of actions can be said to have created the unforeseen consequence of an antiblack world, it is unclear how, without escaping these human dynamics into the realm of metaphysics, the Afropessimist can presume, a priori, to predict the whole range of possible outcomes of interpenetrating complex systems of scientific research, global governance, economic markets, cultural production, climate change, and more. Indeed, given that we are on the cusp of absorbing innovations like artificial intelligence, space travel, gene editing, quantum computing, cloning, and advanced robotics, it seems especially overconfident to hang political judgment on such precarious predictions.

This stance toward the future is self-undermining in another way. To substantiate the claim that all political struggles to overcome or even substantively ameliorate the perpetually restructuring condition of antiblackness will be defeated requires that people continue to engage and experiment with political action to try to do so. Yet Afropessimists, in their recommendation that people do not, would foreclose a range of various strategies, ideals, and possibilities untested against changing social facts. Indeed, the discontent that motivates Afropessimism itself emerges from the longing for total revolution in which black movements would engage with an eye toward a sustained, intergenerational resistance of an unspecified character.

The pessimist, in both heaping scorn on past traditions and counseling withdrawal from the practice of politics, would, if successful, dissolve the possibility of its own reproduction. The pain of oppression and the isolated fact of antiblackness are not enough to lead one to the Afropessimist view—as Afropessimists themselves know quite well by the fact that the broader black tradition of letters disagrees with them. If the rejoinder is that past forms of resistance can never die and are exemplary events inscribed into the memory of peoples, galvanizing them to something other than abjection, then this appears to cast further doubt on their theses that treat social death as the sine qua non of black life.

Adorno rightly charges the advocates of such totalizing pessimism with "self-righteous profundity," and it is impossible to avoid the sense in which the most extreme blend of ironic history and pessimistic prophecy is extraordinarily flattering to the supposed oracular and cognitive gifts and moral purity of its proselytizers. Indeed, given the underwhelming grounds for Afropessimists' confident claims about all future worlds, it strikes me that Warren's defense of apostasy turns more on a commitment to a metaphysics of purity and permanence than any facts about history; the facts of history are organized and narrated (ironically) in light of these commitments. It is yet another iteration of the view that Friedrich Nietzsche criticized long ago, that because "our highest values cannot be realized in this world, and . . . there is no other world in which they can," we should live in nihilistic despair.[116]

Like Schopenhauer's ascetic, Warren treats (black) suffering as the crucial evil of existence and, seeing no way to eliminate suffering altogether or to change the world, he suggests withdrawing altogether to minimize the worldly hopes, strivings, and desires that engender suffering instead. Indeed, like Schopenhauer, Warren's view must lead him to the conclusion that it would be preferable if the world simply did not exist. This view, embedded in his narrative forms, entails that the past is too catastrophic to be redeemed, the present an enduring catastrophe, and the future already foreclosed as anything other than the repetition of this traumatic "present-past."[117] When tied to, or ostensibly justified by, appeal to historical narrative, despair can seem like the only reasonable assessment of the historical facts at hand and as the only rational stance toward the future.

Beyond Pessimism

Part of why I emphasize the narrative modes of historiography is to unsettle the conceit that the relationship between historical reflection, contemporary judgment, and imagined future flows naturally and inevitably in that order. In reality, these hang together far more messily; Warren's remarks on the civil rights movement are as much about the murdered eighteen-year-old Michael Brown as they are about Martin Luther King. Where writers like Wilderson tell us that they have divined a history "beyond the grasp of narration" we should be suspicious of what that foreclosure means for our political practice, imagination, and judgment.[118] As Joshua Dienstag writes, "the independent act of narration is the first, necessary step in opposing those who would control our future by controlling our understanding of the past . . . an inability to narrate . . . is an impediment that must be overcome on the path to freedom."[119]

The question that philosophical reflection on African American history and the interrogation of the role that such historical imaginings play in political philosophy must pursue if it is to enhance political freedom rather than retreat into nihilism are, in some respects, neo-Nietzschean questions: Can black suffering be revalued without falling into romanticism? Can we devalue the presuppositions of purity that give ironist history and pessimism its moral claims? What generic forms can sustain historical imaginings requisite to these tasks? Can we find ways to maturely affirm (black) life and (antiracist) political action in a contingent world without the promise of impending reconciliation or unyielding abjection? And, as Nietzsche asked of the "ascetic priests" and Schopenhauer, Why are people attracted to the lure of pessimism?

These are questions I will pursue in Chapter 8, but the last is worth addressing here. One of the most seductive things about Afropessimism is that in its inflation of antiblackness to the level of metaphysical totality and, in Warren's terms, "ontological terror," it transfigures nearly everything black people do under such conditions into a kind of heroism. Jesse McCarthy, in his brilliant critique of Afropessimism, asks why Wilderson reaches for hyperbole in descriptions of banal racial incidents in his National Book Award–winning memoir. For instance, as McCarthy writes of Wilderson's anecdote about a friend's mother asking him how it felt to be black, "Wilderson says that this was a learning moment for his mother about the lengths whites might go to injure a Black person, in this instance by psychologically attacking their children. 'She knew now how it must feel to be killed by a guided missile,' Wilderson comments. I don't doubt the psychological violence of the incident in question, but that doesn't make moving into Kenwood *like* having a Hellfire missile hit you in the Gaza Strip."[120] The allure of hyperbole here is that it *symbolically* raises the stakes of every crevice of bourgeois social life to an occasion for heroism while obscuring its practical banality and mundanity.

The structure of feeling that Afropessimism taps into goes far beyond the general despair of left melancholia and reflects the intellectual canonization and practical foreclosure of a set of collective scripts regarding heroism, achievement, and meaning. It is not often enough admitted, but one of the most deep-seated cultural legacies of the strange career of Jim Crow was that any number of otherwise mundane things a black person might do—becoming the local postmaster or buying a home in a suburban neighborhood—was consecrated as a heroic achievement by communal ritual (especially in the black press).

Such practices invited scorn on occasion. E. Franklin Frazier, in *Black Bourgeoisie,* derided it as part of "a world of make-believe," and Malcolm X, discussing professional black people he saw growing up in Boston, wrote, "I'd guess that eight out of ten of the Hill Negroes of Roxbury, despite the impressive-sounding job titles they affected, actually worked as menials and servants. 'He's in banking,' or 'He's in securities.' It sounded as though they were discussing a Rockefeller or a Mellon—and not some gray-headed; dignity-posturing bank janitor, or bond-house messenger. . . . It has never ceased to amaze me how so many Negroes, then and now, could stand the indignity of that kind of self-delusion."[121]

The end of Jim Crow dealt a crippling blow to this cultural tendency, but the election of Barack Obama killed it for the foreseeable future. The first black president, an idea that absorbed the most sustained and widespread burst of African American political energies in American history, represented, in a sense, the last first black who mattered. Afterward, especially as the Obama administration's limits led to profound disillusionment with romantic narratives of African American history, the prevailing stance toward "first black" honorifics shifted from pride to disdain, disgust, and embarrassment at their belated character: it should have happened already.[122] The draining of this shallow-end heroism, and the far more spectacular collapse of late twentieth-century black freedom struggles, converged to place their inherited scripts of heroism into crisis.

For those who yearn for a life of bourgeois endurance to be imbued with the drama of a heroic black past, the Afropessimist worldview offers a surprisingly amenable blend of solipsism, pathos, and fatalism. Paving the way for a leveling down of heroism through its ironic critique of all-preceding history, it then transfigures the heroic into something closer to make-believe than "worldmaking."[123]

This is especially intoxicating, one imagines, for black intellectuals, who, at least since W. E. B. Du Bois, have inherited a sense of the vocation of black intellectualism as heroic, with a conception of African American politics as a practice of group leadership and rule by those who share an identity with the folk.[124] The central story of black politics and identity in the post–Jim Crow era has been the sense of fragmentation around divisions of class, gender, sexuality, and ethnicity (e.g., with unprecedented waves of black immigrants), not to mention reasonable political disagreements about "where do we go from here." This fracturing of even the reliable mythos of a black collective subject to being represented, spoken for, and interpreted has occasioned much serious reflection across African American studies, but it would be surprising if it did not provoke anxiety and bad faith evasion as well.

What Afropessimism offers, then, is a way of beginning from this sense of crisis about black representation, but instead of abandoning the purported task to speak on behalf of black people to the wider world, it plunges beneath the prima facie divisions of black life to rediscover unity via ontology. In doing so it restores to its theorists the lost treasure of the past: interpretive authority over every permutation of black life. This is what makes sense of Wilderson's striking talk of Afropessimism as having a mandate to speak on behalf of "black people at their best" and the striking vignette at the opening of Warren's *Ontological Terror,* where he coldly disparages an older black woman in a panel audience for chastening his bleak nihilism. It was, he says, his "nihilistic responsibility" to deliver to her and the audience the terrible truth that there is "no solution to the problem of antiblackness" and that hope only produces more "pain and disappointment."[125] But it is not nihilism that commits Warren to inform his fellow black people of their slaveness—"nihilistic responsibility" appears an unbridgeable contradiction—it is his attachment to the traditional task of (heroic) black intellectualism. After all, the true nihilist would be as indifferent to the ruminations of the herd as they would be to the continued persistence of the world.

In the end, the price of this reforging of the unified mass of black people is that eschatology replaces politics. Yet, as Reinhart Koselleck warned, "The moment the figures of the apocalypse are applied to concrete events or instances, the eschatology has disintegrative effects. The End of the World is only an integrating factor so long as its politico-historical meaning remains indeterminate."[126] The rediscovery of black intellectual authority is, in other words, deeply precarious, and the underlying reality of social divisions strain not only at the seams of the rhetoric of slaveness and blackness but at the traditional aura of the vocation itself.

From Irony to Tragedy

If Du Bois perhaps leads us somewhat astray in our conception of vocation of black intellectuals, he proves more promising as a guide to taking Afropessimism seriously without succumbing to its confusions. In chapter 11, "Of the Passing of the First Born," of *The Souls of Black Folk,* Du Bois channel's Schopenhauer's legendary, world-negating challenge that no person in full grasp of the depth of human suffering would rationally choose to reproduce given the sentence to which they would condemn their offspring. Du Bois invests this abstraction with the concrete horror of his own child, Burghardt's, death, as well as the terror that any black child he would bring into the world would have to be raised in a racist society, one organized to cruelly crush their aspirations, degrade their self-respect, and steal their life, over the arbitrary myth of "race."[127] Riding home from the funeral, Du Bois narrates his apprehension of pessimism: "There sat an awful gladness in my heart. . . . No bitter meanness now shall sicken his baby heart till it die a living death, no taunt shall madden his happy boyhood. Fool that I was to think or wish that this little soul should grow choked and deformed within the Veil! . . . Better far this nameless void that stops my life than a sea of sorrow for you."[128]

The language and imagery of the "nameless void" is crucial here. In deploying a rendering of death as nothingness so absolute that it negates even the venture of anticipatory description, Du Bois underscores the terrible truth of life on the underside of the "Negro Problem" by refusing to seek refuge in the consolation and comfort of heaven. In *Darkwater* (1920) Du Bois lifts the veil to reveal that this Schopenhauerian challenge is one that routinely haunts African Americans, writing that "the mothers and fathers and the men and women of my race must often pause and ask . . . Ought children be born to us? Have we any right to make human souls face what we face today?" How black people answer such a question is freighted with extraordinary consequence for Du Bois, because it is "in the treatment of the child [that] the world foreshadows its own future and faith." It is the child, he writes, that represents "that vast immortality and the wide sweep of infinite possibility" that underwrites hope in justice and the good.[129]

Such assertions resonate with Hannah Arendt's treatment of "the fact of natality." Taking birth as both metaphor and world-disclosing phenomenon, Arendt argues not only that "with each birth something uniquely new comes into the world," but that this underwrites and corresponds with the human capacity for action—the ability to introduce something "unexpected" and "improbable" into the world. Natality, "the birth of new men and the new beginning, the action they are capable of by virtue of being born," continuously introduces not only the possibility of "interrupting" forms of life as they presently exist but also the possibility of trying to sustain them through storytelling and solidarity. Arendt contrasts this emphasis on contingency, possibility, and a shared world beyond any individual life with the necessity, regularity, and fatality of "natural processes."[130]

Given that natality presupposes that we are born into a world alongside others who precede us and that we live alongside others who in all likelihood will survive us, it is perhaps best understood as a way of speaking intelligibly about a kind of human freedom—namely, the freedom to cooperatively and collaboratively make judgments about what forms of life we want to disavow or preserve, the latter being the shared ground of Arendt's and Du Bois's invocations of "immortality."[131] Natality, Arendt sweepingly proclaims, is "the miracle that saves the world, the realm of human affairs, from its normal, 'natural' ruin." It is natality that "can bestow upon human affairs faith and hope," because it allows for the unmaking of ignoble worlds, the forging of new bonds of solidarity in pursuit of the good, and the discovery of new forms of meaning by which to make sense of our fate together—none of which can be fully anticipated or determined.[132]

For Du Bois, the most pressing hope is that the capacities to create something new will be realized in the transfiguration or revaluation of the ignoble inheritance of chattel slavery and Jim Crow. In grasping the "shame-full" evil of white racial domination and the "glory" and "lofty ideal" embodied in the intergenerational struggles against it, he argues that our children's children may be furnished with a grand "life motive"—"a power and impulse toward good" put to service in the "great battle of human right against poverty, disease, and color prejudice."[133] This indeterminate hope, as Richard Rorty might put it, involves "the ability to believe that the future will be unspecifiably different from, and unspecifiably freer than, the past."[134]

That it is only possible and not guaranteed, however, is important; in this respect, natality and tragedy are entangled. As Cornel West puts the point, "The decline and decay in American life *appears,* at the moment, to be irreversible; yet it may not be. This slight possibility—the historic chance that a window of opportunity can be opened by our prophetic thought and action—is, in part, what keeping faith is all about."[135] This faith comes from seeking those narratives capable of bearing both the evil that provokes ironic retreat and the beauty that the romantic pretends is permanent, to instead hold them in tension with appreciation for their mutual fragility. In this redescription of the past, we hope to tell a story of our inheritance that does not disparage the nonsovereign, fragile, and finite strivings toward justice and, while keeping track of their failure, as a story that nevertheless does not use that failure to abstain from caring for the plurality, agency, and natality that makes life—even black life—worth living and the world worth our concern rather than our rejection.[136]

CHAPTER 8

THE TRAGIC VISION

The Meaning of Long Civil Rights Movement History

IF MY CRITICISMS OF both the romantic and ironic pessimist visions of the civil rights movement are compelling, we nevertheless remain in search of another way of envisioning and representing this history that might provide a genuinely critical orientation toward the past and future. This is especially true for those in political theory or politics. We find ourselves entangled with an economy of civil rights exemplarity whose influence over concepts, norms, and other judgments has largely unfolded within, or been anchored to, the terms set by a romantic vision now in the throes of collapse. The goal, for political philosophy and criticism *writ large,* is to seek out a way of rendering this history that can integrate the partial truths of romance and irony, as well as incorporate what neither of these visions can—namely, the essential questions of contingency and the structure of opportunity, agency, and responsibility; social conflict and the plurality of goods; and the relationship between discrete forms of progress and the existence and persistence of the irreparable—severe injustice, death, and defeat. I believe that tragedy is, when carefully understood, where we must turn to pursue this work.

This may already be confusing. Many use *tragedy* as a kind of synonym for *awful* or treat it as a discourse of determinism that leads toward unrelenting despair or hopelessness. Indeed, in the wake of Aristotle's definition of tragedy in his *Poetics,* the contours of what might be said to be a tragic vision of human history or the human condition have been a recurrent and hotly debated topic in the history of philosophy. In this conversation I am decidedly on the side of those who see tragedy as bound up with a clear-eyed grasp of the suffering in the world yet nevertheless commensurate with a peculiar kind of hope. In my view, a tragic vision draws together, above all, four consistent themes: the centrality of *serious conflict,* the potential *significance of defeats,* the *contingency of history,* and the *responsibility* of historical actors. These make it a mode of narration especially incisive for interpreting and judging social and political life.

This chapter advances a tragic vision of history as a critical intervention in both civil rights historiography and political theory. Against the romantic evasion of loss and the paralyzing skepticism of irony, I argue that tragedy offers a more philosophically serious and politically demanding mode of narrating black freedom struggles—one that foregrounds the reality of conflict, the contingency of action, the irreversibility of loss, and the weight of responsibility. Tragedy, as I develop it here, is not despairing. It is a discipline of judgment: a way of seeing and feeling that does not deny hope, but refuses easy optimism. It reckons with the moral ambiguity of means and ends, the partiality of all victories, and the possibility that even the most courageous struggles can end in defeat without rendering their aims meaningless or their insights obsolete. Long civil rights historiography, at its most incisive, operates within this tragic mode. It seeks not merely to extend timelines or diversify our memory but to excavate submerged political possibilities—particularly those forged in the crucible of internationalism, labor radicalism, and left-liberal reconstructionism—and to understand the conditions under which they were abandoned or foreclosed.

My argument here is that this tragic historiographical sensibility opens urgent new terrain for political theory. I suggest how a tragic reading might help recover the lost realism of civil rights internationalism—a realism rooted not in moralist universalism or a cosmopolitanism of color but in hardheaded assessments of geopolitical constraint, American empire, and the limits of moral suasion. I trace this realism through a dialectic of race and nation inspired by Nikhil Pal Singh. I then turn to the work of A. Philip Randolph to show how his work might help us reframe existing, commonsense debates about "integrationism" as involving what he called "reconstruction." This reconstructionist vision was shaped not only by leftist commitments and trade union praxis but also by a tragic understanding of American history, the fragility of democratic advance, and the importance of democratic constitutionalism. Randolph's work confronts the structural compromises of the New Deal, the reactionary consolidation after Reconstruction, and the weakness of classical liberal rights discourse for meeting the challenge of black disadvantage. Both turns, I suggest briefly, also help reframe our thinking of Martin Luther King Jr., especially in King's emphasis on economic justice and international solidarity, marking an underappreciated current of tragic thinking in the civil rights movement.

This tragic vision also furnishes the philosophical resources to challenge efforts—like Richard Rorty's—to conscript civil rights history and figures like Randolph into a national romance. Rorty's call to replace despairing critique with patriotic pride depends on a vision of history that erases precisely the conflicts, contradictions, and betrayals that tragedy insists we confront. His sentimental recovery of Randolph as a figure of "hopeful reform" elides the extent to which Randolph's politics were animated by confrontation, sober reckoning with structural entrenchment, and the knowledge that America's democratic institutions have repeatedly required pressure, disruption, and sacrifice to live up to even a fraction of their promise. A truly tragic reading of civil rights history resists the demand to transform exemplary figures into fables of national uplift. Instead, it retrieves their thought and action as sites of judgment—where moral clarity and political realism do not neatly align, and where memory becomes a battleground over the meaning of defeat, the residue of lost struggles, and the unfinished possibilities they leave behind.

Serious Conflict

Tragedy deals above all with serious conflict that is not easily (or perhaps ever) reconciled.[1] In the Aristotelian account of tragedy, conflict occurs primarily between individuals who are related in some respect through familial ties or friendship.[2] Let us take as an example Sophocles's classic tragedy *Antigone,* which tells the story of the conflict between Creon, the ruler of a post–civil war Thebes, and Antigone, a woman from Thebes who is betrothed to Creon's son Haemon.

In the opening of the play, Creon has declared that Antigone's brother, Polyneices, who fought for the defeated rebel forces against Creon and Thebes, will be denied the burial customary for citizens of Thebes and has prohibited anyone from administering these holy rites to his body, which is ordered to be left to the appetites of scavenging animals and ignoble rot by the forces of nature. On penalty of death, Antigone nonetheless administers these rituals to her brother's body and, when captured, she confronts Creon in contentious ethical debate over the justice of his edict before being sentenced to a live burial. Creon's son Haemon, who is to be married to Antigone, is torn between dutiful support of his father and sympathy for his condemned betrothed, a sentiment that is widely shared in the city-state of Thebes. Haemon, like Tiresias, the blind prophet of Thebes, tries to persuade Creon to relent in his vengeful order against Polyneices and punishment of Antigone, but both are rebuked by the ruler in fits of obstinacy. In the last act, the ruler is beseeched by the chorus, a conventional feature of Greek drama, to relent or risk the punishment of the gods. Creon is eventually convinced to change his edict by burying the body of Polyneices, but it is too late; Antigone has killed herself and

Creon's son Haemon has followed suit in suicide. To compound the tragedy, Creon's wife, Eurydice, also commits suicide on learning of the death of her son, casting aspersions on her husband's name in her final moments.

Even if this is understood primarily as a conflict between individuals and principally between Antigone and Creon, the seriousness of the dispute is evident. Tragedy is not concerned with frivolity or easily reconciled matters but with conflicts over weighty questions like those regarding moral responsibility, meaningful relationships, ethics, and character. The prevalence of death in tragic literature conveys this sense of seriousness through its emergence into the horizon of possible consequences for what we do. Actors in a tragic scenario move within a horizon of significance indelibly shaped by the ineradicable possibility and presence of death, figured both as limit and consequence to human action. That Antigone, for instance, is willing to face death for her actions means that her brother's burial is not a matter open to easy concession or bargaining compromise—it strikes at the very heart of her self-conception, her sense of virtue and moral responsibility. In this, Antigone signifies that a life, and our individual senses of self-worth and personal integrity, can be bound to principles for which we are willing to die.

Dramatic death also conveys this sense of seriousness through its utter finality, from which comes the emotional, moral, and narrative force of the tragedy. Even within worldviews that posit life after death, physical death represents the cessation of a realm of recognizably human possibilities within the world and a continuity of conscious embodiment. If, for example, Creon had recourse to supernatural powers of resurrection, coupled with a power to forget, the drama could lose its tragic dimension.[3] That Creon is bounded by the consequences of immutable earthly law and memory means that he must live with the emotional and moral consequences of what he has wrought and is fated to pass these on to his heirs. This is the essential dimension of the tragedy, and one should expect to see unalloyed confrontation with death in tragic art and discourse.

Part of what makes social conflict ineliminable in this view stems from limitations to human beings' capacities for knowledge, reason, rationality, and will. There will always be information we do not know or do not understand, and as powerful as the capacities of human reason and rationality are, they can falter in the heat of the moment. David Scott articulates this dimension of the tragic vision: "Tragedy raises doubts about the salience of the Platonist vision of the hyperrational ideal and the Kantian belief in the sufficiency and autonomy of the self. . . . The strategy of tragedy is not to dismiss out of hand the claims of reason, but to honor the contingent, the ambiguous, the paradoxical, and the unyielding in human affairs in such a way as to complicate our most cherished notions about the relation between identity and difference, reason and unreason, blindness and insight, action and responsibility, guilt and innocence."[4] These inevitable epistemological limits mean that even in a world where people act according to good intentions, there remains a possibility that their actions, especially collectively, might produce negative consequences or that we might act in ways we ourselves would find objectionable if we had more information.

This knowledge problem is loosely related to a corollary ethical concern with virtuous character. For Aristotle a key dimension of tragedy's aesthetic and ethical force comes from the character imparted to the agents in the story. He defines character as the ascription of certain qualities to the agents of the story, "which reveals moral purposes, showing what kind of things a man chooses or avoids."[5] In traditional Greek tragedy, therefore, tragedy's moral import comes from the archetypes of character represented by each actor in the play. In simplistic renderings of human character, we can see how this maps readily onto Aristotle's larger concern about the relationship between virtues and vices, the former of which are situated at the mean of human character and activity in particular realms of action or feeling.

In tragic literature there is often an excessive or deficient character trait, frequently hubris, that leads the main character toward a tragic reversal of fortune. A character trait may be defined as "a stable disposition to act in distinctive ways" with the practical knowledge to "use the relevant skills" involved in such actions "in the relevant way."[6] This age-old concern with "good" and "bad" character was given richer, more complex life by the Freudian discovery of the unconscious, which gives depth and dynamism to character traits in reflexive emotions, impulses, and "drives." Like limitations on knowledge, our dispositions can involve tendencies and compulsions that we are not always fully conscious of and—in a tragic scenario—directly or indirectly undermine our conscious attempts at realizing a good.

A tragedy, therefore, can best illustrate for Aristotle how a virtue like courage, which sits at the mean of the sphere of human activity concerned with fear and confidence, can, through certain characterizations of the story's agents, become rashness in its excess or cowardice in its deficiency.[7] Thus, tragic drama can become a moral tale capable of educating the audience, especially concerning the inevitability of unintended consequences and impure motivations when understanding human action.

Part of the consequence of what economists have called the problem of "imperfect information" is that we, as actors, must usually act without knowing every pertinent fact and sometimes without even knowing what facts are pertinent.[8] This is to say nothing of the terribly limited predictive capacities of human imagination given that our actions occur within what must be considered complex systems, including markets, societies, the physical earth, and our own human biology. Thus, although we often act in ways motivated by conscious intentions, a distance between our intentions and their realization in the world is often inevitable and can quickly become a chasm as our intentions and actions become more complex.

In tragic literature the problem of limited and asymmetrical information is often central to the dramatic reversal that gives the story its import. Perhaps the most famous example is Sophocles's tragedy *Oedipus Rex,* a prequel to *Antigone* in his trio of Theban plays, where Oedipus slays a man in a road dispute and is later named king of Thebes and granted the hand in marriage of the Theban queen Jocasta, only later to discover that the man whom he killed was his father and woman he married was his mother.

In political philosophy, this concern with unintended consequences most influentially undergirds the thought of the British statesman-intellectual Edmund Burke. "There is not, there never was," Burke argued, "a principle of government under heaven, that does not, in the very pursuit of the good it proposes, naturally and inevitably lead into some inconvenience, which makes it absolutely necessary to counterwork and weaken the application of that first principle itself . . . in order to prevent also the inconveniences, which have arisen from the instrument of all the good you had in view."[9] Burke used this argument to undergird his pleas against both radicalism in the service of abstract theory and corrosive attacks on traditional authority because of the possible tragic consequences of such a politics.[10] One can, however, reject Burke's pessimism (after all, things could turn out better than expected and strengthen a principle) while still conceding his basic point about the inevitability of unintended consequences as a matter of political sociology and, if one were so inclined, a matter of consequential evaluation in ethics.[11]

While Aristotle focused, given the dramatic material of his inquiry, on the intimate relationships between individuals, modern readings of tragedy move beyond individuals to speak, as the great Shakespearean critic A. C. Bradley writes, "of the passions, tendencies, ideas, principles, [and] forces which animate these persons or groups."[12] In their manifestation, articulation, or revelation of certain ideals, the characters can transcend their individual context and narratively exemplify a broader conflict or signify a contest with universal implications. Hence, in G. W. F. Hegel's interpretation of Antigone in his *Phenomenology of Spirit,* Antigone's admission of guilt represents a crucial moment in his philosophy of history—when the private realm of kinship and its associated feminine virtues as represented by Antigone are overcome by law, rationality, and the city-state, all embodied in the form of Creon.[13]

This raises the problem of value pluralism in social and political life, a condition philosophers describe as arising from the fact that we are guided by a wide array of values (e.g., humility, dignity, justice, equality, liberty, and mercy) that are often in some kind of tension or even direct conflict when we attempt to realize them. These values, shaped by community and conscience, are often defended with great conviction and sacrifice and not always easily reconciled in concrete historical and political moments. While many philosophers and political thinkers dream of transcending or dissolving these conflicts, or diffusing them with various schemes of education, management, discipline, or subsumption, it is one implication of tragedy to see them as an unavoidable feature of our life in common. In some accounts, like Isaiah Berlin's, this is an irreducible feature of the human condition; for others, like Max Weber, this is simply our plight after the disenchantment of modernity.[14] This fascinating debate need not lead us astray. The point is simply to note the resonance between strong theories of value pluralism and approaches to tragedy that reject its association with reconciliation. Where value pluralism is at work, conflict takes an especially urgent character. This is because certain values, or at least any prospect for their real-world realization, can also suffer from a sort of death. By the metaphor of death, I mean only some amalgamation of the decisive defeat of the practical aspirations that embody said values, the discrediting of the philosophical and spiritual programs that valorized them, and the loss of historical memory that such values once moved the hearts of men at all.

Contingency, Not False Necessity

This leads directly into a second theme of tragedy, often unstated: that these defeats *matter*. That defeats serve as the pivotal plot points of the plot of tragedy is an implicit claim to their significance, a value that is not easily granted in the romantic or ironic modes. "Tragedy implies value, even if it also puts it into question," Terry Eagleton reminds us. "We do not grieve over the loss of what we regard as worthless . . . the ultimate tragedy would be a condition in which we were so careless of human value that we would no longer be able to mourn."[15]

This significance, however, fits best with an axiomatic view of the world and history as *contingent:* sometimes the reasonable, the good, and the right can be partially or utterly defeated by the unreasonable, the bad, and the unjust. This, of course, means that the tragic understanding of the ethical and moral conflicts between human beings is opposed to romanticism and can never be subsumed under the aphoristic optimism of "the arc of the moral universe." But it also means that tragedy should not be subsumed under radical pessimism or self-assured irony. Its greatest poignancy instead relies on the existence of hopes that are not "fruitless from the outset."[16]

Instead tragedy forces us to live with an embrace of the contingency of social outcomes, representing history as "a broken series of paradoxes and reversals in which human action is ever open to unaccountable contingencies—and luck."[17] In this vein, Christophe Menke has rightly criticized the first generation of critical theorists in the Frankfurt school for their interpretation of tragedy as necessarily inculcating a passivity and resignation to the world under a false apprehension of necessity.[18] What this generation of theorists failed to realize, he argues, is that the crux of tragic emplotment, at least in its modern form, turns on the narrative revelation that, had the principal agents acted differently, there could have been a different outcome. Thus, tragedy reflects commitment to the possibilities of human action, even if significantly chastened by death, our lack of sovereignty, irrationality, and more.[19] It is this commitment that underwrites the tragic. A. C. Bradley underscores this insight:

> No amount of calamity which merely befell a man, descending from the clouds like lightning, or stealing from the darkness like pestilence, could alone provide the substance of [tragedy]. Job was the greatest of all the children of the east, and his afflictions were well-nigh more than he could bear; but even if we imagined them wearing him to death, that would not make his story tragic. . . . The calamities of tragedy do not simply happen, nor are they sent; they proceed mainly from actions, and those the actions of men. . . . These actions beget others, and these others beget others again, until this series of inter-connected deeds leads by an apparently inevitable sequence to a catastrophe. The effect of such a series on imagination is to make us regard the sufferings which accompany it, and the catastrophe in which it ends, not only or chiefly as something which happens to the persons concerned, but equally as something which is caused by them.[20]

Another way of putting this is that it is easy to be misled by the focus on "fate" or "necessity" in tragic literature, exemplified by William Shakespeare's Roman soothsayer, who warns Julius Caesar to "beware the ides of March," or by blind Tiresias's warning to Creon that citywide disorder and the death of his family members will come from his tyranny in Antigone. These prophetic warnings, which come true in the course of the plays, can appear in retrospect as the determining laws of fate exerting their control over the vagaries of humankind. If one is attentive to the unfolding of their respective plots, however, it is not only the contingent interaction of individuals and their own personal judgment that lead the principal characters to their demise but also an act of arrogance in the face of these warnings. The warnings of fate may be profitably read as the tragic portrait of the paradoxical character of human action. Or, as Eagleton makes the point, "freely undertaken actions are bound to breed effects which are uncontrollable, and which may then come to confront the agent himself as a form of destiny . . . so it is that freedom gives rise to servitude, a paradox that only a dialectical form of thought"—like the tragic play—"can grasp."[21]

If action is ontologically rooted in the human capacity for imagination and beginning and communication and cooperation, it nevertheless must be instantiated in a world where opportunities to act in certain *ways* or under certain descriptions are rarely enduring. They are, instead, often path-dependent, and always limited by features of the world beyond our sovereign control. What appears as individual tragic fate may be recast sociologically as an increasingly suffocating and constraining web of social structures, patterns of behavior, and opportunity structures for action that finally close out the possibilities, in a given historical moment, to effectively act in a given way, under certain descriptions. As Raymond Williams brilliantly argues, readers of tragedy and society alike commonly abstract "necessity" and imagine it subordinating human will, but the real "character of necessity, insofar as it can be generalised in this culture and these [tragic] plays, is that *its limits on human action are discovered in real actions, rather than known in advance or in general:* the precise qualities that now characterise Necessity and are translated as determinism and fatalism."[22]

Defeat and Significance

This understanding of historical contingency and human action reflects an understanding of the world at work in tragedy's implicit account of significance. This is the contention that practical defeat, in and of itself, cannot serve as a decisive reason to render judgment against an individual, reject a political program, dismiss a theoretical insight, repudiate a moral belief, or concede historical obsolescence in the course of historical reflection. A tragic emplotment of history suggests that these features of the historical landscape might be highly valuable explanatory-analytical, cultural, political, or ethical resources despite their practical defeat or subsequent historical obsolescence. In its abstract form, this claim is not as controversial to philosophers, who tend to be more interested in the internal logic and perspicacious insight of various thinkers and their works when they turn to the history of intellectual thought. Even political theorists, who might—as with critics of Marxism—weigh heavily the exploits of the historical-political champions of a set of ideas against the ideas themselves, tend not to claim an ability to dismiss the possible significance of the defeated.

This, historians might respond, is just fine for philosophy and political theory, whose explicit normative aims set them apart from the discipline of history; but to impart such designs to historical writing would be a travesty. The historian Edward Carr criticizes those for whom "knowledge is knowledge for some purpose," as their instrumental orientation toward history writing leads them to "extravagant interpretation" that rides "roughshod over facts." These historians, he charges, are guilty of writing a kind of "propaganda or historical fiction" that merely uses the past to "embroider a kind of writing that has nothing to do with history."[23] Invoking the ever-unsettling specter of Friedrich Nietzsche, Carr quotes his infamous *Beyond Good and Evil,* in which the German philosopher seduces the historian down the slippery slope toward fiction and myth: "The falseness of an opinion is not for us any objection to it. . . . The question is, how far an opinion is life-furthering, life-preserving, species-preserving, perhaps species-rearing, and we are fundamentally inclined to maintain that the falsest opinions (to which the synthetic judgments *a priori* belong), are the most indispensable to us."[24]

This conception of history, which might justify even deliberately fictive historical mythology, serves for Carr as the foreboding Charybdis of the discipline. His Scylla, on the other side, is the diametrically opposed yet "untenable theory of history as an objective compilation of facts" that appear to the historian in pure, objective form waiting to be told. As we have covered at length in Chapter 3, and as Carr concedes, the historian's work is inevitably interpretive, imaginative, and incomplete and indelibly influenced by the situation of their present. Carr grasps the centrality of interpretation (or what I have called the hermeneutic situation) to historical writing, but he does not seem to fully grasp the import of this concession.

Carr writes elsewhere that historical facts are "not at all like fish on the fishmonger's slab" but instead like "fish swimming about in a vast and sometimes inaccessible ocean; and what the historian catches will depend partly on chance, but mainly on what part of the ocean he chooses to fish in and what tackle he chooses to use—these two factors being, of course, determined by the kind of fish he wants to catch."[25] The problem with his pseudo-hermeneutic circle approach, however, is that it cannot account for political unconscious of history and the horizons of significance that undergird what appears meaningful, ethically gripping, politically relevant, and so on. Perhaps, to stay with the metaphor, we are not talking bait and tackle, but the boat itself.

Let's take an example close to my preoccupations: "American political development," the most proudly and self-consciously historical field in the contemporary study of American politics in professional political science. Stephen Skowronek, arguably the dean of the field, has set its agenda as charting durable shifts in patterns of political authority in the United States. This approach, which unapologetically focuses on the winners in the battle for governing authority, keeps at arm's length much of what interests contemporary historians. As we shall see, much of what concerns long civil rights movement historiography—including efforts to organize transnational black solidarities against racism and imperialism, communist organizing in the Deep South, the National Association for the Advancement of Colored People's (NAACP's) abandoned litigation strategies, or black nationalist community control projects—are of cursory interest or worse. The political science belligerent in the back of the historians' conference session might impolitely insist that these events, however meaningful they may have been for the people who wasted their lives participating in them, are essentially distractions from the truly significant arenas of action in American politics.

Yet the dogged insistence on the significance of these events reflects a deeper *philosophical* conflict about the aims of history and historical judgment. The Pulitzer Prize–winning historian Gordon Wood may be a surprising ally here in explaining my point, given his criticism of "an obvious kind of presentism, which at worst becomes indoctrination by historical example" or skepticism toward "instrumentalist" approaches to history concerned with "multicultural" empowerment and identity, but he draws a helpful distinction worth dwelling on.[26] Wood distinguishes between historical recoveries that make exaggerated claims for "the *original* way [certain ideas] were used in the past," versus those like Hannah Arendt's, which emphasize the ways that time has allowed these to crystallize in new configurations, become strange again, and light up features of *our* present.[27] History of political thought and praxis on these terms, Wood concedes, is "a quite legitimate endeavor," and the historically informed political theorist, then, can comb through the so-called dustbin of history to find those ideas, events, and individuals that can speak powerfully to the present through a tragic narrative that projects them into the realm of appearances.

The significance of what political theorists excavate, therefore, comes mainly from what the hermeneutic fusion allows for these newly recovered fragments to accomplish in terms of enlarging our capacities for judgment, enriching our resources for critique, and educating a sensibility to the world that is more cognizant of the fleetingness of opportunity and the obstacles to the aspirations of human action. This tragic vision looks to the defeated in a hope "to do justice to the memory of the dead by telling the story of history in terms of their failed hopes and efforts."[28] "Under the weight of failure, in tragedy that could have been avoided but was not avoided," as Raymond Williams insists, a new "structure of feeling is now struggling to be formed," one that is life-affirming against death, and as knowledgeable about suffering as joy.[29]

Diverging from the tragic vision of historically informed political and critical theory, Wood also articulates a tragic sensibility for history that he considers more appropriate for the disciplinarily bound historian and which provides us with another foundation to defend claims of tragic historical significance. He concedes that it is only "natural for historians to want to relate the past to the needs and problems of the present," and he thinks that this search for the historical origins of contemporary problems or situations is unproblematic. There, then, is an explanatory interest that might be appealed to for significance.

Wood warns, however, against anachronism, which he identifies as the subordination of the project of explicating "the complicated context of past events" to present criteria and aims.[30] What, then, are we to make of those events plotted in historical narratives that are not necessarily or obviously crucial to *explaining* the evolution of today's social problems? After all, much of this work is increasingly performed with exceeding precision in historical sociology and economic history.[31] What do we do with *stories* whose main import is that they change our descriptions of the world, our ethical and political judgment of the past, and our response to ethical-existential dilemmas?

Here Wood explicitly articulates a tragic vision of history (invoking the tragic fiction of George Eliot, Thomas Hardy, and Henry James) as guided by a "realization that the participants [in our historical narratives] were limited by forces they did not understand or were even aware of" and the "tension that existed between the conscious wills and intentions of the participants in the past and the underlying conditions that constrained their actions and shaped their future." History offers us, in Wood's argument, a "way of coming to terms with an anxious present and an unpredictable future" with "wisdom and humility and indeed a tragic sense of life . . . a sense of the limitations of life."[32] Our turn toward the "failed hopes and efforts" of the past orients us to the significance in those events and figures that can best convey this tragic sensibility about the contingencies and limits that frustrate human action but which are also its conditions for possibility. Moreover, this tragic vision also directs the historian's vision at those ideas, events, personalities, and other historical phenomena that have had an impact or influence on other, more conventionally significant events woven into the complex web of historical actions and consequences.

A Tragic Ethic of Responsibility

This coheres with the ethical response that tragedy, as a dramatic form, attempts to evoke in its audience. Often lost in tragedy's translation from a dramatic theatrical form to a mode of narrative emplotment is the centrality of the chorus and the audience in its original Greek iteration, the focus of much of Aristotle's *Poetics*. The misguided notion of tragedy as counseling reconciliation with the inevitability of defeat or human impotence in the face of fate denies tragedy's original recognition of the potential ethical relationship between an event, its recounting, and its audience. Against this view we can recognize, with Hayden White, that "the fall of the protagonist and the shaking of the world he inhabits which occur at the end of the Tragic play are not regarded as totally threatening to those who survive the agonic test . . . [for there] has been a gain in consciousness for the spectators of the contest."[33] We can change "our own repertoire of responses to pain in ourselves or each other," when we watch tragedy. The point is not to intervene or redeem the past, but to change ourselves and the future.[34]

In one such tragic vision of "long" civil rights history, dramatized on Broadway in the musical *The Scottsboro Boys* (2010), the communist- and (later) NAACP-led organizing around the various trials of nine African American boys falsely accused of rape in 1931 in Jim Crow Alabama failed to accomplish its immediate goal of freeing all nine boys. It nonetheless served as a crucible of organizational and intellectual activity that would greatly shape African American life in the twentieth century. Rosa McCauley, later to become Rosa Parks, was introduced to her husband and civil rights activism alike through the Scottsboro case, and the increased profile of communism in black communities was an obvious influence on the leading lights of black arts and letters (Harold Cruse, Ralph Ellison, Paul Robeson, Richard Wright, etc.).[35] *The Scottsboro Boys* dramatized this relationship through the onstage presence during the entire play of a silent black female witness, seemingly invisible to the other characters, who in the play's conclusion, a split-second reenactment of her dramatic stand on a bus in Montgomery, Alabama, is revealed to be Rosa Parks.

Martha Nussbaum has distilled arguably the most powerful gain in understanding that moral and political agents gain from the encounter with tragedy: an appreciation of tragic choices. This is qualitatively distinct from the obvious question that concerns most applied ethics: "What ought agent X do in situation Y"? This question can be complicated, difficult, and confusing, but it is not necessarily tragic. Tragic questions, instead, are forced by a distinct situation where all the alternatives available to the actor involve "serious moral wrongdoing."[36]

These tragic dilemmas, Nussbaum argues, cannot be readily resolved with cost-benefit analysis. This, she argues, would require an illusory picture of the world as one where our moral principles only come into prima facie, not thoroughgoing, conflict. Or worse, it involves a reduction of our deeply held moral principles to exchange values that can be discarded in the face of various contingencies. The rhetoric of romance treats values in these ways to dissolve conflict without remainder; ironic history treats the values in the world as illusory or corrupted, reducing matters as if the one truly valuable choice is, as in Ta-Nehisi Coates's invocation of Richard Wright, "between the world and me": whether we will reject the world or, in bad faith, reconcile ourselves to its subjection.[37]

Against these dilemmas Nussbaum argues for an ethics that recognizes that choice in a tragic situation does not absolve the actor of responsibility for the implications of their choice. To that end, a sense of tragedy counsels reconciliatory responses to tragic choices like reparations for devastating acts of war (i.e., the bombing of Hiroshima). Moreover, in recognizing the dire internal conflict that tragic choices occasion, a broader social ethics would encourage societies, organizations, and states to be arranged such that these choices, like those between religious obligation and civic duty or parental responsibility and professional responsibility, do not unnecessarily befall people as best we can avoid.[38]

Although Nussbaum's discussion of tragic dilemmas is largely restricted to conflicts between states and citizens or to similar cases involving authority, this problem has also long been central to the philosophical and political concerns of those who seek to dismantle forms of domination or oppression. In a remarkably wide-ranging study of radical democrats in the twentieth-century United States, Marc Stears rebukes contemporary democratic theorists for ignoring the normative questions—usually derisively relegated to the realm of "nonideal theory"—emerging from persistent concerns about the proper relationship of political ends to political means. While Stears does not use the language of tragedy, his concluding remarks seem to suggest a deep appreciation of the messiness of political choices, particularly against what he calls a "backdrop of extreme injustice or exclusion." Above all, this is rooted in an ineradicable divergence between the principles and virtues that are likely consonant with ideal theory (i.e., democratic justice) and those principles and virtues that are appropriate to the political struggle to bring a just society into being from a nonideal one. To this end he expresses skepticism of possibility of "sweeping rules in democratic theory as to the acceptability of particular political strategies at all times and in all places," emphasizing instead the importance therefore of reflective judgment.[39] Stears acknowledges, then, that these two sets of deeply held—and, in some sense, right—principles may be in irreconcilable philosophical conflict, while a particular situation of oppression forces practical choices between them that may bring about genuine wrongs, including acts of violence.

The theologian and philosopher Reinhold Niebuhr, in *Moral Man and Immoral Society* (1932), takes this line of argument to its extreme conclusion, which is an understanding of all politics as tragic. Niebuhr argued, in a Weberian vein, that "all social co-operation on a larger scale than the most intimate social group requires a measure of coercion," by which he means the imposition through violence, social pressure, propaganda, or economic exploitation of one person's or group's will on another who would presumably otherwise behave differently.[40] This claim is rooted in a philosophical anthropology that claims that human beings, especially when organized into collectivities, are ultimately going to display characteristics of selfishness, the vices of an endemic will to power, and inherent limits to their individual and collective intelligence and rationality. To keep these various destructive characteristics in check, societies rely on some mixture of moral suasion, political compromise, and multiple forms of coercion.

Where Niebuhr's relative originality lies, however, is in his tragic sensibility. Unlike Weberian social science, which makes similar claims about the coercive organization of society but insists on value neutrality, Niebuhr demands that we recognize these forms of coercion as *social injustices.* The implication, therefore, is that without injustice, there is no cohesive society. The depth of his tragic vision is greater still when he advances the more controversial claim that those political efforts that attempt or even succeed in destroying forms of injustice are also coercive and thus potential sources of moral wrongs. Consequently, Niebuhr argues, an a priori moral distinction between competing forms of coercion cannot be made, relegating judgment to the grounds of evaluation concerning whether the acts in question can be said to truly advance the long-term cause of social justice or commit one to some intolerable social evil.[41]

Even nonviolent resistance, which Niebuhr discusses at length through the case of Mahatma Gandhi in India, is deemed coercive insofar as it "places restraints upon the freedom of the objects of its discipline and prevents them from doing what they desire to do" and is potentially positively harmful if its boycotts "rob a whole community of its livelihood" or "imperil the life of a whole community which depends upon some vital service with which the strike interferes." And although Niebuhr is loath to use the word *injustice,* his discussion of nonviolent coercion includes people he identifies as innocent—namely, those workers and capitalists, and their communities, who might be called the collateral damage of nonviolent boycotts. "The innocent are involved with the guilty in conflicts between groups by the very group character of the conflict," Niebuhr argues. Specifically, he cites those whom he claims are peripherally connected to unjust societies or actions through the exchange relations instantiated by global capitalism. "The cotton spinners of Lancashire are impoverished by Gandhi's boycott of English cotton," he proclaims—with a self-assurance that would no doubt evoke the ire of today's advocates of consumer and corporate citizenship—"though they can hardly be regarded as the authors of British imperialism."[42]

Arguably the most famous reader of Niebuhr, and *Moral Man and Immoral Society* in particular, was Martin Luther King Jr., who was deeply influenced by Niebuhr's account of the sinfulness of man in social collectives and the inevitability of coercion in politics. Channeling the famed theologian, King thought that while it remained indispensable to appeal, through persuasion, to others' moral or ethical sense, we would never "get by coercion totally because of man's capacity for evil." This fact makes "an element of coercion necessary."[43] In describing his politics as "moral, non-violent coercion," King wants to acknowledge the ethical dilemmas of coercion *and* retain the Niebuhrian distinctions between the intentions, spirit, and likely consequences that attend to violent versus nonviolent resistance. His argument may be restated as follows: *when leveraged against injustice and resentment, leavened with a spirit of goodwill and forgiveness, and articulated through a willingness to take on more suffering than one's opponent, moral, nonviolent coercion is justified.* Indeed, it is the mode of politics most effective for defending one's dignity in the face of oppression, while also remaining capable of creating a "mutual friendship based on complete equality" without the "aftermath of hatred and bitterness that usually follows a violent campaign."[44] And, as I have argued elsewhere, this acceptance of the necessity of *coercion* goes a long way toward explaining the rapid radicalization of King's thought and rhetoric regarding political resistance over the course of his career. In the 1950s, while King defended the coercive power of the boycott, his justifications of nonviolent protest turned primarily on its capacity to elicit shame, spiritual conversion, and social transformation. By 1963 in Birmingham, Alabama, however, faced with the "massive resistance" of segregationists, he began to accent the more baldly coercive and "realist" dimensions of nonviolent direct action. "The purpose of our direct-action program," he proclaimed, "is to create a situation so crisis-packed that it will inevitably open the door to negotiation."[45]

This search for a "crisis-packed" situation occasioned by direct action in 1963 actually helps illustrate the potential "tragic dilemmas" that may emerge in the conflict between means and ends in a campaign against injustice, even with nonviolent methods. Birmingham, although most remembered in philosophical circles for King's passionate defense of civil disobedience and expansive conception of the moral responsibility to protest injustice in his famous "Letter from a Birmingham Jail," has other philosophical questions to pose that are best approached through the lens of tragedy.

Less popularly remembered about Birmingham is that it came on the heels of King's tactical defeat in 1962 at the hands of Albany, Georgia, police chief Laurie Pritchett. Pritchett, a pioneer of contemporary methods of policing civil disobedience, read King's *Stride Toward Freedom* (1958) closely and studied the tactics of the 1961 Freedom Rides—the direct-action campaign organized by the Congress of Racial Equality (CORE) and the Student Nonviolent Coordinating Committee (SNCC) to force compliance with desegregation decisions in interstate transportation. From his research Pritchett understood how King and other civil rights activists were able to garner media attention and a decisive intervention by federal authorities only after police brutality and mob violence erupted. Sensing an opportunity, he departed radically from the preferred response of other Southern law enforcement: vicious, violent repression.[46] As King explained in a private letter,

> Public relations is a very necessary part of any protest of civil disobedience. . . . The public at large must be aware of the inequities involved in such a[n] [unjust] system. In effect, in the absence of justice in the established courts of the region, nonviolent protesters are asking for a hearing in the court of world opinion. Without the presence of the press, there might have been untold massacre in the South. The world seldom believes the horror stories of history until they are documented via mass media. Certainly, there would not have been sufficient pressure [during the Freedom Rides] to warrant a [pro-desegregation] ruling by the ICC [Interstate Commerce Commission] had not the situation been so well-publicized.[47]

What Pritchett realized, bequeathing to future generations of law enforcement, was that if he could prevent mob attacks and discipline his officers to avoid violence, he would discourage media coverage and thus remove the main incentive for federal interventions that would topple local segregation. Combining his ingenuous media strategy with a masterful manipulation of divisions between national civil rights organizations and local black leadership, Pritchett succeeded in enforcing segregation in "every phase of Albany's life." Most devastatingly, he even "won widespread praise in the national media" for his handling of the situation. This tactical defeat led the SCLC to regroup and direct its direct action protest efforts to Birmingham, where black community divisions were expected to be less fractious, the specific and vulnerable targets of department store and church segregation could be challenged, and—more important—the legendarily hot-tempered and brutal public safety commissioner Eugene "Bull" Connor would be less likely to respond with the patient cunning of Sheriff Pritchett.[48]

This context is important for the tragic dilemma at the heart of Birmingham because it illustrates just how crucial dramatic, sympathetic media coverage was to the effectiveness of nonviolent resistance during the civil rights movement. Unfortunately for the SCLC, Pritchett's example was well noted throughout the South, and Bull Connor hired him as a consultant on the announcement of the SCLC's Birmingham campaign. For the first month of the Birmingham conflict, Connor showed uncharacteristic restraint and media coverage dried up as King spoke to increasingly smaller crowds at local churches between trips to jail and court. The protest army gathered by the SCLC was dwindling quickly under the pressures of prolonged imprisonment brought about by the lack of SCLC funds and a creeping feeling of inevitable defeat. Desperately in need of troops for their nonviolent army and sympathetic media coverage, James Bevel, a reverend and activist who cut his direct-action teeth in the 1960 sit-ins that launched the SNCC before moving to the SCLC as Mississippi's field secretary, made the decision—with King's tacit consent but not his explicit authorization—to recruit hundreds of black children to march on downtown Birmingham.

Herein lay the tragic choice, in Nussbaum's sense, faced by the leaders of the SCLC. None of them was naive about the dangers of direct-action protests in Birmingham. King's close confidant Stanley Levinson recalled King's warning at the SCLC strategy session where the Birmingham campaign was agreed on: "There are something like eight people here assessing the type of enemy we're going to face. I have to tell you in my judgment, some of the people sitting here today will not come back alive from this campaign."[49] The question of whether to use their moral authority and social stature to persuade children, some as young as elementary school age, to participate in nonviolent resistance was therefore unavoidably a question about whether to risk children's lives. Thus, the leaders of the SCLC were forced to measure their responsibilities, as adults and pastors, to the children of Birmingham against the responsibility to protest the moral wrong of racial segregation within a tactical situation that pushed this moral conflict to the further into tragic choices.

If the SCLC continued to rely only on Birmingham's adults, the movement would likely have deteriorated, media coverage would have evaporated, and the moral wrong of segregation in Birmingham would possibly remain in place for an unknown period of time. Failure might also discredit nonviolent direct action and civil rights radicalism in American politics. Even in 1962, King's ostensible allies in SNCC were increasingly critical. As Julian Bond said with barely concealed enthusiasm at the time, "[King] has been losing since he left Montgomery. . . . I think he's been losing for a long time. And I think eventually that more Negroes and more white Americans will become disillusioned with him, and find that he after all is only another preacher who can talk well."[50] If the SCLC decided to not act and to cancel the protest, it may have been devastating for the appeal of nonviolence and King's stature, making the defeat of Albany pale in comparison. It would also leave the harm of segregation intact. The last option, Bevel and other SCLC leaders thought, was to encourage the children to protest and, in doing so, to place them in potentially fatal danger.

Numerous parents objected to the use of children in such dangerous protests, as did President John F. Kennedy, who lamented that "an injured, maimed or dead child is a price that none of us can afford to pay," and Malcolm X, who derisively declared, "Real men don't put their children on the firing line."[51] And despite Bevel's rhetorical flourishes claiming that children would "get more education in five days in the city jail than they will get in five months in a segregated school," the harm these children faced—police dogs, high-pressure fire hoses, beatings, and a torrent of racial insult—are indeed genuine harms for which SCLC leadership judged they would bear some degree of responsibility.

There are few contemporary observers, with the blessing of knowing how the campaign eventually was "victorious," who condemn or criticize the SCLC's decision. And this seems entirely appropriate. My point is not that it might be clear as a matter of applied ethics what King and the SCLC should have done. Some tragic choices are clear enough to considered judgment, but the clarity of what must be done does not reduce their tragedy. The point is that if we are investigating this scenario for an option that does not involve "serious moral wrongdoing," we are likely to be disappointed. We instead face a tragic set of circumstances that we can imagine tormented King, who spent hours "closeted in his motel suite . . . unable to make up his mind . . . [and] racked with doubts" about whether to send in the children.[52]

The significance of King's moral paralysis is that it illustrates the crushing sense of responsibility that he felt for his choice in this tragic situation. Far from encouraging total resignation to forces beyond our control, a tragic sensibility insists on the importance of human action and choice. It tempers this sense of responsibility for action and its consequences with humility and resilience derived from the careful consideration of our lack of sovereignty over their consequences.

This insistence on lingering intently on, and reconstructing in full, the genuine possibilities of human action and choice in a moment of judgment leads to an emphasis on responsibility that has certain consequences for tragic emplotments of history. Above all, this tragic sense of responsibility fosters an analytical orientation that seeks to hold in consideration not only the choices made by historical actors but also *the roads not taken,* where what Nussbaum calls the "residuum of tragedy at the heart of human life" resides.[53] Tragedy renders significant these crossroads and dilemmas in a way that irony or romance never could, haunting *what is* with *what might have been.*

Irony sees these choices and possibilities as too illusory; romance sees them as too easily reconciled and redeemed in the sweep of history. The ultimate aim of tragic history is to either return to these crossroads in the form of normative judgment and reflect on the wisdom of a decision or the possible lost treasures to be found by the wayside, or to pursue Wood's narrower project of reflecting, through eyes educated by tragic thought, on the various ways that human beings have attempted to deal with the problems of living together in a world that resists our control.

The Tragic Vision of Long Civil Rights Historiography

Having advanced this account of tragedy, we can turn squarely to the possibility of a "tragic" vision in civil rights history. Taken collectively, the historians laboring under the appellation "long civil rights movement" historiography manifest this sort of tragic vision through their modes of emplotment in narrating the history of the civil rights movement. I turn to this historiography in order to substantiate my view that there is a defensible alternative within our economy of exemplarity to romantic histories that lead to complacent forms of liberalism and ironic histories that lead to passively nihilistic Afropessimism. This long civil rights movement historiography is the seedbed, I think, of a *new* exemplarity, on which we can rethink major questions in black critical thought without evading the crisis of authority that is our predicament.

Every narrative mode in historical discourse has its rhetorical and stylistic strategies of representation. In tragedy, it is often contextualism: expanding the periodization to rethematize and rethink an exemplary event by recovering the difficult choices and lost opportunities that led to the concretization of "necessity." Thus, nearly every major work in this tradition begins with an assault on the "master narrative" of civil rights, or what I have called the romantic emplotment, in the Montgomery-to-

Memphis narrative. Casting doubt on the celebratory tone of romance, these histories recall Hayden White's characterization of tragedy as a belief that "there are no festive occasions, except false and illusory ones."[54]

Thomas Sugrue, for instance, sees his entrée into long civil rights movement historiography as a challenge to "the tired clichés of recent books that fixate on the 1960s as the fundamental turning point in the history of race in modern America." Regarding the Montgomery-to-Memphis narrative he offers only the backhanded compliments that it is "powerful for its simplicity" and "has been influential in shaping national politics." In his final judgment, what I have described as the romantic narrative is "terribly incomplete."[55] Jacquelyn Dowd Hall, in an article that waved the rallying flag for this self-conscious historiographical turn, criticizes what I call the romantic narrative as a "journalistic 'rough draft of history'" that depicts the movement as if it, and the white backlash to it, has "no precedents, no historical roots." A broader contextualization of the civil rights activism, Hall argues, will show its "truer" relationships to the "liberal and radical milieu of the late 1930s," the migration patterns of African Americans, the various mid-twentieth-century interests of the federal government, and deep organizing traditions in black political life, all while destabilizing the tidy geography of racial discord that dominates the American imagination.[56] Nikhil Pal Singh levels a similar critique, arguing that "the contemporary reversals of prior movements toward racial equality reveal the gains of the short civil rights era as provisional codifications of a more complex social reality, temporary achievements of longer-fought and still-persisting social conflicts." The victory posited by the triumphalism of romanticism in "the formal conquest of citizenship rights by African Americans" appears to Singh as "a less than partial victory" when one considers the longer narrative proposed by long civil rights movement historiography.[57]

There is no doubt that contemporary politics plays a tremendous role in this historiographical critique. Aside from the current collapse of the authoritative pillars of black political life and the persistence of racial inequality and black marginalization that would inevitably shape the hermeneutic horizon of any contemporary historical investigation into civil rights history, long civil rights movement historians are also explicitly opposed to neoconservative appropriations of the history of civil rights in service of "color blindness." Hall is most explicit here, railing against the "New Right" and its allies—corporate power brokers, disillusioned liberals turned neoconservatives, and "old-style" conservative intellectuals.[58] They are responsible, in her account, for formulating a narrative that turns King's wish that Americans be "judged not by the color of their skin, but by the content of their character" first into the singular aim of the entire civil rights movement and then into a comprehensive ideology that forbids race-conscious public policy; places unjustified faith in formal legal equality and market rationality to secure justice; and tends to explain the persistence of racial inequality in terms of African American cultural pathologies with regard to family, labor, crime, and education.[59] For Singh, the current triumph of color blindness and its twin beliefs that "any race-based amelioration constitutes a form of reverse discrimination" *and* eliminating racism is equivalent to "eliminating racial reference within juridical discourse and public policy" are unmistakable evidence that the reforms of the civil rights era were built on "shaky political, institutional, and ideological foundations."[60] In the face of this color-blind assault, Hall proclaims a desire to "reinforce the moral authority" of civil rights activists and make their story "harder to simplify, appropriate, and contain."[61]

Recalling Carr's critique of the dangerously slippery slope traversed by the incorporation of instrumental, political projects into the discipline of history, we should be wary of relying only on normative arguments against contemporary political actors to make the case for a certain interpretation of history. If long civil rights movement historiography is going to be compelling *as* history and against competing interpretations, it will have to appeal to some grounds appropriate to professional historical practice. Here, as Charles Taylor has argued in other contexts of science, social science, and moral philosophy, the superiority of one paradigm over another can be assessed by whether a transition between them represents a gain or loss in understanding.

To perform this sort of reflective judgment, Taylor suggests, we might deploy comparative judgments: How does one conception account for the existence of another? We might also discuss how they deal with the overlapping issues that necessarily arise from the common concerns they share, their internal measurements of explanatory success, and their expansion or foreclosure of our practical abilities to effect intentional purpose in the world. Finally, we may even be able to see the superiority of one conception over another because of a transition that is intrinsically error reducing in that it supersedes one-sided interpretations and incorporates the best insights of its competitors while also taking account of facts like agency, contingency, natality, and loss that are not sufficiently present in others.[62]

The claims of this approach are somewhat narrow. Superiority is always comparative and never forecloses on a more compelling interpretation that comes along. In the case of civil rights historiography, however, we are on relatively promising ground. None of these interpretive modes of emplotment—romance, irony, or tragedy—denies, for example, that communists were very active in organizing African Americans for the Scottsboro trials in the 1930s. Nor does any interpretation deny that *Brown v. Board of Education* was indeed decided in 1954 and the court opinion whose textual record we have today is authentic. The difference lies in interpretation.

What is the significance of communist activism for later, more familiar civil rights activists? Was *Brown* the crucial turning point for the civil rights movement, or was it a largely empty symbolic gesture? The answers to these sorts of interpretive and explanatory questions are accomplished in history through narrative and historical judgment. The emplotment gives us a sense of the values that inhere in these judgments, which are exercised in ways structured by disciplinary fidelity to notions of referential validity adjudicated by the archive. Aside from its broadsides against color blindness, long civil rights movement historiography also proclaims a particular, historical superiority as an interpretive frame based on the claim that it offers a gain in understanding when compared to other approaches.

At the theoretical level, this claim is undergirded by the arguments that long civil rights movement historians offer. They claim to provide a more reasonable explanation of the origin and outcome of those events that the romantic narrative is concerned with, a more compelling explanation of the romantic narrative than what its narrators can provide for themselves, and an "intrinsically error-reducing" account insofar as it contains the broadest amount of historical material possible—chronologically and geographically—without tipping into such infinite regress that it would undermine the very aspiration to explanation, like the cartographers in Jorge Luis Borges's famous 1946 short story, "The Exactitude of Science."[63]

Yet these historians also freely avail themselves of the language of moral judgment, perhaps in ways that raise again the concern with *presentism* or *politicization.* Here they side—rightly, in my view—with W. E. B. Du Bois, who criticizes the idea that scholars should research slavery and segregation "impartially." Du Bois assails "mechanistic interpretation" for missing "the real plot of the story, for the clear mistake and guilt of rebuilding a new slavery of the working class in the midst of a fateful experiment in democracy; for the triumph of sheer moral courage and sacrifice in the abolition crusade; and for the hurt and struggle of degraded black millions in their fight for freedom and their attempt to enter democracy. Can all this be omitted and half suppressed in a treatise that calls itself scientific?"[64] For Du Bois, the "scientific" study of history does not preclude moral knowledge, including the knowledge that particular historical moments were shot through with tragic choices.[65]

Building on these implicit theoretical foundations, which are manifest in narrative form, long civil rights movement historians coalesce around a common architecture that frames their intervention and critique. While the primary period of emphasis of much long civil rights movement work, and the focus of most critiques of this approach, is the late 1930s and

1940s, both Glenda Gilmore and Thomas Sugrue begin instead with the first great wave of Northern and urban migration by African Americans following World War I and concurrent with the Bolshevik Revolution of 1917. This is followed by the explosion of left-labor organizing by communists, socialists, civil rights organizations, and others from the 1920s until the 1940s, which reaches its highest point in the New Deal and early modern consumer capitalism era before collapsing under the weight of popular anticommunism, divisions within and between organizations on the left, and the choices and actions of various historical figures. World War II and the immediate postwar era figures largely as the geopolitical context—the specter of the Holocaust, the formation of the United Nations (UN) and human rights discourse, the Cold War, and anticolonial struggles—within which more conventional civil rights actors (the SNCC, the SCLC, etc.) are moving and events (*Brown*) are taking place. Thus, while the conventional narrative from *Brown* in 1954 to the assassination of King in 1968 undergoes little overhaul in archival details, its situation within the new historiography's preferred mode of tragic emplotment reveals different accents and emphases, opens the door to new voices, and compels a distinct understanding of civil rights victories.

In the rest of this chapter, I will synthesize the claims of long civil rights historiography by focusing on their points of narrative emphasis in light of the arguments concerning tragedy advanced above before turning to discussions of internationalism and "integrationism" opened up by this alternative narrative of civil rights exemplarity.

The Dialectic of Race and Nation: Rethinking Regionalism, Nationalism, and Internationalism

The South as Our Country, the South as Another Country: Great Migration

Between 1915 and 1930, more than 1.5 million black people moved from the South to the North. To put this staggering migration in context, the entire black population of the United States in 1910 was roughly 9.8 million.[66] Steven Hahn powerfully captures its transformative impact on American politics and society: "Once overwhelmingly southern, the African American population would become national; once overwhelmingly rural and agricultural, it would become urban and industrial; once overwhelmingly subject to formal and informal repression, coercion, and exclusion, it would find precious new space for civic and political activism."[67] This era also saw the first significant wave of voluntary Afro-Caribbean immigration to the United States and the expansive urbanization of the black population as a whole.[68] These were the early tremors of a political earthquake.

Black migrants were motivated by a combination of push-and-pull factors. On the side of the former, there were the severely limited economic prospects offered by sharecropping and the frequent consumer exploitation that accompanied it, the similarly meager opportunities and increased sexual vulnerability inherent in domestic labor for black women, the mechanization of Southern agriculture, poor schooling, humiliating Jim Crow laws, political disenfranchisement, and racist violence.[69] On the side of the latter were the relative increase in personal freedom and political power offered in the North, the cultural allure of clusters of creative artists, and, above all ,the economic opportunities opened in the industrial and service economies by the increased productive capacity of American industrial capitalism, the material needs of the war effort, the job vacancies left by soldiers, and the severe restrictions on Asian and European immigration (the Immigration Act of 1917, the Emergency Quota Act of 1921, and the Immigration Act of 1924) enacted in the wake of war-fueled isolationist and nativist sentiment.[70]

In long civil rights movement historiography, the invocation of the Great Migration as origin serves a few key narrative and conceptual purposes. First, it destabilizes the conventional geography of the romantic civil rights narrative. Against the implicit notion that the borders of the former Confederacy served as the exclusive territory of racial subordination, long civil rights movement historians articulate the features of racial inequality and white supremacy found outside the South. As Sugrue contends, even though "northern communities did not erect signs to mark separate black and white facilities; only some northern schools were segregated by law; and black voters were not systematically disenfranchised in the North," black people nonetheless lived "as second-class citizens . . . trapped in an economic, political, and legal regime that seldom recognized them as equals." Black migrants, he goes on to show, were met in Northern cities with restrictive covenants that legally forbade African Americans from buying or renting homes in certain neighborhoods, rampant housing discrimination, segregated schools, and the shocking resurgence of the Ku Klux Klan.[71] This is to say nothing of the unsanitary conditions for black migrants in the cities, which led to extraordinary health problems and pandemic-level casualty rates for decades.[72]

The spectacular mob violence of the South is thus, conceptually reconnected with a broader national story of political violence, especially against de facto "integrationists" living in white neighborhoods or in close proximity to white people. Although this mob violence may be said to have reached its zenith in the bloody Red Summer of 1919, when riots consisting mostly of organized white assaults against African Americans broke out across the country, including Northern cities like New York, Philadelphia, and, most spectacularly, Chicago, African Americans continued to be the targets of mob intimidation, assault, and bombing, mostly in retaliation for integrating white neighborhoods.[73]

Glenda Gilmore takes these insights to *conceptually* deconstruct the dialectic of racial, regional, and national geography upholding the romantic narrative through a clever reading of the idea of Dixie. She invokes the African American literary reappropriation and critique of the Confederate ideal of the South as "another country, with its own political and social institutions, upheld by a white supremacist regime," to interpretively reframe post–Great Migration black politics.[74] If Dixie was indeed a "mythical country," then we might profitably think of those who fled its borders and rejected its white supremacist social compact as expatriates, outside agitators, and governments in exile. The revelatory power of this discursive move is grounded not only in a deep sensitivity to the historical trajectory of key figures in both time and space but also in a sociological recognition of the importance of interpersonal networks and the expansive contours of the multiracial public sphere and the black counterpublic sphere.[75] "Jim Crow's black daughters and sons," Gilmore claims, "established beachheads in the North and around the world to gain safe ground from which to fire back at those occupying their country," and in order to grasp this truth, we must imaginatively plot civil rights narratives as "national, even international" stories.[76] Such theoretical interventions are, as we have seen in my reading of John Rawls (see Chapter 6), helpful for breaking from some of the axiomatic descriptions that ideologically fetter philosophers' interpretive judgments about the United States and the import of its authoritarian enclaves for qualitative judgments about what kind of society we inhabit.

Second, the Great Migration draws our attention to a more complicated understanding of African American political and intellectual history. In the conventional civil rights narrative, the ghetto as a political terrain of historical significance arrives fully formed, thoroughly dysfunctional, and on fire in the mid-1960s. Northern black people in the orbit of civil rights, therefore, enter largely as celebrity cameos (e.g., Harry Belafonte and James Baldwin lending their support to Southern activists), NAACP lawyers, and, most fully, the movement's veritable spoilers—the black nationalists, rioters, race relations bureaucrats, and ghetto dwellers whose collective pathologies and excesses would derail the movement's redemptive trajectory. Against this interpretive chronology, long civil rights historians argue for the long-standing importance of Northern ghettoes, both as externally imposed social-institutional formations that circumscribed freedom and equality for black people and as relatively buffered spaces for public discourse, political activity, and minor economic accumulation. This shift in spatial awareness leads not only to more comprehensive and precise understanding of the ghetto and its origins in public policy but also draws out a variety of the political aims and philosophical approaches formed in the course of black political life, often involving organizations and actors we thought we were familiar with. This expanding discursive space is crucial; it is difficult, as we saw with civil disobedience, to understand the formative questions animating political thought and praxis without reconstructing this expansive discursive context and its problem-space first.[77]

Third, the Great Migration is meant to signal a cultural transformation inspired by black soldiers' service in World War I. There was an increased militancy in the face of antiblack violence and oppression, underwritten by the sense that the blessings of equal citizenship should flow reciprocally from the demonstration of martial virtue and patriotic duty. This surge in militancy is said to have inspired not only the political militancy of the "New Negro" intellectuals and frequent acts of collective self-defense but also the flourishing of civil rights organizations like the NAACP. Economists Desmond Ang and Sahil Chinoy show that black men who were induced to enlist in the armed forces were three times more likely to join the NAACP than their counterparts.[78]

This analysis was pioneered long ago by W. E. B. Du Bois in his "Essay Toward a History of the Black Man in the Great War":

> On the Negroes this double experience of deliberate and devilish persecution from their own countrymen, coupled with a taste of real democracy and world-old culture, was revolutionizing. They began to hate prejudice and discrimination as they had never hated it before. . . . Far from filling them with a desire to escape from their race and country, they were filled with a bitter, dogged determination never to give up the fight for Negro equality in America. If American color prejudice counted on this war experience to break the spirit of the young Negro, it counted without its host. A new, radical Negro spirit has been born in France, which leaves us older radicals far behind. Thousands of young black men have offered their lives for the Lilies of France and they return ready to offer them again for the Sun-flowers of Afro-America.[79]

This reveals a tragic paradox of African American protest of significance for contemporary political theory on race, war, and empire. To the extent that protest justified itself with the rhetoric of what Aziz Rana calls "national security citizenship," or the idea that a member of a marginalized minority "can shows one's worthiness for membership by supporting—and being willing to fight and die for—the security policies of the state," it appeared to follow that the state could legitimately extract participation in military adventure, if not outright obedience, even if it involved ritual humiliation (e.g., segregation in the armed forces), racial exploitation (see Chapter 6), and racial justifications of neocolonialism that had a boomerang effect on ideological formations and recognition respect for minority populations back home. In our contemporary world, similar questions may arise where military service remains an attractive alternative to the viable economic options of immigrants, residents of indigenous reservations, or members of nongoverning territories.[80]

The Dialectic of Race, Nation, and Realism

A key part of this cultural transformation, related to the impact of World War I on the black political imagination, was an increasingly international consciousness among African Americans. Much of this was driven by Jamaican-born Marcus Garvey's Universal Negro Improvement Association (UNIA), the largest popular mass movement in black political history. The UNIA appropriated the symbols of Great War–era militarism and European nationalism and integrated them into a black nationalist, Pan-African political philosophy that managed to attract over a million followers. Although the Northern urban branches of the UNIA, especially the New York headquarters, have attracted what limited scholarly attention has been devoted to Garveyism, the UNIA established outposts in such far-flung locales as southern and western Africa, Brazil, Canada, the islands of the Caribbean, Ecuador, Panama, and Venezuela.[81] This unprecedented international appeal was enabled by Garvey's ability to rhetorically and symbolically represent the entirety of African-descended peoples around the globe—"400,000,000 Negroes," as he often put it—as a cohesive group unified by nature and political circumstance alike.[82] He presented the litany of particular abuses suffered by "the Negro" (particularly American lynchings, mob violence, and Jim Crow; exploitative Caribbean labor regimes; and the colonial partitioning of Africa in the 1919 Treaty of Versailles) around the globe as incontrovertible evidence of the truth of his worldview, which essentially blended a universal racialist ontology with a realist theory of international relations.

This vision of a world divided by races, where political peace and "global justice" might arise only from a precarious balance of material and tactical power between these vast human families, had a paradoxical impact on black political life. On the one hand, it encouraged African Americans to see themselves as global citizens with reciprocal obligations to other groups beyond the claims of American nationality and white supremacist practices in the United States as part of a global pattern of racial oppression. On the other hand, it accomplished this through a particularistic and racialist vision that expressed deep skepticism toward such cosmopolitan aspirations as voluntary self-ascription or the normative ideal of egalitarian multiracial, multicultural democracy.

Perhaps because of these illiberal dimensions and its authoritarian commitments, Garveyism has not figured largely in long civil rights scholarship that has sought to portray African American politics as developing certain global concerns in the early twentieth century. Despite the vast influence of Garveyism as the most popular black political movement in history, long civil rights movement historians have sought instead to emphasize an alternate, more obviously cosmopolitan (and socialist) genealogy said to be more intimately related to the civil rights movement's internationalist concerns. This is less a decision about documented popular influence on black political life than interpretive priorities that arise narratively from their tragic vision of civil rights history as a series of lost promises, missed opportunities, and forgotten discourses that are to be found more readily in leftist black activism than Garvey's comparably conservative Pan-Africanism.

Central to this alternate genealogy is that it displaces Garvey's Pan-Africanism with his rival W. E. B. Du Bois's more palatable (and less popular) cosmopolitan version as the font of a post–World War I international consciousness. Nikhil Pal Singh creates a kind of détente by subsumption, pressing Garvey and Du Bois, after the fact, into a thin agreement concerning the necessity of a global vision—he, too, rethinks the notion of "another country" by thinking through the idea of *black* as a country.

I want to raise one reconstructive and normative worry about Singh's specific rendering of this move, sympathetic though I am to its political significance. In short, while I admire the ways that the reading dialectically engages black nationalism to show how readily (and routinely) it evolves into forms of radical cosmopolitanism, I worry that what gets lost in the abstract enthusiasm for internationalism that the narrative conveys is a robust sense of the *realism* that makes nationalist thought of all varieties so distinctive on questions of geopolitics. Ironically, one consequence of taking this feature more seriously as part of the dialectic is that it reconnects Garvey's preoccupation with realism in black internationalist political thought to Martin Luther King's and other activists' navigation of Cold War geopolitics, which could be redescribed as "another realism," to borrow a phrase from Karuna Mantena's similar treatment of Gandhi.[83]

The overarching argument of Singh's book is that twentieth-century black political thought, at its most insightful, dealt primarily with a dialectical tension between the concepts of *race* and *nation* to imagine black peoplehood as a discursive space capable of producing an immanent critique of white supremacy in both the United States and around the world. This, in Singh's view, generated more philosophically expansive and globally inclusive visions of democratic justice and egalitarianism than those philosophical traditions that are tied to American nationalism (liberalism, republicanism, neoliberalism, and color-blind socialism). Garvey, as a critic of democracy, is a poor fit for this story, despite being the central figure within what Singh calls "the beginning of a sustained period of radicalization and adversarial internationalization for black politics as socialists and black nationalists entered the field of racial struggle in significant numbers for the first time."[84]

To substantiate his argument, Singh rejects the interpretive utility of familiar binary opposition between "racial particularity" and "national universality" and the familiar debates between liberalism and civic republicanism as a framework for understanding black politics in the twentieth century. Whereas Rogers Smith considers American politics to be driven by a conflict between three major traditions of thought—liberalism, republicanism, and ascriptive hierarchy (white supremacy, patriarchy, etc.)—Singh sees race as functioning as the persistent mediator, or "metalanguage," of the inherent tensions between liberalism and republicanism in a capitalist society. It is the unique character of race, he argues—namely, that it possesses a "double optic . . . both as an inscription of embodied particularity and as an abstract universality"—that allows it this peculiar place in American society.[85]

Democratic republicanism, Singh claims, often posits an abstract, homogeneous egalitarianism founded in constitutional principles as the ideal of national citizenship. In the United States, however, this abstraction drew its animating power and substantive content for those included, not only from the historical practices of racial domination (e.g., slavery, Jim Crow, the Chinese Exclusion Acts, etc.) but also from the implicit invocation of race as "a particular, putatively 'real' sensuous precedent" that is the silent subject of republicanism's *overcoming* that renders intelligible such sentiments as "our society is color-blind." Liberalism, on the other hand, works from an axiomatic belief in the "infinitely differentiated realm of private individuality." Yet the anthropological content of this differentiation, or the ideological context that shapes its phenomenological recognition, is a racialized worldview that makes whiteness (and other qualities) normative. "Behind the liberal notion of universal human capacity," Singh argues (recalling our discussion of Charles Mills in Chapter 6), "has been a thicket of delimiting 'social credentials'—cultural, historical, material, biological, and psychological 'preconditions'—for which race (and gender) have proved to be highly durable shorthand and broadly disseminating rubrics." The market, therefore, although often conceived by liberals as a space of individual freedom and "private" exchange, is actually provided at the outset with "reliable mechanisms of value-differentiation" in the form of race that render certain forms of racial discrimination, labor exploitation, resource appropriation, and consumer marketing rational and intuitive within a racialized, particularly white supremacist, context.[86] This is the kind of link between race and market value that makes the controversial concept of "racial capitalism" appealing to scholars attempting to understand ongoing dynamics of inequality in liberal market societies.[87]

Crucially, Singh argues that this mediating function of race also holds in the international arena. Here the "herrenvolk republicanism" and color-coded "universal" liberalism in domestic politics find their corollaries in foreign policy and Americans' global consciousness. In the period of ruthless American expansion under the banner of Manifest Destiny, which saw US soldiers and settlers conquer vast expanses of territory from American Indians, Cubans, Filipinos, Hawaiians, Mexicans, Puerto Ricans, and others, naked imperialism was recast as the dual prerogative of white supremacist American nationalism and rational, capitalist expansion to appropriate the lands, resources, and labor of the lesser races of the globe. The denial of formal citizenship rights and the opportunity to participate in political institutions, as well as the exploitation of labor that characterized much of African American life within the United States, were reproduced in similar forms of racially justified domination in newly conquered territory.[88]

This international racial domination, moreover, came into being at the same time as a burgeoning claim to international leadership was being pressed by "progressives" who, victorious in World War I, sought to lead a new global order through the League of Nations. This claim to leadership was to be justified by the success of the American example in creating a democratic republic that had supplanted the divisions of race and ethnicity with the liberal principles of the Declaration of Independence and the promise of personal liberty and economic opportunity. "I have been preaching it year after year as the great thing that lay in the future for the United States to show her wit and skill and enterprise and influence in every country in the world," President Woodrow Wilson proclaimed in his 1916 National Press Club address. The source that justified this universal influence, according to Wilson, was that America was founded "to vindicate the rights of men": "We did not name any differences between one race and another. We did not set up any barriers against any particular people. We opened our gates to all the world and said, 'Let all men who wish to be free come to us and they will be welcome.'"[89]

This presentation of American history was not just sanguine but callously hypocritical. Wilson himself established Jim Crow segregation in the federal government in the nation's capital. Like Mills's unmasking criticism, this prima facie hypocrisy only leads us back to Singh's contention that the work being done by race here was deeper and more complex. Wilson could order the segregation of the nation's capital and proclaim America's world-historical significance as realizing the liberal promise of individual liberty and universal citizenship over particularistic racial identities only through relying on the implicit normativity of whiteness and race hierarchy that provided the anthropological boundaries and content of the relationship between difference and universality he was invoking.

Thus, as Singh argues, "the mediation performed by the US nation-state . . . has not been between ethnos and species . . . but between honored individuals and communities within the nation-state and a privileged series of 'family resemblances' and 'special relationships' beyond national borders" largely bounded by the idea of a "supranational lineage originating in northern or western Europe."[90] It was this bounded, European/intrawhite difference that was the referent of Wilson's approval of immigration, and it also helped underwrite his acquiescence to the partitioning of African colonies in the Treaty of Versailles despite his rhetoric figuring national self-determination as the basis of global justice. Indeed, Wilson's final address in support of the League of Nations insisted on the injustice of denying the Boer rulers of South Africa the rights of international recognition and self-government, free from British colonial administration. There he argued for the proposition that to deny South African generals Louis Botha and Jan Smut the "right to stand up in the parliament of the world and say something concerning the affairs of mankind would be absurd"—never once publicly considering the putative self-determination rights of native South Africans or the injustice of the racial apartheid regime that Smut advocated and helped establish.[91]

Part of Singh's critique, therefore, of what I call the romantic narrative of the civil rights movement stems from its narrative amputation of black politics' explicit internationalist concerns and elision of the philosophical significance of the discursive spaces conjured by various invocations of "black peoplehood." He thinks this promotes a false redemptive story unbounded by the imaginative limits of American nationalism and unburdened by the racial metalanguage distorting American liberalism and civic republicanism. This intervention has the consequence of shifting the philosophical import of black nationalism's relationship to the civil rights movement beyond the former's age-old narrative role, as in Branch's work, as reactionary critics of integration, nonviolence, and Christianity.

Singh treats black nationalism as "the imagination of black communal autonomy arrayed against the primacy of US nationalist discourse and political culture." Black nationalism is the primary discursive form that the invocations of black peoplehood that Singh is concerned with will take in order to dramatize the productive tension between race and nation in black nationalists' political imagination. The dialectical transformation of black nationalism he wants to chart moves from the recognition of the vast cultural, geographic, class, and gender heterogeneity "arrayed and negotiated under the sign 'Negro,' or 'black'" to a negation of the lack of biological grounds for racial categorization. This unfolds toward a "widening of the means and scope of intraracial and interracial communication" driven by a recognition of global forms of oppression, exploitation, and domination with shared ideological and political underpinnings.[92]

To illustrate this, Singh turns to the midcareer writings of Du Bois, because the movement of his thought over time plausibly maps the general trajectory of imaginative possibility that Singh posits for black nationalism as a whole. In 1897 Du Bois published the influential essay "The Conservation of Races," which aspires to defend a historical-sociological conception of race as "a vast family of human beings, generally of common blood and language, always of common history, traditions and impulses, who are both voluntarily and involuntarily striving together for the accomplishment of certain more or less vividly conceived ideals of life."[93] By defining race in this fashion, Du Bois seeks to avoid what he recognizes, very early on, is the fallacy of racial categorization by physiognomy or consanguinity.[94] Du Bois sees instead common history, traditions, impulses, and strivings toward ideals of life as the necessary and sufficient conditions for a group to be a race, whereas blood, language, and physical resemblance are surmised to be secondary, perhaps even parasitic, features of races.[95] This has led some prominent intellectual historians to describe this era of his thinking as culturally nationalist.[96]

Like Garvey, the early Du Bois sees the history of the world as the history of races, but unlike the UNIA founder, Du Bois understands this less as a realist struggle for dominance and security between competing race interests and more as the friction of various "race" (or, cultural) ideals that, through proper governing and economic arrangements, can—indeed, *must*—be reconciled so that civilization may march forward with the full diversity of mankind's most significant cultural gifts contributing to the perfection of human civilization over time: Du Bois's regulative ideal of the "Kingdom of Culture."[97]

This places Du Bois in a unique position from which he is arguing against both assimilationist black intellectuals and ardent black nationalists—assimilationists by exhorting the imperative of developing "race organizations" (e.g., colleges, newspapers, businesses, literary and artistic traditions, and a public sphere of cultural criticism and intellectual thought) and black nationalists by insisting on the ultimate aspiration of "human brotherhood" and racial harmony realized through cultural exchange.[98] Contemporary philosophers, including Anthony Appiah and Robert Gooding-Williams, have criticized Du Bois's essay for its circular reasoning about race, which relies on an implicit racial essentialism masked by such turns of phrase as *common history* or by his geographic demarcations, as well as the alleged distinctiveness of the "gifts" of the Negro.[99] I am concerned less, however, with the logical consistency of Du Bois's argument than with its place in a series of imaginings of black peoplehood that follow Singh's dialectical pattern. From that vantage point, what is most interesting about Du Bois's early theory of race is not its particularity and essentialism but its persistent attempt to deploy race in understanding and realizing *universalist ends.*

By the early 1920s Du Bois had abandoned much of the mystical and idealist language of race that he had inherited from his studies of G. W. F. Hegel and Johann Gottfried von Herder in Germany.[100] In Du Bois's 1923 essay "The Superior Race," written as a dialogue between a first-person black narrator and his "friend," a white interlocutor arguing for white supremacy, Du Bois's narrator concludes a lengthy debate on racial realism and the question "Who is black?" with a new definition of *blackness* that is narratively emplotted as decisive to the argument: "I recognize it quite easily and with full legal sanction: the black man is a person who must ride 'Jim Crow' in Georgia."[101]

But this shift in emphasis toward social (rather than cultural) constructivism in his philosophy of race had fascinating consequences for Du Bois's Pan-Africanism. His 1919 reconvening of the Pan-African Congress in Paris—a body he first convened nearly two decades earlier, in 1900 in London—produced less speculative philosophical anthropology, and instead focused on the overlapping ideological substrate and forms of domination that connected imperialism and Jim Crow.[102] Thus, Du Bois's understanding of global white supremacy moved further away from the idealist realm of the suprasensible friction of racial gifts to the materialist terrain of the dynamics of global capitalism and the domestic politics of Western societies. The origins of imperialism and Jim Crow were now said to be grounded in the converging interests of Euro-American capitalists in the exploitation of material resources and cheap labor and the Euro-American working classes, who are also "given a chance for exploitation on an immense scale for inordinate profit" as both the active agents and passive beneficiaries of colonial expropriation. The wealth accrued through imperialism, its utility as an outlet for superfluous labor, and the psychological goods afforded by the ritual enactment of global white supremacy all create a definite interest in the white working class in colonial subjugation and racism that also serves the social function of easing the domestic tensions between white people arising from material inequality.[103]

Not surprisingly, this sort of political definition of race and imperialism leads Du Bois right through Pan-Africanism into other internationalist solidarities and sympathies with China, India, Ireland, and other nations. In this vein, Du Bois argues in a manner reminiscent of Immanuel Kant's concept of "unsocial sociability" in his "Idea for a Universal History from a Cosmopolitan Point of View," where such horrors as "slavery, peonage, rape, theft, and extermination" serve the process of "slowly uniting humanity . . . [in] economic unity and cultural solidarity."[104] The difference is that this unity is based on resistance to conquest, not capitulation to it. It thus retains an explicit antagonist and the seriousness of conflict, rather than the expectation of imminent reconciliation. With this complex, global interdependence discovered and established, Du Bois argues that we must reject the limited scope of Garveyite Pan-Africanism for a "super-diplomacy of race politics" that uses its *material* foundation in interdependence to build "cultural sympathy, spiritual tolerance, and human freedom." This commitment leads Du Bois to oscillate between the proto–Third Worldism conjured by phrases like "the darker races" and the global socialism of early twentieth-century leftism.[105]

Despite Singh's brilliant dialectical treatment of black nationalism's relation to subversive cosmopolitanism, he unfortunately stops short of reengaging Garveyism in the light of its earlier negation. Having moved beyond Garvey's romantic racialism via Du Bois's subversive cosmopolitanism, might we now see more clearly the powerful *realism* also at the heart of Garveyite internationalism and trace its unlikely circulation?

Garvey distrusted the power of moral suasion and cultural production absent strategic leverage on behalf of African Americans in economics, political violence, statecraft, and geopolitical conflict. His obsession with the idea of African empire reflected both a sense of how difficult it was to secure tractable transnational solidarity without the compulsory and protective force of sovereign government *and* that the fate of black citizenship in the West would turn, in decisive ways, on straightforwardly realist considerations about the geopolitical balance of power and the fate of United States interests within that arrangement. These questions, when not fought in open warfare or trade policy, were fought—as Garvey understood—in the relatively fragile institutions of global governance and what we would now call "soft power" wars of propaganda and spectacle.

Surprisingly, while Du Bois's cosmopolitanism remained the rhetorical and imaginative language for internationalist civil rights movement activists like King, their political *practice* hewed closer to a keen sense of geopolitical realism, which Garvey (despite his fetishizing of World War I–era imperialism) might have been said to pioneer in Afro-modern thought. This dialectical possibility, which would have been difficult to pose outside of the revised exemplarity of long civil rights history and the collapse of the nationalist-integrationist binary, is a question that needs urgent interrogation in a period where what Adom Getachew calls the "new black internationalism" attracts such activist and scholarly energy.[106] The enthusiasm in some corners for this internationalism is in danger of backsliding into romantic racialism and Third Worldism, forgetting this other tradition of realist reflection and judgment manifest not only in black nationalism but, as we saw in Chapter 6, the geopolitics of the civil rights movement.

Civil rights realism, if we may call it that, saw the rise of Nazism, with its trenchant (Jim Crow–inspired) doctrines of white supremacy, racial purity, and anti-Semitism as "a mirror to hold up to Jim Crow's visage."[107] Singh argues that one of the major phenomena that produced the long civil rights era was the ability of black social movements to constitute "the social fact of racial inequality as a symbolic index against which the achievement of US civic ideals could be measured and the legitimacy of US global aspirations could be assessed."[108] Thus, while the emergence of modern Pan-Africanism and communism in black political life served as a persistent source of indictments of white supremacy against a global context of human rights discourses, anti-imperialism, black nationalism, and socialism, perhaps the single most powerful rhetorical trope was the comparison with Nazi Germany.[109]

It was not only critics of Jim Crow and Nazism who drew the connection between the two white supremacist ideologies; so, too, did Adolf Hitler and his party. Gilmore relates a former Nazi's account of a 1933 dinner with Hitler during which he is reported to have praised the prevalence of lynching as the existence of "popular justice" and Jim Crow as a whole as "an assurance that the sound elements of the United States will one day awaken as they have awakened in Germany." Julius Streicher, the anti-Semitic publisher of *Der Sturmer,* proclaimed to an audience of Nazis in 1935 that "the treatment of Negroes in America [is] far worse than that accorded Jews by the Nazis and America's criticism should be turned in that direction rather than toward Germany."[110]

Less popularly remembered is the resistance to the Italian Fascist regime's aggressive military campaign against Ethiopia in 1935. Robin Kelley argues that the "defense of Ethiopia did more than any other event in the 1930s to internationalize the struggles of black people in the United States."[111] Riots broke out between Italians and African Americans in New York, and boycotts of Italian-owned bars in Harlem led to a number of them closing. The National Negro Congress (NNC) advocated a boycott of Italy and issued a denunciation of Benito Mussolini. Black intellectuals took to public forums, magazines, church pulpits, and other venues to denounce not only the Fascists but the League of Nations and the erstwhile champions of self-determination and antifascism around the world that sat idly by as Mussolini made his play for Ethiopian land.[112] Ethiopia had powerful and unique cultural resonance for African Americans. It had long been a touchstone for early black intellectual projects of racial vindicationism that sought to defend "the Negro" from charges of heathenism and barbarism with the Ethiopian example, which was one of the first Christian countries in the world and the only country in Africa that had eluded the colonial yoke.[113] The reference to Ethiopia in Psalms 68:31 ("Princes shall come out of Egypt; Ethiopia shall soon stretch out her hands unto God") had also been consistently featured in black nationalist thought, including by Marcus Garvey, as biblical prophecy of the coming redemption of Africa and the role of African Americans as the chosen people in that redemption.[114]

By the time the hostilities that would eventually develop into the World War II broke out in Europe, African American leftists and liberals had coalesced around a politics that tried to keep the increasing opportunity to press the global significance of their struggle at the forefront by linking it to antifascist concerns.[115] Liberals and the noncommunist Left also moved to support the war effort as a part of what the *Pittsburgh Courier* would eventually label the Double V Campaign in 1942, meaning a victory "against fascism abroad and racism at home."[116] As George Schuyler, the idiosyncratic *Courier* columnist often referred to as the black H. L. Mencken, recalled the campaign,

> It was very obvious that the Negro was called upon to sacrifice like everybody else in the wartime, and yet he did not have complete citizenship. So this was a reminder to people that there were two wars going on: there was one going on abroad and there was another one going on here, that had been going on for nearly a century. We wanted that war won, and it could be won, and failure to win it would make this thing across the seas practically a phony; because we were talking about making the world safe for democracy, and the Atlantic Charter, and all the rest of that gruel that they put out at that time—which was quite insincere, but people took it seriously, around the world.[117]

The justifications for war advanced by President Franklin Delano Roosevelt and other American officials became sources of moral authority, or at least opportunities to embarrass the government at home and abroad, potentially shaming enough citizens and officials into supporting the antiracist measures proposed by black activists. The 1941 Atlantic Charter and Roosevelt's speech on the Four Freedoms all "set out general principles of self-determination, social equality, personal liberty, and economic security now believed to extend from the United States to the entire world."[118] Sugrue echoes this contention, claiming that "few presidential speeches have ever had such currency" and that Roosevelt's passionate defense of freedom of religion, freedom of speech, freedom from fear, and freedom from want, pushed American political discourse toward a notion of positive liberty and the activist government necessary to achieve it.[119]

Arguably the most influential navigator of these dialectical political movements of nationalism and geopolitics was A. Philip Randolph, who vies only with Du Bois in his ubiquity across the grand sweep of long civil rights narratives. As a leader of the NNC, Randolph made a temporary peace with the communists in his fold, despite his long-standing philosophical, political, and personal objections to their creed. In the wake of the Molotov-Ribbentrop Pact, however, when NNC communists maneuvered the organization into adopting it as official policy, Randolph resigned his leadership position to avoid collaboration with Nazism. With his impeccable anticommunist and principled antifascist credentials intact, Randolph took the outbreak of war and the pronouncements of the president to launch a new black coalition, the March on Washington Movement (MOWM), to press the Roosevelt administration for action to desegregate the war industries that were then kicking into high gear.

World War II represented an enormous economic opportunity for black citizens. A million men were drafted in 1941 alone, adjusting the labor market favorably toward those who remained in it, and the vast government spending to prosecute the war effort jump-started the lagging economy into an enormous boom. Discrimination, however, threatened to lock black people out of these gains, with nearly one in three black workers in the Midwest and Northeast unemployed and 70 percent of black women relegated to service work as late as 1940.[120] The NAACP and the Urban League had already pressed the issue of discrimination in war industries through Roosevelt's unofficial "Negro cabinet," but to no avail. In response, these groups organized protests across the country and pursued a press campaign in mainstream and black print forums.

Nothing, however, had the immediate impact of Randolph's MOWM, which drew on his immense grassroots popularity to mobilize black workers across the country, the extensive information networks along the railways he had organized to spread his protest message, and the new political reality hanging over the head of the Democratic president: the suddenly significant black vote concentrated in Northern urban centers that had broken from its loyalties to Republicans (the party of Lincoln) to support his campaigns. With the threat of one hundred thousand black people (Randolph insisted the march be all black) marching on the nation's capital to protest racial discrimination in the midst of war preparations for a battle ostensibly against racist fascism and the haunting memory of the disastrous Bonus Army march of 1932 that devastated Herbert Hoover's political career, Roosevelt capitulated. In 1941, mere days before the march was to be held, Roosevelt issued Executive Order 8802 banning racial discrimination by defense contractors and establishing the Committee on Fair Employment Practices.[121]

Disappointing some of his more militant allies, Randolph called off the march and declared victory, having created an invaluable template for future black protest and civil rights activism that would arguably reach its apex in the 1963 March on Washington for Jobs and Freedom, which Randolph also organized. For long civil rights movement historians, Randolph's victory, although limited, is the first wave of political successes at the federal level, including President Harry S. Truman's executive order to desegregate the military in 1948, that have been criminally overlooked. So, too, has the significance of the conventional civil rights narrative's moral climax having its origins in leftist labor organizing and geopolitical leverage seeking and realism.

Institutionalization and Ideological Constraint

Notably, the long civil rights movement historians do not celebrate what I am calling this realist praxis and its successes unequivocally. They raise—notably, for today's often-utopian internationalists—two central issues: *institutionalization* and *ideological constraint.*

The cessation of hostilities between the Allied and Axis Powers in World War II ushered in a geopolitical context that long civil rights movement historians argue had grand implications for the civil rights struggle. First, in the wake of the profound evil of the Holocaust, there emerged a more robust discourse of human rights and a growing international consensus against biological racism. Although human rights have been quite controversial as a philosophical concept, it is nonetheless true that many African Americans, among other oppressed minorities and colonial subjects around the world, found the ideal intuitively appealing and politically useful.[122] The possible redefinition of the so-called Negro Problem as a human rights problem presented an opportunity for leftist and liberal activists to appeal to UN documents that endorsed "not just freedom from political and legal discrimination but also the right to education, health care, housing, and employment."[123] As early as the UN Charter Conference in San Francisco in 1945, black civil rights activists—including an NAACP delegation sponsored by Eleanor Roosevelt and representatives from the still communist-influenced Council on African Affairs and the NNC—were pressing the nascent organization to act against American Jim Crow, South African apartheid, and African colonialism.

The internationalist vision in black politics thought it had found a potential institutional base from which to pursue its multifaceted program of antiracism and anti-imperialism and sought substantive and symbolic alliances with so-called Third World countries like China and India. Singh captures these aspirations perfectly by imagining black people "as the key diplomatic, technical, and professional intermediaries between US world-ordering ambition and a global, anti-imperialist politics."[124] Yet this precarious middle ground was rapidly eroding from beneath them, even as the NNC and NAACP both delivered petitions to the new UN Human Rights Commission in 1946 and 1947, respectively, pleading the case of black people in the United States and comparing their treatment to other forms of oppression (including that perpetrated by Nazi Germany) and calling for a UN commitment to democracy, self-determination, and anti-colonialism around the globe.[125]

The United States, which wielded immense agenda-setting, financial, and military power within the UN, was able to keep the petitions concerning domestic issues of American racism from being acted on to preserve US authority and political sovereignty. Moreover, the domestic politics of anti-communism were forcefully arrayed against black activists. Not only were the chief architects of the petitions, W. E. B. Du Bois (of the NAACP) and Max Yergan (of the NNC), rumored communists (true in the second case, and soon to be true in the first), but any African American organization that hoped to appeal successfully to international opinion in a body that often seemed to break along Cold War lines between Soviet and US allies would likely have to win Soviet backing in an atmosphere of virulent anti-communism.[126] These attempts were so thoroughly defeated in the late 1940s that by the time Malcolm X began to propose the idea of taking "the case of the black man in this country before the nations in the UN" in 1964, many observers, particularly in the Black Power movement, seemed to consider the idea a novel one.[127]

This escalation of anticommunism hangs heavily over the interpretive judgments of this historiography and gives it its most influentially tragic tone. There had long been trenchant opposition to socialism and communism in the United States on capitalist, religious, white supremacist, nativist, conservative, and liberal grounds alike.[128] An atmosphere of paranoia and repression exploded into the tumult known as the first Red Scare, which began the 1918 trials of 101 members of the militant socialist International Workers of the World union for interfering with the war effort through industrial strikes and ended with the infamous Palmer Raids of 1919–1920, which deported hundreds of immigrants while persistently overstepping the law in a veritable witch hunt for subversives.[129]

The embarrassment of the Palmer Raids, a growing acceptance of ethnic white people, and the Great Depression briefly created a more favorable climate for the American Left, including communists, by the 1930s. In the post–World War II period, however, US anticommunism began the upward trajectory that would reach its heights in spectacle with the US Senate's Internal Security hearings led by Senator Joseph McCarthy and his counterparts on the House Un-American Activities Committee (HUAC). Richard Lingeman describes the 1945–1955 "heyday of anticommunism" as "something of a quasi-evangelical national revival meeting led by the most vocal anticommunist politicians and professional red-hunters and dedicated to cleansing the nation of political heretics."[130] Far from a federal government prerogative, anticommunism was enmeshed in a series of overlapping techniques across private enterprise, state and municipal governments, and civil society.[131] The main event, as it were, of anticommunism was, however, the McCarthy and HUAC hearings, which Victor Navasky has called "degradation ceremonies" and usually consisted of aggressive interrogation, ritual humiliation, and coerced confession and cooperation—the "naming names" that would keep McCarthyites busy chasing various leads for a decade.[132]

Long civil rights movement historiography focuses so intently on this moment for two reasons. First, it has appropriated the general argument about the Cold War's impact on the civil rights movement made by a series of law and politics scholars, including Derrick Bell, Thomas Borstelmann, Mary Dudziak, Michael Klarman, and John Skrentny, among others.[133] As we discussed in Chapter 6's exploration of the geopolitics of civil disobedience, this argument contends that the federal interventions on behalf of the civil rights claims of African Americans, particularly in the judicial and executive branches, were strongly influenced by Cold War domestic and international interests, and especially the struggle for the allegiances of newly independent postcolonial countries in Africa, Asia, the Caribbean, and Latin America (the so-called Third World), as well as in the divided Germany.

In this geopolitical situation, these scholars argue, civil rights liberalism became "a Cold War imperative."[134] The United States, while waging World War II and the early days of the Cold War, had taken the step of presenting itself, through formal decree and covert propaganda, as the beacon of liberty, justice, and opportunity for the world. The long history of African American social movements and intellectual thought, however, had long ago made manifest in political discourse the proposition that "the social fact of racial inequality would be a symbolic index against which the achievement of US civic ideals could be measured and the legitimacy of US global aspirations could be assessed."[135] As then–Vice President Richard Nixon put it on returning from Ghana in 1957, "We cannot talk equality to the peoples of Asia and Africa and practice inequality in the United States."[136] What made the black freedom struggle so especially significant was that by the mid-1950s the global audience was composed largely of the African, Asian, Latin American, and Middle Eastern "domino" states that had been colonized under the justification of similarly white supremacist ideologies and were, due to the work of figures like Du Bois and Garvey, now interpretively linked to African American oppression in black internationalist and anticolonial discourse.

Black intellectuals and activists pressed the realist advantage. A. Philip Randolph proclaimed Jim Crow "the greatest single propaganda and political weapon in the hands of Russia and international communism."[137] NAACP national secretary Walter White, in *How Far the Promised Land,* his 1955 book that mobilizes the Exodus metaphor and romantic narrative to defend the United States against communist propaganda, described the Cold War dilemma presented by racism as follows:

> Americans know that it is not the purpose of the United States to subjugate the colored peoples of the world, yet it is difficult to say this convincingly to a member of one of the dark-skinned races of the East, when at the same time one must answer yes to such questions as: "Is it not true that Negroes have the worst housing in America; that they almost invariably are forced to live in segregated areas; that they are excluded from many restaurants and schools; that it is almost impossible for them to make any significant headway in some occupations; that there is still violence against them?"[138]

This rhetoric produced genuine international effect. When President Truman's secretary of state, James F. Byrnes, criticized the Soviet Union for denying voting rights in the Balkans, for example, the Soviet Union responded with a cutting remark about how the same policy was true for black people in Byrnes's home state of South Carolina.[139] As the fight for the allegiances of Third World countries intensified, so, too, did the Soviet Union and their allies' attempts to portray the United States as irredeemably racist and racism and capitalism as indelibly linked. When the Cold War turned hot and US troops were deployed to Korea and Vietnam, black soldiers and prisoners of war were targeted by communist troops for propaganda meant to undermine their commitment to the war effort and turn their loyalties for intelligence purposes.[140] So widespread was this phenomenon that Russian speakers long used the phrase, "A u vas negrov linchuyut!" (And you lynch Negroes!) to satirize someone who hypocritically distracts from their own ills by indicting others.[141]

Judgment in the Light of Cold War/ Civil Rights Historiography

From this vantage point, the civil rights milestones of the classical phase take on a different meaning. The Cold War foreign policy interests identified by the executive branch were, for example, pressed in an amicus curiae brief submitted by the US Department of Justice in *Brown,* and two arguments in particular concerning American interests stand out. First is the embarrassment that racial segregation poses for diplomacy in the postcolonial world. The "shamefulness and absurdity" of segregation, the brief argued, is highlighted by those situations where "foreign officials are often mistaken for American Negroes and refused food, lodging and entertainment," and on the realization that they are not American, subsequently accommodated.[142] Second, the Justice Department asked that the court consider "the problem of racial discrimination" in the context of "the present world struggle between freedom and tyranny," where it "furnishes grist for the Communist propaganda mills, and it raises doubts even among friendly nations as to the intensity of our devotion to the democratic faith."[143]

Outside the courtroom, the dramatic direct-action protests that shape our collective memory of the civil rights movement are also interpretively transformed. The earnest young students and religious leaders whose political impact is usually phrased in pseudo-evangelical terms retain their spiritual and moral authority, but this is now augmented with a recognition of their geopolitical savvy, more often conceded to diplomats and statesmen from the UN than from the Southern preachers in the SCLC. Indeed, the importance of the ethical discourse provided by African American Christianity similarly becomes transformed from the mere vehicle of American liberal political philosophy identified by secular political theorists or the sociological mechanism for collective action identified by social scientists and instead becomes the crucial mode of presentation for civil rights activism in a staunchly anticommunist era. Finally, the persistent internationalism in black political thought is retrieved from those who would dismiss black reflections on Africa, Asia, China, Latin America, and the Soviet Union as escapist romanticism or meaningless historical curiosities and placed front and center as part of a politics that operates beyond the imaginative, discursive, and juridical boundaries of the US nation-state.

In a tragic register, however, even this discovery of geopolitical leverage is revealed to entail loss at the heart of victory. The political possibilities pioneered in the 1930s and 1940s—civil rights unionism; an interpenetrating analysis of race and class; welfare state reform; and grassroots, working-class politics—are severely burdened in this account by the dictates of anticommunist hysteria and the class-biased understanding of white supremacy as state-enforced racial stigma or intentional, malicious discrimination.

The contention of long civil rights movement historians is that their counterparts in the Cold War/civil rights camp are guilty of producing a narrative that is romantic insofar as it does not attend to loss, and is not contextual enough to recognize what has not been assimilated into the "victory." In other words, they think the paradigm "inflates the Cold War's contributions and discounts its costs."[144] The anticommunist wave may have set the stage for federal intervention, but it was only on behalf of specific forms of de jure racial discrimination based on racial stigma and not those areas where race and class disadvantage was compounded. Also, while anticommunism elevated those civil rights activists who—whether through public displays of religious faith, like Martin Luther King, or through active collaboration with McCarthyism, like Walter White and Whitney Young of the NAACP—displayed their commitment to anticommunism, it marginalized those who fell outside of the new strictures of Cold War liberalism. Leading African American intellectuals, artists, and activists—W. E. B. Du Bois, Langston Hughes, Pauli Murray, Paul Robeson, Bayard Rustin, and Coleman Young—were denied jobs, denounced from the Senate floor, and, most humiliatingly, dragged in for testimony in front of HUAC or McCarthy himself. Both Du Bois and Robeson had their passports revoked and were victims of extensive government surveillance and harassment, and both men, on having their passports reinstated, lived in exile for years—Du Bois in Ghana and Robeson in London.[145]

Apart from these individual persecutions, the long civil rights movement historians say that the Cold War had a chilling effect on those civil rights elements that fell outside the bounds of Cold War liberalism.[146] Central to this case is a critique of Gunnar Myrdal's *An American Dilemma*. Commissioned by the Carnegie Foundation, Myrdal, a Swedish economist, oversaw a team of dozens of social scientists, many of them leading African American scholars like Ralph Bunche and E. Franklin Frazier, in an intensive investigation of the so-called Negro problem. His central conclusion was that the Negro problem was actually a white problem—racial inequality was caused largely by antiblack prejudicial beliefs and attitudes among white people. These prejudices, however, were not more deeply held than the American Creed, an Enlightenment-inspired liberal doctrine committed to freedom, equality, and justice, and the rule of law. Thus, there was a tension in the moral psychology of white Americans between what Myrdal argued were their deeper held beliefs in the American Creed and their racist beliefs, the latter of which could not withstand the deeper national trend toward rationalism and liberalism, particularly with a positive program of education and moral suasion.[147] The trajectory of American history, therefore, would, with some social engineering, be toward greater assimilation and the eradication of the cultural markers of racial difference.

The social scientific legitimacy of the romantic narrative, as we saw in Chapter 1, turns in part on the success of Myrdalism, and long civil rights movement historians, following contemporary critiques by Herbert Aptheker, Oliver Cromwell Cox, and Ralph Ellison, have long assailed its ideological foundations for conflating American values with those of the white public, discursively removing black leftist, nationalist, and internationalist politics to the realm of irrationalism; misrecognizing the persistence and depth of white supremacist ideology in American history; misunderstanding the interpenetration of white supremacy and economic exploitation; and denying the creative and interpretive capacities of African American intellectual life and culture.[148] The convergence in the Cold War era of virulent anticommunism and Myrdalian racial liberalism is implicated by long civil rights historiography in "the collapse of the left-civil rights alliance" and the channeling of civil rights activism "down the narrower path that had been blazed by Myrdal."[149] In the spirit of Hannah Arendt (see Chapter 3) these revisionist historians want to compel us to rethink what we have come to know as "successful" in conventional categories of evaluation or leading accounts of the processes of historical development and, on reflective judgment, refuse our unqualified affirmation. Our retrieval and memory of these roads not taken, as a practice of anamnestic reason, becomes the aperture through which we can envision and judge both our history and present differently.

The Left and the Negro Question: A. Philip Randolph's Tragic Vision

Given this concern with the way that the histories of the civil rights movement perform a "narrowing" function on our imagination and judgment by retrospectively anchoring judgments of "victory" in what was achieved in policy rather than carefully reconstructing what was possible, or what the aims of leading actors were, it should not be surprising that they also focus on the intensive period of labor and civil rights activism from 1919 to the 1940s. A consideration of this period, they hope, will broaden our recognition of the breadth of issues (fair housing, labor rights, lynching, desegregation, anti-imperialism, etc.) that were common concerns for African Americans and the organizations (the Communist Party USA [CPUSA], the Socialist Party of America, the UNIA, etc.) that were crucial actors in the domain of civil rights. Many of the major works in long civil rights movement historiography focus primarily on this period, partly to set up a story about the "roads not taken" and tragic compromises and offer new judgments of familiar history.

Once viewed from a tragic vantage point, widely celebrated legislative and cultural victories not only look more partial, making their inability to more sweepingly change the foundations of racial inequality in economic life clearer, but our celebration of these moments looks like a kind of *failure of responsibility,* a desire on the part of we inheritors to celebrate progress as if there is no remainder or no need to attend to the defeats within the victories.

It is true that long civil rights historians have been accused of romanticism of their own, celebrating short-lived union mobilizations or labor actions as if they were triumphant, but I see their focus as quite strikingly tragic in that they are wrestling with two major questions: how to think about the roads not taken among liberal, leftist, and black nationalist ideas and struggles and how to make judgments about law and politics in the wake of their critique of the New Deal's tragic compromises with racial domination and exploitation.[150] I want to follow these paths by taking up the connected question of the architect of the 1963 March on Washington, A. Philip Randolph, and the underappreciation of his political legacy and historical exemplarity as a thinker concerned with tragic history, nonsovereignty, and the possibility of thinking through loss to revive the power of judgment. Through Randolph we can retrieve insight into the possibility of a form of "reconstructionist" thought that is critical of both strong black nationalism and liberal integrationism while also thinking critically and creatively about what foregrounding the tragic choice dilemmas of the New Deal—at once the greatest moment of progressive political transformation *and* a political and policy alliance that upheld Jim Crow segregation and racial domination—allows us to rethink in the realm of legal-political theory and jurisprudence.

Rorty, Randolph, and the Trouble with Romance: Toward a Tragic Vision

Surprisingly enough, there was a little-remembered attempt at the recovery of A. Philip Randolph in political philosophy, offered by one of the few philosophers who also foregrounded the question of narrative genre for political thinking: Richard Rorty. The grandson of the great social gospel theologian Walter Rauschenbusch, Rorty greatly admired Randolph as an exemplar of an indigenous American leftist tradition rooted in moral idealism, pragmatic hope, and practical reform. As a boy, he ran errands for Randolph at his Harlem office, and marveled at his ability to hold together the central struggles of the age.[151] By the time he would compile *Achieving Our Country* (1998), a book dedicated to Randolph and written toward the end of a neoliberal turn noticeably hostile to New Deal and civil rights politics, Rorty urged the era's beleaguered American Left to pursue revival through the emulation of figures like Randolph. Indeed, he went so far as to take the step of arguing, scandalously for a professor of philosophy and comparative literature, that "it would be a good thing if the next generation of American leftists found as little resonance in the names of Karl Marx and Vladimir Ilyich Lenin as in those of Herbert Spencer and Benito Mussolini," and even better if names such as Randolph's "were more familiar to these leftists than they were to the students of the 60's."[152]

This was mischief-making, for sure, but not entirely disingenuous. Rorty not only admired Randolph's stewardship of the Brotherhood of Sleeping Car Porters and Maids, involvements in labor and civil rights struggle, and democratic socialist principles but saw him as a possible symbol of national pride and loyalty when placed in the right symbolic constellation. After all, a central commitment of Rorty's political philosophy in this period is a call for the Left to abandon what he sees as the cynicism, nihilism, pessimism, and anti-Americanism fashionable among leftist academics in the "years of theory" for the more promising high ground of a hopeful and patriotic story about national progress and a conception of America as quintessentially forward looking and capable of pursuing new "democratic vistas," to invoke Walt Whitman, another Rorty touchstone.[153]

Only the latter posture, Rorty argues, is commensurate with and conducive to national pride, offering the maxim that "national pride is to countries what self-respect is to individuals: a necessary condition for self-improvement." Why improve what you cannot take pride in or feel no loyalty toward? Who can be inspired, Rorty wonders, by a politics of "self-disgust"?[154] Rorty judges the exhaustion and pessimism bred by ironic histories of the sort I criticized in Chapter 7 as leading to self-satisfied disdain for the ready-at-hand work of genuine reform and criticism that might improve real people's lives in the here and now. This spectatorial stance simply abdicates the age-old responsibilities of the Left.

Rorty dutifully acknowledges that "too much national pride can produce bellicosity and imperialism, just as excessive self-respect can produce arrogance" but urges the reader that this is no reason to abandon the ideal. The goal is to somehow balance what our nation "can take pride in as well as what it should be ashamed of."[155] The reformist American Left must narrate a pageantry of progress, worthy of our possibilities as a "country of hope" and replete with exemplary episodes and characters that deserve our ongoing emulation. This kind of story, Rorty thinks, will inspire a more patriotic commitment to doing our part to improve our society—especially if it is a *national* story, one that abandons the preoccupation with the politics of difference and identity for a recommitment to what we, as a nation, might share in solidarity.

Lying powerfully underneath these broader claims about politics and social theory is a claim that *narrative* is, for most of us, *prior to political philosophy:* "The result of a loss of hope—or, more specifically, of an inability to construct a plausible narrative of progress" is rooted in "a turn away from narration and utopian dreams toward philosophy." That turn, Rorty adds, "seems to me a gesture of despair. . . . I think we are now in a situation in which resentment and frustration have taken the place of hope among politically concerned intellectuals, and that the replacement of narrative by philosophy is a symptom of this unhappy situation."[156] In *Philosophy and Social Hope* (1999), Rorty argues (familiarly to the reader who has made it thus far in *Shattered Dreams*) that our imagined futures, political longings, and practical judgments are inextricably shaped by inherited historical narratives and the images and symbols in which they are sedimented. It is through these narratives, he argues, that we cultivate and constitute our sense of peoplehood, the *we* that makes sense of our life in common. He goes so far as to suggest that political persuasion and leadership in a democratic society is, in the main, "a competition between differing stories about a nation's self-identity, and between differing symbols of its greatness."[157]

Accordingly, the Left would be better served by artists and orators like Randolph and Whitman, figures whom Rorty thinks could speak powerfully to this need, rather than the imposing and obscurantist language of contemporary critical social theory imported from either side of the Rhine River. The aim is to achieve our country, not critique it ad nauseum in translation. Unsurprisingly, given the similarities to others I have grouped under the label, Rorty even at times used the language of "national romance" to describe the blend of progressive history, reformist sensibilities, reasonable hope, and prophetic openness toward the future improvement of the country that he saw as constitutive of the best way forward.[158] Given my view that tragedy and hope are not inimical, however, I hope to suggest that Randolph might play a productive role in a different kind of narrative mode, one that more candidly confronts evil, loss, and memory with critique but does not fall into the paralysis or nihilist solipsism that Rorty rightly decries.

There are good reasons to think that A. Philip Randolph is a poor fit for the kind of project Rorty wants to champion. Migrating from Florida to Harlem in 1911, Randolph became well known as editor of *The Messenger,* a radical monthly, with his friend and collaborator Chandler Owen. They were also considered part of the "new crowd" of New Negro leaders, enamored with labor and political militancy and hostile to black leaders who preached a gospel of moderation. Breaking with the elitist conceptions of Booker T. Washington's brokerage politics and racial bossism, as well as the early W. E. B. Du Bois's dream of an aristocratic class of missionary leaders he called the "Talented Tenth," Randolph instead aspired to organize working people—especially black workers and their allies in the black community—in a united front against capitalist exploitation and race prejudice.[159] The magazine was a vehicle for socialist ideas, often reflecting the program of the Socialist Party of America, and it consistently argued that racism was driven by class exploitation and ideological mystification, often manipulated by elites that could use race division to prevent interracial and international labor solidarity.[160]

In the September 1920 issue of *The Messenger,* however, Randolph and Owen explicitly engage the question of "Americanism" so central to Rorty. "When we speak of a man's Americanism," they write, "we speak to his attitude toward the ideals of the nation." Their assessment of "Americanism" raises worries about the plausibility of Rorty's conscription of Randolph into a cheerful and patriotic narrative mode of national romance. In their editors' analysis, the "*real* ideals [of a people] are the ones that assert themselves and give force and direction to the affairs of government," not whatever is "professed." This leads Randolph and Owen to emphasize (contra Rorty) "the stamp of hypocrisy" placed by the Founding Fathers on "the brow of the new born nation," leaving a "hideous heritage . . . still predominant in our present day national life." The "beautiful structure" that many judge as the truth of American government and civic life rests, they argue, "on a foundation of quicksand that almost collapsed in 1861" and remains in need of "deeds" and "dignity" to reconstruct it rather than more "lofty words" and "hypocrisy."[161]

But while Randolph endorses this critique of "Americanism" and general socialist principles about internationalism, he is not reflexively "anti-American," in Rorty's pejorative characterization of his enemies. Lost in a haze of retrospective romanticism about the so-called Greatest Generation, ordinary Americans have lost grasp of the divisive and contentious arguments about the period of fascist ascendency and European conflict before the United States officially entered World War II. Many on the right, including prominent figures like Charles Lindburgh, offered their support for fascism; on the left, partisan communists blew up the premise of so-called popular front politics by dutifully following the party line from the Soviet Union on the Molotov-Ribbentrop Pact. Amid these warring voices, Randolph offered a vicious retort, and his characteristic reflections are worth quoting at length:

> During this World War in which two powerful forces are in conflict; namely democracy and totalitarianism, the Negro—[an] oppressed and exploited minority—has no other choice save to throw his lot in with the democratic powers and join in an all-out struggle to save the democratic system, however it may be. The Negroes' hope, future and destiny are tied up with the hope, future and destiny of American democracy; and the hope, future and destiny of American democracy are tied up with the hope, future and destiny of the democratic powers of the world. If America goes down, the Negro goes down. . . . Under the totalitarian system, minority groups and labor have no rights for freedom such as assembly and the press, trial by jury, right of petition and freedom of worship . . . the salvation of an oppressed minority lies in its opportunity to present its cause to the world. This can only be done within the framework of a democratic state.[162]

These commitments also undergirded Randolph's hostility to the Soviet Union and the CPUSA, which—especially after the Molotov-Ribbentrop Pact—he saw as unduly subordinate to Stalinist dictates from Moscow. Again, Randolph's fidelity to America lies in commitments to principles, albeit unrealized, of *constitutional liberty* and the *democratic ideal.*

These are manifest in a political culture and legal order that sustains and protects agonistic democratic practice, granting its members what Randolph calls "the right to fight for their rights." "The most ardent American patriot must admit the shortcomings, limitations, inconsistencies, contradictions and failures in the great American enterprise of democracy," Randolph warns, this admission must be nested in the recognition that, "by virtue of the Bill of Rights and our traditions of a free way of life," Americans—even African Americans—"*possess the right to fight for their rights.* This is priceless, for the only way to get rights and hold them is to fight for them."[163]

While Randolph believes that the basic foundation of rights is "God-given," and "primarily because of one's being human," our rights are only given reliable recognition, protection, and elaboration within the framework of "civil rights" within a given state and its spaces of agonistic political contestation. The same powers that make state-based civil rights the guarantor of our human rights (as well as our citizenship), however, also render each of us vulnerable to state infringement. Civil rights, therefore, are also meant to "prevent even the state, such as a Mississippi, from interfering with the privilege of individuals to exercise their human rights."[164] This classic paradox of political theory is one that Randolph attempts to resolve, as many leftists influenced by republicanism do, with the need for a vigilant citizenry, collectively organized into social groups that exercise powers of participation, persuasion, noncooperation, and resistance in defense of their rights.[165]

It is remarkable that, as a labor leader who mostly composed short speeches and essays, Randolph persistently devotes large swaths of his intellectual production to historical narrative. He turns to historical exemplarity and narrative to both substantiate the analysis above and to offer guidance about what to do in response to this condition. Across countless speeches, Randolph frequently situates his arguments in long historical context or makes comparative reference to historical events he judges to be exemplary: key periods of labor movement struggle, the French Revolution, and above all, Reconstruction.[166] His approach, however, is often *tragic*. It tries to train political judgment by disclosing a pattern of exemplarity that treats conflict as serious and irreconcilable, understands the role of contingency, attends to the gains of knowledge and insight amid "defeat," and insists on a kind of tragic responsibility in the face of our nonsovereignty as actors embedded in history and interdependency.

Randolph appeals to his supporters to understand that conflict and antagonism is inevitable and not likely to be reconciled by appeals to good and evil. "Every state is both accommodative and repressive in its nature," Randolph explains in his planning for the MOWM in 1942, and the United States is no different. States, at every level of jurisdiction, attempt to "accommodate the interests of conflicting groups in the interest of maintaining a measure of social, economic and political equilibrium, and to prevent any social explosion that may constitute a peril to the state."[167] This broadly pluralist view of politics is undergirded by a decidedly realist account of power, the inequalities of power's exercise, and the bounded rationality of partisan politics. The "action and decisions of the government are not based on moral grounds of justice and right," Randolph argues; instead, "heads of government respond only to pressure . . . [and] move in the direction of the pressure of the greatest challenge." Invoking histories of the organized labor movement (e.g., the militant, sometimes violent campaigns for gains like the eight-hour workday) to suggest that egalitarian struggles have the *contingent* possibility of winning genuine gains, Randolph insists "that Negroes, like labor and farmers, must resort to the strategy and technique of using mass pressure" to influence parties and other institutions. One of the great keywords of Randolph's thinking is *pressure,* a term that captures a range of contentious forms of politics, including negotiation, political campaigning, propaganda, lobbying, boycott, protest demonstrations, and civil disobedience.[168]

Translated to the vocabulary of Rawlsian thinking, this is a politics that dispenses with the romantic idea of an overlapping consensus (unity in the process of becoming) that eliminates modus vivendi settlements in politics. Yet this need not be pejoratively anti-American, as Rorty worries. What Randolph endorses as "the very tradition of America," and the reason to defend it in World War II, is its "*fighting tradition*"—the kind of antagonism of organized groups exemplified in the Revolutionary War, the Civil War, women's suffrage, and labor. "If Negroes get racial equality in America," Randolph argues, "they will have to take it. . . . If white men have to fight other white men for decent wages, hours of work, the right to organize trade unions, freedom, justice and democracy, how can the black man, whom nobody likes anyway, expect to get justice, freedom, and democracy any differently."[169]

It does not even tend to indulge in the imaginative projection of consensus through the rhetoric of anachronism, framing its opponents as always already defeated remnants of the past (see Chapter 4). Randolph counsels that "counterrevolution . . . follows a revolution as reaction follows action." Any action that aspires to dramatic social change will invite serious and organized resistance based on competing interests. This does not lead him to the pessimistic conclusion that no victories may be won, but it does lead him to the *tragic* judgment that even great victories "may not be permanently secure," a problem he calls the "crisis in victory."[170]

The reasons are twofold. First, while the proponents of romantic history like Rorty often insist that people are only emboldened and bolstered in pride by the narration of victory, Randolph—the veteran organizer—argues that victories entail a paradox: they can lead "into a debilitating state of psychological and emotional relaxation" that undermines the morale of activists and rank-and-file members, weakening "organizational structure." Judging this "probably as inevitable as the night following the day," Randolph appeals to the exemplarity of New Deal–era labor struggles. He reminds his audience of the "labor revolution" that broke out in the 1930s, including the sit-down strikes that were exemplars for the 1960s sit-in protests, and the violent Republic Steel "massacre" of striking workers. These events ushered in the Wagner Act ("the Magna Carta of the workers") establishing collective bargaining rights and the Fair Labor Standards Act permitting restrictions on minimum wage and work hours. Tragically, the very growth and success of the labor movement "provoked a sense of relaxation and weakened the will to struggle," sapping its spirit of "evangelism" and the moral fervor behind its claim "to be the conscience of the country." It became "richer in body but poorer in spirit," eventually unable to fend off devastating impositions like the Taft-Hartley Act (permitting antiunion "right-to-work" laws at the state level) and to meet the inevitable challenge of counterrevolution. This raises the complex problem of educating a *disposition,* what John Dewey called "an attitude not to this and that thing nor even to the aggregate of known things, but to the considerations which govern conduct" across a wide range of contexts and engagements with the world.[171] Social movement pedagogy and criticism must seek to cultivate a disposition that is less prone to this perpetual pattern of long-term struggle.

Second, all great egalitarian struggles for the expansion and consolidation of "rights" eventually run into the problem of political economy and economic power.[172] As Michael McCann argues, "the contradiction between economic inequality in market society and the promises of citizen equality in the political sphere" was central to Randolph's thinking, and he insisted that "with unequal material control of property came economic, social, and political dominance." This domination can only be undermined with economic democracy, not simply with the formal establishment of rights, which are—under such conditions—shot through with "the spirit of inequality, injustice, and prejudiced administration."[173] This is a familiar argument for leftists, who have long argued that while formal liberties and opportunities "provide *some* protection from threats to dignity, they are of limited value to those who possess them if these persons are poor. . . . Real freedom and opportunity must be accompanied by sufficient means to take advantage of them."[174] These means, for Randolph, involve not only material sufficiency secured by redistribution but reliable, sustain forms of countervailing *power:* Genuine economic democracy is more than "the dispersal of equality and power among individual citizens in a liberal, political democratic system"; it requires "the dispersal of equality and power among the citizen-workers."[175]

No account of domination, racial or otherwise, which evades this fact through moralizing language is long successful. In Randolph's judgment, the great exemplar of this fact was Reconstruction, which he understood in a tragic register:

> The failure of Reconstruction to provide Negroes with an economic base—the tragedy of the period—foredoomed all efforts at [achieving] political democracy in the South. Even as the Negro was enjoying the fullest participation in political life, helping to maintain Republican power in the South, the stage had been set for the time when, a score [of] years after Reconstruction, his landlord would march him to the polls with voting instructions, and later disenfranchise him altogether. Few examples in history so vividly illustrate the fragility of political freedom unmoored in economic security. Thus the Negro found himself cut adrift into the Gilded Age, the nadir of Big Business morality, the pinnacle of its speculative and exploitative irresponsibility.[176]

Crucially, however, the exemplarity of Reconstruction is not solely a negative lesson about the limits of a narrow, classically liberal construal of civil rights without economic democracy. Its invocation, and Randolph's careful explication throughout his career of the missed opportunities and tragic compromises of that moment, are meant to recover the demands of the past to reorient our judgments of normativity of past settlements and consolidations of civic life. He aims to expand our imaginations concerning what must be demanded and realized in the present.

This underscores, once again, the significance of narrative form. Contra Richard Rorty's call for romantic national narratives and celebratory myths of progressive realization, Randolph narrates in a tragic mode. His speeches and writings are filled not only with policy prescriptions but with long, historical reflections on labor defeats, Reconstruction's betrayal, the partial victories of civil rights law, and the reactionary consolidations that followed each. These are not digressions. They are integral to his political pedagogy. He tells stories of "defeat in victory" and "lost promises" not to wallow in pessimism or cynicism but to cultivate a disposition attuned to the irreversibility of some social harms, the vulnerability of democratic achievements, and the structural tendency of American politics to allow for reform with one hand and reaction with the other.

To narrate in this tragic key is to resist two forms of political forgetfulness: first, the reification of past settlements as if they were without remainder and, second, the dismissal of prior efforts as failures without understanding the ideals that animated them. It is to insist that even victories contain partiality and loss, and that defeats are not always without residue. In this mode, historical memory of exemplary events becomes a site of judgment. We do not simply commemorate or denounce exemplarity; we revisit, reconstruct, and reimagine.

Reconstructionism

Indeed, Randolph makes Reconstruction so exemplary that, early in his career, he transforms it into a *concept* meant to inspire an egalitarian political project and guide political judgment. In the March 1919 *Messenger* supplement titled "The Negro and the New Social Order," Randolph and Owen take the occasion of the coming end of World War I to offer a comprehensive program in the spirit of "Reconstruction." In it they revisit the failures of the earlier period to defend a sprawling vision involving the abolition of peonage and company store exploitation, the replacement of tenant farming by cooperative land ownership and union organization, protections against child labor and for maternity leave, antidiscrimination laws in hiring, free public education, and progressive taxes on income and inheritance. They also suggest a strikingly prescient vision that anticipates much of the drama of late twentieth-century progressivism, including not only the demand for the "rigid enforcement of the 13th, 14th and 15th amendments," which would entail the reduction of congressional representation in states that disenfranchise African Americans, passage of the federal antilynching law, and the abolition of Jim Crow segregation laws, but also—in a dramatic expansion of the federal bureaucracy—the creation of reformist-minded departments of education, prisons, recreation and amusement, health, housing, fuel, and transportation.[177] Reconstruction, through this transfiguration, transforms from historical example back into a practice of tragic vision and emulation (not imitation) that attempts to respond to a new era of war and constitutional crisis. This is a clear instance of being engaged with the afterlife of slavery, but in a way that sees that inheritance as generating both ongoing catastrophe *and* critical insight and opportunity.

Part of what makes Randolph's long career of leftist and left-liberal thinking and organizing fascinating in our own moment is that it helps us retrieve and clarify for contemporary political and public philosophy, a prominent tendency in African American political thought that was long obscured by the hegemonic power of the integrationist-nationalist interpretive binary and which remains muddled in recent talk of a "black radical tradition." This is the tradition of leftist integrationism, or—following Randolph—what we might call "reconstructionism." By this I mean to draw an important distinction between those families of political thinking that see "racial integration" as requiring, or as a constitutive part of, the dramatic egalitarian transformation of the basic structure of society (i.e., its political economy) and those who view integration as "not requiring . . . not demanding that the social system, the power system, be changed fundamentally" but "merely . . . that it include the Negro."[178] Less interested in the politics of social democracy, or certainly anything to the left of that, this latter variant of integrationism focuses instead on formal legal desegregation and antidiscrimination and promotes either the equality of opportunity, narrowly construed, or a more robust program of affirmative action policies meant to establish proportionate representation across a range of economic, educational, and government domains.

It is one of the unfortunate legacies of integrationist-nationalist binary that the commitment to "integrationism" is seen as quintessentially liberal, while nationalism is seen as radical, perhaps because of its unapologetically confrontational rhetoric, propensity to endorse violence, and willingness to countenance separatism are frightening to white audiences. The binary opposition seems to make the key interpretive questions in the study of black political thought about whether one celebrates or disavows an ideal of interracialism (in politics *and* culture); whether one sees certain postures of persuasion, protest, and identification as *undignified supplication* rather than appropriate *reconciliation to interdependency across race;* and whether one finds certain vocabularies useful and meaningful (e.g., America is *inherently, systematically, permanently racist or a white man's country*) or whether one thinks that vocabulary is not especially helpful in solving key political and interpretive problems surrounding black disadvantage and how to redress it. It is clear how questions of political economy and the precise justifications or purposes of "integration" might be lost amid such lines of inquiry.

Even within the long civil rights movement scholarship that helps us rediscover Randolph's long career, this may be a problem. Take, for example, Glenda Gilmore's discussion of the labor campaign led by the CPUSA in a segregated textile factory town compound in Gastonia, North Carolina, with abominable labor and living conditions. The campaign itself was largely a disaster, poorly organized and financed, and it never won an agreement with the factory but was likely a significant cause in its eventual bankruptcy. For Gilmore, however, the import of the Gastonia campaign was less its immediate material impact on factory conditions or even the local political economy of labor in Gastonia but in its implications for a CPUSA that steadfastly enforced its commitment to social equality and multiracial leadership in the face of more expedient options that would make the organizing of white people more feasible.[179] Her account of the power of the stories of interracial cooperation that came out of Gastonia, even if in reality they were aberrations from the norm in a largely defeated campaign, was that they sustained imaginative possibilities that communists used to establish Southern party branches and districts of operation, recruit more black workers, and continue to place the plight of black workers at the center of the party's American political efforts in places like Alabama, the Carolinas, and Virginia.[180] This activism, Gilmore contends, reached its peak with the stalwart defense of the nine Scottsboro Boys who were falsely accused of rape in Alabama.[181]

Gilmore waving the banner of the memory of the splendid failure of interracialist struggle in the communist movement raises the question of Harold Cruse's contention in *The Crisis of the Negro Intellectual* that the integrationist and nationalist divide evacuated leftist politics in the United States of meaningful distinctions between factions on the question of race, subsuming even the dreaded communist into "integrationism," de facto racial liberalism, and popular front politics. The confusion of Cruse's provocation, now more clearly visible amid the collapse of the authoritative integrationist-nationalist binaries, is that his diagnosis reflects a reification of a failure among liberals and leftists to sustain and pass down the difficult work of refining "integrationism" as substantive political theory. That the hard questions of integrationism remain largely underdeveloped in philosophy and popular politics is partly a problem of bad judgment in the Arendtian sense, a refusal to make perspicacious distinctions. Chief among these are distinctions about the precise *ends, justifications,* and *exemplars* animating various accounts of what racial integrationism is for, and what particular pathways or processes it ought to follow. This evasion, unsurprisingly, leads to the proliferation of suspicious (even cynical) readings of figures like Randolph or King for their opposition to communist and black nationalist tendencies.[182]

For instance, Randolph's commitment to "integration" is twofold. The first aim is that forms of segregation are always an imposition of separation and stigmatization, meant to make one's group as socially inferior.[183] Therefore, segregation involves the question of *equal dignity,* the sense of self-respect and reliable recognition respect from others, that gives one assurance and confident comportment as a moral equal to others. In Randolph's view, race segregation, like all forms of segregation undermine dignity and facilitate "the perpetration of palpable injustices, whether upon the weak by the strong, upon the ignorant by the educated, [or] upon the laborer by the capitalist." In his 1924 essay "Segregation in the Public Schools," Randolph writes that after the abolition of slavery, segregation became a tool to impose docility and suppress resistance among newly emancipated black workers. He argues that "cheap labor can be exacted only from docile, subservient human beings . . . beings who will not protest, organize labor unions and strike for a living wage."[184] Segregation, enforced through vagrancy laws, lynching, and terror, functioned to prevent black dignity and the collective power that might emerge from it.

The assault on dignity works by undermining our sense of equality, propagating "the fiction of inherent, inescapable, eternal fundamental difference" until habit and duration inculcates a broad social psychology of superiority and inferiority complexes. Randolph, contrary to the black nationalist arguments that emphasize the fragility of the black psyche in intimate contact with white people, argues that hierarchical ideologies (e.g., divine right of kings, oligarchy, and white supremacy) are difficult to maintain in proximity. "Familiarity," he writes, "breeds contempt," and "contact tends to strip one of his self-acclaimed, god-like, superior attributes, to expose his weaknesses, his commonplaceness and similarities to the so-called common people."[185] Randolph even associates the hysteria around school integration during the "massive resistance" to *Brown v. Board of Education* as anxious projection: "Hysterical with fear of the rise and progress of Negro Americans . . . little men in politics, press and pulpit in Mississippi and some other sections of the deep South, would use the primitive weapons of discrimination, hatreds, mob violence and lynch-law to block the path of advancement of the Negro, fearing lest competition in the arena, spirit, and the mind may expose their pretentious preachments about the white man's superiority to be a hollow farce."[186] In short, integration undermines both sides of the social psychological complexes and dispositions that make equal dignity elusive.

The second aim is to attain the end goal of social or economic democracy, which, Randolph rightly notes, requires the creation of a collective agent of change capable of realizing that aim against organized resistance.[187] In Randolph's account of the origins and evils of segregation, this looms especially large. He places much of the blame for the origins of segregation on the machinations of capital, arguing, "If the employers can keep the white and black dogs, on account of race prejudice, fighting over a bone, the yellow capitalist dog will get away with the bone—the bone of profits."[188] Randolph and Owen thought it incumbent on black militants to disclose the foundations of racial hierarchy in economic exploitation and class antagonism. They saw lynching, for example, as primarily caused by the capitalist system, where it served the purpose of terrorizing black workers into submitting to wildly exploitative labor arrangements and encouraged white workers to avoid common cause against capitalists through the illusion of superiority.[189]

Segregation, likewise, erects enormous obstacles—politically, culturally, psychologically, and intellectually—to the cultivation of broad solidarity, the recognition of mutual interests and moral duties, and the creation of organized political institutions capable of leveraging pressure. "White workers," Randolph argues, "have been negligent and recreant to their duty with respect to the organization of their black brothers. They, unfortunately, have allowed the virus of race prejudice to poison their minds. This has divided the ranks of the workers, thereby enabling the master class to rob both more easily. Yes, black workers should join white unions and white unions should organize black workers."[190] This integrationism focuses, therefore, on sites for the project theorized as conducive to broad-based social power (e.g., unions) rather than educative institutions to resocialize the young elite (e.g., colleges), justifying that primacy within a broader view about the importance of economic democracy for the fair value of our rights, the kinds of collective agents and forms of social organization that could further those ends, and the need for a solidarity of self-interest that does not rely as heavily on moral suasion and rectitude. This vision puts Randolph and his inheritors, like King, at odds with more classically liberal views that are less interested in the sprawling social democracy advocated via the Freedom Budget for All Americans or the participatory parity of working and poor people embodied in the Poor

People's Campaign of 1968—visions of emancipation that cannot be secured by freedoms of contract, association, and movement.

This vision also puts Randolph in ambivalent and critical relation to views that might be described as "strong" black nationalism or projects enamored with the idea of distinctively black forms of self-determination.[191] It is surely correct that Randolph was most vulnerable to the arguments of black nationalists when debating the prospects for interracial cooperation among the working class. Especially in the early years of Randolph's career, union locals (especially craft unions) formally and informally excluded African Americans, while national leaders largely abetted, or acquiesced to, entrenched racism among their members.

In response, prominent black intellectuals and leaders across the political spectrum often characterize unions in baldly antagonistic terms and exhorted black people to become strikebreakers on the grounds of race loyalty. This is especially true of nationalists: Garvey, for instance, argues that "the group of whites from whom Communists are made, in America, as well as trade unionists and members of the Worker's party, is more dangerous to the Negro's welfare than any other group." He charges white workers and unions with being the main participants in lynch mobs and pogroms and as hypocrites cynically looking to use the social power of African Americans to win concessions before turning around to defend white racial privilege. The dream of interracial socialism is an "impossible dream of equality that shall never materialize . . . and [is] never intended." For the UNIA leader, "the only convenient friend the Negro worker or laborer has, in America, at the present time, is the white capitalist." This is because the alleged self-interest of capitalists in cheap labor is more reliable than the goodwill of leftist labor, leading Garvey to recommend that black workers organize deliberately to undercut white workers' wages and build up their own wealth. If socialism is simply the *ressentiment* of white workers, thinly layered over white supremacy and opportunity hoarding, Randolph and his ilk are "distracting the Negro from the real solution and objective of securing nationalism."[192]

Labor union leaders were not especially helpful in proving Garvey wrong. Some offered up apologias for the horrifying violence that organized workers subjected black people to during strikes, work stoppages, and pogroms. These actions in defense of opportunity hoarding and psychic privilege were justified as necessary for the cultivation of labor solidarity and preventing strikebreaking and wage diminishment. In 1905 American Federation of Labor president Samuel Gompers threatened black people with "a race hatred worse than any ever known" as "Caucasian civilization will serve notice that its uplifting process is not to be interfered with" by "the colored man . . . lend[ing] himself to the work of tearing down what the white man has built up" by strikebreaking.[193]

Surveying this sordid history in 1933, W. E. B. Du Bois declared, "Colored labor has no common ground with white labor. No soviet of technocrats would do more than exploit colored labor in order to raise the status of whites. No revolt of a white proletariat could be started if its object was to make black workers their economic, political and social equals. It is for this reason that American socialism for fifty years has been dumb on the Negro problem, and the communists cannot even get a respectful hearing in America unless they begin by expelling Negroes."[194] This led Du Bois to controversially endorse provisional and experimental forms of black institutional autonomy:

> With the use of their political power, their power as consumers, and their brain power, added to that chance of personal appeal which proximity and neighborhood always give to human beings, Negroes can develop in the United States an economic nation within a nation, able to work through inner cooperation, to found its own institutions, to educate its genius, and at the same time, without mob violence or extremes of race hatred, to keep in helpful touch and cooperate with the mass of the nation. . . . If the economic and cultural salvation of the American Negro calls for an increase in segregation and prejudice, then that must come. . . . Control of their own education, which is the logical and inevitable end of separate schools, would not be an unmixed ill; it might prove a supreme good. Negro schools once meant poor schools. They need not today; they must not tomorrow. Separate Negro sections will increase race antagonism, but they will also increase economic cooperation, organized self-defense and necessary self-confidence.[195]

This argument, with its confusing uses of the term "segregation," invited such hostility from his colleagues in the more classically liberal integrationist leadership of the NAACP that Du Bois was compelled to resign.

Randolph, however, had already successfully clarified the distinction between segregation and autonomy *and* pioneered a way of thinking about the relationship of black solidarity and institutional autonomy to egalitarian struggles. In the Brotherhood of Sleeping Car Porters and Maids and other institutions, Randolph showed a principled and strategic commitment to the justifiability of autonomous black institutions—unions, newspapers, schools—as part of the long struggle for dignity and democracy. Where such institutions were necessary for generating effective pressure and countervailing force to domination, African Americans should support them. As early as 1920, *The Messenger* advocated that "wherever white unions discriminate against the Negro worker, then the only sensible thing to do is to form independent unions to fight both the white capitalists for more wages and shorter hours, on the one hand, and white labor unions for justice, on the other."[196] Randolph would later follow just this course in 1925, organizing black railroad workers into the Brotherhood of Sleeping Car Porters and Maids with a struggle lasting more than a decade to win a charter from the discriminatory American Federation of Labor, recognition from the National Mediation Board, and—in 1937—a collective bargaining agreement with the Pullman Company.

To mistake these institutions for "segregation," however, was, in Randolph's mind, to badly confuse categories and mangle concepts. Anticipating Malcolm X's well-known distinction between segregation and separation, Randolph defined segregation as an imposition by superiors onto inferiors for their unjust benefit.[197] The structure of segregation was, for him, a structure of domination, reflecting the exercise of power upon those lacking the resources, social organization, status, or temerity to effectively resist.[198] Separate institutions created and maintained by black people for self-defense and resistive political agency, however, did not fall under this determination. Quite the contrary, they were indispensable tools in the moral and political transformation of society.

But autonomy was not the destination. It was a strategy, a form of self-respect and collective discipline under conditions of rejection. Randolph was emphatic that black workers must not build separate institutions as ends in themselves. In the 1919 *Messenger* supplement on Reconstruction, he and Owen made this point clear: "Where unions refuse black workers admission . . . the black workers should organize separate unions of their own; but where white unions are sufficiently enlightened . . . we recommend that the Negro workers combine with the white workers."[199] The ultimate goal, in other words, was to bring about a progressive movement capable of generating the social pressure to advance the cause of economic democracy. But this interracial solidarity could not be achieved through black supplication or passivity. It had to be compelled—built through strength, not begged for in weakness. Crucially, a presupposition of this view is that where black institutions no longer seem commensurate or congruent with these ends, it is likely prudent to abandon or deemphasize them.

While this perhaps lacks the romantic enthusiasm of the obstinate interracialism that Gilmore recovers from Gastonia, it seems far more coherent as a schema of judgment than either that brief moment in North Carolina, or the self-undermining and contradictory commitments the CPUSA eventually evolved on the "Negro Question" under the leadership of Harry Haywood. Haywood, drawing on Stalinist notions of national minorities with rights of self-determination and the prediction that American capitalism was fast collapsing and revolution imminent, consolidated CPUSA Negro Question policy around ideals of nationality and black self-determination. In a position paper presented to the Sixth Congress of the Communist International (COMINTERN), Haywood articulated what became known as the Black Belt Thesis, an argument that African Americans met Stalin's definition of an oppressed national minority, largely concentrated in the Black Belt region of the South, with rights to self-determination (including its expression in an independent state) that black people should have the opportunity to exercise in the course of socialist revolution.[200] The endorsement of the thesis in 1930–1931 by the COMINTERN inspired an increased focus by American communists on "Negro work" in the South, and the persistent emphasis on "social equality" as organizational culture and political program, as well as national self-determination as a realistic utopia.[201]

One understands historians like Gilmore celebrating the party's attempt to take black self-determination seriously and to organize sharecroppers in the Jim Crow South when few others dared to, but the deep ambiguity or incoherence of the ideological commitments must not be lost. The CPUSA offered little guidance about how its Black Belt nationalism was supposed to relate to the projected communist future of proletarian interracialism. Was the "nation within a nation" to be an enduring political form, a project of cultural conservation, or a transient mobilization strategy? If theoretical resolution to these tensions was hard to deliver, even more daunting was the project of connecting that theoretical resolution to practical judgment in politics. As a result, the commitment to black self-determination often vacillated wildly between what seemed to be a racialist commitment to permanent black nationality based on claims of cultural continuity or the inorganic imposition of party line policies of national self-determination and plebiscites on a population without much organic enthusiasm for, or practical orientation around, the idea beyond its expressive value as a costly signal of commitment to the Negro.

Randolph's strategies across his career—whether in the reconstruction plan of 1920, the MOWM, the campaign for a permanent Fair Employment Practices Committee, or the pressure on Truman to desegregate the military—were built on a theory of agonistic, democratic constitutionalism from the left, understanding constitutional democracy as a terrain of contestation to occupy, pressure, and transform the basic structure of society, including the legal order. Randolph's "integrationism," therefore, was not a politics of simple incorporation or reverence in what exists; it was a politics that aspired to *reconstruction*. It demanded the fair value of formal rights and their substantive realization across even the economic domain through organized power, including the power to disobey the law and bring about social crisis in service of refounding the constitutional and political order.

In an era when the term *integration* has lost much of its orienting and authoritative character and *integrationism* has largely been captured—as

Danielle Allen has argued—by a picture that is only aesthetic or distributional rather than concerned with "predistribution" (e.g., ownership, assets, and decisionmaking authority) or "power sharing," the distinction between classically liberal integrationism and "reconstructionism" seems productive across a wide range of philosophical and political questions.[202] Here I will simply gesture toward two: political praxis and law.

In the first, I take inspiration from Aziz Rana's "Our Segregation Problem," an important recent essay that represents, I think, one of the more ambitious and forthright attempts to defend the kind of reconstructionist vision I've attributed to Randolph.[203] Rana argues, persuasively, that persistent racial segregation remains one of the most significant and underappreciated barriers to the formation of a durable, democratic Left in the United States. He reframes segregation not primarily as a problem of moral injustice or distributive inequality but as a structural impediment to social democratic transformation. Segregation, in Rana's view, isolates individuals from the relationships and institutions that make the kind of collective agency and solidarity necessary to transform the basic structure of American society possible. It fragments the social bases of collective life, separating people not only geographically but also experientially and epistemologically. The result is a civic order in which cross-racial identification is difficult to cultivate, democratic sensibilities are unequally distributed, and the organizational preconditions for effective political action are systematically undermined. What makes this problem especially acute for the Left, Rana argues, is that building cross-racial class coalitions requires more than persuasive appeals to shared material interests. It requires a *cultural infrastructure*—shared institutions and associational spaces—where solidaristic political consciousness can be developed and sustained. Here Rana's work dovetails, in many respects, with democratic theorists like Elizabeth Anderson, who in *The Imperative of Integration* contends that integration is essential to realizing democratic equality because it creates the conditions under which people can relate to one another as equals and break down stereotypes.[204]

In Rana's account, union halls and integrated workplaces once functioned as partial correctives—spaces where poor white and black workers could form political ties in the context of shared struggle. But with the weakening of organized labor and the retrenchment of desegregation efforts since the 1970s, these spaces have declined precipitously and residential integration has stagnated in many respects.[205] These patterns help produce concentrated disadvantage, wealth inequality, and dramatic inequalities in political participation in the present.[206] They are not just remnants of past injustice but active constraints on our imagined futures and the kinds of self-descriptions we can imagine acting politically under.

Assessing this state of affairs, Rana argues that the Left cannot simply speak in the language of redistribution without also engaging the language of integration—or what I have called reconstruction. In his view, schools and housing are especially central, insofar as they both drive the mechanisms of segregation, *and* each, at least in principle, can be articulated as a "public" or "common" good. Since Rana's essay first appeared, there are now promising efforts to think through questions of affordable housing, school reform, and civic distrust through frameworks of "abundance liberalism," "power-sharing liberalism," and "anti-oligarchic" politics.[207] This ferment is exciting insofar as it raises the possibility that the hard questions of integrationism may find intellectual resurgence in preparation for a more favorable hour: the legitimacy and permanence of municipal boundaries, the discriminatory politics of mass transit and high-density housing, the politics of college admissions, the justice and utility of minority set-asides in development and affirmative action in construction, and how old interpretive frameworks of race and culture are changing in light of post-1968 immigration patterns, just to name a few initiatives. The complexity of the problem also permits wildly different points and levels of entry. State governments have expansive powers to impose punishments on towns and cities that resist high-density housing clustered around mass transit. Elite universities, even after the demise of affirmative action, have the power to privilege students from racially and socioeconomically integrated public schools for admission. Unions, as Rana notes, can emphasize bargaining for the common good rather than the narrow benefits of workers in a specific firm or organization.[208] I am less interested, at least in this book, in specifying the exact policy prescriptions; I only mean to underscore the possibility of an underlying vision of "reconstruction" whose goals are in service of building solidarities and forms of institutionally based pressure that might promote economic democracy and a richer sense of flourishing for working citizens over time.

This leads to a final point regarding law, which is both the occasion for much of the ills of modern segregation and a limit on our remedies at present. I have discussed at length Randolph's propensity for tragic narration. He wants to prevent two interpretive failures: the romanticization of partial victories, and the erasure of defeated hopes and ideals. Tragedy allows him to resist both. He names the limits of past victories, the compromises that gutted Reconstruction, the betrayals of the New Deal—and he insists these are *not grounds for despair.* They are grounds for retrospective judgment and reactivated struggle.

This has important implications for constitutional thinking. The American legal imagination tends to congeal historical exemplarity into precedent and prevailing stories into authoritative interpretation. What Randolph permits us to think through, by contrast, is to resist this closure and seek out a *reconstructive* and *agonistic* jurisprudence—a vision of law shaped by a tragic mode of historical imagination and animated by popular mobilization. In 1919, surveying the defeat of the constitutional revolution of Reconstruction, Randolph treats "reconstruction" as a promising practice that can be reanimated and recollected, calling for the retheorization of the Thirteenth, Fourteenth, and Fifteenth Amendments to the US Constitution to leverage their potential not only against segregation but against peonage, labor exploitation, civic domination, and unjust political representation.

What does this mean for those of us doing work in legal and political theory? As the New Deal and civil rights revolutions in constitutional order are increasingly under crisis, we face a choice. Will we treat the civil rights movement as a completed episode, or will we radicalize its long memory, bolstered by a new historiography, into a new standard of critique and action? Randolph invites us to do the latter in the name of reconstructive transformation.

This would, at bottom, mean embracing what Daphna Renan calls "a more political constitutionalism . . . that depends on the institutions of representative democracy, rather than the power of a supreme judicial tribunal, to build political equality on the ground." Renan, too, draws on the history of Reconstruction and nineteenth-century abolitionism to develop a "kind of constitutionalism [that] understands our founding document as a site for political contestation, dissensus, power sharing, and community building . . . [and] recognizes that our constitutional rights are only as secure as our politics can make them."[209] To this the Randolph-King continuum would add the enduring importance of civil disobedience and organized protest movements that can raise the necessity and plausibility of alternative interpretations and incubate different visions of what American public philosophy in law and jurisprudence might be. Randolph's own example—threatening mass protest to force executive action on jobs and desegregation—reminds us that constitutional interpretation is not the monopoly of courts. The pressure politics of the MOWM and the demand for economic rights rooted in Reconstruction-era amendments show us another way to think constitutionally: through the exercise of collective social and political power, not just Supreme Court justices parsing text.

Part of the source of revision is the memory of the tragic choices of the past. Here again the long civil rights movement historiography is useful. Risa Goluboff, for example, traces the competing litigation strategies of the Civil Rights Section (CRS) of the Department of Justice and the NAACP. The CRS used complaints from black agricultural workers to push for expansive interpretations of the Thirteenth Amendment and New

Deal statutes to confront the interpenetration of race and class injustice, while the NAACP, in part because of class bias and the constraints of fundraising from elites, moved away from the concerns of agricultural workers toward the singular focus on the stigma of state classifications that reached its pinnacle in *Brown.* Goluboff offers a critique of the NAACP, through comparative and longitudinal study, as never being significantly interested in agricultural laborers and moving from creative and important litigation efforts on behalf of industrial workers in defense industries through the Fair Employment Practices Committee and the National Labor Relations Act in the early 1940s to a narrower assault on de jure segregation and racial stigma, particularly in education.[210] These are, she argues, the "lost promise" of civil rights.

Setting aside the substance of the various jurisprudential claims that Goluboff defends, I simply want to underscore the way that her reimagining of civil rights litigation is occasioned by intensive focus on the tragic choices structured by the New Deal. While nearly all acknowledge that the New Deal era brought about some impressive gains for black people, including a marked increase in the power of the black vote in Northern cities, over one million jobs provided by the Works Progress Administration, and a host of important social programs, long civil rights movement historians are more interested in the racial inequalities enshrined within the New Deal's social protections and how they shape the terrain of twentieth-century racial politics.

For example, the Civilian Conservation Corps' camps and the Tennessee Valley Authority's planned communities were both segregated, relief employment in the South was notoriously discriminatory, the Agricultural Adjustment Administration refused to punish white landlords for stealing black sharecroppers' crop support payments, and the National Recovery Administration's wage codes institutionalized lower pay rates for industries where black people were concentrated. The Wagner Act refused to outlaw union practices of racial discrimination, and the Social Security Act, which established old-age insurance and unemployment insurance, excluded agricultural and domestic workers—the majority of black people—from access to these funds.[211]

The New Deal programs that receive the most vituperative appraisal, however, are those concerned with housing policy. In 1933 the National Industrial Recovery Act was passed, authorizing "the use of federal funds to finance the construction of low cost housing, for slum clearance, for homesteading, and for the development of Greenbelt towns."[212] The establishment of the Home Owner's Loan Corporation (HOLC) in 1933 followed, providing "funds for refinancing urban mortgages in danger of default" and granting "low-interest loans to former owners who had lost their homes through foreclosure to enable them to regain their properties." With the development of the HOLC the federal government became irrevocably involved in the US housing industry. But in an attempt to keep white citizens and the real estate industry amiable to the administration, the federal government adopted the practices of racist realtors and institutionalized them, effectively making residential segregation federal policy.

The HOLC largely relied on redlining, which grew out of a mortgage risk evaluation rating system.[213] Through racialized redlining practices, "HOLC mortgage funds were invariably channeled away from established black areas and were usually redirected away from neighborhoods that looked as though they might contain blacks in the future."[214] Moreover, individual black families were prevented from receiving federal funds for mortgages to move into any neighborhood in which they would threaten the racial composition. This is largely because "the staff . . . decided that these homes [in white neighborhoods] would more than likely lose their fair market share if African American families moved into them."[215] By no means did the HOLC "invent standards of racial worth in real estate," but it did bureaucratize and apply them on "an exceptional scale" while giving all the "power, prestige, and support of the federal government to the systematic practice of racial discrimination in housing." Thus, in the 1930s and 1940s, the HOLC "was also responsible for a much larger and more significant disinvestment in black areas by private institutions" that used its redlining practices and maps as a business model.[216]

The loan programs created by the National Housing Acts of 1934 and 1937 further "reshaped the residential housing market of the United States and pumped millions of dollars into the housing industry during the postwar era."[217] The primary goal of the Housing Acts was to stimulate the housing industry by encouraging homebuilding and mortgage lending with federal funds.[218] Thus, a major part of the legislation was the creation of a program that used federal funding to help private banks insure home mortgages that they would otherwise be unable to issue because of the prevalent risk of foreclosure.[219] Since this eliminated much of the risk to private banks, they were able to issue more mortgages and to lower interest rates, thereby stimulating homeownership to unprecedented levels. Between 1934 and 1969 the portion of families living in owner-occupied dwellings rose from 44 percent to 63 percent.[220] Unfortunately, with the Federal Housing Administration (FHA) adopting the racist underwriting practices of the HOLC, these owner-occupied dwellings were largely unoccupied by black people and located away from black neighborhoods. Robert Weaver of the NAACP estimated in 1953 that approximately nine million new dwelling units were constructed by private enterprise during the years 1935–1950, but of that total, no more than one hundred thousand, or slightly over 1 percent, were available to nonwhite people.[221]

The FHA wholeheartedly "recommended the use and application of racially restrictive covenants as a means of ensuring the security" of neighborhoods where it insured property—a recommendation that the US Supreme Court found unconstitutional in 1948 but that carried on nonetheless for years due to executive indifference. This adherence to racialized underwriting practices, coupled with antiurban guidelines that set minimum lot sizes, setback lengths, and property sizes for FHA-insured loans, amounted to a massive investment in the largely white suburbs at the expense of the predominately black inner cities. In some locales, like Camden and Paterson, New Jersey, entire cities were declared ineligible for FHA-insured loans because black people and Latinos constituted a majority of the population.[222]

Surveying the massive impact on American society that these policies had, Jacqueline Hall argues that race-coded New Deal reforms had the ideological effects of making race "increasingly specialized, rendering invisible to white people the accumulated race and class privileges that undergirded what suburbanites came to see as the rightful fruits of their own labor": the political effects of fostering a "suburban frontier" politics of low tax rates, property rights, neighborhood autonomy, and limited social responsibility that was generative of modern conservatism and propelled the structural effects of compounding marginalization and disadvantage for black urban residents.[223] The result was, essentially, tragic: "The ability of the New Deal to confront the era's most heinous dictatorships by reshaping liberal democracy required accommodating the most violent and illiberal part of the political system, keeping the South inside the game of democracy. . . . The triumph, in short, cannot be severed from the sorrow. Liberal democracy prospered as a result of an accommodation with racial humiliation and its system of lawful exclusion and principled terror."[224]

Keeping track of these tragic choices, and the serious harm they caused even as they did good, allows us to not only to think through exemplary instances for our own tragic choices but also to raise the question of tragic responsibility through the legal and political practice of reparation based on the Jim Crow–era racial order. The institutional infrastructure of the New Deal is a far more proximate and easily adjudicated site of direct government injury on the basis of race, offering an opportunity to raise claims of compensatory justice, educate citizens (especially first- and second-generation immigrants) about patterns of discrimination, and justify policies meant to redress the legacy of segregation in pursuit of democratic equality.

Finally, in the realm of race scholarship in the legal academy, this turn toward tragic responsibility would supplant much of the language of *irony* and *ontological pessimism* that is the legacy of Derrick Bell in critical race theory. Drawing on black nationalist criticism, Bell powerfully diagnosed many of the failures of desegregation and racial redress in the law, particularly for the black poor. Yet he was prone to moving without warrant from a critique of the sufferings of black poor and working-class citizens to sweeping deployments of the concept of "black interests" and categorical concepts like permanent *racial* subordination. A more promising approach to legal theory and criticism, at least in this era, is to move from critical race theory's traditional association with the epistemological foci of critical legal studies (e.g., language, method, and knowledge claims) toward one that emphasizes hermeneutical recovery of black progressive thinking about law and political economy. This means reading the long civil rights historiography as provocation, not pessimism.

Underneath Gilmore's lament that "in the simplified stories that the media told of the movement, civil rights came to mean school integration, access to public accommodations, and voting rights" we find a barely concealed *normative-political* plea to recover "radical desegregation" and "the complexity of a drive to eliminate the economic injustices wrought by slavery, debt peonage, and a wage labor system." Gilmore's suggestion is to turn to those "connections among civil liberties, labor rights, and civil rights that liberals and radicals had carefully forged."[225] From Singh we find the mournful argument that "many of the valuable insights derived from the ethics and politics of living and overcoming Jim Crow are now being squandered" by a "national forgetting of what Frederick Douglass called the standpoint of the victims in American history" and "the state-sanctioned thinning of the field of robust and independent black public interaction that had been developing since the 1930s."[226] Goluboff worries that romantic myths about the legal strategy leading to *Brown* will continue to "limit our imaginations . . . about the possibilities for constitutional redress of material inequalities" and obscure the "alternatives that black working-class clients and their lawyers once proposed."[227] Hall sums this all up succinctly: "Seen through the optic of the Long Civil Rights Movement, . . . civil rights look less like a product of the Cold War and more like a casualty."[228] Yet we know from tragedy that death is an occasion for critical reflection, not cowardice.

CONCLUSION

> Pessimism is cowardice. The man who cannot frankly acknowledge the "Jim-Crow" car as a fact and yet live and hope is simply afraid either of himself or of the world. There is not in the world a more disgraceful denial of human brotherhood than the "Jim-Crow" car of the southern United States; but, too, just as true, there is nothing more beautiful in the universe than sunset and moonlight on Montego Bay in far Jamaica. And both things are true and both belong to this our world, and neither can be denied. . . . From such heights of holiness men turn to master the world. All the pettiness of life drops away and it becomes a great battle before the Lord.[1]

These provocative sentences appear in "Of Beauty and Death," the penultimate chapter in W.E.B. Du Bois's criminally underappreciated 1920 book *Darkwater: Voices from Within the Veil,* released roughly at the beginning of the long civil rights movement. Taking the segregated railcar as synecdoche, not just for the vast edifice of racial domination consolidated in the aftermath of World War I but also of the "denial of human brotherhood" itself, Du Bois concedes that the existence and endurance of such evils are a profound challenge to our most fundamental judgments about the worth of hope, the meaning of life, and the value of our care for the world. These trials often drive us to despair.[2] That others do not respond with similar angst or indignation only adds to the burden of our seeming abandonment.

Strikingly, among Du Bois's most direct responses to these encounters with pessimism is an essay on beauty and death, turning to the realm of conventionally "aesthetic" judgment in service of existential and political philosophy. What is at issue, he seems to suggest, is not so much the knowledge of the intricacies of inequality that are the province of the sociologist, but a sensibility from which to judge injustice and the struggle against it. Here the intervention is one interested in a change of perspective and disposition, one whose interpretive angle of approach can cultivate virtues of courage and hope without falling into delusion. The challenge, as Du Bois puts it, is to avoid any "pert and easy word of encouragement" or "merely dark despair." We must somehow see the world and "grant all its ugliness and sin—the petty, horrible snarl of its putrid threads," without losing our grip on the acknowledgment that "the beauty of this world is not to be denied."[3] For Du Bois, something in this insight that ugliness and evil are devastatingly real but not the totality of all that exists, especially as we explain social reality and narrate history, steels us for the "great battle" of human emancipation. This is particularly so in dark and uncertain times.

One key to understanding Du Bois's vision—a *tragic* vision—lies in the same chapter, among the densest and most opaque of his voluminous writings.[4] Immediately after these statements on pessimism, Du Bois makes a jarring turn to detail his aesthetic response to the Grand Canyon. While Du Bois's leading interpreter, Robert Gooding-Williams, has recently offered a careful reconstruction of Du Bois's theory of beauty (especially natural beauty) and its relationship to his broader political philosophy, I want to draw attention to his still lesser-known use of the sublime to dramatize these questions of perspective and disposition that remain urgent over a century after *Darkwater.*[5]

Describing a cross-country trip of over seven thousand miles through the Rocky Mountains, California, Texas, and beyond, Du Bois declares that he "saw but one thing that lived and will live eternal in my soul,—the Grand Cañon."[6] Published during a formative wave of conservation activism, the year after the Grand Canyon National Park Act was signed into law by President Woodrow Wilson, *Darkwater* echoes the breathless awe that so characterized the response of turn-of-the-century American audiences. Theodore Roosevelt, whom Du Bois introduced for his last public address in 1918, famously described the canyon's "sublimity" in 1903 as "the one great sight which every American should see," a wonder "beyond comparison—beyond description; absolutely unparalleled throughout the wide world."[7]

Du Bois, too, takes up the rhetoric of sublimity to describe the Grand Canyon, but for weightier existential, ethical, and political purposes. For the philosopher who once waxed rhapsodically about his childhood in the hills of New England, his encounter with this gargantuan natural wonder entailed an aesthetic education on perspective and judgment. Relating his approach from the canyon's rim, we see the imposing landscape that sprawls before Du Bois's eyes as overpowering, violent, and horrifying: "It is a sudden void in the bosom of the earth, down to its entrails—a wound where the dull titanic knife has turned and twisted in the hole, leaving its edges livid, scarred, jagged, and pulsing over the white, and red, and purple of its mighty flesh, while down below—down, down below, in black and severed vein, boils the dull and sullen flood of the Colorado."[8]

In a text notable for its spectacular depictions of lynching and Jim Crow's ritual mutilations, the canyon is apprehended first as violence and viscera, then as senselessness and disorder, magnified by an overwhelming absurdity of scale: "The earth and sky gone stark and raving mad. The mountains up-twirled, disbodied, and inverted, stand on their peaks and throw their bowels to the sky. Their earth is air; the ether blood-red rock engreened. You stand upon their roots and fall into their pinnacles, a mighty mile." Almost surrealist in Du Bois's rendering, it seems impossible to orient oneself in a world where such strange phenomena are possible. One's ability to draw distinctions or exercise discernment—key elements of judgment—are overwhelmed ("Is yonder wall a hedge of black or is it the rampart between heaven and hell? I see greens,—is it moss or giant pines?"). We confront, through this phenomenon, the limits of our powers, faculties, and capacities ("One throws a rock into the abyss. It gives back no sound. It falls on silence"). Indeed, it mocks our finitude, casting disparaging light even on the grand traditions of our gods and the scribbled testaments of their prophets with "the shading of eternity." If we listen closely, Du Bois implores, we will hear the alien "accents of that gorge which mutters: 'Before Abraham was, I am.'"[9]

Du Bois's recounting of the canyon, it is essential to note, comes immediately on the heels of an extended description of the humiliations and oppressions of the segregated Jim Crow railcar. The juxtaposition, puzzling at first glance, is meant to disclose the existential, experiential, and epistemic convergence between the racial order and the canyon. Du Bois gives us, through the sublime, an intimation of race oppression's absurdity in the fullest philosophical sense: the bewildering scale and scope of its impositions, its disorienting and damaging effect on our basic certainties about the normative order and rationality of the world, and our faith in whether it will be possible to find ourselves at home in a world scarred this way.

Here, however, Du Bois makes a quintessentially Kantian turn. Immanuel Kant, too, in *Critique of the Power of Judgement,* depicts the experience of the sublime as beginning with the apprehension of how natural phenomena like "threatening cliffs, thunder clouds towering up into the heavens, bringing with them flashes of lightning and crashes of thunder, volcanoes with their all-destroying violence, hurricanes with the devastation they leave behind, the boundless ocean set into a rage, a lofty waterfall on a mighty river, etc., make our capacity to resist into an insignificant trifle in comparison with their power." Yet this is not the last word. The experience of the sublime also will "elevate the strength of our soul above its usual level, and allow us to discover within ourselves a capacity for resistance . . . which gives us the courage to measure ourselves against the apparent all-powerfulness of nature." The sense of "physical powerlessness" we discern is real and self-evident, but so too is our ability to judge those interests we fear would be destroyed (e.g., material goods, health, or life itself) as ultimately "trivial, and hence to regard [nature's] power (to which we are, to be sure, subjected in regard to these things) as not the sort of dominion over ourselves and our authority to which we would have to bow if it came down to our highest principles and their affirmation or abandonment."[10] Or, as Martin Luther King Jr. more plainly put the point, there are "some things so dear, some things so eternally true, some things so precious that they are worth dying for. And if a man has not discovered something that he will die for, in a sense he is not fit to live."[11]

For Kant, our vocation as moral agents and this ability to judge and act on principle over life itself is a source of sublime feeling even in comparison with nature's most imposing wonders. The Du Boisian sublime echoes this sense of the grandeur of our moral vocation, but in *Darkwater,* the traditional transition from physical powerlessness to spiritual elevation is not characterized by an innate reflex of reason and imagination. The occasion and source of our elevation comes, in crucial respects, from outside of us. The challenge is whether we can achieve a perspectival shift that allows us to recognize these moments, and seize them as opportunities to achieve new descriptions of, and orientation toward, the traditions we inherit, the finitude that is our burden, and the world that we are fated to act within. This, Du Bois appears to think, is a pathway back to political action and political hope, and it remains a pressing one to consider.

Reading in this light, we linger upon the fact that Du Bois's breathless narration of the frightening canyon culminates in the squinting awareness of a dawning light that transforms his sight. We find, in the "blue and brilliant morning," that his initial portrait of the canyon was colored by the night and its surreal dreamscapes.[12] Daybreak, an occasion that is no artifact of the human will, nevertheless allows for a clearer grasp of what is unreal or "but shadows"—ideology, perhaps—permitting a better sense of how to orient ourselves in time and space.

Crucially, this occasion makes possible a new mode of action: his travel from the towering canyon rim down to the roiling Colorado River's dark waters. Of this passage Du Bois writes,

> I have been down into the entrails of earth—down, down by straight and staring cliffs—down by sounding waters and sun-strewn meadows; down by green pastures and still waters, by great, steep chasms—down by the gnarled and twisted fists of God to the deep, sad moan of the yellow river that did this thing of wonder,—a little winding river with death in its depth and a crown of glory in its flying hair.

> I have seen what eye of man was never meant to see. I have profaned the sanctuary. I have looked upon the dread disrobing of the Night, and yet I live. Ere I hid my head she was standing in her cavern halls, glowing coldly westward—her feet were blackness: her robes, empurpled, flowed mistily from shoulder down in formless folds of folds; her head, pine-crowned, was set with jeweled stars. I turned away and dreamed—the cañon,—the awful, its depths called; its heights shuddered. Then suddenly I arose and looked. Her robes were falling. At dim-dawn they hung purplish-green and black. Slowly she stripped them from her gaunt and shapely limbs—her cold, gray garments shot with shadows stood revealed. Down dropped the black-blue robes, gray-pearled and slipped, leaving a filmy, silken, misty thing, and underneath I glimpsed her limbs of utter light.[13]

Du Bois offers a rapid succession of familiar metaphors for "enlightenment," or the dawning of truth: the disrobed female body yielding itself to his gaze, the eye moving from downcast avoidance to courageous investigation, "illumination" by daybreak and sunlight.[14] The language of Enlightenment and courage is not accidental. In Kant's banner-wielding 1784 essay, "What Is Enlightenment?," he identifies "Sapere Aude!" (Dare to Know!) as "the motto of enlightenment": "Have courage to use your own understanding!"[15] Throughout his career, Kant defends courage—often treating it as constitutive of maturity—as a paramount intellectual and existential virtue. It is required, as Susan Neiman writes, "to live with the rift that will run through our lives, however good they may be: ideals of reason tell us how the world should be; experience tells us that it rarely is." Maturity "requires confronting the gap between the two—without giving up on either one." "For the Stoic," Neiman adds, "refusal to accept the world as it's given is a matter of human weakness that may be cured by changing your emotions. For Kant that refusal is precisely human strength. Later writers held that our inability to accept reality stems from infantile wishes that we ought to grow out of. For Kant it stems from the voice of critical reason, and it's a voice that needs to be heard."[16] But what drives the emboldening experience of the sublime, and its enlargement of Du Bois's courage, is only the journey toward the "little winding river with death in its depth." How does the yellow Colorado occasion a newfound courage (recall, pessimism is alleged cowardice) and enhance our insight and agency? What disposition does this aesthetic judgment seek to cultivate? And what does it mean to pay tribute to the "death" in these dark waters?

I take Du Bois's depiction of the Colorado River that carved "this thing of wonder" to be his early metaphorical intimation of what he would later call the "long siege"—the enduring, intergenerational social movement and accumulation of power required to overcome the oppressed social condition of African Americans. Two elements of the long siege are essential.

The first and more familiar is that Du Bois's experiences in political struggle and study led him to increasingly understand that the social condition of African Americans was a tangled knot of overlapping forces whose interpenetrating order would not collapse swiftly. The injustice of the American racial order hangs together not simply on plain ignorance, vicious ill will, suffocating propaganda, and violent subjection. Further, and more obstinately, it also reflects falsely rationalized economic interests and a morass of psychological "complexes sunk now largely to unconscious habit and irrational urge."

The second is that the concept of the long siege names a distinctive disposition toward political and social movement temporality. It tries to woo us away from a competing disposition whose orientation and practice of judgment is based on the expectation that "a series of brilliant immediate assaults" will bring about emancipation.[17] Instead egalitarian politics requires an affective, epistemological, political, and existential adjustment to the long duration and intergenerational character of a struggle of this magnitude. This reeducation of matters of politics and existence requires courage, of course, but of an increasingly unfamiliar sort.

The river represents, therefore, the contingent currents of human action, but with an acknowledgment that their accumulated significance may only be dimly perceptible or easily dismissed from a distance. Only a shift in perspective, dramatized as going down the canyon, can give lie to pessimism. Yet, this picture of the world is not one that licenses the sunny optimism of popular proverbs. The detailed sublimity of the canyon image foregrounds Du Bois's sense of the enormous scale and disorienting character of the vast and cumulative social problems that confront egalitarian political struggles. The relation between river and canyon represents Du Bois's insistence that even the imposing landscape of domination has been painstakingly reshaped by the often-obscure agency of oppressed and ordinary peoples. To see the accumulated traces and impact of these efforts, or to grasp their possible meaning and significance, one cannot remain on "the rim" in the spectatorial remove of a third-person standpoint content to understand human action through mechanistically causal or other externally imposed forms of explanation.[18] One must go down to the river, so to speak, to try to think from the first-person, normative, and evaluative standpoint of others and refuse a fully objectifying stance toward one's own exercises of judgment and action.

This is eerily reflected in the canyon itself. The nature writer Craig Childs, studying the impact of the river's floods, notes how "every physical element of a canyon network is mercurial, with no hard givens, no solid obstacles." Even something as seemingly solid as the "unflagging walls of the Supai Formation were simply another moving part," and the very shape of the canyon "is defined by an alertness to even the most trivial tension." Noting that the "flexible aspects of a flood" are called "*degrees of freedom,*" of all things, Childs draws our notice to the way this concept measures the rate "at which objects give way to pressure: the quick erosion of sand, the steady wearing back of stone walls, and the instant recoil of water hitting a boulder." In the canyon, "everything changes shape."[19]

Translated from geology to politics, these insights about spectatorial remove and the complexity of change were also central to Raymond Williams's pathbreaking account of the *revolutionary* potential of tragedy:

> Elevating ourselves to spectators and judges, we suppress our own real role in any such action, or conclude in a kind of indifference, that what has happened was inevitable and that there is even a law of inevitability. We see indeed a certain inevitability, of a tragic kind, as we see the struggle to end alienation producing its own new kinds of alienation. But, while we attend to the whole action, we see also, working through it, a new struggle against the new alienation: the comprehension of disorder producing a new image of order; the revolution against the fixed consciousness of revolution, and the authentic activity reborn and newly lived. What we then know is no simple action: the heroic liberation. But we know more also that simple reaction, for if we accept alienation, in ourselves or in others, as a permanent condition, we must know that other men, by the very act of living will reject this, making us their involuntary enemies, and the radical disorder is then most bitterly confirmed. . . . We follow the whole action: not only the evil, but the men who have fought against evil; not only the crisis, but the energy released by it, the spirit learned in it. We make the connections, because that is the action of tragedy, and what we learn in suffering is again revolution, because we acknowledge others as men and any such acknowledgment is the beginning of struggle, as the continuing reality of our lives. Then to see revolution in this tragic perspective is the only way to maintain it.[20]

This approach to history is given aesthetic foundation in Du Bois's "Of Beauty and Death," which ends with an otherwise obscure reflection on the nature of ugliness and beauty:

> Ugliness to me is eternal, not in the essence but in its incompleteness; but its eternity does not daunt me, for its eternal unfulfillment is a cause of joy. There is in it nothing new or unexpected; it is the old evil stretching out and ever seeking the end it cannot find; it may coil and writhe and recur in endless battle to days without end, but it is the same human ill and bitter hurt. But Beauty is fulfilment. It satisfies. It is always new and strange. It is the reasonable thing. Its end is Death—the sweet silence of perfection, the calm and balance of utter music. Therein is the triumph of Beauty. So strong is the spell of beauty that there are those who, contradicting their own knowledge and experience, try to say that all is beauty. They are called optimists, and they lie. All is not beauty. Ugliness and hate and ill are here

> with all their contradiction and illogic; they will always be here—perhaps, God send, with lessened volume and force, but here and eternal, while beauty triumphs in its great completion—Death. We cannot conjure the end of all ugliness in eternal beauty, for beauty by its very being and definition has in each definition its ends and limits; but while beauty lies implicit and revealed in its end, ugliness writhes on in darkness forever.[21]

This statement is not just a philosophy of aesthetics; it is also one of politics and historical judgment. It insists that "there is no evil which men have created, of this or any other kind, which other men have not struggled to end," and it counsels us, in light of that fact, to not take only the former part of this relation and "call it absolute or transcendent."[22] Yet it does so without losing its grasp on the fact that it is death that colors the waters.

Du Bois offers not just a critique of what I have called romantic histories (here, "optimism") for evasion of ugliness and social evil. Instead, from his ruminations on Alexander Crummell to John Brown to Reconstruction to his autobiographical reflections on his own scholarly-political efforts, Du Bois returns again and again to mourning, lingering over the wounds, defeats, and lost causes (especially economic justice struggles) of black emancipatory struggle. Against those (the radical ironists and pessimists) who insist that ugliness is the totality, the excavation of these defeated struggles—their "death," as it were—is motivated by three sensibilities. The first is that their significance is not determined by their defeat; these "splendid failures" can be returned to, in their novelty and uncanniness, to inspire our own struggles and sharpen our sense of judgment and possibility. Second is that their existence is a part of what makes ugliness and injustice incomplete. From the vantage of these stories, we can reopen what looks settled or what gets celebrated as "progress," or critique what appears inevitable. It is, in part, our persistence in struggle that staves off the finality of defeat. And third is that sustained investigation and reconstruction of these historical moments reveals the contingency and opportunity structures that are not visible from a distance, renewing our sense that things could have turned out differently, and better. This subjunctive thinking trains judgment to seek out such opportunities in the present and act decisively to seize them with principled action.

This work requires, to use a philosophical term of art, the exercise of *anamnestic reason*.[23] This "reason endowed with memory" seeks a kind of "remembrancing" that refuses to "repress and forget, or idealistically overcome [*aufheben*] humanity's history of suffering."[24] It does so on the grounds that certain species of forgetfulness, or particularly illicit separations of past from present, lead to errors on top of errors. In other words, when we lose the "inexhaustible epistemological potential" of "the vanquished," we lose our grip on critique and instead cultivate an insensitivity to our present injustices, self-undermining ideas of "progress," and a distorted sense of who we are and what our situation demands.[25]

This is a melancholic view, as even its defenders note, but one that resists despair by aiming at obligation not abdication. As Jürgen Habermas powerfully argued amid the *Historikerstreit* (historians' dispute) concerning the place of Nazism and genocide in German identity and historiography, "melancholy in view of the victims whose sufferings cannot be made good . . . places us under an obligation." This duty, as Habermas spells it out, is that we "bear a greater responsibility than ever for the proportion of continuity and discontinuity in the forms of life we pass on," making judgments about the continuation or disavowal of our traditions in light of this remembrance of past suffering. Indeed, such memory leaves one at odds with those who would "rely on a triumphal national history, on the unbroken normality of what has come to prevail."[26]

As Du Bois warned in his magisterial *Black Reconstruction in America* (1935), battles over representations of the past are persistent sites of struggle against propaganda and ideology (in the pejorative sense). His declared object in writing a counterhistory of post–Civil War Reconstruction was to resist the "propaganda" of history on offer, representations of the past he thought distorted, contradicted, and revised the truth until it "changed to any convenient fairy tale that the masters of men wish."[27] Against this, Du Bois modestly described his goal as "simply to establish the Truth, on which Right in the future may be built."[28] This faith in history as a source of inoculation against ideology is rooted in a notion that historical thinking and narrative is indispensable for *explaining* social structures and patterns, as well as for *understanding* the culture, action, and patterns of thought of others we encounter—two contextual insights necessary for clear-eyed moral judgment.[29]

The unmasking critique of American politics, culture, and history-writing is not without its costs. To expose, as Du Bois does, the gruesome histories of "orgy, cruelty, barbarism, and murder done to men and women of Negro descent" in "the name of Civilization, Justice, and Motherhood" is inevitably to cast some skepticism on the worth of the very words and ideals in which such evils can take up rhetorical or ideological residence.[30] The question, however, is to what extent our ethical vocabularies and political traditions are exhausted by these uses. What other interpretations, attempts at practice, or forms of contestation remain available as a usable past that "might re-inspire confidence in the possibility, the hope for, a future different from the past?"[31]

For Du Bois, the answer involves tending to those strivings or ideals among history's defeated and, on occasion, its discredited. His work shows a persistent fascination with those efforts—the Freedman's Bureau, John

Brown's raid, Reconstruction, the consumer cooperative—that are retrospectively dismissed or disavowed in progressive narratives, modus vivendi political settlements, or triumphalist judgments of "success" and "progress." Recovering these strivings allows the imaginative space to redescribe the balance of competing forces and constituencies at a given conjuncture, grasp a broader range of the possibilities generated in that moment, and allow the roads not taken to inform our judgments of past, present, and future. Tragedy's task is "to persuade us that at some significant level we have *never* really known [familiar histories]; that there is no finished narration but only the continuing exposure of ourselves to ever-new perspectives on the danger concealed in where and who we think we are."[32]

Similar sentiments have a venerable history in black political life traceable at least to the epochal debate between Alexander Crummell and Frederick Douglass in the 1880s. Crummell, the Cambridge University–educated Episcopalian priest and founder of the American Negro Academy, lamented to a Storer College commencement audience in 1885 what he saw as "an irresistible tendency in the Negro mind in this land to dwell morbidly and absorbingly upon the servile past." The incessant "recollection" of the history of bondage—for Crummell, recollection described an intentional, active stance toward narrating the past—would leave the group unreceptive to "changed circumstances [that] bring to us an immense budget of new thoughts, new ideas, new projects, new purposes, new ambitions, of which our fathers never thought."[33]

In Crummell's account, Frederick Douglass, the legendary veteran of abolitionist struggle, rose from the audience to meet these claims with "his emphatic and most earnest protest," delivering objections later elaborated in speeches that, unlike his remarks at the West Virginia college, survive in the archives. At an 1888 celebration of emancipation in Washington, DC, for example, Douglass defended the subversive power of historical memory to inspire contemporary protest, protect us from propaganda and ideology, and fulfill our duties to the dead. "The nation," he warned, "may forget; it may shut its eyes to the past, and frown upon any who may do otherwise, but the colored people of this country are bound to keep fresh a memory of the past till justice shall be done to them in the present."[34]

Tragic history, given its focus on human agency, even in the midst of epistemological limitations, unintended consequences, serious defeat, and the fleeting opportunity structure for particular actions, can recover—as Du Bois demonstrates—this sense of expansive political imagination and empowerment. It can bear more easily accounts of history that emphasize the unstable interpenetration and semiautonomous logics of various political practices (e.g., antiblack racism, capitalism, sexism, and colonialism) rather than inflating one axis to a comprehensive, seamless totality and explaining all social life in reference to it.

Tragic history trains our judgment to better notice the opportunities for action that emerge through the interpenetration of systems of power and their emergent properties. Contingency is crucial. The hopes embodied in struggles are only possible; they are not guaranteed. Natality and tragedy must be held in tandem. Nevertheless, the recognition of the interrelation helps steel us against both the fetishism for spectacular eruptions that dominate romantic narrations and the paralyzing disappointment that governs irony. Narrating the complex, long-term web of actions that together constitute important ideals or partial victories helps orient political struggles to the kinds of dispositions needed for the long siege.[35]

A tragic vision seeks perspicacious judgment about partial victories in light of the depth and complexity of sociopolitical conflict. It is wary of how determinant rules and certain narrative modes may lead us to confuse modest gains for human freedom and flourishing with either the completion of struggle or the abject failure of a "nonevent." It achieves this by cultivating a subversive memory of "dead" and defeated struggles as a standpoint from which to judge. It does so not because it is "attached more to a particular [past] political analysis or ideal . . . than to seizing the possibilities for radical change in the present" but because the animating hopes of the past can help us beat back ideological attempts to reconcile us to catastrophic defeat and misname the present an age of victory or rationality.[36] That this is even possible is rooted in the indeterminate status of the past.

The tragic, on this neo–Du Boisian view, refuses the conflation of the real and rational and uses historical narrative to disclose the disjuncture. It transforms despair into what Cornel West once called "revolutionary patience," a disposition that acknowledges the persistence and expanse of evil as such, while working doggedly and "against overwhelming odds" to defeat particular evils in the present.[37] Again, our action and our historical judgments are related. We can remake the meaning of the past out of its indeterminacy and need for narration, "not simply by choosing to read it in a certain way but by virtue of our actions." Put more succinctly, "The meaning of past events lies ultimately in the guardianship of the present. . . . The dead cannot be resurrected; but there is a tragic form of hope whereby they can be invested with new meaning, interpreted otherwise, woven into a narrative which they themselves could not have foretold."[38]

If this vision can do the work of persuasion—or "conversion," as Cornel West might prefer—it must gaze unflinchingly into the death- and defeat-colored waters of intergenerational struggle. "To long," Fredric Jameson writes, "is not necessarily to find," and thus he counsels that a philosophy of the sort I am offering "remains a dead letter unless it comes to terms in one way or another with death itself," personally, politically, and ontologically. The "most urgent question" of radical egalitarian politics, Jameson argues, "remains that of individual sacrifice, and of the renunciations made by present generations for the benefit of generations in a future they will not themselves see."[39]

Something like this challenge must have been on Du Bois's mind as he drew close to his final days. On June 26, 1957, he composed a "final message to the world" that he gave to his wife, the intellectual and activist Shirley Graham Du Bois, to release on his passing. "I have loved my work," he writes. "I have loved people and my play, but always I have been uplifted by the thought that what I have done well will live long and justify my life; that what I have done ill or never finished can be handed on to others for endless days to be finished, perhaps better than I could have done."

Du Bois died on August 27, 1963, hours before the March on Washington for Jobs and Freedom. With uncanny Mosaic resonance, Du Bois would not live to see the moral authority of the long civil rights movement crystallized in the witness of the world. A telegram bearing the message above was sent to the organizers' tent at the march, and Roy Wilkins, the head of the National Association for the Advancement of Colored People, begrudgingly announced Du Bois's death with a moment of silence before the assembled throng.[40] Later that afternoon, King delivered his famed "I Have a Dream" speech, which would become the exemplary text in the public political memory of the civil rights movement and the ever-generative source of romantic rhetoric of dreams and dreaming that critique struggles to resist or repurpose.

Taking this weighty inheritance seriously, a tragic vision of the civil rights movement might proceed by suggesting a different interpretive key, one found in King's largely ignored sermon, sometimes delivered as "Unfulfilled Hopes" but published in *Strength to Love* as "Shattered Dreams" in 1963, the same year as the march.[41] What does it mean that the author of "I Have a Dream" released, in the same year, a book of sermons that argues that "shattered dreams are a hallmark of our mortal life" and "one of the most agonizing problems within our human experiment"? What does it mean that King insists that "few, if any, of us live to see our fondest hopes fulfilled" and that we must "determine how to live in a world where our highest hopes are not satisfied"?[42]

Asking such questions leads us toward a King who, like David Scott, is concerned with "the temporality of the aftermaths of political catastrophe, the temporal disjunctures involved in living *on* in the wake of past political time, amid the ruins . . . as though time had found itself *betrayed* by history, or that history now confronted us as inauthentic time, the irreversibly lapsed time of our former anticipations of political futurity."[43] While many Americans can quote King's stanzas about holding hands across the color line, it is arguably more crucial to his political philosophic practice that his speech *begins*—as was his disposition—with the shattered dreams of emancipation and the bitter marking of 1963 as a time when, a century after the Emancipation Proclamation, "the Negro is still languished in the corners of American society and finds himself in exile in his own land."

In King's view, the question that is utterly fundamental to the philosophical problem space of the civil rights movement is whether this judgment of shattered dreams should authorize philosophies of bitterness and ressentiment, withdrawal and detachment from the world, or a "paralyzing determinism" or fatalism. Do these philosophies of pessimism deny fundamental truths about human freedom or the substance of our humanity? Do they treat particular narratives of the past as finished or closed, unable to be reinterpreted or invested with new meaning? Knowing and reflecting on the unfulfilled hopes of the past, how can we still go on in an affirmative and expectant stance toward the future?[44] Put most sharply, how are we preparing ourselves for political sacrifice and the kinds of shattering and unfulfillment that may follow from our action?

King's response, from which the title of this book is drawn, asks "our willing acceptance of unwanted and unfortunate circumstances even as we still cling to a radiant hope, [and] our acceptance of finite disappointment even as we adhere to infinite hope." This demand, I think, can be taken in two directions. The first is unapologetically metaphysical. If we die without receiving "the earthly promise" of our fulfilled hopes, King suggests that God "shall lead us down that mysterious road called death and at least to that indescribable cry he has prepared for us." "Our earthly life," he declares, "is a prelude to a glorious new awakening, and our death is an open door that leads us into life eternal."[45]

This is not the pageantry of progress familiar to those who repeat King's citation of Theodore Parker, with those well-known claims about the alleged moral arc of the universe bending toward justice. It is, nevertheless, a conception of politics based on faithful fidelity to Christian principles and the ecstatic anticipation of God's eschatological breaking of human history. As Terry Eagleton powerfully argues, the idea of the future "Kingdom of God" works in a surprising fashion "given that the most glaringly obvious fact about the Messiah is that he does not come." In the energetic space of this expected arrival, a prophetic and radical commitment among the faithful regularly seems to emerge, as some passionate group insists that it is only through their action, and their divine dissatisfaction with oppression, that the Lord can appear. The kind of cultural transfiguration and historical consciousness provoked by this commitment "runs against the grain of what one might call the central plot" of human oppression and misery to reveal "a coded pattern of hope."[46]

Even if this religious rhetoric manages to provide *some* motivation to struggle for justice, convincing us to risk our lives in effect by offering us something greater in our afterlives, some might reasonably worry that this mode of faith devalues *this life* and ultimately weakens our sense of what is at stake in the here and now, and truly worth sacrificing for.[47] In the imagined glow of heavenly repose, the grinding suffering and struggle of politics, even of the extraordinary sort, seems unlikely to elicit the kind of deep attachment and attention that seems crucial to sustained care for the moral and political world.

This an argument trenchantly pressed by Malcolm X, who mocked the afterlife concepts of heaven and hell in African American Christianity: "This blue-eyed devil has twisted his Christianity, to keep his foot on our backs . . . to keep our eyes fixed on the pie in the sky and heaven in the hereafter . . . while he enjoys his heaven right here . . . on this earth . . . in this life."[48] It is the nature of such metaphysical arguments, perhaps, that only the inaccessible experience of death itself could provide their fullest adjudication. Yet one can readily see the force of Malcolm's critique, even just where it concerns earthly questions of motivation and struggle. His words call us back to the value of our fragile life in common and the horror that we might lose the possibility of a freer, more fulfilling existence by indulging our longing for something too beautiful to be true. With Malcolm, who replaced this theology with the Nation of Islam's idiosyncratic gospel of black sovereignty and divine retribution, it is perhaps easiest to see the slippery slope from faith to fantasy, from ethical injunction to the evasion of loss.

Yet King's account of shattered dreams has another dimension with a different valence, whose import we should not overlook. This is not a religious faith that seeks to absolve us of loss or inure us to the crosses we must bear. It is instead a faith that is stridently political and strengthens one's resolve to struggle alongside others in the face of the threats of isolation, abandonment, and mounting oppression. It provides a measure of peace, in King's words, "amid the howl and rage of outer storm" and represents the essential political core of both early Christianity and the Christianity reinvented by enslaved African Americans, both forged in the crucible of oppression and bondage as "living examples of peace that passeth all understanding." In other words, they sustain the "hope of freedom" in a "seemingly hopeless situation."

At times, King's conception of hope seems to be based squarely on Christian metaphysics. In one sermon from *Strength to Love,* King gives a sweeping, metaphysical view of human history that permits romantic narration: "In a sense, the history of man is the story of the struggle between good and evil. All of the great religions have recognized a tension at the very core of the universe. . . . Each realizes that in the midst of the upward thrust of goodness there is the downward pull of evil. Christianity clearly affirms that in the long struggle between good and evil, good eventually will emerge as victor. Evil is ultimately doomed by the powerful, inexorable forces of good." In discussing the demise of the evil of colonialism, King argues that these "changes are not mere political and sociological shifts. They represent the passing of systems that were born in injustice, nurtured in inequality, and reared in exploitation. They represent the inevitable decay of any system based on principles that are not in harmony with the moral laws of the universe."[49] Or we might take "Remaining Awake through a Great Revolution," where King repeats his oft-cited claim that "the arc of a moral universe is long, but it bends toward justice."[50]

Almost immediately, however, we recognize a tension. While King speaks forthrightly of "a God of power" who can cut down "giants of injustice" wherever they emerge, he is always profoundly clear that it is human action that must bring this about. King retreats from the strongest formulations of inevitable progress or a theodicy that works entirely behind the backs of human beings. "Perhaps if God dealt with evil in the overbearing way that we wish," King argues, "he would defeat his ultimate purpose. . . . By endowing us with freedom, God relinquished a measure of his own sovereignty and imposed certain limitations upon himself. If his children are free, they must do his well by a voluntary choice. . . . If through sheer omnipotence God were to defeat his purpose, he would express weakness rather than power."[51]

Historical time, King tells us, is neutral on its own; the forces of good or evil may use it more effectively in any given moment. But, while for King, "human progress never rolls in on the wheels of inevitability," it is possible for it to come "through the tireless efforts and the persistent work of dedicated individuals who are willing to be co-workers with God."[52] In a sense, King inhabits the relationship to history and redemption that Terry Eagleton identifies as the radicalism of the New Testament. In absence of the Messiah's immediate return, Eagleton argues, Christians understand themselves as exercising, in the interregnum, "a small portion of his power on behalf of the oppressed, bringing the poor to power in the hope of hastening his advent."[53] In this way, a decisive measure of the task of redeeming history is placed in the hands of humanity.

Beneath the sweeping pronouncements concerning the moral arc, therefore, King has a remarkable insistence on contingency and freedom against fatalism and determinism. "Fatalism," King argues, "implies that everything is foreordained and inescapable. People who subscribe to this philosophy succumb to an absolute resignation to that which they consider to be their fate. . . . To sink in the quicksands of fatalism is both intellectually and psychologically stifling. Because freedom is a part of the essence of man, the fatalist, by denying freedom, becomes a puppet, not a person."[54]

To buttress this argument, King speaks of the unexpected political victories over feudalism, chattel slavery, colonialism, and, now, Jim Crow. "Today when progress has abruptly stalled and hope withers under bitter backlashing," King proclaims, "Negroes can remember days that were incomparably worse."[55] Eagleton puts the point more flippantly. Who, he asks, would like to return to an era of "witch burning, slave-owning, twelfth century sanitation, or pre-anesthetic surgery?"[56] Yet, King is not romantic about "Progress," with a capital *P,* as if all technological, moral, and political developments move hand in hand toward ethical perfection. "All progress is precarious," he notes, "and the solution of one problem brings us face to face with another problem."[57]

But the partial character of hard-won victories should not leave us in total despair. The crippling of forms of domination like colonialism and slavery, King reminds us in *Where Do We Go from Here?,* did not come in one fell swoop of immediacy. They were the hard work of oppressed peoples and their allies exercising their freedom to accumulate partial victories over time: "A final victory is an accumulation of many short-term encounters. To lightly dismiss a success because it does not usher in a complete order of justice is to fail to comprehend the process of achieving full victory. It underestimates the value of confrontation and dissolves the confidence born of a partial victory by which new efforts are powered." The worst thing, King warns, is to lose confidence in the face of obstacles simply because one imagines that progress is a straight line.[58]

The key is to keep struggles on behalf of justice and the heroic efforts to bring us closer to "the Kingdom of God" alive and honored in memory. Such a kingdom, King argues, "may remain not yet as a universal reality in history, in the present it may exist in such isolated forms as in judgment, in personal devotion, and in some group life."[59] In *The Trumpet of Conscience* King discusses the Underground Railroad, which, he admits, never saved many African Americans. Its greatest contribution was symbolic: "It symbolized hope when freedom was almost an impossible dream," reminding black people and their allies that "some small part of [freedom] is in our hands, as collective praxis and intergenerational treasure."[60] The mere act of being able to imagine an alternative future, as Eagleton puts the point, may distance and relativize the present, loosening its grip on us to the point where the future we are striving for becomes more feasible and hope more rational.[61]

In other words, hope, for King, is related to practices of critique and resistance in the past and present that reveal the contingency of various forms of social oppression and contribute to their defeat. As Eagleton helpfully puts the point, for Christians who evoke faith in the "Kingdom of God" or "beloved community" as an ultimate ideal, their hope may have a more profound relationship to critique and revolution than it appears at first glance. Such faith "divests all times to come of their false appearance as absolute futures," making enemies of "political complacency [as well] as metaphysical despair."[62]

Yet this raises an important political and ethical question. King describes his prophetic Christian faith and broader commitment to hope as a kind of "refusal to be stopped, 'courage to be,' [and] determination to go on 'in spite of.'" "The man who has made this discovery," King argues, "knows that no burden can overwhelm him and no wind of adversity can blow his hope away. He can stand anything that can happen to him."[63] But should we seek out this kind of endurance that can bear any burden in the realm of the politics of racial and economic justice? When King brings his metaphysical speculations down to Earth—or, more specifically, down to the bloody soil of the United States—is this faith or hope politically reasonable? Might it not be a kind of cruel optimism, attaching us further to an abusive social order that counts on, and puts to good use, the naive forbearance of its oppressed groups? When King declares that "we're going to win our freedom because both the sacred heritage of our nation and the eternal will of the almighty God are embodied in our echoing demands," how can we even affirm the bequest of such prophesies over five decades later in the polarized, decadent, and contentious country we have inherited?

I confess that my answer is, simply, another question: How can we *not?*

* * *

There are dark days ahead. There is a reason that even Elizabeth Alexander, once recruited to deliver the inaugural poem for the nation's first African American president, bestowed on the black youth who grew to adulthood during his ascendency the epithet of the Trayvon Generation rather than name them after the politician for whom she wrote "Praise Song for the Day."[64] We must come to terms with the fact that we are approaching the end of the time of romance with regard to civil rights memory.

This book deals principally with the consequences of this crisis of romantic narrative for liberals and the Left, and criticism of the nihilism and pessimism that ironic history elicits. In the long years of composing these arguments, however, I have come to think of these battles as preparation for a more epochal contest.

The genuflections that conservatives once routinely performed in honor of the romantic narrative of the civil rights movement have also become more embattled in recent years. Prominent right-wing intellectuals are venturing more sweeping, comprehensive criticism of the jurisprudential and legal canon that emerged from the movement. The journalist Christopher Caldwell, for example, begins a recent book acknowledging the fact of civil rights exemplarity, suggesting that "in and outside the government, [the civil rights movement] became a doctrinal institution, analogous to established churches in pre-democratic Europe." Yet he judges this a profound mistake at the heart of a roiling crisis of constitutional order, democratic life, and national identity—the source of a rival vision of America that must be defeated.[65] Other leading right-wing intellectuals and propagandists have sought to delegitimize the 1964 Civil Rights Act by connecting it genealogically to what they argue are the intolerable excesses of affirmative action and so-called wokeness.[66]

The US Supreme Court, the most antidemocratic branch of US government, has accelerated the attack on civil rights exemplarity in American jurisprudence. Under the leadership of Chief Justice John Roberts and his mantra that "the way to stop discriminating on the basis of race is to stop discriminating on the basis of race," the court has laid waste to constitutional precedents around affirmative action in college admissions, outlawed even voluntary school integration plans, and narrowed the disparate impact standards by which we judge racial domination in the absence of explicit, proven discriminatory intent.[67]

Most infamously, the Roberts court vivisected the long-besieged 1965 Voting Rights Act, amputating its enforcement mechanisms and making space for a flood of voter disenfranchisement efforts and gerrymandering.[68] The work of voter disenfranchisement, as Jacob Grumbach and Robert Mickey have painstakingly demonstrated, was central to the construction, during the Jim Crow era, of "authoritarian enclaves" in the South: state governments characterized by one-party dominion, concerted repression of competitors and dissenters, and elite expropriation of governmental power to drive down labor costs, control resources, and seek out other forms of profiteering.[69] In contemporary legislatures, especially across the Midwest and South, single-party-controlled legislatures are perfecting the art of racialized, partisan gerrymandering to exercise power with impunity, even going so far as to remove elected officials and prosecutors from the opposition party and threaten vote totals with invalidation.[70] The absurd proliferation of segregationist statutes, whose minute partitioning of the races across every cognizable sphere of human interaction seemed to know no end, was made possible by this unique structure of government and its near-total lack of actionable dissent or legislative friction.[71] All manner of injustice may be visited upon vulnerable and stigmatized populations that live under such regimes.

Political scientists are increasingly waking from their dogmatic slumber regarding both the limited extent of democratization in American history and the democratic "backsliding" that is the chief countermovement to the partial victories of the long civil rights struggle. Leading scholars have sounded the alarm about affective partisan polarization and the growing American tolerance for political violence, explicit repression, and rhetorical demonization.[72] In the public sphere, where participatory access to the communicative pathways that stitch together society in an aspirationally democratic society are a vital matter of legitimacy, well-funded and organized interests have taken advantage of weakened antimonopoly laws to buy up local media outlets, marginalize dissent, and impose their picture of the world.[73] This is to say nothing of high-profile propaganda efforts to demonize scholars and scholarship on questions of race and racial justice (as well as gender, colonialism, and sexuality). These have, in some cases successfully, prevailed on local and state officials to ban authors, books, and themes from libraries, school and university curricula, and other public spaces.[74] Surely, the book you hold in your hands may be among them. Even where these efforts stall out legally, their chilling effect on, and stigmatization of, scholars who do the sort of work I undertake here is a significant and unjust imposition on democratic life.

Attracting less attention but also severely consequential is the convergence between post-9/11 security state measures and more recent authoritarian tendencies that have dramatically curtailed the spaces of appearance and legal protections for public protest. Under the banner of spurious claims of security or public order, police departments and other institutions more routinely deny access to public or communal spaces, bring militarized resources to bear on protestors, and use techniques of surveillance and "postdisciplinary control to track and manage [known and suspected] protestors and other people."[75] State courts, moreover, have become bolder in their attempts to allow once-unthinkable penalties and punishments for protestors.[76] This drive back toward a less permissive environment for speech and dissent has been accompanied, despite its appeals to ostensible "security" concerns, by an extremely permissive legal regime around gun possession and "self-defense," including both open and concealed carrying of weapons.[77] This volatile mix has already led to violent, even fatal, clashes between protestors, counterdemonstrators, and self-styled vigilantes, some of whom have gone on to become conservative movement celebrities.[78]

In the face of such developments, political scientists' increasingly frantic paeans to multiracial democracy, welcome as they may be, have a paradoxical character. The very dangers they outline both dramatize and render daunting our democratic nonsovereignty—our entanglement, as King put it, "in a single garment of destiny."[79] The flourishing of democracy remains dependent on what many other individuals and organized groups do, and it cannot be willed otherwise. Yet, as these political scientists speak passionately to the urgent need to defend democracy against its surging opponents, they presume a natural sympathy among the historically disinherited that never quite faces up to the anxieties of entanglement from the vantage of the abyssal depths of skepticism circulating among the ghettoized poor and working class and often only given public voice in popular culture. The watchword of contemporary liberalism is that "democracy is at stake," but the rejoinder from the dark ghetto might well be that democracy has never existed, and nor should exhortations to its purported arrival elicit any sacrifice on my part.

This is why, I think, it is necessary to speak forthrightly and forcefully about the practice of tragic hope. The opposite of hope is self-determination and sovereignty. "What need is there for hope," Eagleton asks, "when one can be the author of oneself?. . . . To say 'I hope to do so' is to concede that there are limits to one's power. Hope and humility are in this sense bedfellows."[80] We must attend to our interdependency, finitude, and contingency with virtues of maturity and responsibility that acknowledges where we have long fallen short. Our reopening of the past to new descriptions and new judgments must be guided by a thread that shows, in fragmentary form if necessary, that such action and ideals have genuinely been possible and can be woven into a living tradition that can nourish our critical sensibilities with a revived historical imagination.

This stance of tragic hope does not, however, evade the depth of death and defeat but recovers it through a sense of meaningful possibility—or value—*and* contingency. It is the fact that *valuable* ideas, practices, and above all, *people* will meet defeat and loss in the pursuit of our aims that grounds a tragic vision. The pessimist, in the last instance, diminishes the significance of this judgment and the sense of value and worth that undergirds it with every scornful claim to "know" the impossibility of change and the inherent foolishness of the attempt. Tragedy makes no commensurate promise or guarantee of what will follow from our acts or in what manner, but this unpredictability lays bare our tremendous responsibilities to the past and the future for passing on what we want to survive and disavowing what we do not.

Most challenging of all, tragic hope takes seriously the possibility that we are not, yet, in the worst of all worlds, and it is part of our responsibility to prevent further catastrophe from coming into being. As Michael Dawson writes, a "great lesson of the civil rights movement is that ultimately progressive politics is about change—a deep commitment that the world *must* change, and that we must be the ones to change it." Courageously, he implores us to hold fast to this lesson, even while recognizing, in the wake of what I have called the collapse of authority, "that the fantasy of being reassured, of knowing fully toward what ends we march, is forever dead."[81]

Du Bois speaks, in "Of Beauty and Death," of a "great battle before the Lord." I know not what cosmic significance the crystallizing struggle with authoritarianism portends, but as we hurtle toward it, we cannot despair of the exemplarity of the civil rights movement simply because the romantic narrative no longer holds the quasi-religious authority it once did. Its collapse, despite all the disorientation it entails, is also an opportunity. It allows us, in Hannah Arendt's phrase, to think without banisters, revisiting the experiences and events of the past to remake our stories of peoplehood, retrain our judgment, and remake the concepts we use to think the world in new light. It allows us to move, as Kant might put it, from our increasingly exhausted "imitation" of the civil rights movement to an "emulation" of the movement in ways that will make us worthy of the profound moral and political inheritances that still lie within. In the spirit of Du Bois's "great battle," we might learn that this particular ending, these ruins of our present, can become the occasion for a new opening—a sublime summons to the ever-unfinished work of resisting the ugliness of authoritarianism, and defiance of the cruelty, corruption, and domination that continue to stake their shameful claims upon our world.

NOTES

Introduction

1. The term *touchstone* originally referred to a fine-grained dark stone used for the construction of monuments or as testing material to assay the purity or authenticity of precious metals brought into contact with it. See Louis E. Lord, "The Touchstone," *Classical Journal* 32, no. 7 (1937): 428–431; and *Oxford English Dictionary,* "touchstone," https://www.oed.com.
2. Alessandro Ferrara, *The Force of the Example: Explorations in the Paradigm of Judgment* (New York: Columbia University Press, 2008), ix–x, 1–3.
3. See the discussion of the lived experience of "facticity" in Jean-Paul Sartre, *Being and Nothingness: An Essay on Phenomenological Ontology* (New York: Philosophical Library, 1956), 481–552.
4. For a persuasive reconstruction of Emile Durkheim's concept of "social facts," see Paul Carls, "The Social Fact in Durkheim's Late Work: Structural Hermeneutics, Positive Sociology, and Causality," *Journal of Classical Sociology* 22, no. 2 (2022): 222–246.
5. Ferrara, *The Force of the Example,* ix–x, 2–3 (emphasis added).
6. For a compelling catalog of the ways that people argue through civil rights history in the present, see Jeanne Theoharis, *A More Beautiful and Terrible History: The Uses and Misuses of Civil Rights History* (Boston: Beacon, 2019), 3–30.
7. David Burner, *Making Peace with the 60s* (Princeton, NJ: Princeton University Press, 1996), 8.
8. On the morphology of moral actions, see Saba Mahmood, *Politics of Piety: The Islamist Revival and the Feminist Subject* (Princeton, NJ: Princeton University Press, 2011), 22–24.
9. Hajar Yazdiha, *The Struggle for the People's King: How Politics Transforms the Memory of the Civil Rights Movement* (Princeton, NJ: Princeton University Press, 2023).
10. "Video Recap: NAACP Tackles Black & Gay Tensions at National Convention," *Metro Weekly* (Washington, DC), August 2, 2011, https://www.metroweekly.com/news/last_word/2011/08/video-recap-naacp-tackles-blac.html. In May 2012 the NAACP itself followed the lead of its former chairman by issuing a national resolution endorsing the right of same-sex

couples to marry; see https://www.latimes.com/news/nation/nationnow/la-na-nn-naacp-gay-marriage-20120519,0,2217856.story.

11. On "self-reassurance," see Jurgen Habermas, *The New Conservatism: Cultural Criticism and the Historian's Debate,* ed. and trans. Shierry Weber Nicholson (Cambridge: Polity, 1994), 263.
12. Barack Obama, "Remarks by the President at the Martin Luther King, Jr. Memorial Dedication," October 11, 2016, https://obamawhitehouse.archives.gov/the-press-office/2011/10/16/remarks-president-martin-luther-king-Jr-memorial-dedication.
13. Cynthia Young, "Black Ops: Black Masculinity and the War on Terror," *American Quarterly* 66, no. 1 (2014): 35–67; Erica R. Edwards, *The Other Side of Terror: Black Women and the Culture of US Empire* (New York: New York University Press, 2021).
14. On how "the mythical space of normative theory" relies on epic narratives of history, including the civil rights movement, see Partha Chatterjee, *Lineages of Political Society: Studies in Postcolonial Democracy* (New York: Columbia University Press, 2011), 1.
15. Friedrich Nietzsche, "On the Uses and Disadvantages of History for Life," in *Untimely Meditations,* ed. Daniel Breazeale (Cambridge: Cambridge University Press, 1997), 67.
16. Luke 24:5.
17. Albena Azmanova, *The Scandal of Reason: A Critical Theory of Political Judgment* (New York: Columbia University Press, 2021), 12–13.
18. Nikolas Kompridis, "Introduction: Turning and Returning; The Aesthetic Turn in Political Thought," in *The Aesthetic Turn in Political Thought,* ed. Nikolas Kompridis (New York: Bloomsbury Academic, 2014), xvii, xix–xx. On commonsense empiricism, see Hayden White, *The Practical Past* (Evanston, IL: Northwestern University Press, 2014), 16.
19. Thomas McCarthy, *Race, Empire, and the Idea of Human Development* (Cambridge: Cambridge University Press, 2009), 40–41.
20. See, for example, Charles W. Mills, *Blackness Visible: Essays on Philosophy and Race* (Ithaca, NY: Cornell University Press, 2018); Lucius T. Outlaw Jr., *Critical Social Theory in the Interests of Black Folks* (Lanham, MD: Rowman and Littlefield, 2005).
21. Cornel West, *Prophesy Deliverance! An Afro-American Revolutionary Christianity* (Philadelphia: Westminster, 1982), 22.
22. W. E. B. Du Bois, *The Souls of Black Folk: Essays and Sketches* (Chicago: A. C. McClurg, 1903), 265.
23. Ludwig Wittgenstein, *On Certainty,* ed. G. E. M. Anscombe and G. H. von Wright, trans. G. E. M. Anscombe (New York: Basil Blackwell, 1969), para. 141–142.
24. Wendy Brown, *Politics out of History* (Princeton, NJ: Princeton University Press, 2001), 4–5.
25. Alexis de Tocqueville, *Democracy in America,* 7th ed., trans. Henry Reeve (New York: Edward Walker, 1847), 352.
26. Leigh Raiford and Renee C. Romano, "Introduction," in *The Civil Rights Movement in American Memory,* ed. Renee C. Romano and Leigh Raiford (Athens: University of Georgia Press, 2006), xii.

27. I adapt this formulation from Gerald L. Bruns, "What Is Tradition?," *New Literary History* 22, no. 1 (1991): 3.
28. See, for example, Robert J. Norrell, "One Thing We Did Right: Reflections on the Movement," in *New Directions in Civil Rights Studies,* ed. Armstead L. Robinson and Patricia Sullivan (Charlottesville: University Press of Virginia, 1991), 65–80; and Harold Cruse, *Plural but Equal: A Critical Study of Blacks and Minorities and America's Plural Society* (New York: William Morrow, 1987).
29. Adolph Reed, *The South: Jim Crow and Its Afterlives* (New York: Verso Books, 2022), 5–9.
30. On the civil rights movement and the sources of black disadvantage, see Glenn C. Loury, *One by One from the Inside Out: Essays and Reviews on Race and Responsibility in America* (New York: Free Press, 1995); Cornel West, "The Paradox of the Afro-American Rebellion," *Social Text* 9, no. 10 (1984): 44–58; William J. Wilson, *The Truly Disadvantaged: The Inner City, the Underclass, and Public Policy,* 2nd ed. (Chicago: University of Chicago Press, 2012); Lani Guinier and Gerald Torres, *The Miner's Canary: Enlisting Race, Resisting Power, Transforming Democracy* (Cambridge, MA: Harvard University Press, 2002); and Thomas Sowell, *Civil Rights: Rhetoric or Reality?* (New York: William Morrow, 1984). On questions of social and political "progress" and evaluative standards that draw on civil rights movement interpretations, see Orlando Patterson, *The Ordeal of Integration: Progress and Resentment in America's "Racial" Crisis* (Washington, DC: Civitas/Counterpoint, 1998); Tommie Shelby, *Dark Ghettos: Injustice, Dissent, and Reform* (Cambridge, MA: Belknap Press of Harvard University Press, 2016); Stephan Thernstrom and Abigail M. Thernstrom, *America in Black and White: One Nation, Indivisible* (New York: Simon and Schuster, 1997); Philip A. Klinkner and Rogers M. Smith, *The Unsteady March: The Rise and Decline of Racial Equality in America* (Chicago: University of Chicago Press, 1999); and Fredrick C. Harris, *The Price of the Ticket: Barack Obama and the Rise and Decline of Black Politics* (New York: Oxford University Press, 2012). For debates about protest, see DeRay McKesson, *On the Other Side of Freedom: The Case for Hope* (New York: Viking, 2018); Russell Rickford, "Black Lives Matter: Toward a Modern Practice of Mass Struggle," *New Labor Forum* 25, no. 1 (2016), 34–42; Adam Szetela, "Black Lives Matter at Five: Limits and Possibilities," *Ethnic and Racial Studies* 43, no. 8 (2020): 1358–1383; Barbara Ransby, *Making All Black Lives Matter: Reimagining Freedom in the Twenty-First Century* (Berkeley: University of California Press, 2018); and Alicia Garza, *The Purpose of Power: How We Come Together When We Fall Apart* (New York: One World, 2020).
31. Robert C. Smith, *We Have No Leaders: African Americans in the Post–Civil Rights Era* (Albany: State University of New York Press, 1996); Bill E. Lawson, ed., *The Underclass Question* (Philadelphia, PA: Temple University Press, 1992); Maulana Karenga, "The Crisis of Black Middle Class Leadership: A Critical Analysis." *Black Scholar* 13, no. 6 (1982): 16–32; Floyd B. McKissick Sr., "Black Leadership in America: The Legacy and the Current Crisis," *Howard Law Journal* 30, no. 4 (1987): 1083–1094; Cornel

West, "The Crisis of Black Leadership," in *Race Matters,* 25th anniversary ed. (Boston: Beacon, 2017), 33–46.

32. John Rawls, *Justice as Fairness: A Restatement,* ed. Erin Kelly (Cambridge, MA: Harvard University Press, 2001).
33. For the classic and compelling account of political peoplehood, see Rogers M. Smith, *Stories of Peoplehood: The Politics and Morals of Political Membership* (Cambridge: Cambridge University Press, 2003).
34. Bruns, "What Is Tradition?," 2.
35. See, for example, Martin Luther King Jr., *Where Do We Go from Here? Chaos or Community* (Boston: Beacon, 2010), much of which is written in response to the kinds of arguments advanced in Stokely Carmichael and Charles V. Hamilton, *Black Power: The Politics of Liberation* (New York: Vintage, 1992).
36. Herbert J. Storing, *Toward a More Perfect Union: Writings of Herbert J. Storing,* ed. Joseph M. Bessette (Washington, DC: AEI, 1995), 207.
37. Robert Gooding-Williams, "History of African American Political Thought and Antiracist Critical Theory," in *The Oxford Handbook of Philosophy and Race,* ed. Naomi Zack (New York: Oxford University Press, 2016), 235–246.
38. Bruns, "What Is Tradition?," 8.
39. Rahel Jaeggi, *Critique of Forms of Life,* trans. Ciaran Cronin (Cambridge, MA: Belknap Press of Harvard University Press, 2018).
40. Bruns, "What Is Tradition?," 9.
41. I borrow the phrase "the Negro in vogue" from the tragicomic account of the Harlem Renaissance in Langston Hughes, *The Big Sea: An Autobiography* (New York: Hill and Wang, 1940), 223.
42. On Afro-modern political thought as a genre of political philosophy preoccupied with these themes, see Robert Gooding-Williams, *In the Shadow of Du Bois: Afro-Modern Political Thought in America* (Cambridge, MA: Harvard University Press, 2009), 3.
43. The most important historicization of the restrictive character of postwar political philosophy is arguably Katrina Forrester, *In the Shadow of Justice: Postwar Liberalism and the Remaking of Political Philosophy* (Princeton, NJ: Princeton University Press, 2019). See also Katrina Forrester, "Liberalism and Social Theory After John Rawls," *Analyse und Kritik* 44, no. 1 (2022): 1–22.
44. Alisdair MacIntyre, "Epistemological Crises, Dramatic Narrative and the Philosophy of Science," *Monist* 60, no. 4 (1977): 453–472.
45. Nikolas Kompridis, *Critique and Disclosure: Critical Theory Between Past and Future* (Cambridge, MA: MIT Press, 2006), 15–16.
46. Gooding-Williams, *In the Shadow of Du Bois.* The idea of "Jim Crow North" has been powerfully recovered by historians; for example, Brian Purnell and Jeanne Theoharis, "Introduction: Histories of Racism, Seen and Unseen: How and Why to Think About the Jim Crow North," in *The Strange Careers of the Jim Crow North: Segregation and Struggle outside of the South,* ed. Brian Purnell and Jeanne Theoharis with Komozi Woodard (New York: New York University Press, 2019), 9, argue that

"using a Jim Crow frame" to describe residential and school segregation, economic discrimination, and discrimination in public accommodations "reveals how northern racism worked *as a racial system* with its own ideologies, rules, cultures, and practices, refuting the idea that racism outside the South was haphazard, transplanted, or resulting from private prejudices."

47. Eddie S. Glaude, *In a Shade of Blue: Pragmatism and the Politics of Black America* (Chicago: University of Chicago Press, 2007), 207.
48. Glaude, *In a Shade of Blue,* 132.
49. Mark Anthony Neal, *Soul Babies: Black Popular Culture and the Post-Soul Aesthetic* (New York: Routledge, 2002), 3.
50. Nelson George, "Buppies, B-Boys, Baps, and Bobos," *Village Voice,* March 17, 1992, https://www.villagevoice.com/buppies-b-boys-baps-bohos/.
51. Paul C. Taylor, "Taking Postracialism Seriously: From Movement Mythology to Racial Formation," *Du Bois Review: Social Science Research on Race* 11, no. 1 (2014): 18. Another way of registering this coincidence is to insist that if so-called postmodernism represents an incredulity toward grand narrative or the crisis of paradigms that once claimed exclusivity of knowledge and insight, central to any such account should be the crisis of authority befalling the white supremacist ideologies and metanarratives forged in the creation of the modern world.
52. Taylor, "Taking Postracialism Seriously," 18.
53. On the role of the church, see West, *Prophesy Deliverance!;* Cornel West, *Democracy Matters: Winning the Fight Against Imperialism* (New York: Penguin, 2004), 145–173; R. Drew Smith, ed., *Long March Ahead: African American Churches and Public Policy in Post–Civil Rights America* (Durham, NC: Duke University Press, 2004); and Eva T. Thorne and Eugene F. Rivers III, "Beyond the Civil Rights Industry," *Boston Review,* April–May 2001, https://www.bostonreview.net. On racial solidarity, see Tommie Shelby, *We Who Are Dark: The Philosophical Foundations of Black Solidarity* (Cambridge, MA: Harvard University Press, 2007); Eddie Glaude Jr., *In a Shade of Blue: Pragmatism and the Politics of Black America* (Chicago: University of Chicago Press, 2007); Andrew Valls, "A Liberal Defense of Black Nationalism," *American Political Science Review* 104, no. 3 (2010): 467–481; and Lawrence Blum, "Three Kinds of Race-Related Solidarity," *Journal of Social Philosophy* 38, no. 1 (2007): 53–72. On the "ordeal" of integration, see Patterson, *The Ordeal of Integration;* and Elizabeth Anderson, *The Imperative of Integration* (Princeton, NJ: Princeton University Press, 2010). On patriarchy and political leadership, see Cathy Cohen, *The Boundaries of Blackness: AIDS and the Breakdown of Black Politics* (Chicago: University of Chicago Press, 1999); and E. Frances White, *Dark Continent of Our Bodies: Black Feminism and the Politics of Respectability* (Philadelphia: Temple University Press, 2001). On the role of protest and formal politics, see Adolph Reed Jr., *Stirrings in the Jug: Black Politics in the Post-Segregation Era* (Minneapolis: University of Minnesota Press, 1999); Cedric Johnson, *Revolutionaries to Race Leaders: Black Power and the Making of African American Politics* (Minneapolis:

University of Minnesota Press, 2007); and Michael C. Dawson, *Not in Our Lifetimes: The Future of Black Politics* (Chicago: University of Chicago Press, 2011).

54. Eric Holder, quoted in James Forman, *Locking Up Our Own: Crime and Punishment in Black America* (New York: Farrar, Straus and Giroux, 2017), 195.
55. Forman, *Locking Up Our Own,* 195.
56. *The Boondocks,* season 1, episode 9, "Return of the King," written by Aaron McGruder and Yamara Taylor, directed by Kalvin Lee, aired January 15, 2006, on the Cartoon Network.
57. Forrester, *In the Shadow of Justice.*
58. Charles W. Mills, *Black Rights/White Wrongs: The Critique of Racial Liberalism* (New York: Oxford University Press, 2017), 139.
59. Charles W. Mills, "Rawls on Race/Race in Rawls," *Southern Journal of Philosophy* 47, no. S1 (2009): 161.
60. Toni Morrison, *Playing in the Dark: Whiteness and the Literary Imagination* (Cambridge MA: Harvard University Press, 1992), 5, 15.
61. Morrison, *Playing in the Dark,* 64–65.
62. Indeed, Morrison suggests this more expansive interpretation in an earlier version of the essay, delivered as the William H. Massey lectures. There she answers the above query:

    > In what public discourse can the reference to black people be said not to exist? It is there in every moment of the nation's mightiest struggles. The presence of black people not only lies behind the framing of the Constitution, it is also in the battle over enfranchising unpropertied citizens, women, and the illiterate. In the construction of a free and public school system, in the balancing of representation in legislative bodies, in jurisprudence and the legal definitions of justice. In theological discourse, in the memoranda of banking houses, in the concept of manifest destiny and the narrative that accompanies the initiation of every immigrant into the community of American citizenship.

    Toni Morrison, "Black Matter(s)," in *The Source of Self-Regard: Selected Essays, Speeches, and Meditations* (New York: Borzoi Books, 2019), 159.
63. John Rawls, *A Theory of Justice,* rev. ed. (Cambridge, MA: Belknap Press of Harvard University Press, 1999), 320n19.
64. On King's political philosophy, see Tommie Shelby and Brandon M. Terry, eds., *To Shape a New World: Essays on the Political Philosophy of Martin Luther King, Jr.* (Cambridge, MA: Belknap Press of Harvard University Press, 2018).
65. Bernard R. Boxill, *Blacks and Social Justice,* rev. ed. (Lanham, MD: Rowman and Littlefield, 1992), 205–225; David Lyons, "Moral Judgment, Historical Reality, and Civil Disobedience," *Philosophy and Public Affairs* 27, no. 1 (1998): 31–49.
66. Erin Pineda, "Civil Disobedience and Punishment: (Mis)Reading Justification and Strategy from SNCC to Snowden," *History of the Present* 5, no. 1 (2015): 1–30; Karuna Mantena, "The Power of Nonviolence," Aeon, 2016, https://aeon.co; Guy Aitchison, "Domination and Disobedience: Protest,

Coercion and the Limits of an Appeal to Justice," *Perspectives on Politics* 16, no. 3 (2018): 666–679; Candice Delmas, *A Duty to Resist: When Disobedience Should Be Uncivil* (New York: Oxford University Press, 2018); Alexander Livingston, "Power for the Powerless: Martin Luther King Jr.'s Late Theory of Civil Disobedience," *Journal of Politics* 82, no. 2 (2020): 700–713; Melissa Schwartzberg, ed., *Protest and Dissent* (New York: New York University Press, 2020); Alex Gourevitch, "Strikes, Civil Rights, and Radical Disobedience: From King to Debs and Back," *Contemporary Political Theory* 22, no. 2 (2023): 143–164.

67. John Rawls, *Political Liberalism,* expanded ed. (New York: Columbia University Press, 2005), 213. On early formulations of "public speech" and the "duty to civility," see Rawls, *A Theory of Justice,* 312, 21.
68. Rawls, *Political Liberalism,* 247n36.
69. Rawls, *Political Liberalism,* 250–251.
70. Michael J. Sandel, review of *Political Liberalism,* by John Rawls, *Harvard Law Review* 107, no. 7 (1994): 1765–1794.
71. John Rawls, "The Idea of Public Reason: Postscript," in *Deliberative Democracy: Essays on Reason and Politics,* ed. James Bohman and William Rehg (Cambridge, MA: MIT Press, 1997), 136.
72. Rawls, *Political Liberalism,* 484. It is a great loss that when portions of Rawls's library were collected by the Harvard University Archives, the curation focused almost exclusively on books of philosophy and economics rather than Rawls's well-known interest in history. The philosopher Samuel Freeman notes that "in his later years Rawls was especially interested in history, particularly books on World War II and on Abraham Lincoln, whom he especially admired as a statesman who did not compromise with evil." Scholars' lack of access to these texts will surely bias the kind of intellectual history scholarship conducted on Rawls going forward. See Samuel Freeman, *Rawls* (New York: Routledge, 2007), 5.
73. See Delmas, *A Duty to Resist;* Martha Craven Nussbaum, *Anger and Forgiveness: Resentment, Generosity, Justice* (New York: Oxford University Press, 2016); Myisha V. Cherry, "Forgiveness, Exemplars, and the Oppressed," in *The Moral Psychology of Forgiveness,* ed. Kathryn J. Norlock (New York: Routledge, 2017), 55–72; Amia Srinivasan, "The Aptness of Anger," *Journal of Political Philosophy* 26, no. 2 (2018): 123–144; Chris Armstrong, "Collapsing Categories: Fraser on Economy, Culture and Justice," *Philosophy and Social Criticism* 34, no. 4 (2008): 409–425; Charles Taylor, *Multiculturalism: Examining the Politics of Recognition,* ed. Amy Gutmann (Princeton, NJ: Princeton University Press, 1994); Kevin Olson, ed., *Adding Insult to Injury: Nancy Fraser Debates Her Critics* (New York: Verso Books, 2008); Michael C. Dawson, *Blacks in and out of the Left* (Cambridge, MA: Harvard University Press, 2013); Shelby, *Dark Ghettos;* Bernard E. Harcourt, *Critique and Praxis: A Radical Critical Philosophy of Illusions, Values, and Action* (New York: Columbia University Press, 2020); Aziz Rana, *The Two Faces of American Freedom* (Cambridge, MA: Harvard University Press, 2010); Stephen Skowronek, Stephen M. Engel, and Bruce A. Ackerman, *The Progressives' Century:*

Political Reform, Constitutional Government, and the Modern American State (New Haven, CT: Yale University Press, 2016); Bruce A. Ackerman, *We the People,* vol. 3, *The Civil Rights Revolution* (Cambridge, MA: Belknap Press of Harvard University Press, 2014); and Christopher Caldwell, *The Age of Entitlement: America Since the Sixties* (New York: Simon and Schuster, 2020).

74. Michèle Lowrie and Susanne Lüdemann, "Introduction," in *Exemplarity and Singularity: Thinking Through Particulars in Philosophy, Literature, and Law,* ed. Michèle Lowrie and Susanne Lüdemann (New York: Routledge, 2015), 2.
75. Lowrie and Lüdemann, "Introduction," 1–3.
76. Alexander Gelley, "Introduction," in *Unruly Examples: On the Rhetoric of Exemplarity,* ed. Alexander Gelley (Stanford, CA: Stanford University Press, 1995), 2.
77. Hannah Arendt, *Lectures on Kant's Political Philosophy* (Chicago: University of Chicago Press, 1982), 85.
78. McCarthy, *Race, Empire, and the Idea of Human Development,* 40.
79. Irene Harvey, "Exemplarity and the Origins of Legislation," in Gelley, *Unruly Examples,* 225.
80. On history and republicanism, see Ferrara, *The Force of the Example,* 100. On history and realism, see Raymond Geuss, *History and Illusion in Politics* (New York: Cambridge University Press, 2001).
81. For related views of African American philosophy that pursue hermeneutics with a critical intent and are concerned with how certain cultural and narrative conditions of self-interpretation can sustain the systematic distortions of racial ideology and domination, see Outlaw, *Critical Social Theory;* and Lorenzo C. Simpson, *Hermeneutics as Critique: Science, Politics, Race, and Culture* (New York: Columbia University Press, 2021).
82. The decision to secure the defeat of imperial Japan through the use of two atomic bombs on civilian populations and the ethical question of war crimes it raises casts such a shadow over the war most routinely cited as a "just" one that the Pacific theater is often diminished in such accounts. See Lesley M. M. Blume, *Fallout: The Hiroshima Cover-Up and the Reporter Who Revealed It to the World* (New York: Simon and Schuster, 2021); John Rawls, "Reflections on Hiroshima: 50 Years After Hiroshima," *Dissent,* Summer 1995, https://www.dissentmagazine.org; and Susan Neiman, "Forgetting Hiroshima, Remembering Auschwitz: Tales of Two Exhibits," *Thesis Eleven* 129, no. 1 (2015): 7–26. The negative exemplarity of Nazism as the great world-historical evil of the twentieth century may now be weakening. The far-right Alternative for Germany (AfD) party and its prominent supporters, including billionaire industrialist Elon Musk, have recently gained popularity attacking what they call the German "cult of guilt" around the Holocaust. At a recent AfD rally, Musk proclaimed that there is "frankly too much of a focus on past guilt and we need to move beyond that." It is an argument he has repeated with reference to American slavery and racial domination. See Rachel Treisman, "Elon Musk Faces Criticism for Encouraging Germans to Move Beyond 'Past Guilt,'" NPR,

January 27, 2025, https://www.npr.org/2025/01/27/nx-s1-5276084/elon-musk-german-far-right-afd-holocaust; and Ruth Umoh, "Elon Musk Says Society Must Move On from the 'Constant Subject' of Racism: 'We Are All Descended from Slaves,'" *Fortune,* March 3, 2024, https://fortune.com/2024/03/20/elon-musk-don-lemon-dei-diversity-slavery-tesla/. See also Lukas Hermsmeier, "Germany's Post-Nazi Taboo Against the Far Right Has Been Shattered," *New York Times,* February 7, 2020.

83. On race and polarization, see Michael Tesler and David O. Sears, *Obama's Race: The 2008 Election and the Dream of a Post-Racial America* (Chicago: University of Chicago Press, 2010); "A 90% Favorability Rating for Martin Luther King Jr. on His 90th Birthday," Ipsos, January 18, 2019, https://www.ipsos.com/en-us/news-polls/90-favorability-rating-martin-luther-king-jr-2019-01-18; and Frank Newport, "Mother Teresa Voted by American People as Most Admired Person of the Century," Gallup, December 31, 1999, https://news.gallup.com/poll/3367/mother-teresa-voted-american-people-most-admired-person-century.aspx.

84. Leigh Coleman, "Mississippi Lawmakers Approve Civil Rights Museum," Reuters, April 5, 2011, https://www.reuters.com; Peter Guinta, "Civil Rights Museum Proposed for Lincolnville," *St. Augustine (FL) Record,* June 12, 2011; Mathew Shaer, "In America's Deep South, a Front Seat for Freedom Riders," *Christian Science Monitor,* July 13, 2011; Owen J. Dwyer and Derek H. Alderman, *Civil Rights Memorials and the Geography of Memory* (Chicago: Center for American Places at Columbia College Chicago, 2008), 10.

85. Dwyer and Alderman, *Civil Rights Memorials,* 13.

86. George W. Bush, "Remarks at Ceremonial Groundbreaking of the Martin Luther King Jr. National Memorial," November 13, 2006, https://georgewbush-whitehouse.archives.gov.

87. George W. Bush, "Address to the Annual NAACP Convention," July 20, 2006, https://georgewbush-whitehouse.archives.gov.

88. Dwyer and Alderman, *Civil Rights Memorials,* 13. This matter-of-factness embedded in the built landscape is, however, a complicated affair (as racial politics in the United States tend to be). On the one hand, the proliferation of public works named after King and, to a lesser extent, other notable African Americans, represents the recognition of (or at least concession to) their individual importance in local or national history. Moreover, underwriting the insistence on the significance of commemorating these individuals, there is often a belief, made much more explicit during peak moments of black cultural nationalist and multiculturalist activism, that such naming rituals constitute a broader form of "recognition," understood here as the state or political community's positive valuation of a particular group's identity, culture, or membership in the polity. Behind the advocacy of these naming practices is often the claim that the "power of the norm" that accrues to the objects bestowed with iconic names is a power that serves a positively valent and inclusive social function in its symbolic interpretation of the significance of the past. On the other hand, despite the aspirations of activists, bureaucrats, and politicians in undertaking these

rituals of naming, the prevailing racial stigmatization of the black poor and the stigmatization of the predominantly black neighborhoods where these particular public works tend to be located, often indelibly shapes their public perception and representation. Paradoxically, these symbolic cultural and political projects, whose aims were originally the positive revaluation of black achievement, identity, and/or culture, are quite easily appropriated for those social and economic practices (e.g., real estate lending) and habituated psychological beliefs (e.g., fear of being victimized by violent crime) invested in the construction and reification of hierarchical or antagonistic symbolic racial and ethnic group boundaries. We can recognize how the names attached to certain streets or parks function as heuristics that reflexively identify these spaces as locations to avoid (or worse, as spaces to seek out in search of "vice" and "deviance"). In one illustrative moment of popular culture performance, the comedian Chris Rock, in his notoriously controversial stand-up routine "Niggas vs. Black People," joked, "You know what's so sad, man? You know what's wild? Martin Luther King stood for nonviolence. . . . Now what's Martin Luther King? A street. And I don't give a f——where you are in America, if you on Martin Luther King Boulevard, there's some violence going down! It ain't the safest place to be! You can't call nobody and tell them you're lost on MLK. [*Imitating a telephone caller:*] 'I'm lost, I'm on Martin Luther King . . .' [*The other person responds:*] 'Run! Run! Run!'" Rock's comedic corpus is long on acerbic wit and short on genuine lament, so when he offers up the uncharacteristic "You know what's so sad, man?" before the joke, he reveals the duality at the core of contention above: even the most pernicious "racial-cum-spatial" stigma has not prevented civil rights movement iconography from ascending to the level of orthodox exemplarity in much of American public life. Chris Rock, "Niggas vs. Black People," track 12 on *Roll with the New,* DreamWorks, 1997.

89. Theoharis, *A More Beautiful and Terrible History,* 2.

90. Julian Bond, quoted in Jeanne Theoharis, "Introduction: What Julian Bond Taught Me," in *Julian Bond's Time to Teach: A History of the Southern Civil Rights Movement* (Boston: Beacon, 2021), xiv.

91. Bruce Ackerman and Jennifer Nou, "Canonizing the Civil Rights Revolution: The People and the Poll Tax," *Northwestern Law Review* 103 (2009): 64, note that in the Supreme Court confirmation hearings of conservative appointees Chief Justice John Roberts and Justice Samuel Alito Jr., the relatively new idea of "superprecedents"—Supreme Court decisions that serve "as fixed parts of the constitutional canon . . . [and] fundamental points of reference for further legal development"—emerged as a central theme of debate. While the conservative judges avoided bestowing such status on the abortion rights decision in *Roe v. Wade,* both agreed that the exemplary superprecedent par excellence was the decision outlawing de jure school segregation in the *Brown* decision. They take this superprecedent theme as a touchstone to argue that other civil rights era laws—namely, the poll tax amendment—should be accorded a similarly exemplary status in American legal and political practice.

92. Hassan Kwame Jeffries, *Understanding and Teaching the Civil Rights Movement* (Madison: University of Wisconsin Press, 2019), 5. See also Orlando Patterson, "Equality," *Democracy* 11 (2009): 9.
93. Raiford and Romano, "Introduction," xii.
94. Pero Gaglo Dagbovie, *Reclaiming the Black Past: The Use and Misuse of African American History in the Twenty-First Century* (New York: Verso Books, 2018).
95. Rogers M. Smith, *Stories of Peoplehood: The Politics and Morals of Political Membership* (Cambridge: Cambridge University Press, 2003).
96. See R. A. R. Edwards, "Deaf Rights, Civil Rights: The Gallaudet 'Deaf President Now' Strike and Historical Memory of the Civil Rights Movement," in Raiford and Romano, *The Civil Rights Movement in American Memory,* 317–345; and John Skretny, *The Minority Rights Revolution* (Cambridge, MA: Belknap Press of Harvard University Press, 2002).
97. Barack Obama, "Read the Full Transcript of Obama's Eulogy for John Lewis," *New York Times,* July 30, 2020.
98. Obama, "Remarks by the President at the Martin Luther King Jr. Memorial Dedication."
99. Andrew Goldman, "Cornel West Flunks the President," *New York Times Magazine,* July 22, 2011. West refers here to Obama's controversial drone warfare program. The political scientist Micah Zenko, "Obama's Final Drone Strike Data," Council on Foreign Relations, January 20, 2017, https://www.cfr.org, estimates that 3,797 people were killed in 542 drone strikes authorized by President Obama, primarily in Pakistan, Somalia, and Yemen. The number of genuine civilian casualties can never be known because the president chose to presume that all military-age males in a strike zone are enemy combatants without countervailing intelligence evidence that proves (posthumously) otherwise. On casualty policy, see Jo Becker and Scott Shane, "Secret 'Kill List' Proves a Test of Obama's Principles and Will," *New York Times,* May 29, 2012.
100. Touré, "Viewpoint: What's Behind Cornel West's Attacks on Obama," *Time,* https://ideas.time.com.
101. Barack Obama, "Remarks by the President at the Acceptance of the Nobel Peace Prize," 2009, https://obamawhitehouse.archives.gov.
102. Lionel K. McPherson, "The Costs of Violence: Militarism, Geopolitics, and Accountability," in Shelby and Terry, *To Shape a New World,* 253–268.
103. Adam Serwer, "All the President's Frenemies," *Prospect,* https://prospect.org.
104. See the interviews in Carol Swain and Russ Nieli, eds., *Contemporary Voices of White Nationalism in America* (Cambridge: Cambridge University Press, 2003), esp. 108–109 and 126–127 (Reno Wolfe), 146–147 (Michael Levin), 172 (David Duke), and 239–241 (Matthew Hale). Even here, Reno Wolfe of the National Association for the Advancement of White People concedes that he thinks Martin Luther King "meant well" (126).
105. Desmond S. King and Rogers M. Smith, *A House Divided: Race and Politics in Obama's America* (Princeton, NJ: Princeton University Press, 2011), 9.
106. Ralph Reed, the executive director of the Christian Coalition, was perhaps the most influential proponent of this view, frequently praising and quoting

King and analogizing the condition of blacks under Jim Crow to contemporary evangelical Christians in such essays as "To the Back of the Bus" and "The New Amos and Andy" contained in his best-selling and aptly titled book *Politically Incorrect: The Emerging Faith Factor in American Politics* (Dallas: Word, 1994). See also David John Marley, "Riding in the Back of the Bus: The Christian Right's Adoption of Civil Rights Movement Rhetoric," in Raiford and Romano, *The Civil Rights Movement in American Memory*, 349, 352.

107. Beck's inflammatory, conspiratorial, and paranoid statements could fill their own book, but worth mentioning is his claim that the Affordable Care Act for health care reform was actually a stealth vehicle for reparations for slavery. See Glenn Beck, "Is Massive Health Care Plan Reparations?," GlennBeck.com, July 23, 2009, https://www.glennbeck.com; and "Glenn Beck: Obama Is a Racist," CBS News, July 29, 2009, https://www.cbsnews.com.

108. Donald J. Trump, "The Inaugural Address," January 20, 2025, The White House, https://https://www.whitehouse.gov/remarks/2025/01/the-inaugural-address/. Trump's support among Hispanic voters far exceeded his support among African Americans, although he did experience growing vote shares among younger black men, and especially those without a college education. These reflect broader dynamics of educational and gender polarization across the Americas and Europe; see Ezra Klein with David Shor, "Democrats Need to Face Why Trump Won," *New York Times,* March 18, 2025.

109. Jacqueline Dowd Hall, "The Long Civil Rights Movement and the Political Uses of the Past," *Journal of American History* 91, no. 4 (2005): 1235.

110. Nikhil Pal Singh, *Black Is a Country: The Unfinished Struggle for Race and Democracy* (Cambridge, MA: Harvard University Press, 2003), 6.

111. This account is based on Tommie Shelby, "Ideology, Racism, and Critical Social Theory," *Philosophical Forum* 34, no. 2 (2003): 153–188; and Shelby, *Dark Ghettos,* 22–24.

112. On the idea of an epistemic critique of ideology, see Sally Haslanger, "Racism, Ideology, and Social Movements," *Res Philosophica* 94, no. 1 (2017): 1–22.

113. This conception of "orientation" is influenced by Rawls, *Lectures on the History of Political Philosophy,* 10. The problem of *misorientation* will be discussed in greater detail in Chapter 1.

114. Jimmy Carter, "Atlanta, Georgia, Remarks Accepting the Martin Luther King, Jr. Nonviolent Peace Prize," January 14, 1979, American Presidency Project, https://www.presidency.ucsb.edu.

115. Carter, "Atlanta, Georgia, Remarks."

116. Ronald Reagan, "Remarks on Signing the Bill Making Birthday of Martin Luther King, Jr., a National Holiday," November 2, 1983, American Presidency Project, https://www.presidency.ucsb.edu.

117. Theoharis, *A More Beautiful and Terrible History,* xxi.

118. Lawrence D. Bobo, James R. Kluegel, and Ryan A. Smith, "Laissez-Faire Racism: The Crystallization of a Kinder, Gentler, Antiblack Ideology," in *Racial Attitudes in the 1990s: Continuity and Change,* ed. Jack Martin and Steven A. Tuch (Westport, CT: Praeger, 1997), 15–42.

119. Eduardo Bonilla-Silva, *Racism Without Racists: Color-Blind Racism and the Persistence of Racial Inequality in the United States* (Lanham, MD: Rowman and Littlefield, 2006).

120. It is important to note that, for Harlan, color-blind constitutionalism is perfectly compatible with white domination through other bases of social and political power. In this sense, laissez-faire racism, as Bobo et. al., "Laissez-Faire Racism," have described it, finds in Harlan an important progenitor. As Harlan writes in his dissent in Plessy v. Ferguson, 163 US 537 (1896),

> The white race deems itself to be the dominant race in this country. And so it is, in prestige, in achievements, in education, in wealth, and in power. So, I doubt not, it will continue to be for all time, if it remains true to its great heritage and holds fast to the principles of constitutional liberty. But in the view of the Constitution, in the eye of the law, there is in this country no superior, dominant, ruling class of citizens. There is no caste here. Our Constitution is color-blind and neither knows nor tolerates classes among citizens. In respect of civil rights, all citizens are equal before the law. The humblest is the peer of the most powerful. The law regards man as man and takes no account of his surroundings or of his color when his civil rights as guaranteed by the supreme law of the land are involved. . . . The arbitrary separation of citizens, on the basis of race, while they are on a public highway, is a badge of servitude wholly inconsistent with the civil freedom and the equality before the law established by the Constitution. It cannot be justified on any legal grounds.

121. Martin Luther King Jr., "I Have a Dream," in *A Testament of Hope,* ed. James Washington (San Francisco: HarperCollins, 1986).

122. Ronald Sundstrom, "The Prophetic Tension Between Race Consciousness and the Ideal of Color-Blindness," in Shelby and Terry, *To Shape a New World,* 127–145.

123. Hall, "The Long Civil Rights Movement," 1262.

124. See, for example, Juliet Hooker, *Black Grief/White Grievance: The Politics of Loss* (Princeton, NJ: Princeton University Press, 2022), 83–126.

125. The idea of a "cruel" affective attachment comes from Lauren Berlant, *Cruel Optimism* (Durham, NC: Duke University Press, 2011). Berlant describes cruel optimism as "a relation of attachment to compromised conditions of possibility whose realization is discovered either to be impossible, sheer fantasy, or *too* possible, and toxic. What's cruel about these attachments, and not merely inconvenient or tragic, is that the subjects who have *x* in their lives might not well endure the loss of their object/scene of desire, even though its presence threatens their well-being" (25).

126. Jaeggi, *Critique of Forms of Life.*

127. On the history of the Ferguson protests, see Wesley Lowery, *They Can't Kill Us All: Ferguson, Baltimore, and a New Era in America's Racial Justice Movement* (New York: Little, Brown, 2016); McKesson, *On the Other Side of Freedom;* and Barbara Ransby, *Making All Black Lives Matter: Reimagining Freedom in the 21st Century* (Berkeley: University of California Press, 2018). On the near-colonial character of Ferguson's exploit-

ative police department, see US Department of Justice, Civil Rights Department, *Investigation of the Ferguson Police Department* (Washington, DC: US Department of Justice, 2015); and Thomas Harvey, John McAnnar, Michael-John Voss, Megan Conn, Sean Janda, and Sophia Keskey, "ArchCity Defenders: Municipal Court White Paper" (ArchCity Defenders, St. Louis, November 23, 2014).

128. Glenn Loury, "Ferguson Won't Change Anything. What Will?," *Boston Review,* January 2, 2015, https://www.bostonreview.net/forum/glenn-loury-ferguson-wont-change-anything-what-will/.
129. Opal Tometi, Alicia Garza, and Patrisse Cullors-Brignac, "Celebrating MLK Day: Reclaiming Our Movement Legacy," *Huffington Post,* March 20, 2015, https://www.huffingtonpost.com.
130. Rahiel Tesfamariam, "How the Modern Civil Rights Struggle Lost Its Religion," *Washington Post,* September 19, 2015. On *ratchet* and its migration from southern black vernacular, see John Ortved, "Ratchet: The Rap Insult That Became a Compliment," The Cut, https://www.thecut.com/2013/04/ratchet-the-rap-insult-that-became-a-compliment.html.
131. Tef Poe, "Ferguson Represents the Shot Heard Around the World . . . ," NewsOne, August 9, 2015, https://newsone.com.
132. Tef Poe, quoted on *Melissa Harris-Perry,* MSNBC, August 30, 2015, https://www.msnbc.com.
133. King, "I Have a Dream." See also Tommie Shelby, "Prisons of the Forgotten," in Shelby and Terry, *To Shape a New World,* 187–204.
134. Martin Luther King Jr., *The Trumpet of Conscience* (Boston: Beacon, 2010), 46–47.
135. *Final Plans for the March on Washington for Jobs and Freedom,* August 28, 1963, Civil Rights Movement Archive, https://www.crmvet.org.
136. Theoharis, *A More Beautiful and Terrible History,* 2.
137. Regarding long civil rights movement historians, I am referring primarily to Glenda Gilmore, *Defying Dixie: The Radical Roots of Civil Rights* (New York: W. W. Norton, 2008); Thomas Sugrue, *Sweet Land of Liberty: The Forgotten Struggle for Civil Rights in the North* (New York: Random House, 2009); Hall, "The Long Civil Rights Movement"; Singh, *Black Is a Country;* and Risa Goluboff, *The Lost Promise of Civil Rights* (Cambridge, MA: Harvard University Press, 2007).
138. On freedom dreams, see Robin D. G. Kelley, *Freedom Dreams: The Black Radical Imagination* (Boston: Beacon, 2002).
139. Gilmore, *Defying Dixie,* 9.
140. Singh, *Black Is a Country,* 57.
141. W. E. B. Du Bois, *Black Reconstruction in America: An Essay toward a History of the Part Which Black Folk Played in the Attempt to Reconstruct Democracy in America, 1860–1880* (New York: Oxford University Press, 2007), 594.
142. Du Bois, *Black Reconstruction in America,* 590. For a devastating account of the sweeping assault on black humanity in response to Reconstruction, see Henry Louis Gates, *Stony the Road: Reconstruction, White Supremacy, and the Rise of Jim Crow* (New York: Penguin, 2020).

143. Du Bois, *Black Reconstruction in America,* 585.
144. This formulation owes a great deal to Harcourt, *Critique and Praxis,* 170–711.
145. Frank R. Wilderson III, *Afropessimism* (New York: Liveright, 2020); Calvin L. Warren, *Ontological Terror: Blackness, Nihilism, and Emancipation* (Durham, NC: Duke University Press, 2018); Calvin L. Warren, "Black Nihilism and the Politics of Hope," *New Centennial Reader* 15, no. 1 (2015): 215–248.
146. Litwack, *How Free Is Free?,* 143.
147. See, especially, Warren, "Black Nihilism and the Politics of Hope."
148. "Editors' Introduction," in *Afro-Pessimism: An Introduction* (Minneapolis: Racked and Dispatched, 2017), 9. The idea of "the nonevent of emancipation" in Afropessimism takes its proximate inspiration from Saidiya Hartman, *Scenes of Subjection: Terror, Slavery, and Self-Making in Nineteenth-Century America* (New York: Oxford University Press, 1997), 116.
149. Frank B. Wilderson III, "Blacks and the Master/Slave Relation," interview with C. S. Soong, *Against the Grain,* KPFA, March 4, 2015.
150. Saidiya Hartman, "Venus in Two Acts," *Small Axe* 12, no. 2 (2008): 12.
151. Hayden V. White, *Metahistory: The Historical Imagination in Nineteenth-Century Europe* (Baltimore: Johns Hopkins University Press, 1973), 5–11.
152. Kompridis, *Critique and Disclosure,* 3, 13.
153. Hayden White, "The Value of Narrativity and the Representation of Reality," *Critical Inquiry* 7, no. 1 (1980): 9–10.
154. White, "The Value of Narrativity," 14.
155. W. B. Gallie, "Narrative and Historical Understanding," in *The History and Narrative Reader,* ed. Geoffrey Roberts (New York: Routledge, 2001), 50.
156. Hayden White, "The Question of Narrative in Contemporary Historical Theory," *History and Theory* 23, no. 1 (1984): 19.
157. For White, the story form of historical narrative is not "found" but intuited or imposed, albeit to varying degrees of consciousness. This is true especially to the extent that story forms demand a beginning, a climax, and an end. White challenges in particular the notion that there are adequately *historical* grounds for these sorts of interpretive decisions. Instead, he argues, claims of "ending" betray a demand or desire "for moral meaning" since "we cannot say, surely, that any sequence of real events actually comes to an end, that reality itself disappears, that events of the order of the real have ceased to happen." See Hayden White, "Narrativity in the Representation of Reality," in *The Content of the Form: Narrative Discourse and Historical Representation* (Baltimore, MD: Johns Hopkins University Press, 1990), 10, 23.
158. Martha Nussbaum, "Form and Content, Philosophy and Literature," in *Love's Knowledge: Essays on Philosophy and Literature* (New York: Oxford University Press, 1990), 3.
159. Ralph Cohen, "History and Genre," *New Literary History* 17, no. 2 (1986): 203–218.
160. Ralph W. Rader, "The Concept of Genre in Eighteenth-Century Studies," in *Fact, Fiction, and Form: Selected Essays,* ed. James Phelan and David H. Richter (Columbia: Ohio State University Press, 2011), 63.

161. White, *Metahistory*, 8–9, 150.
162. Fredric Jameson, *The Political Unconscious: Narrative as Socially Symbolic Act* (Ithaca, NY: Cornell University Press, 1981), 146.
163. Cornel West, "Philosophy and the Afro-American Experience," in *A Companion to African American Philosophy*, ed. Tommy L. Lott and John P. Pittman (Malden, MA: Blackwell, 2003): 11.
164. Joshua Foa Deinstag, "The Example of History and the History of Examples in Political Theory," *New Literary History* 48, no. 3 (2017): 484.
165. Immanuel Kant, "Idea for a Universal History with a Cosmopolitan Purpose," in *Political Writings*, 2nd ed., ed. H. S. Reiss, trans. H. B. Nisbet (Cambridge: Cambridge University Press, 1991), 53.
166. Deinstag, "The Example of History," 492.
167. Denis Diderot, *The Encyclopedia of Diderot and d'Alembert: Collaborative Translation Project*, trans. Philip Stewart (Ann Arbor: University of Michigan Library, 2002), under "encyclopedia."
168. Hannah Arendt, *The Human Condition*, 2nd ed. (Chicago: University of Chicago Press, 1998), 5.
169. Immanuel Kant, *Critique of Pure Reason*, trans. and ed. Paul Guyer and Allen W. Wood (Cambridge: Cambridge University Press, 1998), 268–269.
170. Immanuel Kant, *Groundwork of the Metaphysics of Morals*, ed. Mary J. Gregor and Jens Timmermann (Cambridge: Cambridge University Press, 1998), 21.
171. Kant, *Groundwork of the Metaphysics of Morals*, 21.
172. Immanuel Kant, "An Answer to the Question: 'What Is Enlightenment?,'" in *Political Writings*, 54. See also David Lloyd, "Kant's Examples," *Representations* 28 (1989): 24–54.
173. Immanuel Kant, *Critique of the Power of Judgment*, ed. Paul Guyer, trans. Eric Matthews (New York: Cambridge University Press, 2000), 121.
174. Michel Chaouli, *Thinking with Kant's Critique of Judgment* (Cambridge, MA: Harvard University Press, 2017), 71.
175. Kant, *Critique of the Power of Judgment*, 67.
176. Kant, *Critique of the Power of Judgment*, 387–388n19.
177. Gelley, "Introduction," 2.
178. Nikolas Kompridis, "Introduction: Turning and Returning; The Aesthetic Turn in Political Thought," in *The Aesthetic Turn in Political Thought*, ed. Nikolas Kompridis (New York: Bloomsbury, 2014), xix.
179. See Ferrara, *The Force of the Example*, 3.
180. Hannah Arendt, "Some Questions of Moral Philosophy," in *Responsibility and Judgment*, ed. Jerome Kohn (New York: Schocken, 2003), 139–140.
181. Hannah Arendt, "Understanding and Politics," in *Essays in Understanding, 1930–1954: Formation, Exile, Totalitarianism*, ed. Jerome Kohn (New York: Schocken, 1994), 309–310.
182. Hannah Arendt, "Remarks," in *Thinking Without a Banister: Essays in Understanding, 1953–1975*, ed. Jerome Kohn (New York: Schocken Books, 2018), 481–482.
183. Arendt, "Some Questions of Moral Philosophy," 143–145.
184. Hannah Arendt, *The Life of the Mind* (New York: Harcourt, 1977), 216.

185. Hannah Arendt, "Truth and Politics," in *Essays in Understanding, 1930–1954*, 243.
186. Kompridis, *Critique and Disclosure*, 20, 15.
187. Linda M. G. Zerilli, *A Democratic Theory of Judgment* (Chicago: University of Chicago Press, 2016). See also Hannah Arendt, *Between Past and Future: Eight Exercises in Political Thought*, enlarged ed. (New York: Penguin, 1977), 219.
188. Azmanova, *The Scandal of Reason*, 12–13.
189. I take inspiration here from Zerilli, *A Democratic Theory of Judgment.*
190. I take this closing phrase from Joshua Bennett's extraordinary poem "Theodicy," in *The Sobbing School* (New York: Penguin, 2016), 10.

1. On Exemplarity and Disclosure

1. Hannah Arendt, "Thinking and Moral Considerations," in *Responsibility and Judgment*, 6th ed., ed. Jerome Kohn (New York: Schocken Books, 2003), 160.
2. Hannah Arendt, *The Human Condition*, 2nd ed. (Chicago: University of Chicago Press, 1998), 5.
3. Samuel Fleischacker, *A Third Concept of Liberty: Judgment and Freedom in Kant and Adam Smith* (Princeton, NJ: Princeton University Press, 1999), 211, 212.
4. Martin Heidegger, *Being and Time*, trans. John MacQuarrie and Edward Robinson (Oxford: Blackwell, 1962), §1:3, 98–99.
5. Seyla Benhabib, *The Reluctant Modernism of Hannah Arendt*, 2nd ed. (Lanham, MD: Rowan and Littlefield, 2003), 52.
6. On the notion of a "step back," see Martin Heidegger, *Being and Time* (Oxford: Basil Blackwell, 1962), 197. I am indebted to Robert Gooding-Williams for drawing my attention to this formulation. See also Tobias Keiling, "Step Back (*Schritt zurück*)," in *The Cambridge Heidegger Lexicon*, ed. Mark A. Wrathall (New York: Cambridge University Press, 2021), 703–704.
7. Arendt, *The Human Condition*, 5.
8. *Oxford English Dictionary*, "example," https://www.oed.com.
9. See Manning Marable, *Malcolm X: A Life of Reinvention* (New York: Penguin, 2011).
10. The "ought" claim expressed here can be understood in many ways, including as a moral judgment about good and bad leadership qualities generally, as a bounded claim about what ethical values should govern leadership in the unique environment of the United States, or as an instrumentally rational judgment about what qualities might make leaders "successful" in a this particular context.
11. Orlando Patterson, *Slavery and Social Death: A Comparative Study* (Cambridge, MA: Harvard University Press, 1982), 1–17. On the notion of recognition respect, see Stephen Darwall, *The Second-Person Standpoint: Morality, Respect, and Accountability* (Cambridge, MA: Harvard University Press, 2009).

12. For Patterson, it seems that preemancipation Jamaica is this sort of exemplar, given its merging of the extreme, naked violence of West Indian plantation discipline, the hereditary transmission of slave status, and the generalized dishonor of legalized racial hierarchy—all extreme manifestations of the constituent elements of slavery. See Orlando Patterson, *Enslavement: Past and Present* (Hoboken, NJ: Polity, 2025), chapter 8.
13. See, for example, Jack Goldstone, *States, Parties, and Social Movements* (New York: Columbia University Press, 2003). We see the same sort of exemplarity invoked in literary theory and art history, where genres of artistic production or schools of artistic convention are often understood by reference to exemplary works that, for example, seem to manifest the family resemblances of a given tradition (e.g., detective stories) or school (e.g., romance novels) in the greatest degree. This is the terrain on which we meet familiar claims that Mary Shelley's *Frankenstein* is an exemplary gothic novel or Frederick Douglass's *Narrative of the Life of Frederick Douglass* is an exemplary slave narrative. See, for example, the retrospective construction of a black literary tradition in Henry Louis Gates Jr., *Figures in Black: Words, Signs, and the 'Racial' Self* (New York: Oxford University Press, 1989), 3–58.
14. Alessandro Ferrara, *The Force of the Example: Explorations in the Paradigm of Judgment* (New York: Columbia University Press, 2008), 3.
15. Ferrara, *The Force of the Example,* 3.
16. David Burner, *Making Peace with the 60s* (Princeton, NJ: Princeton University Press, 1996), 8.
17. Michael Jordan, to take a familiar example, had plenty of exemplary performances throughout his storied basketball career that serve as models for contemporary athletes. But to claim that we could find some a priori rule like "score as many points as possible" or "lead the team to victory" as the source of this virtuosity in the game of basketball would be misguided in the former and underdetermining in the latter.
18. Takeshi Kanno—the physician who rescued dozens of patients in the Shizugawa Public Hospital in Minamisanriku, Japan, as it was struck by the deadly 2011 earthquake and tsunami and tended nonstop to their needs for days until evacuation helicopters could rescue them—fits this description well. See Krista Mahr, "Time 100: Takeshi Kanno, Doctor," *Time,* April 21, 2011, https://www.time.com.
19. Charles Guignon, "Introduction," in *The Cambridge Companion to Heidegger,* ed. Charles Guignon (New York: Cambridge University Press, 1993), 8.
20. Lawrence Scanlan, *The Horse God Built: The Untold Story of Secretariat, the World's Greatest Racehorse* (New York: Macmillan, 2010).
21. Alasdair C. MacIntyre, *After Virtue: A Study of Moral Theory* (Notre Dame, IN: University of Notre Dame Press, 2007), 187.
22. Ferrara, *The Force of the Example,* 3 (emphasis added).
23. Émile Durkheim, *The Rules of Sociological Method and Selected Texts on Sociology and Its Method,* ed. Steven Lukes, trans. W. D. Halls (New York: Simon and Schuster, 1982).

24. Arendt, *The Human Condition,* 1–2.
25. Nikolas Kompridis, *Critique and Disclosure: Critical Theory Between Past and Future* (Cambridge, MA: MIT Press, 2006), 216.
26. Ferrara, *The Force of the Example,* 3.
27. Kompridis, *Critique and Disclosure,* 74–75.
28. Nikolas Kompridis, "World Disclosure (*Welterschließung*)," in *The Cambridge Habermas Lexicon,* ed. Amy Allen and Eduardo Mendieta (New York: Cambridge University Press, 2019), 468–469.
29. Kompridis, *Critique and Disclosure,* 35–36.
30. Kompridis, *Critique and Disclosure,* 13.
31. See Alasdair MacIntyre, "Epistemological Crises, Dramatic Narrative, and the Philosophy of Science," *Monist* 60, no. 4 (1977): 453–472.
32. Cass Sunstein, "What the Civil Rights Movement Was and Wasn't (with Notes on Martin Luther King Jr. and Malcolm X)," *University of Illinois Law Review* 191 (1995): 192, 209, 193. Sunstein goes so far as to call the civil rights movement "Burkean," in reference to the eighteenth-century conservative thinker and British member of Parliament Edmund Burke, who extolled the virtues of tradition (specifically, English common law, traditional mores, and constitutional monarchy) as repositories of genuine wisdom and warned against the revolutionary impulse to realize abstract ideals like liberty and equality at the expense of existing, historically evolved, forms of government and social life. See Edmund Burke, *Reflections on the Revolution in France* (New York: Penguin, 1982).
33. Gunnar Myrdal, *An American Dilemma: The Negro Problem and Modern Democracy,* vol. 1 (New York: Harper and Bros, 1944), xlvii.
34. See Myrdal, *An American Dilemma,* especially the introduction and 3–26.
35. Myrdal, *An American Dilemma,* 60–61. See also Maria Krysan, "From Color Caste to Color Blind, Part 1: Racial Attitudes in the United States During World War II, 1939–1945," in *The Oxford Handbook of African American Citizenship, 1865–Present,* ed. Henry Louis Gates Jr., Claude Steele, Lawrence D. Bobo, Michael Dawson, Gerald Jaynes, Lisa Crooms-Robinson, and Linda Darling-Hammond (New York: Oxford University Press, 2012), 184–190. Jane Dailey, *White Fright: The Sexual Panic at the Heart of America's Racist History* (New York: Basic Books, 2020), argues that the defense of racial hierarchy in the United States has been animated as much by sexual hysteria, fantasies of purity, and libidinal economies of desire and disgust as by formal ideologies or economic interests. In Dailey's telling, white anxieties about interracial intimacy—particularly fears of Black male desire and the specter of miscegenation—supplied the moral and emotional energy for some of the most brutal and enduring structures of racial domination, from lynching to segregation to massive resistance. Her work demands that we see racism not simply as a system of legal exclusions or social practices but as a visceral, often eroticized commitment to preserving white identity and self-conception that bleeds into lawmaking, politics, and social life.
36. Myrdal, *An American Dilemma,* xlviii–xlix. This argument, it bears noting, simply misconstrues the ethical valence in the United States of

claims to white racial dominion construed as "freedom" or the fact that Myrdal's dismissiveness of appeals to "tradition" reflects a conventionally liberal misunderstanding of the complex bundles of claims about philosophical anthropology, what is worth desiring or passing on to the next generation, what counts as practical reason, and what makes someone virtuous and with good character that constitute tradition-based reason. On the first point, see Jefferson Cowie, *Freedom's Dominion: A Saga of White Resistance to Federal Power* (New York: Basic Books, 2022). On the second, see Alasdair MacIntyre, *Ethics in the Conflicts of Modernity: An Essay on Desire, Practical Reasoning, and Narrative* (New York: Cambridge University Press, 2016).

37. Myrdal, *An American Dilemma,* xlix.
38. Myrdal, *An American Dilemma,* lii, 784, 786.
39. Myrdal, *An American Dilemma,* 13, 746–749, 836. See also E. Franklin Frazier, *Black Bourgeoisie* (New York: Free Press, 1997), 173.
40. Charles Taylor, "Lichtung or Lebensform: Parallels Between Heidegger and Wittgenstein," in *Philosophical Arguments* (Cambridge, MA: Harvard University Press, 1997), 69.
41. On the critique of Myrdal's picture of race and American politics, see Rogers Smith, *Civic Ideals: Conflicting Visions of Citizenship in US History* (New Haven, CT: Yale University Press, 1997); and Marc Stears, "The Liberal Tradition and the Politics of Exclusion," *Annual Review of Political Science* 10 (2007): 85–101. For a complex account of the quest for inclusion as a metanarrative of American political life, see Judith Shklar, *American Citizenship: The Quest for Inclusion* (Cambridge, MA: Harvard University Press, 1991).
42. Davide Panagia, *The Poetics of Political Thinking* (Durham, NC: Duke University Press, 2006), 2.
43. Danielle S. Allen, *Talking to Strangers: Anxieties of Citizenship Since Brown v. Board of Education* (Chicago: University of Chicago Press, 2006), 17.
44. Danielle Allen, "Invisible Citizens: Political Exclusion and Domination in Arendt and Ellison," in *Political Exclusion and Domination,* ed. Melissa S. Williams and Stephen Macedo (New York: New York University Press, 2004), 31.
45. Allen, "Invisible Citizens," 55. See also Danielle Allen, "A Reply to Bader and Orwin," in Williams and Macedo, *Political Exclusion and Domination,* 179.
46. Allen, *Talking to Strangers,* 115.
47. Stephen A. Berrey, *The Jim Crow Routine: Everyday Performances of Race, Civil Rights, and Segregation in Mississippi* (Chapel Hill: University of North Carolina Press, 2015), 11.
48. Martin Luther King Jr., quoted in Robert Penn Warren, *Who Speaks for the Negro?,* ed. David Blight (New Haven, CT: Yale University Press, 2014), 218.
49. Roy Wilkins, quoted in Stephen Drury Smith and Catherine Ellis, eds., *Free All Along: The Robert Penn Warren Civil Rights Interviews* (New York: New Press, 2019), 228.

50. Kenneth B. Clark, *Social Power and Social Change in Contemporary America* (Washington, DC: Equal Employment Opportunity Commission, 1966), 15–16. North Carolina–born Floyd McKissick was a veteran lawyer and activist in the civil rights struggle who was the successful plaintiff in a Thurgood Marshall–led lawsuit against the University of North Carolina to integrate the state's flagship law school. After a notable career as a civil rights lawyer, McKissick began to endorse Black Power when he became chairman of CORE in 1966. As a Black Power figure, he publicly broke with King on the question of nonviolence and advocated forms of "community control" and self-determination in black communities. It is this transition that Clark means to mark. See "Interview with Floyd B. McKissick, Sr., December 6, 1973," Interview A-0134, Southern Oral History Program Collection, https://docsouth.unc.edu/sohp/html_use/A-0134.html.
51. Krysan, "From Color Caste to Color Blind," 190.
52. Allen, *Talking to Strangers,* 9–10.
53. James Baldwin, "The Fire Next Time," in *Collected Essays,* ed. Toni Morrison (New York: Library of America, 1998), 341–342.
54. Allen, *Talking to Strangers,* 114–116.
55. Ralph Ellison, "An American Dilemma: *A Review,*" in *Shadow and Act* (New York: Random House, 1964), 317.
56. Whitney Young, quoted in Smith and Ellis, *Free All Along,* 228.
57. Ellison, "An American Dilemma: *A Review,*" 314–315.
58. Allen has since developed a comprehensive and important set of interventions on justice, citizenship, and political economy in the twenty-first century. A sustained account of where these conflict with her earlier work is beyond the scope of this book but would be a worthy endeavor. See, above all, Danielle Allen, *Justice by Means of Democracy* (Chicago: University of Chicago Press, 2023).
59. Shatema Threadcraft, *Intimate Justice: The Black Female Body and the Body Politic* (New York: Oxford University Press, 2016), 8–9 (emphasis added).
60. This formulation of crisis-driven learning draws from Rahel Jaeggi, *Critique of Forms of Life,* trans. Ciaran Cronin (Cambridge, MA: Belknap Press of Harvard University Press, 2018), 272–290.
61. For a characteristic statement of the integrationist-nationalist paradigm, see Bernard Boxill, "Two Traditions in African American Political Philosophy," in *African-American Perspectives and Philosophical Traditions,* ed. John Pittman (New York: Routledge, 1996), 119–135.
62. For an invocation of exemplarity in this vein, see Barack Obama, "A More Perfect Union (March 18, 2008)," *Politico,* March 18, 2008, https://www.politico.com.
63. Martin Luther King Jr., "A Testament of Hope," in *A Testament of Hope: The Essential Writings and Speeches of Martin Luther King,* ed. James M. Washington (New York: HarperCollins, 1991), 315.
64. Seyla Benhabib, *Critique, Norm, and Utopia: A Study of the Foundations of Critical Theory* (New York: Columbia University Press, 1986), 19, 226. Benhabib's account of Koselleck's argument draws on Reinhart Koselleck, *Kritik und Krise* (Frankfurt: Suhrkamp, 1976).

65. Kompridis, *Critique and Disclosure,* 3. "Crisis theory," if one insists on a label, has been most readily identified with Marxism over the past century, but this simply obscures the depth and breadth of self-conscious intellectual reflection on various crises while suggesting an inherent relationship to Karl Marx's interest in the cyclical recessions and depressions of capitalism that crisis theory cannot be reduced to, given Friedrich Nietzsche's interest in a crisis of morality, Søren Kierkegaard's crisis of Christian faith, and Arnold's crisis of high culture, to name just three other towering figures of the nineteenth century. See Søren Kierkegaard, *The Present Age: On the Death of Rebellion* (New York: HarperCollins, 2010); Friedrich Nietzsche, *Toward a Genealogy of Morals,* ed. Keith Ansell-Pearson, trans. Carol Diethe (New York: Cambridge University Press, 2007); and Karl Marx, "Capital," in *Karl Marx: Selected Writings,* 2nd ed., ed. David McLellan (New York: Oxford University Press, 2000).
66. See Charles Taylor, *The Ethics of Authenticity* (Cambridge, MA: Harvard University Press, 1992); and Ferrara, *The Force of the Example,* especially chapters 3, 6, and 8.
67. Kompridis, *Critique and Disclosure,* 215.
68. Hannah Arendt, "Understanding and Politics (The Difficulties of Understanding)," in *Essays in Understanding: Formation, Exile, and Totalitarianism* (New York: Schocken Books, 1994) 307–327.
69. James Baldwin, "Faulkner and Desegregation," in *Collected Essays,* ed. Toni Morrison (Washington, DC: Library of America, 1998), 209.
70. Ian Hacking, "Making Up People," in *Historical Ontology* (Cambridge, MA: Harvard University Press, 2004). Hacking argues for the social constructivist thesis that the existence of "human kinds" is made possible by the very invention of the labels under which they are categorized. "The claim of dynamic nominalism," he writes, "is not that there was a kind of person who came increasingly to be recognized by bureaucrats or by students of human nature, but rather that a kind of person came into being at the same time as the kind itself was being invented." The philosophical foundation for Hacking's project is G. E. M. Anscombe's famous argument about action and intention, the contention that intentional human actions must be "actions under a description" and shaped by concepts embedded in our ideas or practices. It follows, according to Hacking, that "if a particular description is not there, then intentional actions under that description cannot be there either . . . [and] if new modes of description come into being, new possibilities for action come into being in consequence." This is, for instance, the substance of the objection persistently and persuasively lodged against the clumsier proponents of Afrocentrism who write about the denizens of ancient Africa using categories of racial identity or Pan-African identity that are creations of modernity unknown to premodern subjects. Mansa Musa, the fourteenth-century ruler of Mali, and the twentieth-century activist Marcus Garvey both desired to rule mighty empires headquartered in West Africa, but only the latter could be said to be a *black* nationalist interested in a *black* empire on this account.

71. Ella J. Baker, "Bigger Than a Hamburger," in *The Eyes on the Prize Civil Rights Reader,* ed. Clayborn Carson, David J. Garrow, Gerald Gill, Vincent Harding, and Darlene Clark Hine (New York: Penguin, 1991), 120.
72. Shklar, *American Citizenship,* 1–11.
73. Rebecca J. Scott, "Discerning a Dignitary Offense: The Concept of Equal "Public Rights" During Reconstruction," *Law and History Review* 38, no. 3 (2020): 519–553; Samuel R. Bagenstos, "The Unrelenting Libertarian Challenge to Public Accommodations Law," *Stanford Law Review* 66, no. 6 (2014): 1205–1240.
74. Perry Mullen, "Reactions Have No Pattern," *Atlanta Journal,* April 28, 1960.
75. Traci Parker, *Department Stores and the Black Freedom Struggle: Workers, Consumers, and Civil Rights from the 1930s to the 1980s* (Chapel Hill: University of North Carolina Press, 2019).
76. On habits and deep rules of citizenship, see Allen, *Talking to Strangers,* 9–10. On notions of social standing and citizenship (albeit restricted to political rights and dignified labor), see Shklar, *American Citizenship.*
77. Martin Luther King Jr., "The Burning Truth in the South (May 1960)," in *A Testament of Hope,* 96.
78. Pauli Murray, *States' Laws on Race and Color* (Athens: University of Georgia Press, 2016), 5.
79. This is illustrated in the early negotiations in the Knoxville, Tennessee, sit-in movement. See Merrill Proudfoot, *Diary of a Sit-In* (Chapel Hill, NC: University of North Carolina Press, 1962).
80. Malcolm X with Alex Haley, *The Autobiography of Malcolm X* (New York: Ballantine, 1965).
81. Elizabeth Abel, *Signs of the Times: The Visual Politics of Jim Crow* (Berkeley: University of California Press, 2010); Victoria W. Wolcott, *Race, Riots, and Roller Coasters: The Struggle over Segregated Recreation in America* (Philadelphia: University of Pennsylvania Press, 2012); Parker, *Department Stores and the Black Freedom Struggle.*
82. On the politics and economics of sharecropping, see W. E. B. Du Bois, "The Economics of Negro Emancipation in the United States," *Sociological Review* 4, no. 3 (1911): 303–313; Gerald D. Jaynes, *Branches Without Roots: Genesis of the Black Working Class in the American South, 1862–1882* (New York: Oxford University Press, 1986); Douglas A. Blackmon, *Slavery by Another Name: The Re-Enslavement of Black Americans from the Civil War to World War II* (New York: Anchor Books, 2008); Deirdre Bloome, James Feigenbaum, and Christopher Muller, "Tenancy, Marriage, and the Boll Weevil Infestation, 1892–1930," *Demography* 54, no. 3 (2017): 1029–1049; and Christopher Muller, "Freedom and Convict Leasing in the Postbellum South," *American Journal of Sociology* 124, no. 2 (2018): 367–405.
83. David Halberstam, "Good City Gone Ugly (March 1960)," in *Reporting Civil Rights,* vol. 1, *American Journalism, 1941–1963* (New York: Library Classics of the United States, 2003), 442.

84. Proudfoot, *Diary of a Sit-In,* 7.
85. Martin Luther King Jr., "The Time for Freedom Has Come," in *A Testament of Hope,* 165. Political theorists have recently attempted to rethink the relationship between the sit-down and sit-in movements. See William E. Scheuerman, "From Labor Sit-Downs to Civil Rights Sit-Ins: A Genealogy of Liberal Civil Disobedience," *Review of Politics* 86, no. 3 (2024): 355–379; Alex Gourevitch, "Strikes, Civil Rights, and Radical Disobedience: From King to Debs and Back," *Contemporary Political Theory* 22, no. 2 (2023): 143–164.
86. Ezell Blair Jr., quoted in "Tape 1: Transcript of Taped Conversation with Stokeley [*sic*] Carmichael, Izell [*sic*] Blair, Lucy Thornton and Jean Wheeler, and Mr. Robert Penn Warren at Howard University—March 4, 1964," in Robert Penn Warren, *Who Speaks for the Negro: An Archival Collection,* https://whospeaks.library.vanderbilt.edu.
87. Doug McAdam, *Political Process and the Development of Black Insurgency, 1930–1970* (Chicago: University of Chicago Press, 1999), 130–138; Ted Dienstfrey, "A Conference on the Sit-Ins," in Carson et al., *The Eyes on the Prize Civil Rights Reader,* 122–124.
88. King, "The Time for Freedom Has Come," 161.
89. Ludwig Wittgenstein, *On Certainty,* ed. G. E. M. Anscombe and G. H. von Wright, trans. G. E. M. Anscombe (New York: Basil Blackwell, 1969), para. 117.
90. Claude Sitton, "Negro Sitdowns Stir Fear of Wider Unrest in South," in *Reporting Civil Rights,* 1:433; Halberstam, "Good City Gone Ugly," 445. The panty raid was a mid-twentieth-century collegiate ritual wherein groups of male students would enter women's dormitories to steal underwear—an act often treated at the time as harmless fun but now widely disavowed as actionable harassment and a gendered assertion of power. For portrayals of this phenomenon in popular culture, see *Animal House,* directed by John Landis (Universal Pictures, 1978); and *Revenge of the Nerds,* directed by Jeff Kanew (Twentieth Century Fox, 1984).
91. Patricia Hill Collins uses the term "controlling images" to describe the set of stereotypical images that portray black women in restrictive, demeaning roles in order to justify their continued subordination. In *Black Feminist Thought* she highlights figures such as the "mammy" (the faithful, obedient domestic servant), the "Jezebel" (the hypersexual black woman portrayed as sexually immoral), and the "welfare queen" (the lazy, greedy mother living off public assistance) as key examples of these controlling images. These stereotypical caricatures function as ideological weapons of oppression and stigmatization, making forms of injustice, cruelty, or disgust directed toward them (or justified by reference to them) seem natural or deserved. Patricia Hill Collins, *Black Feminist Thought: Knowledge, Consciousness, and the Politics of Empowerment,* 2nd ed. (New York: Routledge, 2000), 69–96.
92. James Baldwin, interviewed in *The Negro Protest: James Baldwin, Malcolm X, and Martin Luther King, Jr. Talk with Kenneth B. Clark* (Boston: Beacon, 1963), 10–11.

93. Sue Campbell, "Dominant Identities and Settled Expectations," in *Racism and Philosophy,* ed. Susan E. Babbitt and Sue Campbell (Ithaca, NY: Cornell University Press, 1999), 216–324.
94. Wittgenstein, *On Certainty,* para. 142.
95. Hannah Arendt, *On Revolution* (New York: Penguin, 2006).
96. King, "The Burning Truth in the South," 97–98.
97. Arendt, *On Revolution,* 11, 32.
98. Burke, *Reflections on the Revolution in France,* 117.
99. This dilemma is particularly acute where the extant regime attempts to draw, or once drew, its authority from transcendental religion, and the emergent regime must "step into the shoes of the old absolute that derived from a God-given authority . . . [and] the notion of an incarnation of God on earth." Thus, the American and French Revolutions, as they unfolded, eventually sought to altogether overthrow the proprietary claims of European monarchs and the "divine right" principle that was said to legitimate their rule. In their stead, they sought to establish resolutely antimonarchical forms of government founded on republican principles of popular sovereignty, expansively enumerated systems of basic liberties, and the exclusion of titled nobility, not to mention various political experiments in federalism and the separation of powers. Arendt, *On Revolution,* 29; David Abernethy, *The Dynamics of Global Dominance: Europe and Its Overseas Empires, 1415–1980* (New Haven, CT: Yale University Press, 2002), 73.
100. Arendt, *On Revolution,* 196.
101. To be fair, the brief remarks here on originalism apply most straightforwardly to the "jurisprudence of original intention," original meaning, and conservative objective textual meaning variants of originalist theory. For more on these distinctions, see Thomas B. Colby and Peter J. Smith, "Living Originalism," *Duke Law Journal* 59, no. 1 (2009): 239–308. Constitutional fundamentalism is defined here, following Douglas S. Massey, "Doing Social Science in Anti-Scientific Times," *American Sociologist* 37, no. 2 (2006): 90, as taking the US Constitution essentially as "a holy text, not to be modified or expanded but to [be] applied strictly according to the original intent of the men who wrote it, notwithstanding the fact one of the original intents was to preserve the institution of chattel slavery."
102. For a critique of those forms of originalism that are, in essence, rationalizations for conservatism, see Richard H. Fallon Jr., "Are Originalist Constitutional Theories Principled, or Are They Rationalizations for Conservatism?" *Harvard Journal of Law and Public Policy* 34, no. 1 (2011): 5–28.
103. For a defense of this conception of freedom, see Arendt, *The Human Condition;* and Arendt, *On Revolution.*
104. If an artistic analogy may be invoked, it seems similar to the difference between my composing my own drawing based on an exemplary artistic object and my tracing the object itself with careful precision to create a perfect facsimile.
105. Thus, while we might intelligibly argue that for both Roger B. Taney and Frederick Douglass the founding and the ratification of the Constitution

were key exemplary moments in US history, it seems that Douglass is more attuned to the innovative dimension of the example, at least where citizenship for African Americans is concerned. One can, of course, insist on many plausible arguments for why this might be so, but the focus here is one important dimension. Where Taney insists that racial hierarchy and black subordination are the necessary legal foundations for American jurisprudence given the white supremacist views of the Founding Fathers in the late eighteenth century, Douglass allows himself the same interpretive and political freedom within the soft boundaries of inspiration and exemplarity to appropriate and revise inherited traditions that he heralds in the actions and thought of America's founders. See Frederick Douglass, "The Constitution of the United States: Is It Pro-Slavery or Anti-Slavery? Speech Delivered in Glasgow, Scotland, March 26, 1860," in *Frederick Douglass: Selected Speeches and Writings,* ed. Philip S. Foner and Yuval Taylor (Chicago: Lawrence Hill, 1999), 379–389.

106. Adom Getachew, *Worldmaking After Empire: The Rise and Fall of Self-Determination* (Princeton, NJ: Princeton University Press, 2019).

107. Consider, for example, Jay-Z's "Off That" (2009), in which he responds to criticisms from conservative media elites Rush Limbaugh and Bill O'Reilly that he perceives as racist by narrating an arc of racial progress and integration that collapses the individual and the collective, refracting African American history through his own accumulation of a personal fortune, corporate endorsements, and other accoutrements of wealth:

> This ain't black vs. white, my nigga we off that
> Please tell Bill O'Reilly to fall back
> Tell Rush Limbaugh to get off my balls
> It's 2010, not 1864
> Uhh, yeah we come so far
> So I drive around town, hard top [convertible] and it's off
> Uhh, in my TriBeCa loft
> With my high brow art, and my high yellow broad
> Uhh, and my dark-skinned sis
> And my best white mate, say what's up to Chris [Martin of the British band Coldplay]
> Uhh, how's that for a mix?
> Got a black president [Obama], got green presidents
> Blueprint's in my white iPod
> Black diamonds in my Jesus piece, my God.

Jay-Z, "Off That," track 8 on *The Blueprint 3*, Roc Nation, 2009. Or, if one prefers brevity, perhaps the joie de vivre of Lil Wayne's "A Milli" (2008) might convey the point:

> I open the Lamborghini
> Hoping them crackers see me
> Like, "Look at that bastard Weezy!"

Lil Wayne, "A Milli," track 3 on *Tha Carter III,* Cash Money Records, 2008. For an extended argument with similar conclusions, see Fumi Okiji,

"Onanism, Handjobs, Smut: Performances of Self-Valorization," in *The Routledge Companion to Performance Philosophy,* ed. Laura Cull Ó Maoilearca and Alice Lagaay (New York: Routledge, 2020), 404–414.

2. Between Aesthetics and History

1. All parenthetical in-text citations in this chapter refer to Immanuel Kant, *Critique of the Power of Judgment,* ed. Paul Guyer, trans. Paul Guyer and Eric Matthews (New York: Cambridge University Press, 2000).
2. For a wonderful account of the origins of Picasso's painting that emphasizes its emulation of certain aesthetic innovations in African art, see Suzanne Preston Blier, *Picasso's "Demoiselles": The Origins of a Modern Masterpiece* (Durham, NC: Duke University Press, 2019).
3. William Wordsworth, "Poetry as a Study," in *The Prose Works of William Wordsworth,* vol. 2, *Aesthetical and Literary,* ed. Rev. Alexander B. Grosart (London: Edward Moxon, Son, and Company, 1876), 125.
4. Wendy Brown, *Nihilistic Times: Thinking with Max Weber* (Cambridge, MA: Harvard University Press, 2023), 37. Brown's reinterrogation of charisma comes from her superb engagement with Max Weber's famous lecture, commonly known as "Politics as a Vocation." See Max Weber, "Politics as a Vocation," in *From Max Weber: Essays in Sociology,* ed. H. H. Gerth and C. Wright Mills (New York: Oxford University Press, 1946), 77–128. Weber's larger sweep of writings on charisma are collected in Max Weber, *On Charisma and Institution Building: Selected Writings,* ed. S. N. Eisenstadt (Chicago: University of Chicago Press, 1968).
5. Michel Chaouli, *Thinking with Kant's Critique of Judgment* (Cambridge, MA: Harvard University Press, 2017), xv.
6. Christian Helmut Wenzel, *An Introduction to Kant's Aesthetics: Core Concepts and Problems* (New York: Blackwell, 20005), 78–79.
7. Linda M. G. Zerilli, *A Democratic Theory of Judgment* (Chicago: University of Chicago Press, 2016), 10, 17.
8. Hannah Arendt, *Lectures on Kant's Political Philosophy,* ed. Ronald Beiner (Chicago: University of Chicago Press, 1982).
9. Dabney Townsend, *Taste and Experience in Eighteenth-Century British Aesthetics: The Move to Empiricism* (New York: Bloomsbury, 2022).
10. Edmund Burke, *A Philosophical Enquiry into the Origins of the Sublime and Beautiful and Other Pre-Revolutionary Writings,* ed. David Womersley (New York: Penguin, 1998), 49–200.
11. The search for a science of beauty remains an obsession in some corners, even as it breaks with eighteenth-century British assumptions. See, for example, the "neuroaesthetics" movement encapsulated in Anjan Chatterjee and Eileen R. Cardillo, eds., *Brain, Beauty, and Art: Essays Bringing Neuroaesthetics in Focus* (New York: Oxford University Press, 2021).
12. Immanuel Kant, *Critique of Pure Reason,* ed. Paul Guyer and Allen W. Wood (New York: Cambridge University Press, 1999), §1:A21/B35.
13. Weber, "Science as a Vocation," 142 (emphasis added).
14. Max Weber, *The Protestant Ethic and the Spirit of Capitalism* (New York: Routledge, 1992), 27. See also Jürgen Habermas, *The Theory of*

Communicative Action: Reason and the Rationalization of Society, vol. 1, trans. Thomas McCarthy (Boston: Beacon, 1985); and Jürgen Habermas, "A Genealogical Analysis of the Cognitive Content of Modernity," in *The Inclusion of the Other: Studies in Political Theory,* ed. Ciaran Cronin and Pablo De Grieff (Cambridge, MA: MIT Press, 1998), 3–47. On the axial transformation of religious consciousness, see Jürgen Habermas, *Also a History of Philosophy,* vol. 1, *The Project of a Genealogy of Postmetaphysical Thinking,* trans. Ciaran Cronin (Hoboken, NJ: Polity, 2023), parts 2 and 3.

15. Habermas, *The Theory of Communicative Action,* 1:15.
16. Stephen Mulhall, *Stanley Cavell: Philosophy's Recounting of the Ordinary* (New York: Oxford University Press, 1998), 26.
17. For the field-defining philosophical account of such debates, see Paul C. Taylor, *Black Is Beautiful: A Philosophy of Black Aesthetics* (New York: Routledge, 2016), 77–103.
18. Stanley Cavell, *Must We Mean What We Say?,* 2nd ed. (New York: Cambridge University Press, 2002), 91.
19. This thought experiment draws on the excellent account of "hedonic discrimination" between judgments of agreeableness and beauty in Samantha Matherne, "Kant on Aesthetic Autonomy and Common Sense," *Philosophers' Imprint* 19, no. 24 (2019): 1–22.
20. Branka Spehar, Colin W. G. Clifford, Ben R. Newell, and Richard Taylor, "Universal Aesthetic of Fractals," *Computers and Graphics* 27, no. 5 (2003): 813–820.
21. See Charles Taylor, *The Ethics of Authenticity* (Cambridge, MA: Harvard University Press, 1992), especially 1–12, 55–70. See also Max Weber, "Religious Rejections of the World and Their Directions," in *From Max Weber,* 323–362.
22. Michael Oakeshott, *On History: And Other Essays* (Indianapolis, IN: Liberty Fund, 1983), 19, 48, 20.
23. Oakeshott, *On History,* 18–19.
24. F. R. Ankersmit, *Sublime Historical Experience* (Stanford, CA: Stanford University Press, 2005), xv.
25. Hannah Arendt, "What Is Authority?," in *Between Past and Future: Eight Exercises in Political Thought* (New York: Penguin, 1968), 97.
26. Zerilli, *A Democratic Theory of Judgment,* xii–xiii, 42.
27. Kant wants to resist what might be said to be two other subjectivist approaches to aesthetics. For David Hume, the extent to which aesthetic value is simply the expression of subjectively held sentiment seemed to paradoxically tie "taste" to variances in individual psychology and physiology that are idiosyncratic and not susceptible to rational disputation. Wanting to retain the widely held belief that matters of aesthetic judgment can still, in principle, go awry, Hume insisted on a hierarchy of taste that a cultivated elite of talented critics might, over time, somehow distill into a set of rules that might discipline the untutored judgment and sensibility of the mass (and which might be anchored in sentiment-inducing effects of the objects themselves). The other tradition, closely associated with Johann

Gottfried von Herder and German romanticism, also championed the place of subjective feeling in aesthetics but made claims for it that Kant found epistemologically extravagant, politically dangerous, and personally irritating. This tradition exalted subjective feeling as capable of providing access to metaphysical and other truths that rationalist argument was incapable of accessing or evaluating. These subjective experiences of intense feeling and revelation were best understood as founts of wisdom for "genius" (a label that many of the prominent thinkers in this tradition claimed for themselves) and prerequisites for, or constitutive of, accurate and educated judgment on behalf of audiences exposed to their revelations. Grafted onto this conception of aesthetics was a philosophical anthropology that recognized the existence of distinct cultural groups (created, in the main, by linguistic differences) with divergent aesthetic standards and that criticized the prevailing Enlightenment practice of hierarchically ranking cultures or evaluating them according to extrinsic criteria. Aesthetics was understood, much to Kant's dismay, as the discernment of the forms of artistic genius developed in various cultures—a project that, in the hands of Herder, seemed to insulate the purveyors of such "genius" from rational criticism while implying sharp limits on universality, commensurability, and rationality. See David Hume, "Of the Standard of Taste," in *Essays: Moral, Political and Literary,* vol. 1, ed. T. H. Green and T. H. Grose (London: Longmans, Green, 1875), 266–286; Johann Gottfried Herder, "On the Cognition and Sensation of the Human Soul (1778)," in *Philosophical Writings,* ed. Michael N. Forster (New York: Cambridge University Press, 2002), 187–245; and Johann Gottfried Herder, "On the Change of Taste (1766)," in *Philosophical Writings,* 247–256. See also John H. Zammito, *The Genesis of Kant's Critique of Judgment* (Chicago: University of Chicago Press, 1992). This latter tradition exercised extraordinary influence on African American aesthetic thought through its impact on W. E. B. Du Bois. See Kwame Anthony Appiah, *Lines of Descent: W. E. B. Du Bois and the Emergence of Identity* (Cambridge, MA: Harvard University Press, 2014), 45–82.

28. Chaouli, *Thinking with Kant's Critique of Judgment,* 56.
29. Chaouli, *Thinking with Kant's Critique of Judgment,* xv.
30. Zammito, *The Genesis of Kant's Critique of Judgment,* 46–47. As Charles Taylor, "The Validity of Transcendental Argument," in *Proceedings of the Aristotelian Society* 79, no. 1 (1978–1979), 151, 159, writes, transcendental arguments "start from some feature of our experience which they claim to be indubitable and beyond cavil" before moving to "a stronger conclusion, one concerning the nature of the subject or his position in the world . . . by a regressive argument, to the effect that this stronger conclusion must be so if the indubitable fact about experience is to be possible." Taylor characterizes these "chains of apodeictic indispensability claims which concern experience" as "articulating an insight we have into our own activity"—particularly its purposes, and the constitutive conditions for those purposes.
31. Chaouli, *Thinking with Kant's Critique of Judgment,* 11 (emphasis added).

32. Chaouli, *Thinking with Kant's Critique of Judgment,* 18.
33. Zammito, *The Genesis of Kant's Critique of Judgment,* 92 (emphasis added).
34. Zerilli, *A Democratic Theory of Judgment,* 69.
35. When this occurs, Kant claims, we experience a peculiar "sensation of the effect that consists in the facilitated play of both powers of the mind (imagination and understanding), enlivened through mutual agreement" (§9:219).
36. Kirk Pillow, *Sublime Understanding: Aesthetic Reflection in Kant and Hegel* (Cambridge, MA: MIT Press, 2003), 48.
37. Zammito, *The Genesis of Kant's Critique of Judgment,* 95–96. See also Arendt, *Lectures on Kant's Political Philosophy,* 13. The inability to think through the distinction between purposiveness as a regulative idea for understanding complex phenomena and purposiveness as an attribution of will to individual or collective agents (with all the moral implications that follow) continues to bedevil discussions of functionalist claims in social theory and criticism. A very important text for helping students think through this problem is Tommie Shelby, "A Broken System? Racism and Functional Critique," in *The Idea of Prison Abolition* (Princeton, NJ: Princeton University Press, 2022), 87–119.
38. Chaouli, *Thinking with Kant's Critique of Judgment,* 60.
39. As Matherne, "Kant on Aesthetic Autonomy and Common Sense," 5, argues, "Kant introduces common sense as part of his discussion of the distinctive type of necessity involved in judgments of the beautiful. There he argues that judgments of the beautiful have 'exemplary' necessity: when one makes a judgment of the beautiful, she holds up her judgment as an example that she thinks others 'should' follow. . . . And Kant thinks that what puts one in this normative position is that she regards the ground of her judgment as being 'common to all.'" In other words, the judging subject takes their judgment of beauty to "be grounded in the disinterested pleasure that results from free play that anyone in her situation should be able to feel as well" and thus is correct to treat these judgments "as examples that others should follow."
40. Chaouli, *Thinking with Kant's Critique of Judgment,* 66, 157–158.
41. Zammito, *The Genesis of Kant's Critique of Judgment,* 95, 220, 290–293.
42. In the following discussion, for ease of understanding I will ignore more complicated problems of empirical entailment.
43. Kant, *Critique of Pure Reason,* A141. If we follow the suggestion in Brett Kalar, *The Demands of Taste in Kant's Aesthetics* (London: Continuum, 2006), 44, and view Kantian concepts "concretely and dynamically, rather than abstractly and statically," we recognize the concept itself (i.e., *dog*) as a "law-like mental act" that "unifies" the various intuitive impressions we have of a family of objects into "one integral figure" and disciplines the imagination's representational powers into a state of regularity.
44. Kalar, *The Demands of Taste,* 47.
45. Pillow, *Sublime Understanding,* 20.
46. Pillow, *Sublime Understanding,* 21, 319n5 (emphasis added).
47. This is not because *book* is some sort of "transcendental" eternal concept like a Platonic form. The emergence of tablet computers and the bur-

geoning sales of ebooks and audiobooks, as well as the expansive availability of books as online images through Google Books and other sites, may radically alter (if it has not already) the conceptual schema of *book* over time.

48. The parenthetical suggestions of what else I might judge a book to be—sculpture or spirit repository—help underscore an overarching point that Kant was unwilling to draw from his investigations in aesthetics. In allowing the imagination to be emancipated from the determinant rules that govern it through a subservient relationship to the understanding, aesthetic judgment allows a freer play with concepts that can engender new perspectives on objects of our judgment and clear space for us to pursue cognitive insights that would have been foreclosed in our intuitive acceptance of the prevailing conceptual categories. Aesthetic judgments need not deny that the object at hand is, in some sense, what determinant judgment claims it to be (e.g., a book); they simply allow us to pursue other interpretive paths of imagining and understanding what *else* or what *more* this particular object might be. For example, deploying the concept of *sculpture*—in the barest definition of a visual art medium operating in three dimensions—in an aesthetic judgment of a particular book might attune us to significant features that are present for analysis in the way that the book itself is bound and decorated, lending possible insights to the textual material inside the book or to the critical assessment of decorative art traditions in book publishing. For a study of the aesthetic and sociopolitical importance of decorative art in the emergence of book printing, see Lucien Febvre and Henri-Jean Martin, *The Coming of the Book: The Impact of Printing, 1450–1800* (New York: Verso Books, 1997), especially chapter 3.

Likewise, Henry Louis Gates Jr., among other scholars of African American literature, has identified a literary trope common to African American slave narratives involving a "talking book." In five of the earliest published slave narratives, ex-slave authors all report their early recognition of the link between white domination and literacy through an erroneous belief that the books themselves (or spirits within them) literally spoke to their white masters and told them, and them alone, secrets that secured their power. The ex-slaves, of course, all eventually discard this belief and become literate, but the trope serves, for Gates, a key narrative and symbolic purpose. It affirms the connection between literacy and autonomy, as well as human equality and literary tradition, characteristic of broader Western intellectual tradition and the vindicationist project of Afro-modern literature. Through sustained consideration of this symbolic-metaphorical characterization, Gates is able to develop an entire theory of "signifying," or intertextual references, in African literature and to explore the belief that governed much of African American literature until relatively recently: that a book might "speak" for an entire "race" of people and thereby do the crucial cultural work of proving or at least defending their humanity. See Henry Louis Gates Jr., *The Signifying Monkey: A Theory of African-American Literary Criticism* (New York: Oxford, 1989), chapter 4.

49. Maurizio Passerin D'Entreves, "Hannah Arendt's Theory of Judgment," in *The Cambridge Companion to Hannah Arendt,* ed. Dana Villa (New York: Cambridge University Press, 2000), 250–251 (emphasis added).
50. On the inescapability of concept-based cognition, see Kalar, *The Demands of Taste,* 43–45.
51. Samuel Fleischacker, *A Third Concept of Liberty: Judgment and Freedom in Kant and Adam Smith* (Princeton, NJ: Princeton University Press, 1999), 24.
52. Pillow, *Sublime Understanding,* 24.
53. "Duchamp's Urinal Tops Art Survey," BBC News, December 1, 2004, https://www.bbc.com/news.
54. On the importance of institutional settings and norms for defining art, see Arthur Danto, "The Artworld," *Journal of Philosophy* 61, no. 19 (1964): 571–584.
55. Christian Helmut Wenzel, *An Introduction to Kant's Aesthetics: Core Concepts and Problems* (New York: Blackwell, 2005), 9.
56. This last account is the view in Amiri Baraka, "Aime Cesaire," in *Daggers and Javelins: Essays, 1974–1979* (New York: William Morrow, 1984), 189.
57. A koala, for example, is perplexing to many who encounter it for the first time, and the concept of *bear* is often deployed to help make sense of what one is seeing. A more substantial knowledge of the biological foundations of animal classification, coupled with more information on the biology of koalas, however, would eventually lead the perplexed koala watcher to understand that the koala is better classified, according to the scientific convention, as a marsupial, given its divergent reproductive organs, short gestation period, and the offspring-carrying pouches of the female koala, where most of the early growth occurs. In discovering this acceptable classificatory rule, reflective judgment becomes determinant judgment.
58. Zammito, *The Genesis of Kant's Critique of Judgment,* 132.
59. Henry Allison, "Teleology and History in Kant," in *Kant's Idea for a Universal History with a Cosmopolitan Aim: A Critical Guide,* ed. Amélie Oksenberg Rorty and James Schmidt (New York: Cambridge University Press, 2009), 38.
60. Susan Neiman, *Evil in Modern Thought: An Alternative History of Philosophy* (Princeton, NJ: Princeton University Press, 2004), 83.
61. Kant himself suggested that his teleological approach might lead to more critically and cognitively sophisticated judgments on the possible counterintuitive benefits ("counter-purposive") of things we tend to view with fear and disgust: vermin, mosquitos, parasites, and the like (§67:379). Although Kant pursued the argument that such pests might serve as inducements toward modernization or civilization for "backwards" peoples, modern ecological and environmental sciences have generated tremendous insight through the adoption of something close to this regulative principle (shorn of its anthropocentrism) where a holistic conception of an environment is axiomatic and the operative assumption is that organisms are, prima facie, organically purposive, contributing something to the stability of their ecosystem.

    Take, for example, the gray wolf in the United States. Long considered a threat to humans and livestock agriculture, wolves were hunted and poisoned in extraordinary numbers, virtually vanishing from parts of the country where they once flourished. Ecological research on wolves, however, emphasizes the importance of their role as apex predators in maintaining an ecological equilibrium, and scientists and activists have been successful in reestablishing successful wolf populations in the northern United States. Unfortunately, many vocal constituencies still hold erroneous views about wolves, and there are many cross-cutting efforts to remove federal protections for the species. See Jeremy T. Bruskotter, Eric Toman, Sherry Enzler, and Robert H. Schmidt, "Letters: Gray Wolves Not out of the Woods Yet," *Science* 327, no. 5961 (2010): 30–31.

62. Immanuel Kant, "Idea for a Universal History with a Cosmopolitan Purpose," in *Political Writings,* 2nd ed., ed. H. S. Reiss, trans. H. B. Nisbet (Cambridge: Cambridge University Press, 1991), 42, 43.
63. Kant, "Idea for a Universal History," 43, 44.
64. Kant, "Idea for a Universal History"; Immanuel Kant, "Perpetual Peace: A Philosophical Sketch," in *Political Writings,* 2:93–110. See also Thomas McCarthy, *Race, Empire, and the Idea of Human Development* (New York: University of Cambridge, 2009), 56–57.
65. McCarthy, *Race, Empire, and the Idea of Human Development,* 55–59 (emphasis added). McCarthy helpfully situates Kant within a coterie of eighteenth-century intellectuals, including Bernard Mandeville, Rousseau, and Adam Smith; Rousseau also invoked what McCarthy calls a "dialectic of progress": the "inextricable entanglement of good and evil in human development."
66. Immanuel Kant, "A Renewed Attempt to Answer the Question: Is the Human Race Continually Improving? From *The Contest of Faculties,*" in *Political Writings,* 2:177.
67. Hayden White, "The Politics of Historical Interpretation: Discipline and De-Sublimation" in *The Content of the Form: Narrative Discourse and Historical Representation* (Baltimore: Johns Hopkins University Press, 1990), 72.
68. Friedrich Schiller, quoted in White, "The Politics of Historical Interpretation," 69.
69. Edmund Burke, "On the Sublime and Beautiful," in *Edmund Burke: Harvard Classics Edition,* ed. Charles W. Eliot (New York: P. F. Collier and Son, 1937), 35, 49, 58.
70. Burke, "On the Sublime and Beautiful," 54.
71. Zammito, *The Genesis of Kant's Critique of Judgment,* 283.
72. Kant, "A Renewed Attempt," 177.
73. Kant, "A Renewed Attempt," 177.
74. Kant is not clear if these leaders are suffering from something like what some critics call false consciousness.
75. Kant, "A Renewed Attempt," 189.
76. White explicitly suggests this essay as a precursor to his "metahistorical" approach in "The Politics of Historical Interpretation," 65.
77. Kant "A Renewed Attempt," 178–180, 181 (emphasis added).
78. Karl Marx, "The Holy Family," in *Karl Marx: Selected Writings,* 2nd ed. (Oxford: Oxford University Press, 2000), 265, famously criticizes G. W. F.

Hegel, Immanuel Kant, and their followers for believing that "the demands of the first French Revolution were . . . the demands of 'Practical Reason' in general, and the utterance of the will of the revolutionary French bourgeoisie . . . the laws of pure Will" and not the interests of a bourgeois class in abolishing feudalism.

79. Kant, "A Renewed Attempt," 182, 183–184.
80. Kant, "A Renewed Attempt," 182.
81. Kant, "A Renewed Attempt," 184 (emphasis added).
82. Kant, "A Renewed Attempt," 185.
83. Ralph Ellison, "Introduction to the Thirtieth Anniversary Edition of *Invisible Man*," in *Collected Essays of Ralph Ellison*, ed. John F. Callahan (New York: Modern Library, 2003), 483.
84. Ellison, "Introduction," 484.
85. Ellison, "Introduction," 483.

3. The Defeated Cause

1. See, for example, Seyla Benhabib, *The Reluctant Modernism of Hannah Arendt*, new ed. (Lanham, MD: Rowman and Littlefield, 2003); Lisa Disch, *Hannah Arendt and the Limits of Philosophy* (Ithaca, NY: Cornell University Press, 1994); Maurizio Passerin d'Entrèves, *The Political Philosophy of Hannah Arendt* (New York: Routledge, 1994); Dana Villa, *Politics, Philosophy, Terror: Essays on the Thought of Hannah Arendt* (Princeton, NJ: Princeton University Press, 1996); Andrew Norris, "Arendt, Kant, and the Politics of Common Sense," *Polity* 29, no. 2 (1996): 165–191; Richard J. Bernstein, "Judging—The Actor and the Spectator," in *Philosophical Profiles: Essays in a Pragmatic Mode* (Philadelphia: University of Pennsylvania Press, 1986), 221–237; Elizabeth Young-Bruehl, *Why Arendt Matters* (New Haven, CT: Yale University Press, 2006); David L. Marshall, "The Origin and Character of Hannah Arendt's Theory of Judgment," *Political Theory* 38, no. 3 (2010): 367–393; Linda Zerilli, *A Democratic Theory of Judgment* (Chicago: University of Chicago Press, 2016); and Alessandro Ferrara, *The Force of the Example: Explorations in the Paradigm of Judgment* (New York: Columbia University Press, 2008).
2. See, for example, the relatively recent efforts in Jonathan Peter Schwartz, *Arendt's Judgment: Freedom, Responsibility, Citizenship* (Philadelphia: University of Pennsylvania Press, 2016); and Martin Blumenthal-Barby, *Arendt, Kant, and the Enigma of Judgment* (Evanston, IL: Northwestern University Press, 2023).
3. Hannah Arendt, "Preface: The Gap Between Past and Future," in *Between Past and Future* (New York: Penguin, 1968), 5.
4. Schwartz, *Arendt's Judgment*, 22. Recall the argument in Hannah Arendt, *Lectures on Kant's Political Philosophy*, ed. Ronald Beiner (Chicago: University of Chicago Press, 1982), 85, that "most concepts in the historical and political sciences . . . have their origin in some particular historical incident, and we then proceed to make it 'exemplary'—to see in the particular what is valid for more than one case."

5. Arendt, "Preface," in *Between Past and Future,* 5. For the poem, see Percy Bysshe Shelley, "Ozymandias," in *Poems of Shelley,* ed. Stopford A. Brooke (New York: Macmillan, 1887), 66.
6. Wendy Brown, *Nihilistic Times: Thinking with Max Weber* (Cambridge, MA: Harvard University Press, 2023), 12.
7. Hannah Arendt, "Understanding and Politics (The Difficulties of Understanding)," in *Essays in Understanding: Formation, Exile, and Totalitarianism,* ed. Jerome Kohn (New York: Schocken Books, 1994), 321.
8. Hannah Arendt, "Hannah Arendt on Hannah Arendt," in *Thinking Without a Banister,* ed. Jerome Kohn (New York: Schocken Books, 2018), 473.
9. Hannah Arendt, quoted in Elisabeth Young-Bruehl, *Hannah Arendt: For Love of the World* (New Haven, CT: Yale University Press, 1982), 325.
10. Arendt, *Lectures on Kant's Political Philosophy,* 19.
11. Hannah Arendt, "The Crisis in Culture: Its Social and Political Significance," in *Between Past and Future,* 216.
12. For a sustained criticism of Arendt's reading of Kant, see Matthew C. Weidenfeld, "Visions of Judgment: Arendt, Kant, and the Misreading of Judgment," *Political Research Quarterly* 66, no. 2 (2012): 254–266.
13. Arendt, *Lectures on Kant's Political Philosophy,* 13–15, 65–68, 79–80.
14. David Cesarani, *Becoming Eichmann: Rethinking the Life, Crimes, and Trial of a "Desk Murderer"* (Cambridge, MA: De Capo, 2007).
15. These questions included whether Israel had legitimate jurisdiction to punish Eichmann, whether a government official could be punished for carrying out the legal orders of their polity, and the appropriateness of possible charges. Should we understand "crimes against the Jewish people" in a way distinct from "crimes against humanity"? What would it mean to charge a bureaucrat who orchestrated and organized wholesale slaughter with over six million murders?
16. Hannah Arendt, "Some Questions of Moral Philosophy," in *Responsibility and Judgment,* ed. Jerome Kohn (New York: Random House, 2003), 49–146.
17. Hannah Arendt, "Tradition and the Modern Age," in *Between Past and Future,* 26.
18. Hannah Arendt, *Eichmann in Jerusalem: A Report on the Banality of Evil* (New York: Penguin, 2006), 273. See also Leora Bilsky, "Between Justice and Politics: The Competition of Storytellers in the Eichmann Trial," in *Hannah Arendt in Jerusalem,* ed. Steven E. Ascheim (Berkeley: University of California Press, 2001), 232–252.
19. Seyla Benhabib, "Hannah Arendt and the Redemptive Power of Narrative," in *Hannah Arendt: Critical Essays,* ed. Lewis P. Hinchman and Sandra K. Hinchman (Albany: State University of New York Press, 1994), 118.
20. Arendt, "Tradition and the Modern Age"; Hannah Arendt, "The Tradition of Political Thought," in *The Promise of Politics,* ed. Jerome Kohn (New York: Schocken Books, 2007), 40–62. Robert Gooding-Williams has influentially extended this notion of the dominance of the politics of rule to the Afro-Modern tradition; see Robert Gooding-Williams, *In the Shadow of*

Du Bois: Afro-Modern Political Thought in America (Cambridge, MA: Harvard University Press, 2009).

21. In book 7 of *The Republic,* Plato famously depicts Socrates leading his interlocutor, Glaucon, through a thought experiment meant to dramatize Plato's conception (articulated, of course, through Socrates) of truth and his assessment of its role—and, by extension, the philosopher's role—in human affairs. In Socrates's description of the cave, it contains a group of prisoners who have lived in it since birth, restrained in such a way that they are forced to stare at the back wall of the cave. Behind them, outside the cave, there is a fire, and as the people outside the cave walk back and forth in front of this fire, they cast shadows on the cave's back wall that the prisoners in the cave take for reality and organize their lives around. Socrates then proposes that one of the prisoners be unchained and forcibly dragged out of the cave into the light above and that this person would—after initially resisting the blinding truth—eventually realize that the figures on the wall were but shadows of real beings and objects. Finally, Socrates suggests that this person would be ashamed of his former ignorance, and if he were ever to return to the cave and try to tell his former mates in bondage about their illusory world, their ignorance would lead them to turn on him in fear and violence. Plato, *The Republic,* ed. G. R. F. Ferrari, trans. Tom Griffith (Cambridge: Cambridge University Press, 2000).
22. This tendency presents itself even in traditions prone to populist or egalitarian, democratic arguments. W. E. B. Du Bois has been criticized for characterizing the African American "masses" as ignorant "of the world about them, of modern economic organization, of the function of government, of individual worth and possibilities," and, elsewhere, "of life itself." This ignorance, in his view, famously was part of the warrant for a natural aristocracy of talented leadership, the Talented Tenth, who would serve the purposes of "uplift" (or cultural and social reformation), artistic creativity in service of "group ideals," and political leadership—especially organizing for the promotion of black group interests and the amelioration of racial ideology and domination. See W. E. B. Du Bois, *The Souls of Black Folk* (Chicago: A. C. McClurg, 1903), 97, 143. For prominent criticisms of Du Bois on this point, see Robert Gooding-Williams, *In the Shadow of Du Bois: Afro-Modern Political Thought in America* (Cambridge, MA: Harvard University Press, 2009); and Cornel West, "Black Strivings in a Twilight Civilization," in *The Cornel West Reader* (New York: Basic Books, 1999), 87–118.
23. Hannah Arendt, *The Human Condition,* 2nd ed. (Chicago: University of Chicago Press, 1998), 226, 230–231.
24. Jerome Kohn, "Introduction," in Arendt, *The Promise of Politics,* xxvii.
25. Arendt, *The Human Condition,* 220. Arendt's concern to affirm and reconcile us to human plurality and interdependency as constitutive of freedom, action, and thinking is also a critical response to the ambiguous but often condemnatory account of being in the midst of *das Man* ("the they" or "the anyone") or the public as "distantiality, averageness, and leveling down" in her teacher Martin Heidegger's *Being and Time,* trans.

John MacQuarrie and Edward Robinson (New York: Harper and Row, 1962), 150–169. One of Arendt's major contributions to philosophy, therefore, is that she retains the Heideggerian insight of the human condition as being constituted by being-with-others in the world—what she deems plurality—while undermining Heidegger's claim that the public realm is essentially frustrating to self-realization or self-understanding. To the contrary, the realm of appearances underwritten by human plurality and judgment is the condition of anything like self-realization and self-understanding.

26. Bernard Harcourt, *Critique and Praxis* (New York: Columbia University Press, 2021), 203–226.
27. Arendt, *The Human Condition,* 234.
28. The persistence of Stoicism as a response to this problem will concern us in Chapter 7.
29. Arendt, *The Human Condition,* 222–223.
30. On Arendt's fragmentary historiography of the concept of *rule,* see Patchen Markell, "The Rule of the People: Arendt, Archê, and Democracy," *American Political Science Review* 100, no. 1 (2006): 1–14.
31. Simon Critchley, "Tragedy's Philosophy," in *Performing Antagonism: Theatre, Performance and Radical Democracy,* ed. Tony Fisher and Eve Katsouraki (London: Palgrave Macmillan, 2017), 25–42.
32. Arendt, *The Human Condition,* 222–224. Arendt does not, however, take this in any of the directions profitably pursued by late twentieth-century feminist theory critiquing the negative consequences and epistemic missteps occasioned by the pervasiveness of this model of the family in political thought and the assumptions of political philosophy and political practice. For an excellent collection of feminist engagements with Hannah Arendt, see Bonnie Honig, ed., *Feminist Interpretations of Hannah Arendt* (University Park: Penn State University Press, 1995).
33. For Arendt, these thinkers are central. In trying to save Christian faith from skepticism, Kierkegaard inadvertently lodged doubt and existential choice into its heart; in revealing the "life-denying" and illusory foundations of Western morality, Nietzsche ended up furthering the nihilism he sought to teach his (best) readers how to overcome; and in trying to critique G. W. F. Hegel's metaphysical theory of history and solve the problem of philosophy's relation to politics, Marx ended up dissolving philosophy into political praxis and inverting Hegel's hierarchy of idealism and materialism. "Reversal and inversion," Arendt contends, "carry their own extraordinary significance. They imply that the traditional hierarchy of values, if not necessarily their content, is established arbitrarily, or willfully . . . and in such a way that everything previously considered true now assumes the aspect of a perspective, over against which there must be the possibility of a multitude of equally legitimate and equally fruitful perspectives." Hannah Arendt, "From Hegel to Marx," in *The Promise of Politics,* 72. It is important to note that Arendt does not argue that these thinkers *caused* the collapse of tradition: "To hold the thinkers of the modern age, especially the nineteenth-century rebels against tradition, responsible for the structure and conditions of the twentieth century is even

more dangerous than it is unjust. The implications apparent in the actual event of totalitarian domination go far beyond the most radical or adventurous ideas of any of these thinkers. Their greatness lay in the fact that they perceived their world as one invaded by new problems and perplexities which our tradition of thought was unable to cope with." Arendt, "Tradition and the Modern Age," 26–27.

34. Arendt, "Tradition and the Modern Age," 26. See also Linda M. G. Zerilli, *Feminism and the Abyss of Freedom* (Chicago: University of Chicago Press, 2020), 125–164.
35. Linda M. G. Zerilli, "Castoriadis, Arendt, and the Problem of the New," *Constellations* 9, no. 4 (2002): 540–553.
36. Hannah Arendt, "What Is Freedom?," 163–165. See also Zerilli, "Castoriadis, Arendt, and the Problem of the New," 542.
37. Zerilli, "Castoriadis, Arendt, and the Problem of the New," 545, 547.
38. Hannah Arendt, "Preface to the First Edition," in *The Origins of Totalitarianism* (New York: Harcourt Brace Jovanovich, 1973), viii–ix.
39. Arendt, *The Origins of Totalitarianism,* 444.
40. It is interesting that in the frequent screeds against Arendt's supposed nostalgia for the Greek polis, which often criticize her for not being critical enough of these societies for being slaveholding societies, do not interrogate her remarks on evil for clues to her reticence on the topic. If slavery is not evil, why not?
41. See Arendt, *The Origins of Totalitarianism,* 443–444, 459. Beyond the singular phenomenon of the concentration camp, the Nazi regime as a whole achieved this spectacular evil in its large-scale treatment as utterly superfluous an enormous swath of humanity—its own party members, as well as its victims—through a profound congruence of totalitarian ideology and the administrative instruments of warmongering and extermination.
42. Cesarani, *Becoming Eichmann,* 2–3; Cesarani's reference to "psychological theories of Fascism and Nazism" includes, by his own account, works by the Frankfurt school of critical theory such as Theodor Adorno, Else Frenkel-Brunswik, Daniel J. Levinson, and R. Nevitt Sanford, *The Authoritarian Personality* (New York: Harper and Row, 1950); and Erich Fromm, *Escape from Freedom* (New York: Farrar and Reinhart, 1941). See also the key psychoanalytic text on fascism and sexual repression, Wilhelm Reich, *The Mass Psychology of Fascism* (New York: Farrar, Straus and Giroux, 1946); and, later, Yale University psychologist Stanley Milgram's famous Eichmann-inspired experiments on "obedience," *Obedience to Authority: An Experimental View* (New York: Harper and Row, 1974), which tested participants' willingness to administer electric shocks to other people (played by actors) under the supervision of an authority figure (the "teacher/researcher"). With the notable exception of Milgram, these psychological theories are derived from an appropriation of Freudian psychoanalysis and attempt to root authoritarianism in personality defects caused by repressed sexual desires, internalized anger at familial relationships, or anxieties about the lack of control. Thus, it is no surprise, as Cesarani notes, that Eichmann's libertine sexual proclivities became a central theme

of these works. Milgram's analysis of his experiment, on the other hand, tended to emphasize what was a shocking tendency of individuals to acquiesce to perceived authorities, even when knowingly harming others *and* a general conformity with the actions of peers.

43. Arendt, *Eichmann in Jerusalem,* 276.
44. Benhabib, *The Reluctant Modernism,* 67; Cesarani, *Becoming Eichmann,* 327.
45. Hannah Arendt, "Answers to Questions Submitted by Samuel Grafton," in *The Jewish Writings,* ed. Jerome Kohn and Ron H. Feldman (New York: Schocken Books, 2008), 475.
46. Arendt, *Eichmann in Jerusalem,* 287. See also, for example, *The Devil's Confession: The Lost Eichmann Tapes,* directed by Yariv Mozer (KAN/MGM, 2022); and Bettina Stangneth, *Eichmann Before Jerusalem* (New York: Alfred A. Knopf, 2014). For accounts of the controversy surrounding Arendt's Eichmann writings, see Cesarani, *Becoming Eichmann,* 344–356; Young-Bruehl, *Hannah Arendt,* 328–378; and Seyla Benhabib, "Arendt's *Eichmann in Jerusalem,*" in *The Cambridge Companion to Hannah Arendt,* ed. Dana Villa (New York: Cambridge University Press, 2006), 65–85.
47. Christopher Browning, quoted in Jennifer Schuessler, "Book Portrays Eichmann as Evil but Not Banal," *New York Times,* September 2, 2014.
48. Arendt, *The Human Condition,* 5, 49.
49. Arendt, *Eichmann in Jerusalem,* 53–54, 82. See also Hannah Arendt, "Organized Guilt and Universal Responsibility," in *Essays in Understanding,* 128–129.
50. Hannah Arendt, "A Letter to Gershom Scholem," in *The Jewish Writings,* 471.
51. Arendt, *Eichmann in Jerusalem,* 52, 85, 105–106, 252.
52. Arendt is not always clear on her social theoretic claims in *Eichmann.* There are gestures toward some of the ideological culprits Arendt fingered in *Origins*—the Nazi's teleological theories of global racial conflict and Germanic-Aryan supremacy and the instrumental rationality of state bureaucracy and state sovereignty—but sometimes the problem of thoughtlessness is seemingly unmoored from these broader social or institutional formations. One emphasis is on linguistic manipulation. By giving the tasks of the "final solution" the veneer of heroic burdens, superhuman deeds, or movements of history; or, by obscuring the utter violence of the Nazi project through obfuscating euphemisms (i.e., *final solution, evacuation, special treatment,* and *resettlement*), the Nazi regime was able to cultivate the thoughtlessness needed to reproduce itself. Again, we are supposed to see this as continuous with broader modern trends. Arendt would identify the "public relations" functionaries of government, consumer society advertising, and many social scientists as potential manufacturers of similar "deceptions." The idea that Eichmann is motivated by "personal advancement" like the bourgeois citizen in a modern corporate firm or state bureaucracy is also at play. See Arendt, *Eichmann in Jerusalem,* 52; and Hannah Arendt, "Lying in Politics," in *Crises of the Republic* (New York: Harcourt Brace Jovanovich, 1972), 1–48.

53. Adolf Eichmann, quoted in the appendix to Bryan Garsten, "The Elusiveness of Arendtian Judgment," *Social Research* 74, no. 4 (2007): 1100, 1102.
54. Arendt, *Eichmann in Jerusalem,* 136–137.
55. Garsten, "The Elusiveness of Arendtian Judgment," 1074, 1078.
56. Arendt, "Some Questions of Moral Philosophy," 54, 50.
57. Arendt, "Some Questions of Moral Philosophy," 78.
58. Martin Luther King Jr., "Love, Law, and Civil Disobedience," in *A Testament of Hope,* ed. James Washington (San Francisco: HarperCollins, 1986), 50.
59. Hannah Arendt, *Life of the Mind* (New York: Harcourt Brace Jovanovich, 1977), 5.
60. Zerilli, *A Democratic Theory of Judgment,* 30.
61. All parenthetical in-text citations in this chapter refer to Immanuel Kant, *Critique of the Power of Judgment,* ed. Paul Guyer, trans. Paul Guyer and Eric Matthews (New York: Cambridge University Press, 2000).
62. Rudolf A. Makkreel, *Orientation and Judgment in Hermeneutics* (Chicago: University of Chicago Press, 2015), 2.
63. Makkreel, *Orientation and Judgment in Hermeneutics,* 102.
64. Zerilli, *A Democratic Theory of Judgment,* 77.
65. Michel Chaouli, *Thinking with Kant's Critique of Judgment* (Cambridge, MA: Harvard University Press, 2017), 164.
66. Samantha Matherne, "Kant on Aesthetic Autonomy and Common Sense," *Philosophers' Imprint* 19, no. 24 (2019): 4.
67. Matherne, "Kant on Aesthetic Autonomy," 4–5. For a sympathetic account of the idea of "transcendental psychology," see Patricia Kitcher, *Kant's Transcendental Psychology* (New York: Oxford University Press, 1990).
68. Paul Guyer, "Editor's Introduction," in Kant, *Critique of the Power of Judgment,* xxx.
69. The discussion of sensus communis herein borrows heavily from Brett Kalar, *The Demands of Taste in Kant's Aesthetics* (London: Continuum, 2006), 140–145. Recall that Kant uses the distinction of "pure," idealized judgments of beauty from judgments about "the agreeable" or "the good" to theorize judgments of beauty at their most "disinterested" and, on his account, most free. To be disinterested, in Kant's view, is not to primarily relate to something as an object of desire or obligation.
70. Since our feelings of the relationship between our cognitive faculties remains subjective, we cannot demand or compel agreement. Only those who share (or can be persuaded to share) something like our subjective response in a given reflection can ultimately come to agree with our judgment concerning aesthetic matters. Kant insists that despite the empirical fact of vast differences in taste and judgments of beauty, human beings share a capacity to feel a spontaneous accord between their imaginations and their understandings, especially when apprehending purposiveness without purpose. If this proper functioning is possible to discern and communicate in aesthetic judgments of beauty, this subjective feeling of harmonious accord between faculties allows us to recognize that our judgments of beauty *consist in spontaneous harmony in the first place.*

71. Matherne, "Kant on Aesthetic Autonomy," 11.
72. Matherne, "Kant on Aesthetic Autonomy," 15.
73. Arendt, *Lectures on Kant's Political Philosophy,* 75.
74. Arendt, *Lectures on Kant's Political Philosophy,* 67.
75. Arendt, *The Human Condition,* 176.
76. Maurizio Passerin D'Entrèves, "Arendt's Theory of Judgment," in Villa, *The Cambridge Companion to Hannah Arendt,* 253.
77. Arendt, "The Crisis in Culture," 217 (emphases added).
78. Zerilli, *A Democratic Theory of Judgment,* 9–10.
79. Arendt, *Lectures on Kant's Political Philosophy,* 73.
80. George Kateb, "Fiction as Poison," in *Thinking in Dark Times: Hannah Arendt on Ethics and Politics,* ed. Roger Berowitz, Thomas Keenan, and Jeffrey Katz (New York: Fordham University Press, 2009), 34–36.
81. Arendt, "The Crisis in Culture," 219.
82. Arendt, *The Human Condition,* 23.
83. Arendt, *Lectures on Kant's Political Philosophy,* 75–85.
84. Metaphors, for example, conjoin themes, language, and ideas that, according to strict semantic or cognitive rules, are clearly nonsensical. Allowed some imaginative freedom from these rules, however, language can be deployed in ways that create meaning through unexpected semantic collisions. Metaphors are often clearly incorrect at the level of formal semantic, conceptual correspondence, but as a way of illuminating thematic attributes that are not otherwise easily disclosed, they can usefully convey an analytical and ethical interpretation of relationships not immediately apparent. A metaphor thus presents an interpretation that can then be judged true or false, right or wrong, and so on. Kirk Pillow, *Sublime Understanding* (Cambridge, MA: MIT Press, 2000), 121.
85. Zerilli, *Feminism and the Abyss of Freedom.*
86. Marshall, "The Origin and Character," 375.
87. Arendt, *Lectures on Kant's Political Philosophy,* 77.
88. Zerilli, *Democratic Theory of Judgment,* 68.
89. Arendt, *Lectures on Kant's Political Philosophy,* 75–85.
90. Pillow, *Sublime Understanding,* 120.
91. For instance, as John L. Jackson, *Racial Paranoia: The Unintended Consequences of Political Correctness: The New Reality of Race in America* (New York: Basic Civitas, 2008), 120–123, relates, black racial paranoia about the omnipresence of white racism can take on just this sort of unified, systemic character and develop an expansive reach in its interpretive aims. The psychologist Frances Cress Welsing, whose book *The Isis Papers: The Keys to the Colors* (Chicago: Third World, 1991) Jackson considers an exemplary text of black postwar racial paranoia, advances a theory as impressive in its comprehensiveness as it is absurd in its conclusions. The book is based on a perversion of the Darwinist-Mendelian synthesis in evolutionary biological theory and claims that "whiteness" (understood biologically as melanin deficiency) is a recessive genetic trait, a mutation at perpetual risk of annihilation by the reproduction of nonwhite, and especially black, people. Driven by the innate desire for group survival

but dimly cognizant of their genetic inferiority, white people seek to implement forms of domination that circumscribe the reproductive capacity of black people. As readers of even mainstream evolutionary biology know, the array of social formations that can be "explained" by reference to a genetic interest in reproductive success are massive. For Welsing, familiar forms of domination like segregation and labor discrimination obviously fit the bill, but she also sees such purposes manifest in the existence of male homosexuality, the promotion of abortion rights, and even the implicit symbolism of sports and games. It is no mere coincidence, for Welsing, that in American sports, the largest balls (e.g., basketballs, footballs, bowling balls) are usually dark, and the smaller balls (e.g., baseballs and golf balls) are white, or that the former are usually thrown at a white object (e.g., a basketball net, bowling pins) and the latter are hit with dark sticks. The seemingly innocuous equipment of modern athletics is "revealed" to be a subconscious symbolic field rooted in the psychosexual fears of white people, with balls standing in for testicles, nets standing in for white female genitalia, and so forth.

92. Herbert Marcuse, *Negations: Essays in Critical Theory,* trans. Jeremy J. Shapiro (London: Mayfly, 2009), 47.
93. Arendt, "Truth and Politics," in *Between Past and Future,* 241.
94. Arendt, *Lectures on Kant's Political Philosophy*, 163.
95. Iris Marion Young, "Asymmetrical Reciprocity: On Moral Respect, Wonder, and Enlarged Thought," in *Intersecting Voices: Dilemmas of Gender, Political Philosophy, and Politics* (Princeton, NJ: Princeton University Press, 1997), 38–59.
96. Hannah Arendt, "Reflections on Little Rock," in *Responsibility and Judgment,* reprint ed. (New York: Schocken Books, 2005), 193–213. The literature on Arendt's Little Rock essay is now immense. Especially important are the extremely critical Kathryn T. Gines, *Hannah Arendt and the Negro Question* (Bloomington: Indiana University Press, 2014); the Ralph Ellison-inspired critique offered in Danielle S. Allen, *Talking to Strangers: Anxieties of Citizenship Since Brown v. Board of Education* (Chicago: University of Chicago Press, 2006); and the important recent essay by Ainsley LeSure, "The White Mob, (In)equality Before the Law, and Racial Common Sense: A Critical Race Reading of the Negro Question in 'Reflections on Little Rock,'" *Political Theory* 49, no. 1 (2021): 3–27.
97. There is a long-standing conception of black testimony, refracted through cultural production and political striving, as a "gift" to American civilization. See, for example, W. E. B. Du Bois, *The Gift of Black Folk: The Negroes in the Making of America* (Boston: Stratford, 1924) for an influential account of African American cultural and intellectual production as a gift that emerges from black cultural and political particularity but which Du Bois thinks can (and self-consciously *should*) make an ethical, aesthetic, and epistemological impact on other groups as part of world "civilization." See also Chike Jeffers, "What Counts as a Collective Gift? Culture and Value in Du Bois's 'The Gift of Black Folk.'" *Royal Institute of Philosophy Supplements* 93 (2023): 99–116.

98. These sorts of arguments, which reflect Young's immersion in activist-intellectual defenses of standpoint epistemology, have grown increasingly familiar in recent years. For a wonderfully precise and tightly argued account of the limited "epistemic advantages" that come from being oppressed, see Lidal Dror, "Is There an Epistemic Advantage to Being Oppressed?," *Noûs* 57, no. 3 (2023): 618–640. Arguably the most influential statement of standpoint theory is Patricia Hill Collins, *Black Feminist Thought: Knowledge, Consciousness, and the Politics of Empowerment,* 30th anniversary ed. (New York: Routledge, 2022).
99. Garsten, "The Elusiveness of Arendtian Judgment," 1095, 1096.
100. Zerilli, *Feminism and the Abyss of Freedom,* 159.
101. Zerilli, *A Democratic Theory of Judgment,* 67–68.
102. Zerilli, *Feminism and the Abyss of Freedom,* 171, 163.
103. Arendt, "Some Questions of Moral Philosophy," 166. In the French folktale popularized by Charles Perrault, Bluebeard is a wealthy and violent nobleman who murders his successive wives for disobeying his command not to enter a forbidden room. The tale is often interpreted as a cautionary story about curiosity, patriarchal control, and the dangers hidden within domestic life. See Charles Perrault, "Bluebeard," in *The Great Fairy Tale Tradition: From Straparola and Basile to the Brothers Grimm,* ed. Jack Zipes (New York: W. W. Norton, 2001), 732–736.
104. Garsten, "The Elusiveness of Arendtian Judgment," 1088–1089, 1099.
105. Arendt, *Lectures on Kant's Political Philosophy,* 26, 77.
106. Arendt, *Lectures on Kant's Political Philosophy,* 126.
107. Schwartz, *Arendt's Judgment,* 49
108. Benhabib, *The Reluctant Modernism.*
109. Hannah Arendt, "Walter Benjamin, 1892–1940," trans. Harry Zohn, in Arendt, *Men in Dark Times* (New York: Houghton Mifflin Harcourt, 1970), 205–206.
110. Benhabib, *The Reluctant Modernism,* 88
111. Benhabib, *The Reluctant Modernism,* 88.
112. Arendt, "Preface," in *Between Past and Future,* 14.
113. Leslie Paul Thiele, *The Heart of Judgment: Practical Wisdom, Neuroscience, and Narrative* (New York: Cambridge University Press, 2006), 273.
114. Paul Ricoeur, "Life in Quest of Narrative," in *On Paul Ricoeur: Narrative and Interpretation,* ed. David Wood (New York: Routledge, 1991), 26. This theory of interpretation is opposed to the familiar claim that the meaning of a text lies solely in authorial intent. The authorial intent model of interpretation promotes a methodology and attitude that attempts to recreate the original context of the text, encourages the reader to make an imaginative leap into the self-understanding of the author, and treats the reader's own context as a source of prejudices and assumptions that serve largely as impediments to authentic understanding.
115. Hans-Georg Gadamer, *Truth and Method* (New York: Continuum, 2004).
116. Paul Ricoeur, "Life As Narrative," in *On Paul Ricoeur,* 26.
117. Ricoeur, "Life as Narrative," 28–29.
118. Ricoeur, "Life as Narrative," 28–29.

119. Charles Taylor, *The Sources of the Self: The Making of the Modern Identity* (New York: Cambridge University Press, 1989), 37.
120. Theresa Rundstedler, "Visible Men: African American Boxers, the New Negro, and the Global Color Line," *Radical History Review* 103 (2009): 59–81.
121. Thomas McCarthy, "Reason and Rationalization: Habermas's 'Overcoming' of Hermeneutics," in *Ideals and Illusions: On Reconstruction and Deconstruction in Contemporary Critical Theory* (Cambridge, MA: MIT Press, 1993), 45–46.
122. Hayden White, "The Value of Narrativity in the Representation of Reality," *Critical Inquiry* 7, no. 1 (1980): 9.
123. Glenda Elizabeth Gilmore, *Defying Dixie: The Radical Roots of Civil Rights, 1919–1950* (New York: W. W. Norton, 2008), 15–67.
124. White, "The Value of Narrativity," 10.
125. White, "The Value of Narrativity," 15, 14.
126. For a philosophical history of the Haitian occupation and its consequences, see Patrick Sylvain, "Haiti and Being: Vodoun, Zombies and the Plantation Continuum" (PhD diss., Brandeis University, 2022).
127. Woodrow Wilson, "The Reconstruction of the Southern States," *Atlantic Monthly,* January 1901, 1–15.
128. Gilmore, *Defying Dixie,* 6–8.
129. Rogers M. Smith, *Stories of Peoplehood: The Politics and Morals of Political Membership* (New York: Cambridge University Press, 2003).
130. White, "The Value of Narrativity," 18, 24.
131. Smith, *Stories of Peoplehood,* 20, 44.
132. Smith, *Stories of Peoplehood,* 133–134.
133. Hayden White, "The Question of Narrative in Contemporary Historical Theory," *History and Theory* 3, no. 1 (1984): 19.
134. Hayden White, "Narrativity in the Representation of Reality," in *The Content of the Form: Narrative Discourse and Narrative Representation* (Baltimore, MD: Johns Hopkins University Press, 1990), 10, 23.
135. W. B. Gallie, "Narrative and Historical Understanding," in *The History and Narrative Reader,* ed. Geoffrey Roberts (New York: Routledge, 2001), 50.
136. Noël Carroll, "Interpretation, History, and Narrative," *Monist* 73, no. 2 (1990): 134–136.

4. The Romance of Civil Rights

1. Julian Bond, quoted in Jeanne Theoharis, "Introduction: What Julian Bond Taught Me," in *Julian Bond's Time to Teach: A History of the Southern Civil Rights Movement* (Boston: Beacon, 2021), xiv.
2. Hayden White, *Metahistory: The Historical Imagination in Nineteenth-Century Europe* (Baltimore: Johns Hopkins University Press, 1973), 8–9, 150.
3. Alan Soble, "The Unity of Romantic Love," *Philosophy and Theology* 1, no. 4 (1987): 374–397.
4. Doris Sommer, *Foundational Fictions: The National Romances of Latin America* (Berkeley: University of California Press, 1991).

5. Taylor Branch, *Parting the Waters: America in the King Years, 1954–1963* (New York: Simon and Schuster, 1988); Taylor Branch, *Pillar of Fire: America in the King Years, 1963–1965* (New York: Simon and Schuster, 1998); Taylor Branch, *At Canaan's Edge: America in the King Years, 1965–1968* (New York: Simon and Schuster, 2006).
6. Leon R. Kass, *Founding God's Nation: Reading Exodus* (New Haven, CT: Yale University Press, 2021).
7. Michael Walzer, *Exodus and Revolution* (New York: Basic Books, 1985), 149.
8. Eddie S. Glaude Jr., *Exodus! Religion, Race, and Nation in Early Nineteenth-Century Black America* (Chicago: University of Chicago Press, 2000), 12 (emphasis added).
9. Glaude, *Exodus!*, 49, 56.
10. Martin Luther King Jr., "The Death of Evil upon the Seashore," sermon delivered at the Service of Prayer and Thanksgiving, May 17, 1956, https://www.kinginstitute.stanford.edu/king-papers/documents/death-evil-upon-seashore-sermon-delivered-service-prayer-and-thanksgiving.
11. Branch, *Parting the Waters*, xii. On King as Moses, see Scott W. Hoffman, "Holy Martin: The Overlooked Canonization of Dr. Martin Luther King, Jr.," *Religion and American Culture: A Journal of Interpretation* 10, no. 2 (2000): 128–130.
12. Martin Luther King, Jr., quoted in Loudon Wainwright, "Martyr of the Sit-Ins, Reprinted Courtesy of *Life* Magazine," *Negro History Bulletin* 24, no. 7 (1961): 147.
13. On the spiritual discipline against resentment, see Christopher Lasch, *The True and Only Heaven: Progress and Its Critics* (New York: W. W. Norton, 1991), 369–411. On Black Power as the dramatic exemplar of the "bad 1960s," used to redound to what I call a romantic vision, see Peniel E. Joseph, "The Black Power Movement: A State of the Field," *Journal of American History* 96, no. 3 (2009): 751–776.
14. William Brink and Louis Harris, *The Negro Revolution in America* (New York: Simon and Schuster, 1964), 43.
15. I use the term *slay* deliberately. On Northrop Frye's account, the overall biblical narrative structure is "a comic romance, a *commedia* with its recognition scene in the Gospel and a romance that polarizes its characters and has a divine hero or protagonist killing a dragon." See Alvin A. Lee and Jean O'Grady, "Introduction," in Northrop Frye, *The Collected Works of Northrop Frye*, vol. 4, *Northrop Frye on Religion* (Toronto: University of Toronto Press, 2000), xxii.
16. Michael K. Honey, *Going Down Jericho Road: The Memphis Strike, Martin Luther King's Last Campaign* (New York: W.W. Norton, 2007), 473–474, 480–481.
17. On the Fair Housing Act of 1968, Gerald Jaynes and Robin M. Williams, *A Common Destiny: Blacks and American Society* (Washington, DC: National Academies, 1989), 229, report that "virtually all observers concede that the Fair Housing Act of 1968 owes its existence to the assassination of Martin Luther King, Jr., and the subsequent riots . . . and the package was

passed within a week of the national turmoil following King's assassination." For a detailed historical account of the shift in elite college admissions toward higher admission rates of blacks occasioned by the King assassination, see Jerome Karabel, *The Chosen: The Hidden History of Admission and Exclusion at Harvard, Yale, and Princeton* (Boston: First Mariner Books, 2006), 401–402, 406–407. On racial attitudes, Robert Riley and Thomas Pettigrew, "Dramatic Events and Attitude Change," *Journal of Personality and Social Psychology* 34, no. 5 (1976), 1004–1015, argue that King's assassination had a liberalizing impact on white Texans, particularly in metropolitan areas. Others claim that there is a "liberal leap" in white racial attitudes from 1970 to 1972 that is distinguishable even from the steady liberalization of white racial attitudes more broadly after the end of World War II. See D. Garth Taylor, Paul B. Sheatsley, and Andrew M. Greeley, "Attitudes Toward Racial Integration," *Scientific American* 238, no. 6 (1978): 42–49.

18. Drew Hansen, *The Dream: Martin Luther King, Jr., and the Speech That Inspired a Nation* (New York: HarperCollins, 2003), 208.
19. Branch, *Parting the Waters,* 887.
20. Northrop Frye, *Anatomy of Criticism: Four Essays* (Princeton, NJ: Princeton University Press, 2015), 186.
21. Jana Weiss, "Remember, Celebrate, and Forget? The Martin Luther King Day and the Pitfalls of Civil Religion," *Journal of American Studies* 53, no. 2 (2019): 428–448.
22. Martin Luther King Jr., *The Autobiography of Martin Luther King Jr.* (New York: Warner Books, 1998), 267–268. See also Branch, *Pillar of Fire,* 567–568.
23. Branch, *Pillar of Fire,* 602–605.
24. Ludwig Wittgenstein, *On Certainty,* ed. G. E. M. Anscombe and G. H. von Wright, trans. G. E. M. Anscombe (New York: Basil Blackwell, 1969), §141–142.
25. Jeremiah Wright, "Confusing God and Government (April 13, 2003)," BlackPast, https://www.blackpast.org/african-american-history/2008-rev-jeremiah-wright-confusing-god-and-government/.
26. Barack Obama, "Transcript: Barack Obama's Speech on Race," NPR, March 18, 2008, https://www.npr.org/2008/03/18/88478467/transcript-barack-obamas-speech-on-race.
27. Obama, "Transcript: Barack Obama's Speech on Race."
28. Barack Obama, "Remarks at the Selma Voting Rights March Commemoration, Selma, Alabama," American Presidency Project, March 4, 2007, https://www.presidency.ucsb.edu/documents/remarks-the-selma-voting-rights-march-commemoration-selma-alabama.
29. Melvin Rogers, *The Darkened Light of Faith: Race, Democracy, and Freedom in African American Political Thought* (Princeton, NJ: Princeton University Press, 2023), 143–144.
30. Obama, "Transcript: Barack Obama's Speech on Race."
31. Barack Obama, *The Audacity of Hope: Thoughts on Reclaiming the American Dream* (New York: Crown, 2006), 37.

32. Charles Taylor, "Lichtung or Lebensform: Parallels Between Heidegger and Wittgenstein," in *Philosophical Arguments* (Cambridge, MA: Harvard University Press, 1997), 69.
33. Richard W. Leeman, *The Teleological Discourse of Barack Obama* (Lanham, MD: Lexington Books, 2012), 15.
34. Aziz Rana, *The Constitutional Bind: How Americans Came to Idolize a Document That Fails Them* (Chicago: University of Chicago Press, 2024): 3–6. See also see David E. Pozen, "Structural Biases in Structural Constitutional Law," *New York University Law Review* 97, no. 1 (2022): 1–72.
35. Jacob M. Grumbach, *Laboratories Against Democracy: How National Parties Transformed State Politics* (Princeton, NJ: Princeton University Press, 2022). See also Robert W. Mickey, *Paths Out of Dixie: The Democratization of Authoritarian Enclaves in America's Deep South, 1944–1972* (Princeton, NJ: Princeton University Press, 2015).
36. Obama, "Transcript: Barack Obama's Speech on Race."
37. Obama, "Transcript: Barack Obama's Speech on Race."
38. Brandon Terry, "Racial Politics After Obama," *Dissent,* Summer 2016, https://www.dissentmagazine.org.
39. John Rawls, *Justice as Fairness: A Restatement,* ed. Erin Kelly (Cambridge, MA: Belknap Press of Harvard University Press, 2001), 3.
40. Rawls, *Justice as Fairness,* 3, 4n4, 5.
41. It is perhaps reflective of the broad decline in biblical literacy in American intellectual culture that the figure of Joshua was so easily assimilated to Barack Obama's rhetoric of racial reconciliation, given that Joshua's conquest of Canaan is extraordinarily brutal, including the wholesale slaughter of opposing ethnic groups, including noncombatants.
42. Barack Obama, "Inaugural Address by President Barack Obama," Obama White House Archives, January 21, 2013, https://obamawhitehouse.archives.gov/the-press-office/2013/01/21/inaugural-address-president-barack-obama.
43. Ta-Nehisi Coates, *Between the World and Me* (New York: Spiegel and Grau, 2015).
44. Ta-Nehisi Coates, "Black Pathology and the Closing of the Progressive Mind," *Atlantic,* March 2014.
45. Barack Obama, "Transcript: President Obama's Commencement Address at Howard University," *Politico,* May 7, 2016, https://www.politico.com/story/2016/05/obamas-howard-commencement-transcript-222931.
46. On the possible influence of John Rawls on Obama, see James T. Kloppenberg, *Reading Obama: Dreams, Hope, and the American Political Tradition* (Princeton, NJ: Princeton University Press, 2011): 85–150.
47. Thomas Sowell, *Ever Wonder Why? And Other Controversial Essays* (Stanford, CA: Hoover Institution Press, 2006).
48. Obama, "Remarks at the Selma Voting Rights March Commemoration."
49. Martin Luther King Jr., "I See the Promised Land," in *A Testament of Hope: The Essential Writings and Speeches of Martin Luther King, Jr.*, ed. James Melvin Washington (San Francisco: Harper and Row, 1986), 286.

50. Henry Louis Gates Jr., "In Our Lifetime," *Root,* November 5, 2008, https://www.theroot.com.
51. Barack Obama, *A Promised Land* (New York: Crown, 2020), 397.
52. See Brandon Terry, "A Stranger in Mine Own House: Henry Louis Gates Jr. and the Police in 'Post-Racial' America," *Huffington Post,* July 29, 2009, https://www.huffingtonpost.com.
53. Barack Obama, "Remarks by the President at the 50th Anniversary of the Selma to Montgomery Marches," Obama White House Archives, March 7, 2015, Obama White House Archives, https://obamawhitehouse.archives.gov/the-press-office/2015/03/07/remarks-president-50th-anniversary-selma-montgomery-marches.
54. Rawls, *Justice as Fairness,* 2.
55. Obama, Remarks by the President at the 50th Anniversary of the Selma to Montgomery Marches."
56. Partha Chatterjee, *Lineages of Political Society: Studies in Postcolonial Democracy* (New York: Columbia University Press, 2011), 1–2.
57. Johannes Fabian, *Time and the Other: How Anthropology Makes Its Object* (New York: Columbia University Press, 2002), 31.
58. David A. Graham, "The Wrong Side of 'the Right Side of History,'" *Atlantic,* December 2015, https://www.theatlantic.com/politics/archive/2015/12/obama-right-side-of-history/420462/.
59. Zeeshan Aleem, "The Democrats' Problematic Attitude Toward Voters of Color Hits a Wall," MSNBC, November 12, 2024, https://www.msnbc.com/opinion/msnbc-opinion/democrats-latino-voters-trump-demographics-destiny-rcna179662. The idea of "demography as destiny," promising an enduring liberal majority based on America becoming a "majority-minority" country, was influentially promulgated in John B. Judis and Ruy Teixeira, *The Emerging Democratic Majority* (New York: Scribner, 2002).
60. On Little Rock, see Karen Anderson, *Little Rock: Race and Resistance at Central High School* (Princeton, NJ: Princeton University Press, 2009). On the Children's Crusade and other mass youth protests, see V. P. Franklin, *The Young Crusaders: The Untold Story of the Children and Teenagers Who Galvanized the Civil Rights Movement* (Boston: Beacon, 2021). On armed political resistance in the civil rights movement, see Akinyele Omowale Umoja, *We Will Shoot Back: Armed Resistance in the Mississippi Freedom Movement* (New York: New York University Press, 2013).
61. Owen J. Dwyer and Derek H. Alderman, *Civil Rights Memorials and the Geography of Memory* (Chicago: Center for American Places at Columbia College Chicago, 2008).
62. Taylor Branch, *At Canaan's Edge: America in the King Years, 1965–68* (New York: Simon and Schuster, 2007), 771. Branch seems to suggest that King's quote is taken directly from the nineteenth-century abolitionist Theodore Parker, but this is incorrect. The full Parker quote is as follows: "I do not pretend to understand the moral universe. The arc is a long one. My eye reaches but little ways. I cannot calculate the curve and complete the figure by experience of sight. I can divine it by conscience. And from what I see I am sure it bends toward justice." Theodore Parker, "Of Justice and the

Conscience," in *Views of Religion* (Boston: American Unitarian Association, 1885), 151. King frequently paraphrased this section of Parker's sermon for dramatic effect and for a significantly more assured grasp of transcendental ethical truth and moral direction in history.

63. White, *Metahistory,* 155, 161.
64. On the attack against the civil rights constitution, see Orville Vernon Burton and Armand Derfner, *Justice Deferred: Race and the Supreme Court* (Cambridge, MA: Belknap Press of Harvard University Press, 2021); and Erwin Chemerinsky, *The Conservative Assault on the Constitution* (New York: Simon and Schuster, 2010). On the disorientation of black politics, see Fredrick C. Harris, *The Price of the Ticket: Barack Obama and the Rise and Decline of Black Politics* (New York: Oxford University Press, 2012); and Lester K. Spence, *Knocking the Hustle: Against the Neoliberal Turn in Black Politics* (Brooklyn: Punctum Books, 2015). On democracy, see Craig Calhoun, Dilip Parameshwar Gaonkar, and Charles Taylor, *Degenerations of Democracy* (Cambridge, MA: Harvard University Press, 2022); Steven Levitsky and Daniel Ziblatt, *How Democracies Die* (New York: Crown, 2018); Suzanne Mettler and Robert C. Lieberman, *Four Threats: The Recurring Crises of American Democracy* (New York: St. Martin's, 2020); and Michael J. Sandel, *Democracy's Discontent: A New Edition for Our Perilous Times* (Cambridge, MA: Belknap Press of Harvard University Press, 2022). On the persistence of racial inequality, see Thomas M. Shapiro, *Toxic Inequality: How America's Wealth Gap Destroys Mobility, Deepens the Racial Divide, and Threatens Our Future* (New York: Basic Books, 2017); Patrick Sharkey, *Stuck in Place: Urban Neighborhoods and the End of Progress Toward Racial Equality* (Chicago: University of Chicago Press, 2013); Ellora Derenoncourt, Chi Hyun Kim, Moritz Kuhn, and Moritz Schularick, "Wealth of Two Nations: The US Racial Wealth Gap, 1860–2020," *Quarterly Journal of Economics* 139, no. 2 (2024): 693–750; and Christopher Muller and Alexander F. Roehrkasse, "Racial and Class Inequality in US Incarceration in the Early Twenty-First Century," *Social Forces* 101, no. 2 (2022): 803–828.
65. Stewart Burns, *To the Mountaintop: Martin Luther King Jr.'s Mission to Save America, 1955–1968* (New York: HarperCollins, 2004), 443, 458.
66. Daniel Compagnon, *A Predictable Tragedy: Robert Mugabe and the Collapse of Zimbabwe* (Philadelphia: University of Pennsylvania Press, 2011).
67. David Scott, *Conscripts of Modernity* (Durham, NC: Duke University Press, 2004), 32.
68. Scott, *Conscripts of Modernity,* 2, 41.
69. Scott, *Conscripts of Modernity,* 29.
70. Wendy Brown, *Nihilistic Times: Thinking with Max Weber* (Cambridge, MA: Harvard University Press, 2023).

5. The Tangible Ruins of Our Present

1. Herbert Marcuse, *One-Dimensional Man: Studies in the Ideology of Advanced Industrial Society* (Boston: Beacon, 1964).

2. Ranier Forst, *Normativity and Power: Analyzing Social Orders of Justification* (Oxford: Oxford University Press, 2017).
3. Tommie Shelby, "The Ethics of Uncle Tom's Children," *Critical Inquiry* 38, no. 3 (2012): 514.
4. W. E. B. Du Bois, *The Ordeal of Mansart* (New York: Mainstream, 1957), 151.
5. W. E. B. Du Bois, "Criteria of Negro Art," in *Writings*, ed. Nathan Huggins (New York: Library of America, 1986), 1000–1011.
6. Ralph Ellison, "Working Notes to *Juneteenth*," in *The Collected Essays of Ralph Ellison*, ed. John F. Callahan (New York: Modern Library, 1995), 356.
7. Hannah Arendt, "The Crisis of Authority," in *Between Past and Future: Eight Exercises in Political Thought* (New York: Penguin, 1993), 91–141.
8. For other antiessentialist concepts of black politics, see Adolph Reed Jr., *Stirrings in the Jug: Black Politics in the Post-Segregation Era* (Minneapolis: University of Minnesota Press, 1999); and Tommie Shelby, *We Who Are Dark: The Philosophical Foundations of Black Solidarity* (Cambridge, MA: Harvard University Press, 2005).
9. I take inspiration here from Linda M. G. Zerilli, *Feminism and the Abyss of Freedom* (Chicago: University of Chicago Press, 2005); Ernesto Laclau, *On Populist Reason* (London: Verso Books, 2005); Melvin L. Rogers, "David Walker and the Political Power of the Appeal," *Political Theory* 43, no. 2 (2015): 208–233; and Melvin L. Rogers, *The Darkened Light of Faith: Race, Democracy, and Freedom in African American Political Thought* (Princeton, NJ: Princeton University Press, 2023), 39–63.
10. For an overview of the demographic characteristics of the slave population in the United States, see Peter Kolchin, *American Slavery, 1619–1877* (New York: Penguin, 1995), 49.
11. Following Michael Dawson, *Behind the Mule: Race and Class in African-American Politics* (Princeton, NJ: Princeton University Press, 1994), I use "linked fate" in the sense of individual African Americans conceiving of their own life chances as being tightly connected to the fate of African Americans as a group. On the cotton boom and the expansion of slavery in the Deep South, see Gavin Wright, "Slavery and the Cotton Boom," *Explorations in Economic History* 12, no. 4 (1975): 439–451. For a corrective of the narrative that gives Eli Whitney's invention of the cotton gin rather than cotton prices on the global market pride of place in explanations of the expansion of slavery, see Angela Lakwete, *Inventing the Cotton Gin: Machine and Myth in Antebellum America* (Baltimore: Johns Hopkins University Press, 2003). On the impact of the Haitian Revolution in the United States, see Ed Rugemer, *The Problem of Emancipation: The Caribbean Roots of the American Civil War* (Baton Rouge: Louisiana State University Press, 2008). On black political life in the nineteenth century, see Steven Hahn, *A Nation Under Our Feet: Black Political Struggles in the Rural South, from Slavery to the Great Migration* (Cambridge, MA: Harvard University Press, 2003). And, with a special eye toward the free black press, see Patrick Rael, *Black Identity and Black Protest in the Antebellum North* (Durham, NC: University of North Carolina Press, 2002).

12. Frederick Douglass, "The Anti-Slavery Movement," in *The Frederick Douglass Papers,* ser. 1, *Speeches, Debates, and Interviews,* vol. 5, *1881–1895,* ed. John W. Blassingame and John R. McKivigan (New Haven, CT: Yale University Press, 1992), 484–502. While the slave narrative has become the ur-text for fields of "black literature" and "black political thought" in the academy, it is undeniably true that the mass of nominally free African Americans had their formative encounters with political thought in church or the popular politics (e.g., revivals, rallies, and petitions) of the abolitionist movement. See the extraordinary work by Daniel Carpenter, *Democracy by Petition: Popular Politics in Transformation, 1790–1870* (Cambridge, MA: Harvard University Press, 2021): 164–200, 298–340.
13. Brown, *Nihilistic Times,* 25.
14. Malcolm X, quoted in Richard W. P. McCormick, "The Great Debaters," *Columbia Magazine,* Winter 2021–2022, https://magazine.columbia.edu/article/great-debaters. This debate is part of an electrifying scene starring Denzel Washington in *Malcolm X,* directed by Spike Lee (40 Acres and a Mule Production Company/Warner Brothers Cinema, 1992).
15. Kwame Anthony Appiah, *In My Father's House: Africa and the Philosophy of Culture* (New York: Oxford University Press, 1992), 13.
16. Bernard Boxill, *Blacks and Social Justice,* 2nd ed. (Lanham, MD: Rowman and Littlefield, 1992), 21.
17. Kwame Anthony Appiah, *The Lies That Bind: Rethinking Identity* (New York: Liveright, 2018), 112.
18. Loïc Wacquant, *Racial Domination* (Medford, MA: Polity, 2023).
19. Kwame Anthony Appiah, "Race, Culture, and Identity," in Kwame Anthony Appiah and Amy Gutmann, *Color Conscious: The Political Morality of Race* (Princeton, NJ: Princeton University Press, 1996).
20. See Marcus Garvey, "Race Purity and Desideratum" and "1924 Speech Delivered at Carnegie Hall," in *The Philosophy and Opinions of Marcus Garvey,* vol. 2, ed. Amy Jacques Garvey (Paterson, NJ: Frank Cass, 1925): 62; and Marcus Garvey, "1924 Speech Delivered at Carnegie Hall," in *The Philosophy and Opinions of Marcus Garvey,* 2:101–117.
21. W. E. B. Du Bois, "The Conservation of Races," in *Writings,* 818, 817, 822.
22. W. E. B. Du Bois, "The Talented Tenth Memorial Address," in Henry Louis Gates Jr. and Cornel West, *The Future of the Race* (New York: Vintage, 1996), 164.
23. Stokely Carmichael and Charles V. Hamilton, *Black Power: The Politics of Liberation in America* (New York: Vintage, 1992), 46.
24. Du Bois, "The Conservation of Races," 822.
25. Martin Luther King Jr., *Where Do We Go from Here: Chaos or Community?* (Boston: Beacon, 2010), 42.
26. Eddie S. Glaude Jr., *An Uncommon Faith: A Pragmatic Approach to the Study of African American Religion* (Athens: University of Georgia Press, 2018), 50.
27. Appiah, *In My Father's House,* viii.
28. Appiah, *In My Father's House,* 45.

29. Michelle Brattain, "Race, Racism, and Antiracism: UNESCO and the Politics of Presenting Science to the Postwar Public," *American Historical Review* 112, no. 5 (2007): 1386–1413.
30. Ronald Sundstrom, *The Browning of America and the Evasion of Social Justice* (Albany: State University of New York Press, 2008); Kimberly McClain Dacosta, *Making Multiracials: State, Family, and Market in the Redrawing of the Color Line* (Stanford, CA: Stanford University Press, 2007).
31. Appiah, *Color Conscious,* 68.
32. See, for example, Henry Louis Gates Jr., *Faces of America: How 12 Extraordinary People Discovered Their Pasts* (New York: New York University Press, 2010).
33. Alexander Gusev, "Concepts: Race and Genetic Ancestry," in "A Molecular Genetics Perspective on the Heritability of Human Behavior and Group Differences," https://gusevlab.org/projects/hsq/#h.a4xch8sh53f1. For a contrasting view, see Quayshawn Spencer, "How to Be a Biological Racial Realist," in Joshua Glasgow, Sally Haslanger, Chike Jeffers, and Quayshawn Spencer, *What Is Race? Four Philosophical Views* (Oxford: Oxford University Press, 2019): 85–123.
34. Lionel McPherson, *The Afterlife of Race: An Informed Philosophical Search* (Oxford: Oxford University Press, 2024), 70.
35. David A. Hollinger, *Postethnic America: Beyond Multiculturalism,* 2nd ed. (New York: Basic Books, 2000), 19–51.
36. Orlando Patterson, "Taking Culture Seriously: A Framework and an Afro-American Illustration," in *Culture Matters: How Values Shape Human Progress,* ed. Lawrence E. Harrison and Samuel P. Huntington (New York: Basic Books, 2000), 208.
37. Jafari S. Allen, "Black/Queer/Diaspora at the Current Conjuncture," *GLQ: A Journal of Lesbian and Gay Studies* 18, nos. 2–3 (2012): 211–248; Jeffrey O. G. Ogbar, *Hip-Hop Revolution: The Culture and Politics of Rap* (Lawrence: University Press of Kansas, 2007).
38. Samara Lynn, "Controversial Group ADOS Divides Black Americans in Fight for Economic Equality," ABC News, January 19, 2020.
39. Kwame Anthony Appiah, "Does Truth Matter to Identity?," in *Race or Ethnicity? On Black and Latino Identity* (Ithaca, NY: Cornell University Press, 2007), 33.
40. See Pew Research Center, *Optimism About Black Progress Declines: Blacks See Growing Values Gap Between Poor and Middle Class* (Washington, DC: Pew Research Center, November 13, 2007).
41. Kiana Cox, "Black Voters Support Harris over Trump and Kennedy by a Wide Margin," Pew Research Center, August 22, 2024, https://www.pewresearch.org/short-reads/2024/08/22/black-voters-support-harris-over-trump-and-kennedy-by-a-wide-margin/.
42. Du Bois, "The Talented Tenth Memorial Address"; Fredricka Newton, "Introduction," in Huey P. Newton, *Revolutionary Suicide* (New York: Penguin, 2009), ix.
43. Alicia Garza, *The Purpose of Power: How We Come Together When We Fall Apart* (New York: One World, 2020).

44. See Shelby, *We Who Are Dark;* Robert Gooding-Williams, *In the Shadow of Du Bois: Afro-Modern Political Thought in America* (Cambridge, MA: Harvard University Press, 2009); Paul Gilroy, *Against Race: Imagining Political Culture Beyond the Color Line* (Cambridge, MA: Harvard University Press, 2002); Eddie S. Glaude Jr., *In a Shade of Blue: Pragmatism and the Politics of Black America* (Chicago: University of Chicago Press, 2007); Juliet Hooker, *The Politics of Solidarity: Race, Racism, and Political Belonging* (Oxford: Oxford University Press, 2009); and Shatema Threadcraft, *Intimate Justice: The Black Female Body and the Body Politic* (Oxford: Oxford University Press, 2016).
45. William Brink and Louis Harris, *The Negro Revolution in America: What Negroes Want, Why and How They Are Fighting, Whom They Support, What Whites Think of Them and Their Demands* (New York: Simon and Schuster, 1964), 102.
46. See Kolchin, *American Slavery,* especially 143–148; and Jon Butler, *Awash in a Sea of Faith: Christianizing the American People* (Cambridge, MA: Harvard University Press, 1990), especially 129–164.
47. Hahn, *A Nation Under Our Feet,* 116.
48. Eddie S. Glaude Jr., *Exodus! Religion, Race, and Nation in Early Nineteenth-Century Black America* (Chicago: University of Chicago Press, 2000); Cornel West, *Prophesy Deliverance! An Afro-American Revolutionary Christianity,* 40th anniversary expanded ed. (Louisville, KY: Westminster John Knox, 2022); William R. Jones, *Is God a White Racist? A Preamble to Black Theology* (Garden City, NY: Anchor, 1973).
49. Hahn, *A Nation Under Our Feet.*
50. Martin Delany, quoted in Glaude, *Exodus!,* 19.
51. See Hahn, *A Nation Under Our Feet,* especially part 2, "To Build a New Jerusalem"; and Michelle Mitchell, *Righteous Propagation: African Americans and the Politics of Racial Destiny after Reconstruction* (Chapel Hill: University of North Carolina Press, 2004).
52. On the enforcement of social norms for collective action in black churches, see Doug McAdam, *Political Process and the Development of Black Insurgency, 1930–70* (Chicago: University of Chicago Press, 1999).
53. For the sociological study, see W. E. B. Du Bois, *The Negro Church: Report of a Social Study Made Under the Direction of Atlanta University; Together with the Proceedings of the Eighth Conference for the Study of the Negro Problems, Held at Atlanta University, May 26th, 1903* (Atlanta: Atlanta University Press, 1903). For the "awful" comment, see W. E. B. Du Bois, *The Souls of Black Folk* (Chicago: A. C. McClurg, 1903), 190.
54. W. E. B. Du Bois, "Color and Democracy," in *The World and Africa and Color and Democracy* (New York: Oxford University Press, 2007), 326.
55. Barbara Dianne Savage, "W. E. B. Du Bois and 'The Negro Church,'" *Annals of the American Academy of Political and Social Science* 568, no. 1 (2000): 235–249.
56. Andrew E. Kersten, *Clarence Darrow: American Iconoclast* (New York: Macmillan, 2011), chapter 10.

57. David L. Chappell, *A Stone of Hope: Prophetic Religion and the Death of Jim Crow* (Chapel Hill: University of North Carolina Press, 2004).
58. Mary Dudziak, *Cold War Civil Rights: Race and the Image of American Democracy* (Princeton, NJ: Princeton University Press, 2000).
59. The Nation of Islam first came to true national prominence with the 1959 premiere of *The Hate That Hate Produced,* a five-part documentary that aired on the program *News Beat* on WNTA-TV in New York City and introduced millions of Americans of all races to the theretofore relatively unknown Elijah Muhammad, Louis X (later Louis Farrakhan), and above all, Malcolm X. The entire documentary is now available in streaming video format; see *The Hate That Hate Produced,* produced by Mike Wallace and Louis Lomax (New York: WNTA-TV, 1959), Internet Archive, https://www.archive.org.
60. Darren E. Sherkat and Christopher G. Ellison, "Recent Developments and Current Controversies in the Sociology of Religion," *Annual Review of Sociology* 25 (1999): 368.
61. See, for example, the discussion of religion in Eldridge Cleaver, *Soul on Ice* (New York: Delta, 1999), 50–85; and the account of a meeting with Elijah Muhammad in James Baldwin, *The Fire Next Time* (New York: Delta, 1963), 59–120.
62. Marshall Frady, *Jesse: The Life and Pilgrimage of Jesse Jackson* (New York: Simon and Schuster, 1996); Adolph Reed Jr., *The Jesse Jackson Phenomenon* (New Haven, CT: Yale University Press, 1986).
63. Hannah Arendt, *The Human Condition* (Chicago: University of Chicago Press, 1998).
64. Cathy Cohen, *Boundaries of Blackness: HIV/AIDS and the Breakdown of Black Politics* (Chicago: University of Chicago Press, 1999).
65. Darren E. Sherkat and C. G. Ellison, "The Politics of Black Religious Change: Disaffiliation from Black Mainline Denominations," *Social Forces* 70, no. 2 (1991): 431–454.
66. Cassandra Chaney, "Who Is David and Who Is Goliath? The Eddie Long Scandal and the Black Mega-Church," *Mental Health, Religion and Culture* 16, no. 1 (2013): 58–78; Todne Thomas Chipumuro, "Pastor, Mentor, or Father? The Contested Intimacies of the Eddie Long Sex Abuse Scandal," *Journal of Africana Religions* 2, no. 1 (2014): 1–30.
67. "Black Church Faces Decline in Gen Z Attendance," *New York Times,* September 29, 2024; Pew Research Center, "Faith Among Black Americans," February 16, 2021, https://www.pewresearch.org/religion/2021/02/16/faith-among-black-americans/.
68. Linda M. Chatters, Robert Joseph Taylor, and Karen D. Lincoln, "African American Religious Participation: A Multi-Sample Comparison," *Journal for the Scientific Study of Religion* 38, no. 1 (1999): 133. As Dareen E. Sherkat, "African-American Religious Affiliation in the Late Twentieth Century: Cohort Variations and Patterns of Switching, 1973–1998," *Journal for the Scientific Study of Religion* 41, no. 3 (2002): 490, notes, "The proportion of African Americans who have no religious affiliation is increasing rapidly from switching, and across cohorts—from 1 percent of

the origin in the oldest category (pre-1943) to 8 percent of respondents in the youngest cohort (1944–1980)." Data for the most recent cohort, the so-called millennial generation, is not tabulated, but if trends are consistent, this number may rise significantly.

69. Michael Leo Owens, "The Reverend Floyd Flake: African Methodist Episcopal Church Minister for School Choice," in *Religious Leaders and Faith-Based Politics: Ten Profiles,* ed. Corwin E. Smidt (Lanham, MD: Rowman & Littlefield, 2001), 1–24, explains how Flake's Allen Temple AME Church in Queens, New York, has received government funding and support to create a for-profit corporation that manages a public housing complex for seniors, a Burger King franchise, a vacant home rehabilitation and home improvement arm, and other small enterprises. Michael Leo Owens, *God and Government in the Ghetto: The Politics of Church-State Collaboration in Black America* (Chicago: University of Chicago Press, 2007), is a study of these community development corporations and their ameliorative, if severely limited, effects. Michael Leo Owens and Amy Yuen, "The Distributive Politics of 'Compassion in Action': Federal Funding, Faith-Based Organizations, and Electoral Advantage," *Political Research Quarterly* 65, no. 2 (2012): 422–442, link the electoral politics of black churches with the bureaucratic apparatus developing to channel resources in their direction, unsurprisingly discovering a significant relationship between the percentage of registered black voters in a state's population and the grant allocations awarded by the administration of President George W. Bush's Faith-Based and Community Initiative; they argue that this is an attempt to win political influence by the Bush administration and the Republican Party, noting that black churches are overwhelmingly most likely to apply for public funding and develop programs in response to public funding opportunities. See also Frederick C. Harris, "Black Churches and Civic Traditions: Outreach, Activism, and the Politics of Public Funding of Faith-Based Ministries," in *Can Charitable Choice Work? Covering Religion's Impact on Urban Affairs and Social Services,* ed. Andrew Walsh (Hartford, CT: Pew Program on Religion and the News Media, 2001), 140–156.
70. See Jonathan L. Walton, *Watch This! The Ethics and Aesthetics of Black Televangelism* (New York: New York University Press, 2009), especially chapters 6–7.
71. Hanna Rosin, "Did Christianity Cause the Crash?," *Atlantic,* December 2009.
72. Pew Research Center, "Interviews with Black Pastors," February 16, 2021, https://www.pewresearch.org/religion/2021/02/16/interviews-with-black-pastors/.
73. See Harold Cruse, *The Crisis of the Negro Intellectual* (New York: William Morrow, 1967), especially 4–11.
74. Cruse, *The Crisis of the Negro Intellectual,* 6–7.
75. See Michael Dawson, *Black Visions: The Roots of Contemporary Black Political Ideologies* (Chicago: University of Chicago Press, 2001).
76. Martin Luther King Jr., "The Ethical Demands of Integration," in *A Testament of Hope,* 118.

77. Eugene F. Rivers, "A New Black Nationalism: Beyond the Nationalism of Fools," *Boston Review,* Summer 1995, https://www.bostonreview.net.
78. See, for example, Leah N. Gordon, *From Power to Prejudice: The Rise of Racial Individualism in Midcentury America* (Chicago: University of Chicago Press, 2015), 132–160.
79. Dawson, *Black Visions,* 85.
80. Brandon M. Terry, "Book Review: *The Enigma of Clarence Thomas,* by Corey Robin," *Political Theory* 48, no. 1 (2020): 109–121.
81. King, *Where Do We Go from Here?*
82. Malcolm X, "Not Just an American Problem, but a World Problem (February 16, 1965)," in *Malcolm X, Collected Speeches, Debates, and Interviews (1960–1965),* ed. Sandeep S. Atwal (independently published, 2000), 759.
83. Henry Louis Gates Jr., "Parable of the Talents," in Henry Louis Gates Jr. and Cornel West, *The Future of the Race* (New York: Vintage, 1996), 13.
84. The legal scholar Derrick Bell has been exceptionally critical of the integrationist ethos of civil rights litigation and jurisprudence and has recently suggested that *Brown* would have best been decided by forcing the actual equality of all-black schools instead of pursuing an untenable program of integration that devolved into class privilege at best, tokenism at worse. See Bell's mock decision in Jack M. Balkin, ed., *What "Brown v. Board of Education" Should Have Said: The Nation's Legal Experts Rewrite America's Landmark Civil Rights Decision* (New York: New York University Press, 2001), 185–200.
85. Balkin, *What "Brown v. Board of Education" Should Have Said;* Derrick Bell, *Silent Covenants: Brown v. Board of Education and the Unfulfilled Hopes for Racial Reform* (New York: Oxford University Press, 2004).
86. Ward Churchill and Jim Vander Wall, *Agents of Repression: The FBI's Secret Wars Against the Black Panther Party and the American Indian Movement* (Boston: South End, 2002), 63–102.
87. See Eldridge Cleaver, *Credo for Rioters and Looters* (San Francisco, CA: Black Panther Party, 1969).
88. Whitney M. Young Jr., "We Are in Terrible Danger," in *The City in Crisis* (New York: A. Philip Randolph Educational Fund, 1966), 31, 34.
89. The Black Panther Party was particularly supportive of Van Peebles's film; see Jon Hartmann, "The Trope of Blaxploitation in Critical Responses to *Sweetback,*" *Film History* 6, no. 3 (1994): 382–404.
90. See Doug McAdam, *Political Process and the Development of Black Insurgency, 1930–70* (Chicago: University of Chicago Press, 1999).
91. Adolph Reed Jr., "Black Particularity Reconsidered," in *Is It Nation Time? Contemporary Essays on Black Power and Black Nationalism,* ed. Eddie Glaude Jr. (Chicago: University of Chicago Press, 2002), 39–67.
92. Louis Farrakhan, "P.O.W.E.R. at Last and Forever," in *Modern Black Nationalism: From Marcus Garvey to Louis Farrakhan,* ed. William L. Van Deburg (New York: New York University Press, 1997), 316–327.
93. Robert Singh, *The Farrakhan Phenomenon: Race, Reaction, and the Paranoid Style in American Politics* (Washington, DC: Georgetown University

Press, 1997); Adolph Reed Jr., "False Prophet: The Rise of Louis Farrakhan," in *Class Notes: Posing as Politics and Other Thoughts on the American Scene* (New York: New Press, 2000): 37–60; Barbara Ransby, "Black Feminism at Twenty-One: Reflections on the Evolution of a National Community," *Signs: Journal of Women in Culture and Society* 25, no. 4 (2000): 1215–1221.

94. Douglas S. Massey and Nancy A. Denton, *American Apartheid: Segregation and the Making of the Underclass* (Cambridge, MA: Harvard University Press, 1993).

95. Douglas S. Massey, "Segregation and Stratification: A Biosocial Perspective," *Du Bois Review* 1, no. 1 (2004): 11.

96. Gary Orfield, *Schools More Separate: Consequences of a Decade of Resegregation* (Cambridge, MA: Harvard Civil Rights Project, 2001), https://civilrightsproject.ucla.edu/research/k-12-education/integration-and-diversity/schools-more-separate-consequences-of-a-decade-of-resegregation-1/schools-more-separate_orfield.pdf.

97. William G. Bowen and Derek Bok, *The Shape of the River: Long-Term Consequences of Considering Race in College and University Admissions* (Princeton, NJ: Princeton University Press, 2000).

98. Roland G. Fryer Jr. and Paul Torelli, "An Empirical Analysis of 'Acting White,'" *Journal of Public Economics* 94, nos. 5–6 (2010): 380–396.

99. Lisa Sanbonmatsu, Jeffrey R. Kling, Greg J. Duncan, and Jeanne Brooks-Gunn, "Neighborhoods and Academic Achievement: Results from the Moving to Opportunity Experiment," *Journal of Human Resources* 41, no. 4 (2006): 649–691.

100. Robert D. Putnam, "E Pluribus Unum: Diversity and Community in the Twenty-First Century; The 2006 Johan Skytte Prize Lecture," *Scandanavian Political Studies* 30, no. 2 (2007): 137–174.

101. Parents Involved in Community Schools v. Seattle School District No. 1, 551 US 701 (2007), decided together with Meredith v. Jefferson County Board of Education, 551 US 701 (2007).

102. Orlando Patterson, "Equality," *Democracy: A Journal of Ideas* 11 (2009), https://democracyjournal.org/magazine/11/equality/.

103. Tony Dokoupil, "Cutting Down to Size," *Newsweek,* November 26, 2009, https://www.newsweek.com/how-pittsburgh-managing-population-loss-76973

104. "US Department of Education Awards Promise Neighborhood Planning Grants," press release, US Department of Education, September 21, 2010, https://www.ed.gov/news.

105. Daniel de Vise, "Obama Moves to Bolster HBCUs," *Washington Post,* February 26, 2010.

106. Michael Lackey, ed., *The Haverford Discussions: A Black Integrationist Manifesto for Racial Justice* (Charlottesville: University of Virginia Press, 2013).

107. See, for example, Ralph J. Bunche, *A Brief and Tentative Analysis of Negro Leadership,* ed. Jonathan Scott Holloway (New York: New York University Press, 2005); and Michael C. Dawson, *Black Visions: The Roots of*

Contemporary African-American Political Ideologies (Chicago: University of Chicago Press, 2001).

108. Gene Jarrett, *Representing the Race: A New Political History of African American Literature* (New York: New York University Press, 2011), 5–6.
109. James Baldwin, quoted in Eddie S. Glaude Jr., *Begin Again: James Baldwin's America and Its Urgent Lessons for Our Own* (New York: Crown, 2021), 5.
110. James Weldon Johnson, "Preface to *The Book of American Negro Poetry*," in *James Weldon Johnson: Writings*, ed. William L. Andrews (New York: Library of America, 2004), 688.
111. Jarrett, *Representing the Race*, 6.
112. Ida B. Wells, *Southern Horrors: Lynch Law in All Its Phases* (New York: New York Age, 1892); Jenny Woodley, *Art for Equality: The NAACP's Cultural Campaign for Civil Rights* (Lexington: University Press of Kentucky, 2014).
113. Henry Louis Gates Jr., *Stony the Road: Reconstruction, White Supremacy, and the Rise of Jim Crow* (New York: Penguin, 2019), 252.
114. Sut Jhally, *Enlightened Racism: "The Cosby Show," Audiences, and the Myth of the American Dream* (New York: Routledge, 2019).
115. Alain Locke, "Harlem," in *The New Negro Aesthetic: Selected Writings*, ed. Jeffrey C. Stewart (New York: Penguin Books, 2022), 5.
116. James Weldon Johnson, "Preface," 688.
117. Du Bois, *The Souls of Black Folk;* Kwame Anthony Appiah, *Lines of Descent: W. E. B. Du Bois and the Emergence of Identity* (Cambridge, MA: Harvard University Press, 2014). For the proletariat turn, see Richard Wright, "Blueprint for Negro Writing," in *The Norton Anthology of African American Literature*, 3rd ed., ed. Henry Louis Gates Jr. and Valerie Smith (New York: W. W. Norton, 2014), 1381–1389.
118. Paul C. Taylor, *Black Is Beautiful: A Philosophy of Black Aesthetics* (Malden, MA: Wiley Blackwell, 2016), 5.
119. Richard Iton, *In Search of the Black Fantastic: Politics and Popular Culture in the Post–Civil Rights Era* (New York: Oxford University Press, 2008).
120. Taylor, *Black Is Beautiful*, 18.
121. Daniel T. Rodgers, *Age of Fracture* (Cambridge, MA: Harvard University Press, 2011).
122. Bakari Kitwana, *The Hip-Hop Generation: Young Blacks and the Crisis in African American Culture* (New York: Basic Civitas Books, 2002), 9–21.
123. Todd Boyd, *The New H.N.I.C.: The Death of Civil Rights and the Reign of Hip Hop* (New York: New York University Press, 2003), 10–11.
124. On this notion of populism, see Bart Bonikowski, "Three Lessons of Contemporary Populism in Europe and the United States," *Brown Journal of World Affairs* 23, no. 1 (2016): 9–24.
125. One possible sign of this may be their punitive attitudes toward black people who do appear to conform to such stereotypes. See Hakeem Jefferson, "The Politics of Respectability and Black Americans' Punitive Attitudes," *American Political Science Review* 117, no. 4 (2023): 1448–1464.

126. Christopher Muller and Alexander F. Roehrkasse, “Racial and Class Inequality in US Incarceration in the Early Twenty-First Century,” *Social Forces* 101, no. 2 (2022): 803–828.
127. Orlando Patterson, *Rituals of Blood: Consequences of Slavery in Two American Centuries* (Washington, DC: Civitas/Counterpoint, 1998), chapter 3.
128. Racquel Gates, *Double Negative: The Black Image and Popular Culture* (Durham, NC: Duke University Press, 2018), 12.
129. Taylor, *Black Is Beautiful,* viii.
130. Glaude, *An Uncommon Faith,* 20–39.
131. Friedrich Nietzsche, *On the Genealogy of Morality,* ed. Keith Ansell-Pearson, trans. Carol Diethe (Cambridge: Cambridge University Press, 2007), 119.
132. Raymond Williams, *Modern Tragedy* (London: Verso Books, 2006), 78.
133. Terry Eagleton, *Tragedy* (New Haven, CT: Yale University Press, 2020), 159–160, 182.

6. Beyond Silence and Romance

1. For a stunning account of the impact of Rawls’s work on the center of gravity of professional philosophy and American intellectual life and the metaphor of Rawls’s “shadow,” see Katrina Forrester, *In the Shadow of Justice: Postwar Liberalism and the Remaking of Political Philosophy* (Princeton, NJ: Princeton University Press, 2019).
2. Charles W. Mills, *From Class to Race: Essays in White Marxism and Black Radicalism* (Lanham, MD: Rowman and Littlefield, 2003), 198 (emphasis added).
3. The language of “firm ground” and “righteous position” is borrowed from Bernard Harcourt, *Critique and Praxis: A Critical Philosophy of Illusions, Values, and Action* (New York: Columbia University Press, 2020), 183. Harcourt’s book is, in part, a sustained critique of the desire among critical theorists (I would include Mills among them) for a “final” unmasking of ideology and illusion.
4. Toni Morrison, *Playing in the Dark: Whiteness and the Literary Imagination* (Cambridge, MA: Harvard University Press, 1992), 91.
5. Clay Risen, “Charles W. Mills, Philosopher Who Recast Social Contract Theory, Dies at 70,” *New York Times,* September 27, 2021, https://www.nytimes.com/2021/09/27/us/charles-w-mills-dead.html.
6. Samuel Freeman, “The Cambridge Companion to Rawls” (series introduction), in *The Cambridge Companion to Rawls,* ed. Samuel Freeman (Cambridge: Cambridge University Press, 2003), i. In a comprehensive survey of political theorists, 1,086 respondents ranked John Rawls first among “scholars who have had the greatest impact on political theory in the past 20 years.” He received nearly one out of every four votes and outpaced Jürgen Habermas, who placed second, by 131 votes, a margin of nearly 12 percent of the total votes cast. See Matthew J. Moore, “Political Theory Today: Results of a National Survey,” *PS: Political Science and Politics* 43,

no. 2 (2010): 267, table 4; Thomas Pogge, *John Rawls: His Life and Theory of Justice* (New York: Oxford University Press, 2007); Thomas Nagel, "John Rawls and Affirmative Action," *Journal of Blacks in Higher Education* 39 (2003): 82–84.

7. See, for example, Michael Sandel, *Democracy's Discontent: America in Search of a New Public Philosophy* (Cambridge, MA: Harvard University Press, 1996), 5. As Forrester, *In the Shadow of Justice,* 1–39, notes, the emphasis on Rawls's Americanness, and especially his identification with Great Society liberalism, misses the significance of his immersion in debates on the British Left at a decisive point in his thinking.
8. Kimberlé Crenshaw, Neil Gotanda, Gary Peller, and Kendall Thomas, *Critical Race Theory: The Key Writings that Formed the Movement* (New York: New Press, 1996), xxv, describes the collective project of critical race theory in legal scholarship as "*uncovering* how law was a constitutive element of race itself . . . how law *constructed* race" in order to reckon with the significance of law and the legal order in producing and sustaining white supremacy and other hierarchies. A number of right-wing critics and activists who deploy the term *critical race theory* largely seek to demonize a range of projects including bureaucratic diversity initiatives and the "diversity, equity, and inclusion" trainings familiar from colleges or human resources departments, *and* a wide (perhaps indiscriminate) range of scholarly approaches to the study of race, racial inequality, or racial identity; see, for example, Christopher F. Rufo, "Critical Race Theory: What It Is and How to Fight It," *Imprimis* 50, no. 3 (2021), 1–5. Others focus intensely on what they describe as the "paranoid" style of critical race theory and allege that it promotes cynical pessimism about racial progress, promotes essentialist and discriminatory forms of race consciousness, undermines psychic resiliency and interracial forms of trust by (falsely) positing widespread racial discrimination and injustice, and is indefensibly hostile to classically liberal principles; see, for example, James B. Lindsay and Helen Pluckrose, *Cynical Theories: How Activist Scholarship Made Everything About Race, Gender, and Identity—And Why This Harms Everybody* (Durham, NC: Pitchstone, 2020), 111–134. For a critique of such efforts, see David Theo Goldberg, *The War on Critical Race Theory: Or, the Remaking of Racism* (New York: Polity, 2023).
9. Mills, *From Class to Race,* xvii–xviii.
10. Charles W. Mills, *The Racial Contract* (Ithaca, NY: Cornell University Press, 1999), 1.
11. Charles W. Mills, *Black Rights/White Wrongs: The Critique of Racial Liberalism* (Oxford: Oxford University Press, 2017), 194–195. Surely this statement also represents Mills's own methodological sympathies for those who write in an "analytic" idiom compared to those whose writings draw more unapologetically from phenomenology, existentialism, and pragmatism, traditions largely unthinkable without these categories of analysis.
12. Charles W. Mills, "Rawls on Race/Race in Rawls," *Southern Journal of Philosophy* 47, no. S1 (2009): 161.

13. Charles W. Mills, "Philosophy Raced, Philosophy Erased," in *Reframing the Practice of Philosophy,* ed. George Yancy (Albany, NY: State University of New York Press, 2012), 54.
14. See Mills, *The Racial Contract,* especially 19–40, 109–134; Charles W. Mills, "Ideal Theory as Ideology," *Hypatia* 20, no. 3 (2005): 165–184; Mills, *Black Rights/White Wrongs;* Mills, "Rawls on Race/Race in Rawls"; and Carole Pateman and Charles Mills, *Contract and Domination* (Boston: Polity, 2007), chapters 3, 4, and 8.
15. See, for example, Charles W. Mills, "Occupy Liberalism!," in *Black Rights/White Wrongs,* 11–29.
16. Nikolas Kompridis, "Reorienting Critique: From Ironist Theory to Transformative Practice," *Philosophy and Social Criticism* 26, no. 4 (2000): 28.
17. Charles W. Mills, "Non-Cartesian Sums: Philosophy and the African-American Experience," in *Blackness Visible: Essays on Philosophy and Race* (Ithaca, NY: Cornell University Press, 2018), 1–20.
18. Seyla Benhabib, *Critique, Norm, and Utopia: A Study of the Foundations of Critical Theory* (New York: Columbia University Press, 1987), 13, describes "the politics of fulfillment" as "envisag[ing] that the society of the future attains more adequately what present society has left unaccomplished. It is the culmination of the implicit logic of the present. . . . Within a critical social theory the articulation of norms continues the universalist promise of bourgeois revolutions—justice, equality, civil rights, democracy, and publicity." Contra his chief philosophical interlocutor, Carole Pateman, whose unmasking critique of the social contract tradition led her to reject contractarianism altogether, Mills, *The Racial Contract,* 129, argues instead that the "ideals of contractarianism" are not themselves "necessarily problematic" but instead have been "betrayed by white contractarians."
19. Pateman and Mills, *Contract and Domination,* 247.
20. Thomas McCarthy, "Review: Charles W. Mills, *The Racial Contract,*" *Ethics* 109, no. 2 (1999): 453. For the most important treatment of black Enlightenment liberalism at its early stages, see Keidrick Roy, *American Dark Age: Racial Feudalism and the Rise of Black Liberalism* (Princeton, NJ: Princeton University Press, 2024).
21. John Rawls, *Lectures on the History of Political Philosophy* (Cambridge, MA: Harvard University Press, 2008), 13–14.
22. Jean-Jacques Rousseau, "Discourse on the Origin and the Foundations of Inequality Among Mankind," in *The Social Contract and the First and Second Discourses,* ed. Susan Dunn (New Haven, CT: Yale University Press, 2002), 87.
23. Pateman and Mills, *Contract and Domination,* 81.
24. Mills, *The Racial Contract,* 11.
25. McCarthy, "Review: Charles W. Mills, *The Racial Contract,*" 453.
26. See Emmanuel Chukwudi Eze, *Race and the Enlightenment: A Reader* (Oxford: Blackwell, 1997).
27. This is now a well-developed problem in philosophy and political theory. For illustrative texts, see Uday Singh Mehta, *Liberalism and Empire: A*

Study in Nineteenth-Century British Liberal Thought (Chicago: University of Chicago Press, 1999); Emmanuel Chukwudi Eze, ed., *Philosophers on Race: Critical Essays* (Malden, MA: Blackwell, 2002); Robert Bernasconi and Sybol Cook, eds., *Race and Racism in Continental Philosophy* (Bloomington: Indiana University Press, 2003); Andrew Valls, ed., *Race and Racism in Modern Philosophy* (Ithaca, NY: Cornell University Press, 2005); Jennifer Pitts, *A Turn to Empire: The Rise of Imperial Liberalism in Britain and France* (Princeton, NJ: Princeton University Press, 2005); Thomas McCarthy, *Race, Empire, and the Idea of Human Development* (Cambridge: Cambridge University Press, 2009); and Karuna Mantena, *Alibis of Empire: Henry Maine and the Ends of Liberal Imperialism* (Princeton, NJ: Princeton University Press, 2010).

28. For feminism, see Carole Pateman, *The Sexual Contract* (Stanford, CA: Stanford University Press, 1988). For postcolonial theory, see Uday Singh Mehta, *Liberalism and Empire*. For race, see Frantz Fanon, *The Wretched of the Earth*, anniversary ed., trans. Richard Philcox (New York: Grove, 2021).

29. For Mills, race is socially and politically constructed, and racial categories emerge from practices of domination and exploitation. His contract idea is not meant to treat races as natural facts that precede politics or political convention, nor should any iteration of the relevant racial categories in question be *presumed* fixed and permanent (though they may be difficult to change).

30. Dred Scott v. Sandford, 60 US 393 (406–407) (1856) (emphasis added). For Mills on Taney, see Mills, *The Racial Contract*, 24–25; and Charles W. Mills, "Whose Fourth of July? Frederick Douglass and 'Original Intent,'" in *Frederick Douglass: A Critical Reader*, ed. Bill E. Lawson and Frank M. Kirkland (Malden, MA: Blackwell, 1999), 101–142.

31. See Charles W. Mills, "Kant's Untermenschen," in *Race and Racism in Modern Philosophy*, ed. Andrew Valls (Ithaca, NY: Cornell University Press, 2005), 169–193; and Mills, *Blackness Visible*, chapters 4–5. That the question of Kant's racism has become a vibrant area of philosophical inquiry is yet another element of Mills's field-defining work, even as many scholars disagree with his hard-line criticism. See, for example, Jon M. Mikkelsen, ed., *Kant and the Concept of Race: Late Eighteenth-Century Writings* (Albany: State University of New York Press, 2013); Inés Valdez, "It's Not About Race: Good Wars, Bad Wars, and the Origins of Kant's Anti-Colonialism," *American Political Science Review* 111, no. 4 (2017): 819–834; Oliver Eberl, "Kant on Race and Barbarism: Towards a More Complex View on Racism and Anti-Colonialism in Kant," *Kantian Review* 24, no. 3 (2019): 385–413; Inés Valdez, "Toward a Narrow Cosmopolitanism: Kant's Anthropology, Racialized Character and the Construction of Europe," *Kantian Review* 27, no. 4 (2022): 593–613; Huaping Lu-Adler, *Kant, Race, and Racism: Views from Somewhere* (New York: Oxford University Press, 2023); and Laurenz Ramsauer, "Kant's Racism as a Philosophical Problem," *Pacific Philosophical Quarterly* 104, no. 4 (2023): 791–815.

32. The idea of a herrenvolk ethics draws from Pierre van den Berghe's influential concept of herrenvolk democracy. See Pierre van den Berghe, *Race and Racism: A Comparative Perspective* (New York: Wiley, 1967), 18.
33. On Kant, see Mikkelsen, ed., *Kant and the Concept of Race*. On Locke, see Brad Hinshelwood, "The Carolinian Context of John Locke's Theory of Slavery," *Political Theory* 41, no. 4 (2013): 526–590.
34. This is a theme also in Lawrie Balfour, *The Evidence of Things Not Said: James Baldwin and the Promise of American Democracy* (Ithaca, NY: Cornell University Press, 2000): 1–9; that section of the chapter is appropriately titled "Silences of the Majority."
35. As Sophia Dingli, "We Need to Talk About Silence: Re-Examining Silence in International Relations Theory," *European Journal of International Relations* 21, no. 4 (2015): 721–722, notes, "analyses of silence can be found in the fields of literary theory, psychoanalysis, sociology and history among the works of those scholars who either adopted the deconstructive epistemology of postmodernism or the materialist critique of hegemony found in the work of Antonio Gramsci, or both. Some of the most well-known works to emerge as a result are: Michel Foucault's (1967) study into the structured and eventual confinement of the 'insane' to silence; Luce Irigaray's (1985) investigation into what constitutes a 'woman', where she concluded that 'woman' does not have a voice of her own due to the work of patriarchy; and Edward Said's (1995) study into the co-construction of the 'Occidental Self' and the 'Oriental Other.'" In invoking *silence* as a keyword, I am following Raymond Williams's treatment of various vocabularies of critical practice and his focus on how popularly used words bind together certain patterns of interpretation and criticism, as well as how they might indicate or signify broader commitments in traditions of thought; see Raymond Williams, *Keywords: A Vocabulary of Culture and Society* (New York: Oxford University Press, 1976).
36. Brian Leiter, "The Hermeneutics of Suspicion: Recovering Nietzsche, Marx, and Freud," in *The Future for Philosophy*, ed. Brian Leiter (Oxford: Clarendon Press, 2004), 150–153. For the origins of the "hermeneutics of suspicion" phrase, see Paul Ricoeur, *Freud and Philosophy: An Essay on Interpretation* (New Haven, CT: Yale University Press, 1970), 32–33. For an influential reconstruction of this paradigm, see Rita Felski, "Suspicious Minds," *Poetics Today* 32, no. 2 (2011): 215–234.
37. Charles W. Mills, "Alternative Epistemologies," *Social Theory and Practice* 14, no. 3 (1988): 237–263. Charles W. Mills, "An Illuminating Blackness," *Black Scholar* 43, no. 4 (2013): 33, argues that black philosophy is "the philosophy that develops out of the distinctive experience of racial subordination in modernity—a philosophy that in its effort to understand and end that subordination, illuminates modernity more thoroughly and relentlessly, more free from illusions, than its white antagonist." Black people, he argues, drawing on a revision of feminist standpoint epistemology, are "peculiarly well placed to theorize . . . the actual material and normative topography of this racialized world." For a powerful model of rational reconstruction and sympathetic critique of the claims of standpoint

epistemology, see Lidal Dror, "Is There an Epistemic Advantage to Being Oppressed?," *Noûs* 57, no. 3 (2023): 618–640.

38. Mills, *The Racial Contract,* 94.
39. John Rawls, *Lectures on the History of Political Philosophy,* ed. Samuel Freeman (Cambridge, MA: Harvard University Press, 2008), 13–20.
40. John Rawls, *A Theory of Justice* (Cambridge, MA: Belknap Press of Harvard University Press, 1999), 207.
41. Rawls, "Outline of a Decision Procedure for Ethics" in *Collected Papers,* ed. Samuel Freeman (Cambridge, MA: Harvard University Press, 1999), 5.
42. Rawls, *A Theory of Justice,* 17 (emphasis added).
43. This is especially true given that other contemporary political theorists working within critical race theory have taken as indispensable for philosophical work on racial justice the architecture that Rawls provides for left-liberal thinking about the redistribution of wealth, the inviolability of civil rights, and the deflation of right-libertarian arguments about personal responsibility or the injustice of wealth transfers. Tommie Shelby, for one, has argued in favor the indispensability of Rawls's insights for theorizing about racial justice, emphasizing that they do not require "radical revision" to develop "a nonideal theory of racial justice" as part of a fully comprehensive theory. See Tommie Shelby, "Race and Social Justice: Rawlsian Considerations," *Fordham Law Review* 72, no. 5 (2004): 1697–1714; Tommie Shelby, "Racial Realities and Corrective Justice: A Reply to Charles Mills," *Critical Philosophy of Race* 1, no. 2 (2013): 142–162; Tommie Shelby, "Justice, Deviance, and the Dark Ghetto," *Philosophy and Public Affairs* 35, no. 2 (2007): 126–160; and Tommie Shelby, "Justice, Work, and the Ghetto Poor," *The Law and Ethics of Human Rights* 6, no. 1 (2012): 71–96.
44. Mills, "Non-Cartesian Sums," 3–4.
45. Kimberlé Crenshaw, "Twenty Years of Critical Race Theory: Looking Back to Move Forward," *Connecticut Law Review* 43, no. 5 (2011): 1295.
46. Cornel West, "Foreword," in Crenshaw et al., *Critical Race Theory,* xi.
47. Mills, "Rawls on Race/Race in Rawls," 169.
48. Charles W. Mills, "Retrieving Rawls for Racial Justice? A Critique of Tommie Shelby," *Critical Philosophy of Race* 1, no. 1 (2013): 22.
49. Mills, "Rawls on Race/Race in Rawls," 170.
50. John Rawls, *Justice as Fairness: A Restatement,* ed. Erin Kelly (Cambridge, MA: Belknap Press of Harvard University Press, 2001), 4–7.
51. Charles W. Mills, "'Ideal Theory' as Ideology," *Hypatia* 20, no. 2 (2005): 165–183; Mills, "Rawls on Race/Race in Rawls," 163.
52. Mills, "Rawls on Race/Race in Rawls," 161.
53. Nancy Fraser, "What's Critical About Critical Theory?," in *Fortunes of Feminism: From State-Managed Capitalism to Neoliberal Crisis* (New York: Verso Books, 2013): 42.
54. Shelby, "Race and Social Justice: Rawlsian Considerations"; Shelby, "Racial Realities and Corrective Justice: A Reply to Charles Mills"; Shelby, "Justice, Deviance, and the Dark Ghetto."
55. Rawls and his allies hoped to influence President Lyndon B. Johnson's newly appointed Marshall Commission and the changes they would rec-

ommend to the Selective Service system. John Rawls, "Talk II May 1968: Grounds for Conscientious Refusal," Folder 2, Box 24, John Rawls Papers (Hum 48), Harvard University Archives (hereafter, Rawls Papers); and John Rawls, "Outlines: Introductory Remarks on 2nd Resolution [1967]," Folder 3, Box 24, Rawls Papers.

56. John Rawls, "Docket for Harvard Faculty of Arts and Sciences Meeting, Tuesday, December 6, 1968," Folder 2, Box 24, Rawls Papers.
57. Robert J. Samuelson, "Faculty Shelves Draft Resolution After Hour and Half," *Harvard Crimson,* January 11, 1967, https://www.thecrimson.com/article/1967/1/11/faculty-shelves-draft-resolution-after-debating/.
58. See, for example, Pogge, *John Rawls,* 19–20.
59. Rawls, *A Theory of Justice,* 266.
60. Unlike the more general enlistments of World War II, the 1960s military had a larger population to draw from and fewer needs for personnel. This permitted a narrow pool of draftees and more discrimination. At least 68 percent of Vietnam veterans had working-class backgrounds, and only 23 percent had fathers with professional/technical or managerial positions—significantly out of proportion with the general male population of their generation. Educational attainment reflected the class-biased composition of the military as well, with 80 percent of Vietnam veterans having received only a high school education or less, in an era where more than half of Americans ages eighteen to twenty-one attended college. See Christopher Appy, *Working-Class War: American Combat Soldiers and Vietnam* (Chapel Hill, NC: University of North Carolina Press, 1993): 18, 25; and Arthur Egendorf, Charles Kadushin, Robert S. Laufer, George Rothbart, and Lee Sloan, *Legacies of Vietnam: Comparative Adjustments of Veterans and Their Peers* (Washington, DC: US Government Printing Office, 1981), 99, 105.
61. Appy, *Working-Class War,* 35.
62. The "channeling" statement was procured and publicized by the American Friends Service Committee as part of its antiwar activism; see "The 'Channeling' Memo from the Selective Service System (1965)," Draft Resistance News, n.d., https://hasbrouck.org/draft/channeling.html. See also Appy, *Working-Class War,* 35; "Student Deferment Urged," *Science News-Letter* 58, no. 20 (1950): 306.
63. Rawls, "Docket for Harvard Faculty of Arts and Sciences Meeting." See also Rawls, *A Theory of Justice,* 333n1.
64. Rawls, "Docket for Harvard Faculty of Arts and Sciences Meeting." Rawls's appreciation of the burdens and risks of military service was influenced by his service in the Pacific Theater during World War II, an experience that also occasioned a dramatic crisis of religious faith. See John Rawls, "On My Religion," in *A Brief Inquiry into the Meaning of Sin and Faith,* ed. Thomas Nagel (Cambridge, MA: Harvard University Press, 2009), 259–270.
65. Such critics were also, invariably, opponents of the war itself as unjust. See, for example, Malcolm X, "See for Yourself, Listen for Yourself, Think for Yourself [1/1/1965]," in *Malcolm X Talks to Young People: Speeches in the U.S., Britain, and Africa,* ed. Steve Clark (New York: Pathfinder,

1991). See also Student Nonviolent Coordinating Committee, "SNCC Statement on Vietnam," January 6, 1966, https://snccdigital.org/inside-sncc/policy-statements/vietnam/. A major impetus for the statement was the murder of Sammy Younge Jr., an SNCC activist and veteran who was slain in a dispute over the use of a "white" designated bathroom at a service station in Tuskegee, Alabama; Clayborne Carson, *In Struggle: SNCC and the Black Awakening of the 1960s* (Cambridge, MA: Harvard University Press, 1981), 188.

66. Martin Luther King Jr., "The Casualties of the War in Vietnam," in *A Single Garment of Destiny: A Global Vision of Justice,* ed. Lewis V. Baldwin (Boston: Beacon, 2012), 150–164.
67. Appy, *Working-Class War,* 19–20; Lisa Hsiao, "Project 100,000: The Great Society's Answer to Military Manpower Needs in Vietnam," *Vietnam Generation* 1, no. 2 (1989): 23.
68. Martin Luther King Jr., "A Time to Break Silence," in *A Testament of Hope: The Essential Writings of Martin Luther King, Jr.,* ed. James Melvin Washington (San Francisco: Harper and Row, 1986), 233. See also Brandon M. Terry, "The Casualties of War: Taking Up King's Fight Against Militarism," *Plough* 16 (2018): 56–65.
69. Mills, "Rawls on Race/Race in Rawls," 161.
70. John Rawls, "Notes on the Draft," Folder 2, Box 24, Rawls Papers, 2–3. In Rawls's account, black Americans were subjected to violations of the fair value of their basic political liberties, undeserved and unjust inequalities of opportunity, disproportionate poverty, and racial discrimination.
71. John Rawls, "An Outline of the 2-S Question," Folder 2, Box 24, Rawls Papers, 2–3. Among the reasons for this, Rawls argues, is "the direct and indirect denial of the franchise to the un or undereducated, the poor, and the non-white."
72. US Department of Defense estimates suggest that of all potential candidates examined, almost 50 percent of nonwhite people between the ages of twenty-six and twenty-nine in 1964 had been found unfit for service, compared to just twenty-five percent of white people. See National Advisory Commission on Selective Service, *In Pursuit of Equity: Who Serves When Not All Serve? Report of the National Advisory Commission on Selective Service* (Washington, DC: US Government Printing Office, 1967), 22.
73. Appy, *Working-Class War,* 19–21.
74. John Rawls, "Questions Re the 2-S Resolution (suggestions only) [1966]," Folder 2, Box 24, Rawls Papers (emphasis added).
75. Rawls, *A Theory of Justice,* 6.
76. See, for example, Pamela Barnhouse Walters, "Educational Access and the State: Historical Continuities and Discontinuities in Racial Inequality in American Education," *Sociology of Education* 74 (2001): 35–49.
77. John Rawls, "Re: 2-S + Rank List: Draft," Folder 2, Box 24, Rawls Papers, 3.
78. Rawls, *A Theory of Justice,* 63, 91–92. Rawls also insisted that the basic structure has immense influence over subjective domains like our personal aims, aspirations, and character that allow us to make effective use of op-

portunities. Thus, even if the controversial claim that African Americans disproportionately came to devalue education during the Jim Crow era is true, the proliferation of these dispositions would *still* raise questions of injustice for Rawls. On the relationship between economic history, attitudes toward education, and racial domination, see Frank Samson, "Reconstruction: The Foundations of Economic Citizenship," in *The Oxford Handbook of African American Citizenship, 1865–Present,* ed. Henry Louis Gates Jr., Claude Steele, Lawrence D. Bobo, Michael C. Dawson, Gerald Jaynes, Lisa Crooms-Robinson, and Linda Darling-Hammond (New York: Oxford University Press, 2012), 286–296. For an important study of efforts to fight racist injustice in American schooling, see Jarvis R. Givens, *Fugitive Pedagogy: Carter G. Woodson and the Art of Black Teaching* (Cambridge, MA: Harvard University Press, 2021).

79. John Rawls, "Proposal for a Military Recruitment Policy," Folder 2, Box 24, Rawls Papers, 7.
80. In the latter case, deferments would be dramatically limited to cases of significant disability, a small number of occupational exemptions for persons whose work was instrumental to military success (e.g., some scientists and engineers), and perhaps other categories like last surviving sons. Rawls's persistent suggestion of a "last surviving sons" exemption from the draft as possibly legitimate, I think, shows how deeply his unreflective patriarchal conceptions of the family went. He did not broach the subject of expanding women's eligibility for the draft outside of a small nursing provision.
81. This definition of racial exploitation is structured to permit a number of plausible conceptions of the broader exploitation concept. See Ruth J. Sample, *Exploitation: What It Is And Why It's Wrong* (Lanham, MD: Rowman and Littlefield, 2003); Tommie Shelby, "Parasites, Pimps, and Capitalists: A Naturalistic Conception of Exploitation," *Social Theory and Practice* 28, no. 3 (2002): 381–418; Nicholas Vrousalis, "Exploitation, Vulnerability, and Social Domination," *Philosophy and Public Affairs* 41, no. 2 (2013): 131–157; Matt Zwolinski, "Structural Exploitation," *Social Philosophy and Policy* 29, no. 1 (2012): 154–179; and Robert Mayer, "What's Wrong with Exploitation?," *Journal of Applied Philosophy* 24, no. 2 (2007): 137–150.
82. Mills, *Black Rights/White Wrongs,* 122, 125.
83. Mills, *Black Rights/White Wrongs,* 118, 125.
84. Patricia M. Shields, "The Burden of the Draft: The Vietnam Years," *Journal of Political and Military Sociology* 9, no. 2 (1981): 215–229.
85. On the changing black class dynamics of this period, see William J. Wilson, *The Declining Significance of Race: Blacks and Changing American Institutions,* 3rd ed. (Chicago: University of Chicago Press, 2012), 122–182.
86. John Rawls, "Notes on the Draft (1966)," Folder 2, Box 24, Rawls Papers, 2.
87. See G. A. Cohen, *Rescuing Justice and Equality* (Cambridge, MA: Harvard University Press, 2008), especially chapter 8.
88. Some philosophers stipulate that exploitation *must* harm; see, for example, Allen E. Buchanan, *Ethics, Efficiency, and the Market* (Totowa, NJ:

Rowman and Littlefield, 1985): 87. But compare Matt Zwolinski, "Dialogue on Price Gouging: Price Gouging, Non-Worseness, and Distributive Justice," *Business Ethics Quarterly* 19, no. 2 (2009): 295–306.

89. Edward C. Banfield, *The Unheavenly City Revisited* (Boston: Little, Brown, 1974), especially chapters 3–4 and 10–12.
90. Edward Banfield to John Rawls, 1966, Folder 2, Box 24, Rawls Papers.
91. Daniel P. Moynihan, "The Negro Family: A Case for National Action," in *The Moynihan Report and the Politics of Controversy: A Trans-Action Social Science and Public Policy Report*, ed. Lee Rainwater and William L. Yancey (Cambridge MA: The MIT Press, 1967), 86, cited failure on the test as "the ultimate mark of inadequate preparation for life" and lamented that over 50 percent of black men fell below its minimal standards. See also United States President's Task Force on Manpower Conservation, *One-Third of a Nation: A Report on Young Men Found Unqualified for Military Service* (Washington DC: US Government Printing Office, 1964); and Moynihan, "The Negro Family," 62.
92. Appy, *Working-Class War*, 32–33.
93. Hsiao, "Project 100,000."
94. John Rawls, "A Proposal for a Military Recruitment Policy," n.d. [1966?], Folder 2, Box 24, Rawls Papers, 8–9 (emphasis added).
95. Rawls, *A Theory of Justice*, 220.
96. Rawls, *Justice as Fairness*, 47.
97. Rawls, *A Theory of Justice*, 216–217.
98. John Rawls, "Docket for Harvard Faculty of Arts and Sciences Meeting." This holds for all compulsory forms of "national service" as well, a view Rawls reiterated in 2001, quoting verbatim from his 1966 critique of draft deferments; Rawls, *Justice as Fairness*, 47.
99. Rawls, "A Proposal for a Military Recruitment Policy." This provides more evidence for the persuasiveness of Shelby's application of Rawlsian thought to ghetto poverty and cultural reform projects in Tommie Shelby, *Dark Ghettos: Injustice, Dissent, and Reform* (Cambridge, MA: Harvard University Press, 2016), chapter 3.
100. Rawls, *A Theory of Justice*, 302, 312.
101. Stanley Cavell, *Conditions Handsome and Unhandsome: The Constitution of Emersonian Perfectionism* (Chicago: University of Chicago Press, 1990): 101–126.
102. Michael Phillips, "Reflections on the Transition from Ideal to Non-Ideal Theory," *Noûs* 19, no. 4 (1985): 551–570; Rawls, *A Theory of Justice*, 7–8, 215–216; Andrew March, "Taking People as They Are: Islam as a 'Realistic Utopia' in the Political Theory of Sayyid Qutb," *American Political Science Review* 104, no. 1 (2010): 192.
103. To this end, Rawls introduces a further commitment, which other ideal theorists, including G. A. Cohen, have rejected to varying degrees: that ideal theories of justice must also be fact sensitive in critical respects. This, principally, means that ideal theory, deal as it must in abstraction, should nonetheless consider realistic notions of moral psychology, certain facts about the functioning of basic institutions (e.g., imperfect administration),

structuring assumptions like the existence of something akin to David Hume's scarcity-dependent "conditions of justice," and problems like stability. This is a point often neglected in arguments that attempt to downplay the significance of full compliance in ideal theory out of concern that they remove questions of institutional design, socialization, preference formation, and moral education from political theory. The assumption of full compliance does not necessarily dissolve the theorists' responsibility to persuasively account for reasons that might motivate, sustain, and restore compliance.

104. Rawls, *A Theory of Justice,* 215–216.
105. Shelby, "Racial Realities and Corrective Justice," 150–51 (emphasis added).
106. Paul Weithman, *Why Political Liberalism? On John Rawls's Political Turn* (Oxford: Oxford University Press, 2013), 44–46, 361–62.
107. Weithman, *Why Political Liberalism?,* 363, 8.
108. Weithman, *Why Political Liberalism?,* 363.
109. Rawls, *Lectures on the History of Moral Philosophy,* ed. Barbara Herman (Cambridge, MA: Harvard University Press, 2000), 319.
110. Shelby, "Racial Realities and Corrective Justice," 160.
111. Mills, *Black Rights/White Wrongs,* 75. This, however, does not seem quite right as a complete definition of nonideal theory. It is not clear why modeling noncompliance or serious injustices need to necessarily model actually existing social ills or enduring injustices. Nonideal theory seems also to include attempts to generate principles of action, institutional design, or other ethico-political judgments drawn from purely speculative or fictional models of social injustice and adversity. See, for example, Derrick Bell, "The Space Traders," in *The Derrick Bell Reader,* ed. Richard Delgado and Jean Stefancic (New York: New York University Press, 2005), 57–72, a story about the arrival of slave traders from outer space that is meant to illuminate Bell's "interest convergence" and permanent racism theses. See also A. John Simmons, "Ideal and Nonideal Theory," *Philosophy and Public Affairs* 38, no. 1 (2010): 5–36.
112. Mills, *The Racial Contract,* 129.
113. Amaryta Sen, *The Idea of Justice* (Cambridge, MA: Harvard University Press, 2009).
114. Susan Moller Okin, *Justice, Gender, and the Family* (New York: Basic Books, 1991).
115. Mills, "Rawls on Race/Race in Rawls," 161.
116. Rawls, *Justice as Fairness,* 29.
117. John Rawls, "The Independence of Moral Theory," in *Collected Papers,* 289.
118. This distinction is covered at length in Chapter 2 of the present volume.
119. Sandel, *Democracy's Discontent.*
120. On orientational *phronesis,* see Albena Azmanova, *The Scandal of Reason: A Critical Theory of Political Judgment* (New York: Columbia University Press, 2021). On civil rights movement as the terrain for political philosophic disagreement, see Michael J. Sandel, "The Constitution of the Procedural Republic: Liberal Rights and Civic Virtues," *Fordham Law Review* 66 (1997): 1–20; David Lyons, *Confronting Injustice: Moral History*

and Political Theory (Oxford: Oxford University Press, 2013); and Bernard R. Boxill, *Blacks and Social Justice* (Lanham, MD: Rowman and Littlefield, 1992).

121. Irene Harvey, "Exemplarity and the Origins of Legislation," in *Unruly Examples: On the Rhetoric of Exemplarity,* ed. Alexander Gelley (Stanford, CA: Stanford University Press,1995), 225 (emphasis added).
122. Rawls again cites the Birmingham letter, as well as the "I Have a Dream" speech and a speech on voting rights to invoke King as an exemplar of public reason and to describe a real-world instance of an appeal to a possible "overlapping consensus" to recognize claims of justice. In his notes for his original paper on civil disobedience, however, it is clear that Rawls was influenced much more broadly by civil rights and antiwar activists, particularly in his list of paradigm cases of civil disobedience. John Rawls, "CD [Civil Disobedience] + The Complications of Our Federal System," Box 7, Folder 6, Rawls Papers, 4.
123. Hugo Adam Bedau, ed., *Civil Disobedience: Theory and Practice* (New York: Pegasus, 1969).
124. Rawls, *A Theory of Justice,* 320n19.
125. Rawls, *A Theory of Justice,* 308. Rawls is at pains to quickly rule out one defense of civil disobedience that seems prima facie plausible to ardent defenders of the freedom of conscience who want to preserve individuals' right to not be a party to injustice or submit to unjust law. This is the claim that "we are never required to comply in these cases," which he dismisses as a "mistake."
126. Rawls, *A Theory of Justice,* 320.
127. Rawls, *A Theory of Justice,* 337 (emphasis added).
128. As Rawls, *A Theory of Justice,* 96, notes, "The main idea is that when a number of persons engage in a mutually advantageous cooperative venture according to rules, and thus restrict their liberty in ways necessary to yield advantages for all, those who have submitted to these restrictions have a right to a similar acquiescence on the part of those who have benefited from their submission."
129. Rawls, *A Theory of Justice,* 309, 310. If the "course of action to be followed depends largely on how reasonable the accepted doctrine is and what means are available to change it," it is not straightforward how civil disobedience on behalf of an aggrieved party would work in a scenario where the (unreasonable) doctrine of justice in a given society was largely congruent with the (unjust) institutions it fosters. These sorts of societies, like feudal societies or inegalitarian theocracies would require a deeper uprooting of the entire order—moral and political—than civil disobedience aims toward in Rawls's conception.
130. Rawls, *A Theory of Justice,* 319, 321 (emphasis added).
131. Rawls, *A Theory of Justice,* 311.
132. Rawls, *A Theory of Justice,* 312.
133. John Rawls, "The Justification of Civil Disobedience," in *Collected Papers,* 182.
134. Forrester, *In the Shadow of Justice.*

135. Rawls, *A Theory of Justice,* 320–321.
136. Rawls, *A Theory of Justice,* 321.
137. John Rawls, *Political Liberalism,* expanded ed. (New York: Columbia University Press, 2005), 247n36, 250–251; Michael J. Sandel, review of *Political Liberalism* by John Rawls, *Harvard Law Review* 107, no. 7 (1994): 1765–1794; John Rawls, "The Idea of Public Reason: Postscript," in *Deliberative Democracy: Essays on Reason and Politics,* ed. James Bohman and William Rehg (Cambridge, MA: MIT Press, 1997), 136.
138. John Rawls, "The Idea of Public Reason Revisited," *University of Chicago Law Review* 64, no. 3 (1997): 776–777. Political values, properly speaking, exist in all sorts of political arrangements—including "aristocracy and corporate oligarchy," but Rawls is concerned with those "political conceptions that are reasonable for a constitutional democratic regime."
139. Rawls, *A Theory of Justice,* 312; Rawls, *Political Liberalism,* 149.
140. Rawls, *Political Liberalism,* 156.
141. Take, for example, Martha Nussbaum, "Introduction," in *Rawls's Political Liberalism,* ed. Thom Brooks and Martha Craven Nussbaum (New York: Columbia University Press, 2013), 9, which argues that overlapping consensus is a "new concept that Rawls develops" in that later text. As Nussbaum rightly notes, "Overlapping consensus is, in effect, the ultimate answer to the question of stability. Because citizens will see that the political conception respects them, both by respecting their liberties and opportunities and by respecting their comprehensive doctrines, they will give it more than grudging allegiance." Yet Rawls already appeals to the idea of an overlapping consensus in the discussion of civil disobedience and uses it there to make a similar distinction between conscientious objectors who appeal to religion and those who engage in civil disobedience who appeal to political ideals. See Rawls, *A Theory of Justice,* 337.
142. Rawls, *A Theory of Justice,* 326–327.
143. See the discussion on refocusing in Chapter 1 of the present volume.
144. Gunnar Myrdal, *An American Dilemma: The Negro Problem and Modern Democracy,* vol. 1 (New York: Harper and Brothers, 1944), lxxxii, lxxx, xlviii–xlix.
145. Gunnar Myrdal, *An American Dilemma: The Negro Problem and Modern Democracy,* vol. 2 (New York: Harper and Brothers, 1944), 1021.
146. Lyndon B. Johnson, "Commencement Address at Howard University: 'To Fulfill These Rights,'" June 4, 1965, American Presidency Project, https://www.presidency.ucsb.edu/documents/commencement-address-howard-university-fulfill-these-rights.
147. Rawls, *A Theory of Justice,* 323–330.
148. Hayden White, *Metahistory: The Historical Imagination in Nineteenth-Century Europe* (Baltimore: Johns Hopkins University Press, 1973), 135–162.
149. It is a frequent criticism, especially outside the United States, that Rawls is manifestly arguing for an "ideal" society suspiciously based on the United States. John Horton, "Rawls in Britain," *European Journal of Political Theory* 1, no. 2 (2002): 147–161.
150. See Rawls, "CD [Civil Disobedience]" (emphasis added).

151. John Rawls, "Nature of Political and Social Thought and Methodology (1960–1964)," Box 35, Folder 10, Rawls Papers, 5–7.
152. Forrester, *In the Shadow of Justice,* 157.
153. Aziz Rana, *The Constitutional Bind: How Americans Came to Idolize a Document That Fails Them* (Chicago: University of Chicago Press, 2024), 11. There are, it must be admitted, other interpretations available. Rawls, *A Theory of Justice,* 198–199, does argue that "one of the main defects of constitutional government has been the failure to insure the fair value of political liberty. The necessary corrective steps have not been taken, indeed, they never seem to have been seriously entertained. Disparities in the distribution of property and wealth that far exceed what is compatible with political equality have generally been tolerated by the legal system." Rawls then, however, argues that such questions belong to "political sociology" and a "theory of the political system," not his work in "the theory of justice." One difficulty with this judgment is that if no existing constitution has ever achieved the fair value of political liberty, such an elusive standard cannot therefore be the one at work when he describes various constitutional orders as "nearly just." Far more plausible is the traditional creedal constitutionalist account which separates the constitutional expression of just principles from statutory law and the description of social inequality.
154. Weithman, *Why Political Liberalism?*
155. Mills, *From Class to Race,* 198 (emphasis added).
156. Karuna Mantena, "Another Realism: The Politics of Gandhian Nonviolence," *American Political Science Review* 106, no. 2 (2012): 455–470.
157. As a Christian moral realist, King does treat these commitments as metaphysically prior in the sense that the creedal affirmation of human rights reflects truth, right, and God's love and will. This, I think, accounts for his riff on America returning "home" to "one nation, indivisible, with liberty and justice for all." Further warrant for this reading is that King immediately says that the destruction of racial domination will give the democratic creed "a new *authentic* ring." Martin Luther King Jr., *Where Do We Go From Here: Chaos or Community?* (Boston: Beacon, 2010), 89.
158. King, *Where Do We Go from Here?,* 72.
159. King, *Where Do We Go from Here?,* 72–73, 76–77.
160. William E. Scheuerman, "Civil Disobedience in the Shadows of Postnationalization and Privatization," *Journal of International Political Theory* 12, no. 3 (2015): 237–257.
161. Thomas Borstelmann, *The Cold War and the Color Line: American Race Relations in the Global Arena* (Cambridge, MA: Harvard University Press, 2001).
162. Nikhil Pal Singh, *Black Is a Country: Race and the Unfinished Struggle for Democracy* (Cambridge, MA: Harvard University Press, 2004).
163. King, *Where Do We Go from Here?,* 200.
164. Martin Luther King Jr., *All Labor Has Dignity* (Boston: Beacon, 2010), 95.
165. Martin Luther King Jr., *The Trumpet of Conscience* (Boston: Beacon, 2010), 34.
166. King, *Where Do We Go from Here?*

167. John Rawls, *A Theory of Justice,* 321 (emphasis added).
168. Stephen Darwall, *The Second-Person Standpoint: Morality, Respect, and Accountability* (Cambridge, MA: Harvard University Press, 2009).
169. King, *Where Do We Go from Here?,* 127.
170. Martin Luther King Jr., *Why We Can't Wait* (Boston: Beacon, 2010), 87.
171. King, *Where Do We Go from Here?,* 212; King, *Why We Can't Wait,* 34.
172. Shame, here, is understood as the affective state that accompanies the awareness that we have fallen short of our integral ideals in an objectionable and irresponsible way. Although he does not draw out this connection, Christopher Lebron approaches the question of racial injustice in a similar fashion in *The Color of Our Shame: Race and Justice in Our Time* (New York: Oxford University Press, 2013).
173. Frederick Douglass, "British Influence on the Abolition Movement in America: An Address Delivered in Paisley, Scotland, on April 17, 1846," in *The Frederick Douglass Papers,* ser. 1, *Speeches, Debates, and Interviews,* vol. 1, *1841–46,* ed. John Blassingame (New Haven, CT: Yale University Press, 1979), 215.
174. Cornel West, *Prophesy Deliverance! An Afro-American Revolutionary Christianity,* 40th anniversary expanded ed. (Louisville, KY: Westminster John Knox, 2022), 31.
175. King, *Where Do We Go from Here?*
176. Cavell, *Conditions Handsome and Unhandsome,* 110–114.
177. Stanley Cavell, *Cities of Words: Pedagogical Letters on a Register of the Moral Life* (Cambridge, MA: Harvard University Press, 2004), 186.
178. Cavell, *Conditions Handsome and Unhandsome,* 110–112.
179. Rawls, *A Theory of Justice,* 312.
180. Cavell, *Conditions Handsome and Unhandsome,* 110, 46.
181. Martin Luther King Jr., "Beyond Vietnam: A Time to Break Silence," in *A Single Garment of Destiny,* 208.
182. Blending King's diagnosis and Rawls's analytical categories, the argument would insist that racism is often a controlling ideology within an outlaw state's practices, domestically and on the world stage. "Racism," King argues in *Where Do We Go from Here?,* 185, "and its perennial ally—economic exploitation—provide the key to understanding most of the international complications of this generation." Citing US support for racist regimes in South Africa and Rhodesia, the corporate cartels dominating Latin American societies, and US military efforts to usurp Vietnamese self-determination, from supporting French colonialism to prosecuting their military endeavor, King sees the United States and many of its allies as engaged in "racism in its more sophisticated form—neocolonialism."
183. John Rawls, *The Law of Peoples: With "The Idea of Public Reason Revisited"* (Cambridge, MA: Harvard University Press, 1999), 6–7; King, "Beyond Vietnam"; Joshua Bloom and Waldo E. Martin, *Black Against Empire: The History and Politics of the Black Panther Party* (Berkeley: University of California Press, 2013), 102–111.
184. Martin Luther King, "The Trumpet of Conscience (1968)," in *A Testament of Hope,* 646–647.

185. Richard Rorty, *Achieving Our Country: Leftist Thought in Twentieth Century America* (Cambridge, MA: Harvard University Press, 1998).
186. King, *Where Do We Go from Here?*, 141.
187. King, *Where Do We Go from Here?*, 141.
188. Rawls, *A Theory of Justice*, 321 (emphasis added).
189. J. M. Bernstein, "Promising and Civil Disobedience: Arendt's Political Modernism," in *Thinking in Dark Times: Hannah Arendt on Ethics and Politics*, ed. Roger Berkowitz (New York: Fordham University Press, 2009), 216.
190. King, *Where Do We Go from Here?*, 53, 52.
191. King, *The Trumpet of Conscience*, 49–50.
192. King, *Why We Can't Wait*, 92, 36.
193. Reinhold Niebuhr, *Moral Man and Immoral Society*, 2nd ed. (Louisville, KY: Westminster John Knox, 2013), 139. In *Moral Man*, Niebuhr was among the first to suggest the applicability of Gandhian *satyagraha* (passive political resistance) to the African American civil rights struggle.
194. King, *Why We Can't Wait*, 125.
195. Indeed, in a militaristic culture like the United States, which, King argues in *Why We Can't Wait*, 35, "worships the frontier tradition" and whose "heroes are those who champion justice through violent retaliation against injustice," it becomes critical even for the survival of a disposition toward *nonviolent* civil disobedience that prevailing conceptions of "bravery," "strength," and "virtue" undergo a kind of redescription and revaluation.
196. Hannah Arendt, *Crises of the Republic* (New York: Harcourt Brace Jovanovich, 1972), 55.
197. Shelby, *Dark Ghettos*.
198. Bertrand Russell, "Civil Disobedience and the Threat of Nuclear Warfare," in Bedau, *Civil Disobedience*, 153–159.
199. King, *Why We Can't Wait*, 37
200. King, *Where Do We Go from Here?*, 19.
201. King, *Why We Can't Wait*, 6.
202. Jason Sokol, *There Goes My Everything: White Southerners in the Age of Civil Rights, 1945–1975* (New York: Vintage, 2007), 92.
203. King *The Trumpet of Conscience*, 15.
204. Boris Groys, *On the New*, trans. G. M. Goshgarian (London: Verso Books, 2014).
205. Monique Roelofs, quoted in Paul C. Taylor, *Black Is Beautiful: A Philosophy of Black Aesthetics* (Malden, MA: Wiley-Blackwell, 2016), 21.
206. Elaine Scarry, *The Body in Pain: The Making and Unmaking of the World* (New York: Oxford University Press, 1988), 77.
207. Sianne Ngai, *Our Aesthetic Categories: Zany, Cute, Interesting* (Cambridge, MA: Harvard University Press, 2015), 141.
208. See, for example, the debate forum that the *Boston Review* hosted on Glenn C. Loury, "Ferguson Won't Change Anything. What Will?" *Boston Review*, December 15, 2014, https://www.bostonreview.net/forum/glenn-loury-ferguson-wont-change-anything-what-will/.

209. Robin Celikates, "Constituent Power Beyond Exceptionalism: Irregular Migration, Disobedience, and (Re-)Constitution," *Journal of International Political Theory* 15, no. 1 (2019): 67–81.
210. Judith Butler, *The Force of Nonviolence: An Ethico-Political Bind* (London: Verso Books, 2020), 45. See also Judith Butler, "The Radical Equality of Lives," interview by and Brandon M. Terry, *Boston Review,* October 26, 2016, https://www.bostonreview.net/articles/brandon-m-terry-butler-int/.
211. King, *Why We Can't Wait,* 28.
212. Rawls, *A Theory of Justice,* 322 (emphasis added).
213. Erin Pineda, "Civil Disobedience and Punishment: (Mis)Reading Justification and Strategy from SNCC to Snowden," *History of the Present* 5, no. 1 (2015): 1–30.
214. King, *Why We Can't Wait,* 139.
215. Michael Walzer, *Obligations: Essays on Disobedience, War and Citizenship* (Cambridge MA: Harvard University Press, 1970), 17.
216. King, *Why We Can't Wait,* 27, 119.
217. Teresa Bejan, *Mere Civility: Disagreement and the Limits of Toleration* (Cambridge, MA: Harvard University Press, 2017).
218. There is, of course, an obvious religious foundation for such language. As Martin Luther King Jr., "Nonviolence and Racial Justice," in *A Testament of Hope,* 9, notes, "it is the love of God working in the lives of men. When we love on the *agape* level," he says, "we love men not because we like them, not because their attitudes and ways appeal to us, but because God loves them." We can hate others' deeds while still loving the person behind them. But King also gives more secular descriptions of, and justifications for "love." For *agape* there are no worthy and unworthy people, or distinctions based on contingent qualities—just disinterested goodwill for the sake of others' needs. King also says that love can put an end to cycles of revenge, hatred, and violent retaliation. It is the best approach for turning people who are our enemies at present into friends moving forward. Instead of entrenching the distinction between friend and enemy permanently in culture and politics, love tries to dissolve the enemy altogether, or at least make the position of enemy contingent and capable of being superseded. A politics informed by love, in other words, leaves a way out of conflict beyond annihilation. When we treat our enemy as someone whose needs continue to obligate us in the midst of conflict, as persons for whom we have goodwill, as equals whom we refuse to humiliate or destroy, we may limit the ill feelings and resentments that otherwise structure contentious politics. So much of what makes politics explosive is the fragility of trust and distrust, the emotions at stake, and the opacity of our opponents' intentions. For King, love gives us, perhaps, a way of managing some of the most deadly consequences of these elements of politics, or, better yet, shows us a way out of calcified relations of distrust, resentment, and fear. See Martin Luther King Jr., *Strength to Love* (Minneapolis: Fortress, 2010), 47.
219. Martin Luther King Jr., "Pilgrimage to Nonviolence," in *The Radical King,* ed. Cornel West (Boston: Beacon, 2015), 51.

220. On the morphology of moral actions, see Saba Mahmood, *Politics of Piety: The Islamist Revival and the Feminist Subject* (Princeton, NJ: Princeton University Press, 2011), 22–24.
221. Philip A. Hart, quoted in Arendt, *Crises of the Republic,* 52.
222. Scheuerman, "Civil Disobedience in the Shadows."
223. Scarry, *The Body in Pain.*
224. Friedrich Nietzsche, *On the Genealogy of Morality,* ed. and trans. Maudemarie Clark and Alan J. Swensen (Indianapolis: Hackett, 1998).
225. Kimberley Brownlee, *Conscience and Conviction: The Case for Civil Disobedience* (Oxford: Oxford University Press, 2012).
226. Elijah Anderson, *Code of the Street: Decency, Violence, and the Moral Life of the Inner City* (New York: W. W. Norton, 1999).
227. Wesley Lowery, *They Can't Kill Us All: Ferguson, Baltimore, and a New Era in America's Racial Justice Movement* (New York: Little, Brown, 2016); DeRay Mckesson, *On the Other Side of Freedom: The Case for Hope* (New York: Viking, 2018); Brandon M. Terry, "After Ferguson," *Point,* June 16, 2015, https://thepointmag.com/politics/after-ferguson/.
228. Reasonable faith that these lexically subordinate ends of justice shall be sufficiently redeemed, also to be secured by the expectation that guarantees of equal citizenship, will enable the kinds of formal political participation necessary for this end. Rawls, *A Theory of Justice,* 327.
229. Martin Luther King Jr., "Nonviolence: The Only Road to Freedom," in *A Testament of Hope,* 55.
230. King, *The Trumpet of Conscience,* 13–15.
231. King, *Where Do We Go from Here?,* 87.
232. Jacquelyn Dowd Hall, "The Long Civil Rights Movement and the Political Uses of the Past," *Journal of American History* 91, no. 4 (2005), 1233–1263.
233. King, *The Trumpet of Conscience.*
234. Nikolas Kompridis, *Critique and Disclosure: Critical Theory Between Past and Future* (Cambridge, MA: MIT Press, 2006), 13, 36.
235. King, *The Trumpet of Conscience,* 63.
236. G. A. Cohen, *Rescuing Justice and Equality* (Cambridge, MA: Harvard University Press, 2008), 8.
237. Seana Valentine Shiffrin, "Race, Labor, and the Fair Equality of Opportunity Principle," *Fordham Law Review* 72 (2003): 1643–1675.
238. See the essays in Seyla Benhabib, ed., *Democracy and Difference: Contesting the Boundaries of the Political* (Princeton, NJ: Princeton University Press, 1996).
239. Rawls, *Justice as Fairness,* 1–4.
240. Thomas McCarthy, *Race, Empire, and the Idea of Human Development* (Cambridge: Cambridge University Press, 2009), 36–41.
241. Rawls, *The Law of Peoples,* 91.
242. Aziz Rana, *The Two Faces of American Freedom* (Cambridge, MA: Harvard University Press, 2010).
243. Cavell, *Conditions Handsome and Unhandsome,* 13. On King's own overlap with Cavell, see Paul C. Taylor, "Moral Perfectionism," in *To Shape a New World: Essays on the Political Philosophy of Martin Luther*

King, Jr, ed. Tommie Shelby and Brandon M. Terry (Cambridge MA: Harvard University Press, 2018), 35–57.

244. Myrdal, *An American Dilemma,* 2:1021–1022.

7. The Changing Same

1. James Baldwin, "Introduction to *Notes of a Native Son,* 1984," in *Collected Essays,* ed. Toni Morrison (New York: Library of America, 1998), 810.
2. Lydia Saad, "US Perceptions of White-Black Race Relations Sink to New Low," Gallup News, September 2, 2020, https://news.gallup.com. See also Michael C. Dawson, *Not in Our Lifetimes: The Future of Black Politics* (Chicago: University of Chicago Press, 2011).
3. Corey Robin, *The Enigma of Clarence Thomas* (New York: Henry Holt, 2019). See also Anthea Butler, *White Evangelical Racism: The Politics of Morality in America* (Chapel Hill: University of North Carolina Press, 2021); Carol Anderson, *White Rage: The Unspoken Truth of Our Racial Divide* (New York: Bloomsbury, 2016); Michael J. Gelin, *The White Storm: Racism and the Rise of the Alt-Right* (New York: Lantern, 2023); Philip S. Gorski and Samuel L. Perry, *The Flag and the Cross: White Christian Nationalism and the Threat to American Democracy* (New York: Oxford University Press, 2022); and Jonathan M. Metzl, *Dying of Whiteness: How the Politics of Racial Resentment Is Killing America's Heartland* (New York: Basic Books, 2019).
4. Ta-Nehisi Coates, *Between the World and Me* (New York: Spiegel and Grau, 2015), 103.
5. Jesse McCarthy, "On Afropessimism," *Los Angeles Review of Books,* July 20, 2020, https://lareviewofbooks.org. In the view defended in the present chapter and in McCarthy, it is probably misleading to characterize Hartman as an Afropessimist. Her commitments to a revival of Pan-Africanism in *Lose Your Mother* and her interest in certain practices of redemptive memory and "care" ethics are at odds with a more thoroughgoing and nihilistic pessimism. Taking McCarthy's helpful reconstruction of four pillars of Afropessimism—the exceptionality thesis, immutability thesis, structural antagonism thesis, and abjection thesis—Pan-Africanism seems to undermine immutability and abjection, while the argument in Hartman's *Scenes of Subjection* should be read not as endorsing structural antagonism but as showing that attempts to enact that antagonism in practice, especially via the law, consistently falls into contradiction, crisis, and aporia. This does not mean that there will be some dialectical progression toward inevitable redemption, but it does mean—similarly to Walter Johnson's critique of "dehumanization talk" in the analysis of slavery—that any attempt to erect a binary like black/human as a stable opposition gets entangled in its own impossibility. See Saidiya V. Hartman, *Scenes of Subjection: Terror, Slavery, and Self-Making in Nineteenth-Century America* (New York: Oxford University Press, 1997); Saidiya V. Hartman, *Lose Your Mother: A Journey Along the Atlantic Slave Route* (New York:

Farrar, Straus and Giroux, 2007); and Walter Johnson, "To Remake the World: Slavery, Racial Capitalism, and Justice," *Boston Review* 20 (2018), https://www.bostonreview.net.

6. Calvin L. Warren, "Black Nihilism and the Politics of Hope," *CR: The New Centennial Review* 15, no. 1 (2015): 215–248.
7. Frank B. Wilderson III, *Afropessimism* (New York: Liveright, 2020), 92.
8. See McCarthy, "On Afropessimism"; Michael C. Dawson, "Hidden in Plain Sight: A Note on Legitimation Crises and the Racial Order," *Critical Historical Studies* 3, no. 1 (2016), 143–161; Iyko Day, "Being or Nothingness: Indigeneity, Antiblackness, and Settler Colonial Critique," *Critical Ethnic Studies* 1, no. 2 (2015): 102–121; Greg Thomas, "Afro-Blue Notes: The Death of Afro-Pessimism (2.0)?," *Theory and Event* 21, no. 1 (2018): 282–317; and Susan Neiman, *Left Is Not Woke* (Hoboken, NJ: Polity, 2023).
9. This conception of therapeutic critique owes a great deal to Martha C. Nussbaum, *The Therapy of Desire: Theory and Practice in Hellenistic Ethics* (Princeton, NJ: Princeton University Press, 1994). See also the sympathetic yet critical take in Michael Temelini, *Wittgenstein and the Study of Politics* (Toronto: University of Toronto Press, 2018).
10. On negation as a simple or stable form of irony, see Nehamas, *The Art of Living: Socratic Reflections from Plato to Foucault* (Berkeley: University of California Press, 1998), 53–55. Nehamas makes the important point that negation is but one form of irony. More fundamentally, irony involves strategies of creating distance between what we say and what we mean and may take the form of negation, concealment, refusal, partial silence, or other strategies.
11. Søren Kierkegaard, *The Concept of Irony: With Continual Reference to Socrates,* ed. and trans. Howard V. Hong and Edna H. Hong (Princeton, NJ: Princeton University Press, 1989).
12. Paul de Man, "The Concept of Irony," in *The Aesthetics of Ideology* (Minneapolis: University of Minnesota Press, 1986), 166.
13. This is exploited to great effect, for instance, in Socratic irony. See Nehamas, *The Art of Living.*
14. Joshua Foa Dienstag, *Pessimism: Philosophy, Ethic, Spirit* (Princeton, NJ: Princeton University Press, 2006), 25.
15. Albert O. Hirschman, *The Rhetoric of Reaction: Perversity, Futility, Jeopardy* (Cambridge, MA: Belknap Press of Harvard University Press, 1991), 70.
16. On irony needing an occasion, see Kevin Newmark, *Irony on Occasion: From Schlegel and Kierkegaard to Derrida and De Man* (New York: Fordham University Press, 2012), 8.
17. Dienstag, *Pessimism.*
18. These pillars are racial realism, church vanguardism, the imagined futures of integrationism and black nationalism, and practical faith and normative commitment to the cultural politics of progressive racial representation.
19. Patrick Sharkey, *Stuck in Place: Urban Neighborhoods and the End of Progress Toward Racial Equality* (Chicago: University of Chicago Press, 2013), 4.
20. Sharkey, *Stuck in Place,* 5.

21. David Scott, *Conscripts of Modernity: The Tragedy of Colonial Enlightenment* (Durham, NC: Duke University Press, 2004).
22. Hayden White, *Metahistory: The Historical Imagination in Nineteenth-Century Europe* (Baltimore: Johns Hopkins University Press, 1973), 9. This invocation of death is meant also to figuratively conjure what W. E. B. Du Bois, calls "a death that is more than death"—namely, the defeat and demise of those commitments and collaborations, ideas and ideals that accrue for us the imperative of duty. Du Bois, *The Souls of Black Folk*, 225.
23. Perhaps the leading defender of a moralist explanation for the end of slavery is David Brion Davis; see David Brion Davis, *Inhuman Bondage: The Rise and Fall of Slavery in the New World* (New York: Oxford University Press, 2006).
24. White, *Metahistory*, 231.
25. See Henry Louis Gates Jr., "'Race,' Writing, and Difference," *Critical Inquiry* 12, no. 1 (1985): 1–20. By contrast, see Richard Rorty, *Contingency, Irony, and Solidarity* (New York: Cambridge University Press, 1989), 73, which expresses confidence that "radical and continuing doubts about [a] final vocabulary" can be overcome by searching for alternative ones in a more liberal "ironist" spirit. I do not discuss Rorty's liberal irony in this chapter because his normative account of the appropriate historical narrative with which to understand American and African American history is self-consciously *romantic*. On Rorty and national romance, see Richard Rorty, *Achieving Our Country* (Cambridge, MA: Harvard University Press, 1999).
26. Jonathan Lear, *A Case for Irony* (Cambridge, MA: Harvard University Press, 2011), drawing on Kierkegaard, illuminates this problem as emerging in the awareness of a gap between pretense and ideals in practical activity and identity. Taking Kierkegaard's famous query "In all of Christendom, is there a Christian?" as the paradigmatic statement of irony, Lear helps reveal the intimate relationship between existential anxiety, epistemic crisis, and ironic critique, which calls into doubt the vocation of the historian, critic, and political actor alike.
27. Lear, *A Case for Irony*, 243; White, *Metahistory*, 243.
28. White, *Metahistory*, 232 (emphasis added).
29. H. Gaston Hall, "Aspects of the Absurd," *Yale French Studies* 25 (1960): 26–32.
30. Arthur Schopenhauer, "On History," in *Philosophical Writings*, ed. Wolfgang Schirmacher (New York: Continuum, 1994), 109–110.
31. Derrick Bell, *Faces in the Bottom of the Well: The Permanence of Racism* (New York: Basic Books, 1992), 12.
32. Bell, *Faces in the Bottom of the Well*, 4.
33. Bell, *Faces in the Bottom of the Well*, 8–9.
34. Bell, *Faces in the Bottom of the Well*, 6–7. See also Derrick M. Bell, "*Brown v. Board of Education* and the Interest-Convergence Dilemma," *Harvard Law Review* 93, no. 3 (1980): 518–533. Bell never gives a compelling answer to what counts as an "interest." He often describes interests in ways that suggest that they are *prior* to, or somehow resistant to, the kind

of discursive struggle that cultivates certain self-conceptions and related interests, as well as linkages between discrete issues that can be figured or rendered persuasive as a "group interest." Nor do we get an adequate account of how our (presumably) varied interests are experienced, ranked, and judged. And what makes something a *white* interest as such, rather than the interest of, say, white elites, or elites of all colors, especially in a post–Jim Crow society? Are there tipping points of misery, or cross-cutting cleavages of interest and identity that might reliably fracture white solidarity and explain the dynamics of our moment, that involve a shift toward racial progressivism among many white liberals? And why is it so despairing, anyway, that material and psychological interests are at play in politics? Surely there are forms of triumphalist liberal moralism about racial progress that are self-indulgent and foolish. Yet, isn't the proper response to the unmasking of interests behind moralism simply to abandon moralism as the standard by which to judge politics as well? If there are no pure moral motivations in politics, so be it, but then why hold up the pursuit of interests as an inherent flaw? That simply smuggles the moralism through the back door to feed on existing distrust. Why would we not, for instance, describe cross-class black solidarity as a kind of "interest convergence" as well?

35. Derrick Bell, *Silent Covenants: Brown v. Board of Education and the Unfulfilled Hopes for Racial Reform* (New York: Oxford University Press, 2004). The domino theory argued that in an era of decolonization, where new nation-states were emerging and seeking allies, ceding any nation's political allegiances to communism and Soviet influence would inevitably risk losing that nation's neighbors to communism, and so on. Thus the Cold War between the Soviet Union and the United States played out almost entirely on the terrain of Third World countries as both superpowers sought to limit the expanded influence of the other through diplomacy, propaganda, international aid, espionage, sabotage, military advice and assistance, and, finally, warfare, most spectacularly in Vietnam.

36. Jack M. Balkin, ed., *What "Brown v. Board of Education" Should Have Said: The Nation's Top Legal Experts Rewrite America's Landmark Civil Rights Decision* (New York: New York University Press, 2001). Bell's argument seems bizarrely sanguine about the prospects for equal-funding jurisprudence in the white-dominated bureaucracies and regionally partitioned governmental entities that would be tasked with carrying out such measures. It is tempting to think that budgetary mathematics would provide comparative clarity over the belabored and byzantine efforts at busing and desegregation that halfheartedly followed the implementation decision in *Brown II* (1955), but it seems that such hopes would be similarly dashed by the decision in *Milliken v. Bradley* (1974), which allowed existing municipal boundaries to thwart most efforts at desegregation and metropolitan equality. The "integrationists," for all their faults, at least understood that America's existing civic boundaries remained a major obstacle to any racial egalitarianism.

37. Bell, *Faces in the Bottom of the Well*, 3, 13.

38. Laura Whitehorn, "Black Power Incarcerated: Political Prisoners, Genocide, and the State," *Socialism and Democracy* 28, no. 3 (2014): 101–117.
39. Bell, *Faces in the Bottom of the Well,* x.
40. Frantz Fanon, *Black Skin, White Masks,* trans. Charles Lam Markmann (New York: Grove, 1967), 229.
41. Henry Louis Gates Jr, "Talkin' That Talk," *Critical Inquiry* 13, no. 1 (1986), 203; Cornel West, *Race Matters* (Boston: Beacon, 1993).
42. Henry Louis Gates Jr., *Figures in Black: Words, Signs, and the 'Racial' Self* (New York: Oxford University Press, 1989), 275.
43. Henry Louis Gates Jr., "What's In a Name?: Some Meanings of Blackness," *Dissent,* September 1989, https://www.dissentmagazine.org.
44. Gates, *Figures in Black,* 274, 204–205.
45. See the defense of a self-described "banal postmodernism" in Kwame Anthony Appiah and Amy Gutmann, *Color Conscious: The Political Morality of Race* (Princeton, NJ: Princeton University Press, 1996), 103–104.
46. Nancy Fraser, "Rethinking Recognition," *New Left Review* 3, no. 3 (2000): 107–118.
47. Wilderson, *Afropessimism* (New York: Liveright, 2020), 41.
48. "Introduction," in *Afro-Pessimism: An Introduction* (Minneapolis: Racked and Dispatched, 2017), 7–14.
49. Warren, "Black Nihilism and the Politics of Hope," 226.
50. Wilderson, *Afropessimism,* 14.
51. I am grateful to Robert Gooding-Williams for this point. For ongoing debate about the metaphysics of race, see Joshua Glasgow, Sally Haslanger, Chika Jeffries, and Quayshawn Spencer, *What Is Race? Four Philosophical Views* (New York: Oxford University Press, 2019).
52. McCarthy, "On Afropessimism."
53. As Wilderson, *Afropessimism,* 13, laments, "I let Humanity say, with a sigh of existential relief, 'At least we're not him.'"
54. Wilderson, *Afropessimism,* 16, 40–41.
55. Jared Sexton, quoted in Wilderson, "Introduction," 10; Warren, "Black Nihilism and the Politics of Hope," 226.
56. Wilderson, *Afropessimism,* 96.
57. Wilderson, *Afropessimism,* 226.
58. Wilderson, "Introduction."
59. Warren, "Black Nihilism and the Politics of Hope," 216–217.
60. Wilderson, "Introduction," 10. Afropessimism has appropriated Orlando Patterson's concept of "social death," which was meant to mark the extreme refusal of social recognition that characterizes enslavement, extending not just to generalized social dishonor or susceptibility to violent coercion but even the standing to make legitimate claims on one's ancestors, progeny, and human equals. Afropessimism has picked up on an ambiguity in Patterson's uses of the term to deploy it as a description of lived experience. See Orlando Patterson, *Slavery and Social Death: A Comparative Study* (Cambridge, MA: Harvard University Press, 1992), 1–17. See also

Vincent Brown, "Social Death and Political Life in the Aftermath of Slavery," *American History Review* 114, no. 5 (2009): 1231–1249.

61. Leon Litwack, *How Free Is Free? The Long Death of Jim Crow* (Cambridge, MA: Harvard University Press, 2009), 143.
62. Litwack, *How Free Is Free?*, 95–128.
63. Warren, "Black Nihilism and the Politics of Hope," 217.
64. Wilderson, "Introduction," 9.
65. Frank B. Wilderson III, "Blacks and the Master/Slave Relation," interview by C. S. Soong, in *Afro-Pessimism: An Introduction,* 18.
66. Wilderson, "Introduction," 9.
67. Sadiya Hartman, "Venus in Two Acts," *Small Axe* 12, no. 2 (2008): 12.
68. Frank B. Wilderson III, "Afro-Pessimism and the End of Redemption," Humanities Futures, October 20, 2015, https://humanitiesfutures.org.
69. This argument is laid out at length in Loïc Wacquant, "Deadly Symbiosis: When Prison and Ghetto Meet and Mesh," *Punishment and Society* 3, no. 1 (2001): 95–134.
70. John J. Dilulio Jr., "My Black Crime Problem and Ours," *City Journal,* Spring 1996, https://www.city-journal.org.
71. Wilderson, "Blacks and the Master/Slave Relation," 19, 24.
72. See, for example, David Harvey, *Seventeen Contradictions and the End of Capitalism* (London: Profile Books, 2015).
73. Warren, "Black Nihilism and the Politics of Hope," 239.
74. Wilderson, "Afro-Pessimism and the End of Redemption."
75. Wilderson, "Blacks and the Master/Slave Relation," 30.
76. Warren, "Black Nihilism and the Politics of Hope," 239.
77. Dienstag, *Pessimism,* 7.
78. Lauren Berlant, *Cruel Optimism* (Durham, NC: Duke University Press, 2011).
79. Warren, "Black Nihilism and the Politics of Hope," 243.
80. Warren, "Black Nihilism and the Politics of Hope," 221, 233, 244.
81. Although Warren seems to reduce this broad terrain of "pathology" to nihilism, this need not follow. There is a long tradition of black social thought, from Du Bois and King to Eldridge Cleaver, Huey Newton, and Angela Davis, that suggests more robustly normative and even emancipatory content to such practices as refusal to work, drug abuse, crime, fraud, and so forth.
82. Coates, *Between the World and Me,* 70.
83. Wilderson, *Afropessimism,* 225, 216.
84. For a similar critique of attempts to appeal to antecedent histories to ground postessentialist conceptions of blackness, see Appiah and Gutmann, *Color Conscious;* and Robert Gooding-Williams, *In the Shadow of Du Bois: Afro-Modern Political Thought in America* (Cambridge, MA: Harvard University Press, 2011), chapter 2.
85. For more on a class-conscious critique of Afropessimism, see Dawson, "Hidden in Plain Sight"; and Loïc Wacquant, "Afropessimism's Radical Abdication: Some Sociological Notes," *New Left Review* 144 (2023): 97–109.

86. Wilderson, "Blacks and the Master/Slave Relation," 28–29.
87. Wilderson, "Blacks and the Master/Slave Relation," 21.
88. Frank Wilderson III, "Gramsci's Black Marx: Whither the Slave in Civil Society?," *Social Identities* 9, no. 2 (2003): 229.
89. Wilderson, "Afro-Pessimism and the End of Redemption."
90. Although Wilderson and company claim fidelity to Sadiya Hartman, they strongly differ on this point. On dehumanization and its flaws as an analytic for slavery, see Walter Johnson, "To Remake the World: Slavery, Racial Capitalism, and Justice," *Boston Review,* May 20, 2020, https://www.bostonreview.net/forum/walter-johnson-to-remake-the-world/.
91. Warren, "Black Nihilism and the Politics of Hope," 220.
92. Warren, "Black Nihilism and the Politics of Hope," 219.
93. Seyla Benhabib, *The Reluctant Modernism of Hannah Arendt* (Lanham, MD: Rowman and Littlefield, 2003), 123–124.
94. Warren, "Black Nihilism and the Politics of Hope," 219.
95. Gavin Wright, *Sharing the Prize: The Economics of the Civil Rights Revolution in the American South* (Cambridge, MA: Harvard University Press, 2018), chapter 6; Jeffrey A. Winters, *Oligarchy* (Cambridge: Cambridge University Press, 2011); Jacob Hacker and Paul Pierson, *Winner-Take-All Politics: How Washington Made the Rich Richer—and Turned Its Back on the Middle Class* (New York: Simon and Schuster, 2011).
96. On this point, see Cornel West, *Prophesy Deliverance! An Afro-American Revolutionary Christianity,* 40th anniversary expanded ed. (Louisville, KY: Westminster John Knox, 2002); Angela Davis, *Blues Legacies and Black Feminism: Gertrude "Ma" Rainey, Bessie Smith, and Billie Holiday* (New York: Vintage, 1999); Paul Taylor, *Black Is Beautiful: A Philosophy of Black Aesthetics* (New York: Wiley-Blackwell, 2016); Nick Bromell, *The Time Is Always Now: Black Thought and the Transformation of US Democracy* (Oxford: Oxford University Press, 2013); and Eddie Glaude Jr., ed., *Is It Nation Time? Contemporary Essays on Black Power and Black Nationalism* (Chicago: University of Chicago Press, 2002).
97. W. E. B. Du Bois, *The Souls of Black Folk: Essays and Sketches* (Chicago: A. C. McClurg, 1903), 11.
98. See Danielle Allen, *Talking to Strangers: Anxieties of Citizenship Since "Brown v. Board of Education"* (Chicago: University of Chicago Press, 2006).
99. Charles M. Payne, *I've Got the Light of Freedom: The Organizing Tradition and the Mississippi Freedom Struggle* (Berkeley: University of California Press, 2007), 68. See also Francesca Polletta, *Freedom Is an Endless Meeting: Democracy in American Social Movements* (Chicago: University of Chicago Press, 2002).
100. On "participatory parity," see Nancy Fraser, *Scales of Justice: Reimagining Political Space in a Globalizing World* (New York: Columbia University Press, 2008), chapter 4.
101. Patchen Markell, "The Insufficiency of Non-Domination," *Political Theory* 36, no. 1 (2008): 9–36.
102. Barbara Ransby, *Ella Baker and the Black Freedom Movement: A Radical Democratic Vision* (Chapel Hill: University of North Carolina Press, 2005), 191; Polletta, *Freedom Is an Endless Meeting,* 7.

103. Ella J. Baker, quoted in Ransby, *Ella Baker and the Black Freedom Movement,* 188.
104. The so-called third generation of critical theory emerged out of the New Left and has been deeply engaged with social movements around racial justice and radical democracy more broadly. See Iris Marion Young, *Inclusion and Democracy* (New York: Oxford University Press, 2000); and Seyla Benhabib, ed., *Democracy and Difference* (Princeton, NJ: Princeton University Press, 1996).
105. Tom Hayden, ed., *Inspiring Participatory Democracy: Student Movements from Port Huron to Today* (New York: Routledge, 2015). See also Polletta, *Freedom Is an Endless Meeting,* 127–128.
106. "The Port Huron Statement of the Students for a Democratic Society," in Hayden, *Inspiring Participatory Democracy,* 127–184.
107. On voting as an attempt to achieve nondomination, see Stokely Carmichael and Charles V. Hamilton, *Black Power: The Politics of Liberation* (New York: Vintage, 1992). On voting as expression of dignity, see Derrick Darby, "A Vindication of Voting Rights," in *To Shape a New World: Essays on the Political Philosophy of Martin Luther King, Jr.,* ed. Tommie Shelby and Brandon M. Terry (Cambridge, MA: Belknap Press of Harvard University Press, 2020), 161–184. On voting to avoid complicity with injustice, see King's statement on Barry Goldwater in Martin Luther King Jr., *The Autobiography of Martin Luther King,* ed. Clayborne Carson (New York: Time Warner, 1998), 247.
108. For a fuller account of the complicity argument, see Eric Beerbohm, *In Our Name: The Ethics of Democracy* (Princeton, NJ: Princeton University Press, 2012).
109. Patricia S. Parker, *Ella Baker's Catalytic Leadership: A Primer on Community Engagement and Communication for Social Justice* (Berkeley: University of California Press, 2020), 40.
110. Warren, "Black Nihilism and the Politics of Hope," 222.
111. Wilderson, *Afropessimism,* 223.
112. Hannah Arendt, *The Human Condition,* 2nd ed. (Chicago: University of Chicago Press, 1998).
113. Wilderson, *Afropessimism,* 217.
114. Arendt, *The Human Condition,* 220.
115. Theodor Adorno, "Progress," *Philosophical Forum* 15, no. 1 (1983): 153.
116. Bernard Reginster, *The Affirmation of Life: Nietzsche on Overcoming Nihilism* (Cambridge, MA: Harvard University Press, 2009), 8.
117. The notion of the "present-past" refers to how historical experiences—especially those of racialized oppression like slavery—persist within and shape the political, moral, and emotional life, often in ways that challenge liberal narratives of progress and closure *and* ontological and metaphysical questions about the meaning of "pastness." See Richard Terdiman, *Present Past: Modernity and the Memory Crisis* (Ithaca, NY: Cornell University Press, 1993); Gregory Laski, *Untimely Democracy: The Politics of Progress After Slavery* (New York: Oxford University

Press, 2018); Jack Turner, "Thinking Historically," *Theory and Event* 19, no. 1 (2016); and Lawrie Balfour, *Democracy's Reconstruction: Thinking Politically with W. E. B. Du Bois* (New York: Oxford University Press, 2011).

118. Frank B. Wilderson III, "Social Death and Narrative Aporia in *12 Years a Slave*," *Black Camera: An International Film Journal*, new ser., 7, no. 1 (2015): 134.
119. Dienstag, *Pessimism,* 197.
120. McCarthy, "On Afropessimism."
121. Malcolm X with Alex Haley, *The Autobiography of Malcolm X* (New York: Ballantine, 1965), 49; E. Franklin Frazier, *The Black Bourgeoisie* (New York: Free Press, 1957), 168.
122. I am grateful to Durba Mitra for this point.
123. Adom Getachew, *Worldmaking After Empire: The Rise and Fall of Self-Determination* (Princeton, NJ: Princeton University Press, 2019).
124. Gooding-Williams, *In the Shadow of Du Bois,* 14.
125. Calvin L. Warren, *Ontological Terror: Blackness, Nihilism, and Emancipation* (Durham, NC: Duke University Press, 2018), 3.
126. Reinhart Koselleck, *Futures Past: On the Semantics of Historical Time,* trans. Keith Tribe (Cambridge, MA: MIT Press, 1990), 13.
127. There are few descriptions of the degradations of childhood in a racist society more succinctly powerful than the one that begins Martin Luther King's "Letter from Birmingham Jail" in his *Why We Can't Wait* (Boston: Beacon, 2011), 85–110.
128. Du Bois, *The Souls of Black Folk,* 213.
129. W. E. B. Du Bois, *Darkwater: Voices from Within the Veil* (New York: Harcourt, Brace and Howe, 1920), 202.
130. Arendt, *The Human Condition,* 176–178, 246.
131. Nikolas Kompridis, *Critique and Disclosure: Critical Theory Between Past and Future* (Cambridge, MA: MIT Press, 2006), 14–15, 195–197.
132. Arendt, *The Human Condition,* 246–247.
133. Du Bois, *Darkwater,* 204.
134. Richard Rorty, *Philosophy and Social Hope* (New York: Penguin, 1999), 120.
135. Cornel West, *Keeping Faith* (New York: Routledge, 2008), xvi.
136. For a similar view, see Martin Hägglund, *This Life: Secular Faith and Spiritual Freedom* (New York: Pantheon, 2019).

8. The Tragic Vision

1. This view is, therefore, at odds with many of the approaches in German idealism that emphasize reconciliation. See Terry Eagleton, *Tragedy* (New Haven, CT: Yale University Press, 2020), 155–220.
2. Aristotle, *Poetics,* trans. S. H. Butcher (New York: Macmillan, 1902), 14:2–8, 45–47.
3. David Scott, *Conscripts of Modernity: The Tragedy of Colonial Enlightenment* (Durham, NC: Duke University Press 2004), 134.

4. Scott, *Conscripts of Modernity,* 13.
5. Aristotle, *Poetics,* 6:14–19, 29–31.
6. Gilbert Harman, "Moral Philosophy Meets Social Psychology: Virtue Ethics and the Fundamental Attribution Error," *Proceedings of the Aristotelian Society* 99 (1999): 317. For a criticism of Harman's position, see Nafsika Athanassoulis, "A Response to Harman: Virtue Ethics and Character Traits," *Proceedings of the Aristotelian Society* 100 (2000): 215–221.
7. On courage, see Roger Crisp, "Introduction," in Aristotle, *Nicomachean Ethics,* ed. and trans. Roger Crisp (New York: Cambridge University Press, 2000), xv.
8. Among the most influential proponent of the "imperfect" or "asymmetrical" information paradigm in economics has been the Nobel Prize laureate Joseph Stiglitz, whose theoretical economic insights have been restated in more popularly accessible form and applied to broader questions of political philosophy. See Joseph Stiglitz, *Globalization and Its Discontents* (New York: W. W. Norton, 2002); and Joseph Stiglitz, *Whither Socialism?* (Cambridge, MA: MIT Press, 1996).
9. Edmund Burke, "Speech on a Bill for Shortening the Duration of Parliaments," in *The Works of the Right Honourable Edmund Burke,* vol. 10 (London: F. C. and J. Rivington, 1812), 73.
10. Edmund Burke, *Reflections on the Revolution in France,* ed. Conor Cruise O'Brien (New York: Penguin, 1982).
11. Taking Scott's earlier remarks about how tragedy can severely complicate our familiar notions of guilt and innocence and action and responsibility, we need only turn to the philosophical literature on "moral luck." There unintended consequences, which are considered a domain of "resultant luck" in the framework popularized by Thomas Nagel, have inspired spirited debate about moral judgments of responsibility, the ethics of punishment, and the possibility of deontological ethics altogether. For an introduction to these debates, see Daniel Statman, ed., *Moral Luck* (Albany: State University of New York Press, 1993), which includes Nagel's essay "Moral Luck" as well as the Bernard Williams essay of the same title that inspired it. On consequential evaluation as an alternative formulation of consequentialism, see Amartya Sen, "Consequential Evaluation and Practical Reason," *Journal of Philosophy* 97, no. 9 (2000): 477–502.
12. A. C. Bradley, *Shakespearean Tragedy: Lectures on Hamlet, Othello, King Lear, Macbeth,* 2nd ed. (London: Macmillan, 1922), 17.
13. G. W. F. Hegel, *Phenomenology of Spirit* (New York: Oxford University Press, 1977), 274. Hegel's reading has come under feminist criticism for its patriarchal tone, its insistence on the political expulsion of women from public life, and its philosophical relegation of women to the "doomed phase of the dialectic." But even this criticism underscores our principal point, which is that tragedy can figure in historical writing and represent not only individual but also social, political, philosophical, spiritual, and moral conflict. See, for example, Seyla Benhabib, "On Hegel, Women, and Irony," in *Situating the Self: Gender, Community and Postmodernism in*

Contemporary Ethics (New York: Routledge, 1992), 255–256; Judith Butler, *Antigone's Claim: Kinship Between Life and Death* (New York: Columbia University Press, 2000); and Bonnie Honig, *Antigone, Interrupted* (Cambridge: Cambridge University Press, 2013).

14. Isaiah Berlin, "Two Concepts of Liberty," in *The Proper Study of Mankind: An Anthology of Essays,* ed. Henry Hardy (New York: Macmillan, 2000), 191–242; Max Weber, "Science as a Vocation," in *From Max Weber: Essays in Sociology,* ed. H. H. Gerth and C. Wright Mills (Oxford: Oxford University Press, 1946), 148.
15. Eagleton, *Tragedy,* 20.
16. Eagleton, *Tragedy,* 20.
17. Scott, *Conscripts of Modernity,* 13.
18. Christophe Mencke, "Critical Theory and Tragic Knowledge," in *The Handbook of Critical Theory,* ed. David M. Rasmussen (Malden, MA: Blackwell, 1999).
19. Max Horkheimer, *Critical Theory* (New York: Seabury, 1982).
20. Bradley, *Shakespearean Tragedy,* 11–12.
21. Eagleton, *Tragedy,* 159–160.
22. Raymond Williams, *Modern Tragedy* (London: Verso Books, 2006), 17–18.
23. Edward Hallett Carr, *What Is History?* (New York: Macmillan, 1967), 32–33.
24. Friedrich Wilhelm Nietzsche, *Beyond Good and Evil: Prelude to a Philosophy of the Future,* trans. Helen Zimmern (New York: Macmillan, 1907), 8–9.
25. Carr, *What Is History?,* 26.
26. Gordon S. Wood, *The Purpose of the Past: Reflections on the Uses of History* (New York: Penguin, 2008), 8, 293–294.
27. Wood, *The Purpose of the Past,* 163 (emphasis added).
28. Seyla Benhabib, *The Reluctant Modernism of Hannah Arendt,* 2nd ed. (Lanham, MD: Rowman and Littlefield, 2003), 88.
29. Williams, *Modern Tragedy,* 240
30. Wood, *The Purpose of the Past,* 10.
31. See, for example, Ellora Derenoncourt, Chi Hyun Kim, Moritz Kuhn, and Moritz Schularick, "Wealth of Two Nations: The U.S. Racial Wealth Gap, 1860–2020," *Quarterly Journal of Economics* 139, no. 2 (2024): 693–750; Richard Hornbeck and Suresh Naidu, "When the Levee Breaks: Black Migration and Economic Development in the American South," *American Economic Review* 104, no. 3 (2014): 963–990; and Christopher Muller, "Northward Migration and the Rise of Racial Disparity in American Incarceration, 1880–1950," *American Journal of Sociology* 118, no. 2 (2012): 281–326.
32. Wood, *The Purpose of the Past,* 11, 14.
33. Hayden White, *Metahistory: The Historical Imagination in Nineteenth-Century Europe* (Baltimore: Johns Hopkins University Press, 1973), 9.
34. Williams, *The Tragic Imagination,* 42.

35. See Robin D. G. Kelley, *Hammer and Hoe: Alabama Communists in the Great Depression* (Chapel Hill: University of North Carolina Press, 1990); Glenda Gilmore, *Defying Dixie: The Radical Roots of Civil Rights, 1919–1950* (New York: W. W. Norton, 2009); Mark Solomon, *The Cry Was Unity: Communists and African Americans, 1917–1936* (Jackson: University Press of Mississippi, 1998); Barbara Foley, *Spectres of 1919: Class and Nation in the Making of the New Negro* (Urbana: University of Illinois Press, 2003); and Barbara Foley, *Wrestling with the Left: The Making of Ralph Ellison's "Invisible Man"* (Durham, NC: Duke University Press, 2010).
36. Martha Nussbaum, "The Costs of Tragedy: Some Moral Limits of Cost-Benefit Analysis," *Journal of Legal Studies,* 29, no. 2 (2000): 1007.
37. Ta-Nehisi Coates, *Between the World and Me* (New York: Spiegel and Grau, 2015).
38. Nussbaum, "The Costs of Tragedy," 1010–1017.
39. Marc Stears, *Demanding Democracy* (Princeton, NJ: Princeton University Press, 2010), especially 1–21, 214–219.
40. Reinhold Niebuhr, *Moral Man and Immoral Society: A Study in Ethics and Politics* (New York: Charles Scribner's Sons, 1960), 3.
41. Niebuhr, *Moral Man and Immoral Society,* 169–175.
42. Niebuhr, *Moral Man and Immoral Society,* 231–256. For a popular contemporary defense of an expansive, cosmopolitan consumer ethics, see Naomi Klein, *No Logo: Taking Aim at the Brand Bullies* (New York: Picador, 2009). For a history of consumer activism in the United States, see Lawrence B. Glickman, *Buying Power: A History of Consumer Activism in America* (Chicago: University of Chicago Press, 2009).
43. Martin Luther King, Jr., "Interview by Lester Margolies (March 22, 1961)," in Martin Luther King, Jr., *The Papers of Martin Luther King, Jr.,* vol. 7, *To Save the Soul of America, January 1961–August 1962,* ed. Clayborne Carson and Tenisha Hart Armstrong (Berkeley: University of California Press, 2014), 187.
44. Martin Luther King, Jr., "My Trip to the Land of Gandhi," in *A Testament of Hope,* ed. James Washington (San Francisco: HarperCollins, 1986), 39.
45. Martin Luther King Jr., *Why We Can't Wait* (Boston: Beacon, 2010), 90. By 1968, confronted with the intractability of ghetto poverty, the strength of reactionary conservatism, the crisis of the Vietnam War, and the visceral challenge of Black Power, King argued for a turn toward a program of "mass civil disobedience." This program was distinguished not only by its aspiration to "national" scale or its disdain for party politics but by its refusal to "count on government goodwill" or the moral force of "a statement to the larger society." Instead the need was to deploy "a force that interrupts [society's] functioning at some key point," to "compel unwilling authorities to yield to the mandates of justice"—including economic and reparative justice. Martin Luther King Jr., *The Trumpet of Conscience* (Boston: Beacon, 2011), 14–16. For more on this theme, see Brandon M. Terry, "Requiem for a Dream: The Problem-Space of Black Power," in *To Shape a New World: Essays on the Political Philosophy of Martin Luther*

King, Jr., ed. Tommie Shelby and Brandon M. Terry (Cambridge, MA: Harvard University Press, 2018), 290–324.

46. Sarah Keys v. Carolina Coach Company, 64 MCC 769 (1955); NAACP v. St. Louis-Santa Fe Railway Company, 297 ICC 335 (1955); Boynton v. Virginia, 364 US 454 (1960). On the Freedom Rides, see Raymond Arsenault, *Freedom Riders: 1961 and the Struggle for Racial Justice* (New York: Oxford University Press, 2006).
47. Martin Luther King Jr., "Letter to Harold Courlander, 10/31/1961," quoted in David J. Garrow, *Bearing the Cross: Martin Luther King Jr. and the Southern Christian Leadership Conference* (New York: HarperCollins, 1986), 172.
48. Garrow, *Bearing the Cross,* 217, 227.
49. Garrow, *Bearing the Cross,* 229.
50. Julian Bond, quoted in Garrow, *Bearing the Cross,* 202.
51. Malcolm X, quoted in Burns, *To the Mountaintop: Martin Luther King Jr.'s Sacred Mission to Save America, 1955–1968* (New York: HarperOne, 2003), 196–197.
52. Garrow, *Bearing the Cross,* 191.
53. Nussbaum, "The Costs of Tragedy," 1035.
54. White, *Metahistory,* 9. As regards long civil rights movement historians, I am referring primarily to Gilmore, *Defying Dixie;* Thomas Sugrue, *Sweet Land of Liberty: The Forgotten Struggle for Civil Rights in the North* (New York: Random House, 2009); Jacqueline Dowd Hall, "The Long Civil Rights Movement and the Political Uses of the Past," *Journal of American History* 91, no. 4 (2005): 1233–1263; Nikhil Pal Singh, *Black Is a Country: The Unfinished Struggle for Race and Democracy* (Cambridge, MA: Harvard University Press, 2003); Risa Goluboff, *The Lost Promise of Civil Rights* (Cambridge, MA: Harvard University Press, 2007); Kenneth Mack, "Law and Mass Politics in the Making of the Civil Rights Lawyer, 1931–1941," *Journal of American History* 93, no. 1 (2006): 37–62; Kenneth Mack, "Rethinking Civil Rights Lawyering and Politics in the Era Before *Brown,*" *Yale Law Journal* 115, no. 2 (2005): 256–354; and Kenneth Mack, "Bringing the Law Back into the History of the Civil Rights Movement," *Law and History Review* 27, no. 3 (2009): 657–671.
55. Sugrue, *Sweet Land of Liberty,* xxii.
56. Hall, "The Long Civil Rights Movement," 1234, 1235.
57. Singh, *Black Is a Country,* 12, 216.
58. It is not clear who "old-style" conservatives is meant to point out, but presumably this refers to either Burkeans or paleoconservative elements on the right.
59. Hall, "The Long Civil Rights Movement," 1237.
60. Singh, *Black Is a Country,* 11–12.
61. Hall, "The Long Civil Rights Movement," 1235.
62. Charles Taylor, "Explanation and Practical Reason," in *Philosophical Arguments* (Cambridge, MA: Harvard University Press, 1995), 34–60.
63. For example, long civil rights movement history includes the entire career trajectories of central activists like Ella Baker and Bayard Rustin, which

likely helps us better understand their work in the conventional period of civil rights history but does not stray into tangential topics like the entire intellectual history of Christianity, Marxism, or liberalism. Jorge Luis Borges, "On Exactitude in Science," in *Collected Fictions,* trans. Andrew Hurley (New York: Penguin, 1998), 325, describes an empire that commissions a map at a 1:1 scale, which being an exact replica of its territory is functionally useless rather than clarifying to judgment.

64. W. E. B. Du Bois, *Black Reconstruction in America, 1860–1880* (New York: Harcourt, Brace, 1935), 585.
65. Robert Gooding-Williams, "W. E. B. Du Bois," in *The Stanford Encyclopedia of Philosophy,* ed. Edward N. Zalta and Uri Nodelman, online Summer 2024 ed., last revised December 20, 2023, https://plato.stanford.edu/archives/sum2024/entries/dubois/.
66. Campbell Gibson and Kay Jung, "Historical Census Statistics on Population Totals by Race, 1790 to 1990, and by Hispanic Origin, 1970 to 1990, for the United States, Regions, Divisions, and States," Working Paper No. 56 (US Census Bureau, Population Division, September 2002).
67. Steven Hahn, *A Nation Under Our Feet: Black Political Struggles in the Rural South, from Slavery to the Great Migration* (Cambridge, MA: Harvard University Press, 2003), 465.
68. I am indebted to Gerald Jaynes for this latter point. See also Hahn, *A Nation Under Our Feet,* 468; and Stewart E. Tolnay, "The African-American 'Great Migration' and Beyond," *Annual Review of Sociology* 29 (2003): 209–232, especially 212.
69. On black female vulnerability to rape in the South, particularly as domestic servants in white households, see Darlene Clark Hine, "Rape and the Inner Lives of Black Women in the Middle West," *Signs* 14, no. 4 (1989): 912–290; and Danielle L. McGuire, *At the Dark End of the Street: Black Women, Rape, and Resistance—A New History of the Civil Rights Movement from Rosa Parks to the Rise of Black Power* (New York: Random House, 2010). Stewart E. Tolnay and E. M. Beck, "Racial Violence and Black Migration in the American South, 1910 to 1930," *American Sociological Review* 57, no. 1 (1992): 103–116, shows that when controlled for economic status, black out-migration was significantly higher in counties where more black lynchings had occurred.
70. Tolnay, "The African American 'Great Migration,'" 215.
71. Sugrue, *Sweet Land of Liberty,* xv, 6.
72. Jonathan L Zelner, Christopher Muller, and James J. Feigenbaum, "Racial Inequality in the Annual Risk of Tuberculosis Infection in the United States, 1910–1933." *Epidemiology and Infection* 145, no. 9 (2017): 1797–1804.
73. On the Red Summer, see Mark Robert Schneider, *We Return Fighting: The Civil Rights Movement in the Jazz Age* (Boston: Northeastern University Press, 2002), 20–36. The most famous case of white mob violence against a black homeowner is the case of Ossian Sweet, a well-to-do black physician from Detroit who bought a home in a white working-class neighborhood (at an inflated price, of course) and was subsequently attacked at his home by a mob of white people who wanted to intimidate him into leaving

the neighborhood, if not kill him. Sweet had earlier recruited nine other friends and family members to stand guard inside the house after receiving death threats, and in the course of events, shots fired from inside the home struck two members of the mob, killing one. All eleven people inside the house were charged with murder and were represented in court by the famed lawyer Clarence Darrow, who was hired by the NAACP. After a hung jury, the prosecutors pursued a second trial against Henry Sweet, Ossian's brother, where Darrow won a not-guilty verdict, compelling the state to drop the murder charges against the other ten defendants. This story is told masterfully in Kevin Boyle, *Arc of Justice: A Saga of Race, Civil Rights and Murder in the Jazz Age* (New York: Henry Holt, 2004).

74. Gilmore, *Defying Dixie,* 1–4.
75. With this sort of approach we remember, for example, that *The Messenger,* the socialist newspaper often described as a leading voice of "Northern radicalism," was founded by A. Phillip Randolph only six years after he left Florida with an even more recently arrived partner, Chandler Owen, from North Carolina. On the idea of the black public sphere, see Black Public Sphere Collective, *The Black Public Sphere* (Chicago: University of Chicago Press, 1995); and Michael Dawson, *Black Visions: The Roots of Contemporary African-American Political Ideologies* (Chicago: University of Chicago Press, 2001), especially 1–85.
76. Gilmore, *Defying Dixie,* 4–5.
77. For example, Mack, "Rethinking Civil Rights Lawyering, 288–299, traces the origins of the civil rights lawyering associated with legal-liberalism and the NAACP's campaign against Jim Crow in the South to ideas of intraracial institutional building, racial uplift, and cultural pluralism that were shaped by the experience of the ghetto.
78. Desmond Ang and Sahil Chinoy, "Vanguard: Black Veterans and Civil Rights After World War I," NBER Working Paper No. 33460 (National Bureau of Economic Research, February 2025); Ang and Chino takes inspiration from Chad L. Williams, *Torchbearers of Democracy: African American Soldiers in the World War I Era* (Chapel Hill: University of North Carolina Press, 2010). Black veterans were actively involved in collective self-defense in response to 1919's Red Summer of race riots. An especially noteworthy incident was the Camp Logan Mutiny in Houston, where approximately one hundred black soldiers, in retaliation for local police assaulting a black mother and a fellow soldier, clashed with police and white residents, killing sixteen and losing four of their own; see Schneider, *We Return Fighting,* 218–231.
79. W. E. B. Du Bois, "An Essay Toward a History of the Black Man in the Great War," *Crisis* 18, no. 2 (1919): 76. See also Chad L. Williams, *The Wounded World: W. E. B. Du Bois and the First World War* (New York: Farrar, Straus and Giroux, 2023).
80. As Holly Straut-Eppsteiner, *Foreign Nationals in the U.S. Armed Forces: Immigration Issues,* R48163 (Washington, DC: Congressional Research Service, August 19, 2024), 1, notes, "As of February 2024, more than 40,000 foreign nationals were serving in active and reserve components of

the Armed Forces. An estimated additional 115,000 foreign nationals residing in the United States are veterans who have previously served on active duty. This report focuses on immigration considerations related to foreign nationals in the U.S. Armed Forces, including U.S. citizenship eligibility through military service and the removal of foreign nationals who have served in the Armed Forces."

81. Steven Hahn, *The Political Worlds of Slavery and Freedom* (Cambridge, MA: Harvard University Press, 2009), 124.
82. For example, in the UNIA's "Declaration of the Rights of the Negro Peoples of the World," in *Selected Writings and Speeches of Marcus Garvey,* ed. Bob Blaisdell (Mineola, NY: Dover, 2004), 16–23, Garvey proclaims that "nowhere in the world, with few exceptions, are black men accorded equal treatment with white men, although in the same situations and circumstances, but, on the contrary, are discriminated against and denied the common rights due to human beings for no other reason than their race and color." This foundation of black Pan-African nationalism in common oppression is often accompanied by claims of collective identity, as one finds in Garvey's "Africa for the Africans," in *Selected Writings and Speeches,* 69–73, where he asserts that "everybody knows there is absolutely no difference between the native African and the American and West Indian Negroes, in that we are descendants from one common family stock" and approvingly suggests that "there is no other way to avoid the threatening war of the races that is bound to engulf all mankind . . . than by apportioning every race to its own habitat."
83. Karuna Mantena, "Another Realism: The Politics of Gandhian Nonviolence," *American Political Science Review* 106, no. 2 (2012): 455–70.
84. Singh, *Black Is a Country,* 48.
85. Singh, *Black Is a Country,* 26;
86. Singh, *Black Is a Country,* 26, 28–29; Evelyn Brooks Higginbotham, "African-American Women's History and the Metalanguage of Race," *Signs* 17, no. 2 (1992): 251–274.
87. Justin Leroy and Destin Jenkins, eds., *Histories of Racial Capitalism* (New York: Columbia University Press, 2021); Jodi Melamed, "Racial Capitalism," *Critical Ethnic Studies* 1, no. 1 (2015): 76–85; Nikhil Pal Singh, "Of Racial Capitalism," in *After Marx: Literature, Theory, and Value in the Twenty-First Century,* ed. Colleen Lye and Christopher Nealon (Cambridge: Cambridge University Press, 2022), 23–39. For a critique, see Loïc Wacquant, "The Trap of 'Racial Capitalism,'" *European Journal of Sociology/Archives Européennes de Sociologie* 64, no. 2 (2023): 153–162.
88. Echoing Singh's overarching claim but focusing on a case that he ignores, Gilmore, *Defying Dixie,* 22–23, gives brief treatment of the US military's 1915 occupation of Haiti, where a cadre of white Southern officers and military forces installed by fellow Southerner Woodrow Wilson to protect American financial interests on the restless island instituted the familiar Jim Crow institutions of segregated facilities, vocational education in the style of the Tuskegee Normal and Industrial Institute, and a forced-labor regime upheld through physical coercion and incarceration.

89. Woodrow Wilson, "The President's Inner Self: Remarkable Heart to Heart Talk to Newspaper Men at the National Press Club, May 15, 1916," in *President Wilson's Great Speeches and Other History Making Documents* (Chicago: Stanton and Van Vliet, 1917), 189.
90. Singh, *Black Is a Country,* 35–36.
91. Woodrow Wilson, "Final Address in Support of the League of Nations (Sept. 25, 1919)," American Rhetoric, https://www.americanrhetoric.com.
92. Singh, *Black Is a Country,* 46, 50.
93. W. E. B. Du Bois, "The Conservation of Races," in *Writings* (New York: Library of America, 1986), 817.
94. Lee Baker, *From Savage to Negro: Anthropology and the Construction of Race, 1896–1954* (Berkeley: University of California Press, 1998).
95. Du Bois, "The Conservation of Races," 817–818. Du Bois also asserts the existence of "minor" race groups, of which he gives "The American Indians, the Esquimaux [Inuit/Eskimo], and the South Sea Islanders." He does not explicitly give an account of what makes these groups "minor," but, to be consistent, the distinction should not be based on the mixed blood often attributed to these groups, given that blood is said to be secondary. Nor should this be a result of their conquering by "great" races, as this would disqualify the Negro race, besieged by slavery, colonialism, and Jim Crow, from such greatness. The criteria for distinction, therefore, seems most likely to be a skepticism about the world-historical significance in modernity for the race ideals produced by these civilizations, a skepticism probably rooted in ideas about the backwardness of subsistence societies inherited from nineteenth-century European liberalism's progressive theories of history and theories of private property, where examples of indigenous peoples in the Americas and South Pacific loomed large. See, for example, John Locke, *Two Treatises of Government and a Letter Concerning Toleration,* ed. Ian Shapiro (New Haven, CT: Yale University Press, 2003); and Denis Diderot, "The Supplement au Voyage de Bougainville," in *Political Writings,* ed. John Hope Mason and Robert Wokler (New York: Cambridge University Press, 1992), 31–77.
96. Wilson Jeremiah Moses, *The Golden Age of Black Nationalism, 1850–1925* (New York: Oxford University Press, 1988).
97. Du Bois, "The Conservation of Races," 820.
98. Du Bois, "The Conservation of Races," 822, 825.
99. Kwame Anthony Appiah, "The Uncompleted Argument: Du Bois and the Illusion of Race," *Critical Inquiry* 12, no. 1 (1985): 21–37; Gooding-Williams, *In the Shadow of Du Bois,* 38–66. For a defense, see Chike Jeffers, "What Counts as a Collective Gift? Culture and Value in Du Bois' *The Gift of Black Folk,*" *Royal Institute of Philosophy Supplements* 93 (2023): 99–116.
100. For the influence of German romanticism and idealism on Du Bois, see Shamoon Zamir, *Dark Voices: W. E. B. Du Bois and American Thought, 1888–1903* (Chicago: University of Chicago Press, 1995); and Gooding-Williams, *In the Shadow of Du Bois.*
101. W. E. B. Du Bois, "The Superior Race," *Smart Set* 10, no. 4 (1923): 60.

102. W. E. B. Du Bois, "The Pan-African Congress," *Crisis* 17, no. 6 (1919): 271, 273–274.
103. W. E. B. Du Bois, "The Souls of White Folk," in *Writings,* 932.
104. Adopting a species-level analysis of the development of reason, Immanuel Kant, "Idea for a Universal History with a Cosmopolitan Purpose," in *Political Writings,* 2nd ed., ed. H. S. Reiss, trans. H. B. Nisbet (Cambridge: Cambridge University Press, 1991), 41–44, locates the engine of history in what he calls a natural "unsocial sociability" in mankind. By this he means what he identifies—in a synthesis of Thomas Hobbes's and Jean-Jacques Rousseau's respective accounts of human nature—as the tendency of people "to come together in society, coupled, however, with a continual resistance which constantly threatens to break this society up." The former impulse is rooted in the yearning to develop our fullest capacities in communion with others, while the latter stems from our individual desire for the entire society to conform to our own predilections and preferences. The resistance that we expect from others in our respective quests to establish our own personal visions of society as reality, Kant argues, "awakens all men's powers and induces him to overcome his tendency to laziness." This awakening is that to which Kant attributes the birth of both culture and morality.
105. W. E. B. Du Bois, "Back to Africa," *Century* 150, no. 4 (1923): 536–537.
106. Adom Getachew, "The New Black Internationalism," *Dissent* 68, no. 4 (2021): 92–99.
107. Gilmore, *Defying Dixie,* 168.
108. Singh, *Black Is a Country,* 6.
109. Gilmore, *Defying Dixie,* 167–173, details a litany of references to Germany from African American newspapers in the early 1930s that reference the Ku Klux Klan and the Nazis, or Jim Crow as a whole, in the same breath. Even mainstream papers drew the connection; the *Chicago Tribune*'s Paris edition ran an opinion editorial debate in September 1933 over whether Jews in Germany or African Americans in the South were more oppressed.
110. Adolf Hitler and Julius Streicher, quoted in Gilmore, *Defying Dixie,* 170–171.
111. Robin D. G. Kelley, "African Americans in the Spanish Civil War: 'This Ain't Ethiopia, But It'll Do,'" in *Race Rebels: Culture, Politics, and the Black Working Class* (New York: Simon and Schuster, 1994), 128.
112. Gilmore, *Defying Dixie,* 183–184; Sugrue, *Sweet Land of Liberty,* 38; Adom Getachew, *Worldmaking After Empire: The Rise and Fall of Self-Determination* (Princeton, NJ: Princeton University Press, 2019), 37–70.
113. See Martin R. Delany, *Principia of Ethnology: The Origin of Races and Color, with an Archeological Compendium of Ethiopian and Egyptian Civilization, from Years of Careful Examination and Enquiry,* 2nd ed. (Philadelphia: Harper and Brother, 1880), especially 83–92, 99–105. See also Robin D. G. Kelley, *Freedom Dreams: The Black Radical Imagination* (Boston: Beacon, 2002), 19–20.
114. On the significance of Psalms 68:31 in black nationalist thought, see Eddie S. Glaude Jr., *Exodus! Religion, Race, and Nation in Early*

Nineteenth-Century Black America (Chicago: University of Chicago Press, 2000).

115. Not all elements of the Left met the political challenges of this period. The Communist Party in the late 1930s and early 1940s had many recruiting obstacles: mounting evidence of repression in Russia, the authoritarian restrictions of the Central Committee's organizing directives from abroad, anticommunist suppression and propaganda in the United States, the inherent difficulties of forging a popular position on the politics of race and class, the unpopularity of communist atheism among black people, and African Americans' perceived ambivalence on the Ethiopian situation. Yet perhaps the most important source of fragmentation for the American Left in this period was the Molotov-Ribbentrop Pact of nonaggression, which decimated the antifascist popular front program across the globe. Gilmore, *Defying Dixie,* 300–302, identifies this pact as singularly destructive for the Southern Left, as it undermined the "most powerful single weapon in the southern Left's arsenal": antifascism. The Soviet alliance with Hitler and subsequent CPUSA opposition to America's entry into the war, as well as President Roosevelt's political program more generally, left many African Americans cold—as it did CPUSA membership more generally, which plummeted 15 percent in 1939 alone. See also Dawson, *Black Visions,* 195.
116. Singh, *Black Is a Country,* 123.
117. George S. Schuyler, "Interview by William Ingersoll (November 7, 1960)," in *The Reminiscences of George S. Schuyler* (Alexandria, VA: Alexander Street, 2003), 592
118. Singh, *Black Is a Country,* 103.
119. Sugrue, *Sweet Land of Liberty,* 54. On the distinction between negative and positive liberty, see Berlin, "Two Concepts of Liberty." Negative liberty entails understanding freedom as the noninterference of other human beings—the absence of coercive force levied by others to prevent an actor from undertaking a desired action. In contrast, the so-called positive conception of liberty does not see an absence of interference by other human beings as a sufficient, or even sometimes a necessary, condition of true freedom. This comparatively expansive definition of freedom is often grounded in the ideas of self-mastery and self-determination. Thus, liberty becomes not only access to the resources and skills necessary to act on individual desires but also the capacity to order conflicting desires or overcome crippling thoughts in order to truly understand one's own desires and act on them. Berlin went on to famously argue, against conceptions like those found in Roosevelt's "Four Freedoms" speech and certainly those advocated in most of black political thought, on the grounds that positive liberty places one inexorably on the slippery slope toward totalitarianism, to "forcing people to be free," to paraphrase Jean-Jacques Rousseau's unfortunate phrase. For a compelling critique of Berlin's arguments *against* positive liberty, see Charles Taylor, "What's Wrong with Negative Liberty," in *The Idea of Freedom: Essays in Honour of Isaiah Berlin,* ed. Alan Ryan (Oxford: Oxford University Press, 1979), 175–193. For important critiques of the usefulness of Berlin's distinction altogether, see

Gerald C. MacCallum, "Negative and Positive Freedom," *Philosophical Review* 76, no. 3 (1967): 312–334; and Eric Nelson, "Liberty: One Concept Too Many?" *Political Theory* 33, no. 1 (2005): 58–78.

120. Sugrue, *Sweet Land of Liberty*, 44–45.
121. Sugrue, *Sweet Land of Liberty*, 48–49, 56–57.
122. Carol Anderson, *Eyes off the Prize: The United Nations and the African American Struggle for Human Rights* (New York: Cambridge University Press, 2003).
123. Hall, "The Long Civil Rights Movement," 1250.
124. Singh, *Black Is a Country*, 139.
125. Gilmore, *Defying Dixie*, 405–407; Singh, *Black Is a Country*, 157–158.
126. See Anderson, *Eyes off the Prize*.
127. Malcolm X, "The Ballot or the Bullet (April 3, 1964)," in *Malcolm X Speaks*, ed. George Breitman (New York: Grove, 1965), 34–35.
128. In the United States, the period immediately following the Bolshevik Revolution, from 1917 to 1920, was characterized by a wave of hysteria over the dangers, real and imagined, that leftist and anarchist "subversives"—almost always imagined as "foreign"—posed to the existing social order. With nativist and nationalist sentiment already rampant during and following World War I, the arrival of millions of southern and eastern Europeans and African Americans from the South to urban centers sparked a moral panic rooted in ideas of racial hierarchy and xenophobia. These were exacerbated by the rhetoric of political and economic elites also concerned with the increasingly assertive labor movement and the difficulties of prosecuting the American war effort while maintaining domestic order, as well as the terrorist bombing campaigns undertaken by contemporary anarchists. The era was marked by such legislation as the Sedition Act of 1918, which outlawed the use or distribution of "disloyal, profane, scurrilous, or abusive language" about the United States in wartime, and by various repression campaigns by federal and state law enforcement and intelligence agencies; Sedition Act of 1918 (Pub. L. 65–150, 40 Stat. 553, enacted May 16, 1918).
129. Patrick Renshaw, "The IWW and the Red Scare, 1917–1924," *Journal of Contemporary History* 3, no. 4 (1968): 63–72.
130. Richard Lingeman, "Domestic Containment: The Downfall of Postwar Idealism and Left Dissent, 1945–1950," in *The Columbia History of Post-World War II America*, ed. Mark C. Carnes (New York: Columbia University Press, 2007), 207.
131. According to Lingeman, "Domestic Containment," 207, these include "federal loyalty review boards; congressional, state, and municipal 'Americanism' committees; private employer loyalty boards; law enforcement investigators, from the Justice Department, FBI, State Department, and US military intelligence agencies down through state and local police 'Red Squads'; and private vigilante groups that were in the business of exposing Communists and Communist sympathizers and 'clearing' them—for a price." See also Charisse Burden-Stelly, *Black Scare/Red Scare: Theorizing Capitalist Racism in the United States* (Chicago: University of Chicago Press, 2023).

132. Victor Navasky, *Naming Names* (New York: Hill and Wang, 2003).
133. Mary Dudziak, *Cold War Civil Rights: Race and the Image of American Democracy* (Princeton, NJ: Princeton University Press, 2000); Michael Klarman, *From Jim Crow to Civil Rights: The Supreme Court and the Struggle for Racial Equality* (New York: Oxford University Press 2004); John Skrentny, "The Effect of the Cold War on African-Americans Civil Rights: America and the World Audience, 1945–1968," *Theory and Society* 27, no. 2 (1988): 237–285; Derrick Bell, "Brown v. Board of Education and the Interest Convergence Dilemma," *Harvard Law Review* 93, no. 5 (1980): 518–533.
134. Dudziak, *Cold War Civil Rights.*
135. Singh, *Black Is a Country,* 6.
136. Richard M. Nixon, quoted in Thomas Borstelmann, *The Cold War and the Color Line: American Race Relations in the Global Arena* (Cambridge, MA: Harvard University Press, 2001), 109
137. A. Philip Randolph, quoted in Singh, *Black Is a Country,* 166.
138. Walter White, *How Far the Promised Land* (New York: Viking, 1955), 16.
139. Borstelmann, *The Cold War and the Color Line,* 75.
140. White, *How Far the Promised Land,* 224–226.
141. "Whataboutism—Come Again, Comrade?," *Economist,* January 31, 2008, https://www.economist.com/europe/2008/01/31/whataboutism.
142. Brief for the United States as Amicus Curiae in Brown v. Board of Education of Topeka, Kansas, October 1952, Organization of American Historians, https://archive.oah.org/special-issues/teaching/2008_12/sources/ex1src2.pdf, 5–6.
143. Brief for the United States, 6, 8.
144. Gilmore, *Defying Dixie,* 7.
145. For firsthand accounts, see Paul Robeson, "Set Him Free to Labor On—A Tribute to W. E. B. Du Bois," in *Paul Robeson Speaks: Writings, Speeches, Interviews, 1918–1974,* ed. Philip S. Foner (New York: Citadel, 1978), 268; Paul Robeson, "The House Un-American Activities Committee," in *Paul Robeson Speaks,* 413–435; Paul Robeson, "Our Right to Travel," in *Here I Stand* (New York: Dobson, 1958), 71–81; W. E. B. Du Bois, "Whither Now and Why," *Quarterly Review of Higher Education Among Negroes* 28, no. 3 (1960): 139–141; W. E. B. Du Bois, *The Autobiography of W. E. B. Du Bois: A Soliloquy on Viewing My Life from the Last Decade of Its First Century* (New York: International, 1968), 361–408; and Langston Hughes, *Testimony of Langston Hughes, Accompanied by His Counsel, Frank D. Reeves, March 26, 1953* (Alexandria, VA: Alexander Street, 1953).
146. Adam Fairclough, "Historians and the Civil Rights Movement," *Journal of American Studies* 24, no. 3 (1990): 390.
147. Gunnar Myrdal, *An American Dilemma: The Negro Problem and Modern Democracy,* vol. 1 (New York: Harper and Bros, 1944); Rogers M. Smith, *Civic Ideals: Conflicting Visions of Citizenship in US History* (New Haven, CT: Yale University Press, 1997).
148. Singh, *Black Is a Country,* 141–154; Sugrue, *Sweet Land of Liberty,* 59–63, 80–84.
149. Sugrue, *Sweet Land of Liberty,* 110.

150. See, for example, Eric Arnesen, "Reconsidering the 'Long Civil Rights Movement,'" *Historically Speaking* 10, no. 2 (2009): 31–34.
151. Richard Rorty, *Philosophy and Social Hope* (New York: Penguin, 1999), 6.
152. Richard Rorty, *Achieving Our Country: Leftist Thought in Twentieth-Century America* (Cambridge, MA: Harvard University Press, 1998), 51.
153. Fredric Jameson, *The Years of Theory* (New York: Verso Books, 2024); Walt Whitman, "Democratic Vistas," in *Poetry and Prose,* ed. Justin Kaplan (New York: Library of America, 1996), 929–993.
154. Rorty, *Achieving Our Country,* 3, 4.
155. Rorty, *Achieving Our Country,* 3–4.
156. Rorty, *Philosophy and Social Hope,* 232–233.
157. Rorty, *Achieving Our Country,* 3–4.
158. Richard Rorty, "Unger, Castoriadis, and the Romance of a National Future," *Northwestern University Law Review* 82, no. 2 (1987): 335–351.
159. Michael McCann, "A. Philip Randolph: Radicalizing Rights at the Intersection of Class and Race," in *African American Political Thought: A Collected History,* ed. Melvin L. Rogers and Jack Turner (Chicago: University of Chicago Press, 2021), 290–314.
160. Socialist Party leader Eugene V. Debs spoke famously and, for the party at least, decisively in 1903 of the so-called Negro Question or the social equality of the races. Eugene V. Debs, "The Negro in the Class Struggle," *International Socialist Review* 4, no. 5 (1903): 257–260, famously argues that "the Negro question is pure fraud and serves to mask the real issue, which is not social equality, but ECONOMIC FREEDOM." In human history, Debs proclaimed, there "never was any social inferiority that was not the shriveled fruit of economic inequality," and in the future victory of socialism, with its realization of economic freedom, he was confident that "the burning question of 'social equality' [would] disappear like mist before the sunrise." This framework led him to the practical political position that the only meaningful conflict was between capitalists of all races and labor of all races, and therefore socialists "have nothing special to offer the Negro, and . . . cannot make separate appeals to all the races."
161. "Americanism," *Messenger,* September 1920, 80.
162. A. Philip Randolph, "The Negro, the War, and the Future of Democracy (ca. 1940s)," in *For Jobs and Freedom: Selected Speeches and Writings of A. Philip Randolph,* ed. Andrew E. Kersten and David Lucander (Amherst: University of Massachusetts Press, 2014), 304.
163. A. Philip Randolph, "Should Negroes Help the U.S.A. Win the Cold War Against the U.S.S.R.?," in *For Jobs and Freedom,* 317.
164. A. Philip Randolph, "Commencement Address at Morgan State College (1951)," in *For Jobs and Freedom,* 252.
165. Alex Gourevitch, *From Slavery to the Cooperative Commonwealth: Labor and Republican Liberty in the Nineteenth Century* (New York: Cambridge University Press, 2015).
166. See, for example, A. Philip Randolph, "The Civil Rights Revolution—Origin and Mission (1964)," in *For Jobs and Freedom,* 265; A. Philip

Randolph, "Crisis of Victory (1965)," in *For Jobs and Freedom,* 271–272; and A. Philip Randolph, "Speech at White House, 'To Fulfill These Rights' (1966)," in *For Jobs and Freedom,* 289–290.

167. A. Philip Randolph, "The Negro's Fight for Democracy Now," Address at Union United Church, Speeches and Writings File, September 11, 1942–November 1, 1942, A. Philip Randolph Papers, Manuscript Division, Library of Congress.
168. Randolph, "The Negro's Fight"; A. Philip Randolph, "March on Washington Movement Presents Program for the Negro (1944)," in *For Jobs and Freedom,* 217.
169. A. Philip Randolph, "Address in the Chicago Coliseum, June 26, 1942," Speeches and Writings File, September 11, 1942–November 1, 1942, A. Philip Randolph Papers, Manuscript Division, Library of Congress.
170. Randolph, "Crisis of Victory," 271, 270.
171. John Dewey, *Democracy and Education* (New York: Macmillan, 1916), 379.
172. Randolph, "March on Washington Movement," 214.
173. McCann, "A. Philip Randolph," 307.
174. Tommie Shelby, "Prisons of the Forgotten: Ghettos and Economic Injustice," in Shelby and Terry, *To Shape a New World,* 196.
175. A. Philip Randolph and Chandler Owen, quoted in McCann, "A. Philip Randolph," 308.
176. A. Philip Randolph, "Keynote Address at Negro American Labor Council Convention (1962)," in *For Jobs and Freedom,* 138.
177. A. Philip Randolph and Chandler Owen, "The Negro and the New Social Order: A Reconstruction Program," *Messenger,* March 1919, 3–11.
178. Kenneth B. Clark, *Social Power and Social Change in Contemporary America* (Washington, DC: Equal Employment Opportunity Commission, 1966), 15–16.
179. Gilmore, *Defying Dixie,* 69–105.
180. Kelley, *Hammer and Hoe;* Robert Korstad, *Civil Rights Unionism: Tobacco Workers and the Struggle for Democracy in the Mid-Twentieth Century South* (Chapel Hill: University of North Carolina Press, 2003).
181. Gilmore, *Defying Dixie,* 128–133.
182. A. Philip Randolph, "Why I Would Not Stand for Re-Election for President of the National Negro Congress (1940)," in *For Jobs and Freedom,* 186–189. See also Martin Luther King Jr., *Strength to Love* (Minneapolis: Fortress, 2010), especially chapter 10.
183. A. Philip Randolph, "Segregation in the Public Schools: A Promise or a Menace," *Messenger,* June 1924, 185–186.
184. Randolph, "Segregation in the Public Schools," 185.
185. Randolph, "Segregation in the Public Schools," 185–186.
186. A. Philip Randolph, "Protest Against Mississippi Lynching of Emmett Till (1955)," *For Jobs and Freedom,* 241–242.
187. Ben Laurence, *Agents of Change: Political Philosophy in Practice* (Cambridge, MA: Harvard University Press, 2021).
188. Randolph and Owen, "The Negro and the New Social Order," 5.

189. A. Philip Randolph, *The Truth About Lynching: Its Causes and Effects* (New York: Cosmo-Advocate, 1917).
190. "Should Black Workers Join White Unions?," *Messenger,* September 1920, 82.
191. Tommie Shelby, "Two Conceptions of Black Nationalism: Martin Delany on the Meaning of Black Political Solidarity," *Political Theory* 31, no. 5 (2003): 664–692, makes the helpful distinction that strong black nationalism means to pick out those political philosophies and programs that view "black solidarity and voluntary separation . . . [as] a *worthwhile end in itself,* a constitutive and enduring component of the collective self-realization of blacks as a people."
192. Marcus Garvey, "The Negro, Communism, Trade Unionism and His (?) Friend: 'Beware of Greeks Bearing Gifts,'" in *The Philosophy and Opinions of Marcus Garvey, or Africa for the Africans,* vol. 2, ed. Amy Jacques Garvey (New York: Universal, 1925), 69.
193. Samuel Gompers, "Talks on Labor: Addresses at St. Paul and Minneapolis," *American Federationist* 12 (1905): 638.
194. W. E. B. Du Bois, "Marxism and the Negro Problem (1933)," Abolition Notes, https://abolitionnotes.org/web-dubois/marxism.
195. W. E. B. Du Bois, "A Negro Nation Within the Nation," *Current History* 42 (1935): 269–270. Following Michael Dawson, I define *community nationalism* as a political philosophy that combines a commitment to political and economic control of majority-black areas with a program of institutional autonomy and racial solidarity on many, if not all, political issues (domestic or international). Community nationalists argue for an economic agenda that, notes Dawson, *Black Visions,* 101, promotes "controlling the black segment of the marketplace by attempting to establish black businesses and by 'buy-black' campaigns" and a political platform that "includes the concepts of self-determination, black control of political and economic institutions in the black community, and the building of autonomous black organizations." The primary difference between community nationalism and the other major strains of nationalism is that community nationalists largely reject strong separatist politics and do indeed hold many values that are "consistent with the liberal tradition" in America. For that reason, they are more likely to enter into politically expedient partnerships with other racial or ethnic groups as long as some level of institutional autonomy is maintained and the relationship is perceived as politically or economically advantageous to black people. This is not to understate the inward focus of community nationalism, however, which is, at its core, a doctrine that advances the belief that increasing black people's focus on and support of their own neighborhoods, organizations, and businesses is the most important step to achieving traditional political philosophic concerns of justice, freedom, equality, and self-respect.
196. "The New Negro—What Is He?," *Messenger,* August 1920, 73–74.
197. As Malcolm X, "Twenty Million Black People in a Political, Economic, and Mental Prison (January 23, 1963)," in *Collected Speeches, Debates,*

and Interviews (1960–1965), ed. Sandeep S. Atwal (independently published, 2000), 76, notes,

> Segregation, as we're taught by the Honorable Elijah Muhammad, means that which is forced upon inferiors by superiors. A segregated community is a Negro community. But the white community, though it's all white, is never called a segregated community. It's a separate community. In the white community, the white man controls the economy, his own economy, his own politics, his own everything. That's his community. But at the same time while the Negro lives in a separate community, it's a segregated community. Which means it's regulated from the outside by outsiders. The white man has all of the businesses in the Negro community. He runs the politics of the Negro community. He controls all the civic organizations in the Negro community. This is a segregated community. We don't go for segregation. We go for separation. Separation is when you have your own. You control your own economy; you control your own politics; you control your own society; you control your own everything. You have yours and you control yours; we have ours and we control ours.

198. A. Philip Randolph, "Segregation in the Public Schools (1924)," in *For Jobs and Freedom,* 127.
199. A. Philip Randolph, "Race Workers Turning to the American Federation of Labor, (1929)," in *For Jobs and Freedom,* 82.
200. Dawson, *Black Visions,* 184–185; Gilmore, *Defying Dixie,* 63–65; Kelley, *Freedom Dreams,* 46–49.
201. Gilmore, *Defying Dixie,* 63–65.
202. Danielle Allen, "Integration, Freedom, and the Affirmation of Life," in Shelby and Terry, *To Shape a New World,* 146–160.
203. Aziz Rana, "Our Segregation Problem," *Dissent,* Fall 2022, https://www.dissentmagazine.org.
204. Elizabeth Anderson, *The Imperative of Integration* (Princeton, NJ: Princeton University Press, 2010).
205. Robert D. Putnam, *Our Kids: The American Dream in Crisis* (New York: Simon and Schuster, 2015); Robert D. Putnam, *Bowling Alone: The Collapse and Revival of American Community* (New York: Simon and Schuster, 2000).
206. Empirical studies of contemporary segregation support this analysis. American cities remain starkly divided along racial lines, with residents of predominantly black neighborhoods systematically denied access to high-quality schools, safe streets, and reliable public goods. This separation and the resulting disparities are maintained through policy instruments like exclusionary zoning, regressive property tax regimes, and school funding formulas that reproduce advantage for the privileged while imposing concentrated disadvantage on the marginalized. The result is a political landscape in which democratic participation is uneven and cross-class, cross-racial solidarities are institutionally discouraged. See Sheryll Cashin, *White Space, Black Hood: Opportunity Hoarding and Segregation in the Age of Inequality* (Boston: Beacon, 2021); and Richard Rothstein and Leah

Rothstein, *Just Action: How to Challenge Segregation Enacted Under the Color of Law* (New York: Liveright, 2023).

207. Danielle Allen, *Justice by Means of Democracy* (Chicago: University of Chicago Press, 2023); William E. Forbath and Joseph Fishkin, *The Anti-Oligarchy Constitution: Reconstructing the Economic Foundations of American Democracy* (Cambridge, MA: Harvard University Press, 2022); K. Sabeel Rahman, *Democracy Against Domination* (New York: Oxford University Press, 2017); Ezra Klein and Derek Thompson, *Abundance* (New York: Simon and Schuster, 2025).

208. As BCG Team, "Why Bargaining for the Common Good?," n.d., https://forgeorganizing.org/article/introduction-bargaining-common-good/, explains, "At the center of BCG [Bargaining for the Common Good] campaigns are intentional, long-term alignments between unions and community organizations. Connecting at all levels starting with membership, they build strong, lasting partnerships based on trust and a shared analysis of the systemic problems we are confronting and the solutions necessary to transform our communities. BCG campaigns are centered around joint community-labor planning that brings diverse partners to the table in union bargaining, builds power, and addresses the crises we all face. BCG work centers racial justice because we must collectively confront structural racism to create a powerful, unified movement."

209. Daphna Renan, "Federal Authority Without Judicial Supremacy," February 6, 2023, YouTube, 51 mins., 18 secs., https://www.youtube.com/watch?v=xLaASZH_1Sg&t=352s; Rachel Reed, "We Have to Reject the Idea That Judicial Supremacy Is an Essential Ingredient of Federal Authority," *Harvard Law Today*, https://hls.harvard.edu/today/harvard-law-professor-daphna-renan-says-we-should-give-the-supreme-court-a-little-less-control-over-the-constitution/.

210. See Goluboff, *The Lost Promise of Civil Rights*, especially 184–188, 217–218; and Hall, "The Long Civil Rights Movement," 1250.

211. Phillip Klinkner with Rogers M. Smith, *The Unsteady March: The Rise and Decline of Racial Equality in America* (Chicago: University of Chicago Press, 1999), 126–128; Hall, "The Long Civil Rights Movement," 1241. Sugrue, *Sweet Land of Liberty*, 52, offers the most nuanced appraisal, acknowledging the discrimination of New Deal programs while recognizing the disproportionate benefits that Northern black people received in some states from Aid to Dependent Children and Old Age Assistance.

212. James E. King, *Impact of Federal Housing Policy on Urban African-American Families 1930–1966* (Bethesda, MD: Austin and Winfield, 1997).

213. When evaluating any property for risk, it is imperative to evaluate the value of the neighborhood and the properties that surround it. The problem with HOLC redlining, however, is that it equated property owned by black people and other minorities with an unacceptable level of risk—meaning that federal funds could not legally be funneled into those neighborhoods. HOLC created four neighborhood categories in its rating system, and at each level, race played a central role. See Douglas Massey and Nancy Denton, *American Apartheid: Segregation and the Making of the Under-*

class (Cambridge, MA: Harvard University Press, 1993), 51–52; and King, *Impact of Federal Housing Policy,* 27–31.

214. Massey and Denton, *American Apartheid,* 52.
215. King, *Impact of Federal Housing Policy,* 34.
216. Massey and Denton, *American Apartheid,* 52.
217. Massey and Denton, *American Apartheid,* 53.
218. King, *Impact of Federal Housing Policy,* 35.
219. Before the advent of FHA-insured loans, banks would normally grant mortgages for no more than two-thirds of the appraised value of a home, thus requiring buyers to make a down payment equal to 33 percent of the property's value—a requirement that was, and still is, nigh impossible for most American families. With the FHA-insured loan program, the government would guarantee over 90 percent of the collateral so that down payments of 10 percent became commonplace. The government was also able to extend the mortgage period so that families could pay in low monthly payments that were more affordable. See Massey and Denton, *American Apartheid,* 53.
220. Massey and Denton, *American Apartheid,* 53.
221. Robert C. Weaver, "Excerpts of Remarks at the Open Occupancy Housing Session of the 50th Annual NAACP Convention," *Papers of the NAACP: Supplement to Part 1, 1956–1960* (Bethesda, MD: University Publications of America, 1997), microfilm, reel 11, frame 129.
222. Massey and Denton, *American Apartheid,* 54–55.
223. Hall, "The Long Civil Rights Movement," 1242.
224. Ira Katznelson, *Fear Itself: The New Deal and the Origins of Our Time* (New York: Liveright, 2013).
225. Gilmore, *Defying Dixie,* 9.
226. Singh, *Black Is a Country,* 57, 168.
227. Goluboff, *The Lost Promise of Civil Rights,* 270.
228. Hall, "The Long Civil Rights Movement," 1249.

Conclusion

1. W. E. B. Du Bois, *Darkwater: Voices from Within the Veil* (New York: Harcourt, Brace, and Howe, 1920), 231–232.
2. The temptation of despair, along with doubt and hate, is one of the key existential dilemmas that he describes his mentor, Alexander Crummell (and by extension himself) as facing in life. See Du Bois, "Of Alexander Crummell," in *The Souls of Black Folk: Essays and Sketches* (Chicago: A. C. McClurg, 1903), 215.
3. Du Bois, *Darkwater,* 225.
4. Some evidence of the opacity and confusion of these passages is that even in the voluminous secondary literature on Du Bois, few commentators devote sustained attention to them. For an exception that takes its point of engagement from the concerns of ecocriticism, see John Claborn, "W. E. B. Du Bois at the Grand Canyon: Nature, History, and Race in *Darkwater,*" in *The Oxford Handbook of Ecocriticism,* ed. Greg Garrard (New York: Oxford University Press, 2014), 118–131.

5. Robert Gooding-Williams, *Democracy and Beauty* (New York: Columbia University Press, 2024).
6. Du Bois, *Darkwater,* 237.
7. Theodore Roosevelt, "Presidential Address at the Grand Canyon," May 6, 1903, https://www.americanrhetoric.com.
8. Du Bois, *Darkwater,* 238.
9. Du Bois, *Darkwater,* 238–239.
10. Immanuel Kant, *Critique of Judgment,* ed. Nicholas Walker, trans. James Creed Meredith (New York: Oxford University Press, 2007), §28: 263–264.
11. Martin Luther King Jr., "Convocation Speech at Illinois Wesleyan University (February 10, 1966)," Illinois Wesleyan University, https://www.iwu.edu/. See also Rufus Burrow, *A Child Shall Lead Them: Martin Luther King, Jr., Young People, and the Movement* (Minneapolis: Fortress, 2014), 275.
12. Du Bois, *Darkwater,* 239.
13. Du Bois, *Darkwater,* 239–240.
14. On disrobing and nakedness as metaphors for truth, see Marshall Berman, *All That Is Solid Melts Into Air: The Experience of Modernity* (New York: Verso Books, 1983), 105–110. For an account of ocular tropes in Enlightenment thought, see Martin Jay, *Downcast Eyes: The Denigration of Vision in Twentieth-Century French Thought* (Berkeley: University of California Press, 1994), 83–148. On light as metaphor, see Hans Blumenberg, "Light as a Metaphor for Truth," in *History, Metaphors, Fables: A Hans Blumenberg Reader,* ed. Hannes Bajohr, Florian Fuchs, and Joe Paul Kroll (Ithaca, NY: Cornell University Press, 2020), 129–169.
15. Immanuel Kant, "What Is Enlightenment?," in *Political Writings,* 2nd ed., ed. H. S. Reiss, trans. H. B. Nisbet (Cambridge: Cambridge University Press, 1991), 54.
16. Susan Neiman, *Why Grow Up? Subversive Thoughts for an Infantile Age* (New York: Farrar, Straus and Giroux, 2015), 7, 119.
17. W. E. B. Du Bois, *Dusk of Dawn: An Essay Toward an Autobiography of Race Concept* (New York: Routledge, 1983), 3, 148, 2.
18. Robert Gooding-Williams, "W.E.B. Du Bois," in *The Stanford Encyclopedia of Philosophy,* ed. Edward N. Zalta and Uri Nodelman, online Fall 2020 ed., September 13, 2017, https://plato.stanford.edu/archives/fall2020/entries/dubois/.
19. Craig Childs, "Fear of God," in *The Grand Canyon Reader,* ed. Lance Newman (Berkeley: University of California, 2011), 19–20.
20. Raymond Williams, *Modern Tragedy* (London: Chatto and Windus, 1966), 108.
21. Du Bois, *Darkwater,* 247.
22. Williams, *Modern Tragedy,* 82.
23. Jürgen Habermas, "Israel and Athens, or to Whom Does Anamnestic Reason Belong?," in *The Frankfurt School on Religion,* ed. Eduardo Mendieta (New York: Routledge, 2005), 293–301.
24. Johann Baptist Metz, *A Passion for God: The Mystical-Political Dimension of Christianity,* trans. J. Matthew Ashley (New York: Paulist, 1998), 26.

25. Reinhart Koselleck, *The Practice of Conceptual History: Timing History, Spacing Concepts,* trans. Todd Samuel Presner (Stanford, CA: Stanford University Press, 2002), 83. See also Metz, *A Passion for God,* 64–65.
26. Jürgen Habermas, *The New Conservatism: Cultural Criticism and the Historians' Debate,* ed. and trans. Shierry Weber Nicholsen (Cambridge, MA: MIT Press, 1989), 262–263.
27. W. E. B. Du Bois, *Black Reconstruction in America: An Essay Toward a History of the Part Which Black Folk Played in the Attempt to Reconstruct Democracy in America, 1860–1880* (New York: Harcourt, Brace, 1935), 725–726. For an elaboration of this pejorative conception of ideology, see Tommie Shelby, "Ideology, Racism, and Critical Social Theory," *Philosophical Forum* 34, no. 2 (2003): 153–188.
28. Du Bois, *Black Reconstruction in America,* 725.
29. Perhaps the most compact illustration is the criticism of the "car-window sociologist" in Du Bois, *The Souls of Black Folk,* 154–156. The car-window sociologist is a pejorative description of someone "who seeks to understand and know the South by devoting the few leisure hours of a holiday trip [gazing from the rail car window] to unravelling the snarl of centuries." To underscore his point, Du Bois relays a story about a group of young men transporting a corn crop while letting ear after ear of corn fall off their cart without a care, one fast asleep behind the mule. To the car-window sociologist, this scene is Exhibit A in confirmation of the age-old stereotype, confirming the laziness, shiftlessness, and backwardness of the Negro. Against this view, however, Du Bois seeks to understand the experience of these men with empathy and sympathetic interpretation, bolstered by a comprehensive explanatory grasp on the corrupt political economy and sordid cultural history of the American South. "They are careless," Du Bois writes, "because they have not found that it pays to be careful; they are improvident because the improvident ones of their acquaintance get on about as well as the provident. Above all, they cannot see why they should take unusual pains to make the white man's land better or to fatten his mule, or save his corn." Du Bois moves back and forth from *explaining* vast economic systems to *understanding* human subjectivity and action. Southern capital's "quest [for] the golden fleece" is the context that gives a more plausible interpretive and imaginative rendering of the men's actions than the psychological or racial-cultural attribution of vices like "sloth." Through Du Bois we see their refusal of care in work as a kind of dissent—their rejection of extractive labor in an unjust distribution of economic benefits and burdens. Similar analyses have become familiar in sociological accounts of drug dealing, sex work, or other illicit labor people pursue rather than the low-wage work available to them as formal employment. On more contemporary analyses of dissent against formal work and in the workplace, see Tommie Shelby, *Dark Ghettos: Injustice, Dissent, and Reform* (Cambridge, MA: Harvard University Press, 2016); Robin D. G. Kelley, *Race Rebels: Culture, Politics, and the Black Working Class* (New York: Free Press, 1996), especially 1–102; Cathy J. Cohen, "Deviance as Resistance: A New Research Agenda for the Study of Black Politics,"

Du Bois Review: Social Science Research on Race 1, no. 1 (2004): 27–45; Alex Gourevitch, "Quitting Work but Not the Job: Liberty and the Right to Strike," *Perspectives on Politics* 14, no. 2 (2016): 307–323; Alex Gourevitch, "The Right to Strike: A Radical View," *American Political Science Review* 112, no. 4 (2018): 905–917; and Alex Gourevitch, "Strikes, Civil Rights, and Radical Disobedience: From King to Debs and Back," *Contemporary Political Theory* 22, no. 2 (2023): 143–164.

30. Du Bois, *Darkwater,* 33. See also Frantz Fanon, *The Wretched of the Earth* (New York: Grove, 2004), 8.
31. Nikolas Kompridis, *Critique and Disclosure: Critical Theory Between Past and Future* (Cambridge, MA: MIT Press, 2006), 254.
32. Rowan Williams, *The Tragic Imagination* (Oxford: Oxford University Press, 2016), 27.
33. Alexander Crummell, "The Need of New Ideas and New Aims for a New Era: An Address to the Graduating Class of Storer College," in *Africa and America: Addresses and Discourses* (Springfield, MA: Wiley, 1891), 14, 20.
34. Frederick Douglass, "In Law Free; in Fact, a Slave: An Address Delivered in Washington, DC, on April 16, 1888," in *The Frederick Douglass Papers,* ser. 1, *Speeches, Debates, and Interviews,* vol. 5, *1881–1895,* ed. John W. Blassingame and John R. McKivigan (New Haven, CT: Yale University Press, 1992), 361.
35. Du Bois, *Dusk of Dawn,* 148.
36. Wendy Brown, "Resisting Left Melancholy," *Boundary* 2 26, no. 3 (1999): 20.
37. Cornel West, "Subversive Joy and Revolutionary Patience in Black Christianity," in *The Cornel West Reader* (New York: Basic Books, 1999), 438.
38. Terry Eagleton, *Hope Without Optimism* (Charlottesville: University of Virginia Press, 2015), 32–33.
39. Fredric Jameson, *Marxism and Form: Twentieth-Century Dialectical Theories of Literature* (Princeton, NJ: Princeton University Press, 1971), 134.
40. Jonathan Scott Holloway, "The Soul of W. E. B. Du Bois," *American Quarterly* 49, no. 3 (1997): 603–614.
41. It has long been sermonic convention to blend and borrow homiletic material from other religious figures in the composition of sermons, and King is no exception. As Clayborne Carson and the editorial staff at the Martin Luther King Research Project at Stanford University dutifully demonstrate, the sermon draws from preachers J. Wallace Hamilton, Frederick Meek, Howard Thurman, and Leslie Weatherhead. Martin Luther King Jr., "Draft of Chapter X: 'Shattered Dreams,'" The Papers of Martin Luther King, Jr., n.d. [July 1, 1962–March 31, 1963], https://kinginstitute.stanford.edu/king-papers/documents/draft-chapter-x-shattered-dreams.
42. Martin Luther King Jr., *Strength to Love* (Minneapolis: Fortress, 2010), 87–95.
43. David Scott, *Omens of Adversity: Tragedy, Time, Memory, Justice* (Durham, NC: Duke University Press, 2014), 2.
44. Eagleton, *Hope Without Optimism,* 58.
45. King, *Strength to Love,* 97.

46. Eagleton, *Hope Without Optimism,* 27–28.
47. Martin Hägglund, *This Life: Secular Faith and Spiritual Freedom* (New York: Pantheon Books, 2019).
48. Malcolm X with Alex Haley, *The Autobiography of Malcolm X* (New York: Ballantine Books, 1992), 231.
49. King, *Strength to Love,* 76, 113.
50. Martin Luther King Jr., "Remaining Awake Through a Great Revolution," in *A Testament of Hope: The Essential Writings and Speeches of Martin Luther King, Jr.,* ed. James Melvin Washington (San Francisco: Harper and Row, 1986), 230.
51. King, *Strength to Love,* 9, 84.
52. King, "Remaining Awake," 270.
53. Eagleton, *Hope Without Optimism,* 28.
54. King, *Strength to Love,* 90–91.
55. Martin Luther King Jr., *The Trumpet of Conscience* (Boston: Beacon, 2010), 4.
56. Eagleton, *Hope Without Optimism,* 7.
57. King, *Strength to Love,* 82.
58. Martin Luther King Jr., *Where Do We Go from Here: Chaos or Community?* (Boston: Beacon, 2010), 12–13.
59. King, *Strength to Love,* 82–83.
60. King, *The Trumpet of Conscience,* 4.
61. Eagleton, *Hope Without Optimism,* 85.
62. Eagleton, *Hope Without Optimism,* 69.
63. King, *Strength to Love,* 95.
64. Elizabeth Alexander, *The Trayvon Generation* (New York: Grand Central, 2022); Elizabeth Alexander, "Praise Song for the Day," in *Crave Radiance* (Minneapolis: Greywolf, 2010), 247–248. Trayvon Martin was a seventeen-year-old student killed while visiting his father in Sanford, Florida, by a neighborhood watch captain, George Zimmerman. Zimmerman was acquitted of second-degree murder and other charges and was never prosecuted by the federal government for violating Martin's civil rights. See Lisa Bloom, *Suspicion Nation: The Inside Story of the Trayvon Martin Injustice and Why We Continue to Repeat It* (Berkeley, CA: Counterpoint, 2014).
65. Christopher Caldwell, *The Age of Entitlement: America Since the Sixties* (New York: Simon and Schuster, 2020), 10.
66. Richard Hanania, *The Origins of Woke: Civil Rights Law, Corporate America, and the Triumph of Identity Politics* (New York: HarperCollins, 2023).
67. Parents Involved in Community Schools v. Seattle School District No. 1, 551 U.S. 701 (2007); Ricci v. DeStefano, 557 U.S. 557 (2009); Students for Fair Admissions, Inc. v. President and Fellows of Harvard College, 600 U.S. (2023).
68. Carol Anderson, *One Person, No Vote: How Voter Suppression Is Destroying Our Democracy* (New York: Bloomsbury, 2018); Ari Berman, *Give Us the Ballot: The Modern Struggle for Voting Rights in America* (New York: Farrar, Straus and Giroux, 2015).

69. Jacob M. Grumbach, *Laboratories Against Democracy: How National Parties Transformed State Politics* (Princeton, NJ: Princeton University Press, 2022); Robert Mickey, *Paths out of Dixie: The Democratization of Authoritarian Enclaves in America's Deep South, 1944–1972* (Princeton, NJ: Princeton University Press, 2015).
70. Grumbach, *Laboratories Against Democracy;* Steven Levitsky and Daniel Ziblatt, *Tyranny of the Minority* (New York: Crown, 2023).
71. Pauli Murray, *States' Laws on Race and Color* (Athens: University of Georgia Press, 1997).
72. Aaron Bramson, Patrick Grim, Daniel J. Singer, William J. Berger, Graham Sack, Steven Fisher, Carissa Flocken, and Bennett Holman, "Understanding Polarization: Meanings, Measures, and Model Evaluation," *Philosophy of Science* 84, no. 1 (2017): 116–117; Delia Baldassarri and Andrew Gelman, "Partisans Without Constraint: Political Polarization and Trends in American Public Opinion," *American Journal of Sociology* 114, no. 2 (2008): 408–446; Michael Tesler, *Post-Racial or Most-Racial? Race and Politics in the Obama Era* (Chicago: University of Chicago Press, 2016); Robert Griffin, Mayesha Quasem, John Sides, and Michael Tesler, *Racing Apart: Partisan Shifts on Racial Attitudes over the Last Decade* (Washington, DC: Democracy Fund Voter Study Group, 2021); Joel Olson, "Whiteness and the Polarization of American Politics," *Political Research Quarterly* 61, no. 4 (2008): 704–718; Lilliana Mason, "'I Disrespectfully Agree': The Differential Effects of Partisan Sorting on Social and Issue Polarization," *American Journal of Political Science* 59, no. 1 (2015): 128–145; Lilliana Mason, Julie Wronski, and John V. Kane, "Activating Animus: The Uniquely Social Roots of Trump Support," *American Political Science Review* 115, no. 4 (2021): 1508–1515.
73. Sarah Scire, "'An Immediate Drop in Content': A New Study Shows What Happens When Big Companies Take Over Local News," Nieman Lab, April 12, 2022, https://www.niemanlab.org/2022/04/an-immediate-drop-in-content-a-new-study-shows-what-happens-when-big-companies-take-over-local-news/; Alvin Chang, "Sinclair's Soldiers in Trump's War on Media," Vox, April 3, 2018, https://www.vox.com/2018/4/3/17180020/sinclair-broadcast-group-conservative-trump-david-smith-local-news-tv-affiliate.
74. Jonathan Butcher and Mike Gonzalez, "Rejecting Critical Race Theory: State K-12 Laws," Heritage Foundation, June 9, 2021, https://www.heritage.org/education/report/rejecting-critical-race-theory-state-k-12-laws.
75. Paul A. Passavant, *Policing Protest: The Post-Democratic State and the Figure of Black Insurrection* (Durham, NC: Duke University Press, 2021).
76. See, for example, McKesson v. Doe, 141 S. Ct. 48 (2020); Madeline Johl, "Activism or Domestic Terrorism? How the Terrorism Enhancement Is Used to Punish Acts of Political Protest," *Fordham Urban Law Journal* 50 (2022): 465; Tasnim Motala, "'Foreseeable Violence' & Black Lives Matter: How Mckesson Can Stifle a Movement," *Stanford Law Review Online* 73 (2020): 61; Dawn C. Nunziato, "First Amendment Protections for 'Good Trouble'," *Emory Law Journal* 72 (2022): 1187.

77. Charisse Burden-Stelly, *Black Scare/Red Scare: Theorizing Capitalist Racism in the United States* (Chicago: University of Chicago Press, 2023).
78. District of Columbia v. Heller, 554 U.S. 570 (2008); Becky Sullivan, "Kyle Rittenhouse Is Acquitted of All Charges in the Kenosha Shootings," NPR, November 19, 2021, https://www.npr.org/2021/11/19/1057288807/kyle-rittenhouse-acquitted-all-charges-verdict; Ava Sasani, "Armed and Ready: How Gun Culture Is Changing Protest," *New York Times*, November 26, 2022.
79. Martin Luther King Jr., *In a Single Garment of Destiny: A Global Vision of Justice*, ed. Lewis V. Baldwin (Boston: Beacon, 2012).
80. Eagleton, *Hope Without Optimism*, 69.
81. Michael C. Dawson, *Blacks in and out of the Left* (Cambridge, MA: Harvard University Press, 2013), 209–210.

ACKNOWLEDGMENTS

This book was years in the making, shaped by the love, sacrifices, and wisdom of more exceptional people than I could possibly thank. I am forever grateful to everyone who poured something into this book and my life along the way. It would not have been possible to complete it without the power of family, community, and friendship carrying me forward through bouts of joyous discovery, and the inevitable moments of self-doubt and fatigue. Whatever is good in this text belongs as much to you as it does to me.

At the Edmund and Lily J. Safra Center for Ethics and the Radcliffe Institute for Advanced Study, both at Harvard University, I found much needed research time and community. I want to thank, respectively, Danielle Allen and the Safra Center staff, and Dean Tomiko Brown-Nagin and the Radcliffe staff, for the hard work they devote to sustaining spaces where concentration and creativity are possible. I also want to thank Danielle Allen for being an exemplary colleague, friend, and mentor, as well as a genuine role model as political theorist and citizen in the world.

Pieces of this book received the generous attention of many wonderful audiences across the world, including the Columbia University Law Forum; Boston College Law School; the Edmund and Lily J. Safra Center for Ethics Workshop; the New York University Law and Philosophy Forum; the Philosophy, Politics, and Economics Workshop at Brown University; the Political Philosophy Workshop at Brown University; the Political Theory Colloquium at Goethe-Universität; the Princeton University Center for Human Values; the Stanford University Political Theory Workshop; the Tufts University Philosophy Department; the University of California, Los Angeles, Philosophy Department; the University of Cambridge History of Political Thought Seminar; Ursinus College; the Weatherhead Center Workshop on Inequality; the Williams College English Department; the University of Cambridge; and the Yale University Legal

Theory Workshop: Your rigor and insight shaped this book dramatically, and I appreciate the time and energy you gave to these ideas. I hope to continue the conversation.

My sincerest thanks go to the entire team at Harvard University Press, especially Samantha Mateo and Sharmila Sen. I know I am not the easiest author on the roster, but it is hard to imagine the book without your patience, understanding, and support throughout this process. I am also grateful to Richard Feit, Matt Lord, and Angela Piliouras for their terrific editorial advice and collaboration. And to Lindsay Waters, thank you for your enthusiasm and excitement for the project in its early stages and for persuading me to bring it to the Press.

This work is deeply indebted to Yale University, during what I now even more duly appreciate as a special time and place to study political science and African American studies. I look back with great fondness on the ecumenical spirit, intellectual exhilaration, and true collegiality that was in the air when I first started testing the ideas that evolved into this book, and when I returned during my year as a visiting professor of political science and African American studies in 2021–2022. I especially want to thank Seyla Benhabib, Glenda Gilmore, Gerald Jaynes, and Karuna Mantena; they nurtured this work in its earliest and most fragile stages, and I am truly grateful for their enthusiasm, insight, and example. Thank you for championing my career and giving me the space to develop a voice of my own. I want to thank the interdisciplinary community that allowed me to draw on so many different interlocutors for this idiosyncratic book—in particular, Bruce Ackerman, Jean-Christophe Agnew, Elijah Anderson, Alyssa Battistoni, Monica Bell, Da'Von Boyd, Daphne Brooks, LaMarr Bruce, Hazel Carby, Michelle Clarke, Kathleen Cleaver, Karilyn Crockett, Carmen Dege, Simona De Paolis, Stefan Eich, Lucas Entel, Crystal Feimster, Bryan Garsten, Casey Gerald, Jacqueline Goldsby, Clifton Granby, Kristin Graves, Jacob Hacker, Casiano Hacker-Cordón, Sarah Haley, Jonathan Holloway, Greg Huber, Mie Inouye, Anna Kesson, Dan Kevles, Helene Landemore, David Lebow, Andrew March, Deborah March, David Mayhew, Thomas McCarthy, Paige McGinley, Tracey Meares, Carlos Miranda, Ernest Mitchell, Sam Moyn, Alondra Nelson, Giulia Oskian, Juan Rebolledo, Shana Redmond, Ed Rugemer, Ian Shapiro, Joshua Simon, Anurag Sinha, Stephen Skowronek, Philip Atiba Solomon, Jason Stanley, David Stein, Dawn Teele, Luke Thompson, Adam Tooze, Joy Wang, Calvin Warren, Libby Wood, and my dear friend the late Cecilia Cardenas-Navia. I want to give special thanks to Theresa Bejan for her timely encouragement and support of my work on Rawls at a difficult time for my family.

I completed most of this project while having the wonderful opportunity to be a faculty member in the Department of African and African American Studies and the Committee on Degrees in Social Studies at Harvard University. As an undergraduate at Harvard many years ago, I dreamed of joining these two programs. I am grateful for the opportunity to pay forward what was bestowed on me when I first arrived in Cambridge from Baltimore so many years ago. I want to thank all of my colleagues on the faculty and staff, but especially those who gave advice or feedback on writing along the way, including Kiku Adatto, Emmanuel Akyeampong, David Armitage, Eric Beerbohm, Robin Bernstein, Larry Bobo, Vincent Brown, Glenda Carpio, Bruno Carvalho, Myisha Eatmon, Katrina Forrester, Marla Frederick, Claudine Gay, Jarvis Givens, Daragh Grant, Jona Hansen, Evelyn Brooks Higginbotham, Jennifer Hochschild, Tracey Hucks, Walter Johnson, Randall Kennedy, Jim Kloppenberg, Michèle Lamont, Sarah Lewis, Ken Mack, Angela Maione, Jamie Martin, Jesse McCarthy, Ellis Monk, Marcy Morgan, Vatsal Naresh, Jacob Olupona, Orlando Patterson, Imani Perry, Laurence Ralph, Mattias Risse, Panagiotis Roilos, Michael Rosen, Michael Sandel, Amartya Sen, Gina Schouten, Susanna Siegel, Sandra Smith, Tracy K. Smith, Doris Sommer, Lucas Stanczyk, Ajantha Subramanian Kirsten Weld, Chris Winship, Abby Wolf, Leah Wright-Rigeuer, and the late Anya Bassett.

I want to give special thanks to Elizabeth Hinton, my partner in running the Institute on Policing, Incarceration, and Public Safety at the Hutchins Center, and one of the great historians and scholarly visionaries of our generation. I learned a great deal about tragic history from you, and I hope you find something of use in this work.

Easily the best thing about working at Harvard is the privilege of closely teaching so many incredible students, many of whom leave their imprint on your thinking and scholarship. I want to thank all of the students from Social Studies 10, some of whom may recognize some of the arguments in this book from my lectures. I especially want to thank a handful of former undergraduate and graduate students whose conversations, reading group participation, or research assistance helped this project along the way, including Mafaz al-Suwaidan, Lorenzo Bradford, Olivia Castor, Jaime Cobham, Jalen Daniels, Dante Doig-Acuña, Breond Durr, Emma Ebowe, Kristine Guillaume, Hazim Hardiman, Spencer Hardwick, Jelani Hayes, Christopher Hopson, Jovanna Jones, Sam Klug, Justin McMahan, Mary McNeil, Rayha McPherson, Anwar Omeish, LaKeyma Pennyamon, Justin Porter, Johnny Powell, Sam Reeves, Rachael Riascos, Elizabeth Ross, Keidrick Roy, Robert Rush, and Ajay Singh. These are all names to watch in the world! I must give special thanks and acknowledgment to Kierstan

Kashaul-Carter, with whom I have organized several reading groups, conferences, and classes. She is an indispensable interlocutor who read multiple drafts of chapters and gave extensive feedback on many arguments about black political life over the years.

As a student of African American political thought and critical theory, I know that not every season has been favorable for the kind of scholarship I produce. I feel tremendously blessed that this book was composed in a time of great productivity and creativity on these themes in the fields of African American political thought, history, philosophy, and political theory. I have gained a great deal from my friendship and intellectual exchanges with so many in these fields, including Lawrie Balfour, Martha Biondi, Nick Bromell, Sherwin Bryant, Charisse Burden-Stelly, Chris Chambers, Greg Childs, Cathy Cohen, the late G. A. Cohen, Brittney Cooper, Lauren Coyle, Derrick Darby, Andrew Douglas, David Estlund, Ashley Farmer, John Filling, Megan Ming Francis, Jason Frank, Eddie Glaude, Thavolia Glymph, Robert Gooding-Williams, Farah Jasmine Griffin, Saida Grundy, Ange-Marie Hancock, Bernard Harcourt, Saidiya Hartman, Juliet Hooker, Destin Jenkins, Cedric Johnson, Magana Kabugi, Erin Kelly, Sharon Krause, Chris Lebron, Adriane Lentz-Smith, Alex Livingston, Jared Loggins, Minkah Makalani, Lionel McPherson, Michele Moody-Adams, Khalil Muhammad, Anthony Nadler, Oludamini Ogunnaike, Traci Parker, Tianna Paschel, Jennifer Pitts, Millery Polyné, Melanye Price, Jedediah Purdy, J. T. Roane, Melvin Rogers, Samuel Scheffler, Melissa Schwartzberg, Robbie Shilliam, Lester Spence, Robyn Spencer-Antoine, Ron Sundstrom, Jasmine Syedullah, Paul C. Taylor, Ula Taylor, Mark Christian Thompson, Chip Turner, Jeremy Waldron, Jackie Wang, Vesla Weaver, Chad Williams, Joseph Winters, Deva Woodly, and Jasmin Young. I also want to thank Kendra Field and Kerri Greenidge for the love and labor that has gone into creating a thriving social community of scholars, intellectuals, and artists in Boston through the W. E. B. Du Bois Forum and their many other endeavors. I am sorry that Charles W. Mills did not live to see the release of this book; his generosity when I presented an early version of Chapter 6 was deeply affirming at that stage of my career, and I will miss what I am certain would be a devastating and witty response.

I want to give special thanks to those loving friends and colleagues who provided extensive feedback and devoted many hours and days to reading multiple drafts of this book. To Malcolm Rivers, for many hours of careful editing and aid. To Peniel Joseph, thank you for your review of the manuscript, your belief in what it could become, and your prodigious example in life and scholarship. To Jeff Gonda, thank you for the kind of friendship that shows up when it's hardest and refuses to abandon. It's been an honor to take this journey with you from New Haven, and our ongoing dialogue is one of the great joys in my life; thank you for being the rare person who can make me laugh while turning my ideas upside down. To Adom Getachew: thank you for sharing your brilliance, reading closely, critiquing sharply, and offering your characteristic intellectual generosity at every turn. To Shatema Threadcraft: your friendship, hilarity, and genius have been an endless source of light, laughter, and learning. Thank you for teaching me so much, and helping me bear the unceasing absurdities of academic life.

To Alex Gourevitch, Durba Mitra, Chris Muller, and Aziz Rana, thank you for giving beyond what friendship requires; you read with rigor, listened with care, and spoke with candor. You were the mirror I needed, and the kind of friends and colleagues every scholar hopes for. I have wracked up an impossible debt, and I look forward to paying it down by reading and learning from one extraordinary work of yours after another.

Thank you to the friends and family who checked in, stayed close, and reminded me I wasn't alone with memorable acts of kindness and encouragement along the way: Matt Baker, Joshua Bennett, the Bozza family, Paul Buttenwieser, Brent Carey, Deb Chasman, Brian Clair, Rob Collier, Michael Cornish, Sangu Delle, Kristina Demas, Grant Devine, Matthew Espy, Pierre Francois, Brandon Gayle, Jarvis Givens, Chris Golden, Karin Goodfellow, Chas Hamilton, Cathy Handy, Lenny Howard, Shanti Hubbard, Glenn Hutchins, Anthony Jack, Imari Paris Jeffries, Diana Kim, Brittani Kirkpatrick, Brennan Klein, Kristin Kleisner, Jason Lee, Niles Lichtenstein, Alyssa Liles, Hassan Mansour, Demond Martin, Jeff Mayersohn, DeRay McKesson, Cassandra Mombrun, the Nguyen family, Oludamini Ogunnaike, Kwame Osseo-Asare, Emma Pengelly, the Reid Family, Jacqueline Rivers, Linda Seamonson, Lumumba Seegars, Melissa Simon, Smith and Christine Vioselin, Justin Williams, Enoch Woodhouse, and Jen Wynn. I want to give special thanks to Eugene Rivers for two decades of pastoral care, his example as a person committed to serving the poor and vulnerable, and for his emboldening belief in my potential as a scholar. I also want to give special thanks to Kimberly McClain DaCosta, Domonique Foxworth, Charity Glass, Jason Norman, Kwame Owusu-Kesse, Daryk Pengelly, Salamishah Tillet, and D. A. Wallach for countless hours of conversation and for meeting my most vulnerable moments with a sympathetic ear and profound advice.

No one could possibly deserve the extraordinary mentorship I have been blessed to experience in my career through academia. I would like to especially thank Henry Louis Gates Jr. and Cornel West, whose example, erudition, and encouragement when I first met them at seventeen years old inspired me to become a scholar; their genius is woven throughout this work, and I am honored to be their friend and still their student. To

Tommie Shelby, thank you for the countless hours you dedicated to my development as a scholar, setting high standards and modeling the best of African American studies and philosophy; teaching, learning, and laughing alongside you continues to be a profound gift. To Elizabeth Alexander, thank you for making time to share your brilliance, wit, and wisdom about life and the life of the mind with me in the midst of your work making a world worthy of affirmation; I remain in awe. I also want to thank Danielle Allen, Larry Bobo, Emma Rothschild, Michael Sandel, and Jonathan and Cecily Walton, colleagues who welcomed me to Cambridge with open arms, and from whom I have learned so much about the world in and outside of Harvard's gates.

Finally, I want to thank my beloved family, who have sacrificed more than anyone to bring this book to fruition. To my siblings, uncles, aunts, nieces, nephews, and other relatives, your presence and love never will go unappreciated. To my in-laws, Crystal, Tamerat, Patrick, Jalene, and Menelik, thank you for your extraordinary sacrifices and the love with which you have welcomed me and my work into your lives. To my parents, Avis and Kenneth, my improbable journey to this point is a testament, mainly, to all that you poured into me. I am forever grateful for your boundless love, unwavering faith in me, and dutiful example. To my children, Ayana and Isaiah, you fill my life with joy, wonder, and purpose. Your Daddy loves you more than a book many times as long as this one could say. Thank you for your sweetness, your impressive curiosity, and, yes, your patience. You keep me grounded, but more important, you remind me why this world is worth fighting for.

To my wife, Sheggai, you have made the impossible feel achievable, and your grace steadied me through it all. I am forever in awe of your generosity of spirit. Thank you for helping me find the confidence and courage to write, teach, and appreciate life, even when times of loss and uncertainty made it feel impossible. I hope you can find joy in an achievement that is as much yours as mine.

And finally, to my beloved grandmother, Hattie, who survived Jim Crow; my Uncle Eddie, who made a bet that changed my life forever; Kenneth Terry, Jr., who inspired me to dissent; and Nicole and Danny Green, gone too soon. Rest in peace.

INDEX

End notes are denoted by n and note number following the page number.